T0269163

Data Mining and Data Warehousing

This textbook is written to cater to the needs of undergraduate students of computer science, engineering, and information technology for a course on data mining and data warehousing. It brings together fundamental concepts of data mining and data warehousing in a single volume. Important topics including information theory, decision tree, Naïve Bayes classifier, distance metrics, partitioning clustering, associate mining, data marts and operational data store are discussed comprehensively. The text simplifies the understanding of the concepts through exercises and practical examples. Chapters such as classification, associate mining and cluster analysis are discussed in detail with their practical implementation using Weka and R language data mining tools. Advanced topics including big data analytics, relational data models, and NoSQL are discussed in detail. Unsolved problems and multiple-choice questions are interspersed throughout the book for better understanding.

Parteek Bhatia is Associate Professor in the Department of Computer Science and Engineering at the Thapar Institute of Engineering and Technology, Patiala, India. He has more than twenty years' teaching experience. His current research includes natural language processing, machine learning, and human–computer interface. He has taught courses including, data mining and data warehousing, big data analysis, and database management systems, at undergraduate and graduate levels.

Data Mining and Data Warehousing

Principles and Practical Techniques

Parteek Bhatia

Shaftesbury Road, Cambridge CB2 8EA, United Kingdom

One Liberty Plaza, 20th Floor, New York, NY 10006, USA

477 Williamstown Road, Port Melbourne, VIC 3207, Australia

314–321, 3rd Floor, Plot 3, Splendor Forum, Jasola District Centre, New Delhi – 110025, India

103 Penang Road, #05–06/07, Visioncrest Commercial, Singapore 238467

Cambridge University Press is part of Cambridge University Press & Assessment, a department of the University of Cambridge.

We share the University's mission to contribute to society through the pursuit of education, learning and research at the highest international levels of excellence.

www.cambridge.org
Information on this title: www.cambridge.org/9781108727747

First published 2019

A catalogue record for this publication is available from the British Library

ISBN 978-1-108-72774-7 Paperback

To
my parents, Mr Ved Kumar and Mrs Jagdish Bhatia
my supportive wife, Dr Sanmeet Kaur
loving sons, Rahat and Rishan

Contents

Figures

Tables

Preface

In the modern age of artificial intelligence and business analytics, data is considered as the oil of this cyber world. The mining of data has huge potential to improve business outcomes, and to carry out the mining of data there is a growing demand for database mining experts. This book intends training learners to fill this gap.

This book will give learners sufficient information to acquire mastery over the subject. It covers the practical aspects of data mining, data warehousing, and machine learning in a simplified manner without compromising on the details of the subject. The main strength of the book is the illustration of concepts with practical examples so that the learners can grasp the contents easily. Another important feature of the book is illustration of data mining algorithms with practical hands-on sessions on Weka and R language (a major data mining tool and language, respectively). In this book, every concept has been illustrated through a step-by-step approach in tutorial form for self-practice in Weka and R. This textbook includes many pedagogical features such as chapter wise summary, exercises including probable problems, question bank, and relevant references, to provide sound knowledge to learners. It provides the students a platform to obtain expertise on technology, for better placements.

Video sessions on data mining, machine learning, big data and DBMS are also available on my YouTube channel. Learners are requested to subscribe to this channel https://www.youtube.com/user/parteekbhatia to get the latest updates through video sessions on these topics.

Your suggestions for further improvements to the book are always welcome. Kindly e-mail your suggestions to parteek.bhatia@gmail.com.

I hope you enjoy learning from this book as much as I enjoyed writing it.

Acknowledgments

Writing the acknowledgments is the most emotional part of book writing. It provides an opportunity to pay gratitude to all those who matter in your life and have helped you achieve your dream and aspirations. With the grace of God and three years of effort, I have reached this stage.

I would like to express my gratitude to the many people who saw me through this book, who motivated me directly or indirectly to write this book, to all those who provided support, talked things over, read, wrote, offered comments, and assisted in the editing, proofreading, and design.

Writing a textbook is an enormous task and it requires a great deal of motivation. I appreciate the writings of great authors like Dr A. P. J. Abdul Kalam, Mr Robin Sharma, Mr Shiv Kehra and Mr Jack Canfield, who have inspired me to contribute to the education of our young generation by writing simplified content without compromising on the depth of the subject.

Writing a book is not possible without the support and motivation of one's family. I feel blessed to have Dr Sanmeet Kaur as my wife; she has always been there to support and encourage me, despite all the time it took me, on this project. Since we both belong to the same field and same profession, having long discussions with her on different aspects of the subject is the most beautiful part of learning. These discussions helped me a long way in shaping the contents of the book. Secondly, she has always been there to take care of our whole family during my engagement with this book.

I am blessed to be born into a family of teachers. My parents, Mr Ved Kumar and Mrs Jagdish Bhatia have always provided a guiding path for excellence in life. Their life journey, in itself, is a learning path for me. I thank the almighty for providing me two loving sons, Rahat and Rishan, who filled our life with love and happiness. I thank my parents-in-laws, Mr Dalip Singh and Mrs Joginder Kaur whose daughter Sanmeet filled our home with love and affection. I thank my elder brother Mr Suneet Kumar and *bhabi ji* Mrs Dimple Bhatia, for always showering their love and blessings on me.

I am blessed to have mentors like M. L. Aeri, former Principal, DAV College, Amritsar; Mr O. P. Bhardwaj, former Head, Department of Computer Science, DAV College, Amritsar; Dr R. K. Sharma Professor, DCSE, TIET; Dr Seema Bawa, Professor DCSE, TIET; Dr Maninder Singh, Head CSED, TIET, and Dr Deepak Garg, former Head CSED, TIET, who groomed me as a teacher. I wish to thank my friends Dr Amardeep Gupta and Mr V. P. Singh, who always lend their ears to my thoughts and aspirations. I would like to thank my colleagues at TIET who motivate and provide an excellent environment for growth.

The production of this book involved a lot of help from my team of students consisting of Ms Sujata Singla, Mr Divanshu Singh, Ms Suhandhi, Mr Aditya and Ms Sawinder Kaur, who read the whole manuscript and helped me in editing and refining the text. I acknowledge the contribution of Ms Sujata in implementing the data mining algorithms in R and her assistance in finalizing the contents. There were great insights form Mr Divanshu Singh, who provided feedback and helped me refine the contents in the portions on web mining and search engine.

I would like to express my gratitude to my students at Thapar Institute of Engineering and Technology, Patiala, for their curiosity and zeal for learning which motivated me to write on this topic. I also want to thank the students at other institutes with whom I had the opportunity to interact during my 'invited talks'. They provided much-needed motivation, without which this book would have been impossible.

I want to acknowledge Dr Mark Polczynski, former Director of the MS at Marquette University, USA; Dr Saed Sayad, an Adjunct Professor at the University of Toronto; Mr Martin Fowler, ThoughtWorks, USA, for granting permission to use content from some of their published works.

I thank my publisher, Cambridge University Press, for publishing this book. I thank Mr Gauravjeet Singh of Cambridge University Press and his team for editing, refining and designing the contents, thereby providing life to the manuscript in the form of a book.

1

Beginning with Machine Learning

Chapter Objectives

- ✓ To understand the concept of machine learning and its applications.
- ✓ To understand what are supervised and unsupervised machine learning strategies.
- ✓ To understand the concept of regression and classification.
- ✓ To identify the strategy to be applied to a given problem.

1.1 Introduction to Machine Learning

Machine Learning (ML) has emerged as the most extensively used tool for web-sites to classify surfers and address them appropriately. When we surf the Net, we are exposed to machine learning algorithms multiple times a day, often without realizing it. Machine learning is used by search engines such as Google and Bing to rank web pages or to decide which advertisement to show to which user. It is used by social networks such as Facebook and Instagram to generate a custom feed for every user or to tag the user by the picture that was uploaded. It is also used by banks to detect whether an online transaction is genuine or fraudulent and by e-commerce websites such as Amazon and Flipkart to recommend products that we are most likely to buy. Even email providers such as Gmail, Yahoo, and Hotmail use machine learning to decide which emails are spam and which are not. These are only a few examples of applications of machine learning.

The ultimate aim of machine learning is to build an Artificial Intelligence (AI) platform that is as intelligent as the human mind. We are not very far from this dream and many AI researchers believe that this goal can be achieved through machine learning algorithms that try to mimic the learning processes of a human brain.

Actually, ML is a branch of AI. Many years ago researchers tried to build intelligent programs with pre-defined rules like in the case of a normal program. But this approach did not work as there were too many special cases to be considered. For instance, we can define rules to find the shortest path between two points. But it is very difficult to make rules for programs such as photo tagging, classifying emails as spam or not spam, and web page ranking. The only solution to accomplish these tasks was to write a program that could generate its own rules by examining some examples (also called training data). This approach was named Machine Learning. This book will cover state of art machine learning algorithms and their deployment.

1.2 Applications of Machine Learning

Machine Learning or ML is everywhere. It is a definite possibility that one is using it in one way or the other and doesn't even know about it. Some common applications of machine learning that we come across every day are:

Virtual Personal Assistants

There are many Virtual Personal Assistants such as Siri, Alexa, or Google Assistant that we interact with in our daily life. As the term suggests, they help in discovering information, when asked by voice. You have to train them before asking 'What is my calendar for now?', 'How is climate today', or similar inquiries. For answering, the personal assistant searches for the information over the Internet and recalls your related queries, to solve your request. These assistants can be trained for certain tasks like 'Set an alarm for 5 AM next morning', 'Remind me to visit doctor tomorrow at 6 PM', and so on. Smart Speakers like Amazon Echo and Google Home are the outcomes of this innovation. Above-mentioned assistants use machine learning to achieve these objectives.

Traffic predictions

All of us are familiar with Google maps; it uses machine learning to predict the expected time of arrival at the destination and also to model traffic congestion on real time basis.

Online transportation networks

We all book cabs by using mobile apps like Ola and Uber. These apps estimate the price of the ride by using machine learning. They also use ML to determine price surge hours by predicting the rider's demand.

Video surveillance

CCTV cameras have become common for video surveillance. The manual monitoring of these cameras is a very difficult job and boring as well. This is why the idea of training computers to do this job makes sense and machine learning helps to achieve this objective. ML based video surveillance systems can even detect crime before it happens. It can track unusual behavior in people such as standing motionless for an unnaturally long time, hesitancy, or napping on benches and such-like. The system can thus alert human attendants, for suitable response.

Social media services

Machine learning is also playing a vital role in personalizing news feed in order to better advertisement targeting over social media. Facebook uses machine learning to show news feed to the user based on his or her interests by considering items clicked earlier by that user. Facebook also continuously takes note of the friends that you connect with, the profiles that you often visit, your interests, workplace, and such; and, on the basis of this continuous learning, a list of Facebook users are suggested for you to become friends with.

The Face Recognition feature of Facebook also uses ML to tag the friends in a picture. Facebook checks the poses and projections in the picture, notices the unique features, and then matches them with the people in your friends list. The entire process is performed with the help of ML and is performed so quickly at the backend that it tags the person as soon as we upload his or her picture.

Pinterest also uses ML for computer vision to identify the objects (or pins) in the images and recommend similar pins accordingly.

Email spam and malware filtering

Email spam and malware filters have inbuilt machine learning to identify spam emails. On the basis of emails we earlier marked as spam or not, the system learns and identifies new mail as spam or not, automatically.

Usually, a malware's code is 90–98% similar to its previous versions. The system security programs that incorporate machine learning understand the coding pattern and detect new malware very efficiently and offer protection against them.

Online customer support

Many sites these days offer the surfer the option to talk with them. While doing so, these sites have 'bots' hunting the website internals to come up with an appropriate response. In any case, very few sites have a live official to answer your questions. In most cases, you converse with a chatbot. These bots extract data from the site and present it to clients through machine learning.

Search engine result refining

Google and other search engines use machine learning to improve search results for you. Every time you execute a search, the algorithms at the backend keep a watch on how you respond to the results. If you open the top results and stay on the web page for long, the search engine assumes that the results it displayed were in accordance with the query. Similarly, if you reach the second or third page of the search results but do not open any of the results, the search engine estimates that the results served did not match requirement. This is the way, machine learning trains itself at the backend to improve search results.

Product recommendations

Whenever we make an online purchase on websites such as Amazon or Flipkart or similar, we usually keep receiving emails from them with shopping suggestions. They also recommend us items that somehow match our tastes. This improves the shopping experience and again it is machine learning that makes it happen. On the basis of our behavior on the website or app, past purchases, items liked or added to the cart, brand preferences and other such factors, the product recommendations are made.

Online fraud detection

Machine learning is also helping in making cyberspace more secure and tracking monetary frauds online. For example, Paypal is using ML for protection against money laundering. The company uses a set of ML tools that helps them to compare millions of transactions taking place and distinguish between legitimate or illegitimate transactions taking place between the buyers and sellers.

Medicine

With the advent of automation, medical records are now available in electronic form. The ML algorithms are helping doctors to understand diseases in a better manner by turning the medical records into medical knowledge.

Computational biology

Biologists are also collecting an enormous amount of data about human DNA. The ML algorithms are helping them understand and identify the relationship between various genes and related human features.

Handwriting recognition

ML can not only recognize handwriting but also read different ones. So, it is a versatile tool for many applications. For instance it can be used to route postal mail all over the country once it has been trained to read addresses written in anyone's handwriting.

Machine translation

We use Google Translate that translates text/website instantly between 100 different human languages as if by magic. Available on our phones and smart watches, the technology behind Google Translate is Machine Translation. It has changed the world by allowing people with different language to communicate with each other.

Driverless cars and autonomous helicopters

As pointed out, ML is used for programs in situations for which it is very difficult to define rules. One such application is self-driving cars or autonomous helicopters. It takes years of experience for a person to become a good driver and much of this is intuitive. It is very difficult to define this experience in terms of formulating all the myriad rules which are necessary for a program to drive a car on its own. The only possible solution is machine learning, i.e., having a computer program that can learn by itself how to drive a car or fly a helicopter.

With such enormous scope for employing machine learning there is a corresponding huge demand for machine learning experts all over world. It is one of the top ten most required IT skills.

1.3 Defining Machine Learning

There are two commonly used definitions of machine learning.

Arthur Samuel (1959) coined the term machine learning and defined it as: '*the field of study that gives computers the ability to learn without being explicitly programmed.*' This is an informal and old definition of machine learning.

From this definition, formulated more than half a century ago, it is evident that machine learning is not a new field. But during those times computers were not fast enough to implement the proposed techniques. The concept of machine learning gained popularity in the early 1990s due to the availability of the computers with huge storage space and processing powers.

In 1998, Tom Mitchell redefined the concept of machine learning as '[A] computer program is said to learn from experience E with respect to some class of tasks T and performance measures P, if its performance at tasks in T, as measured by P, improves with experience E.'

For instance, let's say there is an email program which tracks the emails that a person marks as spam or not spam and based on that learns how spam can be filtered in a better way.

Thus, Classification of emails as spam or not spam is the **Task T.**

Tracking the user and marking emails as spam or not spam becomes **Experience E.**

The number of emails correctly classified as spam or not spam is **Performance P.**

1.4 Classification of Machine Learning Algorithms

The classification of machine learning algorithms is shown in Figure 1.1 below.

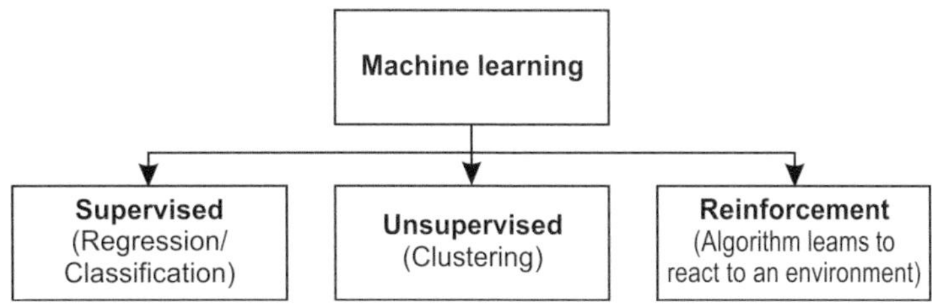

Figure 1.1 Classification of machine learning algorithms

Some examples are given below for better understanding of these classifications. Further definition will follow in a later section.

1.4.1 Supervised learning

Suppose Sonam wants to *accurately* estimate the price of some houses in New Delhi. She first compiles a dataset having covered area of each house with its corresponding price from the city of

New Delhi. She does this for a number of houses of different sizes and plots this data as shown in Figure 1.2. Here, the *Y-axis* represents the price of different houses in lakhs of rupees and the *X-axis* indicates the size of different houses in square feet.

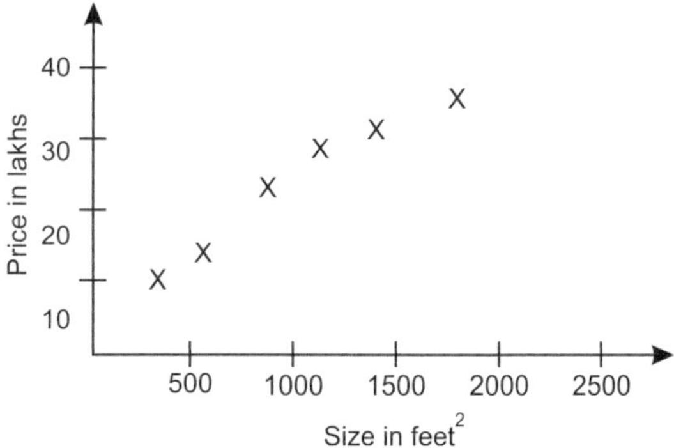

Figure 1.2 Data plot for size of plot and cost

Let's suppose Sonam's friend owns a house that is 850 square feet in size and she wants to know the selling price for the house. In this case, how can a machine learning algorithm help her? An ML algorithm might be able to do so by fitting a straight line through the plotted data and based on the curve obtained it can be observed that house can be sold about approximately 18 lakh rupees as shown in Figure 1.3. But this is just an opening step.

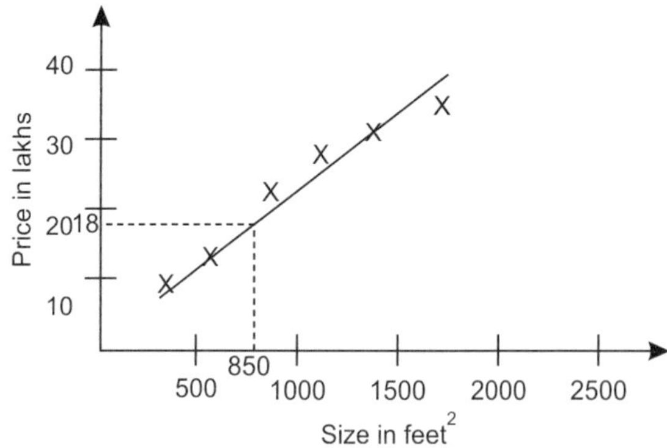

Figure 1.3 Estimation (prediction) of cost of house with a small dataset

As more and more data is added to this dataset, i.e., as the number of experiences plotted are increased, the graph looks as shown in Figure 1.4. Then, instead of fitting a straight line, a second order polynomial will make a better fit for this data. By using a second order polynomial, we get better prediction and it seems that Sonam's friend should expect a price of close to 20 lakhs as shown in Figure 1.4.

It is important to note that, here, by increasing the dataset, i.e., the experience of the machine, the performance of the system for the task 'predicting house price' has improved. And thus, the machine has learnt how to better estimate or predict the prices of houses. The example discussed above is an example of supervised machine learning and the term 'supervised' signifies the fact that the dataset with the 'right answers' is given to the algorithm. The example given above is also a case of regression problem. In a regression problem, the system predicts a continuous–valued output (here, it is the price of the house).

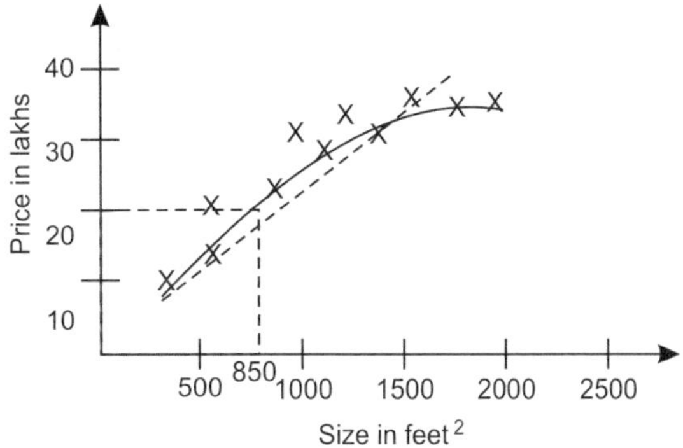

Figure 1.4 Prediction of cost of house with large dataset

Take another example of supervised learning: suppose a doctor looks at a dataset of medical records to try and find out whether a tumour is benign or malignant. A benign tumor is a harmless tumor and a malignant tumor is a tumor that is dangerous and harmful.

Now the doctor wishes to predict whether a tumor is cancerous or not based on the tumor size. For this, the doctor can collect the data of breast tumor patients and plot a graph in which size of the tumor is on X-axis and type of tumor, i.e, cancerous or not, is on Y-axis as shown in Figure 1.5. In this example, we don't try to predict a continuous value but rather try to classify a tumor as being either benign or malignant.

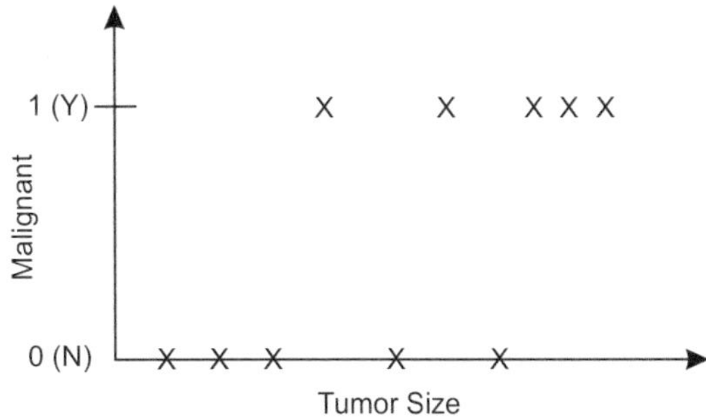

Figure 1.5 Data plot for tumor size and malignancy

In the above plot, we have five examples of malignant or cancerous tumors having value one and five samples of benign or non-cancerous tumors with a value of zero on the Y-axis. Suppose a person has a breast tumor and the size of the tumor is somewhere around the value marked as A as shown in Figure 1.6. The machine learning question here is to predict the chances of that tumor being benign or malignant?

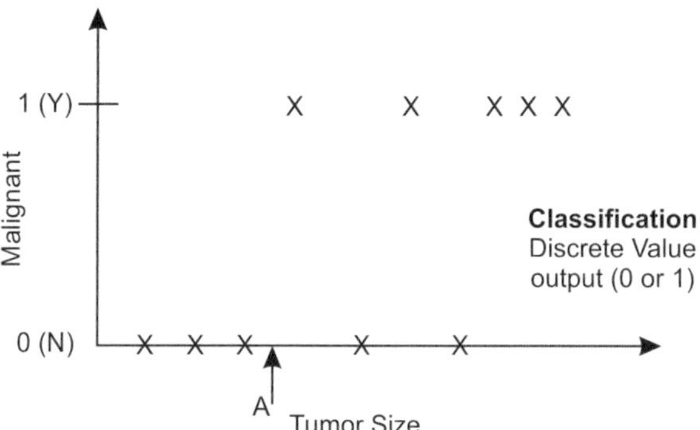

Figure 1.6 Prediction about a tumor of size A

This then is a ***'Classification'*** issue. The term 'classification' signifies that the system has to predict the output as a discrete value, i.e., one or zero (either benign or malignant in the above example). It should be noted that in a classification problem, the output can have more than two possible values. For example, there may be three types of breast cancers and one can try to predict the discrete value, i.e., zero, one or two. Here, zero may represent a benign tumor or not harmful cancer, one may represent type one cancer and the discrete value two may indicate a type two cancer. Hence, in a classification problem, we may have N classes in the output where N is always a finite number.

In this example, only one attribute or feature namely the tumor size has been used with the aim to predict whether the type of tumor is benign or malignant. In other machine learning situations, there can be more than one attribute or feature. For example, the age of the patient can also be considered instead of just knowing the size of tumor only. In that case, our dataset would look like as shown in Figure 1.7.

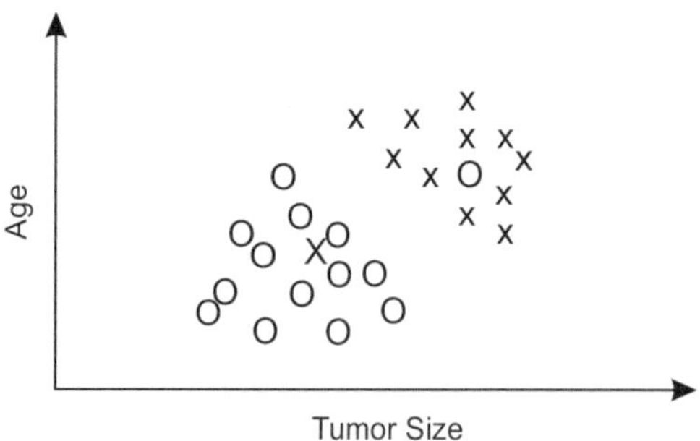

Figure 1.7 Considering tumor size and age as features for classification

Let's suppose a person has a tumour, of size and age as depicted by B in Figure 1.8.

In this dataset, the ML algorithm is able to fit a straight line to separate out the benign tumors from the malignant tumors as shown in Figure 1.9. Thus, according to ML algorithm, a straight line can, hopefully, help us determine a person's tumor by separating out the tumors. And if a person's tumor falls in this benign area then the type of cancer is more likely to be benign than malignant.

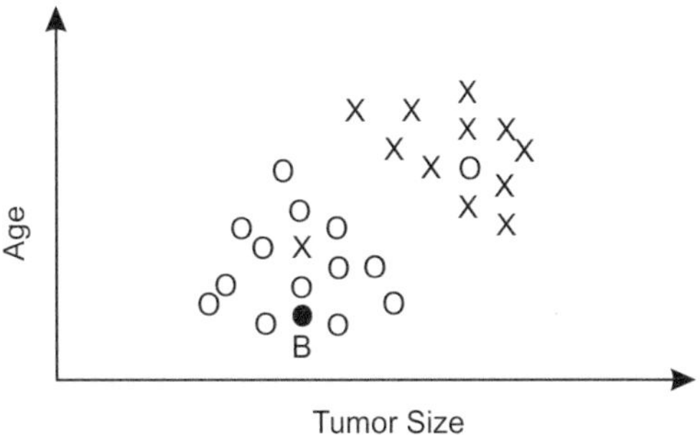

Figure 1.8 Prediction for a tumor of size B

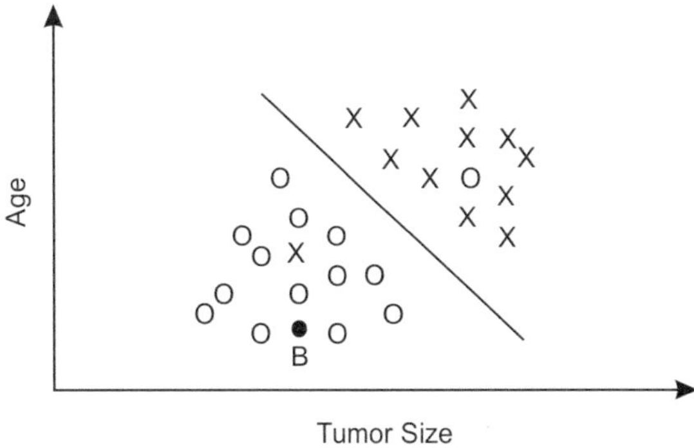

Figure 1.9 Prediction for tumor size B being benign

In this example, two features such as patient's age and tumor size have been considered. However, we can increase the number of features to further increase the accuracy of prediction. It is important to note that as more and more relevant features are added into a model, the model will become more complex but the accuracy may increase. Commonly, machine learning algorithms have more than one feature.

Test your progress

Imagine that you own a company and to address each of its problems, you wish to develop a machine learning algorithm.

Problem 1: For each customer account, you'd like to have a software to check the account and decide if it has been compromised (hacked).

Problem 2: You have a large stock of similar goods. You wish to know that in the next three months how many of these goods will sell.

You have the following options:

(a) Option A: First problem is regression problem and second problem is a classification problem.
(b) Option B: Both are classification problems.

(c) Option C: Both are regression problems.
(d) Option D: First problem is a classification problem and second problem as a regression problem.

The correct answer is option D.

In Problem 1, we have to predict whether the account has been hacked or not. So, if we consider 0 as not hacked and 1 as hacked then we have to predict either 0 or 1. Thus, this is a case of binary classifier (having only two possible outputs). In Problem 2, we have to predict the number of goods that will be sold in next 3 months, so it will be a continuous value, thus it is a case of regression.

Thus, supervised learning problems are categorized into either 'classification' or 'regression' problems. In a regression problem, we try to predict the results within a continuous output. This means that we try to map input variables to some continuous function. In a classification problem instead, we try to predict results in a discrete output. In other words, we try to map input variables into discrete classes or categories.

In the example about predicting the price of houses based on given data about their size: the price as a function of house size is a *continuous* output, so this is a regression problem.

We could turn this example into a classification problem by instead asking whether a house will sell for more than or less than a certain amount. Here, we are classifying the houses based on price into two *discrete* categories.

Further examples should help in better understanding regression and classification. The prediction of marks of a student is a case of regression while prediction about his grades or division is classification. The prediction of a score in a cricket match is an example of regression while to predict if the team will win or lose the match is an example of classification. The prediction about tomorrow's temperature is a case of regression, while to predict whether tomorrow will be cooler or hotter than today is an example of a classification problem.

1.4.2 Unsupervised learning

Unsupervised learning, on the other hand, allows us to approach problems with little or no idea about what the results will look like. We can derive structure from data where we don't necessarily know the effect of the variables.

In unsupervised learning data is not labeled, it means that there is no output attribute. We only have input attributes and on the basis of values of input attributes grouping or clustering is performed on the input data to group them into similar classes.

We can only construct the clusters of data based on relationships among the variables in the data. With unsupervised learning, there is no feedback about the results predicted, i.e., there is no teacher to correct you.

Examples of unsupervised learning

Google news as depicted in Figure 1.10 is an excellent example of clustering that uses unsupervised learning to group news items based on their contents. Google has a collection of millions of news items written on different topics and their clustering algorithm automatically groups these news items into a small number that are somehow similar or related to each other by using different attributes, such as word frequency, sentence length, page count, and so on.

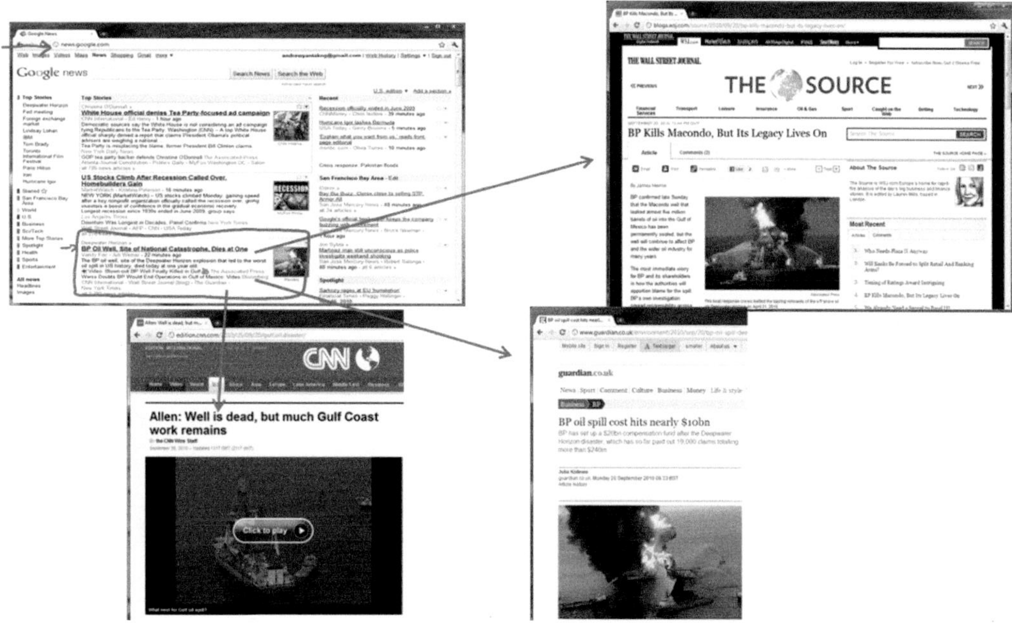

Figure 1.10 Google news

The other examples of unsupervised learning applications are illustrated in Figure 1.11 and are discussed below.

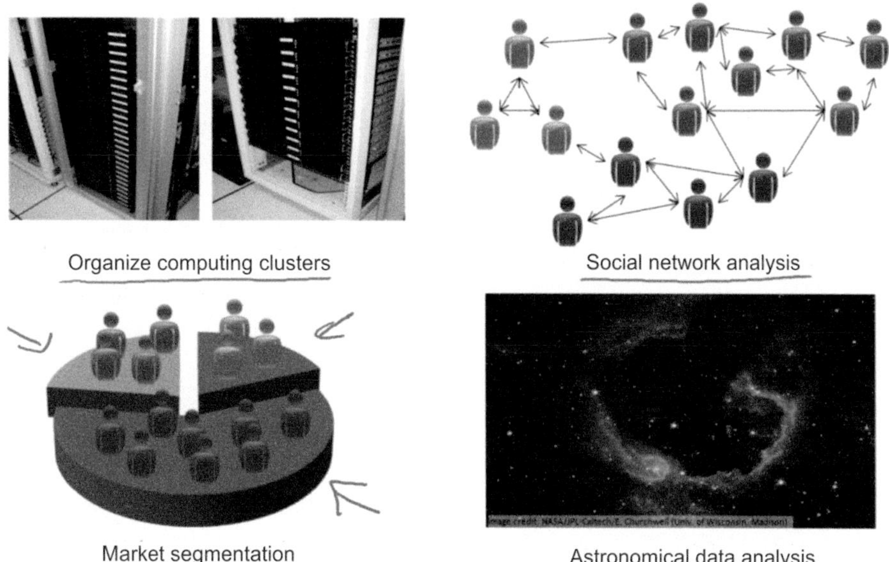

Figure 1.11 Applications of unsupervised learning

Organize computing clusters

The geographic location of servers is decided on the basis of clustering of web requests received from a particular region of the world. The local server will then contain only the data frequently accessed by people of that region.

Social network analysis

Social network analysis is conducted to create clusters of friends based on the frequency of communication among them. Such analysis reveals the links among the users of any social networking website.

Market segmentation

Sales organizations can cluster or group their customers into different segments on the basis of their previous billed items. For example, a big superstore may want to send an SMS about grocery items specifically to its customers of grocery instead of sending that SMS to all its customers. Not only is it cheaper but also better; after all it might be an irrelevant irritant to those who only purchase clothing from the store. The grouping of customers into different segments based on their purchase history will help the store to target the correct customers for increasing sales and improving its profits.

Astronomical data analysis

Astronomers use large telescopes to study galaxies and stars. The patterns in light or grouping of lights received from different parts of the sky help to identify different galaxies, planets, and satellites.

1.4.3 Supervised and unsupervised learning in real life scenario

To understand the difference between supervised and unsupervised learning let us consider the learning process of Adam and Eve who are considered to be the first human beings on Earth according to Biblical texts.

Adam and Eve might have learned by analyzing the attributes or features of the various objects because at that time no item had a name or label attached to it. They might have associated an object to be a part of a group or cluster of items based on their features like colour, shape, size, smell, taste, etc. First, they might have categorized the things into living and nonliving groups. Then they might have further analyzed each group and divided it into subgroups and so on. For example, they might have identified one group as 'animals' which they might have further sub-grouped as a tiger, dog, cat and so on. In simple terms, they performed clustering of objects based on their features and later on with the development of language, they assigned names to these groups and subgroups.

Thus, Adam and Eve learned through unsupervised learning because during that time nothing was labeled and based on their analysis of things they made groups and subgroups and only later did they give names to these groups and subgroups.

On the other hand, in today's world, when a child is born in a family, its learning process is different from Adam and Eve's learning process because now everything has already been labeled, i.e., has a name. We show different items to a child and tell the child what an item's name is, such as a pen, pencil, chair, table, car, bus, and so on. During this learning process along with all the features of an object, the child also gets to know the name or label of that item. The child does not need to see all the pencils in the world to identify it, after being trained on three or four of them; with just an initial few reminders the child will be able to differentiate between pen/pencil/car/bus or whatever. Thus the child's learning is supervised learning because labeled data is provided with all attributes of the items. In supervised machine learning, a system gets trained on some sample data (training data), and whenever it comes across unknown sample data, the system will be able to predict based on experience gained by analyzing training data.

In simple words, when data is labeled, it is considered as supervised learning but when data is unlabeled then it is known as unsupervised learning. In supervised learning, the system makes predictions, i.e., classification or regression and in case of unsupervised learning, clustering is performed based on the features of the object.

As another example, assume you have different kinds of fruits filled in a basket. You have to organize them into different groups. Let's suppose there are 4 types of fruits in the basket, which are as follows – cherry, mango, grapes, and banana.

Supervised learning

From your prior knowledge, you might have learned about the physical characters of the fruits. So, it may be very easy to organize the similar type of fruits into one group. In machine learning, the prior work of analyzing sample data is known as training. As a result of this training, it is able to associate a label with every fruit i.e. FRUIT NAME as shown in Table 1.1.

Table 1.1 Fruit data for supervised learning

No.	*Shape*	*Colour*	*Size*	*Fruit Name*
1	Heart-shaped to nearly globular	Red	Small	Cherry
2	Kidney shaped	Yellow	Big	Mango
3	Round to oval, bunch shaped cylindrical	Green	Small	Grapes
4	Long curving cylinder	Green	Big	Banana

Assume from the basket of fruits, you picked a new fruit and observed the shape, size, and colour of that particular fruit. If the fruit is kidney-shaped, bigger in size and yellow in colour, then the fruit is classified as mango. Similarly, this process is repeated for other fruits present in the basket. This is a case of the classification problem. If any prior knowledge acquired by analyzing training data is then used for making predictions about unseen data then it is known as supervised machine learning.

Unsupervised learning

Let us take the basket that is filled with some distinctive types of fruits and you have to organize them into groups. Assume that this is the first time you have seen these fruits and you don't know anything about them. It means data is not labeled and it will appear like as shown in Table 1.2. This is the same situation that Adam and Eve had when nothing was labeled. So, having no clue about the fruits how will you start the process of organizing them into different groups?

Table 1.2 Fruit data for unsupervised learning

No.	Shape	Colour	Size
1	Heart-shaped to nearly globular	Red	Small
2	Kidney-shaped	Yellow	Big
3	Round to oval, bunch shape cylindrical	Green	Small
4	Long curving cylinder	Green	Big

You may organize them on the basis of their physical characteristics. Assume that you organize them on the basis of their respective size and colour.

Then the groups will be like this.

SMALL SIZE AND RED COLOUR: cherry fruits.

BIG SIZE AND YELLOW COLOUR: mango.

SMALL SIZE AND GREEN COLOUR: grapes.

BIG SIZE AND GREEN COLOUR: banana.

Now, on the basis of colour, the groups will be.

GREEN COLOUR GROUP: grapes and banana.

RED COLOUR GROUP: cherry.

YELLOW COLOUR GROUP: mango.

This example is a case of clustering problem fall under unsupervised learning.

When you don't have any prior knowledge or labeled data then it is called as unsupervised learning.

1.4.4 Reinforcement learning

Reinforcement learning is used in applications like computer games (where the machine plays with a human), driverless cars, robot navigation, etc. It works through trial and error, and the machine selects those actions that yield the greatest rewards. These algorithms have three major components mentioned as follows.

Agent: It is used for learning and decision making. The agent chooses actions that maximize some specified reward metric over a given amount of time.

Environment: It defines the outer world with which the agent interacts.

Actions: It defines the tasks to be performed by the agent.

Thus, reinforcement learning allows machines and software agents to automatically determine the ideal behavior within a specific context, in order to maximize its performance. Simple reward feedback is required for the agent to learn its behavior and this is known as the reinforcement signal. Google's AlphaGo program which defeated the world champion in the game of Go, the self-driving car from Tesla Motors and Amazon's prime air delivery are all based on reinforcement learning.

Remind Me

- Machine Learning (ML) is a field that has grown out of Artificial Intelligence (AI).
- Machine learning is the field of study that gives computers the ability to learn without being explicitly programmed.
- Machine learning algorithms are broadly classified into two classes such as supervised learning and unsupervised learning.

Point Me (Books)

- Mitchell, Tom M. 2017. *Machine Learning.* Chennai: McGraw Hill Education.
- Witten, Ian H., Eibe Frank, Mark A. Hall, and Christopher Pal. 2016. *Data Mining: Practical Machine Learning Tools and Techniques*, 4th ed. Burlington: Morgan Kaufmann.

Point Me (Video)

- Machine Learning Tutorial, Parteek Bhatia, https://youtu.be/K488fqToBbE

Connect Me (Internet Resources)

- http://www.expertsystem.com/machine-learning-definition/
- https://www.techemergence.com/what-is-machine-learning/
- http://dataaspirant.com/2014/09/19/supervised-and-unsupervised-learning/
- https://www.datascience.com/blog/supervised-and-unsupervised-machine-learning-algorithms

Test Me

Answer these multiple choice questions based on what you learnt in this chapter.

1. A computer program is said to learn from experience E with respect to some performance measure P and some task T, if this improves with experience E when its performance on T is measured by P. Let us feed a machine learning algorithm to predict the weather by providing a lot of historical weather data. What would be a reasonable choice for P in this case?
   (a) The process of the algorithm examining a large amount of historical weather data.
   (b) The probability of it correctly predicting a future date's weather.
   (c) The weather prediction task.
   (d) None of these.
2. Suppose you are working on weather prediction and your weather station makes one of given three predictions for each day's weather: Cloudy, Rainy or Sunny. You'd like to use a machine learning algorithm to predict tomorrow's weather. Would you treat this as a regression or a classification problem?
   (a) Regression (b) Classification
3. Assume that you work at a stock trading company and you have to estimate whether or not a particular stock's price will be higher or not on next day than today. You wish to use a machine learning algorithm for this. Would you treat this as a regression or a classification problem?
   (a) Regression (b) Classification
4. Some of the problems given below are best addressed using a supervised machine learning algorithm and the others with an unsupervised machine learning algorithm. In which of the following case would you apply supervised learning? (Select all that apply.) Assume that to learn from each case, some suitable dataset is accessible for your algorithm.

(a) Have a computer inspect an audio clip of music and classify whether or not there are vocals (i.e., a human voice singing) in that audio clip or if it is a clip of only musical instruments (and no vocals).
(b) Find a way to automatically group the essays taken from a group of thousand essays written on the Indian Economy into a small number of groups of essays that are somehow 'related' or 'similar'.
(c) Examine a web page and classify whether the content on that web page should be considered 'child-friendly' (e.g., non-pornographic, etc.) or 'adult'.
(d) To discover if there are sub-types of spam mail, examine a large collection of emails that are labeled as spam email.

5. Which of these is a reasonable definition of machine learning?
   (a) Machine learning means learning from labeled data.
   (b) Machine learning is the field of study that gives computers the ability to learn without being explicitly programmed.
   (c) Machine learning is the science of programming computers.
   (d) Machine learning is the field of allowing robots to act intelligently.
6. What is training data?
   (a) The dataset used to check the accuracy of an algorithm
   (b) The data that algorithm will receive to make predictions in a production environment
   (c) A subset of the whole dataset that we have
   (d) The data generated as output by the algorithm

Answer Keys:

1. (b)	2. (b)	3. (b)	4. (a, c, d)
5. (b)	6. (b)		

2

Introduction to Data Mining

Chapter Objectives

- ✓ To learn about the concepts of data mining.
- ✓ To understand the need for, and the applications of data mining
- ✓ To differentiate between data mining and machine learning
- ✓ To understand the process of data mining.
- ✓ To understand the difference between data mining and machine learning.

2.1 Introduction to Data Mining

In the age of information, an enormous amount of data is available in different industries and organizations. The availability of this massive data is of no use unless it is transformed into valuable information. Otherwise, we are sinking in data, but starving for knowledge. The solution to this problem is data mining which is the extraction of useful information from the huge amount of data that is available.

Data mining is defined as follows:

'Data mining is a collection of techniques for efficient automated discovery of previously unknown, valid, novel, useful and understandable patterns in large databases. The patterns must be actionable so they may be used in an enterprise's decision making.'

From this definition, the important take aways are:

- Data mining is a process of automated discovery of previously unknown patterns in large volumes of data.
- This large volume of data is usually the historical data of an organization known as the data warehouse.
- Data mining deals with large volumes of data, in Gigabytes or Terabytes of data and sometimes as much as Zetabytes of data (in case of big data).

- Patterns must be valid, novel, useful and understandable.
- Data mining allows businesses to determine historical patterns to predict future behaviour.
- Although data mining is possible with smaller amounts of data, the bigger the data the better the accuracy in prediction.
- There is considerable hype about data mining at present, and the Gartner Group has listed data mining as one of the top ten technologies to watch.

2.2 Need of Data Mining

Data mining is a recent buzz word in the field of Computer Science. It is a computing process that uses intelligent mathematical algorithms to extract the relevant data and computes the probability of future actions. It is also known as Knowledge Discovery in Data (KDD).

Although data mining has existed for 50 years, it has become a very important technology only recently due to the Internet boom. Database systems are being used since the 1960s in the Western countries (perhaps, since the 1980s in India). These systems have generated mountains of data. There is a broad agreement among all sources that the size of the digital universe will double every two years at least. Therefore, there will be a 50-fold growth from 2010 to 2020.

Every minute, huge data is generated over Internet as depicted in Figure 2.1. The analysis of this huge amount of data is an important task and it is performed with the help of data mining. This analysis of data has significant potential to improve business outcomes for an organization.

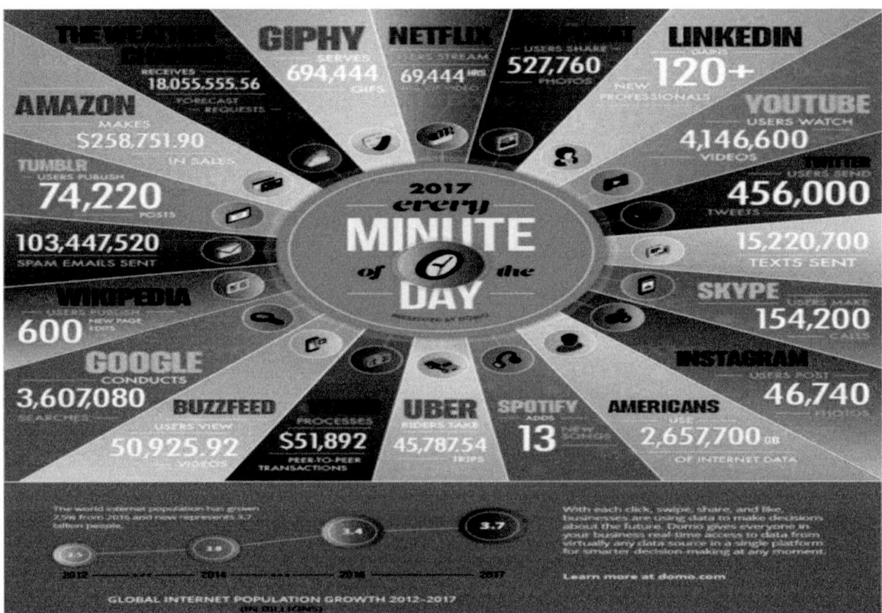

Figure 2.1 Per minute generation of data over the Internet according to a 2017 report

[*Credit*: http://www.iflscience.com/technology/how-much-data-does-the-world-generate-every-minute/]

Some facts about this rapid growth of data are as follows.

- 48 hours of new videos are uploaded by YouTube users every minute of the day.
- 571 new websites are created every minute of the day.
- 90% of world's data has been produced in the last two years.
- The production of data will be 44 times greater in 2020 than it was in 2010.
- Brands and organizations on Facebook receive 34,722 'Likes' every minute of the day.
- 100 terabytes of data is uploaded daily to Facebook.
- In early 2012, there were more than 465 million accounts and 175 million tweets were shared by people on Twitter every day, according to Twitter's own research.
- Every month, 30 billion pieces of content are shared by people on Facebook.
- By late 2011, approximately 1.8 zetta byte of data had been created in that year alone, according the report published by IDC Digital Universe.

The analysis of such huge amounts of data is a challenging task that requires suitable analytics to sieve it for the bits that will be useful for business purposes. From the start, data mining was designed to find data patterns from data warehouses and data mining algorithms are tuned so that they can handle large volumes of data. The boom in big data volumes has led to great interest in data mining all over the world.

The other allied reasons for popularity of data mining are as follows.

- Growth in generation and storage of corporate data
- Need for sophisticated decision making
- Evolution of technology
- Availability of much cheaper storage, easier data collection and better database management for data analysis and understanding
- Point of sale terminals and bar codes on many products, railway bookings, educational institutions, mobile phones, electronic gadgets, e-commerce, etc., all generate data.
- Great volumes of data generated with the recent prevalence of Internet banking, ATMs, credit and debit cards; medical data, hospitals; automatic toll collection on toll roads, growing air travel; passports, visas, etc.
- Decline in the costs of hard drives
- Growth in worldwide disk capacities

Thus, the need for analyzing and synthesizing information is growing in the fiercely competitive business environment of today.

2.3 What Can Data Mining Do and Not Do?

Data mining is a powerful tool that helps to determine the relationships and patterns within data. However, it does not work by itself and does not eliminate the requirement for understanding data, analytical methods and to know business. Data mining extracts hidden information from the data, but it is not able to assess the value of the information.

One should know the important patterns and relationships to work with data over time. In addition to discovering new patterns, data mining can also highlight other empirical observations that are not instantly visible through simple observation.

It is important to note that the relationships or patterns predicted through data mining are not necessarily causes for an action or behavior. For example, data mining may help in determining that males with income between Rs 20,000 and Rs 75,000 who contribute to certain journals or magazines, may be expected to purchase such-and-such a product. This information can be helpful in developing a marketing strategy. However, it is not necessary that the population identified through data mining will purchase the product simply because they belong to this category.

2.4 Data Mining Applications

The applications of data mining exist in almost every field. Some of the important applications of data mining are in finance, telecom, insurance and retail sectors include loan/credit card approval, fraud detection, market segmentation, trend analysis, better marketing, market basket analysis, customer churn and web site design and promotion. These are discussed below.

Loan/Credit card approvals

Banks are able to assess the credit worthiness of their customers by mining a customer's historical records of business transactions. So, credit agencies and banks collect a lot of customer' behavioural data from many sources. This information is used to predict the chances of a customer paying back a loan.

Market segmentation

A huge amount of data about customers is available from purchase records. This data is very useful to segment customers on the basis of their purchase history. Let us suppose a mega store sells multiple items ranging from grocery to books, electronics, clothing et al. That store now plans to launch a sale on books. Instead of sending SMS texts to all the customers it is logical and more efficient to send the SMS only to those customers who have demonstrated interest in buying books, i.e., those who had earlier purchased books from the store. In this case, the segmentation of customers based on their historical purchases will help to send the message to those who may find it relevant. It will also give a list of people who are prospects for the product.

Fraud detection

Fraud detection is a very challenging task because it's difficult to define the characteristics for detection of fraud. Fraud detection can be performed by analyzing the patterns or relationships that deviate from an expected norm. With the help of data mining, we can mine the data of an organization to know about outliers as they may be possible locations for fraud.

Better marketing

Usually all online sale web portals provide recommendations to their users based on their previous purchase choices, and purchases made by customers of similar profile. Such recommendations are generated through data mining and help to achieve more sales with better marketing of their products. For example, amazon.com uses associations and provides recommendations to customers on the basis of past purchases and what other customers are purchasing. To take another example, a shoe store can use data mining to identify the right shoes to stock in the right store on the basis of shoe sizes of the customers in the region.

Trend analysis

In a large company, not all trends are always visible to the management. It is then useful to use data mining software that will help identify trends. Trends may be long term trends, cyclic trends or seasonal trends.

Market basket analysis

Market basket analysis is useful in designing store layouts or in deciding which items to put on sale. It aims to find what the customers buy and what they buy together.

Customer churn

If an organization knows its customers better then it can retain them longer. In businesses like telecommunications, companies very hard to retain their good customers and to perhaps persuade good customers of their competitors to switch to them. In such an environment, businesses want to rate customers (whether they are worthwhile to be retained), why customers switch over and what makes customers loyal. With the help of this information some businesses may wish to get rid of customers that cost more than they are worth, e.g., credit card holders that don't use the card; bank customers with very small amounts of money in their accounts.

Website design

A web site is effective only if the visitors easily find what they are looking for. Data mining can help discover affinity of visitors to pages and the site layout may be modified based on data generated from their web clicks.

Corporate analysis and risk management

Data mining can be used to perform cash flow analysis to plan finance and estimate assets. The analysis of data can be performed by comparing and summarizing the spending and planning of resources. It helps to analyze market directions and monitor competitors to analyze the competition.

Thus, one can conclude that the applications of data mining are numerous and it is worthwhile for an organization to invest in data mining for generating better business revenue. This is the reason that many organizations are investing in this field and there is a huge demand for data mining experts in the world.

2.5 Data Mining Process

Data mining process consists of six phases, as illustrated in Figure 2.2.

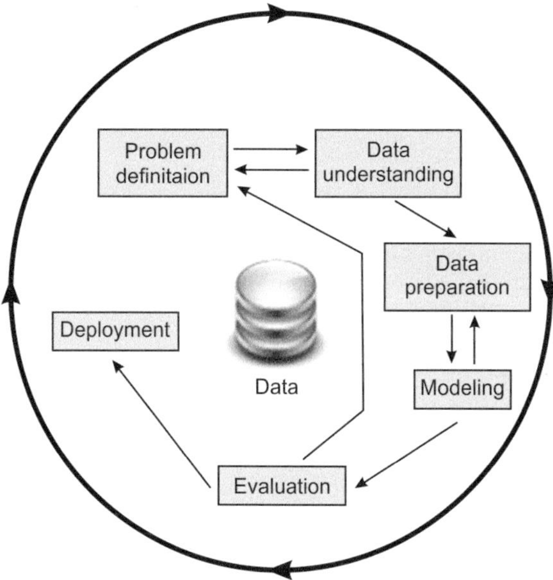

Figure 2.2 Data mining process

A brief description about these phases is as follows.

Problem definition phase

The main focus of the first phase of a data mining process is to understand the requirements and objectives of such a project. Once the project has been specified, it can be formulated as a data mining problem. After this, a preliminary implementation plan can be developed.

Let us consider a business problem such as 'How can I sell more of my product to customers?' This business problem can be translated into a data mining problem such as 'Which customers are most likely to buy the product?' A model that predicts the frequent customers of a product must be built on the previous records of customers' data. Before building the model, the data must be assembled that consists of relationships between customers who have purchased the product and customers who have not purchased the product. The attributes of customers might include age, years of residence, number of children, owners/renters, and so on.

Data understanding phase

The next phase of the data mining process starts with the data collection. In this phase, data is collected from the available sources and in order to make data collection proper, some important activities such as data loading and data integration are performed. After this, the data is analyzed closely to determine whether the data will address the business problem or not. Therefore, additional data can be added or removed to solve the problem effectively. At this stage missing data is also identified. For example, if we require the AGE attribute for a record then column DATE_OF_BIRTH can be changed to AGE. We can also consider another example in which average income can be inserted if value of column INCOME is null. Moreover, new computed attributes can be added in the data in order to obtain better focused information. For example, a new attribute such as 'Number of Times Amount Purchased Exceeds Rs. 500 in a 12 month time period.' can be created instead of using the purchase amount.

Data preparation phase

This phase generally consumes about 90% of the time of a project. Once available data sources are identified, they need to be selected, cleaned, constructed and formatted into the desired form for further processing.

Modeling phase

In this phase, different data mining algorithms are applied to build models. Appropriate data mining algorithms are selected and applied on given data to achieve the objectives of proposed solution.

Evaluation phase

In the evaluation phase, the model results are evaluated to determine whether it satisfies the originally stated business goal or not. For this the given data is divided into training and testing datasets. The models are trained on training data and tested on testing data. If the accuracy of models on testing data is not adequate then one goes back to the previous phases to fine tune those areas that may be the reasons for low accuracy. Having achieved a satisfactory level of accuracy, the process shifts to the deployment phase.

Deployment phase

In the deployment phase, insights and valuable information derived from data need to be presented in such a way that stakeholders can use it when they want to. On the basis of requirements of the project, the deployment phase can be simple (just creating a report) or complex (requiring further iterative data mining processing). In this phase, Dashboards or Graphical User Interfaces are built to solve all the requirements of stakeholders.

2.6 Data Mining Techniques

Data mining can be classified into four major techniques as given below.

- Predictive modeling
- Database segmentation
- Link analysis
- Deviation detection

To briefly discuss each technique:

2.6.1 Predictive modeling

Predictive modeling is based on predicting the outcome of an event. It is designed on a pattern similar to the human learning experience in using observations to form a model of the important characteristics of some task. It is developed using a supervised learning approach, where we have some labeled data and we use this data to predict the outcome of unknown instances. It can be of two types, i.e., classification or regression as discussed in Chapter 1.

Some of the applications of predictive modeling are: predicting the outcome of an event, predicting the sale price of a property, predicting placement of students, predicting the score of any team during a cricket match and so on.

2.6.2 Database segmentation

Database segmentation is based on the concept of clustering of data and it falls under unsupervised learning, where data is not labeled. This data is segmented into groups or clusters based on its features or attributes. Segmentation is creating a group of similar records that share a number of properties.

Applications of database segmentation include customer segmentation, customer churn, direct marketing, and cross-selling.

2.6.3 Link analysis

Link analysis aims to establish links, called associations, between the individual record, or sets of records, in a database. There are three specialisations of link analysis.

- Associations discovery
- Sequential pattern discovery
- Similar time sequence discovery

Associations discovery locates items that imply the presence of other items in the same event. There are association rules which are used to define association. For example, 'when a customer rents property for more than two years and is more than 25 years old, in 40% of cases, the customer will buy a property. This association happens in 35% of all customers who rent properties'.

Sequential pattern discovery finds patterns between events such that the presence of one set of items is followed by another set of items in a database of events over a period of time. For example, this approach can be used to understand long-term customer buying behavior.

Time sequence discovery is used to determine whether links exist between two sets of data that are time-dependent. For example, within three months of buying property, new home owners will purchase goods such as cookers, freezers, and washing machines.

Applications of link analysis include market basket analysis, recommendation system, direct marketing, and stock price movement.

2.6.4 Deviation detection

Deviation detection is a relatively new technique in terms of commercially available data mining tools. It is based on identifying the outliers in the database, which indicates deviation from some previously known expectation and norm. This operation can be performed using statistics and visualization techniques.

Applications of deviation detection include fraud detection in the use of credit cards and insurance claims, quality control, and defects tracing.

2.7 Difference between Data Mining and Machine Learning

Data mining refers to extracting knowledge from a large amount of data, and it is a process to discover various types of patterns that are inherent in the data and which are accurate, new and useful. It is an iterative process and is used to uncover previously unknown trends and patterns in vast amount of data in order to support decision making.

Data mining is the subset of business analytics; it is similar to experimental research. The origins of data mining are databases and statistics. Two components are required to implement data mining techniques: the first is the database and the second is machine learning.

Data mining as a process includes data understanding, data preparation and data modeling; while machine learning takes the processed data as input and performs predictions by applying algorithms. Thus, data mining requires involvement of human beings to clean and prepare the data and to understand the patterns. While in machine learning human effort is involved only to define an algorithm, after which the algorithm takes over operations. Tabular comparison of data mining and machine learning is given in Table 2.1.

Table 2.1 Tabular comparison of data mining and machine learning

Basic for comparison	*Data mining*	*Machine learning*
Meaning	It involves extracting useful knowledge from a large amount of data.	It introduces new algorithm from data as well as past experience.
History	Introduced in 1930 it was initially called knowledge discovery in databases.	It was introduced in 1959.
Responsibility	Data mining is used to examine patterns in existing data. This can then be used to set rules.	Machine learning teaches the computer to learn and understand the given rules.
Nature	It involves human involvement and intervention.	It is automated, once designed it is self-implementing and no or very little human effort is required.

In conclusion the analysis of huge amounts of data generated over Internet or by traditional database management systems is an important task. This analysis of data has the huge potential to improve business returns. Data mining and machine learning play vital roles in understanding and analyzing data. Thus, if data is considered as oil, data mining and machine learning are equivalent to modern day oil refineries that make this data more useful and insightful.

Remind Me

- Data mining is a process of automated discovery of previously unknown patterns in large volumes of data.
- Data mining process consists of six phases, namely problem definition, data understanding, data preparation, modeling, evaluation and deployment.
- The important applications of data mining are in finance, telecom, insurance and retail sectors; and include loan/credit card approval, fraud detection, market segmentation, trend analysis, focused marketing, market basket analysis, customer churn and web-site design.
- There are four main operations associated with data mining techniques, namely, predictive modeling, database segmentation, link analysis and deviation Detection.

Point Me (Books)

- Han, Jiawei, Micheline Kamber, and Jian Pei. 2011. *Data Mining: Concepts and Techniques*, 3rd ed. Amsterdam: Elsevier.
- Gupta, G. K. 2014. *Introduction to Data Mining with Case Studies*. Delhi: PHI Learning Pvt. Ltd.
- Mitchell, Tom M. 2017. *Machine Learning*. Chennai: McGraw Hill Education.
- Witten, Ian H., Eibe Frank, Mark A. Hall, and Christopher Pal. 2016. *Data Mining: Practical Machine Learning Tools and Techniques*, 4th ed. Burlington: Morgan Kaufmann.

Connect Me (Internet Resources)

- https://www.kdnuggets.com/data_mining_course/x1-intro-to-data-mining-notes.html
- https://www.cse.iitb.ac.in/infolab/Data/Talks/datamining-intro-IEP.ppt
- https://tutorials.datasciencedojo.com/data-mining-fundamentals-part-1-3/

Test Me

1. What is the full form of KDD ....
2. Which learning approach is used by Database Segmentation?
   (a) Supervised Learning (b) Unsupervised Learning
3. Links between the individual record, or sets of records in a database is called ....
4. What are the two types of predictive modeling?
   (a) .... (b) ....
5. Deviation detection can be performed by using .... and .... techniques.
6. Predictive Modeling is developed using a supervised learning approach.
   (a) True (b) False
7. Data mining is ....
   (a) The process of automated discovery of previously unknown patterns in large volumes of data.
   (b) The stage of selecting the right data for a KDD process
   (c) A subject-oriented integrated time variant non-volatile collection of data in support of management
   (d) None of these
8. Value prediction uses the traditional statistical techniques of .... and ....
9. Classification falls under which technique of data mining?
   (a) Predictive modeling (b) Database segmentation
   (c) Link analysis (d) Deviation detection.

10. Regression falls under which technique of data mining?
    (a) Predictive modeling (b) Database segmentation
    (c) Link analysis (d) Deviation detection.
11. Clustering falls under which technique of data mining?
    (a) Predictive modeling (b) Database segmentation
    (c) Link analysis (d) Deviation detection.
12. Visualization is core part for which of following data mining technique?
    (a) Predictive modeling (b) Database segmentation
    (c) Link analysis (d) Deviation detection.
13. Association mining falls under which technique of data mining?
    (a) Predictive modeling (b) Database segmentation
    (c) Link analysis (d) Deviation detection.

Answer Keys:

1. Knowledge Discovery in Database; 2. (b); 3. Associations;
4. (a) Classification (b) Value prediction 5. Statistics, Visualization
6. (a); 7. (a); 8. Linear regression, Nonlinear regression;
9. (a); 10. (a); 11. (b); 12. (d);
13. (c).

3

Beginning with Weka and R Language

Chapter Objectives

- ✓ To learn to install Weka and the R language
- ✓ To demonstrate the use of Weka software
- ✓ To experiment with Weka on the Iris dataset
- ✓ To introduce basics of R language
- ✓ To experiment with R on the Iris dataset

3.1 About Weka

In this book, all data mining algorithms are explained with Weka and R language. The learner can perform and apply these algorithms easily using these well-know data mining tool and language. Let's first discuss the Weka tool.

Weka is an open-source software under the GNU General Public License System. It was developed by the Machine Learning Group, University of Waikato, New Zealand. Although named after a flightless New Zealand bird, 'WEKA' stands for Waikato Environment for Knowledge Analysis. The system is written using the object oriented language Java. Weka is data mining software and it is a set of machine learning algorithms that can be applied to a dataset directly, or called from your own Java code. Weka contains tools for data pre-processing, classification, regression, clustering, association rules, and visualization.

The story of the development of Weka is very interesting. It was initially developed by students of University of Waikato, New Zealand, as part of their course work on data mining. They had implemented all major machine learning algorithms as part of lab work for this course. In 1993, the University of Waikato began development of the original version of Weka, which became a mix of Tcl/Tk, C, and Makefiles. In 1997, the decision was made to redevelop Weka from scratch in Java, including implementations of modeling algorithms. In 2006, Pentaho Corporation acquired an exclusive license to use Weka for business intelligence.

This chapter will cover the installation of Weka, datasets available and will guide the learner about how to start experimentation using Weka. Later on we will discuss another data mining tool, R. Let us first discuss the installation process for Weka, step-by-step.

3.2 Installing Weka

Weka is freely available and its latest version can be easily downloaded from https://www.cs.waikato.ac.nz/ml/weka/downloading.html as shown in Figure 3.1.

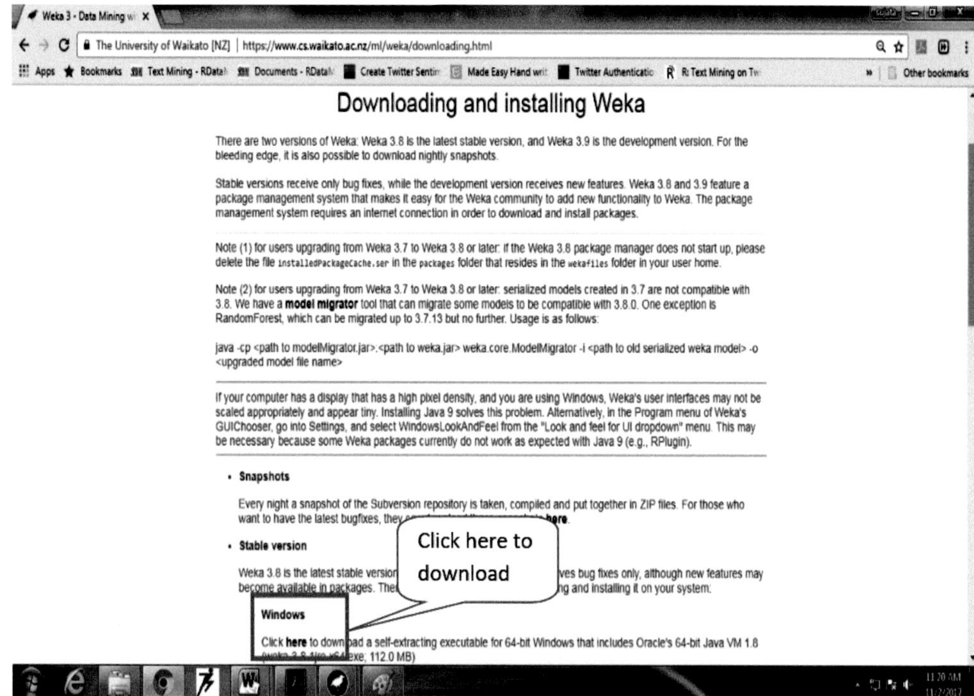

Figure 3.1 Downloading Weka

To work more smoothly, you must first download and install Java VM before downloading Weka.

3.3 Understanding Fisher's Iris Flower Dataset

R. A. Fisher's Iris Flower dataset is one of the most well-known datasets in data mining research. The Iris dataset is commonly used in texts on data mining to illustrate various approaches and tools. Becoming familiar with this dataset will aid you in using the data mining literature to advance your knowledge of the subject. Fisher's Iris dataset is available inside the 'data' folder of the Weka directory as 'iris.arff' or you can find it at link http://archive.ics.uci.edu/ml/datasets/Iris and can be downloaded as shown in Figure 3.2.

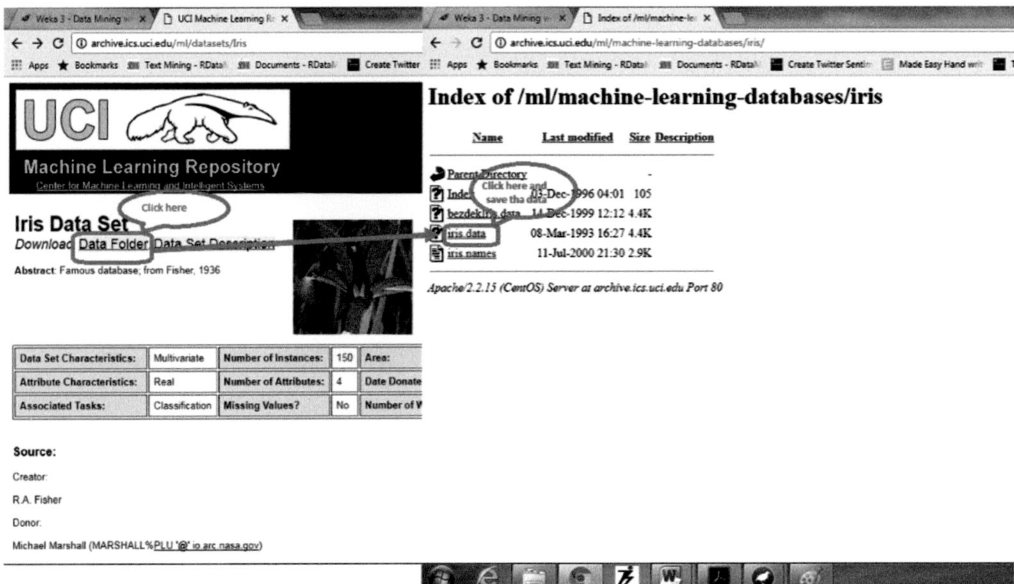

Figure 3.2 Downloading the Iris dataset

The origins of Fisher's dataset can be traced to Anderson's Iris dataset because Edgar Anderson collected the data to quantify the morphologic variation of Iris flowers of three related species. This dataset contains 50 samples of each of the three species, for a total of 150 samples. A sample of the Iris dataset is shown in Figure 3.3.

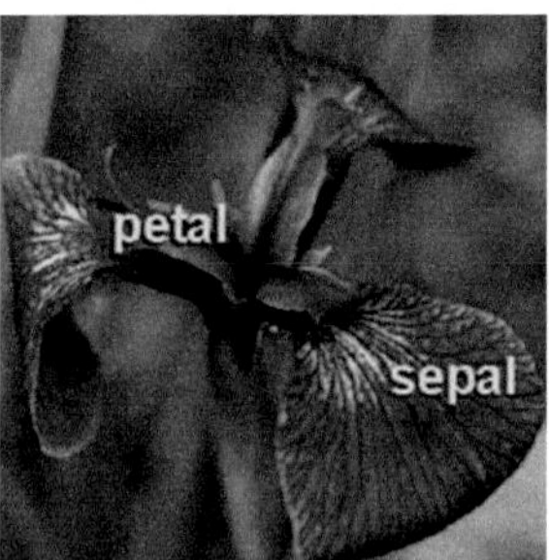

Figure 3.3 Sample of the Iris flower [see colour plate]

Anderson performed measurements on the three Iris species (i.e., Setosa, Versicolor, and Virginica) using four iris dimensions, namely, Sepal length, Sepal width, Petal length, and Petal width. He had observed that species of the flower could be identified on the basis of these four parameters. So, he prepared a dataset for its analysis. In data mining terminology, these four iris dimensions are termed as 'attributes' or 'input attributes'. The three iris species are known as 'classes', or 'output attributes' and each example of an iris is termed as 'sample', or 'instance'.

A section of the Fisher's dataset spreadsheet is given in Figure 3.4, showing the four input attributes and one output attribute, or class. This figure only shows five of the 150 instances, or samples, of irises. For this dataset, the input attributes are numerical attributes, meaning that the attributes are given as real numbers, in this case in centimeters. The output attribute is a nominal attribute, in other words, a name for a particular species of Iris.

Sample | Class

	Input Attributes				Output Attribute
Instance No.	Sepal Length	Sepal Width	Petal Length	Petal Width	Species
1	5.1	3.5	1.4	0.2	setosa
2	4.9	3	1.4	0.2	setosa
3	4.7	3.2	1.3	0.2	setosa
4	4.6	3.1	1.5	0.2	setosa
5	5	3.6	1.4	0.2	setosa

Numerical | Nominal

Figure 3.4 Sample of Fisher's dataset

3.4 Preparing the Dataset

The preferred Weka dataset file format is an Attribute Relation File Format (ARFF) format. Weka also accepts several alternative dataset file formats, one of them being the Comma Separated Values (CSV) file format. Commonly dataset is available in XLS (Excel file) format, and in order to process excel data with Weka, the first step we need to do is convert our XLS file into a CSV file. For this open the dataset spreadsheet by using excel in XLS format, and then choose ***Save As***, and then ***Other Formats.*** On this screen, we choose the file type as CSV as shown in Figure 3.5. When the information box appears, select ***Yes.*** In this way, we can open any XLS file in Weka by first converting it into CSV.

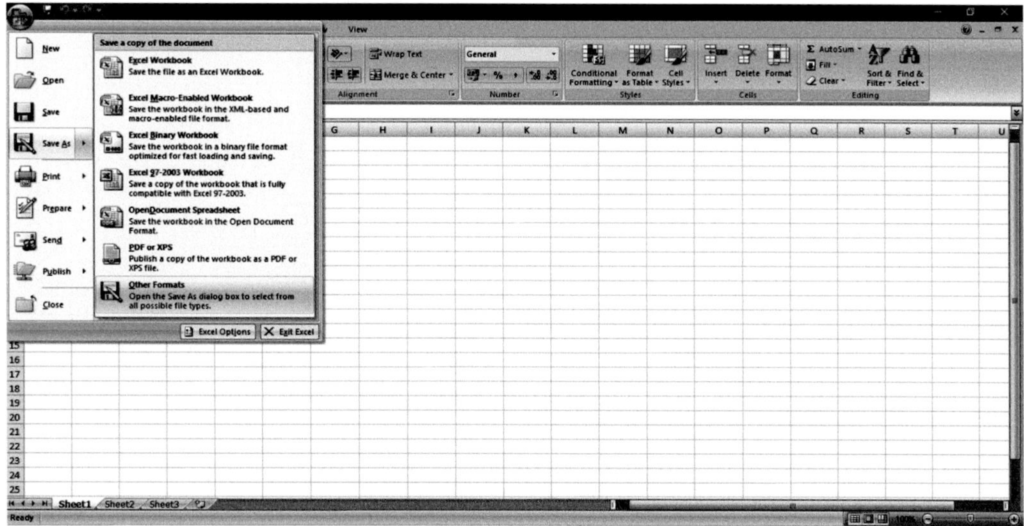

Figure 3.5 Save as 'Other Format'

3.5 Understanding ARFF (Attribute Relation File Format)

An ARFF file is an ASCII text file that describes a list of instances sharing a set of attributes. ARFF files were developed for use with the Weka machine learning software. ARFF files have two distinct sections. The first section is the Header information, which is followed by the Data information as shown in Figure 3.6.

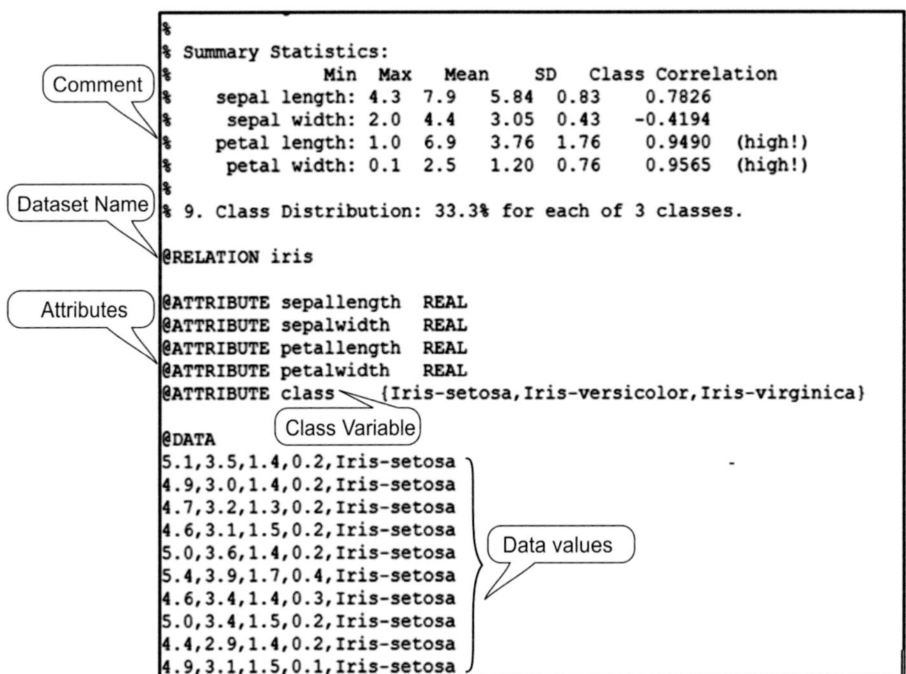

```
%
% Summary Statistics:
%                Min  Max   Mean    SD   Class Correlation
%    sepal length: 4.3  7.9   5.84  0.83    0.7826
%     sepal width: 2.0  4.4   3.05  0.43   -0.4194
%    petal length: 1.0  6.9   3.76  1.76    0.9490  (high!)
%     petal width: 0.1  2.5   1.20  0.76    0.9565  (high!)
%
% 9. Class Distribution: 33.3% for each of 3 classes.

@RELATION iris

@ATTRIBUTE sepallength  REAL
@ATTRIBUTE sepalwidth   REAL
@ATTRIBUTE petallength  REAL
@ATTRIBUTE petalwidth   REAL
@ATTRIBUTE class    {Iris-setosa,Iris-versicolor,Iris-virginica}

@DATA
5.1,3.5,1.4,0.2,Iris-setosa
4.9,3.0,1.4,0.2,Iris-setosa
4.7,3.2,1.3,0.2,Iris-setosa
4.6,3.1,1.5,0.2,Iris-setosa
5.0,3.6,1.4,0.2,Iris-setosa
5.4,3.9,1.7,0.4,Iris-setosa
4.6,3.4,1.4,0.3,Iris-setosa
5.0,3.4,1.5,0.2,Iris-setosa
4.4,2.9,1.4,0.2,Iris-setosa
4.9,3.1,1.5,0.1,Iris-setosa
```


Figure 3.6 ARFF format of IRIS dataset

3.5.1 ARFF header section

The header of the ARFF file contains the name of the relation, a list of the attributes (the columns in the data), and their types. The first line in the ARFF file defines the relation and its format is given as follows.

@relation <relation-name>

Where <relation-name> is a string and if the relation name consists of spaces then it must be quoted. The declaration of attributes includes an ordered sequence of @attribute statements. Each attribute of the dataset is defined by @attribute statement in the ARFF file which uniquely defines the name and data type of attribute. The format for the @attribute statement is given as follows.

@attribute <attribute-name> <datatype>

Where the <attribute-name> must start with an alphabetic character and if attribute-name consists of spaces then it must be quoted. The <datatype> can be of any types such as numeric, string, date and nominal. The keywords numeric, string and date are case insensitive. Numeric attributes can be real or integer numbers and string attributes consist of textual values. Date attribute is declared according to the format given as follows.

@attribute <name> date [<date-format>]

Where <name> represents attribute name and <date-format> is an optional string which represents that how date values should be printed. The default format string is 'yyyy-mm-dd hh:mm:ss' as shown below.

@RELATION Timestamps

@ATTRIBUTE timestamp DATE 'yyyy-mm-dd hh:mm:ss'

@DATA

'2018-05-15 10:15:10'

'2018-05-14 09:50:55'

Nominal values are defined by providing an <nominal-specification> listing the possible values: {<nominal-name1>, <nominal-name2>, <nominal-name3>, ...} as shown below.

For example, the class value of the Iris dataset can be defined as follows:

@ATTRIBUTE class {Iris-setosa, Iris-versicolor, Iris-virginica}

The values that contain spaces must be quoted.

The order sequence of declaration of the attributes indicates the column position of the attribute in the data section of the ARFF file. For example, if an attribute is declared at second position then Weka expects that all that attributes values will be found in the second comma delimited column.

3.5.2 ARFF data section

The ARFF Data section of the file contains the data declaration line and the actual instance lines.

The data declaration line consists of @data statement that is a single line representing the start of the data segment in the ARFF file. Each instance of the dataset is represented on a single line and the end of the instance is specified with carriage return. All the values of the attributes for each instance are delimited by commas and the missing values are represented by a single question mark. The format of the data section of ARFF file is given as follows.

@data

1.4, 2.3, 1.8, 1.5, ABC

The values of string and nominal attributes are case sensitive, and any that contain space must be quoted. For example, the ARFF format of IRIS dataset looks like as shown in Figure 3.6.

3.6 Working with a Dataset in Weka

When you install Weka, you can expect to find a Weka icon on your desktop. When you start up Weka, you will see the ***Weka GUI Chooser*** screen as shown in Figure 3.7.

From Weka Chooser, we can select any of the applications such as Explorer, Experimenter, KnowledgeFlow, Workbench and Simple CLI. The brief description about these applications is given in Table 3.1.

In this chapter, we will cover the application **Explorer** only as we can directly apply data mining algorithms through this option.

Figure 3.7 Weka GUI Chooser screen

Table 3.1 WEKA GUI applications

Application	*Description*
Explorer	It is an environment for exploring data.
Experimenter	This interface is for designing experiments with your selection of algorithms and datasets, running experiments and analyzing the results.
Knowledge Flow	It is a Java-Beans based interface to design configurations for streamed data processing.
Workbench	It is a unified graphical user interface that combines the other three such as Explorer, Experimenter and Knowledge Flow (and any plugins that the user has installed) into one application.
Simple CLI	It provides a simple command-line interface and allows direct execution of Weka commands.

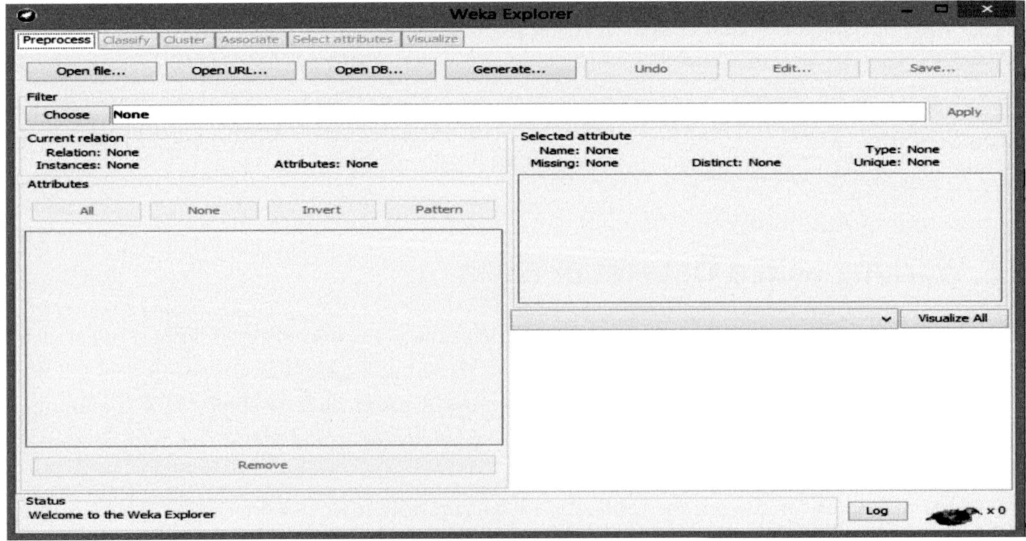

Figure 3.8 Weka Explorer screen

Select the ***Explorer*** application. Selecting the ***Explorer*** application displays the ***Weka Explorer*** screen as shown in Figure 3.8. Select the ***Preprocess*** tab to load the dataset to Weka. On the ***Preprocess*** tab, select ***Open file... and*** then select the ***FishersIrisDataset.csv*** file.

Note that all six attribute columns in our dataset have been recognized, and that all 150 instances have been read as shown in Figure 3.9. For the purpose of analysis, remove the instance number attribute by selecting it in the ***Attributes*** check box, or by clicking on it, as it does not play any role as shown in Figure 3.9.

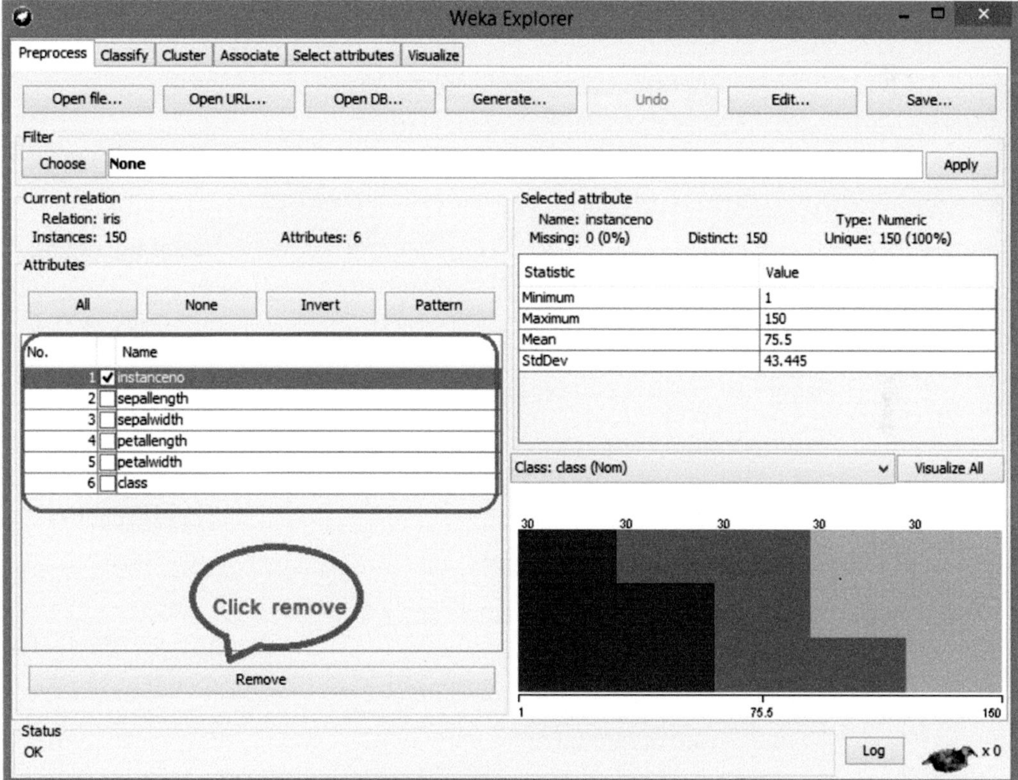

Figure 3.9 Loading Fisher's dataset

3.6.1 Removing input/output attributes

Since we have just removed an attribute, this would be a good point to ***save***. Here, we choose to save our modified dataset in the preferred Weka.arff file format. As expected, we are now working on just 5 total attributes, having removed the 'Instance' attribute as shown in Figure 3.10.

The Explorer Preprocess screen provides several types of information about our dataset. There are three main elements of this screen as shown in Figure 3.11.

i. The class designator,
ii. The attribute histogram,
iii. The attribute statistics.

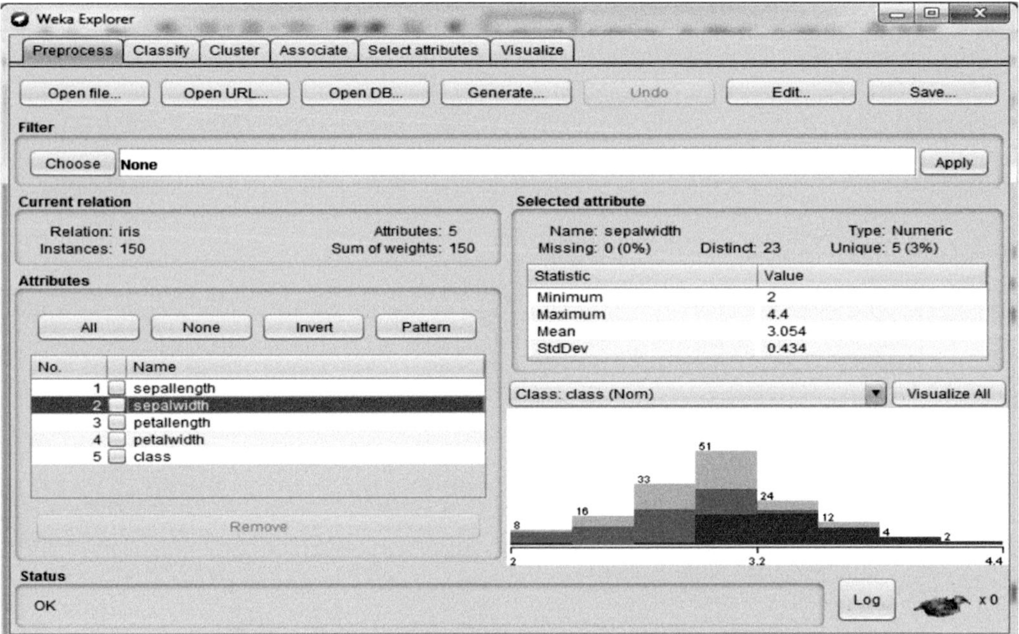

Figure 3.10 Fisher's dataset after removal of instance number

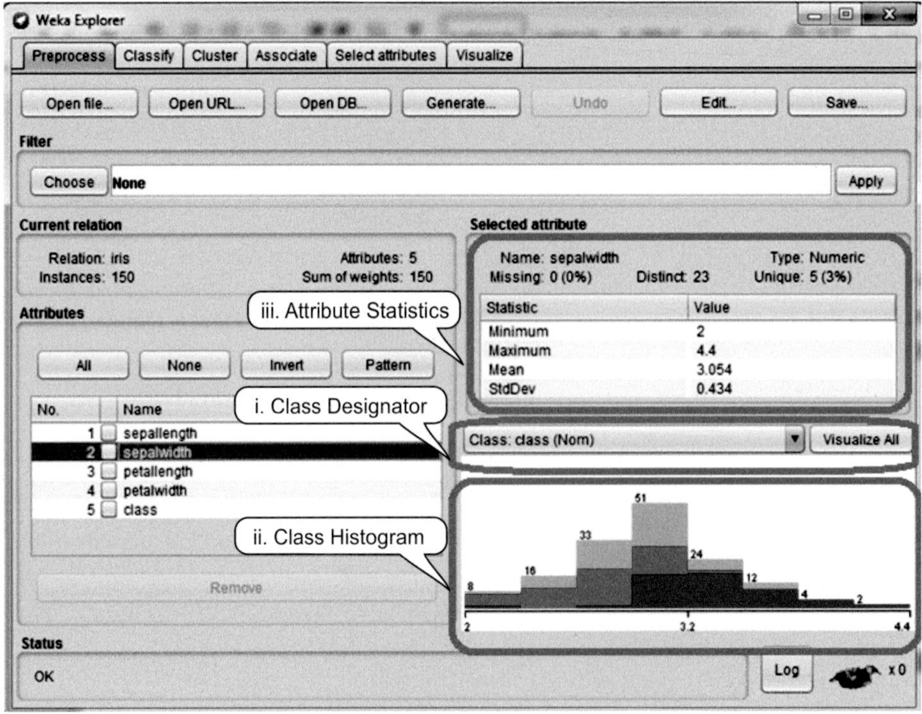

Figure 3.11 Elements of the Explorer screen

Expand the ***Class Designator*** box as shown in Figure 3.12. By default, the last (rightmost) column in the dataset is used as the output attributes, or class attribute. Here, class is by default considered as the output attribute to be used for classifying iris samples. Weka allows you to change the class attribute to any attribute in the dataset.

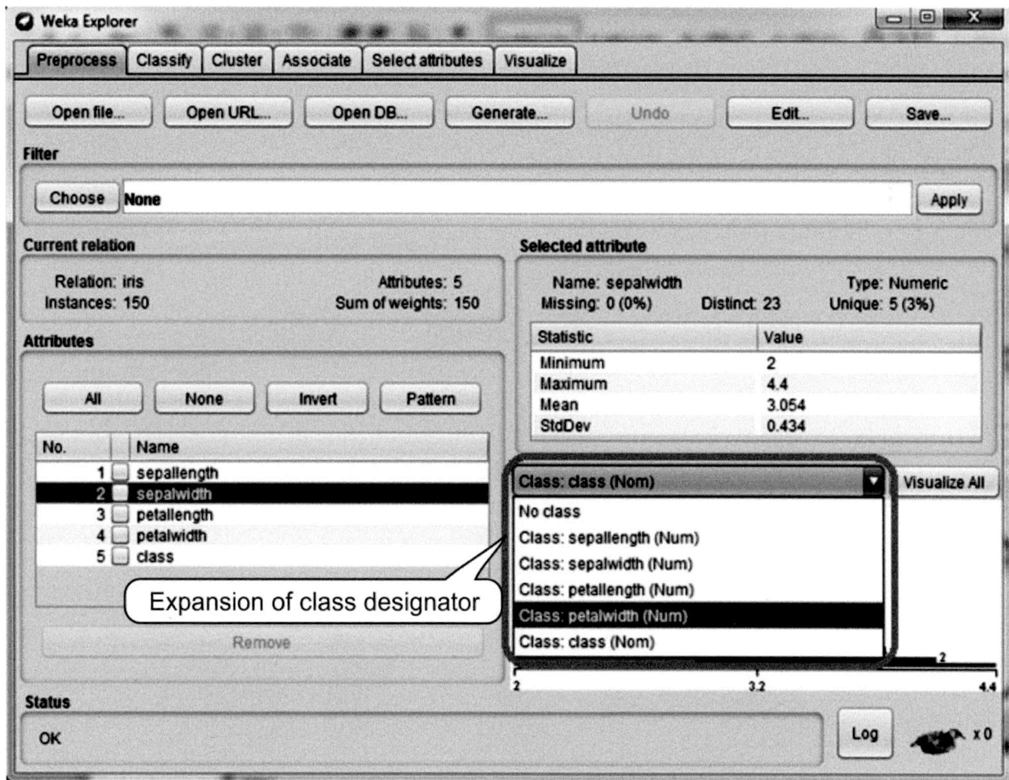

Figure 3.12 Expansion of class designator

3.6.2 Histogram

To see a histogram for any attribute, select it in the ***Attributes*** section of the ***Preprocess*** tab.

Figure 3.13 represents the histogram that shows us the distribution of Petal widths for all three species. As it turns out for this histogram, dark blue is Setosa, red is Versicolor, and bright blue is Virginica. The histogram shows that there are, for example, 49 samples in the lower histogram bin for Petal width, all of which are ***Iris-Setosa***, and shows that there are 23 samples in the highest bin, all of which are Virginica. The histogram also shows that there are 41 samples in the middle bin, in which most of the samples belong to Versicolor irises and rest are Virginica. Now, click on the ***Visualize All*** (as shown in Figure 3.13) button to see the histograms of all the attributes together.

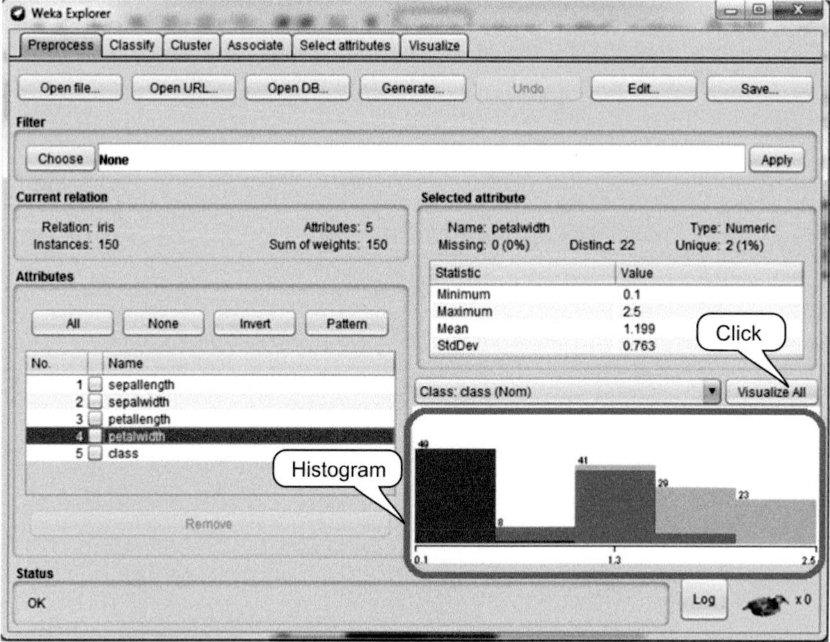

Figure 3.13 Histogram for Petal width [see colour plate]

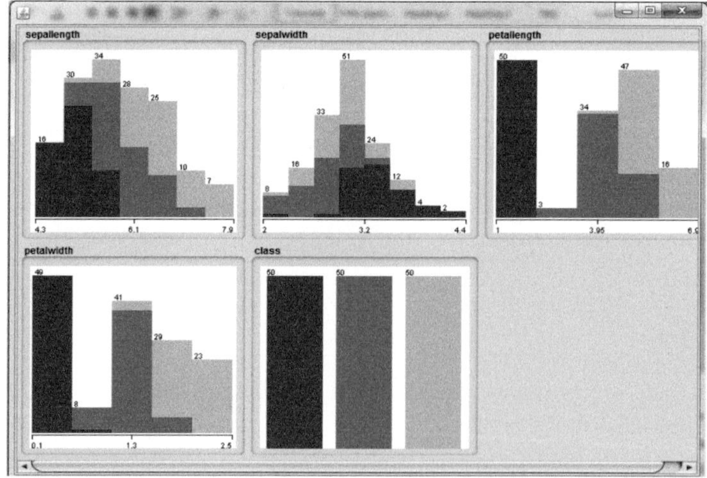

Figure 3.14 Histograms for all attributes of Iris dataset [see colour plate]

Figure 3.14 shows histograms for all input attributes of the iris dataset. By comparing the histograms for all of the input attributes, we can begin to get a sense of how the four input attributes vary with different iris species. For example, it appears that Iris Setosa tends to have relatively small Sepal length, Petal length, and Petal width, but relatively large Sepal width. These are the sorts of patterns that data mining algorithms use to perform classification and other functions. Notice also that the species histogram verifies that we have 50 of each iris species in our dataset.

3.6.3 Attribute statistics

In statistics for attributes, for example in case of Petal width attribute as shown in Figure 3.15, we see that we have no missing data, in other words, there are no instances in the dataset which are without Petal width measurement. It also shows basic statistics of the selected attribute in the form of its minimum, maximum, mean and standard deviation values as shown in Figure 3.15. It also provides values for two characteristics termed ***Distinct*** and ***Unique***.

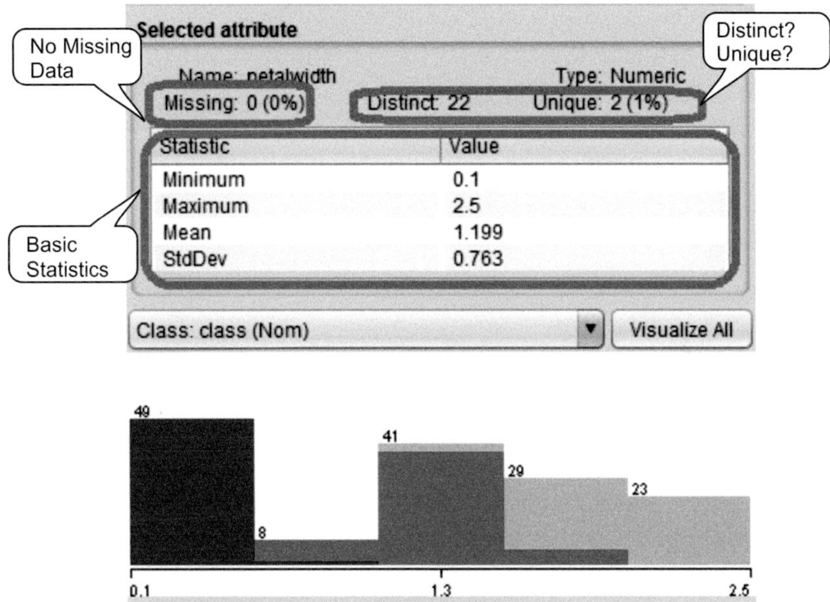

Figure 3.15 Attribute statistics [see colour plate]

First, consider the ***Distinct*** characteristic. The distinct characteristic shows how many different values are taken on by a particular attribute in the dataset. In case of Petal width attribute, we see a segment of the Iris Dataset showing seven of the 150 samples in the dataset as shown in Figure 3.16. For just this segment of seven samples in the iris dataset, we see four distinct values for Petal width, i.e., 0.1, 0.2, 0.6 and 0.3. There are a total of 22 distinct values for Petal width in the entire dataset of 150 samples.

The ***Unique*** characteristic on the Explorer screen tells us the total of Petal measurement values that appear only once in the full dataset, i.e. out of 150 samples. In the case of attribute 'Petal Width' we have three samples with Petal width of 0.1, 0.6 and 0.3 that are unique in selected instances of the dataset as shown in Figure 3.16. However, overall we have only 2 unique samples in the entire dataset of 150 samples as indicated in Figure 3.15.

To practice this concept, let us find distinct and unique values for the following dataset:

23, 45, 56, 23, 78, 90, 56, 34, 90

Solution:

Distinct: 6 (23, 45, 56, 78, 90, 34)

Unique: 3 (45, 78, 34)

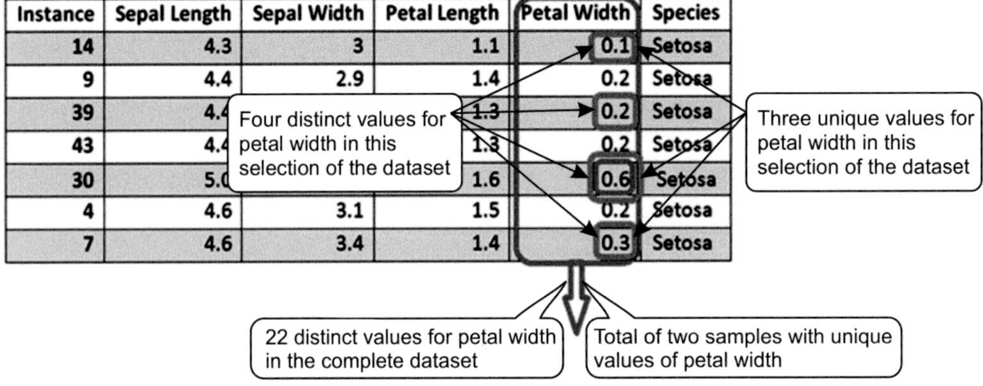

Instance	Sepal Length	Sepal Width	Petal Length	Petal Width	Species
14	4.3	3	1.1	0.1	Setosa
9	4.4	2.9	1.4	0.2	Setosa
39	4.4	[illegible]	1.3	0.2	Setosa
43	4.4	[illegible]	1.3	0.2	Setosa
30	5.0	[illegible]	1.6	0.6	Setosa
4	4.6	3.1	1.5	0.2	Setosa
7	4.6	3.4	1.4	0.3	Setosa

Figure 3.16 Distinct and Unique values

3.6.4 ARFF Viewer

With the ARFF Viewer, we can view the attributes and data of a dataset without loading of the dataset. When the ARFF Viewer opens up, select ***Open***, then find and open the Fisher's Iris dataset file. Figure 3.17 (a) shows how to open the ARFF Viewer from Weka GUI Chooser and further, Figure 3.17 (b) shows how to open a file in ARFF Viewer.

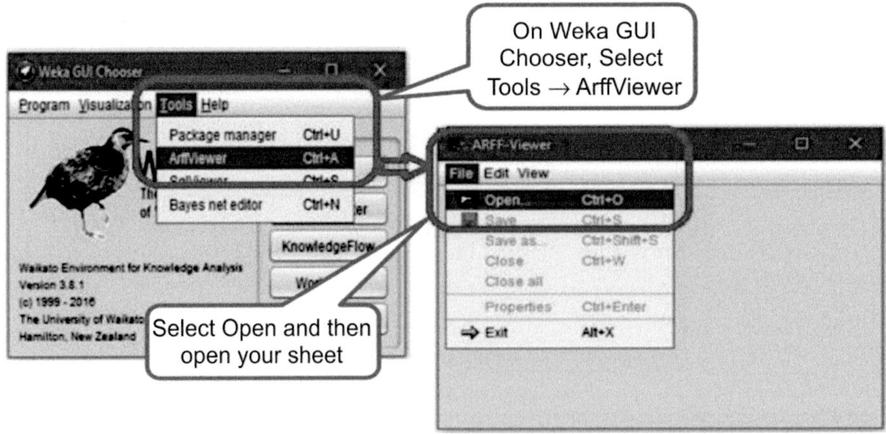

Figure 3.17 (a) Selecting ARFF Viewer from GUI Chooser and (b) opening the file in ARFF Viewer

Note that Weka has identified the Sepal and Petal values as numeric, and species as a nominal attribute. The highlighting of the label 'species' shows that this is specified as the class attribute for the dataset. It is important to note that we can perform a number of operations on the dataset using the AARF Viewer's File, Edit, and View functions. Figure 3.18 shows the ARFF Viewer of Fisher's dataset.

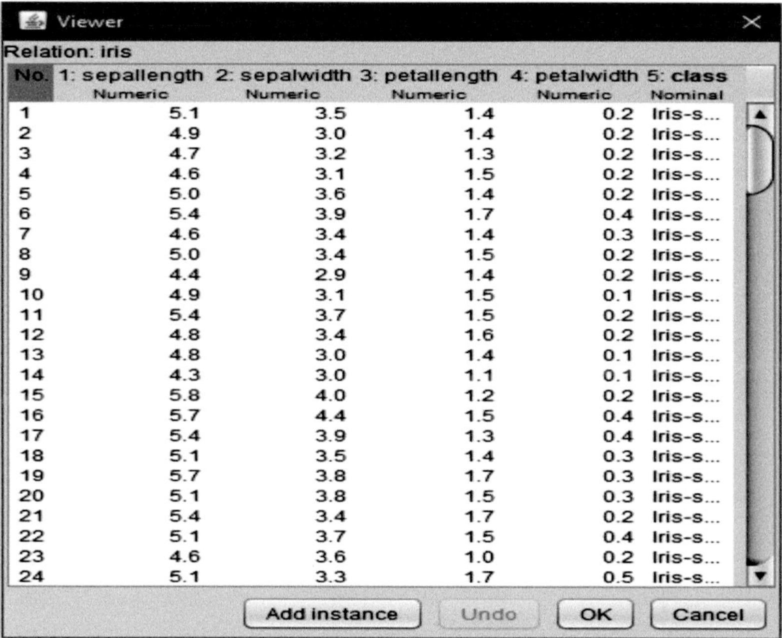

No.	1: sepallength Numeric	2: sepalwidth Numeric	3: petallength Numeric	4: petalwidth Numeric	5: class Nominal
1	5.1	3.5	1.4	0.2	Iris-s...
2	4.9	3.0	1.4	0.2	Iris-s...
3	4.7	3.2	1.3	0.2	Iris-s...
4	4.6	3.1	1.5	0.2	Iris-s...
5	5.0	3.6	1.4	0.2	Iris-s...
6	5.4	3.9	1.7	0.4	Iris-s...
7	4.6	3.4	1.4	0.3	Iris-s...
8	5.0	3.4	1.5	0.2	Iris-s...
9	4.4	2.9	1.4	0.2	Iris-s...
10	4.9	3.1	1.5	0.1	Iris-s...
11	5.4	3.7	1.5	0.2	Iris-s...
12	4.8	3.4	1.6	0.2	Iris-s...
13	4.8	3.0	1.4	0.1	Iris-s...
14	4.3	3.0	1.1	0.1	Iris-s...
15	5.8	4.0	1.2	0.2	Iris-s...
16	5.7	4.4	1.5	0.4	Iris-s...
17	5.4	3.9	1.3	0.4	Iris-s...
18	5.1	3.5	1.4	0.3	Iris-s...
19	5.7	3.8	1.7	0.3	Iris-s...
20	5.1	3.8	1.5	0.3	Iris-s...
21	5.4	3.4	1.7	0.2	Iris-s...
22	5.1	3.7	1.5	0.4	Iris-s...
23	4.6	3.6	1.0	0.2	Iris-s...
24	5.1	3.3	1.7	0.5	Iris-s...

Figure 3.18 ARFF Viewer of Fisher's dataset

3.6.5 Visualizer

It is also possible to do data visualization on our dataset from the Weka GUI Chooser. On the GUI Chooser, choose ***Visualization***, and then ***Plot*** as shown in Figure 3.19.

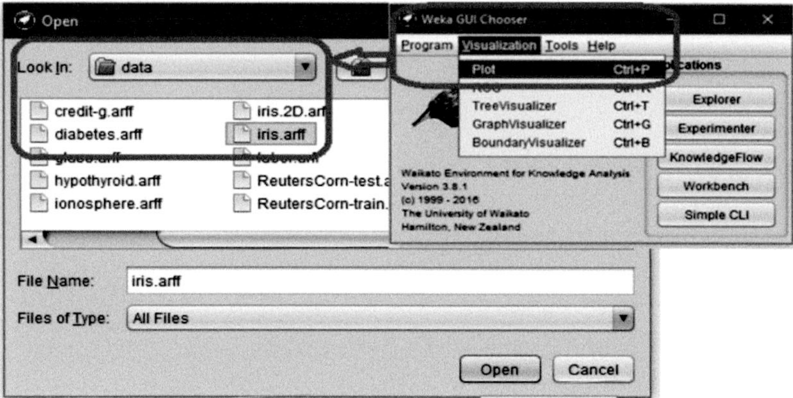

Figure 3.19 Visualization of dataset

Figure 3.20 shows the plot between Sepal length and Sepal width. Here, Sepal length is displayed on the x-axis, and Sepal width on the y-axis. Using the drop-down boxes, we can change the axes to other attributes.

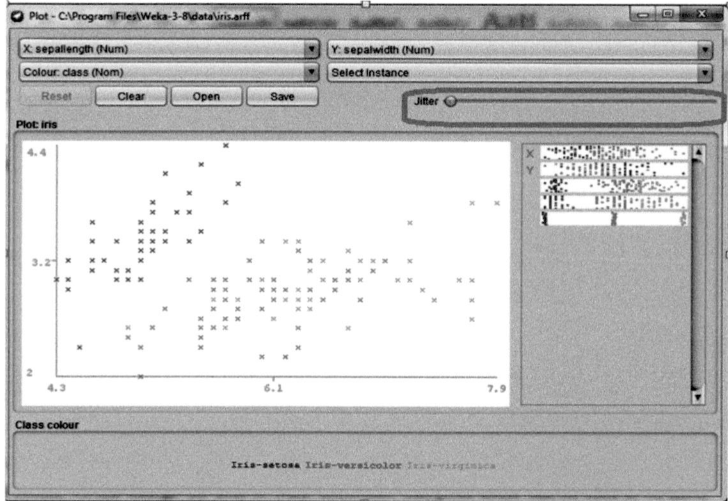

Figure 3.20 Plotting of dataset [see colour plate]

Jitter: Sometimes there are some overlapping data points in the dataset and it becomes difficult to analyze these points, therefore we add artificial random noise to the coordinates of the plotted points in order to spread the data slightly and the process of adding noise is called as Jitter.

In Weka, jitter slider can be used if we have points with the same or similar x-y coordinates. Increasing jitter adds noise to the values, thereby separating overlapping points. The plot screen also shows us which colors are associated with which classes on the various Weka screens. Note that plots of attributes can also be obtained by using the ***Weka Explorer*** option. To do this, switch from the ***Preprocess*** tab to the ***Visualize*** tab. The screenshots of Weka plots can be taken by left-clicking in the plot area that you want to capture. This brings up a Save screen with several file type options. If you want to get a screenshot of the entire screen, you can use your computer's Print Screen feature.

In the next section, the well known programming language **R** for implementing data mining algorithms has been discussed.

3.7 Introduction to R

R is a programming language for statistical computing and graphics. It was named R on the basis of the first letter of first name of the two R authors (Robert Gentleman and Ross Ihaka). It was developed at the University of Auckland in New Zealand. R is freely available under the GNU General Public License, and pre-compiled binary versions are provided for various operating systems like Linux, Windows and Mac.

This section will cover the installation of R, basic operations in R, loading of datasets in R. Let us discuss each process step-by-step.

3.7.1 Features of R

The basic features of R are given as follows.

- R is a well-developed, simple and effective programming language which includes conditionals, loops, user defined recursive functions and input and output facilities.
- R has an effective data handling and storage facility.
- R provides a suite of operators for calculations on arrays, lists, vectors and matrices.
- R provides a large, coherent and integrated collection of tools for classification, clustering, time-series analysis, linear and non-linear modeling.
- R provides graphical facilities for data analysis and display either directly at the computer screen or for printing on paper.

3.7.2 Installing R

R can be downloaded from one of the mirror sites available at http://cran.r-project.org/mirrors.html as shown in Figure 3.21.

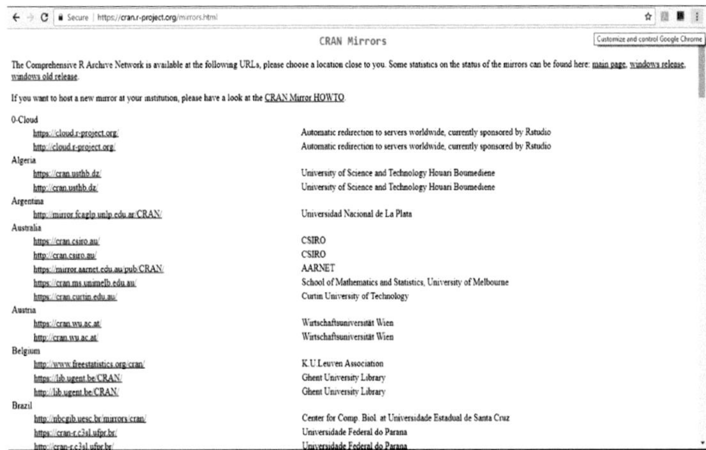

Figure 3.21 Screenshot of download link for R

After installation of R, the console screen of R will look as shown below in Figure 3.22.

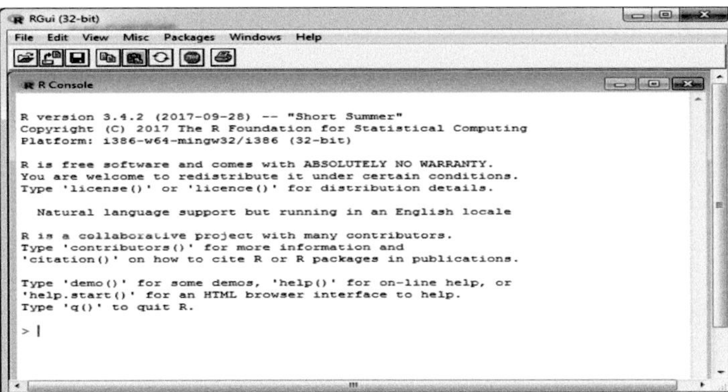

Figure 3.22 Console screen of R

Depending on the needs, you can program either at R command prompt or you can use an R script file to write your program. After R is started, there is a console waiting for input. At the prompt *(>)*, you can start typing your program.

3.8 Variable Assignment and Output Printing in R

In R, a variable name consists of letters, numbers and the dot or underline characters. The variable name starts with a letter or the dot not followed by a number. The variables can be assigned values using leftward, rightward and equal to operator. The values of the variables can be printed using *print( )* or *cat( )* function. *cat( )* function combines multiple items into a continuous print output as shown in Figure 3.23.

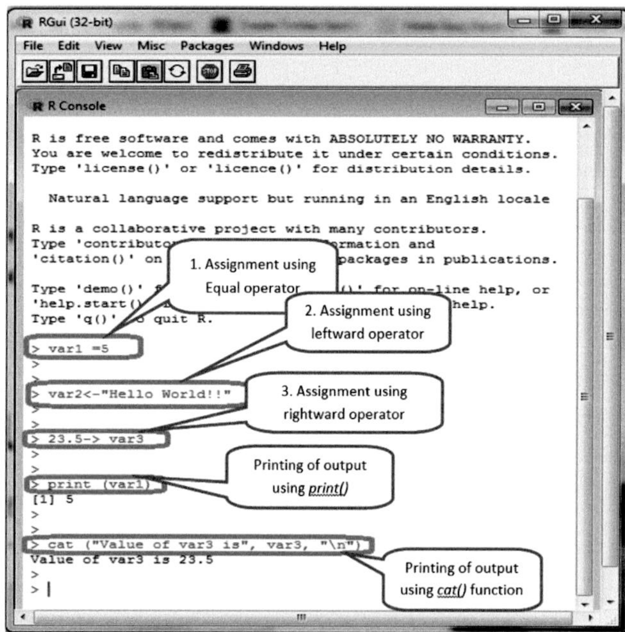

Figure 3.23 Basic syntax in R

3.9 Data Types

In R, there is no need to declare the data type of variables as we do in other programming languages such as Java and C. The variables are assigned with R-Objects and the data type of the R-object becomes the data type of the variable.

The data type of a variable can be identified using the *class( )* function as shown in Figure 3.24. Here, the variables ***var1*** and ***var3*** represent the data type numeric as we have assigned a numeric value 5 and 23.5 to variable *var1* and *var3* respectively. Similarly, ***var2*** represents the data type character as a character string is being assigned to *var2*.

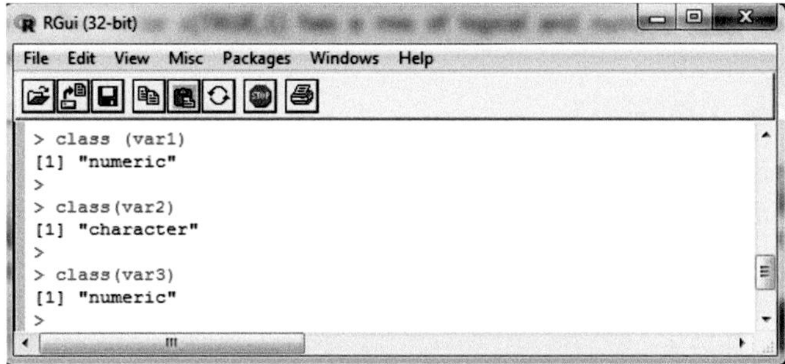

Figure 3.24 Data type of a variable

There are five basic data types in R such as numeric (real or decimal), integer, classic, logical and character. The brief description about these data types with examples is given in Table 3.2.

Table 3.2 Description about basic data types

Data Type	*Description*	*Examples*
Character	A character object is used to represent string values.	'A', 'I am learning programming'
Numeric	Numeric stores the real or decimal values.	10, 25.2
Integer	Integer is used to store integer values.	2L (the L tells R to store this as an integer)
Logical	A logical value is created via comparison between variables.	TRUE, FALSE
Complex	A complex value in R is defined via the pure imaginary value *i*.	2+5*i* (complex numbers with real and imaginary parts)

3.10 Basic Operators in R

R has many operators to carry out different operations and can be classified into the following categories such as arithmetic, relational, logical and assignment operators. These basic operators are summarized in Table 3.3.

Table 3.3 Summary about basic operators of R

Type	*Operators*
Arithmetic	+, -, *, %%, ^
Relational	<. >, <=, >=, !=
Logical	&, |, &&, ||, !
Assignment	=, <-, ->

A brief description about the working of these operators is given as follows.

3.10.1 Arithmetic operators

The arithmetic operators available in R are addition (+), subtraction (-), division (/), multiplication (*), exponent (^) and modulus (%%). Figure 3.25 shows the execution of basic arithmetic operations in the R console.

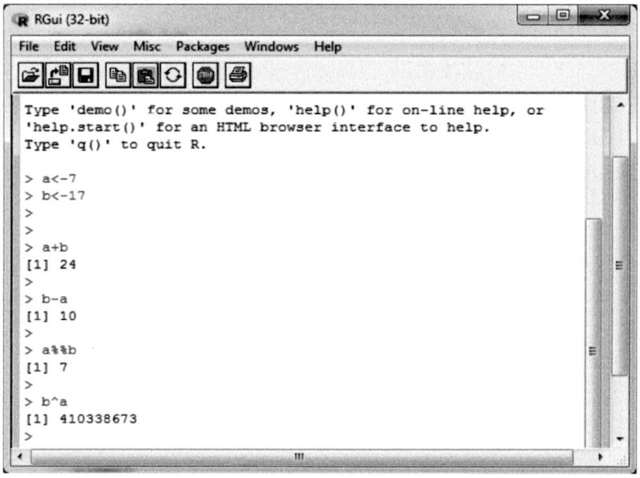

```
RGui (32-bit)
File Edit View Misc Packages Windows Help
Type 'demo()' for some demos, 'help()' for on-line help, or
'help.start()' for an HTML browser interface to help.
Type 'q()' to quit R.

> a<-7
> b<-17
>
>
> a+b
[1] 24
>
> b-a
[1] 10
>
> a%%b
[1] 7
>
> b^a
[1] 410338673
>
```

Figure 3.25 Screenshot of basic arithmetic operators

3.10.2 Relational operators

Relational operators are used to compare values. In R, relational operators are less than (<), greater than (>), less than equal to (<=), greater than equal to (>=) and not equal to (!=). Figure 3.26 shows the working of basic relational operators at R console.

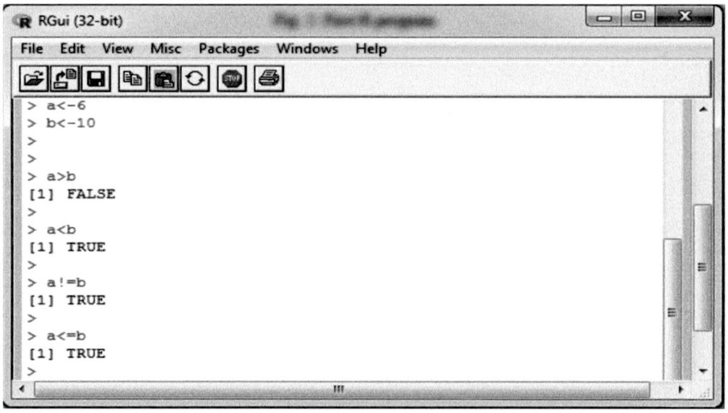

```
RGui (32-bit)
File Edit View Misc Packages Windows Help
> a<-6
> b<-10
>
>
> a>b
[1] FALSE
>
> a<b
[1] TRUE
>
> a!=b
[1] TRUE
>
> a<=b
[1] TRUE
>
```

Figure 3.26 Relational operators in R

3.10.3 Logical operators

In case of logical operators, Zero is considered FALSE and non-zero numbers are taken as TRUE. The basic logical operators are ***logical not*** **(!)**, ***logical AND*** **(&&)**, ***logical OR*** **(||)**, ***element-wise AND*** **(&)** and ***element-wise OR*** **(|)**. Figure 3.27 shows the working of logical operators at R console.

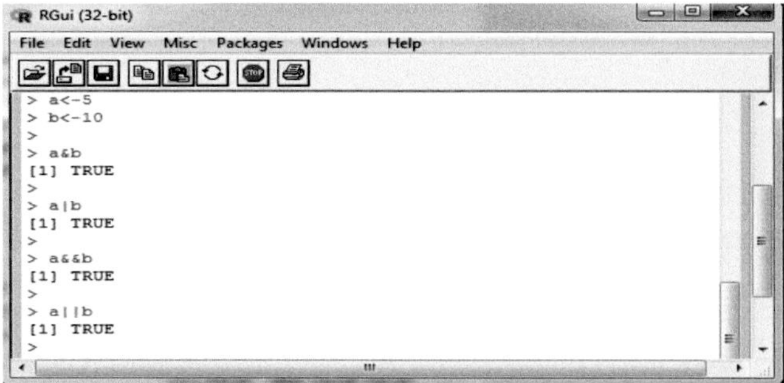

Figure 3.27 Working of logical operators

3.10.4 Assignment operators

The main assignment operators are equal to (=), leftward (<-) and rightward (->) direction. The working of these operators has already been shown in Figure 3.23.

3.11 Installing Packages

R packages are a collection of R functions, compiled code and sample data. They are stored under a directory called 'library' in the R environment. The already installed packages can be checked using the ***library()*** command as shown in Figure 3.28.

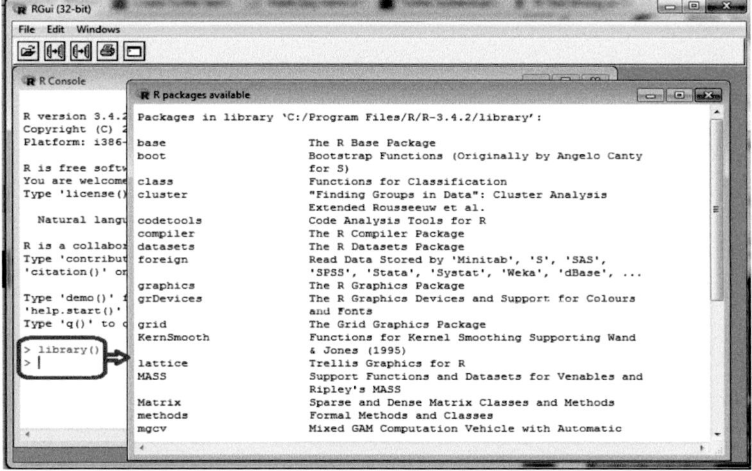

Figure 3.28 Checking of already installed packages

Sometimes, we need additional functionality beyond those offered by the core R library. In order to install an extension package, you should invoke the ***install.packages()*** function at the prompt and follow the instruction. R packages can be installed in two ways,either directly from the CRAN (Comprehensive R Archive Network) directory; Or, by downloading the package to your local system and installing it manually. The most frequently used method is installation from the CRAN directory. So, in this chapter, we will discuss the installation of R packages through this method.

The following command gets the packages directly from CRAN webpage and installs the package in the R environment. You may be prompted to choose a nearest mirror.

```
install.packages("Package Name")
```

When the command ***install.packages ('XML')*** is executed to install the package, a window prompts for the selection of nearest CRAN mirror as shown in Figure 3.29. Then, select any nearest mirror and click ***OK***.

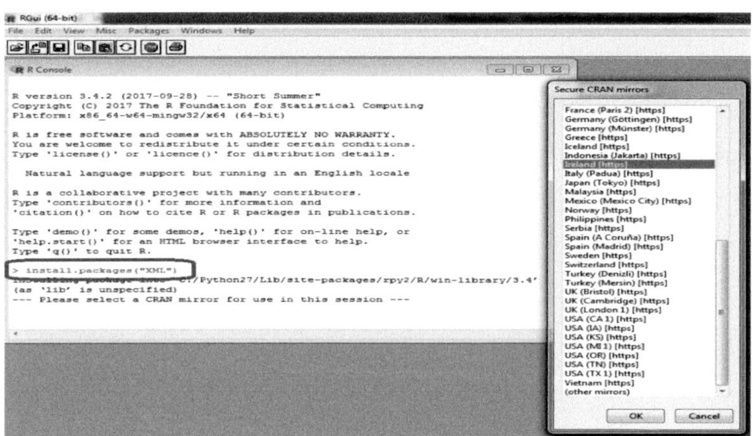

Figure 3.29 Installation of a new package

Figure 3.30 represents the successful installation of package XML.

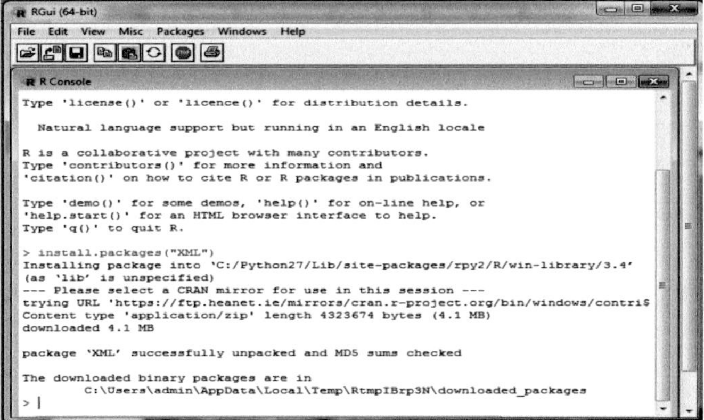

Figure 3.30 Console after successful installation of package

Some of the important machine learning or data mining packages

Table 3.4 provides some of the important machine learning packages along with their description that need to be installed for performing data analysis such as classification, clustering, association mining, etc. More details about these topics will be presented in subsequent chapters.

Table 3.4 Some of the important machine learning packages

Sr. No.	*Package Name*	*Description*
1.	e1071	This package is used for implementing Naïve Bayes (conditional probability), SVM, Fourier Transforms, Bagged Clustering, Fuzzy Clustering, etc.
2.	CORElearn	It is used for classification, regression, feature evaluation and ordinal evaluation.
3.	randomForest	It is used to create large number of decision trees and then each observation is inputted into the decision tree.
4.	Arules	This package is used for Mining Association Rules and Frequent Itemsets.
5.	MICE	This package is used to assign missing values by using multiple techniques, depending on the kind of data.
6.	RPART (Recursive Partitioning and Regression Trees)	It is used to build classification or regression models using a two stage procedure and the resultant models are represented in the form of binary trees.
7.	nnet	This package is used for Feed-forward Neural Networks and Multinomial Log-Linear Models.

Further details about concepts like classification, clustering, association mining and otherswill follow in subsequent chapters.

3.12 Loading of Data

In R, we can upload the data using any file format such as .xls, .csv or .arff format. For this, we can use the function ***readfunction*** from the '***gdata***' package. It reads from an Excel spreadsheet or Comma Separated Values (CSV) or Attribute-Relation File Format (ARFF) format and returns a data frame. The following commands show how to load data named '***mydata***' using any of formats such as .xls, .csv or .arff.

```
>library(gdata)       # load gdata package
>mydata = read.xls("mydata.xls") # read from first sheet
Or
>mydata = read.csv("mydata.csv") # read from csv format
Or
>mydata = read.arff("mydata.arff") # read from arff format
```

3.12.1 Working with the Iris dataset in R

In R, some of the datasets are available in *datasets* library. The *dataset* library is first loaded to include any dataset of your choice. Then use the command ***data*** to load dataset as given below.

```
>library (datasets)          # load datasets package
> data (iris)                # load dataset
> names (iris)               # display attribute names
```

The execution of above commands for the Iris dataset is shown in Figure 3.31.

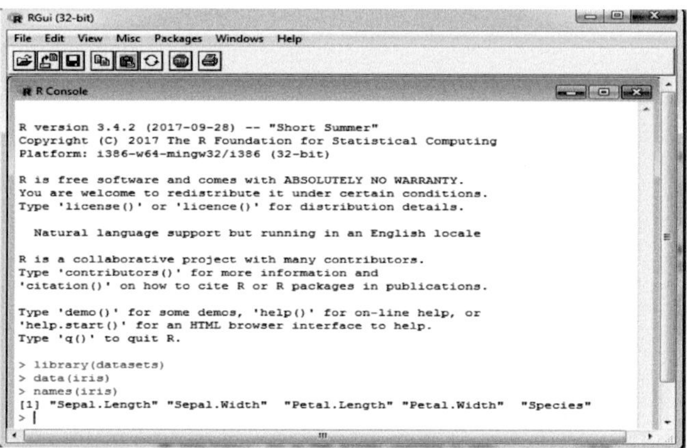

Figure 3.31 Attribute names of a dataset

The statistics of a dataset can be found using the ***summary()*** function. We can find the statistics about the whole dataset as well as of single column as given below. For example, Figure 3.32 shows the statistics of iris dataset as well as statistics of attribute Sepal Length.

```
> summary (iris)
> summary (iris$Sepal.Width)
```

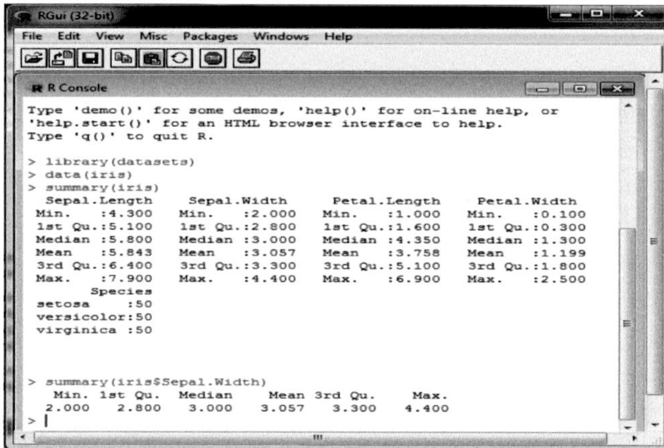

Figure 3.32 Statistics of Iris dataset

The dataset can be viewed using the function ***View()*** as shown in Figure 3.33. This figure shows the first 18 records of the iris dataset.

```
> View(iris) #To view the dataset instances
```

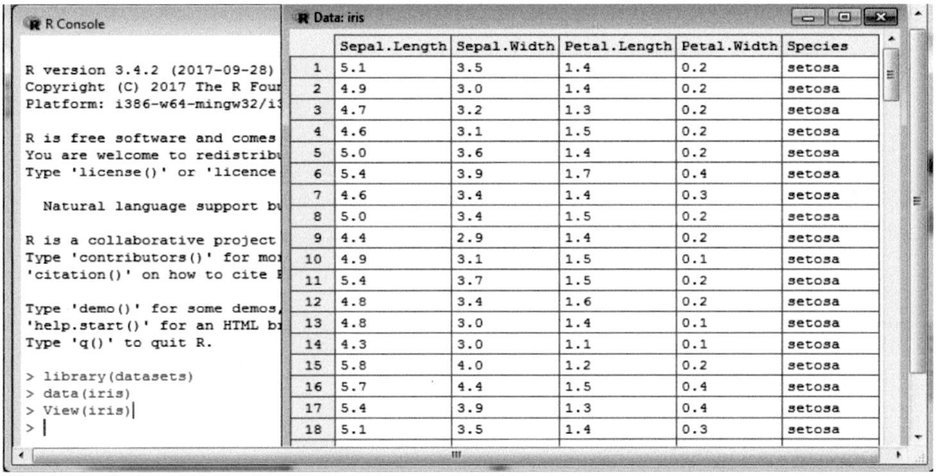

Figure 3.33 Viewing of dataset

We can also find the missing and unique values of an attribute in a dataset by using ***is.na()*** and ***unique()*** functions. Figure 3.34 shows that there are 23 unique values for the column Sepal Width and no missing value.

```
> is.na(iris$Sepal.Width) # To find the missing values
>length(unique(iris$Sepal.Width)) #To find the unique values
```

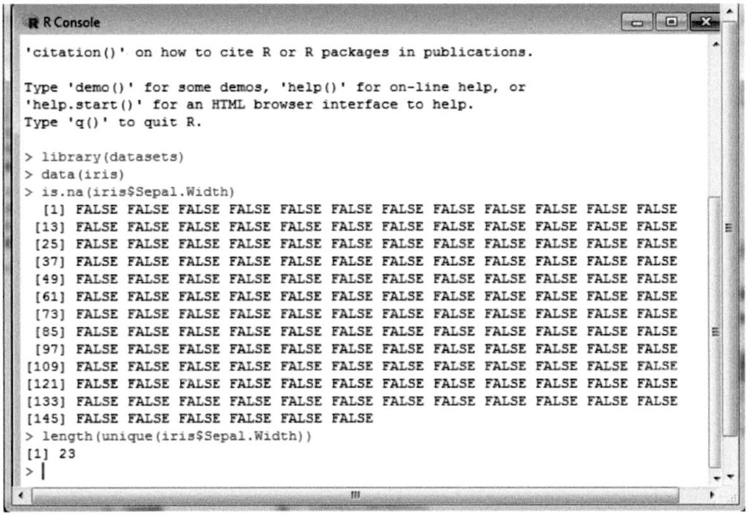

Figure 3.34 Identification of unique and missing values for Sepal width

The graph can be plotted for a dataset using the ***plot()*** function. For example, Figure 3.35 shows the plotting of Iris dataset in R.

```
> plot(iris) #To plot the graph of complete dataset
```

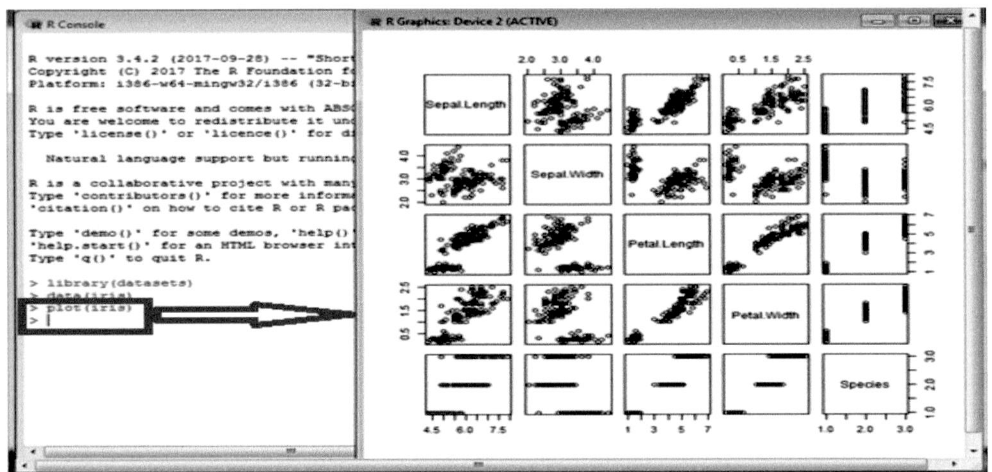

Figure 3.35 Plotting the Iris dataset

Similarly, a graph can also be plotted between any two columns using the ***plot()*** function. For example, Figure 3.36 shows the graph between columns Petal width and Petal length.

```
> plot(iris$Petal.Width, iris$Petal.Length) #To plot the graph of between any two attributes of dataset
```

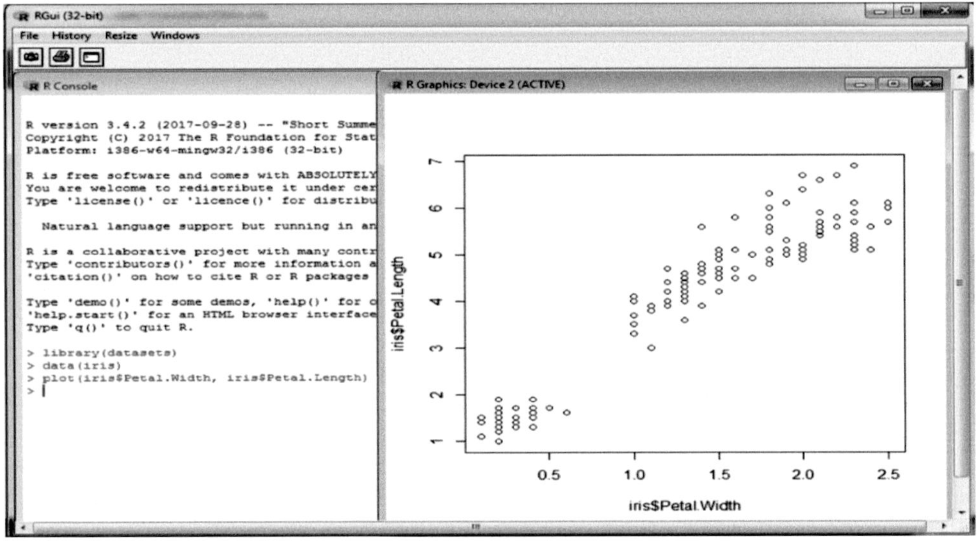

Figure 3.36 Plotting between Petal width and Petal length

We can also draw the histogram in R using the ***hist()*** function as shown in Figure 3.37.

```
> hist(iris$Sepal.Width) #To draw the histogram
```

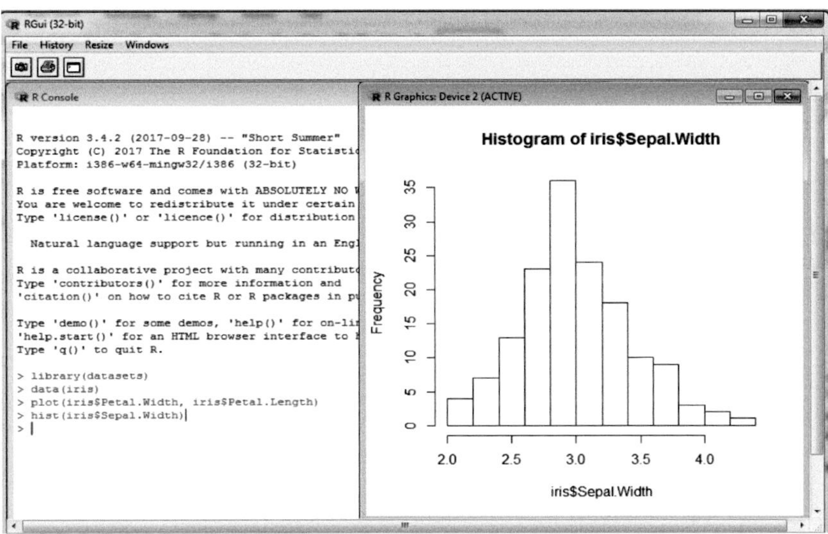

Figure 3.37 Histogram for Sepal width

Remind Me

- WEKA (Waikato Environment for Knowledge Analysis) is open-source software and named after a flightless New Zealand bird.
- Fisher's dataset is sometimes called Anderson's Iris dataset because Edgar Anderson collected the data to quantify the morphologic variation of Iris flowers of three related species.
- Weka accepts Attribute-Relation File Format (ARFF) format but it also accepts several alternative dataset file formats such as Comma Separated Values (CSV) file format.
- The process of adding noise to the coordinates of the plotted points in order to spread the data out a bit is called Jitter.
- R is a programming language for statistical computing and graphics and named on the basis of the first letter of the first name of the two R authors (Robert Gentleman and Ross Ihaka) at the University of Auckland, New Zealand.
- In R, there is no need to declare the data type of variables as we do in other programming languages such as Java and C.
- The five basic data types in R are numeric (real or decimal), integer, classic, logical and character.

Point Me (Books)

- Witten, Ian H., Eibe Frank, Mark A. Hall, and Christopher Pal. 2016. *Data Mining: Practical Machine Learning Tools and Techniques*, 4th ed. Burlington: Morgan Kaufmann.
- Lesmeister, Cory. 2015. *Mastering Machine Learning with R*. Birmingham: Packt Publishing Ltd.

Point Me (Video)

- Introduction to Weka, Parteek Bhatia, https://youtu.be/BxhPtYguXus

Connect Me (Internet Resources)

- https://www.slideshare.net/wekacontent/an-introduction-to-weka-2875221
- https://www.cs.auckland.ac.nz/courses/compsci367s1c/tutorials/IntroductionToWeka.pdf
- https://www.cs.waikato.ac.nz/ml/weka/
- https://onlinecourses.science.psu.edu/statprogram/r
- http://www.r-tutor.com/r-introduction

Do It Yourself

The purpose of this hands-on session is to verify that you have Weka installed and running.

1. Go to www.technologyforge.net/Datasets and download WineQuality.zip.
2. Unzip the folder and read WineQuality.pdf.
3. Convert WineQuality.xls file to .csv format and save as WineQuality.csv.
4. Open WineQuality.csv in Weka Explorer.
5. Save as WineQuality.arff (do not overwrite WineQuality.arff).
6. Using the 'Visualize All' button, display histograms of all attributes on one screen.
7. Perform the same operations by using the R Language.

Test Me

Answer these multiple choice questions based on your learning in this chapter.

1. What is total number of distinct values in the following dataset?

   12, 13, 14, 154, 14, 23, 13

   (a) 5 (b) 3 (c) 7 (d) none of the above
2. What is total number of unique values in the following dataset?

   12, 13, 14, 154, 14, 23, 13

   (a) 5 (b) 3 (c) 7 (d) none of the above
3. What would be the result of following R code?

   ```
   > x<-1
   > print(x)
   ```

   (a) 1 (b) 2 (c) 3 (d) All of the mentioned
4. The primary R system is available from the ____________

   (a) CRAN (b) CRWO (c) GNU (d) All of the mentioned
5. In 1991, R was created by Ross Ihaka and Robert Gentleman in the Department of Statistics at the University of ____________.

   (a) John Hopkins (b) California (c) Harvard (d) Auckland
6. If you explicitly want an integer, you need to specify the ____________ suffix.

   (a) D (b) R (c) L (d) All of the mentioned
7. Which of the following is not an open source data mining tool.

   (a) WEKA (b) R (c) RapidMiner (d) KnowledgeMiner

Answer Keys:

1. (a)	2. (b)	3. (a)	4. (a)
5. (d)	6. (c)	7. (d)	

4

Data Preprocessing

Chapter Objectives

- ✓ To understand the need for data preprocessing.
- ✓ To identify different phases of data preprocessing such as data cleaning, data integration, data transformation and data reduction

4.1 Need for Data Preprocessing

For any data analyst, one of the most important concerns is 'Data'. In fact, the representation and quality of data which is being used for carrying out an analysis is the first and foremost concern to be addressed by any analyst. In the context of data mining and machine learning, 'Garbage in, Garbage out', is a popular saying while working with large quantities of data.

Commonly, we end up having lot of noisy data; as an example, income: -400 i.e. negative income. Sometimes, we may have unrealistic and impossible combinations of data, for example, in a record, Gender-Male may be entered as Pregnant-Yes. Obviously absurd! because males do not get pregnant. We also suffer due to missing values and other data anomalies. Analyzing such sets of data, that have not been screened before analysis can cause misleading results. Hence, data preprocessing is the first step for any data mining process.

Data preprocessing is a data mining technique that involves transformation of raw data into an understandable format, because real world data can often be incomplete, inconsistent or even erroneous in nature. Data preprocessing resolves such issues. Data preprocessing ensures that further data mining process are free from errors. It is a prerequisite preparation for data mining, it prepares raw data for the core processes.

The University Management System Example

For any University Management System, a correct set of information about their students or vendors is of utmost importance in order to contact them. Hence, accurate and up to date student information is always maintained by a university. Correspondence sent to wrong address would, for instance, lead to a bad impression about the respective university.

Millions of Customer Support Centres across the globe also maintain correct and consistent data about their customers. Imagine a case where a call centre executive is not able to identify the client or customer that he is handling, through his phone number. Such scenarios suggest how reputation is at stake when it comes to accuracy of data. But, on the other hand obtaining the correct details of students or customers is a very challenging task. As most of the data is entered by data entry operators who are not paid well and consequently poorly motivated, these operators make a lot of mistakes while feeding the data into the systems, leading to data which is full of errors. Mistakes like same customer or student's entry might be visible twice in the system. These and other mistakes, are quite common due to data entry negligence. Hence, identification and correction of the data entry done by these operators is one of the basic challenges.

As example, let us consider the records of a vendor providing services to a university stored in different forms in different tables.

Table 4.1 Vendor's record extracted from the first source system

Supplier Name	Jugnoo Food Limited
Address	86 Gandhi Road
City	Indore
State	Madhya Pradesh
PIN	452001
Mobile Number	0731-7766028
Fax	0731-77766022
Email	info@jugnoo.co.in
Owner	Samitra nandan Singh
Last updated	7/12/2017

Table 4.2 Vendor's record extracted from the second source system by Supplier ID

Supplier ID	23234
Business name	JF Limited
Address	855 Gandhi Road
City	Indore
State	Madhya Pradesh
PIN	452001
Telephone	0731-77766028
Fax	0731-77766022
Email	info@jugnoo.co.in
Owner	Samitra N. Singh
Last updated	7/06/2018

Table 4.3 Vendor's record extracted from the third source system

Business name	Jugnoo Food Limited
Address	86 Gandhi Road
City	Indore
State	MP
PIN	Null
Telephone	0731-7766028
Fax	0731-7766022
Email	info@jugnoo.co.in
Owner	Samitra nandan Singh
Postal Address	PO Box 124
Last updated	7/12/2017

There are many errors and missing values in the records extracted from three different source systems. Compare with what the record should look like after it has gone through a preprocessing process.

Table 4.4 Vendor's record after pre-processing

Supplier ID	23234
Business Name	Jugnoo Food Ltd.
Address	86 Gandhi Road
City	Indore
State	Madhya Pradesh
PIN	452001
Postal address	PO Box 124
Telephone	0731-7766028
Fax	0731-7766022
Owner	Samitra Nandan Singh
Last updated	7/06/2018

Table 4.4 is the best information which we could derive from Tables 4.1, 4.2 and 4.3. There is still the possibility that it might contain errors, to remove which further information is required.

Data preprocessing is part of a very complex phase known as ETL (Extraction, Transformation and Loading). It involves extraction of data from multiple sources of data, transforming it to a standardized format and loading it to the data mining system for analysis.

4.2 Data Preprocessing Methods

Raw data is highly vulnerable to missing values, noise and inconsistency and the quality of data affects the data mining results. So, there is a need to improve the quality of data, in order to improve mining results. For achieving better results, raw data is pre-processed so as to enhance its quality and make it error free. This eases the mining process.

As depicted in Figure 4.1 the various stages in which data preprocessing is performed.

- Data Cleaning
- Data Integration
- Data Transformation
- Data Reduction

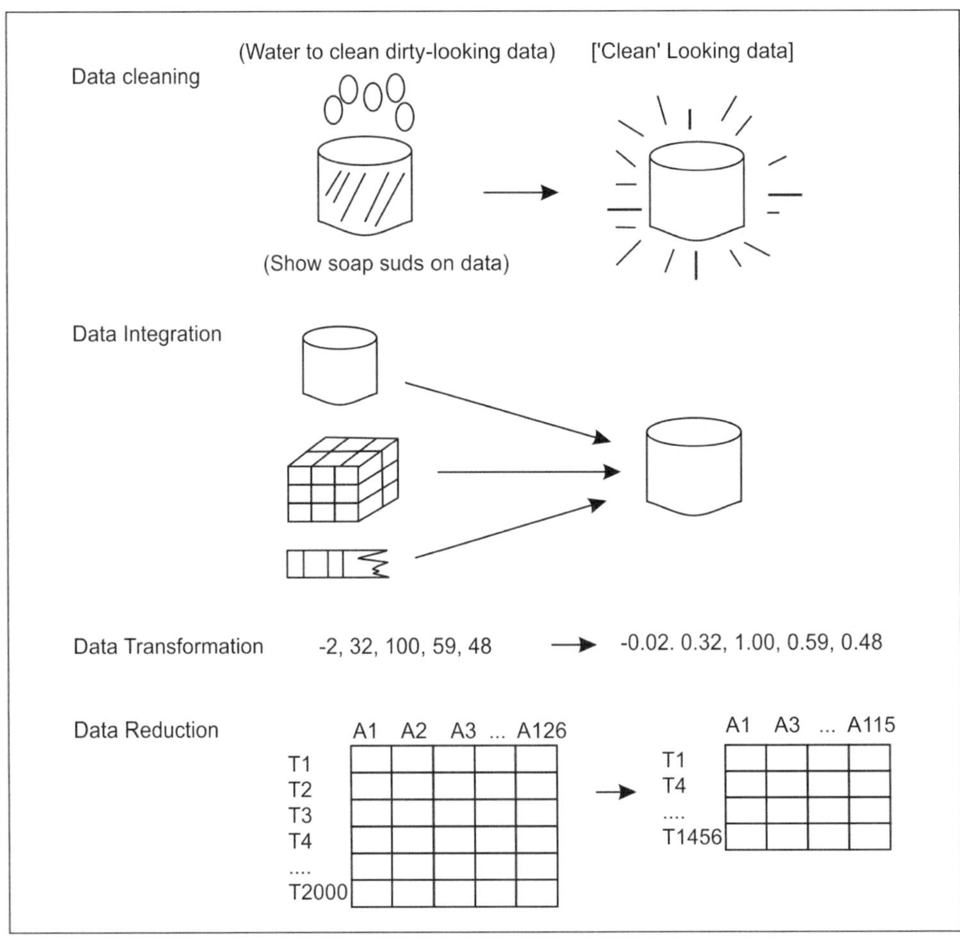

Figure 4.1 Various stages of preprocessing

Let's discuss the details of each phase one by one.

4.2.1 Data cleaning

First the raw data or noisy data goes through the process of cleansing. In data cleansing missing values are filled, noisy data is smoothened, inconsistencies are resolved, and outliers are identified and removed in order to clean the data. To elaborate further:

Handling missing values

It is often found that many of the database tuples or records do not have any recorded values for some attributes. Such cases of missing values are filled by different methods, as described below.

i. *Fill in the missing value manually:* Naturally, manually filling each missing value is laborious and time consuming and so it is practical only when the missing values are few in number. There are other methods to deal with the problem of missing values when the dataset is very large or when the missing values are very many.
ii. *Use of some global constant in place of missing value:* In this method, missing values are replaced by some global label such as 'Unkown' or $-\infty$. Although one of the easiest approaches to deal with the missing values, it should be avoided when mining program presents a pattern due to repetitive occurrences of global labels such as 'Unknown'. Hence, this method should be used with caution.
iii. *Use the attribute mean to fill in the missing value:* Fill in the missing values for each attribute with the mean of other data values of the same attribute. This is a better way to handle missing values in a dataset.
iv. *Use some other value which is high in probability to fill in the missing value:* Another efficient method is to fill in the missing values with values determined by tools such as Bayesian Formalism or Decision Tree Induction or other inference based tools. This is one of the best methods, as it uses most of the information already present to predict the missing values, although it is not biased like previous methods. The only difficulty with this method is complexity in performing the analysis.
v. *Ignore the tuple:* If the tuple contains more than one missing value and all other methods are not applicable, then the best strategy to cope with missing values is to ignore the whole tuple. This is commonly used if the class label goes missing or the tuple contains missing values for most of the attributes. This method should not be used, if the percentage of values that are missing per attribute varies significantly.

So, we can conclude that use the attribute mean to fill in the missing value is most common technique used by most data mining tools to handle the missing values. However, one can always use knowledge of probability to fill these values.

Handling noisy data

Most data mining algorithms are affected adversely due to noisy data. The ***noise*** can be defined as unwanted variance or some random error that occurred in a measurable variable. Noise is removed from the data by the method of 'smoothing'. The methods used for data smoothing are as follows:

i. Binning methods

The Binning method is used to divide the values of an attribute into bins or buckets. It is commonly used to convert one type of attribute to another type. For example, it may be necessary to convert a real-valued numeric attribute like temperature to a nominal attribute with values cold, cool, warm, and hot before its processing. This is also called 'discretizing' a numeric attribute. There are two types of discretization, namely, ***equal interval and equal frequency***.

In equal interval binning, we calculate a bin size and then put the samples into the appropriate bin. In equal frequency binning, we allow the bin sizes to vary, with our goal being to choose bin sizes so that every bin has about the same number of samples in it. The idea is that if each bin has the same number of samples, no bin, or sample, will have greater or lesser impact on the results of data mining.

To understand this process, consider a dataset of the marks of 50 students. . The process divides this dataset on the basis of their marks into, for this example, 10 bins.

In case of equal interval binning, we will create bins from 0-10, 10-20, 20-30, 30-40, 40-50, 50-60, 60-70, 70-80, 80-90, 90-100. If most students commonly have marks between 60 to 80, some bins may be full and most bins may have very few entries e.g., 0-10, 10-20, 90-100.

Thus, it might be better to divide this dataset on the equal frequency basis. It means that with the same 50 students in class and we want to put these into 10 bins on the basis of their marks then instead of creating the bins for marks like 0-10, 10-20 and so on, here we will first sort the records of students on the basis of their marks in descending order (or ascending order as we prefer). The first 5 students having highest marks will put into one bin and next 5 students on the basis of their marks will put into another and so on. If our boundary students have same marks then bin range can be shifted to accommodate students with the same marks into one common bin. For example, let us suppose that after arranging the data in descending order of marks and we found that marks of 5th and 6th students are same of 85. Then we cannot put one student in one bin and other in a different bin because both have the same marks. So, we either shift our bin range may be up (i.e., 86 in this case) to accommodate the first 4 students in one bin and next 5 into another. Similarly, we can shift our bin range down to accommodate first 6 students in one bin (i.e., 85 in this case so that 5th and 6th student falls in same bin) and next 5 into another. Thus, in this case of equal frequency most of bins will have a count of approximately 5, while in case of equal interval some bins will be heavily loaded while most will be lightly loaded.

Thus, the idea of having same number of samples in each bin works better as no bin, or sample, will have greater or lesser impact on the results of data mining.

ii. Clustering or outlier analysis

Clustering or outlier analysis is a method that allows detection of outliers by clustering. In clustering, values which are common or similar are organized into groups or 'clusters', and those values which lie outside these clusters are termed as outliers or noise.

iii. Regression

Regression is another such method which allows data smoothing by fitting it to some function. For example, Linear Regression is one of the most used methods that aims at finding the most suitable line to fit values of two variables or attributes (i.e., best fit). The primary purpose of this is to predict the value of other variable using the first one. Similarly, Multiple Regression is used when more than two variables are involved. Regression allows data fitting which in turn removes noise from data and hence smoothens the dataset using mathematical equations.

iv. Combined computer and human inspection

Using both computers and human inspection one can detect suspicious values and outliers.

Handling of inconsistent data

Many times data inconsistencies are encountered when data is recorded during some transaction. Such inconsistencies can be manually removed by using external references. As an example: errors that have been made at the time of data entry be corrected manually by performing a paper trace operation.

4.2.2 Data integration

A most necessary step to be taken during data analysis is Data Integration. Data integration is a process which combines data from a plethora of sources (such as multiple databases, flat files or data cubes) into a unified data store.

The example of the University Database system discussed under section 4.1 refers to the issues of data integration.

During data integration, a number of tricky issues have to be considered. For example, how does the data analyst or the analyzing machine be sure that student_id of one database and student_number of another database refer to the same entity? This is referred to as the problem of entity identification. Solution to the problem lies with the term 'metadata'. Databases and data warehouses consist of metadata, which is data about data. This metadata is taken as a reference and referred by the data analyst to avoid errors during the process of data integration.

Another such issue which may be caused due to schema integration is redundancy. In the language of database, an attribute is said to be redundant if it is derivable from some other table (of the same database). Mistakes in attribute naming can also lead to data redundancies in the resulting dataset. We use a number of tools to perform data integration from different sources into one unified schema.

4.2.3 Data transformation

When the value of one attribute is small as compared to other attributes, then that attribute will not have much influence on mining of information, since the values of this attribute were smaller than other attributes and the variation within the attribute will also be small.

Thus, data transformation is a process in which data is consolidated or transformed into some other standard forms which are better suited for data mining.

For example, the dataset given in Figure 4.2 is for the chemical composition of wine samples. Note that the values for different attributes cover a range of six orders of magnitude. It turns out that data mining algorithms struggle with numeric attributes that exhibit such ranges of values.

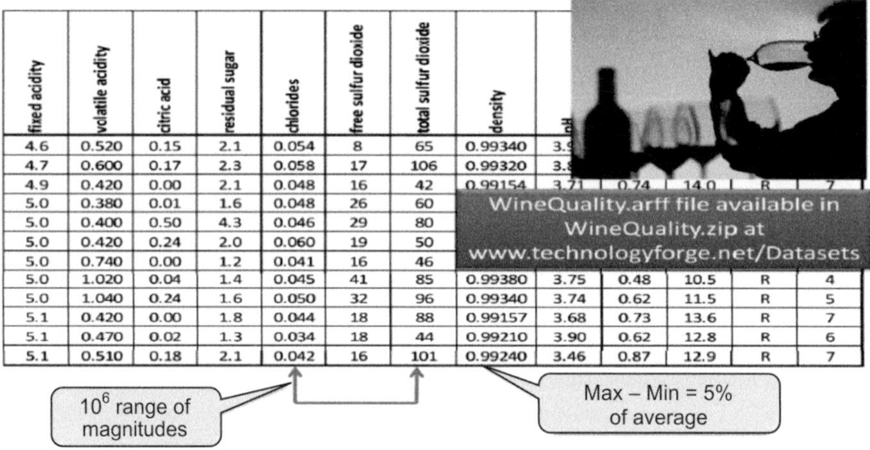

fixed acidity	volatile acidity	citric acid	residual sugar	chlorides	free sulfur dioxide	total sulfur dioxide	density	pH				
4.6	0.520	0.15	2.1	0.054	8	65	0.99340	[illegible]	[illegible]	[illegible]	[illegible]	[illegible]
4.7	0.600	0.17	2.3	0.058	17	106	0.99320	[illegible]	[illegible]	[illegible]	[illegible]	[illegible]
4.9	0.420	0.00	2.1	0.048	16	42	0.99154	3.71	0.74	14.0	R	7
5.0	0.380	0.01	1.6	0.048	26	60	[illegible]	[illegible]	[illegible]	[illegible]	[illegible]	[illegible]
5.0	0.400	0.50	4.3	0.046	29	80	[illegible]	[illegible]	[illegible]	[illegible]	[illegible]	[illegible]
5.0	0.420	0.24	2.0	0.060	19	50	[illegible]	[illegible]	[illegible]	[illegible]	[illegible]	[illegible]
5.0	0.740	0.00	1.2	0.041	16	46	[illegible]	[illegible]	[illegible]	[illegible]	[illegible]	[illegible]
5.0	1.020	0.04	1.4	0.045	41	85	0.99380	3.75	0.48	10.5	R	4
5.0	1.040	0.24	1.6	0.050	32	96	0.99340	3.74	0.62	11.5	R	5
5.1	0.420	0.00	1.8	0.044	18	88	0.99157	3.68	0.73	13.6	R	7
5.1	0.470	0.02	1.3	0.034	18	44	0.99210	3.90	0.62	12.8	R	6
5.1	0.510	0.18	2.1	0.042	16	101	0.99240	3.46	0.87	12.9	R	7

Figure 4.2 Chemical composition of wine samples

All attributes should be transformed to a similar scale for clustering to be effective unless we wish to give more weight to some attributes that are comparatively large in scale. Commonly, we use two techniques to convert the attributes: Normalization and Standardization are the most popular and widely used data transformation methods.

Normalization

In case of normalization, all the attributes are converted to a normalized score or to a range (0, 1). The problem of normalization is an outlier. If there is an outlier, it will tend to crunch all of the other values down toward the value of zero. In order to understand this, let's suppose the range of students' marks is 35 to 45 out of 100. Then 35 will be considered as 0 and 45 as 1, and students will be distributed between 0 to 1 depending upon their marks. But if there is one student having marks 90, then it will act as an outlier and in this case, 35 will be considered as 0 and 90 as 1. Now, it will crunch most of the values down toward the value of zero. In this scenario, the solution is standardization.

Standardization

In case of standardization, the values are all spread out so that we have a standard deviation of 1.

Generally, there is no rule for when to use normalization versus standardization. However, if your data has outliers, use standardization, otherwise use normalization. Using standardization tends to make the remaining values for all of the other attributes fall into similar ranges since all attributes will have the same standard deviation of 1.

4.2.4 Data reduction

It is often seen that when the complex data analysis and mining processes are carried out over humongous datasets, they take such a long time that the whole data mining or analysis process becomes unviable. Data reduction techniques come to the rescue in such situations. Using data reduction techniques a dataset can be represented in a reduced manner without actually compromising the integrity of original data.

Data reduction is all about reducing the dimensions (referring to the total number of attributes) or reducing the volume. Moreover, mining when carried out on reduced datasets often results in better accuracy and proves to be more efficient. There are many methods to reduce large datasets to yield useful knowledge. A few among them are:

i. Dimension reduction

In data warehousing, 'dimension' equips us with structured labeling information. But not all dimensions (attributes) are necessary at a time. Dimension reduction uses algorithm such as Principal Component Analysis (PCA) and others. With the usage of such algorithms one can detect and remove redundant and weakly relevant, attributes or dimensions.

ii. Numerosity reduction

It is a technique which is used to choose smaller forms of data representation for reducing the dataset volume.

iii. Data compression

We can also use data compression techniques to reduce the dataset size. These techniques are classified as lossy and loseless compression techniques where some encoding mechanisms (e.g. Huffman coding) are used.

Remind Me

- Data preprocessing is a data mining technique that involves transformation of raw data into an understandable format.
- The various phases of data preprocessing are data cleaning, data integration, data transformation and data reduction.
- In data cleansing, missing values are filled, noisy data is smoothened, inconsistencies are resolved, outliers are identified and removed in order to clean the data.
- Data integration is a method which combines data from a plethora of sources (such as multiple databases, flat files or data cubes) into a unified data store.
- Data transformation is a process in which data is consolidated or transformed into some other standard forms which are suitable for data mining.
- Using data reduction techniques a large dataset can be represented in a reduced manner without actually compromising the integrity of original data.

Point Me (Books)

- Han, Jiawei, Micheline Kamber, and Jian Pei. 2011. *Data Mining: Concepts and Techniques*, 3rd ed. Amsterdam: Elsevier.
- Gupta, G. K. 2014. *Introduction to Data Mining with Case Studies*. Delhi: PHI Learning Pvt. Ltd.

- Mitchell, Tom M. 2017. *Machine Learning*. Chennai: McGraw Hill Education.
- Witten, Ian H., Eibe Frank, Mark A. Hall, and Christopher Pal. 2016. *Data Mining: Practical Machine Learning Tools and Techniques*, 4th ed. Burlington: Morgan Kaufmann.

Connect Me (Internet Resources)

- https://www.kdnuggets.com/data_mining_course/x1-intro-to-data-mining-notes.html
- https://www.cse.iitb.ac.in/infolab/Data/Talks/datamining-intro-IEP.ppt
- https://tutorials.datasciencedojo.com/data-mining-fundamentals-part-1-3/

Test Me

1. What is the need for a data cleaning phase in any data mining process? Justify your answer with examples.
2. What is the difference between normalization and standardization?
3. What is meant by discretization? Why is it performed?
4. What is the difference between equal interval binning and equal frequency binning? Explain with examples.
5. Explain the different phases of data preprocessing with examples.

5

Classification

Chapter Objectives

- ✓ To comprehend the concept, types and working of classification
- ✓ To identify the major differences between classification and regression problems
- ✓ To become familiar about the working of classification
- ✓ To introduce the decision tree classification system with concepts of information gain and Gini Index
- ✓ To understand the workings of the Naïve Bayes method

5.1 Introduction to Classification

Nowadays databases are used for making intelligent decisions. Two forms of data analysis namely classification and regression are used for predicting future trends by analyzing existing data. Classification models predict discrete value or class, while Regression models predict a continuous value. For example, a classification model can be built to predict whether India will win a cricket match or not, while regression can be used to predict the runs that will be scored by India in a forthcoming cricket match.

Classification is a classical method which is used by machine learning researchers and statisticians for predicting the outcome of unknown samples. It is used for categorization of objects (or things) into given discrete number of classes. Classification problems can be of two types, either binary or multiclass. In binary classification the target attribute can only have two possible values. For example, a tumor is either cancerous or not, a team will either win or lose, a sentiment of a sentence is either positive or negative and so on. In multiclass classification, the target attribute can have more than two values. For example, a tumor can be of type 1, type 2 or type 3 cancer; the sentiment of a sentence can be happy, sad, angry or of love; news stories can be classified as weather, finance, entertainment or sports news.

Some examples of business situations where the classification technique is applied are:

- To analyze the credit history of bank customers to identify if it would be risky or safe to grant them loans.
- To analyze the purchase history of a shopping mall's customers to predict whether they will buy a certain product or not.

In first example, the system will predict a discrete value representing either risky or safe, while in second example, the system will predict yes or no.

Some more examples to distinguish the concept of regression from classification are:

- To predict how much a given customer will spend during a sale.
- To predict the salary-package of a student that he/she may get during his/her placement.

In these two examples, there is a prediction of continuous numeric value. Therefore, both are regression problems.

In this chapter, we will discuss the basic approaches to perform the classification of data.

5.2 Types of Classification

Classification is defined as two types. These are:

- Posteriori classification
- Priori classification

5.2.1 Posteriori classification

The word '*Posteriori*' means something derived by reasoning from the observed facts. It is a supervised machine learning approach, where the target classes are already known, i.e., training data is already labeled with actual answers.

5.2.2 Priori classification

The word '*Priori*' means something derived by reasoning from self-evident propositions. It is an unsupervised machine learning approach, where the target classes are not given. The question is 'Is it possible to make predictions, if labeled data is not available?'

The answer is yes. If data is not labeled, then we can use clustering (unsupervised technique) to divide unlabeled data into clusters. Then these clusters can be assigned some names or labels and can be further used to apply classification to make predictions based on this dataset. Thus, although data is not labeled, we can still make predictions based on data by first applying clustering followed by classification. This approach is known as Priori classification.

In this chapter, we will learn posteriori classification, a supervised machine learning approach to predict the outcome when training dataset is labeled.

5.3 Input and Output Attributes

In any machine learning approach the input data is very important. Data contains two types of attributes, namely, input attributes and output attributes. The class attribute that represents the output of all other attributes is known as an output attribute or dependent attribute, while all other attributes are known as input attributes or independent attributes. For example, the dataset for iris plant's flowers given in Figure 5.1 has Sepal length, Sepal width, Petal length and Petal width as input attributes and species as an output attribute.

Class

Input Attributes				Output Attribute
Sepal Length	**Sepal Width**	**Petal Length**	**Petal Width**	**Species**
5.1	3.5	1.4	0.2	setosa
4.9	3	1.4	0.2	setosa
4.7	3.2	1.3	0.2	setosa
4.6	3.1	1.5	0.2	setosa
5	3.6	1.4	0.2	setosa

Numerical Nominal

Figure 5.1 Input and output attributes

The attributes can be of different types. The attributes having numbers are called numerical attributes while attributes whose domain is not numerical are known as nominal or categorical attributes. Here, input attributes are of numerical type while species, i.e., the output attribute is of nominal type (as shown in Figure 5.1).

During classification, it is important to have a database of sufficient size for training the model accurately. The next section covers how a classification model is built.

5.4 Working of Classification

Classification is a two-step process. The first step is training the model and the second step is testing the model for accuracy. In the first step, a classifier is built based on the training data obtained by analyzing database tuples and their associated class labels. By analyzing training data, the system learns and creates some rules for prediction. In the second step, these prediction rules are tested on some unknown instances, i.e., test data. In this step, rules are used to make the predictions about the output attribute or class. In this step, the predictive accuracy of the classifier is calculated. The system performs in an iterative manner to improve its accuracy, i.e., if accuracy is not good on test data, the system will reframe its prediction rules until it gets optimized accuracy on test data as shown in Figure 5.2.

The test data is randomly selected from the full dataset. The tuples of the test data are independent of the training tuples. This means that the system has not been exposed to testing data during the training phase. The accuracy of a classifier on a given test data is defined as the percentage of test data tuples that are correctly classified by the classifier. The associated class label of each test tuple is compared with the class prediction made by the classifier for that particular tuple. If the accuracy of the classifier is satisfactory then it can be used to classify future data tuples with unknown class labels.

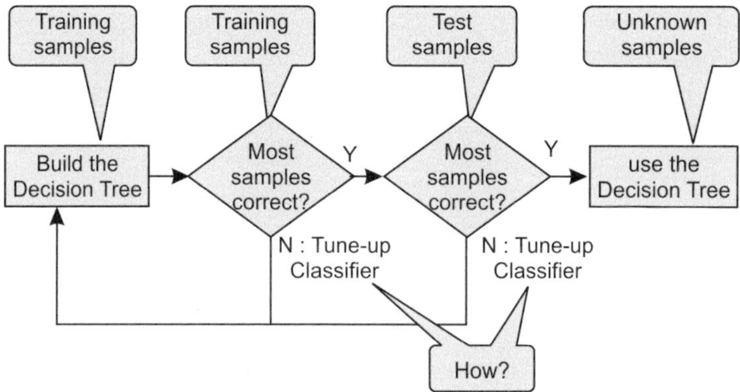

Figure 5.2 Training and testing of the classifier

For example, by analyzing the data of previous loan applications as shown in Figure 5.3, the classification rules obtained can be used to approve or reject the new or future loan applicants as shown in Figure 5.4.

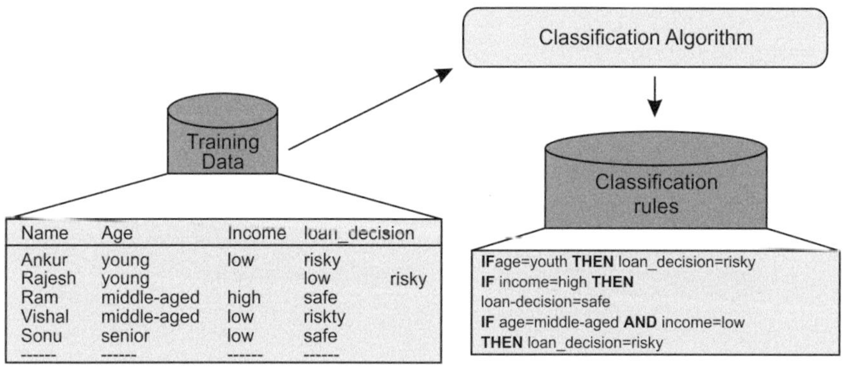

Figure 5.3 Building a classifier to approve or reject loan applications

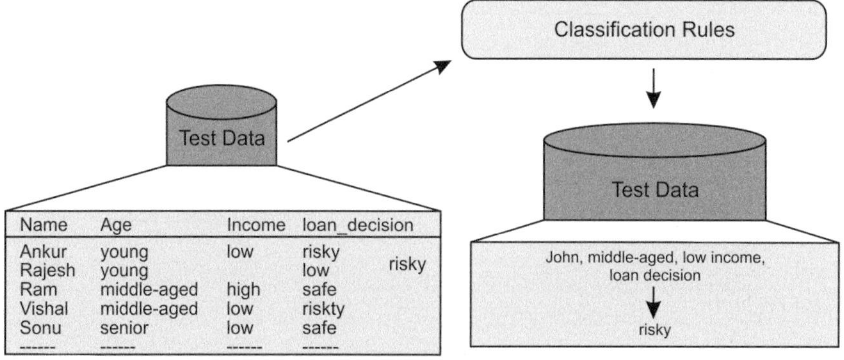

Figure 5.4 Predicting the type of customer based on trained classifier

The same process of training and testing the classifier has also been illustrated in Figure 5.5.

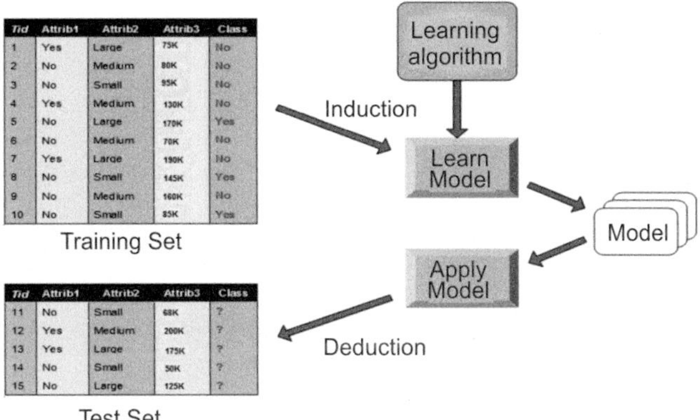

Figure 5.5 Training and testing of the classifier

5.5 Guidelines for Size and Quality of the Training Dataset

There should be a balance between the number of training samples and independent attributes. It has been observed that generally, the number of training samples required is likely to be relatively small if the number of independent or input attributes is small and similarly, number of training samples required is likely to be relatively large if the number of independent or input attributes is large. The quality of the classifier depends upon the quality of the training data. If there are two or more than two classes, then sufficient training data should be available belonging to each of these classes.

Researchers have developed a number of classifiers that include: Decision Tree, Naïve Bayes, Support Vector Machine and Neural Networks. In this chapter, two important classification methods, namely, Decision Tree and Naive Bayes are discussed in detail, as these are widely used by scientists and organizations for classification of data.

5.6 Introduction to the Decision Tree Classifier

In the decision tree classifier, predictions are made by using multiple 'if…then…' conditions which are similar to the control statements in different programming languages, that you might have learnt. The decision tree structure consists of a root node, branches and leaf nodes. Each internal node represents a condition on some input attribute, each branch specifies the outcome of the condition and each leaf node holds a class label. The root node is the topmost node in the tree.

The decision tree shown in Figure 5.6 represents a classifier tasked for predicting whether a customer will buy a laptop or not. Here, each internal node denotes a condition on the input attributes and each leaf node denotes the predicted outcome (class). By traversing the decision tree, one can analyze that if a customer is middle aged then he will probably buy a laptop, if a customer is young and a student then he will probably not buy a laptop. If a customer is a senior citizen and has an excellent credit rating then he can probably buy a laptop. The system makes these predictions with a certain level of probability.

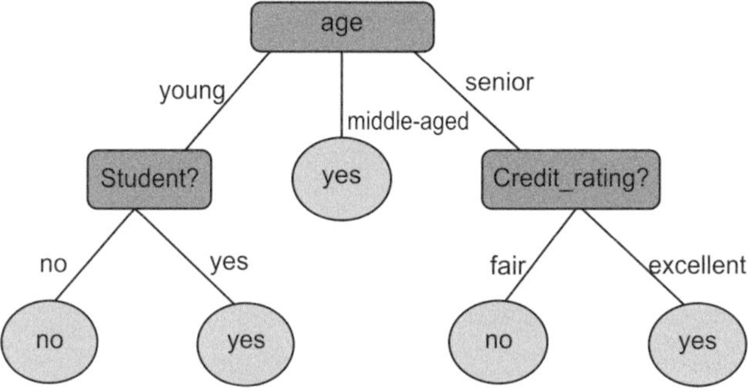

Figure 5.6 Decision tree to predict whether a customer will buy a laptop or not

Decision trees can easily be converted to classification rules in the form of if-then statements. Decision tree based classification is very similar to a '20 questions game'. In this game, one player writes something on a page and other player has to find what was written by asking at most 20 questions; the answers to which can only be yes or no. Here, each node of the decision tree denotes a choice between numbers of alternatives and the choices are binary. Each leaf node specifies a decision or prediction. The training process that produces this tree is known as induction.

5.6.1 Building decision tree

J. Ross Quinlan, a researcher in machine learning, developed a decision tree algorithm known as **ID3 (Iterative Dichotomiser)** during the late 1970s and early 1980s. Quinlan later proposed C4.5 (a successor of ID3), which became a benchmark to which newer supervised learning algorithms are often compared. Decision tree is a common machine learning technique which has been implemented in many machine learning tools like Weka, R, Matlab as well as some programming languages such as Python, Java, *etc.*

These algorithms are based on the concept of Information Gain and Gini Index. So, let us first understand the role of information gain in building the decision tree.

5.6.2 Concept of information theory

Decision tree algorithm works on the basis of information theory. It has been observed that information is directly related with uncertainty. If there is uncertainty then there is information and if there is no uncertainty then there is no information. For example, if a coin is biased having a head on both sides, then the result of tossing it does not give any information but if a coin is unbiased having a head and a tail then the result of the toss provides some information.

Usually the newspaper carries the news that provides maximum information. For example, consider the case of an India-UAE world cup cricket match. It appears certain that India will beat UAE, so this news will not appear on front page as main headlines, but if UAE beats India in a world cup cricket match then this news being very unexpected (uncertain) will appear on the first page as headlines.

Let us consider another example, if in your university or college, there is holiday on Sunday then a notice regarding the same will not carry any information (because it is certain) but if some particular Sunday becomes a working day then it will be information and henceforth becomes a news.

From these examples we can observe that information is related to the probability of occurence of an event. Another important question to consider is, whether the probability of occurrence of an event is more. Then, the information gain will be more frequent or less frequent?

It is certain from above examples that 'more certain' events such as India defeating UAE in cricket or Sunday being a holiday carry very little information. But if UAE beats India or Sunday is working, then even though the probability of these events is lesser than the previous event, it will carry more information. Hence, less probability means more information.

5.6.3 Defining information in terms of probability

Information theory was developed by Claude Shannon. Information theory defines entropy which is average amount of information given by a source of data. Entropy is measured as follows.

$$\text{entropy}\,(p_1, p_2, \ldots, p_n) = -p_1\log(p_1) - p_2\log(p_2) - \ldots - p_n\log(p_n)$$

Therefore, the total information for an event is calculated by the following equation:

$$I = \sum_i \left(-p_i \log p_i\right)$$

In this, information is defined as $-p_i \log p_i$ where p_i is the probability of some event. Since, probability p_i is always less than 1, $\log p_i$ is always negative; thus negating *log pi* we get the overall information gain (*–pi log pi*) as positive.

It is important to remember that the logarithm of any number greater than 1 is always positive and the logarithm of any number smaller than 1 is always negative. Logarithm of 1 is always zero, no matter what the base of logarithm is. In case of log with base 2, following are some examples.

$$\log_2(2) = 1$$

$$\log_2(2^n) = n$$

$$\log_2(1/2) = -1$$

$$\log_2(1/2^n) = -n$$

Let us calculate the information for the event of throwing a coin. It has two possible values, i.e., head (p_1) or tail (p_2). In case of unbiased coin, the probability of head and tail is 0.5 respectively. Thus, the information is

$$I = -0.5 \log(0.5) - 0.5 \log(0.5)$$

$$= -(0.5) * (-1) - (0.5) * (-1) \qquad [\text{As}, \log_2(0.5) = -1]$$

$$= 0.5 + 0.5 = 1$$

The result is 1.0 (using log base 2) and it is the maximum information that we can have for an event with two possible outcomes. This is also known as entropy.

But if the coin is biased and has heads on both the sides, then probability for head is 1 while the probability of tails will be 0. Thus, total information in tossing this coin will be as follows.

$$I = -1 \log(1) - 0 \log(0) = 0 \qquad [\text{As}, \log_2(1) = 0]$$

You can clearly observe that tossing of biased coin carries no information while tossing of unbiased coin carries information of 1.

Suppose, an unbiased dice is thrown which has six possible outcomes with equal probability, then the information is given by:

$$I = 6(-1/6)\log(1/6) = 2.585$$

[the probability of each possible outcome is 1/6 and there are in total six possible outcomes from 1 to 6]

But, if dice is biased such that there is a 50% chance of getting a 6, then the information content of rolling the die would be lower as given below.

$$I = 5(-0.1)\log(0.1) - 0.5\log(0.5) = 2.16$$

[One event has a probability of 0.5 while 5 other events has probability of 0.5, which makes 0.5/5 = 0.1 as the probability of each of remaining 5 events.]

And if the dice is further biased such that there is a 75% chance of getting a 6, then the information content of rolling the die would be further low as given below.

$$I = 5(-0.05)\log(0.05) - 0.75\log(0.75) = 1.39$$

[One event has a probability of 0.75 while 5 other events has probability of 0.25, which makes 0.25/5 = 0.05 as probability of each of remaining 5 events.]

We can observe that as the certainty of an event goes up, the total information goes down.

Information plays a key role in selecting the root node or attribute for building a decision tree. In other words, selection of a *split attribute* plays an important role. Split attribute is an attribute that reduces the uncertainty by largest amount, and is always accredited as a root node. So, the attribute must distribute the objects such that each attribute value results in objects that have as little uncertainty as possible. Ideally, each attribute value should provide us with objects that belong to only one class and therefore have zero information.

5.6.4 Information gain

Information gain specifies the amount of information that is gained by knowing the value of the attribute. It measures the 'goodness' of an input attribute for predicting the target attribute. The attribute with the highest information gain is selected as the next split attribute.

Mathematically, it is defined as the entropy of the distribution before the split minus the entropy of the distribution after split.

Information gain = (Entropy of distribution before the split) – (Entropy of distribution after the split)

The largest information gain is equivalent to the smallest entropy or minimum information. It means that if the result of an event is certain, i.e., the probability of an event is 1 then information provided by it is zero while the information gain will be the largest, thus it should be selected as a split attribute.

Assume that there are two classes, P and N, and let the set of training data S (with a total number of records s) contain p records of class P and n records of class N. The amount of information is defined as

$$I = -(p/s)\log(p/s) - (n/s)\log(n/s)$$

Obviously if $p = n$, i.e., the probability is equally distributed then I is equal to 1 and if $p = s$ or $n = 0$, i.e., training data S contains all the elements of a single class only, then $I = 0$. Therefore if there was an attribute for which all the records had the same value (for example, consider the attribute gender, when all people are male), using this attribute would lead to no information gain that is, no reduction in uncertainty. On the other hand, if an attribute divides the training sample such that all female records belong to Class *A*, and male records belong to Class *B*, then uncertainty has been reduced to zero and we have a large information gain.

Thus after computing the information gain for every attribute, the attribute with the highest information gain is selected as split attribute.

5.6.5 Building a decision tree for the example dataset

Let us build decision tree for the dataset given in Figure 5.7.

Instance Number	X	Y	Z	Class
1	1	1	1	A
2	1	1	0	A
3	0	0	1	B
4	1	0	0	B

X	Y	Z	Class
1 = 3	1 = 2	1 = 2	A = 2
0 = 1	0 = 2	0 = 2	B = 2

Figure 5.7 Dataset for class C prediction based on given attribute condition

The given dataset has three input attributes X, Y, Z and one output attribute Class. The instance number has been given to show that the dataset contains four records (basically for convenience while making references). The output attribute or class can be either A or B.

There are two instances for each class so the frequencies of these two classes are given as follows:

$$A = 2 \text{ (Instances 1, 2)}$$

$$B = 2\text{(Instances 3, 4)}$$

The amount of information contained in the whole dataset is calculated as follows:

I = - probability for Class A * log (probability for class A)
- probability for class B * log (probability for class N)

Here, probability for class A = (Number of instances for class A/Total number of instances) = 2/4
And probability for class B = (Number of instances for class B/Total number of instances) = 2/4
Therefore, I = (-2/4) log (2/4) – (2/4) log (2/4) = 1

Let us consider each attribute one by one as a split attribute and calculate the information for each attribute.

Attribute 'X'

As given in the dataset, there are two possible values of X, i.e., 1 or 0. Let us analyze each case one by one.

For X= 1, there are 3 instances namely instance 1, 2 and 4. The first two instances are labeled as class A and the third instance, i.e, record 4 is labeled as class B.

For X = 0, there is only 1 instance, i.e, instance number 3 which is labeled as class B.

Given the above values, let us compute the information given by this attribute. We divide the dataset into two subsets according to X either being 1 or 0. Computing information for each case,

$$I\ (\text{for } X = 1) = I(X1) = -\ (2/3)\log(2/3) - (1/3)\log(1/3) = 0.92333$$

$$I\ (\text{for } X = 0) = I(X0) = -\ (0/1)\log(0/1) - (1/1)\log(1/1) = 0$$

Total information for above two sub-trees = probability for X having value 1 * I(X1) + probability for X having value 0 * I(X0)

Here, probability for X having value 1 = (Number of instances for X having value 1/Total number of instances) = 3/4

And probability for X having value 0 = (Number of instances for X having value 0/Total number of instances) = 1/4

Therefore, total information for the two sub-trees = (3/4) I(X1) + (1/4) I(X0)
= 0.6925 + 0
= 0.6925

Attribute 'Y'

There are two possible values of Y attribute, i.e., 1 or 0. Let us analyze each case one by one.

There are 2 instances where Y has value 1. In both cases when Y=1 the record belongs to class A and, in the 2 instances when Y = 0 both records belong to class B.

Given the above values, let us compute the information provided by Y attribute. We divide the dataset into two subsets according to Y either being 1 and 0. Computing information for each case,

$$I\ (\text{For } Y = 1) = I\ (Y1) = -\ (2/2)\log(2/2) - (0/2)\log(0/2) = 0$$

$$I\ (\text{For } Y = 0) = I\ (Y0) = -\ (0/2)\log(0/2) - (2/2)\log(2/2) = 0$$

Total information for the two sub-trees = probability for Y having value 1* I(Y1) + probability for Y having value 0 * I(Y0)

Here, probability for Y in 1 = (Number of instances for Y having 1/Total number of instances) = 2/4

And probability for Y in 0 = (Number of instances for Y having 0/Total number of instances) = 2/4

Therefore, the total information for the two sub-trees = (2/4) I(Y1) + (2/4) I(Y0)
= 0 + 0
= 0

Attribute 'Z'

There are two possible values of Z attribute, i.e., 1 or 0. Let us analyze each case one by one.

There are 2 instances where Z has value 1 and 2 instances where Z has value 0. In both cases, there exists a record belonging to class A and class B with Z is either 0 or 1.

Given the above values, let us compute the information provided by the Z attribute. We divide the dataset into two subsets according to Z either being 1 or 0. Computing information for each case,

$$I\ (\text{For } Z = 1) = I\ (Z1) = -\ (1/2) \log(1/2) - (1/2) \log(1/2) = 1.0$$

$$I\ (\text{For } Z = 0) = I\ (Z0) = -\ (1/2) \log(1/2) - (1/2) \log(1/2) = 1.0$$

Total information for the two sub-trees = probability for Z having value 1 * I(Z1) + probability for Z having value 0 * I(Z0)

Here, probability for Z having value 1 = (Number of instances for Z having value 1/Total number of instances) = 2/4

And probability for Z having value 0 = (Number of instances for Z having value 0/Total number of instances) = 2/4

Therefore, total information for two sub-trees = (2/4) I(Z1) + (2/4) I(Z0)

= 0.5 + 0.5

= 1.0

The Information gain can now be computed:

Potential Split attribute	*Information before split*	*Information after split*	*Information gain*
X	1.0	0.6925	0.3075
Y	**1.0**	**0**	**1.0**
Z	1.0	1.0	0

Hence, the largest information gain is provided by the attribute 'Y' thus it is used for the split as depicted in Figure 5.8.

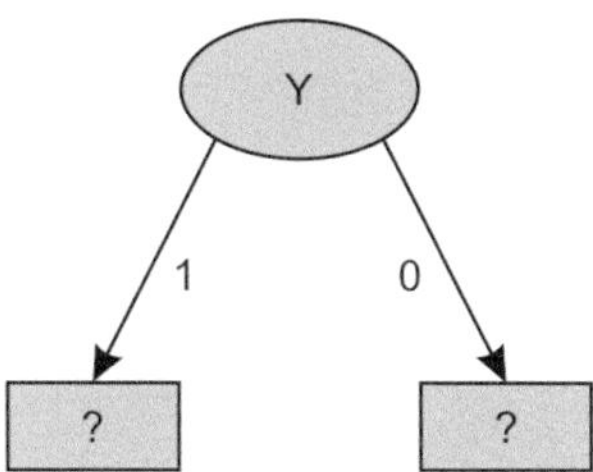

Figure 5.8 Data splitting based on Y attribute

For Y, as there are two possible values, i.e., 1 and 0, therefore the dataset will be split into two subsets based on distinct values of the Y attribute as shown in Figure 5.8.

Dataset for Y = '1'

Instance Number	*X*	*Z*	*Class*
1	1	1	A
2	1	0	A

There are 2 samples and the frequency of each class is as follows.

A = 2 (Instances 1, 2)
B = 0 Instances

Information of the whole dataset on the basis of class is given by

$$I = (-2/2) \log (2/2) - (0/2) \log(0/2) = 0$$

As it represents the same class 'A' for all recorded combinations of X and Z, therefore, it represents class 'A' as shown in Figure 5.9.

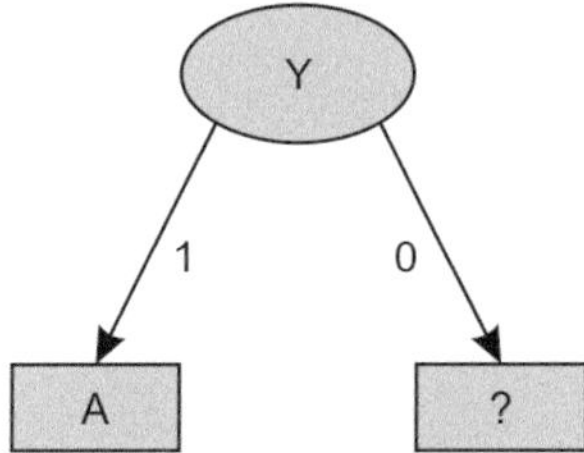

Figure 5.9 Decision tree after splitting of attribute Y having value '1'

Dataset for Y = '0'

Instance Number	X	Z	Class
3	0	1	B
4	1	0	B

For Y having value 0, it represents the same class 'B' for all the records. Thus, the decision tree will look like as shown in Figure 5.10 after analysis of Y dataset.

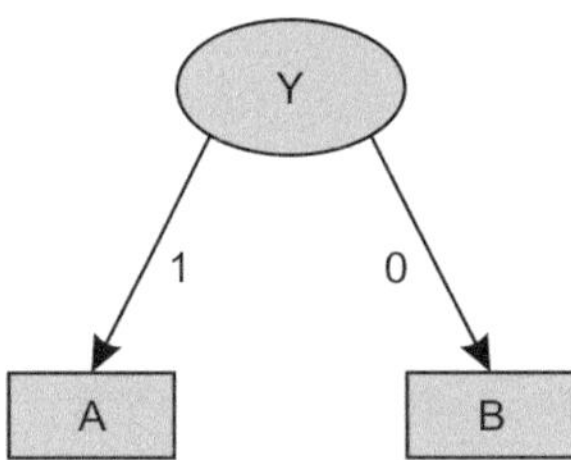

Figure 5.10 Decision tree after splitting of attribute Y value '0'

Let us consider another example and build a decision tree for the dataset given in Figure 5.11. It has 4 input attributes outlook, temperature, humidity and windy. As before we have added instance number for explanation purposes. Here, 'play' is the output attribute and these 14 records contain the information about weather conditions based on which it was decided if a play took place or not.

Instance Number	Outlook	Temperature	Humidity	Windy	Play
1	sunny	hot	high	false	No
2	sunny	hot	high	true	No
3	overcast	hot	high	false	Yes
4	rainy	mild	high	false	Yes
5	rainy	cool	normal	false	Yes
6	rainy	cool	normal	true	No
7	overcast	cool	normal	true	Yes
8	sunny	mild	high	false	No
9	sunny	cool	normal	false	Yes
10	rainy	mild	normal	false	Yes
11	sunny	mild	normal	true	Yes
12	overcast	mild	high	true	Yes
13	overcast	hot	normal	false	Yes
14	rainy	mild	high	true	No

Attribute values and counts

Outlook	Temp.	Humidity	Windy	Play
sunny = 5	hot = 4	high = 7	true = 6	yes = 9
overcast = 4	mild = 6	normal = 7	false = 8	no = 5
rainy = 5	cool = 4			

Figure 5.11 Dataset for play prediction based on given day weather conditions

In the dataset, there are 14 samples and two classes for target attribute 'Play', i.e., Yes or No. The frequencies of these two classes are given as follows:

Yes = 9 (Instance number 3,4,5,7,9,10,11,12,13 and 14)

No = 5 (Instance number 1,2,6,8 and 15)

Information of the whole dataset on the basis of whether play is held or not is given by

I = - probability for play being held * log (probability for play being held) - probability for play not being held * log (probability for play not being held)

Here, probability for play having value Yes = (Number of instances for Play is Yes/Total number of instances) = 9/14

And probability for play having value No = (Number of instances for Play is No/Total number of instances) = 5/14

Therefore, I = - (9/14) log (9/14) – (5/14) log (5/14) = 0.9435142

Let us consider each attribute one by one as split attributes and calculate the information for each attribute.

Attribute 'Outlook'

As given in dataset, there are three possible values of outlook, i.e., sunny, overcast and rainy. Let us analyze each case one by one.

There are 5 instances where outlook is sunny. Out of these 5 instances, in 2 instances (9 and 11) the play is held and in remaining 3 instances (1, 2 and 8) the play is not held.

There are 4 instances where outlook is overcast and in all these instances the play always takes place.

There are 5 instances where outlook is rainy. Out of these 5 instances, in 3 instances (4, 5 and 10) the play is held whereas in remaining 2 instances (6 and 14) the play is not held.

Given the above values, let us compute the information provided by the outlook attribute. We divide the dataset into three subsets according to outlook conditions being sunny, overcast or rainy. Computing information for each case,

$$I\ (\text{Sunny}) = I\ (S) = -\ (2/5)\log(2/5) - (3/5)\log(3/5) = 0.97428$$

$$I\ (\text{Overcast}) = I\ (O) = -\ (4/4)\log(4/4) - (0/4)\log(0/4) = 0$$

$$I\ (\text{Rainy}) = I\ (R) = -\ (3/5)\log(3/5) - (2/5)\log(2/5) = 0.97428$$

Total information for these three sub-trees = probability for outlook Sunny * I(S) + probability for outlook Overcast * I(O) + probability for outlook Rainy * I(R)

Here, probability for outlook Sunny = (Number of instances for outlook Sunny/Total number of instances) = 5/14

And probability for outlook Overcast = (Number of instances for outlook Overcast/Total number of instances) = 4/14

And probability for outlook Rainy = (Number of instances for outlook Rainy/Total number of instances) = 5/14

Therefore, total information for three sub-trees = (5/14) I(S) + (4/14) I(O) + (5/14) I(R)

= 0.3479586 + 0.3479586

= 0.695917

Attribute 'Temperature'

There are three possible values of the Temperature attribute, i.e., Hot, Mild and Cool. Let us analyze each case one by one.

There are 4 instances for Temperature hot. Play is held in case of 2 of these instances (3 and 13) and is not held in case of the other 2 instances (1 and 2).

There are 6 instances for Temperature mild. Play is held in case of 4 instances (4, 10, 11 and 12) and is not held in case of 2 instances (8 and 14).

There are 4 instances for Temperature cool. Play is held in case of 3 instances (5, 7 and 9) and is not held in case of 1 instance (6).

Given the above values, let us compute the information provided by Temperature attribute. We divide the dataset into three subsets according to temperature conditions being Hot, Mild or Cool. Computing information for each case,

$$I\ (\text{Hot}) = I\ (H) = -\ (2/4)\log(2/4) - (2/4)\log(2/4) = 1.003433$$

$$I\ (\text{Mild}) = I\ (M) = -\ (4/6)\log(4/6) - (2/6)\log(2/6) = 0.9214486$$

$$I\ (\text{Cool}) = I\ (C) = -\ (3/4)\log(3/4) - (1/4)\log(1/4) = 0.814063501$$

Total information for the three sub-trees = probability for temperature hot * I(H) + probability for temperature mild * I(M) + probability for temperature cool * I(C)

Here, probability for temperature hot = (Number of instances for temperature hot/Total number of instances) = 4/14

And probability for temperature mild = (Number of instances for temperature mild/Total number of instances) = 6/14

And probability for temperature cool = (Number of instances for temperature cool/Total number of instances) = 4/14

Therefore, total information for these three sub-trees

$$= (4/14)\ I(H) + (6/14)\ I(M) + (4/14)\ I(C)$$
$$= 0.2866951429 + 0.3949065429 + 0.23258957$$
$$= 0.9141912558$$

Attribute 'Humidity'

There are two possible values of the Humidity attribute, i.e., High and Normal. Let us analyze each case one by one.

There are 7 instances where humidity is high. Play is held in case of 3 instances (3, 4 and 12) and is not held in case of 4 instances (1, 2, 8 and 14).

There are 7 instances where humidity is normal. Play is held in case of 6 instances (5, 7, 9, 10, 11 and 13) and is not held in case of 1 instance (6).

Given the above values, let us compute the information provided by the humidity attribute. We divide the dataset into two subsets according to humidity conditions being high or normal. Computing information for each case,

$$I\ (\text{High}) = I\ (H) = -\ (3/7)\log(3/7) - (4/7)\log(4/7) = 0.98861$$

$$I\ (\text{Normal}) = I\ (N) = -\ (6/7)\log(6/7) - (1/7)\log(1/7) = 0.593704$$

Total information for the two sub-trees = probability for humidity high * I(H) + probability for humidity normal * I(N)

Here, probability for humidity high = (Number of instances for humidity high/Total number of instances) = 7/14

And probability for humidity normal = (Number of instances for humidity normal/Total number of instances) = 7/14

Therefore, Total information for the two sub-trees = (7/14) I(H) + (7/14) I(N)

$$= 0.494305 + 0.29685$$
$$= 0.791157$$

Attribute 'Windy'

There are two possible values for this attribute, i.e., true and false. Let us analyze each case one by one.

There are 6 instances when it is windy. On windy days, play is held in case of 3 instances (7, 11 and 12) and is not held in case of remaining 3 instances (2, 6 and 14).

For non-windy days, there are 8 instances. On non-windy days, the play is held in case of 6 instances (3, 4, 5, 9, 10 and 13) and is not held in case of 2 instances (1 and 8).

Given the above values, let us compute the information provided by the windy attribute. We divide the dataset into two subsets according to windy being true or false. Computing information for each case,

$$I\ (True) = I\ (T) = -\ (3/6)\ \log(3/6) - (3/6)\ \log(3/6) = 1.003433$$

$$I\ (False) = I\ (F) = -\ (6/8)\ \log(6/8) - (2/8)\ \log(2/8) = 0.81406$$

Total information for the two sub-trees = probability for windy true * I(T) + probability for windy true * I(F)

Here, The probability for windy being True = (Number of instances for windy true/Total number of instances) = 6/14

And probability for windy being False = (Number of instances for windy false/Total number of instances) = 8/14

Therefore, Total information for the two sub-trees = (6/14) I(T) + (8/14) I(F)

= 0.4300427 + 0.465179

= 0.89522

The information gain can now be computed:

Potential Split attribute	*Information before split*	*Information after split*	*Information gain*
Outlook	0.9435	0.6959	0.2476
Temperature	0.9435	0.9142	0.0293
Humidity	0.9435	0.7912	0.15234
Windy	0.9435	0.8952	0.0483

From the above table, it is clear that the largest information gain is provided by the attribute 'Outlook' so it is used for the split as depicted in Figure 5.12.

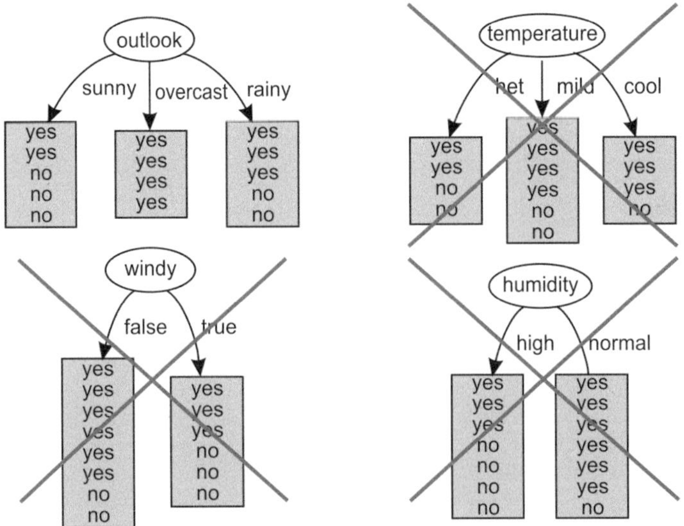

Figure 5.12 Selection of Outlook as root attribute

For Outlook, as there are three possible values, i.e., Sunny, Overcast and Rain, the dataset will be split into three subsets based on distinct values of the Outlook attribute as shown in Figure 5.13.

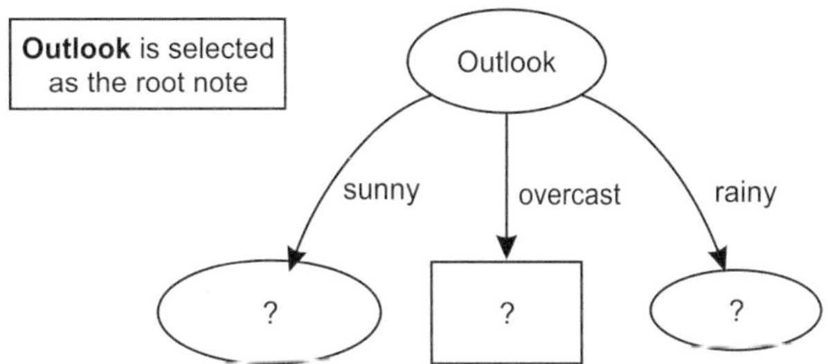

Figure 5.13 Data splitting based on the Outlook attribute

Dataset for Outlook 'Sunny'

Instance Number	*Temperature*	*Humidity*	*Windy*	*Play*
1	Hot	high	false	No
2	Hot	high	true	No
3	Mild	high	false	No
4	Cool	normal	false	Yes
5	Mild	normal	true	Yes

Again, in this dataset, a new column instance number is added to the dataset for making explanation easier. In this case, we have three input attributes Temperature, Humidity and Windy. This dataset consists of 5 samples and two classes, i.e., Yes and No for the Play attribute. The frequencies of classes are as follows:

Yes = 2 (Instances 4, 5)

No = 3 (Instances 1, 2, 3)

Information of the whole dataset on the basis of whether play is held or not is given by

I = - probability for Play Yes * log (probability for Play Yes)
- probability for Play No * log (probability for Play No)

Here, probability for play being Yes = (Number of instances for Play Yes/Total number of instances) = 2/5

And probability for Play being No = (Number of instances for Play No/Total number of instances) = 3/5

Therefore, I = (-2/5) log (2/5) – (3/5) log(3/5) = 0.97

Let us consider each attribute one by one as a split attribute and calculate the information for each attribute.

Attribute 'Temperature'

There are three possible values of Temperature attribute, i.e., hot, mild and cool. Let us analyze each case one by one.

There are 2 instances for temperature hot. Play is never held when the temperature is hot as shown in 2 instances (1 and 2).

There are 2 instances when temperature is mild. Play is held in case of 1 instance (5) and is not held in case of 1 instance (3).

There is 1 instance when temperature is cool. Play is held in this case as shown in instance 4.

Given the above values, let us compute the information provided by this attribute. We divide the dataset into three subsets according to temperature conditions being hot, mild or cool. Computing information for each case,

$$I\ (\text{Hot}) = I\ (H) = -\ (0/2) \log(0/2) - (2/2) \log(2/2) = 0$$

$$I\ (\text{Mild}) = I\ (M) = -\ (1/2) \log(1/2) - (1/2) \log(1/2) = 1.003433$$

$$I\ (\text{Cool}) = I\ (C) = -\ (1/1) \log(1/1) - (0/1) \log(1/1) = 0$$

Total information for these three sub-trees = probability for temperature hot * I(H) + probability for temperature mild * I(M) + probability for temperature cool * I(C)

Here, probability for temperature hot = (No of instances for temperature hot/Total no of instances) = 2/5

And probability for temperature mild = (Number of instances for temperature mild/Total number of instances) = 2/5

And probability for temperature cool = (Number of instances for temperature cool/Total number of instances) = 1/5

Therefore, total information for three subtrees = (2/5) I(H) + (2/5) I(M) + (1/5) I(C)
= 0 + (0.4) * (1.003433) + 0
= 0.40137

Attribute 'Humidity'

There are two possible values of Humidity attribute, i.e., High and Normal. Let us analyze each case one by one.

There are 3 instances when humidity is high. Play is never held when humidity is high as shown in case of 3 instances (1, 2 and 3).

There are 2 instances when humidity is normal. Play is always held as shown in case of 2 instances (4 and 5).

Given the above values, let us compute the information provided by this attribute. We divide the dataset into two subsets according to humidity conditions being high or normal. Computing information for each case,

$$I\ (\text{High}) = I\ (H) = -(0/3) \log(0/3)-(3/3) \log(3/3) = 0$$

$$I\ (\text{Normal}) = I\ (N) = -(2/2) \log(2/2)-(0/2) \log(0/2) = 0$$

Total information for these two sub-trees = probability for humidity high * I(H) + probability for humidity normal * I(N)

Here, probability for humidity high = (Number of instances for humidity high/Total number of instances) = 3/5

And probability for humidity normal = (Number of instances for humidity normal/Total number of instances) = 2/5

Therefore, total information for these two sub-trees = (3/5) I(H) + (2/5) I(N) = 0

Attribute 'Windy'

There are two possible values for this attribute, i.e., true and false. Let us analyze each case one by one.

There are 2 instances when windy is true. On windy days play is held in case of 1 instance (5) and it is not held in case of another 1 instance (2).

There are 3 instances when windy is false. The play is held in case of 1 instance (4) and is not held in case of 2 instances (1 and 3).

Given the above values, let us compute the information by using this attribute. We divide the dataset into two subsets according to windy being true or false. Computing information for each case,

$$I\ (\text{True}) = I\ (T) = -\ (1/2)\log(1/2) - (1/2)\log(1/2) = 1.003433$$

$$I\ (\text{False}) = I\ (F) = -\ (1/3)\log(1/3) - (2/3)\log(2/3) = 0.9214486$$

Total information for these two sub-trees = probability for windy true * I(T) + probability for windy true * I(F)

Here, the probability for windy true = (Number of instances for windy true/Total number of instances) = 2/5

And probability for windy false = (Number of instances for windy false/Total number of instances) = 3/5

Therefore, total information for two sub-trees = (2/5) I(T) + (3/5) I(F)
= 0.40137 + 0.55286818
= 0.954239

The Information gain can now be computed:

Potential Split attribute	Information before split	Information after split	Information gain
Temperature	0.97	0.40137	0.56863
Humidity	0.97	0	0.97
Windy	0.97	0.954239	0.015761

Thus, the largest information gain is provided by the attribute 'Humidity' and it is used for the split. This algorithm can be tuned by stopping when we get the 0 value of information as in this case to reduce the number of calculations for big datasets. Now, the Humidity attribute is selected as split attribute as depicted in Figure 5.14.

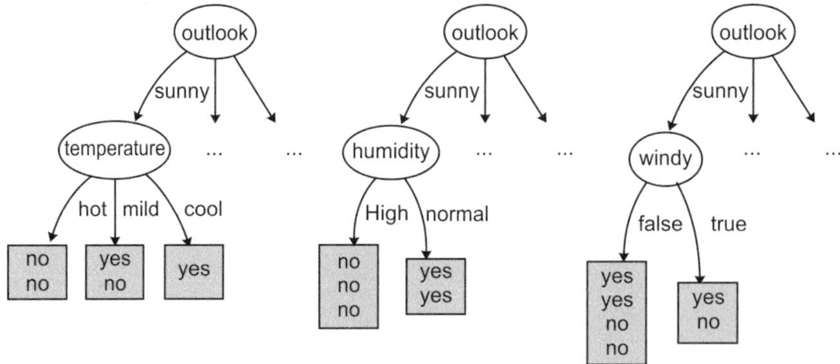

Figure 5.14 Humidity attribute is selected from dataset of Sunny instances

There are two possible values of humidity so data is split into two parts, i.e. humidity 'high' and humidity 'low' as shown below.

Dataset for Humidity 'High'

Instance Number	*Temperature*	*Windy*	*Play*
1	hot	false	No
2	hot	true	No
3	mild	false	No

Again, in this dataset a new column instance number has been introduced for explanation purposes. For this dataset, we have two input attributes Temperature and Windy. As the dataset represents the same class 'No' for all the records, therefore for Humidity value 'High' the output class is always 'No'.

Dataset for Humidity 'Normal'

Instance No	*Temperature*	*Windy*	*Play*
1	cool	false	Yes
2	mild	true	Yes

When humidity's value is 'Normal' the output class is always 'Yes'. Thus, decision tree will look like as shown in Figure 5.15 after analysis of the Humidity dataset.

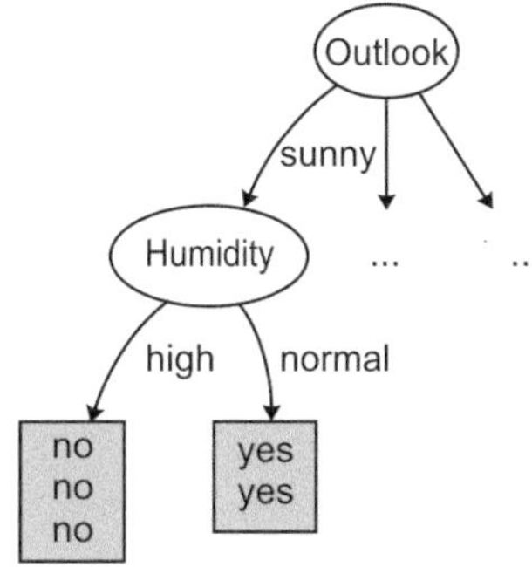

Figure 5.15 Decision tree after spitting of data on Humidity attribute

Now, the analysis of Sunny dataset is over. From the decision tree shown in Figure 5.15, it has been analyzed that if the outlook is 'Sunny' and humidity is 'normal' then play is always held while on the other hand if the humidity is 'high' then play is not held.

Let us take next subset which has Outlook as 'Overcast' for further analysis.

Dataset for Outlook 'Overcast'

Instance Number	*Temperature*	*Humidity*	*Windy*	*Play*
1	hot	high	false	Yes
2	cool	normal	true	Yes
3	mild	high	true	Yes

For outlook Overcast, the output class is always 'Yes'. Thus, decision tree will look like Figure 5.16 after analysis of the overcast dataset.

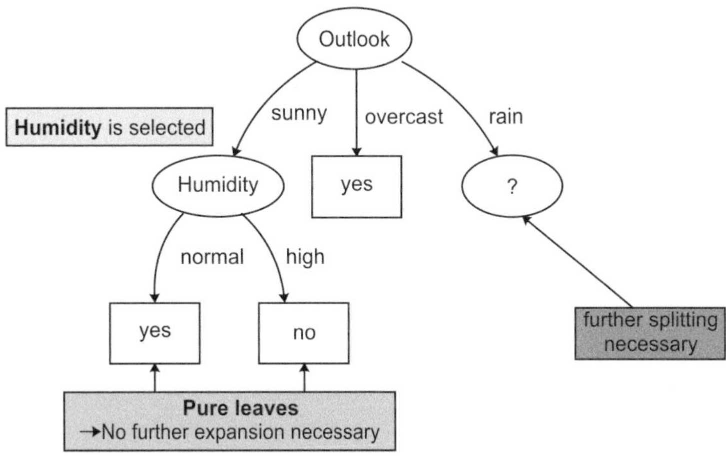

Figure 5.16 Decision tree after analysis of Sunny and Overcast dataset

Therefore, it has been concluded that if the outlook is 'Overcast' then play is always held. Now we have to select another split attribute for the outlook rainy and subset of the dataset for this is given below.

Dataset for Outlook 'Rainy'

Instance Number	Temperature	Humidity	Windy	Play
1	Mild	High	False	Yes
2	Cool	Normal	False	Yes
3	Cool	Normal	True	No
4	Mild	Normal	False	Yes
5	Mild	High	True	No

In the above dataset, a new column for instance numbers has again been added for ease of explanation. This dataset consists of 5 samples having input attributes Temperature, Humidity and Windy; and the single output attribute Play has two classes, i.e., Yes and No. The frequencies of these classes are as follows:

Yes = 3 (Instances 1, 2, 4)

No = 2 (Instances 3, 5)

Information of the whole dataset on the basis of whether play is held or not is given by

I = - probability for Play Yes * log (probability for Play Yes)
- probability for Play No * log (probability for Play No)

Here, probability for Play Yes = (Number of instances for Play Yes/Total number of instances) = 3/5

And probability for Play No = (Number of instances for Play No/Total number of instances) = 2/5

Therefore, I = (-3/5) log (3/5) – (2/5) log (2/5) = 0.97428

Let us consider each attribute one by one as split attributes and calculate the information provided for each attribute.

Attribute 'Temperature'

There are two possible values of Temperature attribute, i.e., mild and cool. Let us analyze each case one by one.

There are 3 instances with temperature value mild. Play is held in case of 2 instances (1 and 4) and is not held in case of 1 instance (5).

There are 2 instances with temperature value cool. Play is held in case of 1 instance (2) and is not held in case of other instance (3).

Given the above values, let us compute the information provided by this attribute. We divide the dataset into two subsets according to temperature being mild and cool. Computing information for each case,

I (Mild) = I(M) = - (2/3) log(2/3) - (1/3) log(1/3) = 0.921545

I (Cool) = I(C) = - (1/2) log(1/2) - (1/2) log(1/2) = 1.003433

Total information for the two sub-trees = probability for temperature mild * I(M) + probability for temperature cool * I(C)

And probability for temperature mild = (Number of instances for temperature mild/Total number of instances) = 3/5

And probability for temperature cool = (Number of instances for temperature cool/Total number of instances) = 2/5

Therefore, total information for three subtrees = (3/5) I(M) + (2/5) I(C)
= 0.552927 + 0.40137
= 0.954297

Attribute 'Humidity'

There are two possible values of Humidity attribute, i.e., High and Normal. Let us analyze each case one by one.

There are 2 instances with high humidity. Play is held in case of 1 instance (1) and is not held in case of another instance (5).

There are 3 instances with normal humidity. The play is held in case of 2 instances (2 and 4) and is not held in case of single instance (3).

Given the above values, let us compute the information provided by this attribute. We divide the dataset into two subsets according to humidity being high or normal. Computing information for each case,

I (High) = I (H) = - (1/2) log(1/2) - (1/2) log(1/2)= 1.0

I (Normal) = I (N) = -(2/3) log(2/3)-(1/3) log(1/3)= 0.9187

Total information for the two sub-trees = probability for humidity high * I(H) + probability for humidity normal * I(N)

Here, probability for humidity high = (Number of instances for humidity high/Total number of instances) = 2/5

And probability for humidity normal = (Number of instances for humidity normal/Total number of instances) = 3/5

Therefore, total information for the two sub-trees = (2/5) I(H) + (3/5) I(N)
= 0.4 + 0.5512 = 0.9512

Attribute 'Windy'

There are two possible values for this attribute, i.e., true and false. Let us analyze each case one by one.

There are 2 instances where windy is true. Play is not held in case of both of the 2 instances (3 and 5).

For non-windy days, there are 3 instances. Play is held in all of the 3 instances (1, 2 and 4).

Given the above values, let us compute the information provided by this attribute. We divide the dataset into two subsets according to windy being true or false. Computing information for each case,

$$I\ (True) = I\ (T) = -\ (0/2)\log(0/2) - (2/2)\log(2/2) = 0$$

$$I\ (False) = I\ (F) = -\ (3/3)\log(3/3) - (0/3)\log(0/3) = 0$$

Total information for the two sub-trees = probability for windy true * I(T) + probability for windy false * I(F)

Here, probability for windy true = (Number of instances for windy true/Total number of instances) = 2/5

And, probability for windy false = (Number of instances for windy false/Total number of instances) = 3/5

Therefore, total information for the two sub-trees = (2/5) I(T) + (3/5) I(F) = 0

The Information gain can now be computed:

Potential Split attribute	*Information before split*	*Information after split*	*Information gain*
Temperature	0.97428	0.954297	0.019987
Humidity	0.97428	0.9512	0.02308
Windy	0.97428	0	0.97428

Hence, the largest information gain is provided by the attribute 'Windy' and this attribute is used for the split.

Dataset for Windy 'TRUE'

Instance Number	*Temperature*	*Humidity*	*Play*
1	cool	normal	No
2	mild	high	No

From above table it is clear that for Windy value 'TRUE', the output class is always 'No'.

Dataset for Windy 'FALSE'

Instance Number	*Temperature*	*Humidity*	*Play*
1	Mild	High	Yes
2	Cool	Normal	Yes
3	Mild	Normal	Yes

Also for Windy value 'FALSE', the output class is always 'Yes'. Thus, the decision tree will look like Figure 5.17 after analysis of the rainy attribute.

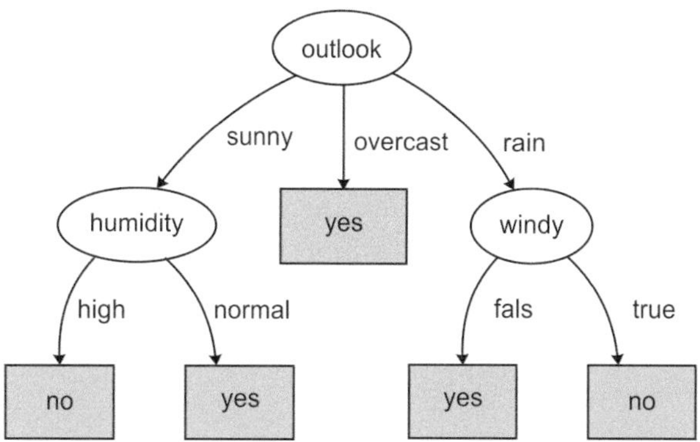

Figure 5.17 Decision tree after analysis of Sunny, Overcast and Rainy dataset

We have concluded that if the outlook is 'Rainy' and value of windy is 'False' then play is held and on the other hand, if value of windy is 'True' then it means that play is not held in that case.

Figure 5.18 represents the final tree view of all the 14 records of the dataset given in Figure 5.11 when it is generated using Weka for the prediction of play on the basis of given weather conditions. The numbers shown along with the classes in the tree represent the number of instances that are classified under that node. For example, for outlook 'overcast', play is always held and there are total 4 instances in the dataset which agree with this rule. Similarly, there are 2 instances in the dataset for which play is not held if outlook is rainy and windy is true.

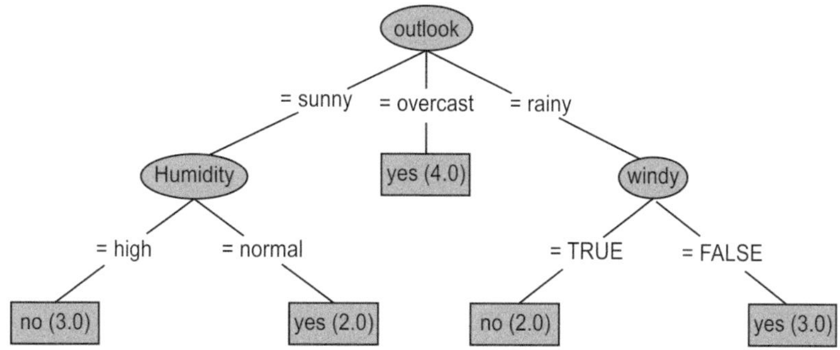

Figure 5.18 Final decision tree after analysis of Sunny, Overcast and Rainy dataset

Suppose, we have to predict whether the play will be held or not for an unknown instance having Temperature 'mild', Outlook 'sunny', Humidity 'normal' and windy 'false', it can be easily predicted on the basis of decision tree shown in Figure 5.18. For the given unknown instance, the play will be held based on conditional checks as shown in Figure 5.19.

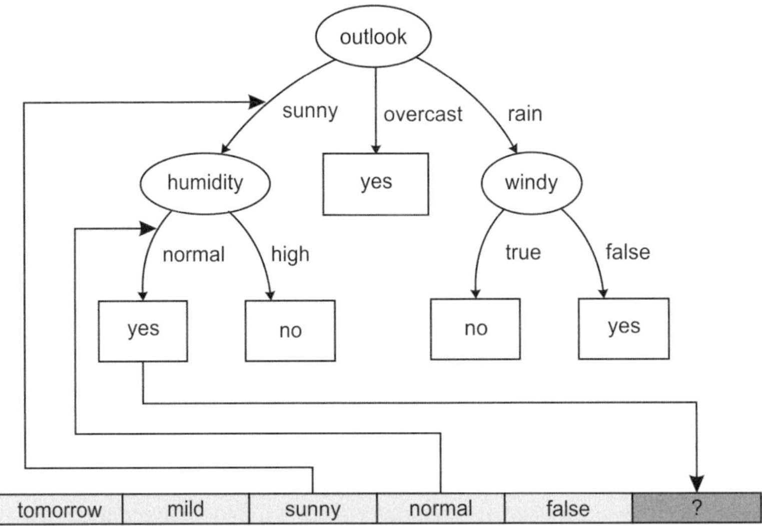

Figure 5.19 Prediction of Play for an unknown instance

5.6.6 Drawbacks of information gain theory

Though information gain is a good measure for determining the significance of an attribute, it has its own limitations. When it is applied to attributes with a large number of distinct values, a noticeable problem occurs. For example, while building a decision tree for a dataset consisting of the records of customers. In this case, information gain is used to determine the most significant attributes so that they can be tested for the root of the tree. Suppose, customers' credit card number is one of the input attributes in the customer dataset. As this input attribute uniquely identifies each customer, it has high mutual information. However, it cannot be included in the decision tree for making decisions because not all customers have credit cards and there is also a problem of how to treat them on the basis of their credit card number. This method will not work for all the customers.

5.6.7 Split algorithm based on Gini Index

The Gini Index is used to represent level of equality or inequality among objects. It can also be used to make decision trees. It was developed by Italian scientist Corrado Gini in 1912 and was used to analyze equality distribution of income among people. We will consider the example of wealth distribution in society in order to understand the concept of the Gini Index. The Gini Index always ranges between 0 and 1. It was designed to define the gap between the rich and the poor, with 0 signifying perfect equality where all people have the same income while 1 demonstrating perfect inequality where only one person gets everything in terms of income and rest of the others get nothing.

From this, it is evident that if Gini Index is very high, there will be huge inequality in income distribution. Therefore, we will be interested in knowing person's income. But in a society where everyone has same income then no one will be interested in knowing each other's income because they know that everyone is at the same level. Thus, the attribute of interest can be decided on the basis that if attribute has a high value Gini Index then it carriers more information and if it has a low value Gini Index then its information content is low.

To define the index, a graph is plotted by considering the percentage of income of the population as the Y-axis and the percentage of the population as the X-axis as shown in Figure 5.20.

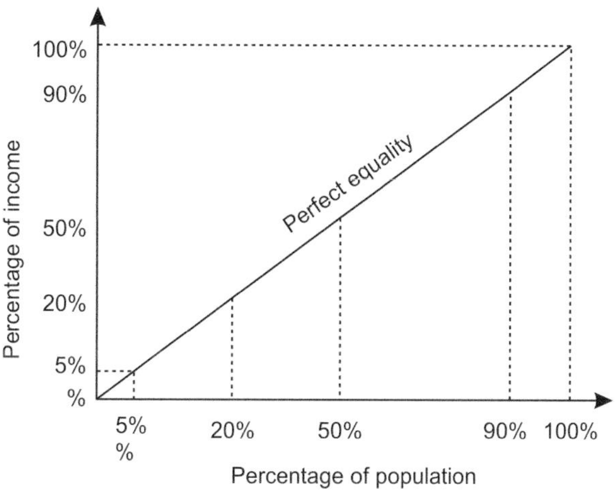

Figure 5.20 Gini Index representing perfect equality

In case of total equality in society, 5% of the people own 5% of the wealth, 20% of the people own 20% of the wealth similarly 90% of people own 90% of wealth. The line at 45 degrees thus represents perfect equal distribution of income in society.

The Gini Index is the ratio of the area between the Lorenz curve and the 45 degree line to the area under the 45 degree line given as follows.

$$\text{Gini Index (G)} = \frac{\text{area between the Lorenz curve and the 45} - \text{degree line}}{\text{area under the 45} - \text{degree line}}$$

As shown in Figure 5.21, the area that lies between the line of equality and the Lorenz curve is marked with A and the total area under the line of equality is represented by $(A + B)$ in the figure. Therefore,

$$G = \frac{A}{(A + B)}$$

Smaller the ratio, lesser is the area between the two curves and more evenly distributed is the wealth in the society.

The most equal society will be the one in which every person has the same income, making $A = 0$, thus making $G = 0$.

However, the most unequal society will be the one in which a single person receives 100% of the total wealth thus making $B = 0$ and $G = A/A = 1$. From this, we can observe that G always lies between 0 and 1.

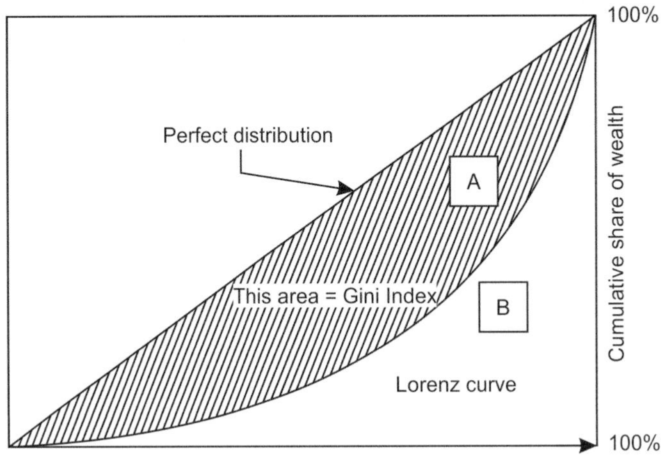

Figure 5.21 Lorenz curve

The more nearly equal a country's income distribution is, the closer is its Lorenz curve to the 45 degree line and the lower is its Gini Index. The more unequal a country's income distribution is, the farther is its Lorenz curve from the 45 degree line and the higher is its Gini Index. For example, as shown in Figure 5.22 (a), the bottom 10% of the people have 90% of total income, therefore Gini Index will be larger as the area between the equality line and the Lorenz curve is larger because there is large inequality in income distribution. Similarly, as shown in Figure 5.22 (b), the bottom 20% of the people have 80% of the total income and the bottom 30% of the people have 70% of the total income is shown in Figure 5.22 (c).

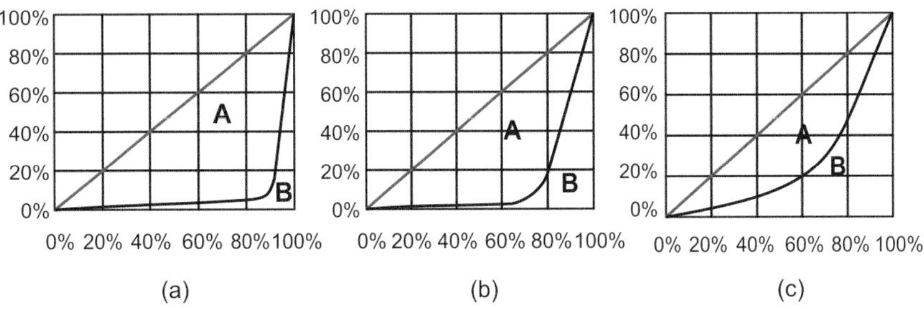

Figure 5.22 Lorenz curves with varying income distributions

From this, it can be concluded that, if income were distributed with perfect equality, the Lorenz curve would coincide with the 45 degree line and the Gini Index would be zero. However, if income were distributed with perfect inequality, the Lorenz curve would coincide with the horizontal axis and the right vertical axis and the index would be 1.

Gini Index can also be calculated in terms of probability and if a dataset D contains instances from n classes, the Gini Index, G(D), is defined as

$$G(D) = 1 - \Sigma(p_i)^{\text{No. of classes}}$$

Here, p_i is the relative frequency or probability of class i in D. *Let us calculate the Gini Index for tossing an unbiased coin.*

$$G = 1 - (\text{Probability of getting head})^{\text{No of classes}} - (\text{Probability of getting tail})^{\text{No of classes}}$$

$$G = 1 - (0.5)^2 - (0.5)^2 = 0.5$$

But if coin is biased having head on both sides, then there is 100% chance of a head and 0% chance of tail then the Gini Index is:

$$G = 1 - (1)^2 = 0$$

As there is no uncertainty about the coin in this case so the index is 0. It is maximum at a value of 0.5 in case of an unbiased coin. If the coin is biased, such that head occurs 60% of the times. then the Gini Index is reduced to 0.48.

Similarly we can calculate the Gini Index for a dice with six possible outcomes with equal probability as

$$G = 1 - 6(1/6)^2 = 5/6 = 0.833$$

If the dice is biased, let us say there is 50% chance of getting 6 and remaining 50% is being shared by other 5 numbers leaving only a 10% chance of getting each number other than 6 then the Gini Index is

$$G = 1 - 5(0.1)^2 - (0.5)^2 = 0.70$$

$$G = 1 - 5(0.05)^2 - (0.75)^2 = 0.425$$

Here, Gini Index has been reduced from 0.833 to 0.70. Clearly, the high value of index means high uncertainty.

It is important to observe that the Gini Index behaves in the same manner as the information gain discussed in Section 5.6.4. Table 5.1 clearly shows that same trend in both the cases.

Table 5.1 Information and Gini Index for a number of events

Event	Information	Gini Index
Toss of a unbiased coin	1.0	0.5
Toss of a biased coin (60% heads)	0.881	0.42
Throw of a unbiased dice	2.585	0.83
Throw of a biased die (50% chance of a 6)	2.16	0.7

5.6.8 Building a decision tree with Gini Index

Let us build the decision tree for the dataset given in Figure 5.23.

It has 3 input attributes X, Y, Z and one output attribute 'Class'. We have added a new column for instance numbers for easy explanation. The dataset contains four records and the output attribute or class can be either A or B.

Instance Number	X	Y	Z	Class
1	1	1	1	A
2	1	1	0	A
3	0	0	1	B
4	1	0	0	B

X	Y	Z	Class
1 = 3	1 = 2	1 = 2	A = 2
0 = 1	0 = 2	0 = 2	B = 2

Figure 5.23 Dataset for class C prediction based on given attribute condition

The frequencies of the two output classes are given as follows:
A = 2 (Instances 1,2)
B = 2 (Instances 3,4)
The Gini Index of the whole dataset is calculated as follows:

$$G = 1 - (\text{probability for Class A})^{\text{No of classes}} - (\text{probability for Class B})^{\text{No of classes}}$$

Here, probability for class A = (No of instances for class I/Total no of instances) = 2/4
And probability for class B = (No of instances for class II/Total no of instances) = 2/4
Therefore, $G = 1 - (2/4)^2 - (2/4)^2 = 0.5$

Let us consider each attribute one by one as split attribute and calculate Gini Index for each attribute.

Attribute 'X'

As given in dataset, there are two possible values of X, i.e., 1, 0. Let us analyze each case one by one.

For X = 1, there are 3 instances namely instance 1, 2 and 4. The first two instances are labeled as class A and the third instance, i.e, record number 4 is labeled as class B.

For X = 0, there is only 1 instance, i.e, instance number 3 which is labeled as class B.

Given the above values, let us compute the Gini Index by using this attribute. We divide the dataset into two subsets according to X being 1 or 0.

Computing the Gini Index for each case,

$$G(X1) = 1 - (2/3)^2 - (1/3)^2 = 0.44444$$

$$G(X0) = 1 - (0/1)^2 - (1/1)^2 = 0$$

Total Gini Index for the two sub-trees = probability for X having value 1 * G(X1) + probability for X having value 0 * G(X0)

Here, probability for X having value 1 = (Number of instances for X having value 1/Total number of instances) = 3/4

And probability for X having value 0 = (Number of instances for X having value 0/Total number of instances) = 1/4

Therefore, total Gini Index for two subtrees = (3/4) G(X1) + (1/4) G(X0)
= 0.333333+0
= 0.333333

Attribute 'Y'

There are two possible values of the Y attribute, i.e., 1 or 0. Let us analyze each case one by one.

There are 2 instances where Y has value 1. In both cases when Y = 1, the record belongs to class A and in 2 instances when Y = 0 both records belong to class B.

Given the above values, let us compute Gini Index by using this attribute. We divide the dataset into two subsets according to Y being 1 or 0.

Computing the Gini Index for each case,

$$G(Y1) = 1 - (2/2)^2 - (0/2)^2 = 0$$

$$G(Y0) = 1 - (0/2)^2 - (2/2)^2 = 0$$

Total Gini Index for two sub-trees = probability for Y having value 1* G(Y1) + probability for Y having value 0 * G(Y0)

Here, probability for Y in 1 = (Number of instances for Y having 1/Total number of instances) = 2/4

And probability for Y in 0 = (Number of instances for Y having 0/Total number of instances) = 2/4

Therefore, Total Gini Index for the two sub-trees = (2/4) G(Y1) + (2/4) G(Y0)
= 0 + 0 = 0

Attribute 'Z'

There are two possible values of the Z attribute, i.e., 1 or 0. Let us analyze each case one by one.

There are 2 instances where Z has value 1 and 2 instances where Z has value 0. In both cases, there exists a record belonging to class A and class B with Z either being 0 or 1.

Given the above values, let us compute the information by using this attribute. We divide the dataset into two subsets according to Z conditions, i.e., 1 and 0.

Computing the Gini Index for each case,

$$G (Z1) = 1 - (1/2)^2 - (1/2)^2 = 0.5$$

$$G(Z0) = 1 - (1/2)^2 - (1/2)^2 = 0.5$$

Total Gini Index for the two sub-trees = probability for Z having value 1 * G(Z1) + probability for Z having value 0 * G(Z0)

Here, probability for Z having value 1 = (Number of instances for Z having value 1/Total number of instances) = 2/4

And probability for Z having value 0 = (Number of instances for Z having value 0/Total number of instances) = 2/4

Therefore, total information for the two subtrees = (2/4) G(Z1) + (2/4) G(Z0)
= 0.25 + 0.25 = 0.50

The Gain can now be computed:

Potential Split attribute	Gini Index before split	Gini Index after split	Gain
X	0.5	0.333333	0.166667
Y	0.5	0	0.5
Z	0.5	0.50	0

Since the largest Gain is provided by the attribute 'Y' it is used for the split as depicted in Figure 5.24.

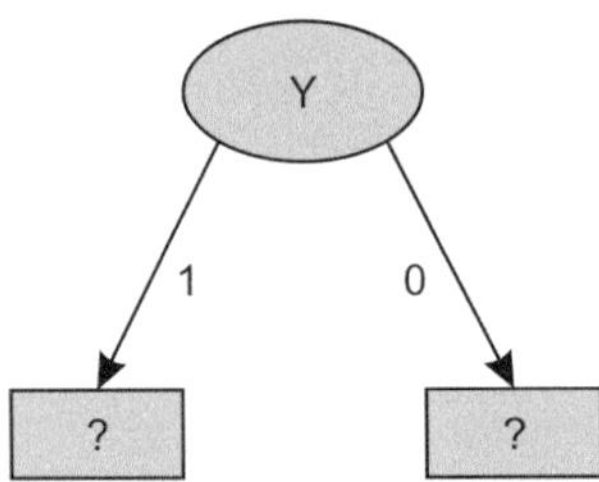

Figure 5.24 Data splitting based on Y attribute

There are two possible values for attribute Y, i.e., 1 or 0, and so the dataset will be split into two subsets based on distinct values of Y attribute as shown in Figure 5.24.

Dataset for Y '1'

Instance Number	X	Z	Class
1	1	1	A
2	1	0	A

There are 2 samples records both belonging to class A. Thus, frequencies of classes are as follows:
A = 2 (Instances 1, 2)
B = 0
Information provided by the whole dataset on the basis of class is given by

$$I = - (2/2) \log (2/2) - (0/2) \log(0/2) = 0$$

As irrespective of value of X and Z both the records belong to class 'A' hence for Y = 1 the tree will classify as class 'A' as shown in Figure 5.25.

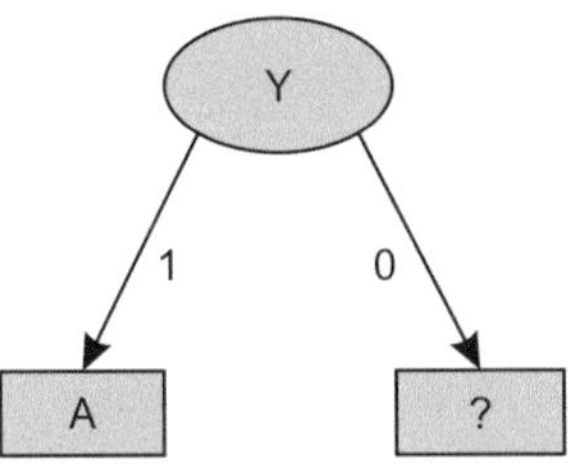

Figure 5.25 Decision tree after splitting of attribute Y having value '1'

Dataset for Y '0'

Instance Number	X	Z	Class
3	0	1	B
4	1	0	B

Here, for Y having value 0, both records are classified as class 'B' irrespective of value of X and Z. Thus, the decision tree will look like as shown in Figure 5.26 after analysis of the Y = 0 subset.

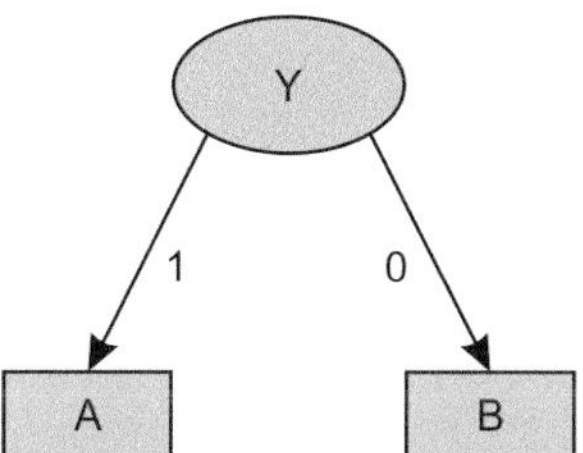

Figure 5.26 Decision tree after splitting of attribute Y value '0'

Let us consider another example to build a decision tree for the dataset given in Figure 5.27. It has four input attributes outlook, temperature, humidity and windy. Instance numbers have been added for easier explanation. Here, 'Play' is the class or output attributes and there are 14 records containing the information if play was held or not, based on weather conditions.

Instance Number	Outlook	Temperature	Humidity	Windy	Play
1	sunny	hot	high	false	No
2	sunny	hot	high	true	No
3	overcast	hot	high	false	Yes
4	rainy	mild	high	false	Yes
5	rainy	cool	normal	false	Yes
6	rainy	cool	normal	true	No
7	overcast	cool	normal	true	Yes
8	sunny	mild	high	false	No
9	sunny	cool	normal	false	Yes
10	rainy	mild	normal	false	Yes
11	sunny	mild	normal	true	Yes
12	overcast	mild	high	true	Yes
13	overcast	hot	normal	false	Yes
14	rainy	mild	high	true	No

Attribute, Values and Counts

Outlook	Temperature	Humidity	Windy	Play
sunny = 5	hot = 4	high = 7	true = 6	yes = 9
overcast = 4	mild = 6	normal = 7	false = 8	no = 5
rainy = 5	cool = 4			

Figure 5.27 Dataset for play prediction based on given day weather conditions

In this dataset, there are 14 samples and two classes for target attribute Play, i.e., Yes and No. The frequencies of these two classes are given as follows:

Yes = 9 (Instances 3,4,5,7,9,10,11,12,13 and 14)

No = 5(Instances 1,2,6,8 and 15)

The Gini Index of the whole dataset is given by

$$G = 1 - (\text{probability for Play Yes})^{\text{No of classes}} - (\text{probability for Play No})^{\text{No of classes}}$$

Here, probability for Play Yes = 9/14

And, probability for Play No = 5/14

Therefore, $G = 1-(9/14)^2 - (5/14)^2 = 0.45918$

Let us consider each attribute one by one as split attributes and calculate the Gini Index for each attribute.

Attribute 'Outlook'

As given in the dataset, there are three possible values of outlook, i.e., Sunny, Overcast and Rainy. Let us analyze each case one by one.

There are 5 instances for outlook having value sunny. Play is held in case of 2 instances (9 and 11) and is not held in case of 3 instances (1, 2 and 8).

There are 4 instances for outlook having value overcast. Play is held in case of all the 4 instances (3, 7, 12 and 13).

There are 5 instances for outlook having value rainy. Play is held in case of 3 instances (4, 5 and 10) and is not held in case of 2 instances (6 and 14).

Given the above values, let us compute the Gini Index by using this 'Outlook' attribute. We divide the dataset into three subsets according to outlook being sunny, overcast or rainy. Computing Gini Index for each case,

$$G(\text{Sunny}) = G(S) = 1- (2/5)^2 - (3/5)^2 = 0.48$$

$$G(\text{Overcast}) = G(O) = 1 - (4/4)^2 - (0/4)^2 = 0$$

$$G(\text{Rainy}) = G(R) = 1 - (3/5)^2 - (2/5)^2 = 0.48$$

Total Gini Index for three sub-trees = probability for outlook Sunny * G(S) + probability for outlook Overcast * G(O) + probability for outlook Rainy * G (R)

The probability for outlook Sunny = (Number of instances for outlook Sunny/Total number of instances) = 5/14

The probability for outlook Overcast = (Number of instances for outlook Overcast/Total number of instances) = 4/14

The probability for outlook Rainy = (Number of instances for outlook Rainy/Total number of instances) = 5/14

Therefore, the total Gini Index for the three sub-trees = (5/14) G(S) + (4/14) G(O) + (5/14) G(R)
= 0.171428+ 0 + 0.171428
= 0.342857

Attribute 'Temperature'

There are three possible values of the 'Temperature' attribute, i.e., Hot, Mild or Cool. Let us analyze each case one by one.

There are 4 instances for temperature having value hot. Play is held in case of 2 instances (3 and 13) and is not held in case of other 2 instances (1 and 2).

There are 6 instances for temperature having value mild. Play is held in case of 4 instances (4, 10, 11 and 12) and is not held in case of 2 instances (8 and 14).

There are 4 instances for temperature having value cool. Play is held in case of 3 instances (5, 7 and 9) and is not held in case of 1 instance (6).

Given the above values, let us compute the Gini Index by using this attribute. We divide the dataset into three subsets according to temperature conditions, i.e., hot, mild and cool. Computing the Gini Index for each case,

$$G\ (Hot) = G\ (H) = 1 - (2/4)^2 - (2/4)^2 = 0.50$$

$$G\ (Mild) = G\ (M) = 1 - (4/6)^2 - (2/6)^2 = 0.444$$

$$G\ (Cool) = G(C) = 1 - (3/4)^2 - (1/4)^2 = 0.375$$

Total Gini Index of 3 sub-trees = probability for temperature hot * G(H) + probability for temperature mild * G(M) + probability for temperature cool * G(C)

Here, probability for temperature hot = (Number of instances for temperature hot/Total number of instances) = 4/14

And probability for temperature mild = (Number of instances for temperature mild/Total number of instances) = 6/14

And probability for temperature cool = (Number of instances for temperature cool/Total number of instances) = 4/14

Therefore, the total Gini Index of the three sub-trees = (4/14) G(H) + (6/14) G(M) + (4/14) G(C)
= 0.44028

Attribute 'Humidity'

There are two possible values of the 'Humidity' attribute, i.e., High and Normal. Let us analyze each case one by one.

There are 7 instances for humidity having high value. Play is held in case of 3 instances (3, 4 and 12) and is not held in case of 4 instances (1, 2, 8 and 14).

There are 7 instances for humidity having normal value. Play is held in case of 6 instances (5, 7, 9, 10, 11 and 13) and is not held in case of 1 instance (6).

Given the above values, let us compute the Gini Index by using this attribute. We divide the dataset into two subsets according to humidity conditions, i.e., high and normal. Computing Gini Index for each case,

$$G\ (\text{High}) = G(H) = 1 - (3/7)^2 - (4/7)^2 = 0.48979$$

$$G\ (\text{Normal}) = G(N) = 1 - (6/7)^2 - (1/7)^2 = 0.24489$$

Total Gini Index for the two sub-trees = probability for humidity high* G(H) + probability for humidity normal * G(N)

Here, probability for humidity high = (Number of instances for humidity high/Total number of instances) = 7/14

The probability for humidity normal = (Number of instances for humidity normal/Total number of instances) = 7/14

Therefore, the total Gini Index for two sub-trees = (7/14) G(H) + (7/14) G(N)
= 0.3673439

Attribute 'Windy'

There are two possible values for this attribute, i.e., true and false. Let us analyze each case one by one.

There are 6 instances for windy having value true. Play is held in case of 3 instances (7, 11 and 12) and is not held in case of another 3 instances (2, 6 and 14).

There are 8 instances for windy having value false. Play is held in case of 6 instances (3, 4, 5, 9, 10 and 13) and is not held in case of 2 instances (1 and 8).

Given the above values, let us compute the Gini Index by using this attribute. We divide the dataset into two subsets according to windy being true or false. Computing Gini Index for each case,

$$G\ (\text{True}) = G(T) = 1 - (3/6)^2 - (3/6)^2 = 0.5$$

$$G\ (\text{False}) = G(F) = 1 - (6/8)^2 - (2/8)^2 = 0.375$$

Total Gini Index for the two sub-trees = probability for windy true * G(T) + probability for windy false * G(F)

Here, The probability for windy true = (Number of instances for windy true/Total number of instances) = 6/14

And the probability for windy false = (Number of instances for windy false/Total number of instances) = 8/14

Therefore, total Gini Index for the two sub-trees = (6/14) G(T) + (8/14) G(F)
= 0.42857

The gain can now be computed as follows:

Potential Split attribute	Gini Index before split	Gini Index after split	Gain
Outlook	0.45918	0.342857	0.116323
Temperature	0.45918	0.44028	0.0189
Humidity	0.45918	0.3673439	0.0918361
Windy	0.45918	0.42857	0.03061

Hence, the largest gain is provided by the attribute 'Outlook' and it is used for the split as depicted in Figure 5.28.

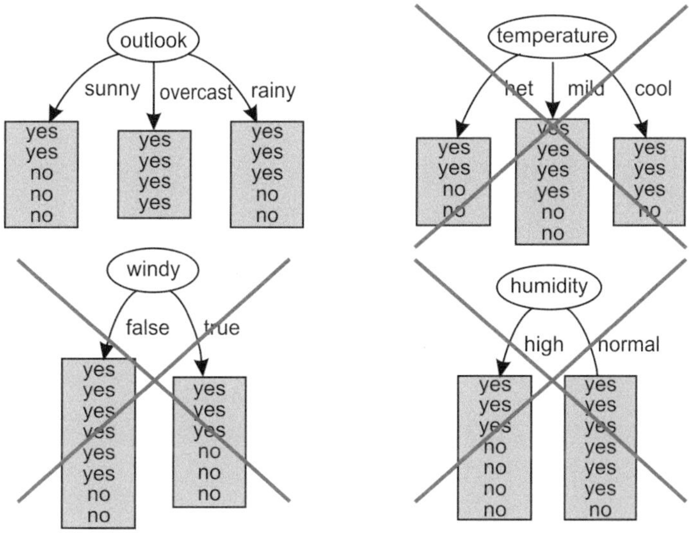

Figure 5.28 Selection of Outlook as root attribute

For Outlook, as there are three possible values, i.e., sunny, overcast and rainy, the dataset will be split into three subsets based on distinct values of the Outlook attribute as shown in Figure 5.29.

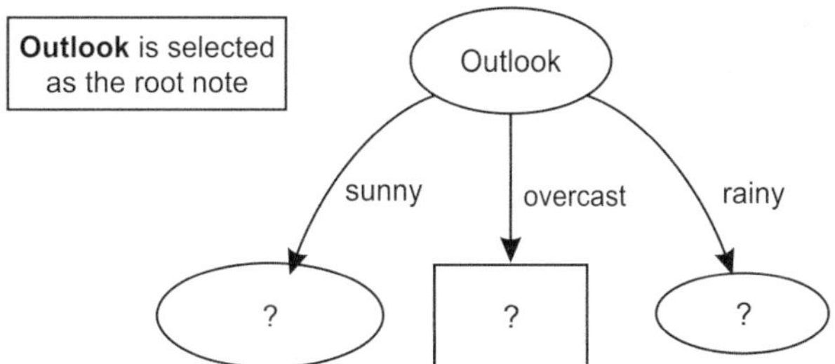

Figure 5.29 Data splitting based on Outlook attribute

Dataset for Outlook 'Sunny'

Instance Number	*Temperature*	*Humidity*	*Windy*	*Play*
1	hot	high	false	No
2	hot	high	true	No
3	mild	high	false	No
4	cool	normal	false	Yes
5	mild	normal	true	Yes

In this case, we have three input attributes Temperature, Humidity and Windy. This dataset consists of 5 samples. The frequencies of the classes are as follows:

Yes = 2 (Instances 4, 5)

No = 3 (Instances 1,2,3)

The Gini Index of the whole dataset is given by

$$G = 1 - (\text{probability for Play Yes})^{\text{Number of classes}} - (\text{probability for Play No})^{\text{Number of classes}}$$

Here, probability for Play Yes = 2/5

And probability for Play No = 3/5

Therefore, $G = 1 - (2/5)^2 - (3/5)^2 = 0.48$

Let us consider each attribute one by one as split attributes and calculate the Gini Index for each attribute.

Attribute 'Temperature'

There are three possible values of Temperature attribute, i.e., hot, mild and cool. Let us analyze each case one by one.

There are 2 instances for temperature having value hot. Play is not held in both of 2 instances (1 and 2).

There are 2 instances for temperature having value mild. Play is held in case of 1 instance (5) and is not held in case of another instance (3).

There is only 1 instance for temperature having value cool. Play is held in this single instance (4).

Given the above values, let us compute the Gini Index by using this attribute. We divide the dataset into three subsets according to temperature being hot, mild or cool. Computing Gini Index for each case,

$$G(\text{Hot}) = G(H) = 1 - (0/2)^2 - (2/2)^2 = 0$$

$$G(\text{Mild}) = G(M) = 1 - (1/2)^2 - (1/2)^2 = 0.5$$

$$G(\text{Cool}) = G(C) = 1 - (1/1)^2 - (0/1)^2 = 0$$

Total Gini Index for the three sub-trees = probability for temperature hot * G(H) + probability for temperature mild * G(M) + probability for temperature cool *G(C)

Here, probability for temperature hot = (Number of instances for temperature hot/Total number of instances) = 2/5

And probability for temperature mild = (Number of instances for temperature mild/Total number of instances) = 2/5

And probability for temperature cool = (Number of instances for temperature cool/Total number of instances) = 1/5

Therefore, total Gini Index for these three sub-trees = (2/5)G(H) + (1/5) G(M) + (2/5) G(C)

= 0 + 0.1 + 0 = 0.1

Attribute 'Humidity'

There are two possible values of Humidity attribute, i.e., High and Normal. Let us analyze each case one by one.

There are 3 instances when humidity is high. Play is not held in any of these 3 instances (1, 2 and 3).

There are 2 instances when humidity is normal. Play is held in both of 2 instances (4 and 5).

Given the above values, let us compute the Gini Index by using this attribute. We divide the dataset into two subsets according to humidity being high or normal. Computing Gini Index for each case,

$$G\ (\text{High}) = G(H) = 1 - (0/3)^2 - (3/3)^2 = 0$$

$$G\ (\text{Normal}) = G(N) = 1 - (2/2)^2 - (0/2)^2 = 0$$

Total Gini Index for the two sub-trees = probability for humidity high * G(H) + probability for humidity normal * G(N)

Here, probability for humidity high = (Number of instances for humidity high/Total number of instances) = 3/5

And probability for humidity normal = (Number of instances for humidity normal/Total number of instances) = 2/5

Therefore, total Gini Index for the two sub-trees = (3/5) G(H) + (2/5) G(N) = 0

Attribute 'Windy'

There are two possible values for this attribute, i.e., true and false. Let us analyze each case one by one.

There are 2 instances when it is windy. Play is held in case of 1 instance (5) and is not held in case of another 1 instance (2).

There are 3 instances when it is not windy. Play is held in case of 1 instance (4) and is not held in case of 2 instances (1 and 3).

Given the above values, let us compute the Gini Index by using this attribute. We divide the dataset into two subsets according to windy being true or false. Computing Gini Index for each case,

$$G\ (\text{True}) = G\ (T) = 1 - (1/2)^2 - (1/2)^2 = 0.5$$

$$G\ (\text{False}) = G\ (F) = 1 - (1/3)^2 - (2/3)^2 = 0.4444$$

Total Gini Index for the two sub-trees = probability for windy true * G(T) + probability for windy false * G(F)

Here, probability for windy true = (Number of instances for windy true/Total number of instances) = 2/5

And probability for windy false = (Number of instances for windy false/Total number of instances) = 3/5

Therefore, total Gini Index for the two sub-trees = (2/5) G(T) + (3/5) G(F) = 0.2 + 0.2666 = 0.4666

The Gain can now be computed:

Potential Split attribute	*Gini Index before split*	*Gini Index after split*	*Gain*
Temperature	0.48	0.1	0.38
Humidity	0.48	0	0.48
Windy	0.48	0.4666	0.014

The largest gain is provided by the attribute 'Humidity' and so, it is used for the split. Here, the algorithm is to be tuned in such a way that it should stop when we get the 0 value of the Gini Index to reduce the calculations for larger datasets. Now, the Humidity attribute is selected as the split attribute as depicted in Figure 5.30.

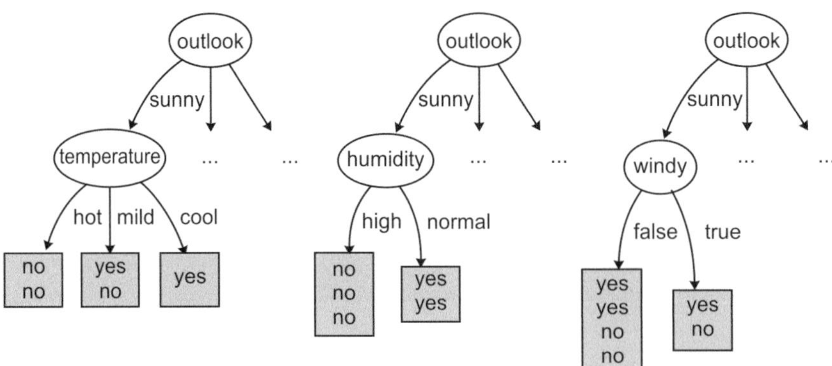

Figure 5.30 Humidity attribute is selected from dataset of Sunny instances

As the dataset consists of two possible values of humidity so data is split in two parts, i.e. humidity 'high' and humidity 'low' as shown below.

Dataset for Humidity 'High'

Instance Number	*Temperature*	*Windy*	*Play*
1	Hot	false	No
2	Hot	true	No
3	Mild	false	No

We can clearly see that all records with high humidity are classified as play having 'No' value. On the other hand, all records with normal humidity value are classified as play having 'Yes' value.

Dataset for Humidity 'Normal'

Instance Number	*Temperature*	*Windy*	*Play*
1	cool	false	Yes
2	mild	true	Yes

Thus, the decision tree will look like as shown in Figure 5.31 after analysis of the Humidity attribute.

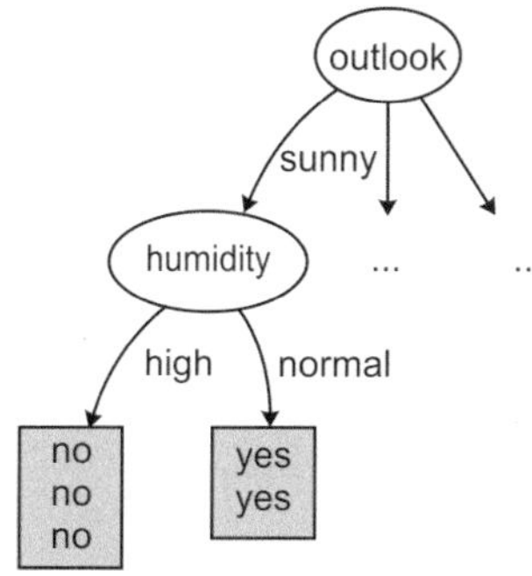

Figure 5.31 Decision tree after spitting data on the Humidity attribute

The analysis of the 'Sunny' dataset is now over and has allowed the the generation of the decision tree shown in Figure 5.31. It has been analyzed that if the outlook is 'Sunny' and humidity is 'Normal' then play will be held while on the other hand if the humidity is 'high' then play will not be held.

Now, let us take next dataset of where Outlook has value overcast for further analysis.

Dataset for Outlook 'Overcast'

Instance Number	*Temperature*	*Humidity*	*Windy*	*Play*
1	hot	high	false	Yes
2	cool	normal	true	Yes
3	mild	high	true	Yes

This dataset consists of 3 records. For outlook overcast all records belong to the 'Yes' class only. Thus, the decision tree will look like Figure 5.32 after analysis of the overcast dataset.

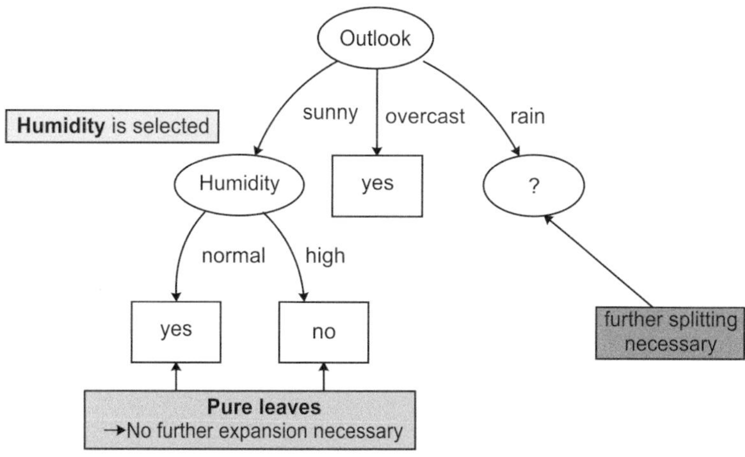

Figure 5.32 Decision tree after analysis of Sunny and Overcast datasets

Therefore, it may be concluded that if the outlook is 'Overcast' then play is held. Now we have to select another split attribute for the outlook rainy and dataset for this is given as follows.

Dataset for Outlook 'Rainy'

Instance Number	*Temperature*	*Humidity*	*Windy*	*Play*
1	Mild	High	False	Yes
2	Cool	Normal	False	Yes
3	Cool	Normal	Ttrue	No
4	Mild	Normal	False	Yes
5	Mild	High	True	No

This dataset consists of 5 records. The frequencies of the classes are as follows:

Yes= 3 (Instances 1,2 and 4)

No= 2 (Instances 3 and 5)

Gini Index of the whole dataset on the basis of whether play held or not is given by

$$G = 1 - (\text{probability for Play Yes})^{\text{Number of classes}} - (\text{probability for Play No})^{\text{Number of classes}}$$

Here, probability for Play Yes = 3/5

And probability for Play No = 2/5

Therefore, $G = 1 - (3/5)^2 - (2/5)^2 = 0.48$

Let us consider each attribute one by one as split attributes and calculate the Gini Index for each attribute.

Attribute 'Temperature'

There are two possible values of Temperature attribute, i.e., mild and cool. Let us analyze each case one by one.

There are 3 instances for temperature having value mild. Play is held in case of 2 instances (1 and 4) and is not held in case of 1 instance (5).

There are 2 instances for temperature having value cool. Play is held in case of 1 instance (2) and is not held in case of another 1 instance (3).

Given the above values, let us compute the Gini Index by using this attribute. We divide the dataset into two subsets according to temperature being mild or cool. Computing Gini Index for each case,

$$G\ (\text{Mild}) = G(M) = 1 - (2/3)^2 - (1/3)^2 = 0.444$$

$$G\ (\text{Cool}) = G(C) = 1 - (1/2)^2 - (1/2)^2 = 0.5$$

Total Gini Index for the two sub-trees = probability for temperature mild * G(M) + probability for temperature cool * G (C)

Here, probability for temperature mild = (Number of instances for temperature mild/Total number of instances) = 3/5

And probability for temperature cool = (Number of instances for temperature cool/Total number of instances) = 2/5

Therefore, Total Gini Index for the two sub-trees = (3/5) G(M) + (2/5) G(C) = 0.2666 + 0.2 = 0.4666

Attribute 'Humidity'

There are two possible values of Humidity attribute, i.e., High and Normal. Let us analyze each case one by one.

There are 2 instances for humidity having high value. Play is held in case of 1 instance (1) and is not held in case of 1 instance (5).

There are 3 instances for humidity having normal value. Play is held in case of 2 instances (2 and 4) and is not held in case of 1 instance (3).

Given the above values, let us compute the Gini Index by using this attribute. We divide the dataset into two subsets according to humidity being high or normal. Computing the Gini Index for each case,

$$G\ (\text{High}) = G(H) = 1 - (1/2)^2 - (1/2)^2 = 0.5$$

$$G\ (\text{Normal}) = G(N) = 1 - (2/3)^2 - (1/3)^2 = 0.4444$$

Total Gini Index for the two sub-trees = probability for humidity high* G(H) + probability for humidity normal * G(N)

Here, probability for humidity high = (Number of instances for humidity high/Total number of instances) = 2/5

And probability for humidity normal = (Number of instances for humidity normal/Total number of instances) = 3/5

Therefore, Total Gini Index for the two sub-trees = (2/5) G(H) + (3/5) G(N) = 0.2 + 0.2666 =0.4666

Attribute 'Windy'

There are two possible values for this attribute, i.e., true and false. Let us analyze each case one by one.

There are 2 instances where windy is true. Play is not held in case of both of 2 instances (3 and 5).

There are 3 instances where windy is false. Play is held in case of all 3 instances (1, 2 and 4).

Given the above values, let us compute the Gini Index by using this attribute. We divide the dataset into two subsets according to windy being true or false. Computing the Gini Index for each case,

$$G\ (\text{True}) = G(T) = 1 - (0/2)^2 - (2/2)^2 = 0$$

$$G\ (\text{False}) = G(F) = 1 - (3/3)^2 - (0/3)^2 = 0$$

Total Gini Index for the two sub-trees = probability for windy true * G(T) + probability for windy false * G(F)

Here, probability for windy true = (Number of instances for windy true/Total number of instances) = 2/5

And probability for windy false = (Number of instances for windy false/Total number of instances) = 3/5

Therefore, total Gini Index for these two subtrees = (2/5) G(T) + (3/5) G(F) = 0

The Gain can now be computed:

Potential Split attribute	Gini Index before split	Gini Index after split	Gain
Temperature	0.48	0.4666	0.0134
Humidity	0.48	0.4666	0.0134
Windy	0.48	0	0.48

Hence, the largest gain is provided by the attribute 'Windy' and it is used for the split. Now, the Windy attribute is selected as split attribute.

Dataset for Windy 'TRUE'

Instance Number	*Temperature*	*Humidity*	*Play*
1	cool	normal	No
2	mild	high	No

It is clear from the data that whenever it is windy the play is not held. Play is held whenever conditions are otherwise.

Dataset for Windy 'FALSE'

Instance Number	*Temperature*	*Humidity*	*Play*
1	mild	high	Yes
2	cool	normal	Yes
3	mild	normal	Yes

Thus, the decision tree will look like Figure 5.33 after analysis of the 'Rainy' attribute.

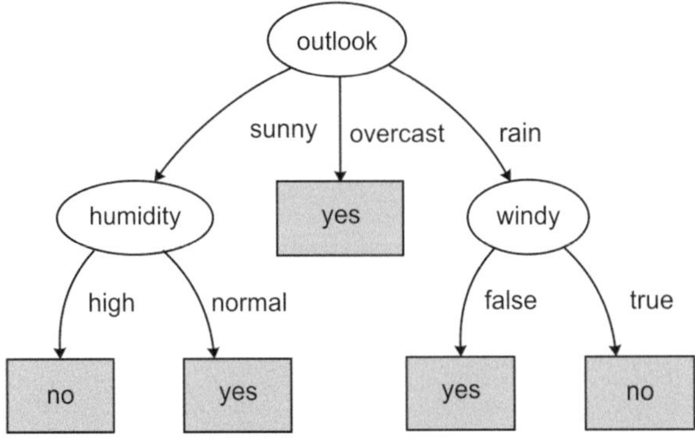

Figure 5.33 Decision tree after analysis of Sunny, Overcast and Rainy datasets

It has been concluded that if the outlook is 'Rainy' and value of windy is 'False' then play will be held and on the other hand, if value of windy is 'True' then the play will not be held.

Figure 5.34 represents the final tree view of all the 14 records of the dataset given in Figure 5.27 when it is generated using Weka for the prediction of play on the basis of given weather conditions. The numbers shown along with the classes in the tree represent the number of instances that are classified under that node. For example, for outlook overcast, play is always held and there are total 4 instances in the dataset which agree with this rule. Similarly, there are 2 instances in the dataset for which play is not held if outlook is rainy and windy is true.

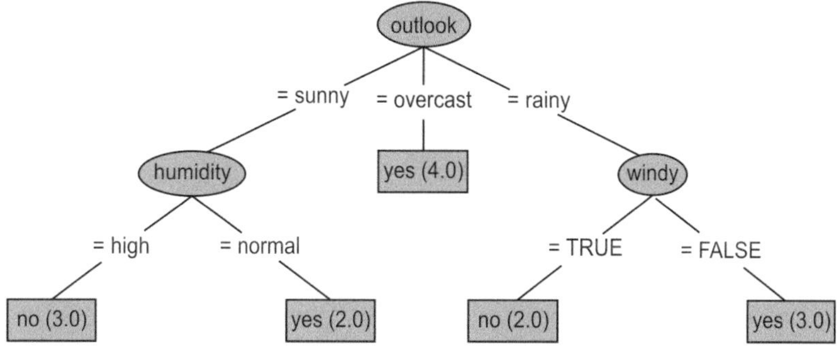

Figure 5.34 Final decision tree after analysis of Sunny, Overcast and Rainy datasets

If we have to predict whether play will be held or not for an unknown instance having Temperature 'mild', Outlook 'sunny', Humidity 'normal' and Windy 'false', it can be easily predicted on the basis of decision tree shown in Figure 5.34. For the given unknown instance, play will be held as shown in Figure 5.35.

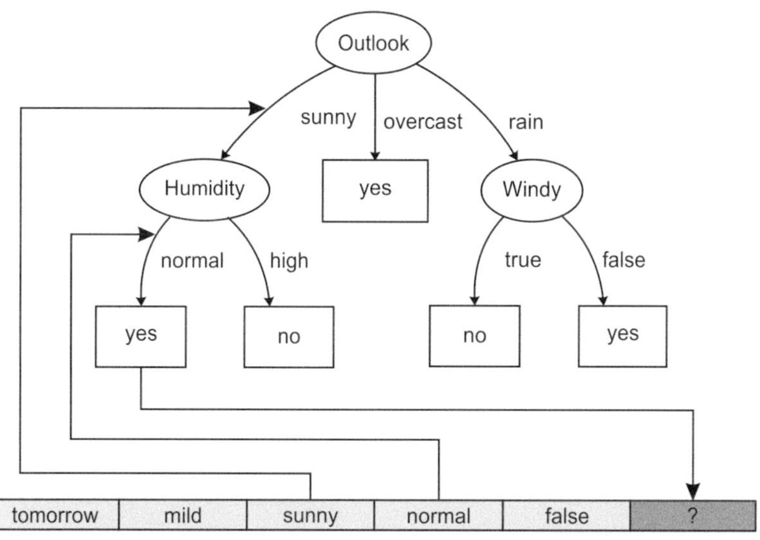

Figure 5.35 Prediction of play for unknown instance

5.6.9 Advantages of the decision tree method

The main advantages of a decision tree classifier are as follows:.

- The rules generated by a decision tree classifier are easy to understand and use.
- Domain knowledge is not required by the decision tree classifier.
- Learning and classification steps of the decision tree are simple and quick.

5.6.10 Disadvantages of the decision tree

The disadvantages of a decision tree classifier can be:

- Decision trees are easy to use compared to other decision-making models, but preparing decision trees, especially large ones with many branches, are complex and time-consuming affairs.
- They are unstable, meaning that a small change in the data can lead to a large change in the structure of the optimal decision tree.
- They are often relatively inaccurate. Many other predictors perform better with similar data.
- Decision trees, while providing easy to view illustrations, can also be unmanageable. Even data that is perfectly divided into classes and uses only simple threshold tests may require a large decision tree. Large trees are not intelligible, and pose presentation difficulties.

The other important classification technique is the Naïve Bayes Method which is based on Bayes theorem. The details of Naïve Bayes method have been discussed in next section.

5.7 Naïve Bayes Method

It is based on Bayes theorem given by Thomas Bayes in middle of the eighteenth century. It is amazing that despite being such an old theorem it has found its way into many modern fields such as AI and machine learning. Classification using Bayes theorem is different from the decision tree approach. It is based on a hypothesis that the given data belongs to a particular class. In this theorem probability is calculated for the hypothesis to be true.

Our understanding of this theorem begins with the fact that the Bayes Theorem in based on probabilities and so it is important to define some notations in the beginning.

$P(A)$ refers to the probability of occurrence of event A, while $P(A|B)$ refers to the conditional probability of event A given that event B has already occurred.

Bayes theorem is defined as follows …

$$P(A|B) = P(B|A)\,P(A)/P(B) \qquad \ldots(1)$$

Let us first prove this theorem.

We already know that

$$P(A|B) = P(A \,\&\, B)/P(B) \qquad \ldots(2)$$

[It is the probability that next event will be A when B has already happened]

Similarly, $$P(B|A) = P\,(B \,\&\, A)/P(A) \qquad \ldots(3)$$

From equation (3):

Thus, $P(B \& A) = P(B|A) * P(A)$

By putting this value of $P(B \& A)$ in equation (2), we get ....

$$P(A|B) = P(B|A)\, P(A)/P(B)$$

This proves the Bayes theorem.

Now let us consider that we have to predict the class of X out of three given classes C_1, C_2 and C_3. Here, the hypothesis is that event X has already occurred. Thus, we have to calculate $P(C_i|X)$, conditional probability of class being C_i when X has already occurred.

According to Bayes theorem:

$$P(C_i\,|X) = P(X|C_i)\, P(C_i)/P(X)$$

In this equation:

$P(C_i|X)$ is the conditional probability of class being C_i when X has already occurred or it is probability that X belongs to class C_i.

$P(X|C_i)$ is the conditional probability of record being X when it is known that output class is C_i

$P(C_i)$ is probability that object belongs to class C_i.

$P(X)$ is the probability of occurrence of record X.

Here, we have already made the hypothesis that X has already occurred so $P(X)$ is 1 so we have to calculate $P(X|C_i)$ and $P(C_i)$ in order to find required value.

To further understand this concept let us consider the following database, where the class of customer is defined based on his/her marital status, gender, employment status and credit rating as shown below.

Owns Home	Married	Gender	Employed	Credit rating	Class
Yes	Yes	Male	Yes	A	II
No	No	Female	Yes	A	I
Yes	Yes	Female	Yes	B	III
Yes	No	Male	No	B	II
No	Yes	Female	Yes	B	III
No	No	Female	Yes	B	I
No	No	Male	No	B	II
Yes	No	Female	Yes	A	I
No	Yes	Female	Yes	A	III
Yes	Yes	Female	Yes	A	III

Here, we have to predict the class of occurrence of X and let us suppose X is as shown below.

Owns Home	Married	Gender	Employed	Credit rating	Class
Yes	No	Male	Yes	A	?

Then we have to calculate the probability for class C_i, when X has already occurred. Thus it is

$$P(C_i \mid Yes, No, Male, Yes, A) = P(Yes, No, Male, Yes, A \mid C_i) * P(C_i)$$

Let us first calculate probability of each class, i.e., $P(C_i)$. Here, we have three classes, i.e., *I*, *II* and *III*. There are total 10 instances in the given dataset and there are three instances for class *I*, three for class *II* and four for class *III*. Thus,

Probability of class *I*, i.e., $P(I) = 3/10 = 0.3$

Probability of class *II*, i.e., $P(II) = 3/10 = 0.3$

Probability of class *III*, i.e., $P(III) = 4/10 = 0.4$

Now, let us calculate $P(X|C_i)$, i.e., $P(Yes, No, Male, Yes, A \mid C_i)$

$P(Yes, No, Male, Yes, A \mid C_i) = P(Owns\ Home = Yes| C_i) * P(Married = No| C_i) * P(Gender = Male| C_i) * P(Employed = Yes| C_i) * P(Credit\ rating = A| C_i)$

Thus, we need to calculate

$P(Owns\ Home = Yes|C_i)$,

$P(Married = No| C_i)$,

$P(Gender = Male|C_i)$,

$P(Employed = Yes|C_i)$,

$P(Credit\ rating = A|C_i)$.

Owns Home	Married	Gender	Employed	Credit rating	Class
No	No	Female	Yes	A	I
No	No	Female	Yes	B	I
Yes	No	Female	Yes	A	I
Yes	**No**	**Male**	**Yes**	**A**	**? [To be found]**
1/3	1	0	1	2/3	Probability of having{Yes, No, Male, Yes, A} Attribute value given the risk Class I
Yes	Yes	Male	Yes	A	II
Yes	No	Male	No	B	II
No	No	Male	No	B	II
Yes	**No**	**Male**	**Yes**	**A**	**? [To be found]**

Contd.

Owns Home	Married	Gender	Employed	Credit rating	Class
2/3	2/3	1	1/3	1/3	Probability of having{Yes, No, Male, Yes, A} Attribute value given the risk Class II
Yes	Yes	Female	Yes	B	III
No	Yes	Female	Yes	B	III
No	Yes	Female	Yes	A	III
Yes	Yes	Female	Yes	A	III
Yes	**No**	**Male**	**Yes**	**A**	**? [To be found]**
1/2	0	0	1	1/2	Probability of having{Yes, No, Male, Yes, A} Attribute value given the risk Class III

Thus, $P(X|I) = 1/3 * 1 * 0 * 1 * 2/3 = 0$

$P(X|II) = 2/3 * 2/3 * 1 * 1/3 * 1/3 = 4/81$

$\mathrm{P(X|III)} = 1/2 * 0 * 0 * 1 * 1/2 = 0$

$P(I \mid Yes, No, Male, Yes, A) = P(Yes, No, Male, Yes, A \mid I) * P(I) = 0*0.3 = 0$

$P(II \mid Yes, No, Male, Yes, A) = P(Yes, No, Male, Yes, A \mid II) * P(II) = 4/81*0.3 = 0.0148$

$P(III \mid Yes, No, Male, Yes, A) = P(Yes, No, Male, Yes, A \mid III) * P(III) = 0*0.4 = 0$

Therefore, *X* is assigned to Class *II*. It is very unlikely in real life datasets that the probability of class comes out to be 0 as in this example.

5.7.1 Applying Naïve Bayes classifier to the 'Whether Play' dataset

Let us consider another example of Naïve Bayes classifier for the dataset shown in Figure 5.36. It has 4 input attributes outlook, temperature, humidity and windy. Play is the class or output attribute. These 14 records contain the information if play has been held or not on the basis of any given day's weather conditions.

Instance Number	Outlook	Temperature	Humidity	Windy	Play
1	sunny	hot	high	false	No
2	sunny	hot	high	true	No
3	overcast	hot	high	false	Yes
4	rainy	mild	high	false	Yes
5	rainy	cool	normal	false	Yes

Contd.

Instance Number	*Outlook*	*Temperature*	*Humidity*	*Windy*	*Play*
6	rainy	cool	normal	true	No
7	overcast	cool	normal	true	Yes
8	sunny	mild	high	false	No
9	sunny	cool	normal	false	Yes
10	rainy	mild	normal	false	Yes
11	sunny	mild	normal	true	Yes
12	overcast	mild	high	true	Yes
13	overcast	hot	normal	false	Yes
14	rainy	mild	high	true	No

Attribute values and counts

Outlook	Temperature	Humidity	Windy	Play
sunny = 5	hot = 4	high = 7	true = 6	yes = 9
overcast = 4	mild = 6	normal = 7	false = 8	no = 5
rainy = 5	cool = 4			

Figure 5.36 Dataset for play prediction based on a given day's weather conditions

From this dataset, we can observe that when the outlook is sunny, play is not held on 3 out of the 5 days as shown in Figure 5.37.

Instance Number	Outlook	Temperature	Humidity	Windy	Play
1	Sunny	Hot	High	False	No
2	Sunny	Hot	High	True	No
8	Sunny	Mild	High	False	No
9	Sunny	Cool	Normal	False	Yes
11	Sunny	Mild	Normal	True	Yes

Figure 5.37 Probability of whether play will be held or not on a Sunny day

Therefore, it can be concluded that there are 60% chances that Play will not be held when it is a sunny day.

The Naïve Bayes theorem is based on probabilities, so we need to calculate probabilities for each occurrence in the instances. So, let us calculate the count for the each occurrence as shown in Figure 5.38.

	Play	
Outlook	**yes**	**no**
sunny	2	3
overcast	4	0
rainy	3	2
TOTAL	9	5

Instance Number	Outlook	Temperature	Humidity	Windy	Play
1	sunny	hot	high	false	No
2	sunny	hot	high	true	No
3	overcast	hot	high	false	Yes
4	rainy	mild	high	false	Yes
5	rainy	cool	normal	false	Yes
6	rainy	cool	normal	true	No
7	overcast	cool	normal	true	Yes
8	sunny	mild	high	false	No
9	sunny	cool	normal	false	Yes
10	rainy	mild	normal	false	Yes
11	sunny	mild	normal	true	Yes
12	overcast	mild	high	true	Yes
13	overcast	hot	normal	false	Yes
14	rainy	mild	high	true	No

	Play			Play			Play			Play			Play
Outlook	**yes**	**no**	**Temp.**	**yes**	**no**	**Humid.**	**yes**	**no**	**Windy**	**yes**	**no**		
sunny	2	3	hot	2	2	high	3	4	false	6	2	yes	9
overcast	4	0	mild	4	2	normal	6	1	true	3	3	no	5
rainy	3	2	cool	3	1								
TOTAL	9	5	TOTAL	9	5	TOTAL	9	5	TOTAL	9	5	TOTAL	14

Figure 5.38 Summarization of count calculations of all input attributes

Now, we can calculate the probability of play being held or not for each value of input attribute as shown in Figure 5.39. For example, we have 2 instances for play not being held when outlook is rainy and there are in total 5 instances for the outlook attribute where play is not held.

Probability for play no given outlook rainy

$$= \frac{\text{occurrences of play no. given outlook = rainy}}{\text{total no. of occurrences for play no. for attribute outlook}} = 2/5 = 0.40$$

	Play			Play			Play			Play			Play
Outlook	**yes**	**no**	**Temp.**	**yes**	**no**	**Humid.**	**yes**	**no**	**Windy**	**yes**	**no**		
sunny	0.22	0.60	hot	0.22	0.40	high	0.33	0.80	false	0.67	0.40	yes	0.64
overcast	0.44	0.00	mild	0.44	0.40	normal	0.67	0.20	true	0.33	0.60	no	0.36
rainy	0.33	0.40	cool	0.33	0.20								

Figure 5.39 Probability of play held or not for each value of attribute

Here, we have to predict the output class for some X. Let us suppose X is as given below.

Outlook	Temperature	Humidity	Windy	Play
sunny	cool	high	true	?

Then, we have to calculate probability of class C_i, when X has already occurred. Thus, it is

$$P(C_i \mid sunny, cool, high, true) = P(sunny, cool, high, true \mid C_i) * P(C_i)$$

Let us first calculate probability of each class, i.e., $P(C_i)$. Here, we have two classes, i.e., Yes and No. There are total 14 instances in the given dataset from which 9 instances are for class Yes and 5 for class No. Thus,

Probability of class Yes, i.e., P(Yes) = 9/14=0.64

Probability of class No, i.e., P(No) = 5/14=0.36

Now, let us calculate $P(X|C_i)$, i.e., $P(sunny, cool, high, true |C_i)$

$$P(sunny, cool, high, true|C_i) = P(outlook = sunny|C_i)*P(Temperature$$
$$= cool|C_i)* P(humidity$$
$$= high|C_i) * P(windy = true|C_i)$$

Therefore, probability of play to be held under these weather conditions is as shown in Figure 5.40.

$P(outlook = sunny|Yes) = 0.22$

$P(Temperature = cool|Yes) = 0.33$

$P(humidity = high|Yes) = 0.33$

$P(windy = true|Yes) = 0.33$

$P(Yes) = 0.64$

	Play			Play			Play			Play			Play
Outlook	**yes**	**no**	**Temp.**	**yes**	**no**	**Humid.**	**yes**	**no**	**Windy**	**yes**	**no**		
sunny	0.22	0.60	hot	0.22	0.40	high	0.33	0.80	false	0.67	0.40	yes	0.64
overcast	0.44	0.00	mild	0.44	0.40	normal	0.67	0.20	true	0.33	0.60	no	0.36
rainy	0.33	0.40	cool	0.33	0.20								

Figure 5.40 Probability for play 'Yes' for an unknown instance

Likelihood of play being held = $P(X|Yes) * P(Yes)$ = 0.22 * 0.33 * 0.33 * 0.33 * 0.64 = 0.0053

Similarly, probability of play not being held under these weather conditions is as shown in Figure 5.41.

$P(outlook = sunny|No) = 0.60$

$P(Temperature = cool|No) = 0.20$

$P(humidity = high|No) = 0.80$

$P(windy = true|No) = 0.60$

$P(No) = 0.36$

	Play			Play			Play			Play			Play
Outlook	yes	no	Temp.	yes	no	Humid.	yes	no	Windy	yes	no		
sunny	0.22	0.60	hot	0.22	0.40	high	0.33	0.80	false	0.67	0.40	yes	0.64
overcast	0.44	0.00	mild	0.44	0.40	normal	0.67	0.20	true	0.33	0.60	no	0.36
rainy	0.33	0.40	cool	0.33	0.20								

Figure 5.41 Probability for play 'No' for an unknown instance

Likelihood of play being held = $P(X|No) * P(No)$ = 0.60 * 0.20 * 0.80 * 0.60 * 0.36 = 0.0206

Now, above calculated likelihoods are converted to probabilities to decide whether the play is held or not under these weather conditions.

Probability of play Yes = Likelihood for play Yes/(Likelihood for play Yes + Likelihood for play No) = 0.0053/(0.0053 + 0.0206) = 20.5%

Probability of play No = Likelihood for play No/(Likelihood for play Yes + Likelihood for play No) = 0.0206/(0.0053 + 0.0206) = 79.5%

From this, we can conclude that there are approximately 80% chances that play will not be held and 20% chances that play will be held. This makes a good prediction and Naïve Bayes has performed very well in this case.

But Naïve Bayes has a drawback to understand which, let us consider another example from this dataset under same weather conditions except that now the outlook is overcast instead of rainy. The problem here is that there is no instance in the dataset when outlook is overcast and play is No which indicates that play is always held on overcast day as shown in Figure 5.38. This result about likelihood of play not being held on overcast days is 0 which causes all the other attributes to be rejected. Simply put, we can say that play is always being held when outlook is overcast, regardless of what the other attributes are. The calculations for this are shown in Figure 5.42.

Therefore, likelihood of play not being held under these weather conditions = 0.00 * 0.20 * 0.80 * 0.60 * 0.36 = 0

	Play			Play			Play			Play			Play
Outlook	yes	no	Temp.	yes	no	Humid.	yes	no	Windy	yes	no		
sunny	0.22	0.60	hot	0.22	0.40	high	0.33	0.80	false	0.67	0.40	yes	0.64
overcast	0.44	0.00	mild	0.44	0.40	normal	0.67	0.20	true	0.33	0.60	no	0.36
rainy	0.33	0.40	cool	0.33	0.20								

Figure 5.42 Probability of play not being held when outlook is overcast

However, we may have reached this result because we may not have enough instances in the dataset especially of cases where play was not held when the outlook was overcast. To solve this issue, a Laplace estimator is used which simply adds a value of 1 to each count of attribute values.

5.7.2 Working of Naïve Bayes classifier using the Laplace Estimator

After adding 1 to each count of attribute values, the modified values are shown in Figure 5.43.

	Play			Play			Play			Play			Play
Outlook	yes	no	Temp.	yes	no	Humid.	yes	no	Windy	yes	no		
sunny	2	3	hot	2	2	high	3	4	false	6	2	yes	9
overcast	4	0	mild	4	2	normal	6	1	true	3	3	no	5
rainy	3	[illegible]	cool	3	1								
TOTAL	9	5	TOTAL	9	5	TOTAL	9	5	TOTAL	9	5	TOTAL	14

Laplace estimator:
Add 1 to each count

Add 1 to count (Laplace estimator)

	Play			Play			Play			Play			Play
Outlook	yes	no	Temp.	yes	no	Humid.	yes	no	Windy	yes	no		
sunny	3	[illegible]	hot	3	3	high	4	5	false	7	3	yes	9
overcast	5	1	mild	5	3	normal	7	2	true	4	4	no	5
rainy	4	3	cool	4	2								
TOTAL	12	8	TOTAL	12	8	TOTAL	11	7	TOTAL	11	7	TOTAL	14

Figure 5.43 Values of attributes after adding Laplace estimator

Now, probability of play being held or not for each modified value of input attribute is recomputed as shown in Figure 5.44.

	Play			Play			Play			Play			Play
Outlook	yes	no	Temp.	yes	no	Humid.	yes	no	Windy	yes	no		
sunny	0.25	0.50	hot	0.25	0.38	high	0.36	0.71	false	0.64	0.43	yes	0.64
overcast	0.42	0.13	mild	0.42	0.38	normal	0.64	0.29	true	0.36	0.57	no	0.36
rainy	0.33	0.38	cool	0.33	0.25								

Figure 5.44 Probability of play held or not for each modified value of attribute

Now, probability of play whether held or not for the given weather conditions such as Outlook = overcast, Temperature = cool, Humidity = high, Windy = true can be calculated from the Figure 5.45.

	Play			Play			Play			Play			Play
Outlook	yes	no	Temp.	yes	no	Humid.	yes	no	Windy	yes	no		
sunny	0.25	0.50	hot	0.25	0.38	high	0.36	0.71	false	0.64	0.43	yes	0.64
overcast	0.42	0.13	mild	0.42	0.38	normal	0.64	0.29	true	0.36	0.57	no	0.36
rainy	0.33	0.38	cool	0.33	0.25								

Figure 5.45 Attribute values for given example instance

Likelihood for play Yes = 0.42 * 0.33 * 0.36 * 0.36* 0.64 = 0.0118

Likelihood for play No = 0.13 * 0.25 * 0.71 * 0.57 * 0.36 = 0.0046

Probability of play Yes = 0.0118/(0.0118+0.0046) = 72%

Probability of play No = 0.0046/(0.0118+0.0046) =28%

From this, it can be concluded that instead of 100% chance of play being held whenever outlook is overcast, we now calculate the probability of 72% for this combination of weather conditions, which is more realistic.

Thus, the Laplace estimator has been used to handle the case of zero probabilities which commonly occurs due to insufficient training data.

5.8 Understanding Metrics to Assess the Quality of Classifiers

The quality of any classifier is measured in terms of True Positive, False Positive, True Negative and False Negative, Precision, Recall and F-Measure.

To understand this concept, let us first consider the story of boy who shouted 'Wolf' to fool the villagers. The story goes as follows.

5.8.1 The boy who cried wolf

Once a boy was getting bored and thought of making fools out of fellow villagers. To have some fun, he shouted out, 'Wolf!' even though no wolf was in sight. The villagers ran to rescue him, but then got angry when they realized that the boy was playing a joke on them. The boy repeated the same prank a number of times and each time the villagers rushed out. They got angrier when they found he was joking.

One night, the boy saw a real wolf approaching and shouted 'Wolf!'. This time villagers stayed in their houses and the hungry wolf turned the flock into lamb chops.

Let's make the following definitions: Here, 'Wolf' is a **positive class** and 'No wolf' is a **negative class.** We can summarize our 'wolf-prediction' model using a 2x2 confusion matrix that depicts all four possible outcomes as shown below.

True Positive (TP): Reality: A wolf threatened. Boy said: 'Wolf.' Outcome: Boy is a hero.	**False Positive (FP):** Reality: No wolf threatened. Boy said: 'Wolf.' Outcome: Villagers are angry at Boy for waking them up.
False Negative (FN): Reality: A wolf threatened. Boy said: 'No wolf.' Outcome: The wolf ate all the flock.	**True Negative (TN):** Reality: No wolf threatened. Boy said: 'No wolf.' Outcome: Everyone is fine.

Now consider a classifier, whose task is to predict whether the image is of a bird or not. In this case, let us assume, 'Bird' is a positive class and 'Not a Bird' is a negative class.

Let us suppose we have a dataset of 15,000 images having 6000 images of birds and 9000 images of anything that is not a bird. The matrix illustrating actual vs. predicted results also known as confusion matrix is given in Figure 5.46 below.

Results for 15,000 Validation Images

(6000 images are birds, 9000 images are not birds)

	Predicted 'bird'	**Predicted 'not a bird'**
Bird	5,450 ***True Positives***	550 ***False Negatives***
Not a Bird	162 ***False Positives***	8,838 ***True Negatives***

Figure 5.46 Confusion matrix for bird classifier

5.8.2 True positive

Those instances where predicted class is equal to the actual class are called as true positive or a true positive is an outcome where the model correctly predicts the positive class.

For example in the case of our bird classifier, the birds that are correctly identified as birds are called true positive.

5.8.3 True negative

Those instances where predicted class and actual class are both negative are called as true negative or a true negative is an outcome where the model correctly predicts the negative class.

For example, in the case of our bird classifier there are images that are not of birds which our classifier correctly identified as 'not a bird' are called true negatives.

5.8.4 False positive

Those instances where predicted class/answer is positive, but actually the instances are negative or a false positive is an outcome where the model incorrectly predicts the positive class.

For example, in case of our bird classifier there are some images that the classifier predicted as birds but they were something else. These are our false positives.

5.8.5 False negative

Those instances where predicted class is negative, but actually the instances are positive or a false negative is an outcome where the model incorrectly predicts the negative class.

For example, in case of our bird classifier there are some images of birds that the classifier did not correctly recognize as birds. These are our false negatives.

In simple words, predicted 'bird' column is considered as Positive and if the prediction is correct then cell is labeled as true positive, otherwise it is false positive. The column where prediction is 'not a bird' is considered as negative and if prediction is correct, the cell is labeled as true negative otherwise it is false negative as shown in Figure 5.46.

5.8.6 Confusion matrix

Confusion matrix is an $N \times N$ table that summarizes the accuracy of a classification model's predictions. Here, N represents the number of classes. In a binary classification problem, $N = 2$. In simple words, it is a correlation between the actual labels and the model's predicted labels. One axis of a confusion matrix is the label that the model predicted, and the other axis is the actual label.

For example, consider a sample confusion matrix for a binary classification problem to predict if a patient has a tumor or not.

	Tumor (predicted)	*No-Tumor (predicted)*
Tumor (actual)	18 (TP)	1 (FN)
No-Tumor (actual)	*6 (FP)*	*452 (TN)*

Figure 5.47 Confusion matrix for tumor prediction

The confusion matrix shown in Figure 5.47 has 19 samples that actually had tumor, the model correctly classified 18 as having tumor (18 true positives), and incorrectly classified 1 as not having a tumor (1 false negative). Similarly, of 458 samples that actually did not have tumor, 452 were correctly classified (452 true negatives) and 6 were incorrectly classified (6 false positives).

Confusion matrices contain sufficient information to calculate a variety of performance metrics, including precision, recall and F-Measure. Instead of just looking at overall accuracy, we usually calculate precision, recall and F-Measure. These metrics give us a clear picture of how well the classifier performed.

5.8.7 Precision

Precision identifies the frequency with which a model was correct when predicting the positive class. It is defined as:

$$\text{Precision} = \frac{\text{True Positive}}{\text{True Positive} + \text{False Positive}}$$

Or we can say that Precision = True Positives/All Positive predicted. In other words, if we predict positive then how often was it really a positive instance.

For example, in case of our bird classifier, it refers to the situation where a bird was predicted, but how often was it really a bird.

For classifier shown in Figure 5.46, the Precision = 5450/(5450 + 162) =5450/5612 =0.9711. In terms of percentage it is 97.11%.

5.8.8 Recall

Recall identifies out of all the possible positive labels, how many did the model correctly identify? In simple word, it refers to what percentage of actual positive instances we are able to find.

For example, In case of our bird classifier, it refers what percentage of the actual birds did we find?

So,
$$\text{Recall} = \frac{\text{True Positive}}{\text{All actual positive instances}} = \frac{\text{True Positive}}{\text{True Positive} + \text{False Negatives}}$$

For classifier shown in Figure 5.46, the Recall = 5450/(5450 + 550) = 5450/6000 = 0.9083 and in terms of percentage it is 90.83%.

The table below shows both precision and recall for the bird classifier discussed above.

Precision *If we predicted 'bird', how often was it really a bird?*	**97.11%** *(True positives ÷ All Positive Guesses)*
Recall *What percentage of the actual birds did we find?*	**90.83%** *(True positives ÷ Total Bird in Dataset)*

In our example of bird classifier, this tells us that 97.11% of the time the prediction was right! But it also tells us that we only found 90.83% of the actual birds in the dataset. In other words, we might not find every bird but we are pretty sure about it when we do find one!

Now, let us consider a multi class classifier, where a classifier has to predict one class out of three classes. Here, we have three classes A, B and C.

		Predicted Class		
		A	B	C
Actual Class	A	25	3	2
	B	2	34	5
	C	2	3	20

Let's calculate Precision and Recall for each predicted class.

For Class A

Precision = True Positives/All Positive Predicted

Precision = 25/29

Recall = True Positive/All actual positive instances = 25/30

For Class B

Precision = True Positives/All Positive Predicted

Precision = 34/40

Recall = True Positive/All actual positive instances =34/41

For Class C

Precision = True Positives/All Positive Predicted

Precision = 20/27

Recall = True Positive/All actual positive instances =20/25

5.8.9 F-Measure

In statistical analysis of binary classification, the F-Measure (also known as F-score or F-1 score) is a measure of a test's accuracy. It considers both the precision p and the recall r of the test to compute the score. Here, p is the number of correct positive results divided by the number of all positive results returned by the classifier, and r is the number of correct positive results divided by the number of all relevant samples (all samples that should have been identified as positive). The F1 score is the harmonic average of the precision and the recall, where, an F1 score reaches its best value at 1 (perfect precision and recall), and its worst at 0.

$$F = 2 \cdot \frac{\text{precision} \cdot \text{recall}}{\text{precision} + \text{recall}}$$

Remind Me

- Classification and regression are two main techniques generally used for data analysis. Classification predicts categorical values, while regression models predict continuous values.
- Classification is further defined as two types that are posteriori classification and priori classification. Posterior classification is supervised machine learning approach, where classes are already given. On

the other hand, priori classification is unsupervised machine learning approach, where classes are not given.

- Information gain measures the quality of an attribute for predicting the class of each sample of the training data. The attribute with the highest information gain is selected as the next split attribute.
- Gini Index was developed by Italian scientist Corrado Gini in 1912. It is basically used to represent level of equality or inequality among objects and it can also be used to develop the decision tree. It always ranges between 0 and 1.
- Bayes theorem was postulated by Thomas Bayes and the classification system using Bayes theorem is based on a hypothesis that the given data belongs to a particular class. In this theorem, probability is calculated for the hypothesis to be true.

Point Me (Books)

- Han, Jiawei, Micheline Kamber, and Jian Pei. 2011. *Data Mining: Concepts and Techniques*, 3rd ed. Amsterdam: Elsevier.
- Gupta, G. K. 2014. *Introduction to Data Mining with Case Studies*. Delhi: PHI Learning Pvt. Ltd.
- Mitchell, Tom M. 2017. *Machine Learning*. Chennai: McGraw Hill Education.
- Witten, Ian H., Eibe Frank, Mark A. Hall, and Christopher Pal. 2016. *Data Mining: Practical Machine Learning Tools and Techniques*, 4th ed. Burlington: Morgan Kaufmann.

Connect Me (Internet Resources)

- https://medium.com/machine-learning-101/chapter-1-supervised-learning-and-naive-bayes-classification-part-2-coding-5966f25f1475
- https://medium.com/machine-learning-101/chapter-3-decision-tree-classifier-coding-ae7df4284e99
- https://www.tutorialspoint.com/data_mining/dm_classification_prediction.htm
- Weka Tutorial 5 - Naive Bayes Classifier By Mark Polczynski

Test Me

Answer these questions based on your learning in this chapter.

1. Suppose you are working on weather prediction, and your weather station makes one of three predictions for each day's weather: Sunny, Cloudy or Rainy. You'd like to use a learning algorithm to predict tomorrow's weather. Identify the type of problem.
   (a) Classification problem (b) Regression problem
2. Suppose you are working on stock market prediction, and you would like to predict whether or not a particular stock's price will be higher tomorrow than it is today. You want to use a learning algorithm for this. Identify the type of problem.
   (a) Classification problem (b) Regression problem
3. Which type of machine learning technique will be used for the following?
   I. Predicting the price of a house.
   II. Predicting the type of a disease.
   III. Predicting tomorrow's temperature.
   IV. Predicting if tomorrow will be cooler or hotter than today.
4. During calculation of probability P(C | X) which probability does not play vital role in working of classifier and why?
5. High False Negative signifies:
   (a) Good classifier (b) Bad classifier

6. Let us suppose that there are 200 pages available on Internet for Machine Learning. The search on this term returns total 210 pages, out of which 190 belongs to Machine Learning, calculate precision and recall for our algorithm.
7. What is the formula for calculation of Gini Index and total information?
8. Draw a decision tree for following database with information theory and Gini Index? Indicate all the intermediate steps.

Day	*Temperature*	*Outlook*	*Humidity*	*Windy*	*Play Golf?*
07-05	hot	sunny	high	false	no
07-06	hot	sunny	high	true	no
07-07	hot	overcast	high	false	yes
07-09	cool	rain	normal	false	yes
07-10	cool	overcast	normal	true	yes
07-12	mild	sunny	high	false	no
07-14	cool	sunny	normal	false	yes
07-15	mild	rain	normal	false	yes
07-20	mild	sunny	normal	true	yes
07-21	mild	overcast	high	true	yes
07-22	hot	overcast	normal	false	yes
07-23	mild	rain	high	true	no
07-26	cool	rain	normal	true	no
07-30	mild	rain	high	false	yes

9. Predict that X will buy the computer or not, for following training database by using Naïve Bayes.

X= (age = 31...40, income = medium, student = yes, credit-rating = fair)

rec	*Age*	*Income*	*Student*	*Credit_rating*	*Buys_computer*
r1	<=30	High	no	Fair	no
r2	≤30	High	no	Excellent	no
r3	30...40	High	no	Fair	yes
r4	>40	Medium	no	Fair	yes
r5	>40	Low	yes	Fair	yes
r6	>40	Low	yes	Excellent	no
r7	30...40	Low	yes	Excellent	yes

Contd.

rec	*Age*	*Income*	*Student*	*Credit_rating*	*Buys_computer*
r8	<=30	Medium	no	Fair	no
r9	<=30	Low	yes	Fair	yes
r10	>40	Medium	yes	Fair	yes
r11	<=30	Medium	yes	Excellent	yes
r12	30...40	Medium	no	Excellent	yes
r13	30...40	high	yes	Fair	yes
r14	>40	Medium	no	Excellent	no

10. Identify the attribute that will act as the root node of a decision tree to predict golf play for following database with Gini Index. Indicate all the intermediate steps.

Outlook	Wind	PlayGolf
rain	strong	no
sunny	weak	yes
overcast	weak	yes
rain	weak	yes
sunny	strong	yes
rain	strong	no
overcast	strong	no

11. What is the role of information theory in building the decision tree?

12. Why is Naïve Bayes called naïve? Explain the working of the NB algorithm by proving the Bayes theorem.

13. Make a decision tree for the following database using Gini Index. Indicate all intermediate steps.

Example	*Colour*	*Shape*	*Size*	*Class*
1	Red	Square	Big	+
2	Blue	Square	Big	+
3	Red	Circle	Big	+
4	Red	Circle	Small	–
5	Green	Square	Small	–
6	Green	Square	Big	–

14. What is the major change made in the Naïve Bayes algorithm to improve its performance?

15. Calculate the information gain when splitting on *A* and *B*. Which attribute would the decision tree induction algorithm choose?

A	B	*Class Lable*
T	F	+
T	T	+
T	T	+
T	F	–
T	T	+
F	F	–
F	F	–
F	F	–
T	T	–
T	F	–

Calculate the gain in the Gini Index when splitting on *A* and *B*. Which attribute would the decision tree induction algorithm choose?

16. What is the need of Laplace estimator? Give examples.

17. Consider the training examples shown in below Table for classification problem.

Gender	*Car Type*	*Shirt Size*	*Class*
M	Family	Small	C0
M	Sports	Medium	C0
M	Sports	Medium	C0
M	Sports	Large	C0
M	Sports	Extra Large	C0
M	Sports	Extra Large	C0
F	Sports	Small	C0
F	Sports	Small	C0
F	Sports	Medium	C0
F	Luxury	Large	C0
M	Family	Large	C1
M	Family	Extra Large	C1
M	Family	Medium	C1
M	Luxury	Extra Large	C1
F	Luxury	Small	C1

Contd.

F	Luxury	Small	C1
F	Luxury	Medium	C1
F	Luxury	Medium	C1
F	Luxury	Medium	C1
F	Luxury	Large	C1

- Apply the split algorithm based on information theory to perform classification of the given dataset. Indicate all intermediate steps properly.

18. During calculation of P(Ci|X) which probability does not play vital role in working of classifier and why?

19. At the Krispie Foods factory, cookies are tested for crispness with the following results:
- For cookies that are really crispy, the test says 'Yes' 90% of the time
- For cookies that are not crispy, the test says 'Yes' 15% of the time

Prepare confusion matrix for the above given results.

Answer Keys:

1. (a) 2. (a)
3. I. Regression II. Calssification III. Regression IV. Classification
5. b. 6. Precision = 190/210 Recall = 190/200

6

Implementing Classification in Weka and R

Chapter Objectives

- ✓ To demonstrate the use of the decision tree
- ✓ To apply the decision tree on a sample dataset
- ✓ To implement a decision tree process using Weka and R

6.1 Building a Decision Tree Classifier in Weka

In this chapter, we will learn how Weka's decision tree feature helps to classify unknown samples of a dataset based on its attribute values. When Weka's decision tree is applied to an unknown sample, the decision tree classifies the sample into different classes such as Class A, Class B and Class C as shown in Figure 6.1.

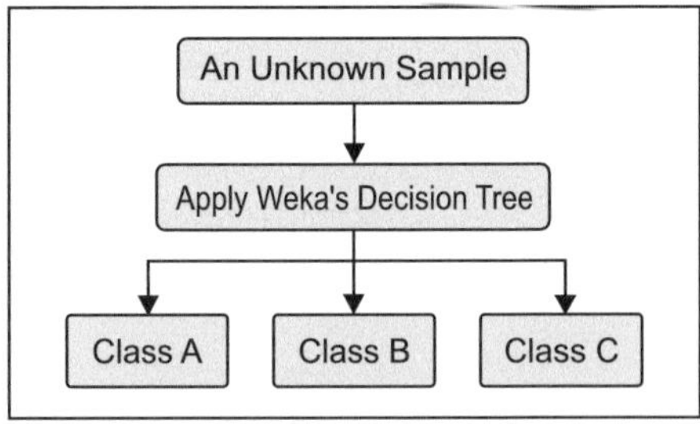

Figure 6.1 Classification using Weka's decision tree

For example, if we want to predict the class of an unknown sample of a flower based on the length and width dimensions of its Sepal and Petal. The first step would be to measure Sepal length and width and Petal length and width of an unknown flower and compare these dimensions to the values of the samples in our dataset of known species. The decision tree algorithm of Weka will help in creating decision rules to predict the class of unknown flower automatically as shown in Figure 6.2.

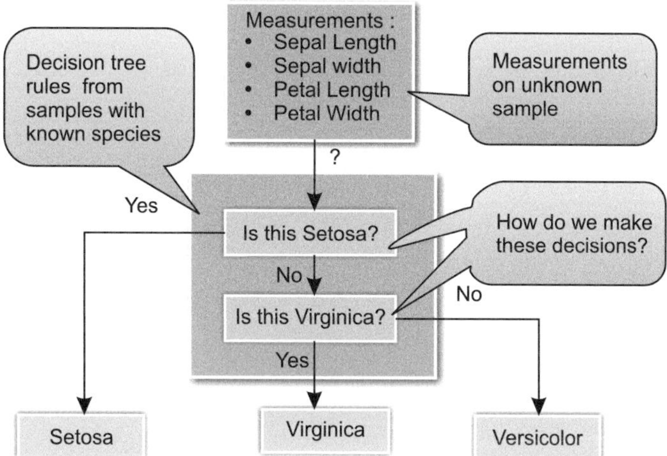

Figure 6.2 Classification of an unknown sample using Weka's decision tree

As shown in Figure 6.2, the dimensions of an unknown sample of flower will be matched with the rules generated by the decision tree. First, the rules will be matched to determine whether the sample belongs to Setosa class or not, if yes, the unknown sample will be classified as setosa. If not, the unknown sample will be checked for being of the Virginica class. If it matches with the conditions of the Virginica class, it will be labeled as Virginica, otherwise Versicolor. It is important to note that it would not be simple to create these rules on the basis of the values of single attribute as shown in Table 6.1. It is clear that for the same Sepal width, the flower may be of Setosa or Versicolor or Virginica, making it unclear which species an unknown flower belongs to on the basis of Sepal width alone. Thus, the decision tree must make its prediction based on all four flower dimensions.

Table 6.1 Iris dataset sample

	Input Attributes				Output Attribute
Instance No.	**Sepal Length**	**Sepal Width**	**Petal Length**	**Petal Width**	**Species**
2	4.9	3.0	1.4	0.2	Setosa
3	4.7	3.2			Setosa
51	7.0	3.2			Versicolor
111	6.5	3.2			Virginica
129	6.4	2.8	5.6	2.1	Virginica

What species is an iris with sepal width of 3.2 cm?

Due to such overlaps, the decision tree cannot predict with 100% accuracy the class of flower, but can only determine the likelihood of an unknown sample belonging to a particular class. In real situations the decision tree algorithm works on the basis of probability.

For example, an unknown sample of flower might be either Setosa, Versicolor or Virginica as shown in Figure 6.3. The probability of belonging to a particular class depends upon the parameters of the unknown sample.

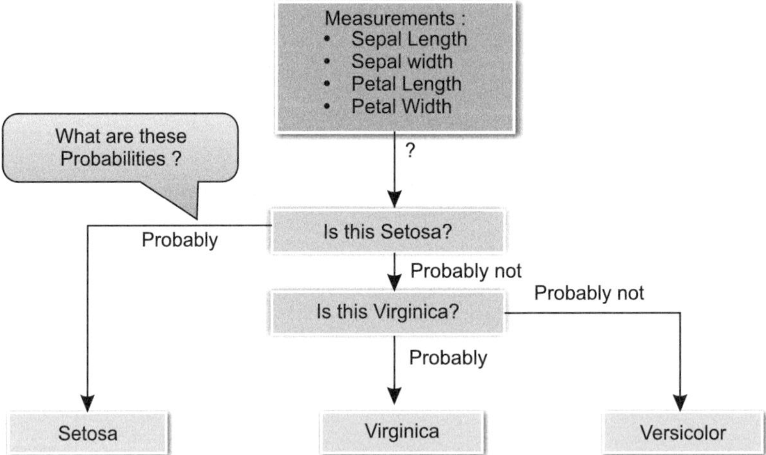

Figure 6.3 Working of the decision tree

Weka operates its decision tree with the J4.8 or J48 decision tree learner, which is based on J. Ross Quinlan's landmark decision tree program called C4.5. Weka operates this algorithm in Java and the current version of this algorithm is 4.8, which is why Weka named its decision tree learner as the J48.

6.1.1 Steps to take when applying the decision tree classifier on the Iris dataset in Weka

The Iris dataset is available in the data folder of Weka for experimentation. We can avail this dataset by following the path: C:\Program Files\Weka_folder\data *[In our case, we have Installed weka-3-6 in C: drive under Program files folder]*. The step-by-step procedure to apply the decision tree classifier is as follows:

1. Start ***Weka Explorer*** and go to the ***Preprocess*** tab.
2. Under ***Open File*** tab, select the data source as given in Figure 6.4

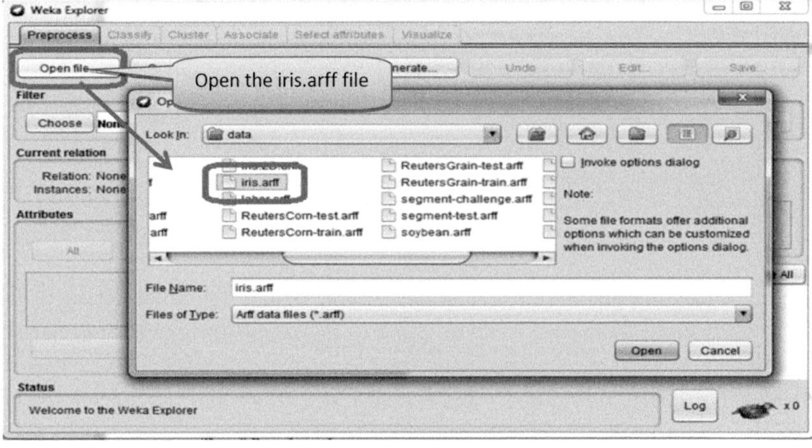

Figure 6.4 Loading the iris.arff file

3. Move from the ***Preprocess*** tab to the ***Classify*** tab. To select the Weka J48 algorithm, click on ***Choose***. Then follow the path:

```
Weka -> classifiers -> trees -> J48
```

After selecting J48, click ***Close*** to return to the ***Classify*** tab as shown in below Figure 6.5.

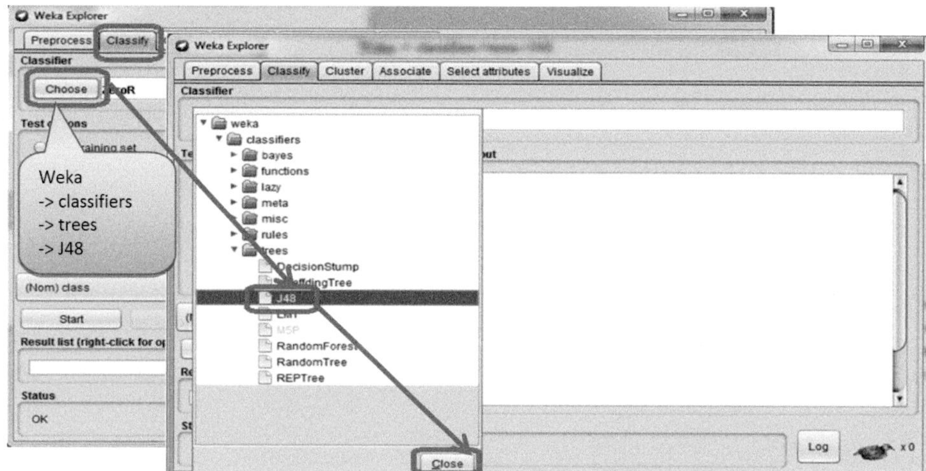

Figure 6.5 Selecting Weka J48 algorithm

4. After loading the J48 decision tree, left-click on J48 to open up the Weka ***Generic Object Editor***. For our first try to build a decision tree, we will accept all of the defaults here, except that we will change ***saveInstanceData*** to ***true***. This will allow us to find out how each iris sample is classified after building the tree. By clicking ***More***, you can find further information on the items.

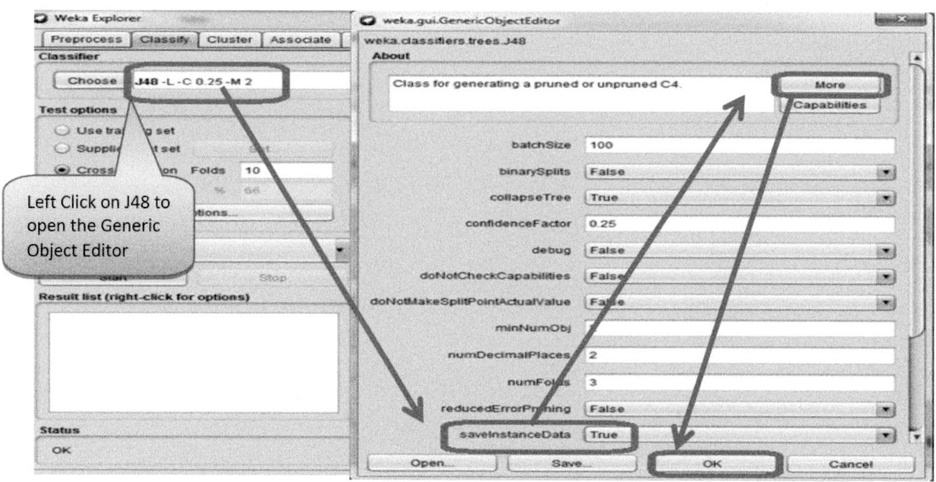

Figure 6.6 Selection of the Weka J48 algorithm

5. Select ***Percentage split*** from test options as shown in Figure 6.7. Keep default value 66%. It means 66% records, i.e., 2/3 of records from whole Iris dataset (containing 150 records), will be used for training purpose and remaining records in the dataset will be used for testing purpose. Since the Iris dataset has a total of 150 records, 99 records will be used for training the decision tree model, while the remaining 51 records will be used to test the decision tree. In other words, the decision tree will be created by examining 99 records of this Iris dataset and will then be evaluated on the remaining 51 records.

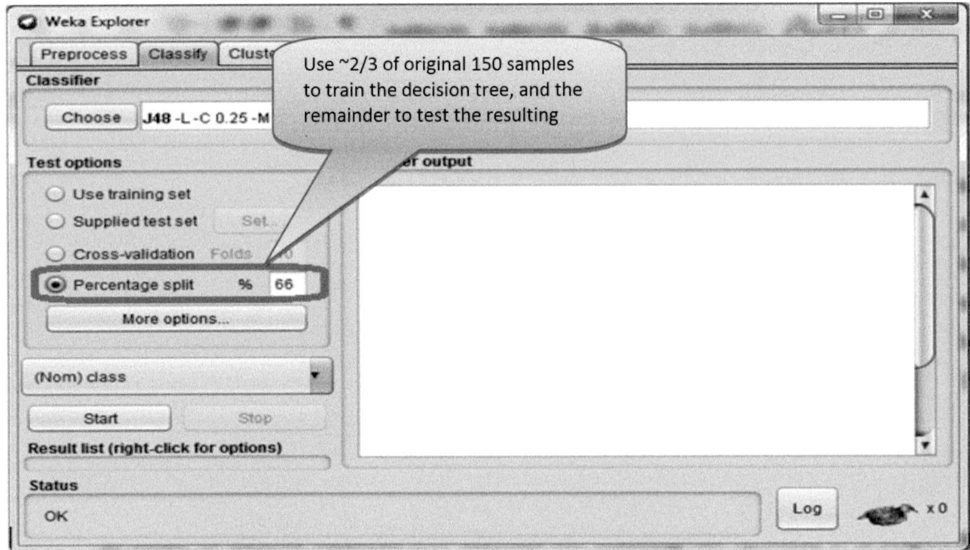

Figure 6.7 Selection of percentage split test option

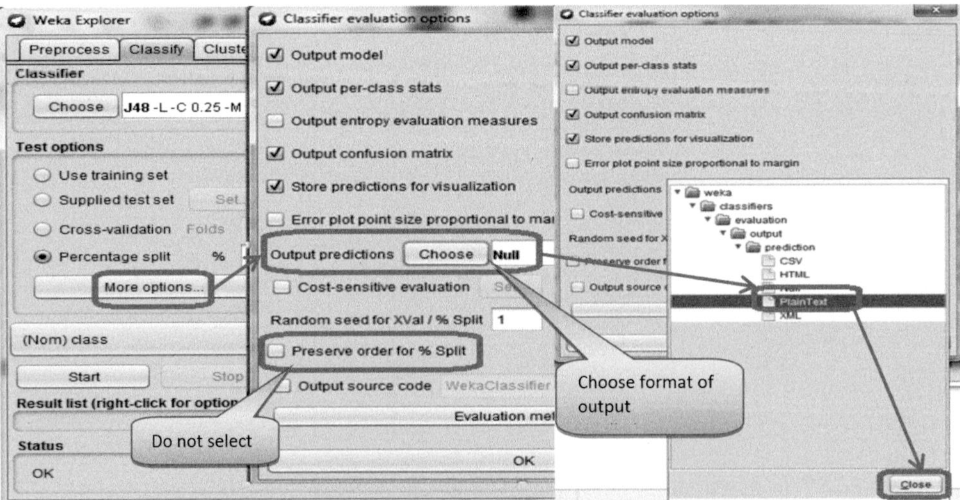

Figure 6.8 Saving output predictions

In order to choose random 99 records for training the system, it is important to unselect ***preserve order for % split*** as shown in below Figure 6.8; otherwise the system will consider first 99 records for training and last 51 records for testing.

Recall that in our original Fisher's Iris Dataset, all the Setosa samples were at the top of the dataset, the VVersicolor samples were in the middle, and the virginica samples were all at the end as shown in Figure 6.9.

Relation: iris

No.	1: sepallength Numeric	2: sepalwidth Numeric	3: petallength Numeric	4: petalwidth Numeric	5: class Nominal
1	5.1	3.5	1.4	0.2	Iris-setosa
2	4.9	3.0	1.4	0.2	Iris-setosa
3	4.7	3.2	1.3	0.2	Iris-setosa
4	4.6	3.1	1.5	0.2	Iris-setosa
5	5.0	3.6	1.4	0.2	Iris-setosa
6	5.4	3.9	1.7	0.4	Iris-setosa
7	4.6	3.4	1.4	0.3	Iris-setosa
8	5.0	3.4	1.5	0.2	Iris-setosa
9	4.4	2.9	1.4	0.2	Iris-setosa
10	4.9	3.1	1.5	0.1	Iris-setosa
11	5.4	3.7	1.5	0.2	Iris-setosa
12	4.8	3.4	1.6	0.2	Iris-setosa
13	4.8	3.0	1.4	0.1	Iris-setosa
14	4.3	3.0	1.1	0.1	Iris-setosa
15	5.8	4.0	1.2	0.2	Iris-setosa
16	5.7	4.4	1.5	0.4	Iris-setosa
17	5.4	3.9	1.3	0.4	Iris-setosa
18	5.1	3.5	1.4	0.3	Iris-setosa
19	5.7	3.8	1.7	0.3	Iris-setosa
20	5.1	3.8	1.5	0.3	Iris-setosa
21	5.4	3.4	1.7	0.2	Iris-setosa
22	5.1	3.7	1.5	0.4	Iris-setosa
23	4.6	3.6	1.0	0.2	Iris-setosa
24	5.1	3.3	1.7	0.5	Iris-setosa
25	4.8	3.4	1.9	0.2	Iris-setosa
26	5.0	3.0	1.6	0.2	Iris-setosa
27	5.0	3.4	1.6	0.4	Iris-setosa
28	5.2	3.5	1.5	0.2	Iris-setosa
29	5.2	3.4	1.4	0.2	Iris-setosa
30	4.7	3.2	1.6	0.2	Iris-setosa
31	4.8	3.1	1.6	0.2	Iris-setosa
32	5.4	3.4	1.5	0.4	Iris-setosa
33	5.2	4.1	1.5	0.1	Iris-setosa
34	5.5	4.2	1.4	0.2	Iris-setosa
35	4.9	3.1	1.5	0.1	Iris-setosa
36	5.0	3.2	1.2	0.2	Iris-setosa
37	5.5	3.5	1.3	0.2	Iris-setosa
38	4.9	3.1	1.5	0.1	Iris-setosa
39	4.4	3.0	1.3	0.2	Iris-setosa
40	5.1	3.4	1.5	0.2	Iris-setosa
41	5.0	3.5	1.3	0.3	Iris-setosa
42	4.5	2.3	1.3	0.3	Iris-setosa
43	4.4	3.2	1.3	0.2	Iris-setosa
44	5.0	3.5	1.6	0.6	Iris-setosa
45	5.1	3.8	1.9	0.4	Iris-setosa
46	4.8	3.0	1.4	0.3	Iris-setosa
47	5.1	3.8	1.6	0.2	Iris-setosa
48	4.6	3.2	1.4	0.2	Iris-setosa
49	5.3	3.7	1.5	0.2	Iris-setosa
50	5.0	3.3	1.4	0.2	Iris-setosa
51	7.0	3.2	4.7	1.4	Iris-versicolor
52	6.4	3.2	4.5	1.5	Iris-versicolor
53	6.9	3.1	4.9	1.5	Iris-versicolor
54	5.5	2.3	4.0	1.3	Iris-versicolor
55	6.5	2.8	4.6	1.5	Iris-versicolor
56	5.7	2.8	4.5	1.3	Iris-versicolor
57	6.3	3.3	4.7	1.6	Iris-versicolor
58	4.9	2.4	3.3	1.0	Iris-versicolor
59	6.6	2.9	4.6	1.3	Iris-versicolor
60	5.2	2.7	3.9	1.4	Iris-versicolor

Figure 6.9 Original Fisher's Iris dataset

Also, note that 1/3 of the samples were Setosa, 1/3 Versicolor, and 1/3 Virginica. Morever, we also specified that Weka is to use 2/3 of the samples to train the classifier, and 1/3 to test the classifier after training is completed. But when Weka splits the original dataset into training and test datasets, we need to have a mixture of species in the training set and also in the test set. If we select ***Preserve order for % Split***, then the training dataset will have only Setosa and Versicolor samples, and the test set would have only Virginica. Regardless of how J48 works, it is obvious that this situation will result in a poor quality decision tree.

6. Now we are ready to run the J48 decision tree learner. Click ***Start*** on the ***Classify*** tab as shown in Figure 6.10. The ***Classifier output*** box shows the results of classification. The portion of the ***Classifier output*** box seen here verifies that we have analyzed the correct dataset.

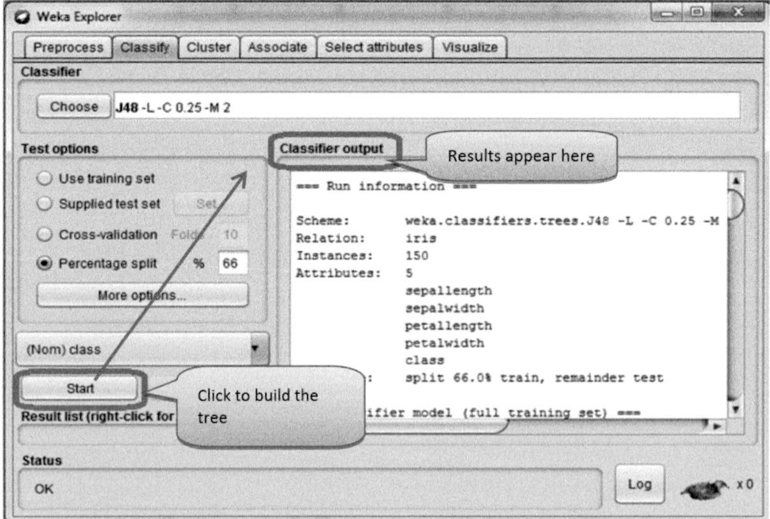

Figure 6.10 Building the decision tree

The classifier's accuracy statistics can be found in the classifier output section as shown in Figure 6.11.

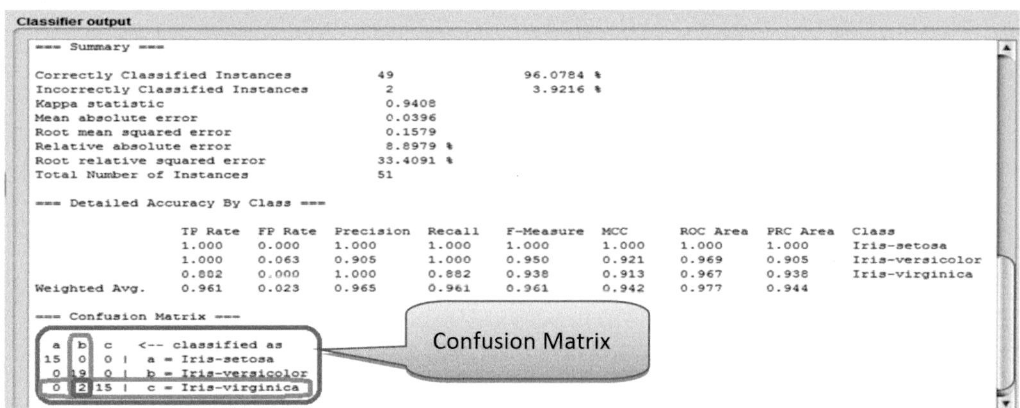

Figure 6.11 Decision tree accuracy statistics [see colour plate]

7. To see the tree, right-click on the highlighted ***Result list*** entry for the tree we just built, and then click ***Visualize tree*** as shown in Figure 6.12.

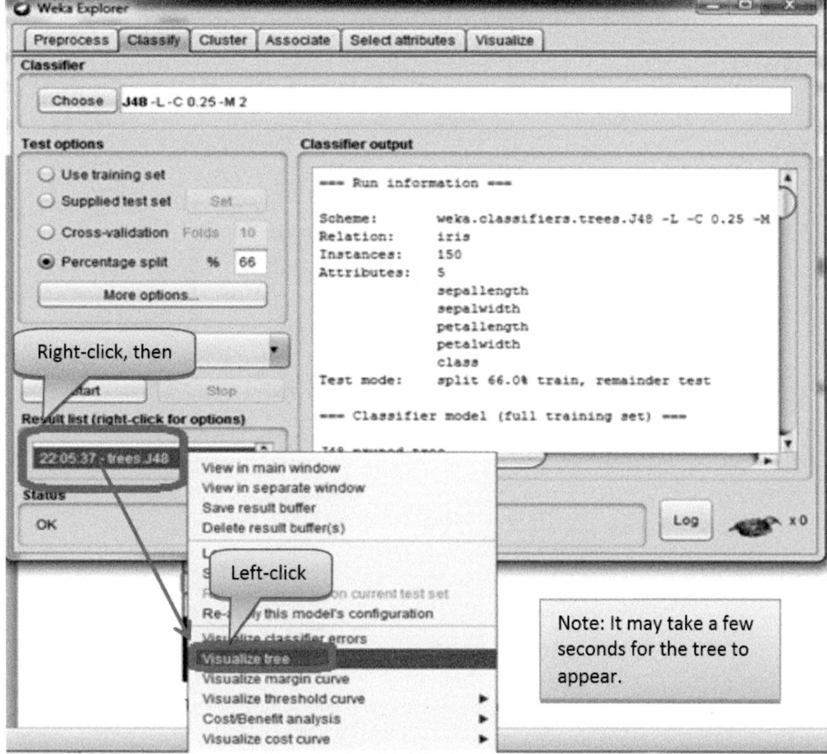

Figure 6.12 Visualization of the tree

8. Finally, we have our long-awaited decision tree for our Fisher's Iris Dataset. As given in Figure 6.13 you can see that it is quite easy to read.

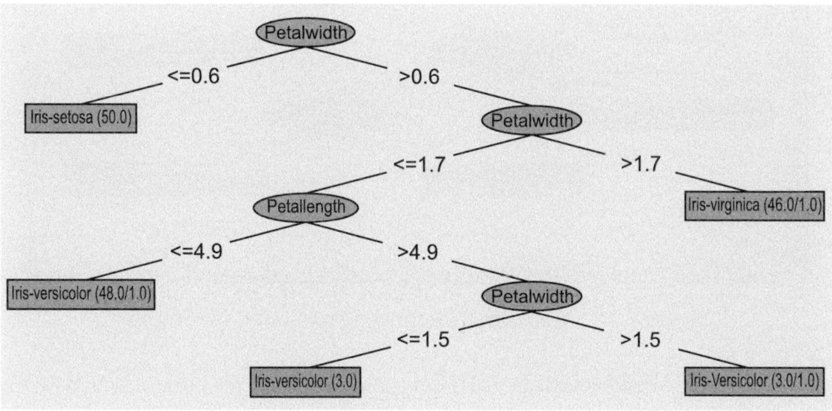

Figure 6.13 Decision tree for the Iris dataset

6.1.2 Understanding the confusion matrix

There are a total of 51 instances for which we have tested using J48. Of these, the confusion matrix shown in Figure 6.14, tells us that us that J48 properly classified 15 Setosa, 19 Versicolor and 15 Virginica. However it classified incorrectly, 2 Virginica as Versicolor as shown in Figure 6.14.

```
=== Confusion Matrix ===

  a  b  c   <-- classified as
 15  0  0 |  a = Iris-setosa
  0 19  0 |  b = Iris-versicolor
  0  2 15 |  c = Iris-virginica
```

Figure 6.14 Confusion matrix [see colour plate]

6.1.3 Understanding the decision tree

Examining the decision tree created by Weka leads us to the following conclusions:

- Starting at the top of the tree, it says that if Petal width is less than or equal to 0.6 cm, then the Iris species is Setosa as shown in Figure 6.15.

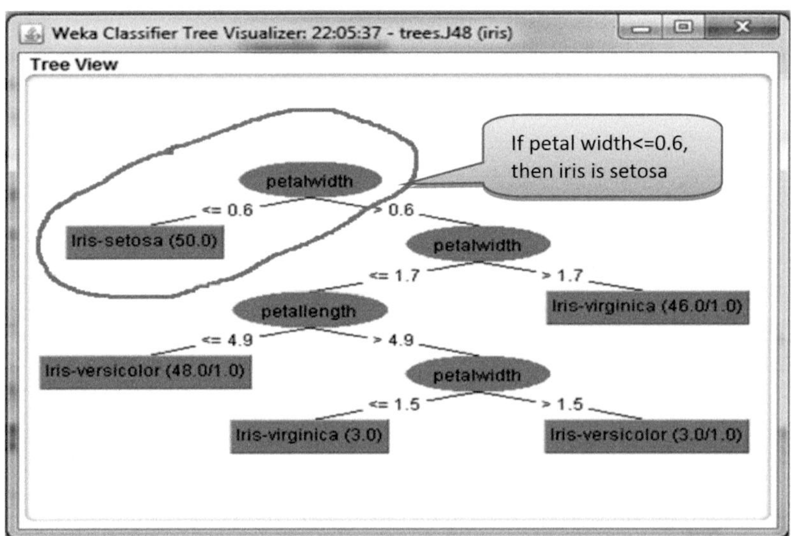

Figure 6.15 Decision tree showing condition for Setosa

- Next, we see that if Petal width is > 0.6 cm, and also > 1.7 cm, then the Iris is Virginica as shown in Figure 6.16.

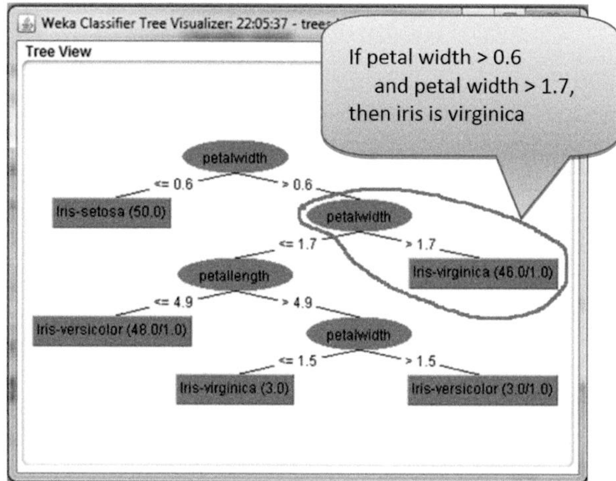

Figure 6.16 Decision tree showing conditions for Virginica

- Now, if Petal width is > 0.6 cm, and Petal width is <= 1.7 cm, we check Petal length. If Petal length is <= 4.9 cm, the Iris is Versicolor as shown in Figure 6.17.

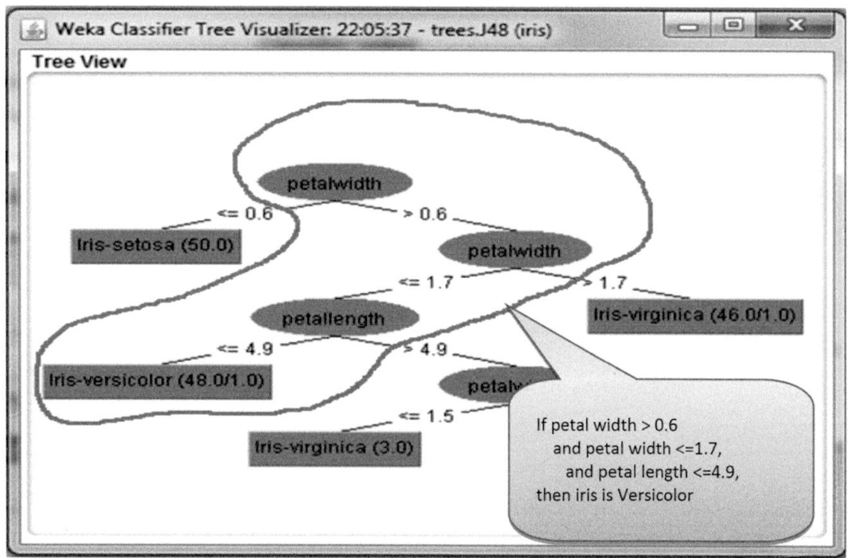

Figure 6.17 Decision tree showing condition for Versicolor

- However, if Petal length is > 4.9 cm, we go back to checking Petal width. Now, if Petal width is <= 1.5 cm, the Iris is Virginica, otherwise it is Versicolor.

6.1.4 Reading decision tree rules

Weka also produces the decision tree structure in terms of rules. Scroll through the ***Classifier output*** box on the ***Classify*** tab to find the rules that govern the tree as shown in Figure 6.18.

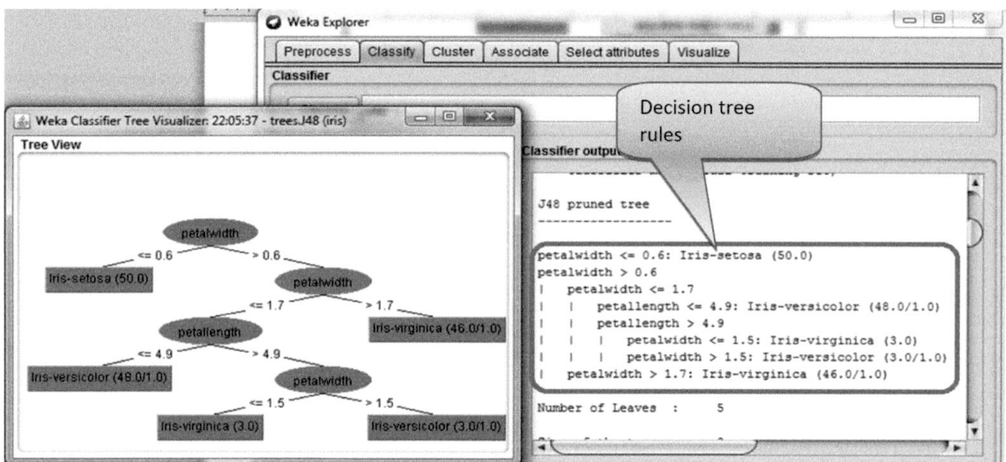

Figure 6.18 Rules identified by the decision tree

Suppose we have an unknown iris with Petal width of 1.6 cm, and Petal length of 5.0 cm. Well, Petal width is > 0.6 cm, and Petal width is <= 1.7 cm. Also, Petal length is > 4.9 cm, and Petal width is > 1.5 cm. So, the Iris is Versicolor according to the rules as shown in Figure 6.19.

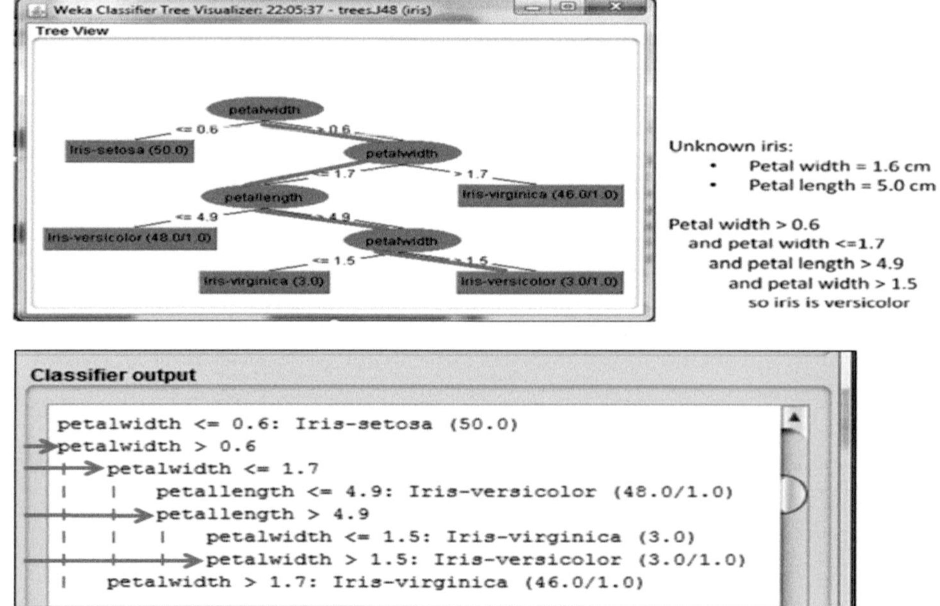

Figure 6.19 Classification of an unknown sample according to decision tree rules

6.1.5 Interpreting results

We see that the tree has 5 leaves, and that the total size of the tree is 9 elements as shown in Figure 6.20.

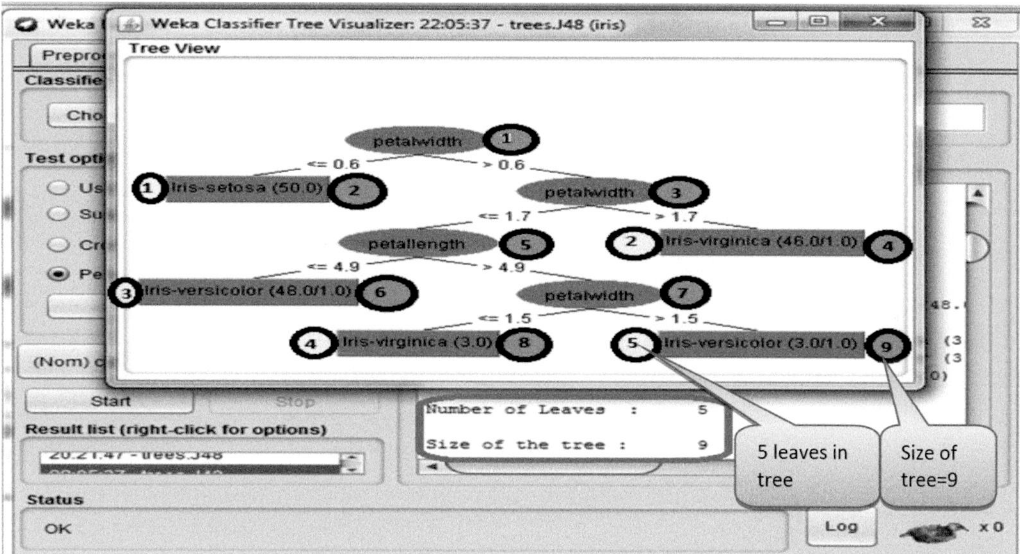

Figure 6.20 Size and leaves of the tree [see colour plate]

6.1.6 Using rules for prediction

The rules shown in Figure 6.18 can be coded into any programming language such as Java, C++, C#, Python and others, and can be used to predict the class of unknown samples. A GUI can be built consisting of text boxes for receiving values of input attributes and a button, namely ***predict***, can be created such that clicking on it will help in displaying the output after applying decision tree rules on input attributes. Thus, we will be able to build applications such as sentiment analysis, financial analysis, agriculture, placement prediction of students and match prediction and such, from the rules built by the decision tree classifier.

6.2 Applying Naïve Bayes

To apply Naïve Bayes on any given dataset, the following steps need to be taken:

1. Start ***Weka Explorer*** and go to the ***Preprocess*** tab.
2. Now select the ***Open file*** tab and select the ***weather.nominal.arff*** as given in Figure 6.21.
3. Now select the ***Classify*** tab and choose ***Naivebayes*** classifier as shown in Figure 6.22.
4. Click on ***More Options*** button and set options in ***classifier evaluation options*** as given in Figure 6.22.
5. Select ***Use Training Set*** option as given in Figure 6.22.

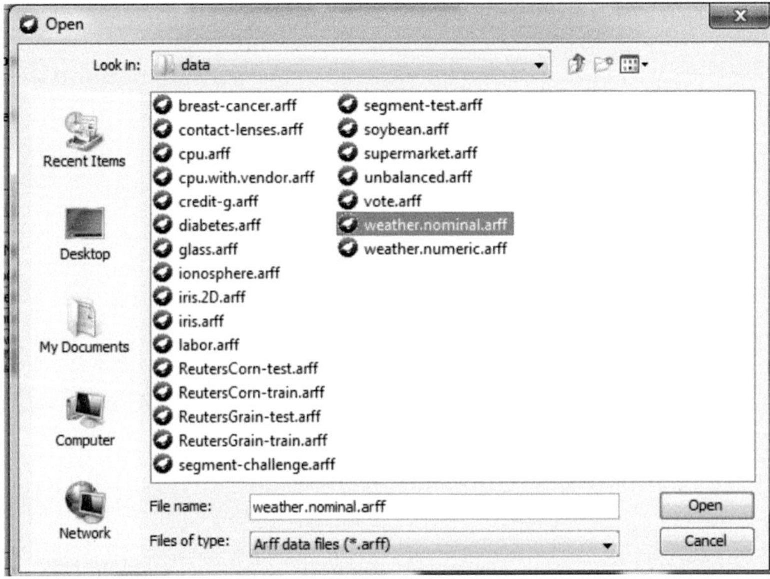

Figure 6.21 Selecting dataset file

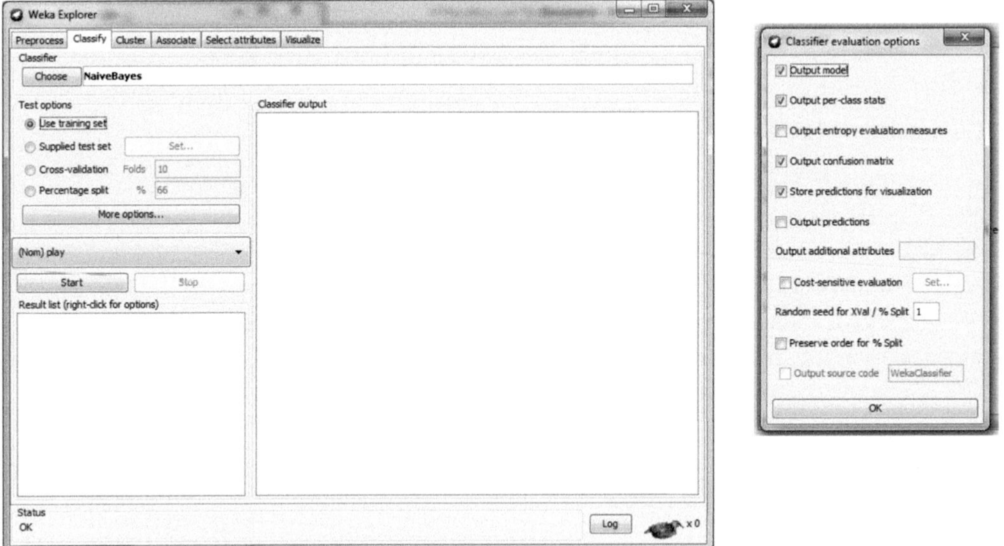

Figure 6.22 Selecting the classifier and setting classifier evaluation options

6. Click on ***Start*** button
   After the processing, the output will appear as shown in Figure 6.23, where it shows that the ***correctly classified instances*** are 13 and ***incorrect instance*** is 1 and the overall result is 92.8571%. The incorrect instance is shown in the above figure as a plus (+) symbol in the error column and is the 6th instance.

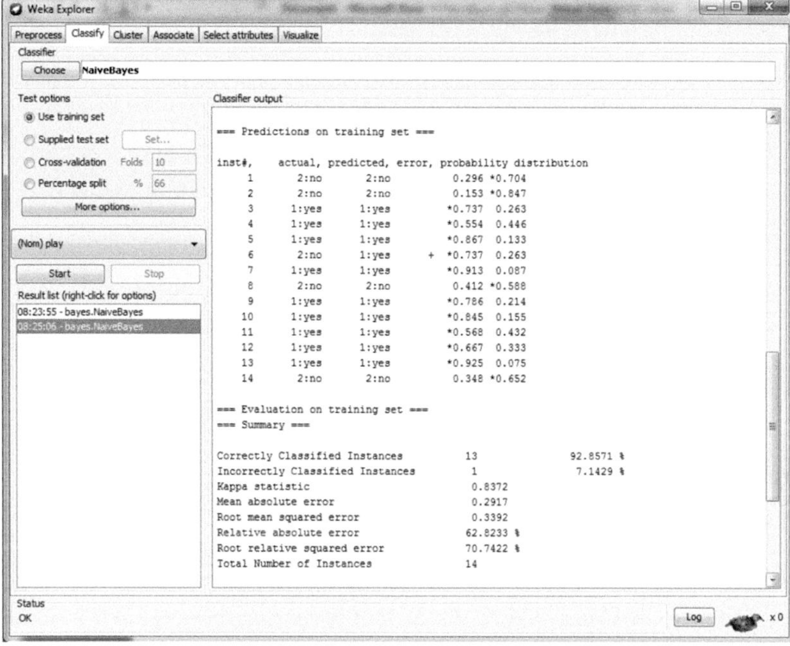

Figure 6.23 Classifier results after processing

This result also shows that the Naïve Bayes classifier of Weka has automatically applied a Laplace estimator as shown in the modified count as given in Figure 6.24.

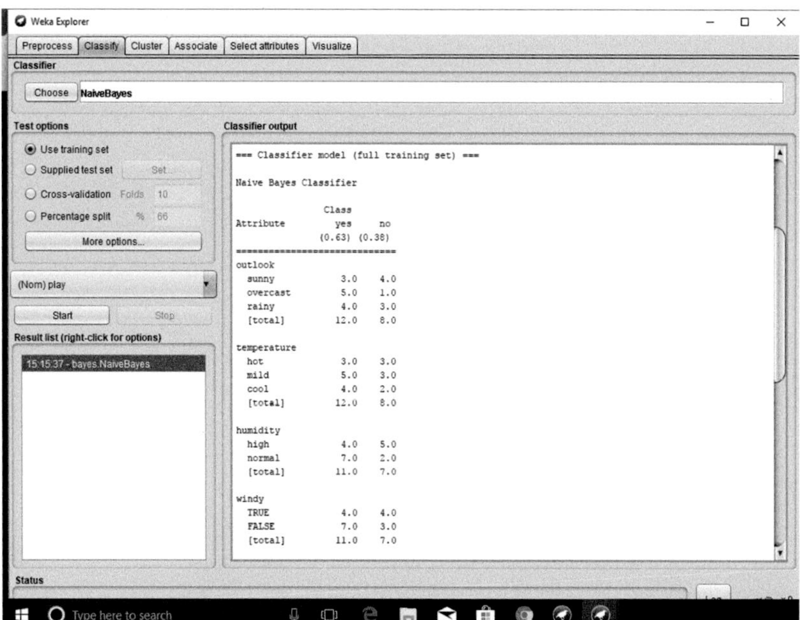

Figure 6.24 Naïve Bayes classifier with Laplace estimator

6.3 Creating the Testing Dataset

To test the classifier on unknown instance(s) we have to create the test data. In this section, a process has been illustrated to create a test dataset from an existing dataset.

In order to create test instance(s) follow the following steps.

1. Click on ***tool*** option in menu tab and select ***ArffViewer*** as shown in Figure 6.25.

Figure 6.25 Selecting ArffViewer option

2. Now click on File → Open → then select the file ***weather.nominal.arff*** as shown in Figure 6.26.

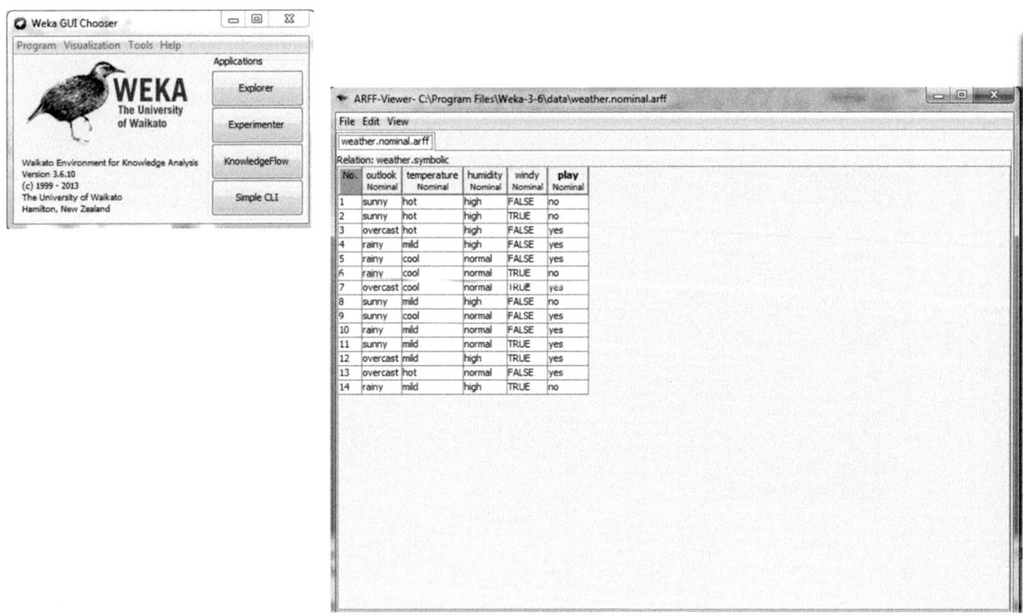

No.	outlook Nominal	temperature Nominal	humidity Nominal	windy Nominal	play Nominal
1	sunny	hot	high	FALSE	no
2	sunny	hot	high	TRUE	no
3	overcast	hot	high	FALSE	yes
4	rainy	mild	high	FALSE	yes
5	rainy	cool	normal	FALSE	yes
6	rainy	cool	normal	TRUE	no
7	overcast	cool	normal	TRUE	yes
8	sunny	mild	high	FALSE	no
9	sunny	cool	normal	FALSE	yes
10	rainy	mild	normal	FALSE	yes
11	sunny	mild	normal	TRUE	yes
12	overcast	mild	high	TRUE	yes
13	overcast	hot	normal	FALSE	yes
14	rainy	mild	high	TRUE	no

Figure 6.26 Opening the arff file

3. Select all of the records in ***ArffViewer*** except one record because we wish to keep that as a testing record instance. In case you want to have *n* records as testing dataset then select all the records except first *n* records.

4. Click on ***Edit → Delete Instances*** as shown in Figure 6.27.

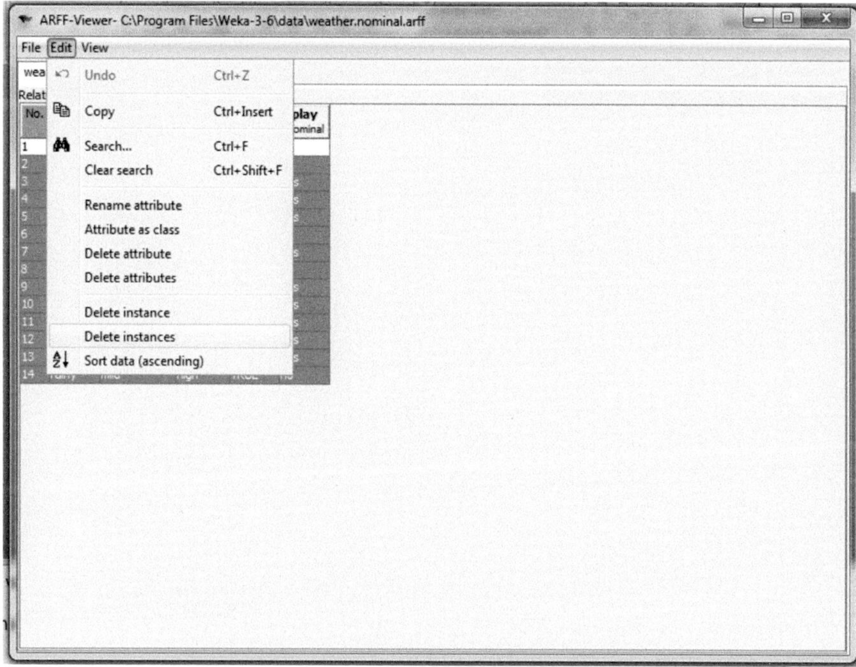

Figure 6.27 Selecting and deleting the rows

5. Now change the values of one record and set it according to values that we want to have for the testing record by using the drop down option for setting the value of the attributes as shown in Figure 6.28.

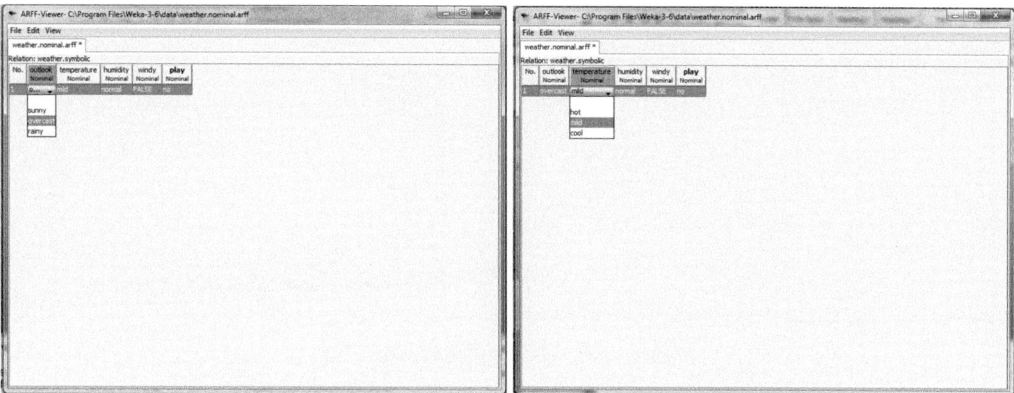

Figure 6.28 Setting the values of the testing record

6. Keep the class attribute blank because we wish to predict its values by the classifier as shown in Figure 6.29.

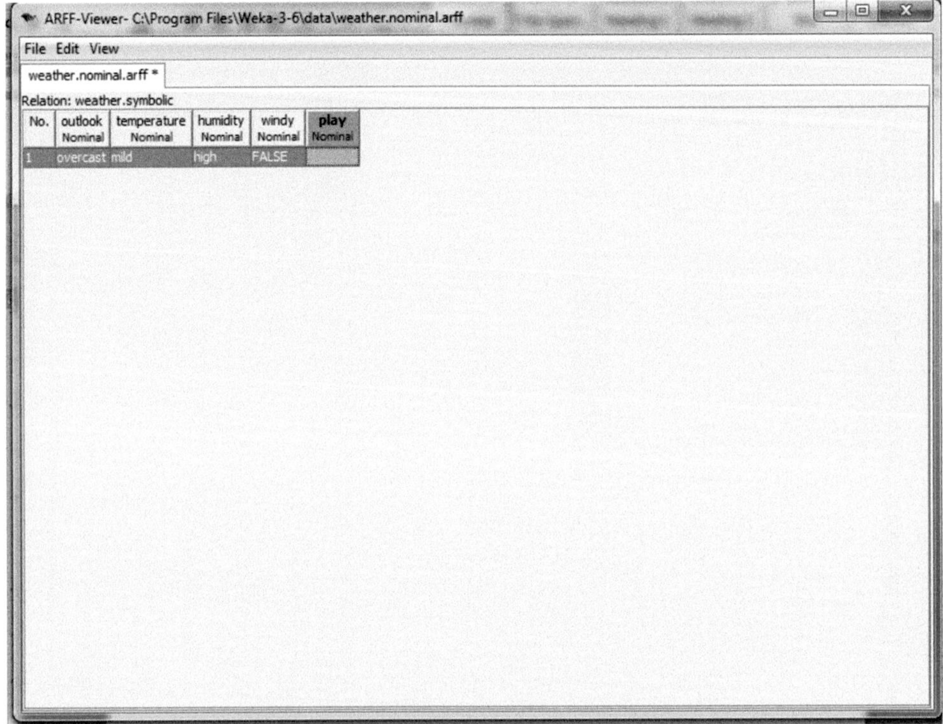

Figure 6.29 Setting class attribute to blank

7. After changing the values of row(s), Save the file as ***test.arff*** as shown in Figure 6.30.

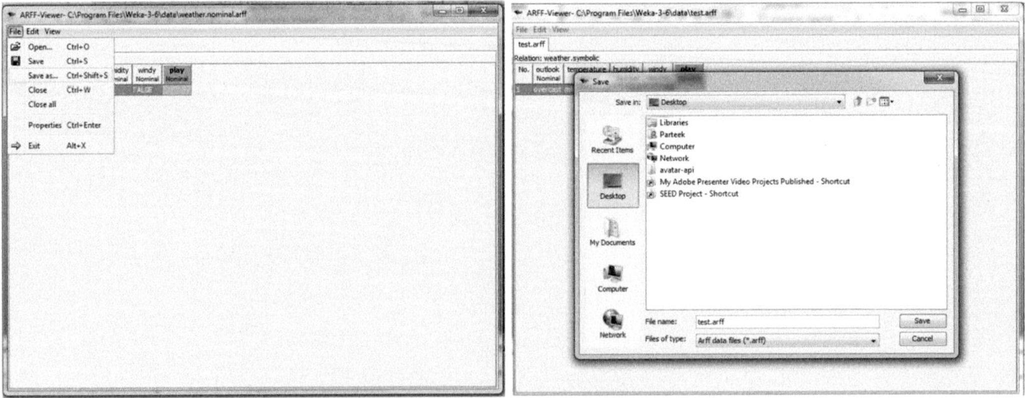

Figure 6.30 Saving the **test.arff** file

8. Now move to ***Preprocess*** tab and click on ***Open file*** option and select the ***weather.nominal.arff*** file as shown in Figure 6.31.

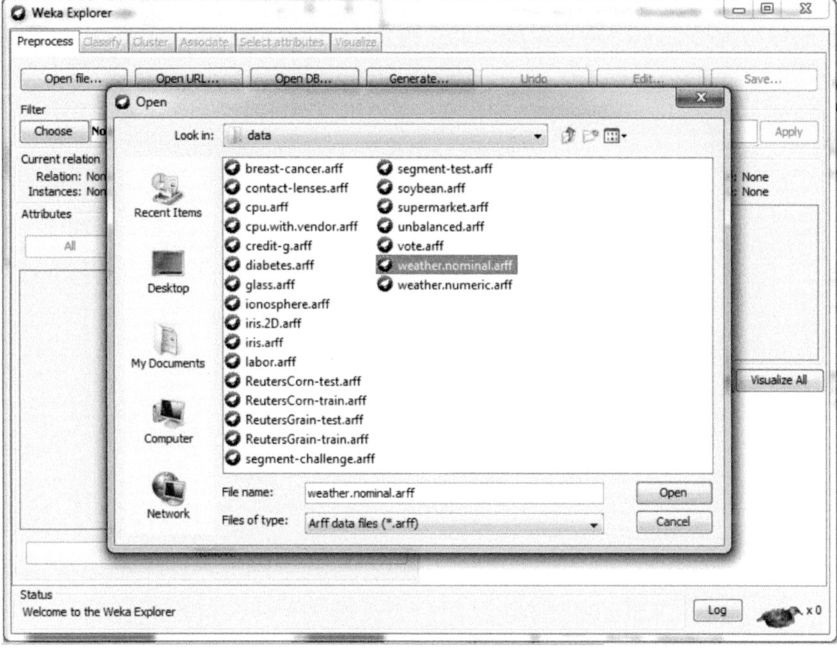

Figure 6.31 Opening the ***weather.nominal.arff*** file

9. Select the ***Classify*** tab and choose ***NaiveBayes*** Classifier.
10. Click on the ***Start*** button, it will build the classifier as shown in Figure 6.32.

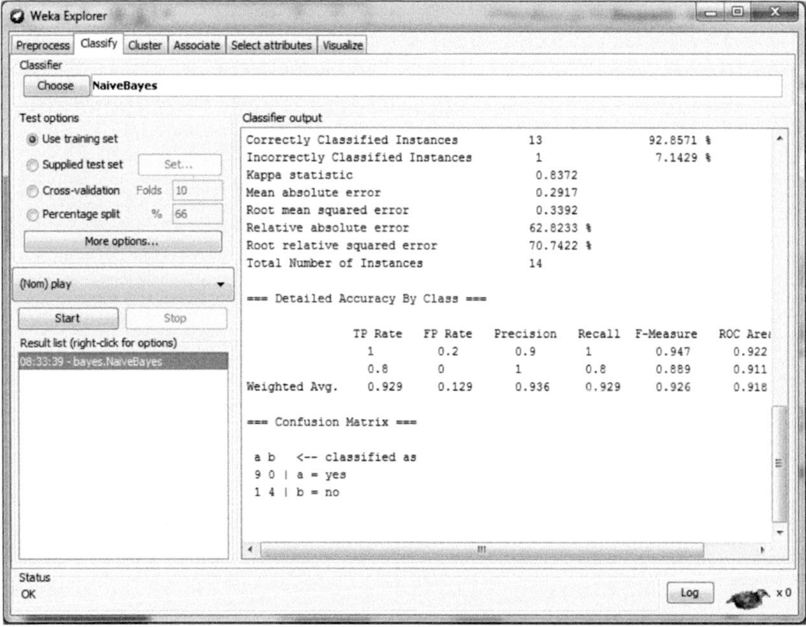

Figure 6.32 Building the Naïve Bayes classifier

11. Now select the ***Supplied test set*** option and click on the ***Set button*** as shown in Figure 6.33.
12. Then ***Open File → select test.arff file.*** Once the test file has been selected, it will show details about file, i.e., name of relation, number of attribute and instances, etc. as shown in Figure 6.33.

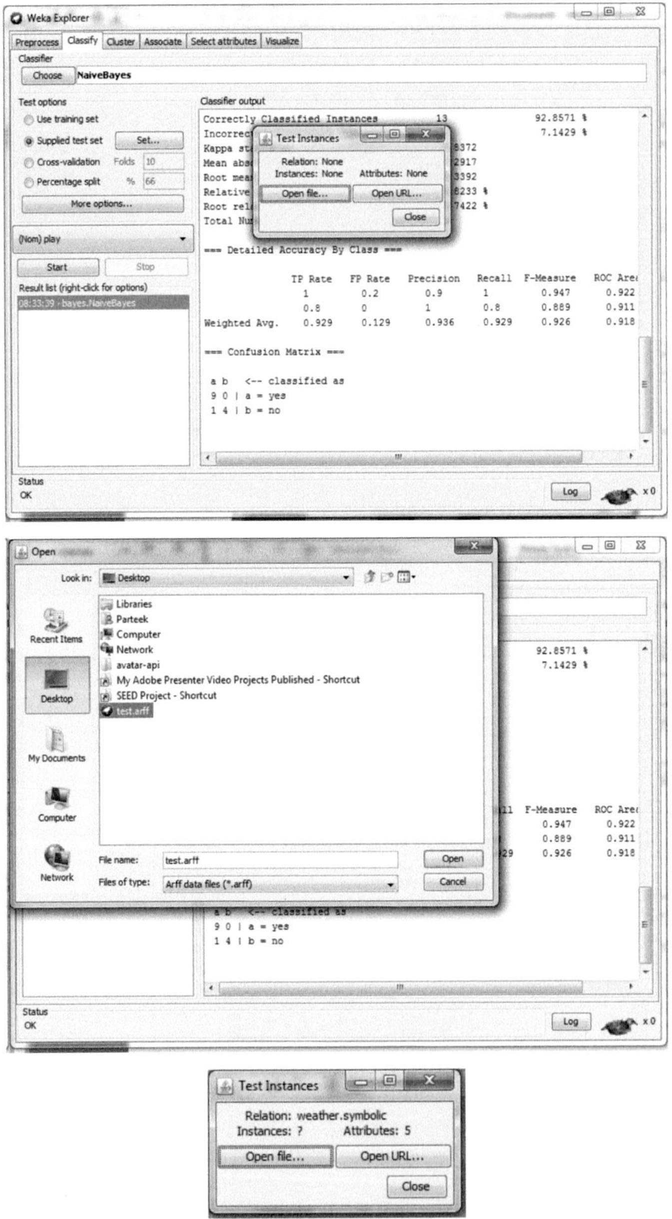

Figure 6.33 Supplying test dataset for predicting the value of known instance(s)

13. Now click on the ***Start*** button and apply the classifier on test instance(s). In this case, classifier has predicted an unkown instance as Play: Yes as shown in Figure 6.34.

In your case, the predicted value may be different as it depends upon the values of attributes set during the creation of the test dataset.

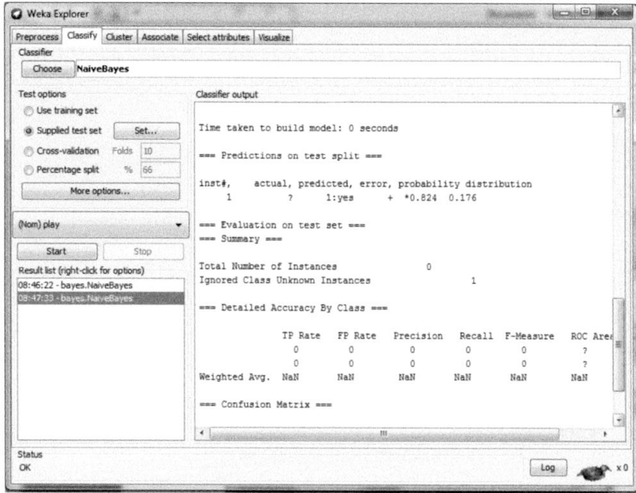

Figure 6.34 Predicting the value of an unknown sample as Play: Yes

Now, let us apply the J48 classifier on this test dataset to verify whether it shows the same prediction or not by performing the following steps.

1. Change the classifier to J48 by using following steps.

   Click on Choose → Weka → classifiers → trees → J48

2. Select the ***Use Training Set*** option and click on ***Start*** button to build the J48 classifier as shown in Figure 6.35.

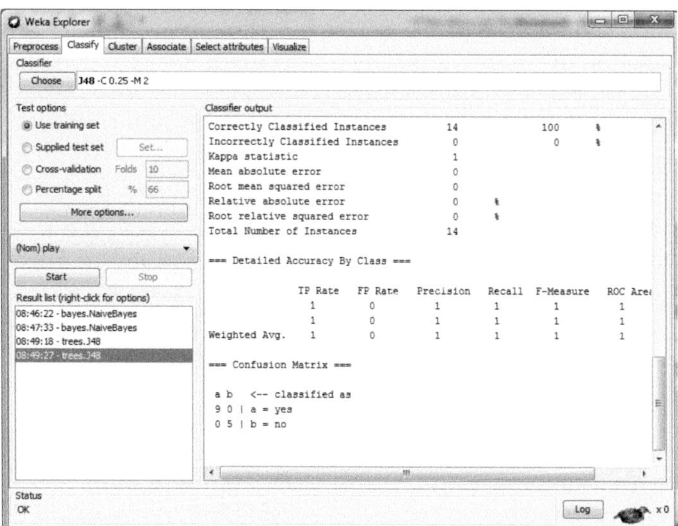

Figure 6.35 Building J48 on the training dataset

3. Now select the ***supplied test set*** option and select the test dataset as ***test.arff*** and then click on the ***start*** button to apply J48 on the test dataset as shown in Figure 6.38. You can verify that J48 has also predicted the value of Play as Yes, which is the same as in the Naïve Bayes Classifier. However, J48 is surer about its prediction as compared to Naïve Bayes as it predicted with the probability of 1.0 while Naïve Bayes predicted the same with probability of 0.824. You can find these values in the output as shown in Figure 6.36 and Figure 6.38.

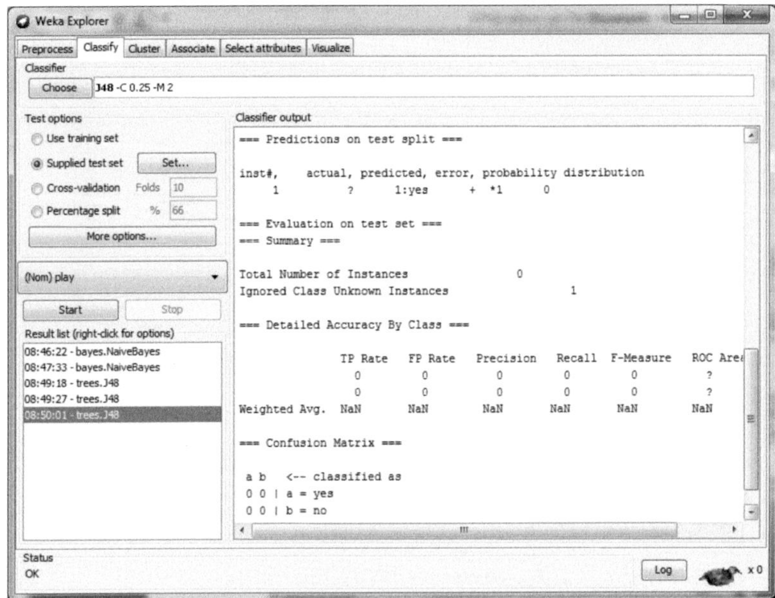

Figure 6.36 Predicting the value of an unknown sample as Play: Yes by J48

6.4 Decision Tree Operation with R

Decision trees in R can be implemented using different packages. Here, we are using the 'party' package to operate the decision tree on the Iris dataset. The function '***ctree***' has been used to build a decision tree on the Iris dataset as given below.

```
> library(party) # Load package party
>
> target = Species ~ Sepal.Length + Sepal.Width + Petal.Length + Petal.Width
>
> cdt <- ctree(target, iris) #Build tree
>
> table(predict(cdt), iris$Species) # Create confusion matrix
```

As given above, first load the '***party***' package to build the decision tree. In the next line, the '***target***' variable specifies that **Species** is the class variable and all other variables are independent variables. Function ***ctree()*** provides some parameters, such as MinSplit, MinBusket, MaxSurrogate and MaxDepth, to control the training of decision trees. Here, we have used the default settings such as it takes two parameters such as the '*target*' variable and the dataset on which it will train the decision tree. In this example, we have used the Iris dataset. In the next line, the ***predict ()*** function is used to check the prediction on trained data itself. Function ***table ()*** creates the confusion matrix and misclassification errors.

Figure 6.37 shows the operation of the decision tree in R. After applying the decision tree, the confusion matrix helps in summarizing the results of testing the algorithm for further inspection. For the Iris dataset, we have a total of 50 Setosa, 50 Versicolor and 50 Virginica. *In the confusion matrix, horizontal rows represent the actual classification and vertical columns show the prediction done by the system.* Here, the confusion matrix tells us that decision tree properly classified 50 Setosa, 49 Versicolor and 45 Virginica. However, it classified 1 Versicolor as Virginica and 5 Virginica as Versicolor.

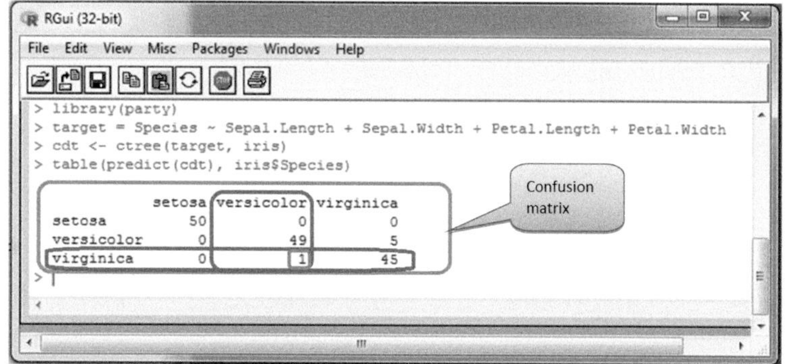

Figure 6.37 Implementation of the decision tree in R [see colour plate]

```
> cdt #To display decision tree rules
```

The rules based on which the decision tree is trained using the ***ctree ()*** function can be checked by just typing the variable name at the console of R. In the above example, we have stored the rules in the *'cdt'* variable.

Figure 6.38 shows the rules based on which classification has been performed by the decision tree.

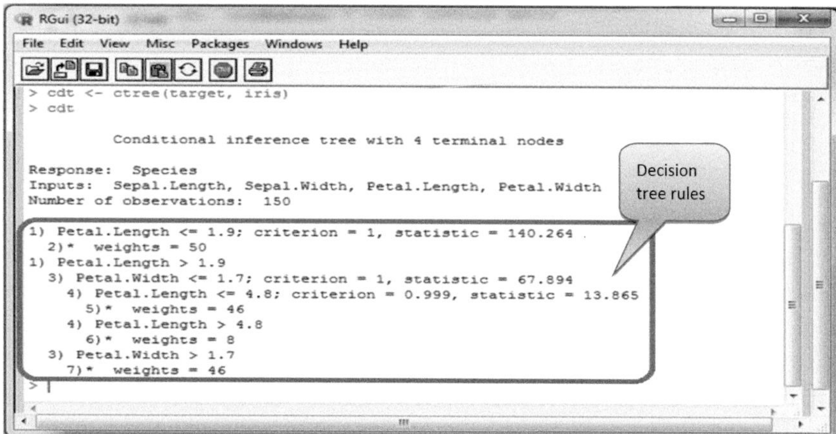

Figure 6.38 Decision tree rules in R

```
> plot(cdt, type="simple") #Plotting of decision tree
```

The decision tree can be plotted using the ***plot ()*** function by passing the results of the built decision tree as an argument as shown in Figure 6.39. The '***type***' parameter is optional.

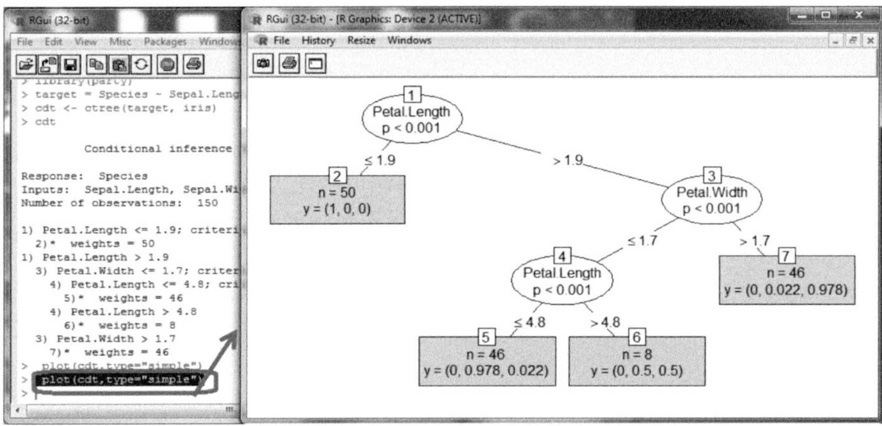

Figure 6.39 Plotting the decision tree

Training and testing of the dataset

Earlier, we trained the whole dataset to implement the decision tree. In this section, suppose we want to train the decision tree on approximately 2/3 of the samples of the dataset and test the built decision tree on the remaining samples. For example, in this case, the dataset has been trained on 99 instances and tested on the remaining 51 samples out of 150 samples in total.

```
> library(party)
>
> indexes = sample(150, 99) #select ~2/3 of the instances of iris dataset
>
> iris_train = iris[indexes,] # training of instances
>
> iris_test = iris[-indexes,] #testing of instances
>
> target = Species ~ Sepal.Length + Sepal.Width + Petal.Length + Petal.Width
>
> cdt <- ctree(target, iris_train) #Training of decision tree
>
> table(predict(cdt, newdata=iris_test), iris_test$Species) # testing of dataset
```

First of all, load the '***party***' package. Then split the samples into training and testing dataset. For this, we used the ***sample ()*** function. This function takes a sample of the specified size from the elements of *x* either with or without replacement. In our case, we selected the 99 samples out of 150 samples in '***indexes***' variable. Then, we used this '***indexes***' variable to retrieve training and testing dataset. ***Iris[indexes,]*** indicates that the random indexes selected by ***sample ()*** are retrieved from the Iris dataset and '-' sign indicates that the remaining samples retrieved from iris dataset are stored for testing. Similarly as previously discussed, the tree is built using the ***ctree()*** function and tested on the test dataset as shown in Figure 6.40.

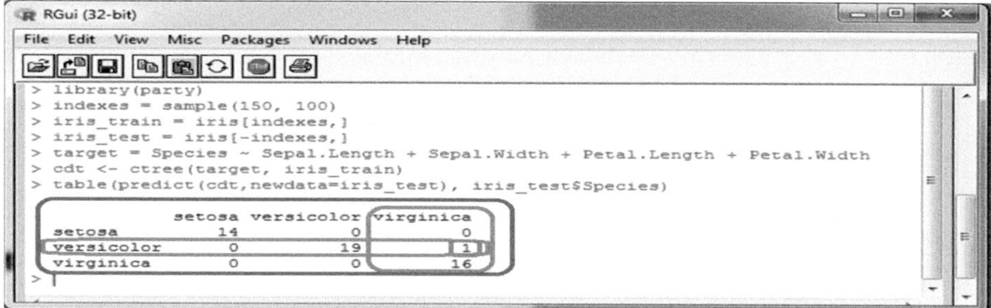

Figure 6.40 Prediction by the decision tree on testing dataset [see colour plate]

```
> summary(iris _ test) #To print summary of results
```

Function ***summary ()*** shows the results of dataset passed as argument. Figure 6.25 shows the summary about the testing dataset. It shows that the testing dataset consists of 14 Setosa, 19 Versicolor and 17 Virginica. When we tested this dataset, it was observed that the decision tree properly classified 14 Setosa, 19 Versicolor and 16 Virginica. However, it classified 1 Virginica as Versicolor as shown in Figure 6.41.

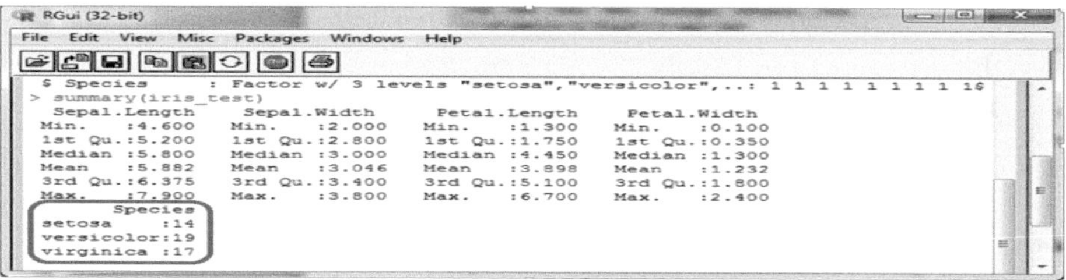

Figure 6.41 Summary of testing the dataset

6.5 Naïve Bayes Operation using R

Naïve Bayes in R can be implemented using different packages. Here, we are using the 'e1071' package to implement Naïve Baycs on a weather dataset. The e1071 package contains the Naïve Bayes function. It allows numeric and factor variables to be used in the Naïve Bayes model. If the package 'e1071' is not installed, then first install the package using the following command.

```
> install.packages("e1071") ##Installation of package "e1071"
```

After installation, load the package using the '***library***' command given as follows.

```
> library("e1071") ##Load the package "e1071"
```

Then, the '**Weather**' dataset may be employed to illustrate how the Naïve Bayes classification can be performed in R. After loading, convert the dataset into a data frame

```
> library("e1071") ##Load the package "e1071"
> data<-read.csv("F:\\dataset\\weather.csv",header=TRUE) ##Load the .csv file of dataset
> weather _ df=as.data.frame(data) #Conversion of dataset into data frame
```

The following command displays the instances of dataset as shown in Fig. 6.42.

```
> weather _ df #To display instances of weather dataset
```

```
> data<-read.csv("F:\\dataset\\weather.csv",header=TRUE)
> weather_df=as.data.frame(data)
> weather_df
   outlook temperature humidity windy play
1  overcast        hot     high FALSE  yes
2  overcast       cool   normal  TRUE  yes
3  overcast       mild     high  TRUE  yes
4  overcast        hot   normal FALSE  yes
5     rainy       mild     high FALSE  yes
6     rainy       cool   normal FALSE  yes
7     rainy       cool   normal  TRUE   no
8     rainy       mild   normal FALSE  yes
9     rainy       mild     high  TRUE   no
10    sunny        hot     high FALSE   no
11    sunny        hot     high  TRUE   no
12    sunny       mild     high FALSE   no
13    sunny       cool   normal FALSE  yes
14    sunny       mild   normal  TRUE  yes
```

Figure 6.42 Instances of Weather dataset

After applying the Naïve Bayes function on weather dataset, the results obtained are shown in Figure 6.43.

```
> Naive _ Bayes _ Model=naiveBayes(play ~., data=weather _ df)
> Naive _ Bayes _ Model
```

```
> Naive_Bayes_Model=naiveBayes(play ~., data=weather_df)
> Naive_Bayes_Model

Naive Bayes Classifier for Discrete Predictors

Call:
naiveBayes.default(x = X, y = Y, laplace = laplace)

A-priori probabilities:
Y
       no       yes 
0.3571429 0.6428571 

Conditional probabilities:
     outlook
Y      overcast     rainy     sunny
  no  0.0000000 0.4000000 0.6000000
  yes 0.4444444 0.3333333 0.2222222

     temperature
Y          cool       hot      mild
  no  0.2000000 0.4000000 0.4000000
  yes 0.3333333 0.2222222 0.4444444

     humidity
Y          high    normal
  no  0.8000000 0.2000000
  yes 0.3333333 0.6666667

     windy
Y         FALSE      TRUE
  no  0.4000000 0.6000000
  yes 0.6666667 0.3333333
```

Figure 6.43 Results of Naïve Bayes on Weather dataset

After applying Naïve Bayes, a confusion matrix can be created which helps in summarizing the results of testing the algorithm for further inspection using the following commands. The confusion matrix is shown in Figure 6.44.

```
> NB _ Predictions=predict(Naive _ Bayes _ Model,weather _ df)
> table(NB _ Predictions,weather _ df$play, dnn=c("Prediction","Actual"))
```

```
> NB_Predictions=predict(nb_laplace1,weather_df)
> table(NB_Predictions,weather_df$play, dnn=c("Prediction","Actual"))
          Actual
Prediction no yes
       no   4   0
       yes  1   9
```

Figure 6.44 The confusion matrix

For the weather dataset, we have a total of 14 instances. Out of which, there are 9 instances that specify that play will be held in the given weather conditions and 5 instances that specify that play will not be held. Here, the confusion matrix tells us that Naïve Bayes properly classified 9 instances for play to be held and 4 instances for play not to be held. However, it classified 1 instance of play into the 'Yes' class that actually belongs to the 'No' play class.

The Naive Bayes function includes the Laplace parameter. Whatever positive integer this is set to will be added into for every class. In this example, we set the Laplace parameter to 1 as given in the following commands.

```
> nb _ laplace1 <- naiveBayes(play~., data=weather _ df, laplace=1)
> laplace1 _ pred <- predict(nb _ laplace1, weather _ df, type="class")
> table(laplace1 _ pred, weather _ df$play,dnn=c("Prediction","Actual"))
```

Acknowledgement

We acknowledge the consent of Mr Mark Polczynski to use the ideas and illustration given in his Weka Tutorial 3 - Classification Using the Decision Tree.

Remind Me

- J48 is used in Weka to apply classification.
- This algorithm can be applied in Weka by selecting Weka–>classifiers–>trees–>J48
- Select Percentage split from test options to use 2/3 of records for training and remaining for testing.
- To see the tree, right-click on the highlighted Result list entry for the tree we just built, and then click Visualize tree.
- Decision tree in R can be implemented using the ***'party'*** package.
- The function ***'ctree'*** can be used to build the decision tree
- The ***predict ( )*** function is used to check the prediction on trained data itself.
- The ***table ( )*** creates the confusion matrix and misclassification errors.
- The decision tree can be plotted using the ***plot ( )*** function
- The ***sample ( )*** function can be used to split the samples into training and testing datasets.
- Function ***summary ( )*** shows the results of dataset passed as argument.

Point Me (Books)

- Witten, Ian H., Eibe Frank, and Mark A. Hall. 2010. *Data Mining: Practical Machine Learning Tools and Techniques*, 3rd ed. Amsterdam: Elsevier.
- Lesmeister, Cory. 2015. *Mastering Machine Learning with R*. Birmingham: Packt Publishing Ltd.

Connect Me (Internet Resources)

- http://technobium.com/decision-trees-explained-using-weka/
- http://www.cs.miami.edu/home/geoff/Courses/COMP6210-10M/Content/DecisionTrees.shtml
- https://machinelearningmastery.com/how-to-run-your-first-classifier-in-weka/
- http://kt.ijs.si/PetraKralj/IPS_DM_0910/HandsOnWeka-Part1.pdf
- http://art.uniroma2.it/basili/MLWM09/002_DecTree_Weka.pdf
- https://www.cs.cmu.edu/afs/cs/academic/class/15381-s07/www/slides/041007decisionTrees1.pdf
- http://www.cs.ukzn.ac.za/~hughm/dm/content/slides06.pdf

Do It Yourself

1. The purpose of this assignment is to verify that you have learnt the concepts of classification. Implement this assignment in both Weka and R to check your learning.
   Task 1. Go to http://www3.dsi.uminho.pt/pcortez/wine/ and download WineQuality.zip.
   Task 2. Unzip the folder and read WineQuality.pdf.
   Task 3. Convert WineQuality.xls file to .csv format and save as WineQuality.csv.
   Task 4. Open WineQuality.csv in Weka Explorer.
   Task 5. Save as WineQuality.arff (do not overwrite WineQuality.arff).
   Task 6. Using the "Visualize All" button, display histograms of all attributes on one screen.
   Task 7. Using all the default settings, apply the J48 classifier to the dataset.
   Task 8. Cut and paste a screenshot of the resulting confusion matrix on the following designated slide.
   Task 9. Perform the decision tree classification on the same dataset in R language.
2. Why is J48 called J48? Justify your answer.

7

Cluster Analysis

Chapter Objectives

- ✓ To comprehend the concept of clustering, its applications, and features.
- ✓ To understand various distance metrics for clustering of data.
- ✓ To comprehend the process of K-means clustering.
- ✓ To comprehend the process of hierarchical clustering algorithms.
- ✓ To comprehend the process of DBSCAN algorithms.

7.1 Introduction to Cluster Analysis

Generally, in the case of large datasets, data is not labeled because labeling a large number of records requires a great deal of human effort. The unlabeled data can be analyzed with the help of clustering techniques. Clustering is an unsupervised learning technique which does not require a labeled dataset.

Clustering is defined as grouping a set of similar objects into classes or clusters. In other words, during cluster analysis, the data is grouped into classes or clusters, so that records within a cluster (intra-cluster) have high similarity with one another but have high dissimilarities in comparison to objects in other clusters (inter-cluster), as shown in Figure 7.1.

The similarity of records is identified on the basis of values of attributes describing the objects. Cluster analysis is an important human activity. The first human beings Adam and Eve actually learned through the process of clustering. They did not know the name of any object, they simply observed each and every object. Based on the similarity of their properties, they identified these objects in groups or clusters. For example, one group or cluster was named as trees, another as fruits and so on. They further classified the fruits on the basis of their properties like size, colour, shape, taste, and others. After that, people assigned labels or names to these objects calling them mango, banana, orange, and so on. And finally, all objects were labeled. Thus, we can say that the first human beings used clustering for their learning and they made clusters or groups of physical objects based on the similarity of their attributes.

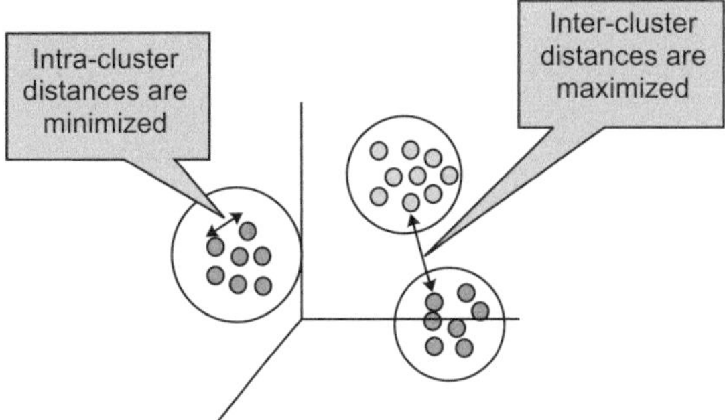

Figure 7.1 Characteristics of clusters

7.2 Applications of Cluster Analysis

Cluster analysis has been widely used in various important applications such as:

- Marketing: It helps marketers find out distinctive groups among their customer bases, and this knowledge helps them improve their targeted marketing programs.
- Land use: Clustering is used for identifying areas of similar land use from the databases of earth observations.
- Insurance: Clustering is helpful for recognizing clusters of insurance policyholders with a high regular claim cost.
- City-planning: It also helps in identifying clusters of houses based on house type, geographical location, and value.
- Earthquake studies: Clustering is helpful for analysis of earthquakes as it has been noticed that earthquake epicenters are clustered along continent faults.
- Biology studies: Clustering helps in defining plant and animal classifications, identifying genes with similar functionalities, and in gaining insights into structures inherent to populations.
- Web discovery: Clustering is helpful in categorizing documents on the web for information discovery.
- Fraud detection: Clustering is also helpful in outlier detection applications such as credit card fraud detection.

7.3 Desired Features of Clustering

The desired feature of an ideal clustering technique is that intra-cluster distances should be minimized and inter-cluster distances should be maximized. Following are the other important features that an ideal cluster analysis method should have:

- ***Scalability:*** Clustering algorithms should be capable of handling small as well as large datasets smoothly.

- ***Ability to handle different types of attributes:*** Clustering algorithms should be able to handle different kinds of data such as binary, categorical and interval-based (numerical) data.
- ***Independent of data input order:*** The clustering results should not be dependent on the ordering of input data.
- ***Identification of clusters with different shapes:*** The clustering algorithm should be capable of identifying clusters of any shape.
- ***Ability to handle noisy data:*** Usually, databases consist of noisy, erroneous or missing data, and algorithm must be able to handle these.
- ***High performance:*** To have a high performance algorithm, it is desirable that the algorithm should need to perform only one scan of the dataset. This capability would reduce the cost of input-output operations.
- ***Interpretability:*** The results of clustering algorithms should be interpretable, logical and usable.
- ***Ability to stop and resume:*** For a large dataset, it is desirable to stop and resume the task as it can take a huge amount of time to accomplish the full task and breaks may be necessary.
- ***Minimal user guidance:*** The clustering algorithm should not expect too much supervision from the analyst, because commonly the analyst has a limited knowledge of the dataset.

In clustering, distance metrics play a vital role in comprehending the similarity between the objects. In the next section, we will discuss different distance metrics that play an important role in the process of clustering of objects.

7.4 Distance Metrics

A distance metric is a function ***d(x, y)*** that specifies the distance between elements of a set as a non-negative real number. Two elements are equal under a particular metric if the distance between them is zero. Distance functions present a method to measure the closeness of two elements. Here, elements can be matrices, vectors or arbitrary objects and do not necessarily need to be numbered.

In the following subsections, important distance metrics used in the measuring similarity among objects have been illustrated.

7.4.1 Euclidean distance

Euclidean distance is mainly used to calculate distances. The distance between two points in the plane with coordinates (x, y) and (a, b) according to the Euclidean distance formula is given by:

$$\text{Euclidean dist}((x, y), (a, b)) = \sqrt{(x - a)^2 + (y - b)^2}$$

For example, the (Euclidean) distance between points (-2, 2) and (2, -1) is calculated as

$$\begin{aligned}\text{Euclidean dist}((-2, 2), (2, -1)) &= \sqrt{(-2 - (2))^2 + (2 - (-1))^2} \\ &= \sqrt{(-4)^2 + (3)^2} \\ &= \sqrt{16 + 9} \\ &= \sqrt{25} \\ &= 5\end{aligned}$$

Let's find the Euclidean distance among three persons to find the similarities and dissimilarities among them, on the basis of two variables. The data is given in Table 7.1.

Table 7.1 Data to calculate Euclidean distances among three persons

	Variable 1	*Variable 2*
Person 1	30	70
Person 2	40	54
Person 3	80	50

Using the formula of Euclidean distance, we can calculate the similarity distance among persons.

The calculation for the distance between person 1 and 2 is:

$$\begin{aligned}\text{Euclidean dist}((30, 70), (40, 54)) &= \sqrt{(30 - 40)^2 + (70 - 54)^2} \\ &= \sqrt{(-10)^2 + (16)^2} \\ &= \sqrt{100+256} \\ &= \sqrt{356} \\ &= 18.86\end{aligned}$$

The calculation for the distance between person 1 and 3 is:

$$\begin{aligned}\text{Euclidean dist}((30, 70), (80, 50)) &= \sqrt{(30 - 80)^2 + (70 - 50)^2} \\ &= \sqrt{(-50)^2 + (20)^2} \\ &= \sqrt{2500 + 400} \\ &= \sqrt{2900} \\ &= 53.85\end{aligned}$$

The calculation for the distance between person 2 and 3 is:

$$\begin{aligned}\text{Euclidean dist}((40, 54), (80, 50)) &= \sqrt{(40 - 80)^2 + (54 - 50)^2} \\ &= \sqrt{(-40)^2 + (4)^2} \\ &= \sqrt{1600+16} \\ &= \sqrt{1616} \\ &= 40.19\end{aligned}$$

This indicates that the persons 1 and 2 are most similar while person 1 and person 3 are most dissimilar. Thus, Euclidean distance is used to determine the dissimilarity between two objects by comparing them across a range of variables. These two objects might be profiles of two persons, e.g., a person and a target profile, or in fact, any two vectors taken across equivalent variables.

In the Euclidean distance, the attribute with the largest value may dominate the distance. Thus, it's important that attributes should be properly scaled before the application of the formula. It is also possible to use the Euclidean distance formula without the square root if one wishes to place greater weightage on large differences. Euclidean distance can also be represented as shown in Figure 7.2.

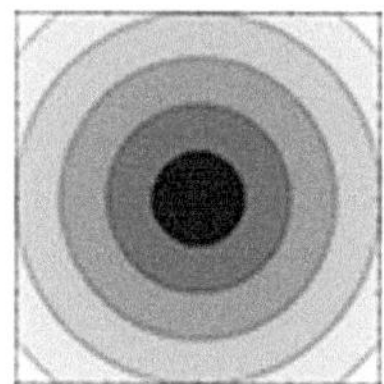

Figure 7.2 Representation of Euclidean distance [see colour plate]

[*Credits*: https://numerics.mathdotnet.com/Distance.html]

7.4.2 Manhattan distance

Manhattan distance is also called L1-distance. It is defined as the sum of the lengths of the projections of the line segment between the two points on the coordinate axes.

For example, the distance between two points in the plane with coordinates (x, y) and (a, b) according to the Manhattan distance formula, is given by:

$$\text{Manhattan dist}((x, y), (a, b)) = | x - a | + | y - b |$$

Let's do the calculations for finding the Manhattan distance among the same three persons, on the basis of their scores on two variables as shown in Table 7.1.

Using the formula of Manhattan distance, we can calculate the similarity distance among persons.

The calculation for the distance between person 1 and 2 is:

$$\begin{aligned}\text{Manhattan dist}((30, 70), (40, 54)) &= |30 - 40| + |70 - 54| \\ &= |-10| + |16| \\ &= 10+16 \\ &= 26\end{aligned}$$

The calculation for the distance between person 1 and 3 is:

$$\begin{aligned}\text{Manhattan dist}((30, 70), (80, 50)) &= |30 - 80| + |70 - 50| \\ &= 50+20 \\ &= 70\end{aligned}$$

The calculation for the distance between person 2 and 3 is:

$$\begin{aligned}\text{Manhattan dist}((40, 54), (80, 50)) &= |40 - 80| + |54 - 50| \\ &= 40+4 = 44\end{aligned}$$

This indicates that the persons 1 and 2 are most similar while person 1 and person 3 are most dissimilar and it produces the same conclusion as Euclidean distance.

Manhattan distance is also called city block distance because like Manhattan, it is the distance a car would drive in a city laid out in square blocks. In Manhattan city, one-way, oblique streets and real streets only exist at the edges of blocks. The Manhattan distance can be represented as shown in Figure 7.3.

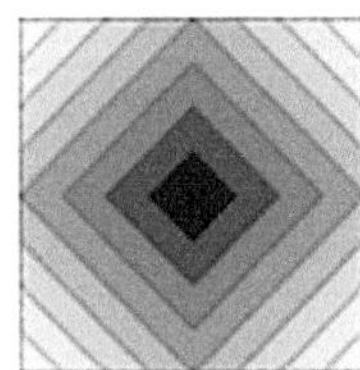

Figure 7.3 Representation of Manhattan distance [see colour plate]
[*Credits*: https://numerics.mathdotnet.com/Distance.html]

In Manhattan distance, the largest valued attribute can again dominate the distance, although not as much as in the Euclidean distance.

7.4.3 Chebyshev distance

It is also called as chessboard distance because, in a game of chess, the minimum number of moves required by a king to go from one square to another on a chessboard equals Chebyshev distance between the centers of the squares. Chebyshev distance is defined on a vector space, where the distance between two vectors is the maximum value of their differences along any coordinate dimension.

Formula of Chebyshev distance is given by:

$$\text{Chebyshev dist}((r1, f1), (r2, f2)) = \max(|r2-r1|,|f2-f1|)$$

Using the formula of Chebyshev distance, let us find the distance between object A and object B.

Features	*Coord1*	*Coord2*	*Coord3*	*Coord4*
Object A	0	1	2	3
Object B	6	5	4	-2

Object A coordinate = {0,1,2,3}
Object B coordinate = {6,5,4,-2}
According to Chebyshev distance formula

$$\begin{aligned} D &= \max(|r2-r1|,|f2-f1|) \\ &= \max(|6-0|,|5-1|,|4-2|,|-2-3)|) \\ &= \max(6,4,2,5) = 6 \end{aligned}$$

Let's compute the calculations for finding the Chebyshev distance among three persons, on the basis of their scores on two variables as shown in Table 7.1.

The calculation for the distance between person 1 and 2 is:

$$\begin{aligned} \text{Chebyshev dist}((30, 70), (40, 54)) &= \max(\ |30 - 40|, |70 - 54|) \\ &= \max(|- 10\ |, |\ 16|) = 16 \end{aligned}$$

The calculation for the distance between person 1 and 3 is:

$$\begin{aligned} \text{Chebyshev dist}((30, 70), (80, 50)) &= \max(|30 - 80|\ , |70 - 50|) \\ &= \max(50,20) = 50 \end{aligned}$$

The calculation for the distance between person 2 and 3 is:

$$= \max(|40 - 80|, |54 - 50|)$$

$$\text{Chebyshev dist}((40, 54), (80, 50)) = \max(40,4) = 40$$

This indicates that the persons 1 and 2 are most similar while person 1 and person 3 are most dissimilar and it produces the same conclusion as Euclidean and Manhattan distance.

The Chebyshev distance can be represented as shown in Figure 7.4.

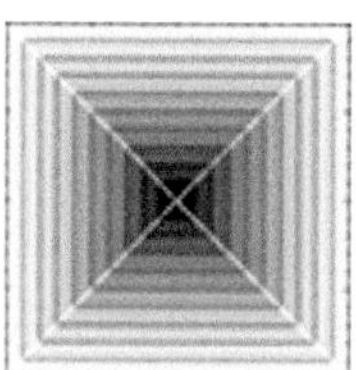

Figure 7.4 Representation of Chebyshev distance [see colour plate]

[*Credits*: https://numerics.mathdotnet.com/Distance.html]

7.5 Major Clustering Methods/Algorithms

Clustering methods/algorithms can be categorized into five categories which are given as follows:

- ***Partitioning method:*** It constructs random partitions and then iteratively refines them by some criterion.
- ***Hierarchical method:*** It creates a hierarchical decomposition of the set of data (or objects) using some criterion.
- ***Density-based method:*** It is based on connectivity and density functions.
- ***Grid based method:*** It is based on a multiple-level granularity structure.
- ***Model based method:*** A model is considered for each of the clusters and the idea is to identify the best fit for that model.

The categorization of clustering algorithms is shown in Figure 7.5.

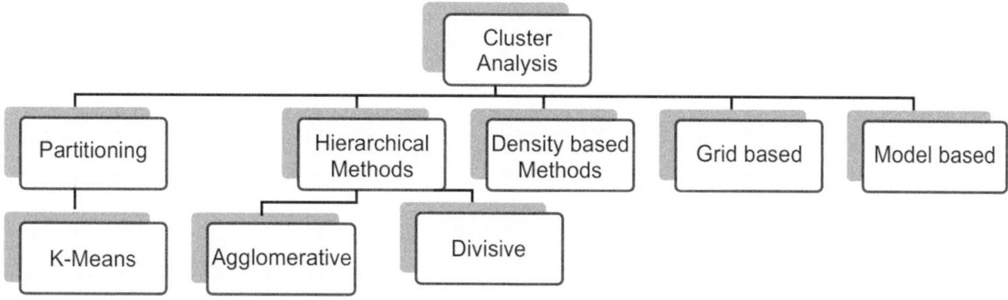

Figure 7.5 Major clustering methods/algorithms

Now, let us understand each method one by one.

7.6 Partitioning Clustering

Clustering is the task of splitting a group of data or dataset into a small number of clusters. For example, the items in a grocery store are grouped into different categories (butter, milk, and cheese are clustered in dairy products). This is a qualitative kind of partitioning. A quantitative approach on the other hand, measures certain features of the products such as the percentage of milk and suchlike, i.e., products having a high percentage of milk would be clustered together.

In the partitioning method, we cluster objects based on attributes into a number of partitions. The k-means clustering is an important technique which falls under partitioning clustering.

7.6.1. k-means clustering

In the k-means clustering algorithm, n objects are clustered into k clusters or partitions on the basis of attributes, where $k < n$ and k is a positive integer number. In simple words, in k-means clustering algorithm, the objects are grouped into 'k' number of clusters on the basis of attributes or features. The grouping of objects is done by minimizing the sum of squares of distances, i.e., a Euclidean distance between data and the corresponding cluster centroid.

Working of the k-means algorithm

The working of k-means clustering algorithm can be illustrated in five simple steps, as given below.

Step 1: Start with a selection of the value of k where k = number of clusters

In this step, the k centroids (or clusters) are initiated and then the first k training samples out of n samples of data are taken as single-element clusters. Each of the remaining (n-k) training samples are assigned to the cluster with the nearest centroid and the centroid of the gaining cluster is recomputed after each assignment.

Step 2: Creation of distance matrix between the centroids and each pattern

In this step, distance is computed from each sample of data to the centroid of each of the clusters. The heavy calculation involved is the major drawback of this step since there are k centroids and n samples, the algorithm will have to compute $n*k$ distances.

Step 3: Assign each sample in the cluster with the closest centroid (minimal distance)

Now, the samples are grouped on the basis of their distance from the centroid of each of the clusters. If currently, the sample is not in the cluster then switch it to the cluster with the closest centroid. When there is no movement of samples to another cluster anymore, the algorithm will end.

Step 4: Update the new centroids for each cluster

In this step, the locations of centroids are updated. Update the location for each centroid of the cluster that has gained or lost a sample by computing the mean of each attribute of all samples belonging to respective clusters.

Step 5: Repeat until no further change occurs

Return to Step 2 of the algorithm and repeat the updating process of each centroid location until a convergence condition is satisfied, which is until a pass through the training sample causes no new changes.

The flow chart of k-means algorithm is illustrated in Figure 7.6.

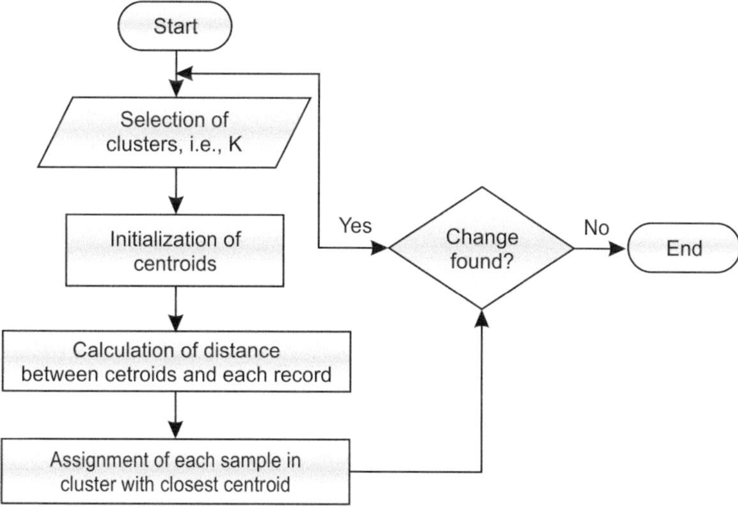

Figure 7.6 Flowchart for k-means algorithm

Example 7.1: Let's understand this procedure through an example; the database for which is given in Table 7.2. Here k=2 (there are just going to be two clusters).

Table 7.2 Database for the k-means algorithm example

Individual	*Variable 1*	*Variable 2*
1	1.0	1.0
2	1.5	2.0
3	3.0	4.0
4	5.0	7.0
5	3.5	5.0
6	4.5	5.0
7	3.5	4.5

Step 1:

The first step will be to choose the value of *k*. In this problem, let's suppose, *k*=2, i.e., we are going to create two clusters C1 and C2 from this database. Let's suppose, record number 1st and 4th are randomly chosen as candidates for clusters (By just browsing the database given in Table 7.2, we can conclude that 1st and 4th are the most dissimilar records or farthest from each other. Otherwise, we can choose any two records as the starting point for initialization of this algorithm).

In this case, the two centroids are: centroid 1 (first record) = (1.0,1.0) and centroid 2 (fourth record) = (5.0,7.0) as shown in Figure 7.7.

Individual	Variable 1	Variable 2
1	1.0	1.0
2	1.5	2.0
3	3.0	4.0
4	5.0	7.0
5	3.5	5.0
6	4.5	5.0
7	3.5	4.5

	Individual	Mean Vector
Group 1	1	(1.0, 1.0)
Group 2	4	(5.0,7.0)

Figure 7.7 Database after initialization

Step 2:

Now, the distance of each object is calculated from the other objects in this database on the basis of Euclidean distance as shown in Table 7.3.

The Euclidean distance of record 2 (1.5,2.0) from centroid 1 and centroid 2 has been given below.

Table 7.3 Database after first iteration

Individual	$Centroid_1$ (1,1) for C1	$Centroid_2$ (5,7) for C2	Assigned Cluster
1 (1.0,1.0)	0	$\sqrt{\|1-5\|^2+\|1-7\|^2}$ $= \sqrt{16+36}$ $= \sqrt{52}$ = 7.21	C1
2 (1.5,2.0)	$\sqrt{\|1.5-1\|^2+\|2.0-1\|^2}$ $= \sqrt{0.25+1}$ $= \sqrt{1.25}$ = 1.12	$\sqrt{\|1.5-5\|^2+\|2.0-7\|^2}$ $= \sqrt{12.25+25}$ $= \sqrt{37.25}$ = 6.10	C1

Contd.

Individual	$Centroid_1$ (1,1) for C1	$Centroid_2$ (5,7) for C2	Assigned Cluster
3 (3.0,4.0)	$\sqrt{\|3-1\|^2+\|4-1\|^2}$ $= \sqrt{4+9}$ $= \sqrt{13}$ $= 3.61$	$\sqrt{\|3-5\|^2+\|4.0-7\|^2}$ $= \sqrt{4+9}$ $= \sqrt{13}$ $= 3.61$	C1
4 (5.0, 7.0)	$\sqrt{\|5-1\|^2+\|7-1\|^2}$ $= \sqrt{16+36}$ $= \sqrt{52}$ $= 7.21$	$\sqrt{\|5-5\|^2+\|7.0-7\|^2}$ $= \sqrt{0}$ $= 0$	C2
5 (3.5, 5.0)	$\sqrt{\|3.5-1\|^2+\|5-1\|^2}$ $= \sqrt{6.25+16}$ $= \sqrt{22.25}$ $= 4.72$	$\sqrt{\|3.5-5\|^2+\|5.0-7\|^2}$ $= \sqrt{2.25+4}$ $= 2.5$	C2
6 (4.5, 5.0)	$\sqrt{\|4.5-1\|^2+\|5.0-1\|^2}$ $= \sqrt{12.25+16}$ $= \sqrt{28.25}$ $= 5.31$	$\sqrt{\|4.5-5\|^2+\|5.0-7\|^2}$ $= \sqrt{0.25+4}$ $= 2.06$	C2
7 (3.5, 4.5)	$\sqrt{\|3.5-1\|^2+\|4.5-1\|^2}$ $= \sqrt{6.25+12.25}$ $= \sqrt{18.5}$ $= 4.30$	$\sqrt{\|3.5-5\|^2+\|4.5-7\|^2}$ $= \sqrt{2.25+6.25}$ $= \sqrt{8.5}$ $= 2.92$	C2

Thus, we obtain two clusters containing: {1,2,3} and {4,5,6,7}.

The updated centroid for cluster 1 will be average of instances 1, 2 and 3 and for cluster 2 it will be average of instances 4, 5, 6 and 7 as shown below.

$$\text{centroid}_1 = \left(\frac{1}{3}(1.0 + 1.5 + 3.0),\ \frac{1}{3}(1.0 + 2.0 + 4.0)\right) = (1.83, 2.33)$$

$$\text{centroid}_2 = \left(\frac{1}{4}(5.0 + 3.5 + 4.5 + 3.5),\ \frac{1}{4}(7.0 + 5.0 + 5.0 + 4.5)\right) = (4.12, 5.38)$$

Now, the distance of each object to the modified centroid is calculated as shown in Table 7.4.

Table 7.4 Database after the second iteration

Individual	$Centroid_1$ (1.83,2.33) for C1	$Centroid_2$ (4.12,5.38) for C2	Assigned Cluster
1 (1.0,1.0)	$\sqrt{\|1.0-1.83\|^2+\|1.0-2.33\|^2} = 1.56$	$\sqrt{\|1.0-4.12\|^2+\|1.0-5.83\|^2} = 4.83$	C1
2 (1.5,2.0)	$\sqrt{\|1.5-1.83\|^2+\|2.0-2.33\|^2} = 0.46$	$\sqrt{\|1.5-4.12\|^2+\|2.0-5.83\|^2} = 4.64$	C1
3 (3.0,4.0)	$\sqrt{\|3.0-1.83\|^2+\|4.0-2.33\|^2} = 2.03$	$\sqrt{\|3.0-4.12\|^2+\|4.0-5.83\|^2} = 2.14$	C2
4 (5.0,7.0)	$\sqrt{\|5.0-1.83\|^2+\|7.0-2.33\|^2} = 5.64$	$\sqrt{\|5.0-4.12\|^2+\|7.0-5.83\|^2} = 1.84$	C2
5 (3.5,5.0)	$\sqrt{\|3.5-1.83\|^2+\|5.0-2.33\|^2} = 3.14$	$\sqrt{\|3.5-4.12\|^2+\|5.0-5.83\|^2} = 1.03$	C2
6 (4.5,5.0)	$\sqrt{\|4.5-1.83\|^2+\|5.0-2.33\|^2} = 3.77$	$\sqrt{\|4.5-4.12\|^2+\|5.0-5.83\|^2} = 0.91$	C2

The clusters obtained are: {1,2} and {3,4,5,6,7}

The updated centroid for cluster 1 will be average of instances 1 and 2 and for cluster 2 it will be average of instances 3, 4, 5, 6 and 7 as shown below.

$centroid_1$ = (1/2 (1.0+1.5), 1/2 (1.0+2.0)) = (1.25,1.5)

$centroid_2$ = (1/5 (3.0+5.0+3.5+4.5+3.5), 1/5 (4.0+7.0+5.0+5.0+4.5)) = (3.9,5.1)

Now, the distance of each object to the modified centroid is calculated as shown in Table 7.5.

Table 7.5 Database after the second iteration

Individual	*$Centroid_1$ (1.25, 1.5) for C1*	*$Centroid_2$ (3.9, 5.1) for C2*	*Assigned Cluster*
1 (1.0,1.0)	$\sqrt{\|1-1.25\|^2+\|1.0-1.5\|^2}$ = 0.56	$\sqrt{\|1-3.9\|^2+\|1-5.1\|^2}$ = 5.02	C1
2 (1.5,2.0)	$\sqrt{\|1.5-1.25\|^2+\|2.0-1.5\|^2}$ = 0.56	$\sqrt{\|1.5-3.9\|^2+\|2.0-5.1\|^2}$ = 3.92	C1
3 (3.0,4.0)	$\sqrt{\|3-1.25\|^2+\|4-1.5\|^2}$ = 3.05	$\sqrt{\|3-3.9\|^2+\|4.0-5.1\|^2}$ = 1.42	C2
4 (5.0, 7.0)	$\sqrt{\|5-1.25\|^2+\|7-1.5\|^2}$ = 6.66	$\sqrt{\|5-3.9\|^2+\|7.0-5.1\|^2}$ = 2.20	C2
5 (3.5, 5.0)	$\sqrt{\|3.5-1.25\|^2+\|5-1.5\|^2}$ = 4.16	$\sqrt{\|3.5-3.9\|^2+\|5.0-5.1\|^2}$ = 0.41	C2
6 (4.5, 5.0)	$\sqrt{\|4.5-1.25\|^2+\|5.0-1.5\|^2}$ = 4.78	$\sqrt{\|4.5-3.9\|^2+\|5.0-5.1\|^2}$ = 0.61	C2
7 (3.5, 4.5)	$\sqrt{\|3.5-1.25\|^2+\|4.5-1.5\|^2}$ = 3.75	$\sqrt{\|3.5-3.9\|^2+\|4.5-5.1\|^2}$ = 0.72	C2

The clusters obtained are: {1,2} and {3,4,5,6,7}

At this iteration, there is no further change in the clusters. Thus, the algorithm comes to a halt here and final result consists of 2 clusters, {1,2} and {3,4,5,6,7} respectively. These instances can be plotted as two clusters as shown in Figure 7.8.

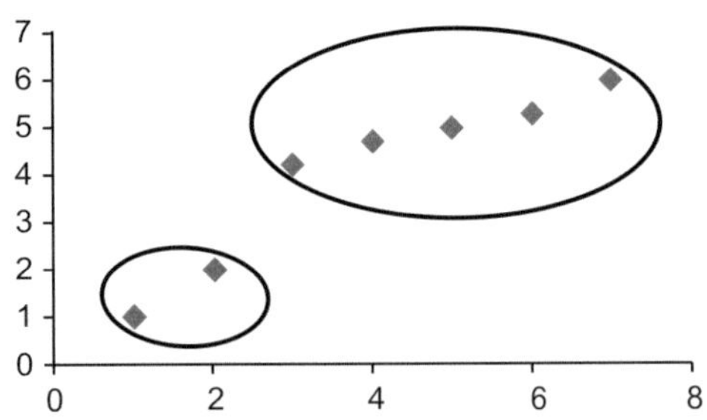

Figure 7.8 Plot of data for k=2 [see colour plate]

Step 3: Implementation of the k-means algorithm (using k=3)

For the same database, if k = 3; it means that there will be three clusters for this database. Let's randomly choose first three records as candidates for clusters. This time, readers are advised to perform the calculations and compare their results with final clusters data given in Table 7.6.

Table 7.6 Initial dataset for k = 3

Individual	Centroid1 = 1	Centroid2 = 2	Centroid3 = 3	Assigned cluster
1	0	1.11	3.61	C1
2	1.12	0	2.5	C2
3	3.61	2.5	0	C3
4	7.21	6.10	3.61	C3
5	4.72	3.61	1.12	C3
6	5.31	4.24	1.80	C3
7	4.30	3.20	0.71	C3

Clustering with initial centroids (1,2,3)

Now, if we calculate the centroid distances as discussed above, the algorithm will stop at the state of the database as shown in Table 7.7, by putting instance 1 in cluster 1, instance 2 in cluster 2 and instances 3,4,5,6 and 7 in cluster 3 as shown below.

Table 7.7 Final assigned cluster for k = 3

Individual	Centroid1(0.56,0.55,3.05) for C1	Centroid2(4.21, 3.10, 0.61) for C2	Centroid3(6.26,5.17,0.56) for C3	Assigned cluster
1	0	1.11	5.02	C1
2	1.12	0	3.92	C2
3	3.61	2.5	1.42	C3
4	7.21	6.10	2.20	C3
5	4.72	3.61	0.41	C3
6	5.31	4.24	0.61	C3
7	4.30	3.20	0.72	C3

The plot of this data for k = 3 is shown below in Figure 7.9.

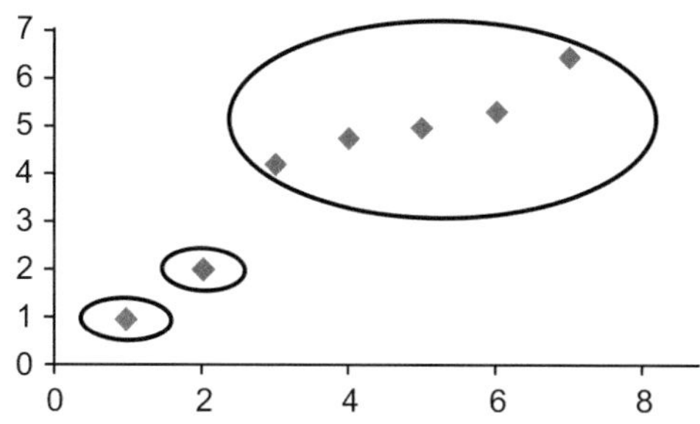

Figure 7.9 Plot of data for k=3 [see colour plate]

Example 7.2: Suppose the visitors visiting a website are to be grouped on the basis of their age given as follows:

15,15,16,19,19,20,20,21,22,28,35,40,41,42,43,44,60,61,65

To perform clustering for the given data, the first step will be to choose the value of k. In this case, let's suppose, k = 2, i.e., we are going to create just two clusters for this database and suppose we randomly choose the 3rd record i.e, 16 and the 9th , i.e., 22 as the initial centroids for the two clusters.

Thus: Centroid for C1 = 16 [16]

Centroid for C2 = 22 [22]

The distances of each record from centroid 1 and centroid 2 is given in Table 7.8. Here, the Manhattan distance has been used to calculate the distance metric which is the absolute distance between the points in this case. It has been used to make the calculations simple.

Table 7.8 Dataset after first iteration

Instances	Centroid 16 for C1	Centroid 22 for C2	Assigned Cluster
15	1	7	C1
15	1	7	C1
16	0	6	C1
19	3	3	C2
19	3	3	C2
20	4	2	C2
20	4	2	C2
21	5	1	C2
22	6	0	C2
28	12	6	C2
35	19	13	C2
40	24	18	C2
41	25	19	C2
42	26	20	C2
43	27	21	C2
44	28	22	C2
60	44	38	C2
61	45	39	C2
65	49	43	C2

Thus, we obtain two clusters containing:

{15, 15, 16} and {19,19,20,20,21,22,28,35,40,41,42,43,44,60,61,65}.

The updated centroid for clusters will be as follows:
Centroid1 = avg(15, 15, 16) = 15.33
Centroid2 = avg(19,19,20,20,21,22,28,35,40,41,42,43,44,60,61,65) = 36.25
Now, the distance of each object to modified centroid is calculated as shown in Table 7.9.
The least actual distances from the instance to the centroid have been highlighted.

Table 7.9 Dataset after second iteration

Instances	Centroid 15.33 for C1	Centroid 36.25 for C2	Assigned Cluster
15	0.33	21.25	C1
15	0.33	21.25	C1
16	0.67	20.25	C1
19	3.67	17.25	C1
19	3.67	17.25	C1
20	4.67	16.25	C1
20	4.67	16.25	C1
21	5.67	15.25	C1
22	6.67	14.25	C1
28	12.67	8.25	C2
35	19.67	1.25	C2
40	24.67	3.75	C2
41	25.67	4.75	C2
42	26.67	5.75	C2
43	27.67	6.75	C2
44	28.67	7.75	C2
60	44.67	23.75	C2
61	45.67	24.75	C2
65	49.67	28.75	C2

Now, we have obtain two fresh clusters containing:

{15,15,16,19,19,20,20,21,22} and {28,35,40,41,42,43,44,60,61,65}.

The updated centroids for these fresh clusters will be as follows:
Centroid 1 = avg(15,15,16,19,19,20,20,21,22) = 18.55
Centroid 2 = avg(28,35,40,41,42,43,44,60,61,65) = 45.9
Next, the distance of each object to the modified centroid is calculated as shown in Table 7.10

Table 7.10 Dataset after third iteration

Instances	*Centroid 18.55 for C1*	*Centroid 45.9 for C2*	*Assigned Cluster*
15	3.55	30.9	C1
15	3.55	30.9	C1
16	2.55	29.9	C1
19	0.45	26.9	C1
19	0.45	26.9	C1
20	1.45	25.9	C1
20	1.45	25.9	C1
21	2.45	24.9	C1
22	3.45	23.9	C1
28	9.45	17.9	C1
35	16.45	10.9	C2
40	21.45	5.9	C2
41	22.45	4.9	C2
42	23.45	3.9	C2
43	24.45	2.9	C2
44	25.45	1.9	C2
60	41.45	14.1	C2
61	42.45	15.1	C2
65	46.45	19.1	C2

Here, we obtain two clusters with still fresher changes containing:

{15,15,16,19,19,20,20,21,22,28} and {35,40,41,42,43,44,60,61,65}.

The updated centroid for clusters will be as follows:
Centroid 1 = avg(15,15,16,19,19,20,20,21,22,28) =19.5
Centroid 2 = avg(35,40,41,42,43,44,60,61,65) = 47.89
Now, the distance of each object to the most recently modified centroids is calculated as shown in Table 7.11.

Table 7.11 Dataset after fourth iteration

Instances	*Centroid 19.50 for C1*	*Centroid 47.89 for C2*	*Assigned Cluster*
15	4.5	32.89	C1
15	4.5	32.89	C1
16	3.5	31.89	C1
19	0.5	28.89	C1
19	0.5	28.89	C1
20	0.5	27.89	C1
20	0.5	27.89	C1
21	1.5	26.89	C1
22	2.5	25.89	C1
28	8.5	19.89	C1
35	15.5	12.89	C2
40	20.5	7.89	C2
41	21.5	6.89	C2
42	22.5	5.89	C2
43	23.5	4.89	C2
44	24.5	3.89	C2
60	40.5	12.11	C2
61	41.5	13.11	C2
65	45.5	17.11	C2

At this iteration, no object has shifted from one cluster to another, i.e., no change has been found between iterations 3 and 4. Thus, the algorithm will stop at fourth iteration and the final clusters will be as follows.

Cluster 1 = [15,15,16,19,19,20,20,21,22,28]

Cluster 2 = [35,40,41,42,43,44,60,61,65]

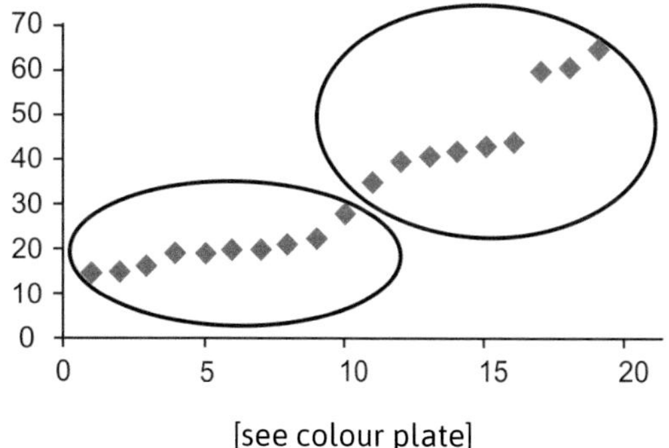

[see colour plate]

Hence, two groups, i.e., 15-28 and 35-65 have been found by using clustering. The output clusters can be affected by the initial choice of centroids. The algorithm is run several times with different starting conditions in order to get a fair view of clusters.

Example 7.3: Clustering of Students record with the k-means algorithm

Let us consider another database containing the result of students' examination in a given course. Here, we wish to cluster the students according to their performance in the course. The students' marks (obtained out of 100) across Quiz1, MSE (Mid Semester Exam), Quiz2, and ESE (End Semester Exam) are given in Table 7.12.

Table 7.12 Record of students' performance

Sr. No	Quiz1	MSE	Quiz2	ESE
S1	8	20	6	45
S2	6	18	7	42
S3	5	15	6	35
S4	4	13	5	25
S5	9	21	8	48
S6	7	20	9	44
S7	9	17	8	49
S8	8	19	7	39
S9	3	14	4	22
S10	6	15	7	32

Steps 1 and 2:

Let's consider the first three students as the three seeds as shown in Table 7.13.

Table 7.13 Seed records

Sr. no	Quiz1	MSE	Quiz2	ESE
S1	8	20	6	45
S2	6	18	7	42
S3	5	15	6	35

Steps 3 and 4:

In this step, calculate the distance using the four attributes as well as the sum of absolute differences for simplicity, i.e., Manhattan distance. Table 7.14 shows the distance values for all the objects, wherein columns 7, 8 and 9 represent the three distances from the three seed records respectively.

On the basis of distances computed, each student is allocated to the nearest cluster, i.e., C1, C2 or C3. The result of the first iteration is given in Table 7.14.

Table 7.14 First iteration-allocation of each object to its nearest cluster

		Quiz1	*MSE*	*Quiz2*	*ESE*	*Distances from Cluster*			*Allocation to the nearest Cluster*
Seed Records	*C1*	*8*	*20*	*6*	*45*				
	C2	*6*	*18*	*7*	*42*				
	C3	*5*	*15*	*6*	*35*	*C1*	*C2*	*C3*	
S1	1	8	20	6	45	(|8-8|+|20-20|+|6-6|+|45-45|) = 0	(|8-6|+|20-18|+|6-7|+|45-42|) = 8	(|8-5|+|20-15|+|6-6|+|45-35|) = 18	C1
S2	2	6	18	7	42	(|6-8|+|18-20|+|7-6|+|42-45|) = 8	(|6-6|+|18-18|+|7-7|+|42-42|) = 0	(|6-5|+|18-15|+|7-6|+|42-35|) = 12	C2
S3	3	5	15	6	35	(|5-8|+|15-20|+|6-6|+|35-45|) = 18	(|5-6|+|15-18|+|6-7|+|35-42|) = 12	(|5-5|+|15-15|+|6-6|+|35-35|) = 0	C3
S4	4	4	13	5	25	32	26	14	C3
S5	5	9	21	8	48	7	13	25	C1
S6	6	7	20	9	44	5	7	19	C1
S7	7	9	17	8	49	10	12	22	C1
S8	8	8	19	7	39	8	6	12	C2
S9	9	3	14	4	22	36	30	18	C3
S10	10	6	15	7	32	21	13	5	C3

Instances in Cluster 1, i.e., C1 are 1, 5, 6 and 7
Instances in Cluster 2, i.e., C2 are 2 and 8
Instances in Cluster 3, i.e., C3 are 3, 4, 9 and 10

The first iteration results in four, two and four students in the first, second and third cluster, respectively.

Step 5:

New centroids for each attribute/column are updated after the first iteration as shown in Table 7.15.

Table 7.15 Updated centroids after first iteration

	Quiz1	*MSE*	*Quiz2*	*ESE*
C1 (record 1,5,6,7)	8.25 Avg(8,9,7,9)	19.5 Avg(20,21,20,17)	7.75 Avg(6,8,9,7)	46.5 Avg(45,48,44,39)
C2 (record 2,8)	7 Avg(6,8)	18.5 Avg(18,19)	7 Avg(7,7)	40.5 Avg(42,39)
C3 (record 3,4,9, 10)	4.5 Avg(5,4,3,6)	14.25 Avg(15,13,14,15)	5.5 Avg(6,5,4,7)	28.5 Avg(35,25,22,32)

It is interesting to note that the mean marks for cluster C3 are significantly lower than for clusters C1 and C2. So, the distances of each object to each of the means using new cluster are again re-computed and allocate each object to the nearest cluster. The results of the second iteration are shown in Table 7.16.

Table 7.16 Second iteration-allocation of each object to its nearest cluster

Seed Records		*Quiz1*	*MSE*	*Quiz2*	*ESE*	*Distances from Cluster*			*Allocation to the nearest Cluster*
	C1	8.25	19.5	7.75	46.5				
	C2	7	18.5	7	40.5				
	C3	4.5	14.25	5.5	28.5	C1	C2	C3	
Student 1	1	8	20	6	45	(|8-8.25|+|20-19.5|+|6-7.75|+|45-46.5|) = 4	(|8-7|+|20-18.5|+|6-7|+|45-40.5|) = 8	(|8-4.5|+|20-14.25|+|6-5.5|+|45-28.5|) = 26.25	C1
Student 2	2	6	18	7	42	(|6-8.25|+|18-19.5|+|7-7.75|+|42-46.5|) = 9	(|6-7|+|18-18.5|+|7-7|+|42-40.5|) = 3	(|6-4.5|+|18-14.25|+|7-5.5|+|42-28.5|) = 20.25	C2
Student 3	3	5	15	6	35	21	12	8.25	C3
Student 4	4	4	13	5	25	35	26	5.75	C3
Student 5	5	9	21	8	48	4	13	33.25	C1
Student 6	6	7	20	9	44	5.5	7	27.25	C1
Student 7	7	9	17	8	49	6	13	30.25	C1
Student 8	8	8	19	7	39	9	3	20.25	C2
Student 9	9	3	14	4	22	39	30	9.75	C3
Student 10	10	6	15	7	32	22	13	7.25	C3

Again, there are four, two and four students in clusters C1, C2 and C3, respectively. A more careful look shows that there is no change in clusters at all. Therefore, the method has converged quite quickly for this very simple dataset. For more clarity, the final assigned cluster has been reproduced in Table 7.17.

Table 7.17 Final allocation

Seed Records		*Quiz1*	*MSE*	*Quiz2*	*ESE*	*Allocation to Cluster*
	C1	*8.25*	*19.5*	*7.75*	*46.5*	
	C2	*7*	*18.5*	*7*	*40.5*	
	C3	*4.5*	*14.25*	*5.5*	*28.5*	
S1	1	8	20	6	45	C1
S2	2	6	18	7	42	C2
S3	3	5	15	6	35	C3
S4	4	4	13	5	25	C3
S5	5	9	21	8	48	C1
S6	6	7	20	9	44	C1
S7	7	9	17	8	49	C1
S8	8	8	19	7	39	C2
S9	9	3	14	4	22	C3
S10	10	6	15	7	32	C3

The membership of clusters is as follows:
Cluster 1, i.e., C1 - 1,5,6,7
Cluster 2, i.e., C2 - 2, 8
Cluster 3, i.e., C3 - 3, 4, 9, 10

It should be noted that the above method was k-median rather than k-means because we wanted to use a simple distance measure that a reader could check without using a computer or a calculator.

Interestingly, when k-means is used, the result is exactly the same and the method again converges rather quickly.

Another point worth noting is about the intra (within) cluster variance and inter (between) cluster variance. The average Euclidean distance of objects in each cluster to the cluster centroids is presented in Table 7.18. The average distance of objects within clusters C1, C2, and C3 from their centroids is 2.89, 1.87 and 5.51, respectively. Although these numbers do not indicate which result is better, they help however, in analyzing that the clustering method has performed well in maximizing inter (between) cluster variance and minimizing intra (within) cluster variance. Here, one can notice that the Euclidean distance between C1 and C2 is 6.89, while it is 44.89 in case of C1 and C3. The intra cluster distance in the case of C1, is the minimum i.e., 2.89 between the instances of C1. Similarly, the intra cluster distance is minimum in case of C2 and C3.

We can get different results with different seed records.

Table 7.18 Within (intra) cluster and between (inter) clusters distance

Cluster	C1	C2	C3
C1	2.89	6.89	19.46
C2	6.52	1.87	13.19
C3	20.02	14.17	5.51

The detail of calculations for the identification of within (intra) cluster and between (inter) cluster variance is shown in Table 7.19.

Table 7.19 Calculations for within-cluster and between-cluster variance using Euclidean distance

Calculation	*Quiz1*	*MSE*	*Quiz2*	*ESE*	*Description*
x_i-y_i for S1 of C1	-0.25 [8-8.25]	0.5 [20-19.5]	-1.75 [6-7.75]	-1.5 [45-46.5]	For Cluster C1
x_i-y_i for S5 of C1	0.75	1.5	0.25	1.5	
x_i-y_i for S6 of C1	-1.25	0.5	1.25	-2.5	
x_i-y_i for S7 of C1	0.75	-2.5	0.25	2.5	
sumsqr(x_i-y_i)	5.625 sumsqr(-0.25,0.5,-1.75,-1.5)	for S1			
sumsqr(x_i-y_i)	5.125 sumsqr(0.75,1.5,0.25, 1.5)	for S5			
sumsqr(x_i-y_i)	9.625	for S6			
sumsqr(x_i-y_i)	13.125	for S7			
avg(1,56,7)	8.375 avg (5.625, 5.125, 9.625, 13.125)	for 1,5,6,7 of c1 from Cluster C1			
sqrt (avg(1,56,7))	**2.893959**	for 1,5,6,7 of c1, Thus within-cluster variance of C1 is 2.89			
x_i-y_i for S1 of C1	1	1.5	-1	4.5	For Cluster C2
x_i-y_i for S5 of C1	2	2.5	1	7.5	
x_i-y_i for S6 of C1	0	1.5	2	3.5	
x_i-y_i for S7 of C1	2	-1.5	1	8.5	

Contd.

Calculation	*Quiz1*	*MSE*	*Quiz2*	*ESE*	*Description*
sqr(x_i-y_i)	24.5	for S1			
sqr(x_i-y_i)	67.5	for S5			
sqr(x_i-y_i)	18.5	for S6			
sqr(x_i-y_i)	79.5	for S7			
avg(1,56,7)	47.5	for 1,5,6,7 of C1 from C2			
sqrt (avg(1,56,7))	**6.892024**	for 1,5,6,7 of C1 from C2 Thus variance between C1 and C2 is 6.89			
x_i-y_i for S1 of C1	3.5	5.75	0.5	16.5	For Cluster C3
x_i-y_i for S5 of C1	4.5	6.75	2.5	19.5	
x_i-y_i for S6 of C1	2.5	5.75	3.5	15.5	
x_i-y_i for S7 of C1	4.5	2.75	2.5	20.5	
sqr(x_i-y_i)	317.8125	for S1 from C3			
sqr(x_i-y_i)	452.3125	for S5 from C3			
sqr(x_i-y_i)	291.8125	for S6 from C3			
sqr(x_i-y_i)	454.3125	for S7 from C3			
avg(1,56,7)	379.0625	for 1,5,6,7 of C1 from C3			
sqrt(avg(1,56,7))	**19.4695**	for 1,5,6,7 of C1 from C3 Thus variance between C1 and C3 is 19.4695			
x_i-y_i for S2 of C2	-2.25	-1.5	-0.75	-4.5	For Cluster C1
x_i-y_i for S8 of C2	-0.25	-0.5	-0.75	-7.5	
sqr(x_i-y_i)	28.125	for S2 of C2 from C1			
sqr(x_i-y_i)	57.125	for S8 of C2 from C1			
avg(2,8)	42.625	for 2,8 of C2 from C1			
sqrt(avg(2,8))	**6.528782**	for 2,8 of C2 from C1 Thus variance between C2 and C1 is 6.52			
x_i-y_i for S2 of C2	-1	-0.5	0	1.5	For Cluster C2
x_i-y_i for S8 of C2	1	0.5	0	-1.5	
sqr(x_i-y_i)	3.5	for S2 of C2 from C2			
sqr(x_i-y_i)	3.5	for S8 of C2 from C2			
avg(2,8)	3.5	for 2,8 of C2 from C2			

Contd.

Calculation	*Quiz1*	*MSE*	*Quiz2*	*ESE*	*Description*
sqrt(avg(2,8))	**1.870829**	for 2,8 of C2 from C2 Thus within cluster variance of C2, i.e. from C2 to C2 is 1.87			
x_i-y_i for S2 of C2	1.5	3.75	1.5	13.5	For Cluster C3
x_i-y_i for S8 of C2	3.5	4.75	1.5	10.5	
sqr(x_i-y_i)	200.8125	for S2 of C2 from C3			
sqr(x_i-y_i)	147.3125	for S8 of C2 from C3			
avg(2,8)	174.0625	for 2,8 of C2 from C3			
sqrt(avg(2,8))	**13.19327**	for 2,8 of C2 from C3 Thus variance between C2 and C3 is 13.19			
x_i-y_i for S3 of C3	-3.25	-4.5	-1.75	-11.5	For Cluster C1
x_i-y_i for S4 of C3	-4.25	-6.5	-2.75	-21.5	
x_i-y_i for S9 of C3	-5.25	-5.5	-3.75	-24.5	
x_i-y_i for S10 of C3	-2.25	-4.5	-0.75	-14.5	
sqr(x_i-y_i)	166.125	for S3 of C3 from C1			
sqr(x_i-y_i)	530.125	for S4 of C3 from C1			
sqr(x_i-y_i)	672.125	for S9 of C3 from C1			
sqr(x_i-y_i)	236.125	for S10 of C3 from C1			
avg(3,4,9,10)	401.125	for 3,4,9,10 of C3 from C1			
sqrt(avg(3,4,9,10))	**20.02811**	for 3,4,9,10 of C3 from C1 Thus variance between C3 and C1 is 20.02			
x_i-y_i for S3 of C3	-2	-3.5	-1	-5.5	For Cluster C2
x_i-y_i for S4 of C3	-3	-5.5	-2	-15.5	
x_i-y_i for S9 of C3	-4	-4.5	-3	-18.5	
x_i-y_i for S10 of C3	-1	-3.5	0	-8.5	
sqr(x_i-y_i)	47.5	for S3 of C3 from C2			
sqr(x_i-y_i)	283.5	for S4 of C3 from C2			
sqr(x_i-y_i)	387.5	for S9 of C3 from C2			
sqr(x_i-y_i)	85.5	for S10 of C3 from C2			
avg(3,4,9,10)	201	for 3,4,9,10 of C3 from C2			

Contd.

Calculation	*Quiz1*	*MSE*	*Quiz2*	*ESE*	*Description*
sqrt(avg(3,4,9,10))	**14.17745**	for 3,4,9,10 of C3 from C2 Thus variance between C3 and C2 is 14.17			
x_i-y_i for S3 of C3	0.5	0.75	0.5	6.5	For Cluster C3
x_i-y_i for S4 of C3	-0.5	-1.25	-0.5	-3.5	
x_i-y_i for S9 of C3	-1.5	-0.25	-1.5	-6.5	
x_i-y_i for S10 of C3	1.5	0.75	1.5	3.5	
sqr(x_i-y_i)	43.3125	for S3 of C3 from C3			
sqr(x_i-y_i)	14.3125	for S4 of C3 from C3			
sqr(x_i-y_i)	46.8125	for S9 of C3 from C3			
sqr(x_i-y_i)	17.3125	for S10 of C3 from C3			
avg(3,4,9,10)	30.4375	for 3,4,9,10 of C3 from C3			
sqrt(avg(3,4,9,10))	**5.517019**	for 3,4,9,10 of C3 from C3 Thus within cluster variance of C3, i.e. from C3 to C3 is 5.51			

7.6.2 Starting values for the k-means algorithm

Normally we have to specify the number of starting seeds and clusters at the start of the k-means algorithm. We can use an iterative approach to overcome this problem. For example, first select three starting seeds randomly and choose three clusters. Once the final clusters have been found, the process may be repeated several times with a different set of seeds. We should select the seed records that are at maximum distance from each other or are as far as possible. If two clusters are identified to be close together during the iterative process, it is appropriate to merge them. Also, a large cluster may be partitioned into two smaller clusters if the intra-cluster variance is above some threshold value.

7.6.3 Issues with the k-means algorithm

There are a number of issues with the k-Means algorithm that should be understood. Some of these are:

- The results of the k-means algorithm intensively depends on the initial guesses of the seed records.
- The k-means algorithm is sensitive to outliers. Thus, it may give poor results if an outlier is selected as a starting seed record.
- The k-means algorithm works on the basis of Euclidean distance and the mean(s) of the attribute values of intra-cluster objects. Thus, it is only suitable for continuous data as it is restricted to data for which there is the notion of a center (centroid).
- The k-means algorithm does not take into account the size of the clusters. Clusters may be either large or small.

- It does not deal with overlapping clusters.
- It does not work well with clusters of different sizes and density.

7.6.4 Scaling and weighting

Sometimes during clustering, the value of one attribute may be small as compared to other attributes. In such cases, that attribute will not have much influence on determining which cluster the object belongs to, as the values of this attribute are smaller than other attributes and hence, the variation within the attribute will also be small.

Consider the dataset given in Table 7.20 for the chemical composition of wine samples. Note that the values for different attributes cover a range of six orders of magnitude. It is also important to notice that for wine density, values vary by only 5% of the average value. It turns out that clustering algorithms struggle with numeric attributes that exhibit such ranges of values.

Table 7.20 Chemical composition of wine samples

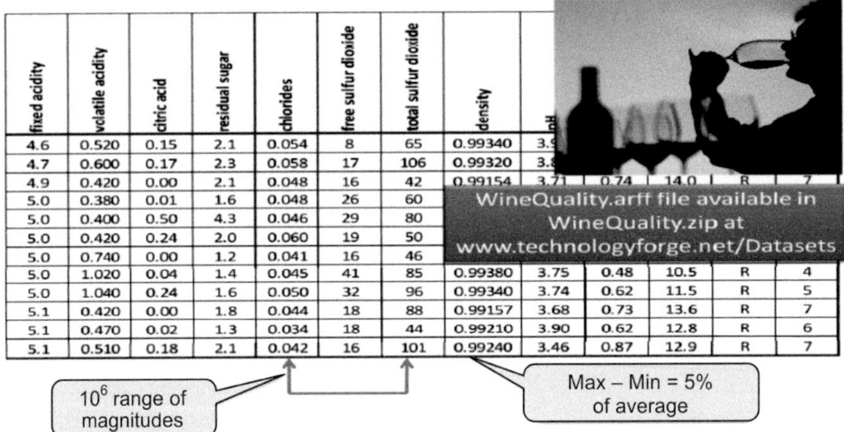

fixed acidity	volatile acidity	citric acid	residual sugar	chlorides	free sulfur dioxide	total sulfur dioxide	density	pH				
4.6	0.520	0.15	2.1	0.054	8	65	0.99340	3.[illegible]				
4.7	0.600	0.17	2.3	0.058	17	106	0.99320	3.[illegible]				
4.9	0.420	0.00	2.1	0.048	16	42	0.99154	3.71	0.74	14.0	R	7
5.0	0.380	0.01	1.6	0.048	26	60						
5.0	0.400	0.50	4.3	0.046	29	80						
5.0	0.420	0.24	2.0	0.060	19	50						
5.0	0.740	0.00	1.2	0.041	16	46						
5.0	1.020	0.04	1.4	0.045	41	85	0.99380	3.75	0.48	10.5	R	4
5.0	1.040	0.24	1.6	0.050	32	96	0.99340	3.74	0.62	11.5	R	5
5.1	0.420	0.00	1.8	0.044	18	88	0.99157	3.68	0.73	13.6	R	7
5.1	0.470	0.02	1.3	0.034	18	44	0.99210	3.90	0.62	12.8	R	6
5.1	0.510	0.18	2.1	0.042	16	101	0.99240	3.46	0.87	12.9	R	7

[*Source*: Witten et. al.]

All attributes should be transformed to a similar scale for clustering to be effective unless we want to give more weight to some attributes that are comparatively large in scale. Commonly, we use two techniques to convert the attributes. These are Normalization and Standardization.

Normalization

In case of normalization, all the attributes are converted to a normalized score or to a range (0, 1). The problem of normalization is an outlier. If there is an outlier, it will tend to crunch all of the other values down toward the value of zero. In order to understand this case, let's suppose the range of students' marks is 35 to 45 out of 100. Then 35 will be considered as 0 and 45 as 1, and students will be distributed between 0 to 1 depending upon their marks. But if there is one student having marks 90, then it will act as an outlier and in this case, 35 will be considered as 0 and 90 as 1. Now, it will crunch most of the values down toward the value of zero. In this scenario, the solution is standardization.

Standardization

In case of standardization, the values are all spread out so that we have a standard deviation of 1.

Generally, there is no rule for when to use normalization versus standardization. However, if your data does have outliers, use standardization otherwise use normalization. Using standardization tends to make the remaining values for all of the other attributes fall into similar ranges since all attributes will have the same standard deviation of 1.

In next section, another important clustering technique, i.e., Hierarchical Clustering has been discussed.

7.7 Hierarchical Clustering Algorithms (HCA)

Hierarchical clustering is a type of cluster analysis which seeks to generate a hierarchy of clusters. It is also called Hierarchical Cluster Analysis (HCA). Hierarchical clustering methods build a nested series of clusters in comparison to partitioned methods that generate only a flat set of clusters.

There are two types of Hierarchical clustering: agglomerative and divisive.

Agglomerative

This is a 'bottom-up' approach. In this approach, each object is a cluster by itself at the start and its nearby clusters are repetitively combined resulting in larger and larger clusters until some stopping criterion is met. The stopping criterion may be the specified number of clusters or a stage at which all the objects are combined into a single large cluster that is the highest level of hierarchy as shown in Figure 7.10.

Divisive

This is a 'top-down' approach. In this approach, all objects start from one cluster, and partitions are performed repeatedly resulting in smaller and smaller clusters until some stopping criterion is met or each cluster consists of the only object in it as shown in Figure 7.10. Generally, the mergers and partitions are decided in a greedy manner.

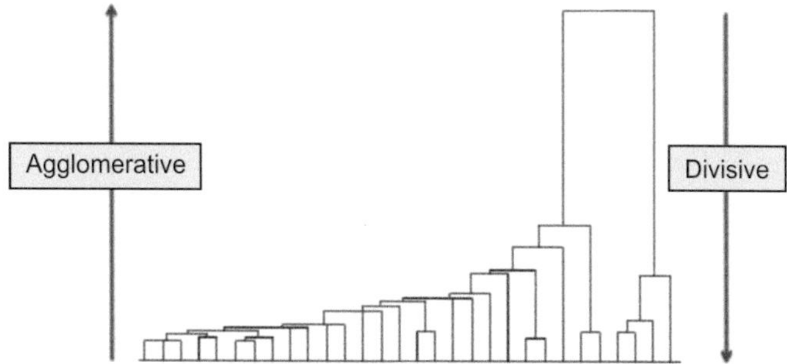

Figure 7.10 Illustration of agglomerative and divisive clustering

[*Credits*: http://chem-eng.utoronto.ca/~datamining/dmc/clustering_hierarchical.htm]

Let's discuss agglomerative and divisive clustering in detail.

7.7.1 Agglomerative clustering

In agglomerative clustering, suppose a set of *N* items are given to be clustered, the procedure of clustering is given as follows:

1. First of all, each item is allocated to a cluster. For example, if there are *N* items then, there will be *N* clusters, i.e., each cluster consisting of just one item. Assume that the distances (similarities) between the clusters are same as the distances (similarities) between the items they contain.
2. Identify the nearest (most similar) pair of clusters and merge that pair into a single cluster, so that now we will have one cluster less.
3. Now, the distances (similarities) between each of the old clusters and the new cluster are calculated.
4. Repeat steps 2 and 3 until all items are merged into a single cluster of size *N*.

As this type of hierarchical clustering merges clusters recursively, it is therefore known as agglomerative.

Once the complete hierarchical tree is obtained, then there is no point of grouping *N* items in a single cluster. You just have to cut the *k-1* longest links to get *k* clusters.

Let's understand the working of agglomerative clustering by considering the following raw data given in Figure 7.11.

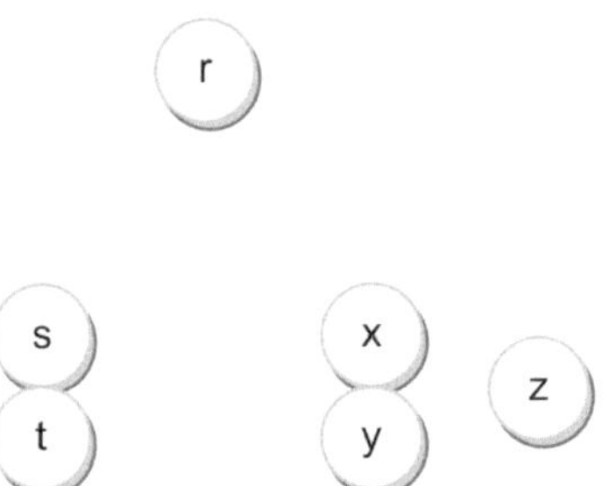

Figure 7.11 Raw data for agglomerative clustering

This method generates the hierarchy by recursively combining clusters from the individual items. For example, there are six items {r}, {s}, {t}, {x}, {y} and {z}. The first step is to identify the items to be combined into a cluster. Normally, the two closest elements are taken on the basis of the chosen distance.

When the tree is cut at a given height, it gives a partitioning clustering at a selected precision. In this case, cutting the tree after the second row produces clusters {r} {s t} {x y} and {z} as shown in Figure 7.12. Cutting the tree after the third row will produce clusters {r} {s t} and {x y z}, which is called as coarser clustering, with a smaller number of clusters, but which are larger in size. The complete hierarchical clustering tree diagram is as given in Figure 7.12.

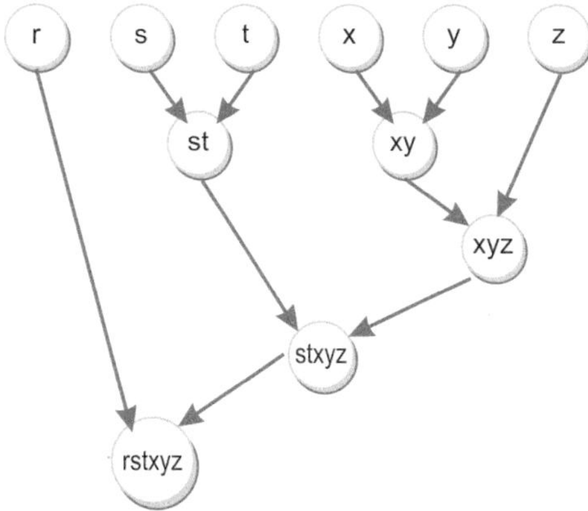

Figure 7.12 Complete hierarchical clustering tree diagram

7.7.1.1 *Role of linkage metrics*

It is required to compute the distance between clusters by using some metrics before any clustering is performed. These metrics are called linkage metrics.

It will be beneficial to identify the proximity matrix consisting of the distance between each point using a distance function.

The important linkage metrics to measure the distance between each cluster are given below:

Single linkage

In single linkage hierarchical clustering, the shortest distance between two points in each cluster is considered as the distance between two clusters. For example, the distance between two clusters 'r' and 's' to the left is equal to the length of the arrow between their two closest points as shown in Figure 7.13 and the formula of calculation of distance using single-linkage hierarchical clustering is given by:

$$L(r,s) = \min(D(x_{ri}, x_{sj}))$$

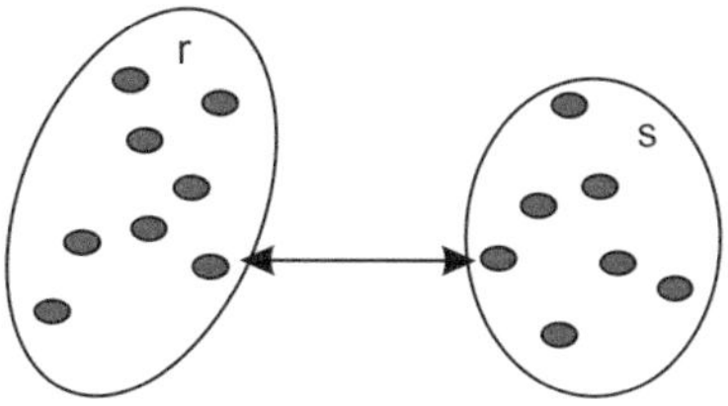

Figure 7.13 Single linkage

[*Credits*: http://chem-eng.utoronto.ca/~datamining/dmc/clustering_hierarchical.htm]

Complete linkage

In complete linkage hierarchical clustering, the longest distance between two points in each cluster is considered as the distance between two clusters. For example, the distance between clusters 'r' and 's' to the left is equal to the length of the arrow between their two farthest points as shown in Figure 7.14 and the formula of calculation of distance using complete linkage hierarchical clustering is given by:

$$L(r,s) = \max(D(x_{ri}, x_{sj}))$$

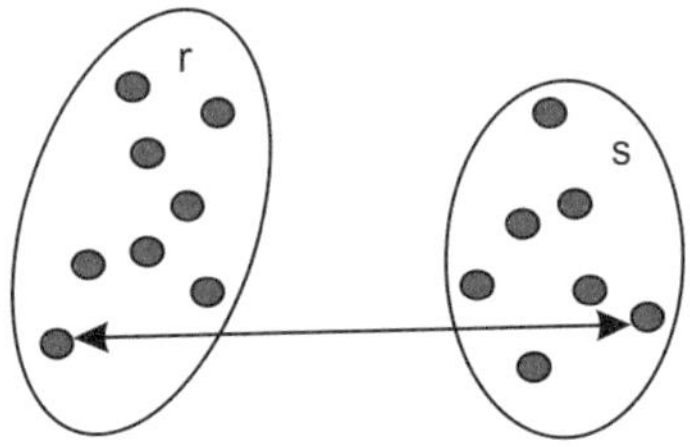

Figure 7.14 Complete linkage

[*Credits*: http://chem-eng.utoronto.ca/~datamining/dmc/clustering_hierarchical.htm]

Average linkage

In average linkage hierarchical clustering, the average distance between each point in one cluster to every point in the other cluster is considered as the distance between two clusters. For example, the distance between clusters 's' and 'r' to the left is equal to the average length of each arrow connecting the points of one cluster to the other as shown in Figure 7.15 and the formula of calculation of distance using average linkage hierarchical clustering is given by:

$$L(r,s) = \frac{1}{n_r n_s} \sum_{i=1}^{n_Y} \sum_{j=1}^{n_S} D\left(x_{ri}, x_{sj}\right)$$

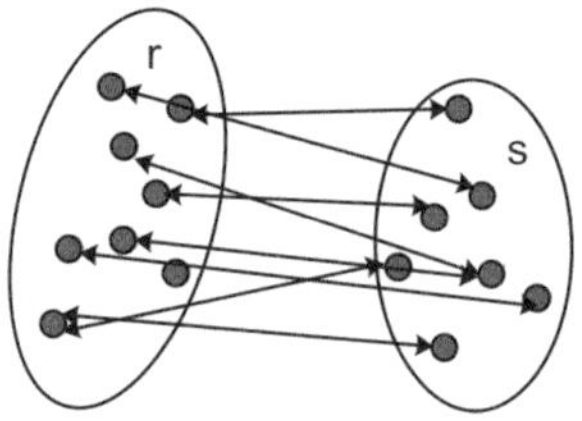

Figure 7.15 Average linkage

[*Credits*: http://chem-eng.utoronto.ca/~datamining/dmc/clustering_hierarchical.htm]

Example of Single-linkage hierarchical clustering

Let's perform a hierarchical clustering of some Indian cities on the basis of distance in kilometers between them. In this case, single-linkage clustering is used to calculate the distance between clusters.

The distance matrix (with a sequence number, m: 0) shown in Table 7.21 represents the distance in kilometers among some of the Indian cities. Suppose initially the level (L) is 0 for all the clusters.

Table 7.21 Input distance matrix (L = 0 for all the clusters)

	Delhi	*Jammu*	*Srinagar*	*Patiala*	*Amritsar*	*Pahalgam*
Delhi	0	575	853	267	452	842
Jammu	575	0	294	359	203	285
Srinagar	853	294	0	627	469	98
Patiala	267	359	627	0	235	610
Amritsar	452	203	469	235	0	456
Pahalgam	842	285	98	610	456	0

The nearest pair of cities is Srinagar and Pahalgam as the distance between them is 98. These cities are combined into a single cluster called 'Srinagar/Pahalgam'. Then, the distance is calculated from this new compound object to all other objects. In case of single link clustering, the shortest distance from any object of the cluster to the outside object is considered as the distance from the compound object to another object. Therefore, distance from 'Srinagar/Pahalgam' to Delhi is picked to be 842, i.e., min(853,842), which is the distance from Pahalgam to Delhi.

Now, the level of the new cluster is L(Srinagar/Pahalgam) = 98 and **m: 1 is the new sequence number**. By following the same method, new distance from the compound object is calculated as shown in Table 7.22 and the description of calculation is given as follows.

*min(853,842) **min(294,285) ***min(627,610)

Table 7.22 Input distance matrix, with m: 1

	Delhi	*Jammu*	*Srinagar/ Pahalgam*	*Patiala*	*Amritsar*
Delhi	0	575	842	267	452
Jammu	575	0	285	359	203
Srinagar/Pahalgam	842*	285**	0	610***	456
Patiala	267	359	610	0	235
Amritsar	452	203	456	235	0

At the level of m:1, the minimum distance (min(Jammu, Amritsar)) in the distance matrix is 203, i.e., the distance between Jammu and Amritsar so, Jammu and Amritsar will be merged into a new cluster called Jammu/Amritsar with new L(Jammu/Amritsar) = 203 and m = 2 as shown in

Table 7.23. The description of the calculation of the new distance from the compound object to other objects is given as follows.

*min(575,452) **min(285,456) ***min(359,235)

Table 7.23 Input distance matrix, with m: 2

	Delhi	*Jammu/Amritsar*	*Srinagar/ Pahalgam*	*Patiala*
Delhi	0	452	842	267
Jammu/Amritsar	452*	0	285**	235**
Srinagar/Pahalgam	842	285	0	610
Patiala	267	235	610	0

At the level of m:2, the minimum distance (min (Jammu/Amritsar, Patiala)) in the distance matrix is 235, i.e., distance between Jammu/Amritsar and Patiala so, Jammu/Amritsar will be merged with Patiala into a new cluster called Jammu/Amritsar/Patiala with L(Jammu/Amritsar/Patiala) = 235

and m = 3 as shown in Table 7.24. The description of the calculation of the new distance from the compound object to other objects is given as follows.

*min(452,267) **min(285,610)

Table 7.24 Input distance matrix, with m: 3

	Delhi	*Jammu/Amritsar/Patiala*	*Srinagar/Pahalgam*
Delhi	0	267	842
Jammu/Amritsar/Patiala	267*	0	285**
Srinagar/Pahalgam	842	285	0

At the level of m:3, the minimum distance (min(Jammu/Amritsar/Patiala, Delhi)) in the distance matrix is 267, i.e., the distance between Jammu/Amritsar/Patiala and Delhi so, Jammu/Amritsar/Patiala will be merged with Delhi into a new cluster called Delhi/Jammu/Amritsar/Patiala with L(Delhi/Jammu/Amritsar/Patiala) = 267 and m = 4 as shown in Table 7.25. The description of the calculation of the new distance from the compound object to other objects is given as follows.

*min(285,842)

Table 7.25 Input distance matrix, with m: 4

	Delhi/ Jammu/Amritsar/Patiala	*Srinagar/Pahalgam*
Delhi/Jammu/Amritsar/Patiala	0	285*
Srinagar/Pahalgam	285	0

Finally, the last two clusters are merged at level 285. The whole procedure is outlined by the hierarchical tree as shown in Figure 7.16.

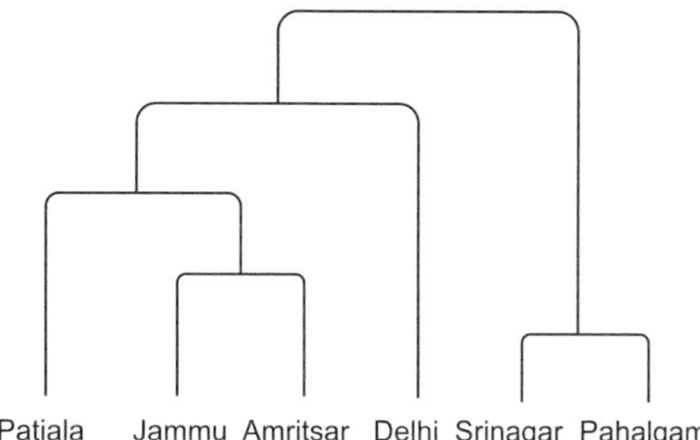

Figure 7.16 Hierarchical tree of clustering of Indian cities on the basis of distance

Example of clustering of students record with the agglomerative algorithm

Let us apply the Agglomerative algorithm on the database containing results of students' examination in a given course (earlier discussed for the k-mean algorithm). The students' performance on the basis of marks obtained out of 100 marks distributed across Quiz1, MSE, Quiz2, and ESE is given again in Table 7.26.

Table 7.26 Record of students' performance

Instances	*Quiz 1*	*MSE*	*Quiz2*	*ESE*
S1	8	20	6	45
S2	6	18	7	42
S3	5	15	6	35
S4	4	13	5	25
S5	9	21	8	48
S6	7	20	9	44
S7	9	17	8	49
S8	8	19	7	39
S9	3	14	4	22
S10	6	15	7	32

Step 1:

In this step, the distance matrix is computed from the above data using the centroid method between every pair of instances that are to be clustered. Due to the symmetric nature of the distance matrix (because the distance between p and q is same as the distance between q and p), only the lower triangular matrix is shown in Table 7.27 as the upper triangle can be filled in by reflection. The distance matrix consists of zeroes on the diagonal because every instance is at zero distance from itself.

The description of some of the calculations for cells of the second and third row of the distance matrix given in Table 7.27 drawn from Table 7.26 is given as follows.

*__Second row S2:__ [S2-S1] = [|6-8|+|18-20|+|7-6|+|42-45|] = 8
**__Third row S3:__ [S3-S1] = [|5-8|+|15-20|+|6-6|+|35-45|] = 18
***__Third row S3:__ [S3-S2] = [|5-6|+|15-18|+|6-7|+|35-42|] = 12

Table 7.27 Distance matrix at m: 0

Instances	S1	S2	S3	S4	S5	S6	S7	S8	S9	S10
S1	0									
S2	8*	0								
S3	18**	12***	0							
S4	32	26	14	0						
S5	7	13	25	39	0					
S6	5	7	19	33	8	0				
S7	10	12	22	36	5	11	0			
S8	8	6	12	26	13	9	14	0		
S9	36	30	18	6	43	37	40	30	0	
S10	21	13	5	13	26	20	23	13	17	0

Step 2:

Apply the agglomerative method on this distance matrix and calculate the minimum distance between clusters and combine them. The minimum distance in the distance matrix is 5. Let's randomly select the minimum distance, i.e., 5 between S7 and S5.

Thus, the instances S7 and S5 are merged into a cluster called C1 and the distance is calculated from this new compound object to all other objects by following the single link hierarchical clustering approach for calculation. To attain a new distance matrix, the instances S5 and S7 need to be removed and are replaced by cluster C1. Since single link hierarchical clustering is used, the distance between cluster C1 and every other instance is the shortest of the distance between an instance and S5; and an instance and S7. The cells involved in merging record number S5 and S7 for the creation of a new cluster are highlighted in Table 7.28.

Table 7.28 Cells involved in C1

Instances	S1	S2	S3	S4	S5	S6	S7	S8	S9	S10
S1	0									
S2	8*	0								
S3	18**	12***	0							
S4	32	26	14	0						
S5	7	13	25	39	0					
S6	5	7	19	33	8	0				
S7	10	12	22	36	5	11	0			
S8	8	6	12	26	13	9	14	0		
S9	36	30	18	6	43	37	40	30	0	
s10	21	13	5	13	26	20	23	13	17	0

The description of the some of the calculations to create a new distance matrix with m:2 is given as follows.

For example, to create a new distance matrix after merging S5 and S7, calculations will be as:

d (S1, S5) = 7 and d (S1, S7) = 10, so d (S1, C1) = min (7, 10) = 7*

Similarly, d (S2, S5) = 13 and d (S2, S7) = 12, so d (S2, C1) = min (13, 12) = 12**

The distance between S6 and C1 will be (minimum of distance between S6-S5 and S7-S6, i.e. min (8, 11), i.e., 8***). By using the highlighted cells, the data in C1 is filled as shown in Table 7.29.

d(S8, S5) = 13 and d(S8, S7) = 14, so d(S8, C1) = min (13, 14) =13****

Similarly, d(S9, S5) = 43 and d(S9, S7) = 40, so d(S9, C1) = min (43, 40) =40*****

The instances with the smallest distance get clustered next.

Table 7.29 Input distance matrix, with m: 2

Instances	S1	S2	S3	S4	C1	S6	S8	S9	S10
S1	0								
S2	8	0							
S3	18	12	0						
S4	32	26	14	0					
C1	7*	12**	22	36	0				
S6	5	7	19	33	8***	0			
S8	8	6	12	26	13****	9	0		
S9	36	30	18	6	40*****	37	30	0	
S10	21	13	5	13	23	20	13	17	0

Step 3: Repeat Step 2 until all clusters are merged.

Combine S3 and S10 clusters into C2 as it has the minimum distance. The cells involved in merging record number 3 and 10 for the creation of C2 have been highlighted in Table 7.30.

Table 7.30 Cells involved in C2

Instances	S1	S2	S3	S4	C1	S6	S8	S9	S10
S1	0								
S2	8	0							
S3	18	12	0						
S4	32	26	14	0					
C1	7	12	22	36	0				
S6	5	7	19	33	8	0			
S8	8	6	12	26	13	9	0		
S9	36	30	18	6	43	37	30	0	
s10	21	13	**5**	13	23	20	13	17	0

The description of the some of the calculations to create a new distance matrix with m:3 is given as follows.

For example, to create a new distance matrix after merging S3 and S10, calculations will be as:

d(S1, S3) = 18 and d(S1, S10) = 21, so d(S1, C2) = min(18, 21) = 18*

Similarly, d(S2, S3) = 12 and d(S2, S10) = 13, so d(S2, C2) = min(12, 13) = 12**

The distance between S4 and C2 will be (minimum of distance between S4-S3 and S10-S4, i.e. min(14,13), i.e., 13***). By using the highlighted cells, the data in C2 is filled as shown in Table 7.30.

d(C1, S3) = 22 and d(C1, S10) = 23, so d(C1, C2) = min (22, 23) = 22****

Similarly, d(S6, S3) = 19 and d(S6, S10) = 20, so d(S6, C2) = min (19, 20) = 19*****

The input matrix at m: 3 is shown in Table 7.31.

Table 7.31 Input distance matrix, with m: 3

Instances	S1	S2	C2	S4	C1	S6	S8	S9
S1	0							
S2	8	0						
C2	18*	12**	0					
S4	32	26	13***	0				
C1	7	12	22****	36	0			
S6	5	7	19*****	33	8	0		
S8	8	6	12	26	13	9	0	
S9	36	30	17	6	40	37	30	0

At the level of m: 3, the minimum distance in the distance matrix is 5 between S6 and S1, so S6 and S1 will be merged into C3. The cells involved in the merging of S6 and S1 for the creation of C3 have been highlighted in Table 7.32.

Table 7.32 Cells involved in creating C3

Instances	S1	S2	C2	S4	C1	S6	S8	S9
S1	0							
S2	8	0						
C2	18*	12**	0					
S4	32	26	13***	0				
C1	7	12	22****	36	0			
S6	5	7	19	33	8	0		
S8	8	6	12	26	13	9	0	
S9	36	30	17	6	40	37	30	0

The description of calculation of some of new distances from compound object C3 to other objects is given below.

d(S2, S1) = 8 and d(S2, S6) = 7 so, d(S2, C3) = min (8, 7) = 7*

d (C2, S1) = 18 and d(C2, S6) = 19 so, d(C2, C3) = min (18, 19) =18**

Similarly, d(S8, S1) = 8 and d (S8, S6) = 9 so, min (S8, C3) = min (8, 9) = 8***

The input matrix at m: 4 is shown in Table 7.33.

Table 7.33 Input distance matrix, with m: 4

Instances	C3	S2	C2	S4	C1	S8	S9
C3	0						
S2	7*	0					
C2	18**	12	0				
S4	32	26	13	0			
C1	7	12	22	36	0		
S8	8***	6	12	26	13	0	
S9	36	30	17	6	40	30	0

At the level of m: 4, the minimum distance in the distance matrix is 6, so S9 and S4 will be merged into C4, and the cells involved in C4 are highlighted in Table 7.34.

Table 7.34 Cells involved in creating C4

Instances	C3	S2	C2	S4	C1	S8	S9
C3	0						
S2	7*	0					
C2	18	12	0				
S4	32	26	13	0			
C1	7	12	22	36	0		
S8	8	6	12	26	13	0	
S9	36***	30	17	**6**	40	30	0

The calculation of some of new distances from the compound object C4 to other objects is given below.

d(C3, S4) = 32 and d(C3, S9) = 36 so, d(C3, C4) = min(32, 36) = 32*

d (C2, S4) = 13 and d(C2, S9) = 17 so, d(C2, C4) = min(13, 17) =13**

Similarly, d(C1, S4) = 36 and d (C1, S9) = 40 so, min(C1, C4) = min(36, 40) = 36***
The input matrix at m: 5 is shown in Table 7.35.

Table 7.35 Input distance matrix, with m: 5

Instances	C3	S2	C2	C4	C1	S8
C3	0					
S2	7	0				
C2	18	12	0			
C4	32*	26	13**	0		
C1	7	12	22	36***	0	
S8	8	6	12	26	13	0

At the level of m: 5, the minimum distance in the distance matrix is 6, so S8 and S2 will be merged into C5, and the cells involved in C5 are highlighted in Table 7.36.

Table 7.36 Cells involved in creating C5

Instances	C3	S2	C2	C4	C1	S8
C3	0					
S2	7	0				
C2	18	12	0			
C4	32*	26	13**	0		
C1	7	12	22	36***	0	
S8	8	6	12	26	13	0

The description of calculation of new distances from compound object C5 to other objects is given below. The input matrix at m:6 is shown in Table 7.37.

*min(12,12) **min(26,26) ***min(12,13)

Table 7.37 Input distance matrix, with m: 6

Instances	C3	C5	C2	C4	C1
C3	0				
C5	7	0			
C2	18	12*	0		
C4	32	26**	13	0	
C1	7	12***	22	36	0

At the level of m: 6, the minimum distance in the distance matrix is 7, so C1 and C3 will be merged into C6, and the cells involved in C6 are highlighted in Table 7.38.

Table 7.38 Cells involved in creating C6

Instances	C3	C5	C2	C4	C1
C3	0				
C5	7	0			
C2	18	12*	0		
C4	32	26**	13	0	
C1	7	12***	22	36	0

The calculation of some of new distances from compound object C6 to other objects is given below. The input matrix at m: 7 is shown in Table 7.39.

*min(12,7) **min(22,18) ***min(36,32)

Table 7.39 Input distance matrix, with m: 7

Instances	C6	C5	C2	C4
C6	0			
C5	**7***	0		
C2	18**	12	0	
C4	32***	26	13	0

At the level of m: 7, the minimum distance in the distance matrix is 7, so C5 and C6 will be merged into C7, and the cells involved in C7 are highlighted in Table 7.40.

Table 7.40 Cells involved in creating C7

Instances	C6	C5	C2	C4
C6	0			
C5	**7***	0		
C2	18** ⟷	12	0	
C4	32*** ⟷	26	13	0

The calculation of some of new distances from compound object C7 is given below. The input matrix at m: 8 is shown in Table 7.41.

*min(12, 18) **min(26,32)

Table 7.41 Input distance matrix, with m: 8

Instances	C7	C2	C4
C7	0		
C2	**12***	0	
C4	26**	13	0

At the level of m:8, the minimum distance in the distance matrix is 12, so C2 and C7 will be merged into C8, and the cells involved in C8 are highlighted in Table 7.42.

Table 7.42 Cells involved in creating C8

Instances	C7	C2	C4
C7	0		
C2	12*	0	
C4	26** ⟷	13	0

The input matrix at m: 9 is shown in Table 7.43.

Table 7.43 Input distance matrix, with m: 9

Instances	C8	C4
C8	0	
C4	13	0

Finally, the last two clusters are merged at level 8. The whole procedure is outlined by the hierarchical tree as shown in Figure 7.17. Thus, all clusters are eventually combined.

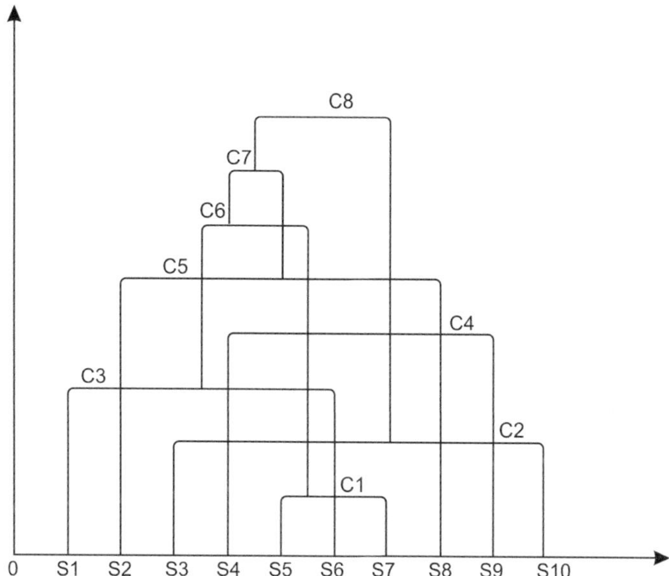

Figure 7.17 Hierarchical tree of clustering of students on the basis of their marks

7.7.1.2 *Weakness of agglomerative clustering methods*

The major weaknesses of agglomerative clustering methods are given as follows:

- Agglomerative clustering methods do not scale well as they have a high time complexity of at least $O(n^2)$ as the algorithm will have to compute $n*n$ distances, where n is the number of total objects.
- There is no undo mechanism to undo what was done previously.

7.7.2 Divisive clustering

As discussed earlier, in divisive clustering, all the objects or observations are assigned to a single cluster and then that single cluster is partitioned into two least similar clusters. This approach is repeatedly followed on each cluster until there is only one cluster for each object or observation.

Let us now apply a divisive algorithm on the same database discussed earlier for k-means and agglomerative clustering that contains the results of student examination in a given course. The students' performance on the basis of marks obtained out of 100 marks distributed across Quiz1, MSE, Quiz2, and ESE is given again in Table 7.44.

Table 7.44 Record of students' performance

Roll no	Quiz1	MSE	Quiz2	ESE
1	8	20	6	45
2	6	18	7	42

Contd.

Roll no	Quiz1	MSE	Quiz2	ESE
3	5	15	6	35
4	4	13	5	25
5	9	21	8	48
6	7	20	9	44
7	9	17	8	49
8	8	19	7	39
9	3	14	4	22
10	6	15	7	32

Step 1:

The distance matrix is calculated in the same way as we did in agglomerative clustering by using the centroid method to calculate the distance between the clusters. For representation, Roll numbers have been converted to Instances S1 to S10. Due to the symmetric nature of the distance matrix, we need to represent only the lower triangular matrix as shown in Table 7.45.

Table 7.45 Distance matrix at m: 0

Instances	S1	S2	S3	S4	S5	S6	S7	S8	S9	S10
S1	0									
S2	8	0								
S3	18	12	0							
S4	32	26	14	0						
S5	7	13	25	39	0					
S6	5	7	19	33	8	0				
S7	10	12	22	36	5	11	0			
S8	8	6	12	26	13	9	14	0		
S9	36	30	18	6	43	37	40	30	0	
S10	21	13	5	13	26	20	23	13	17	0

Step 2:

Pick up the two objects with the largest distance, i.e., 43 in this case between S5 and S9. Now, these two objects become the seed records of two new clusters. Split the entire group into two clusters based on the distances in the distance matrix as shown in Figure 7.18.

The details about some of the calculations of the distance matrix (referring to Table 7.45) for cluster C1 have been shown in Figure 7.18 (b) and similarly, the distances, for instance S9, i.e., C2 from other instances are computed.

(a)

Instances	S1	S2	S3	S4	S5	S6	S7	S8	S9	S10
S1	0									
S2	8	0								
S3	18	12	0							
S4	32	26	14	0						
S5	**7**	**13**	**25**	**39**	**0**					
S6	5	7	19	33	**8**	0				
S7	10	12	22	36	**5**	11	0			
S8	8	6	12	26	**13**	9	14	0		
S9	36	30	18	6	**43**	37	40	30	0	
S10	21	13	5	13	**26**	20	23	13	17	0

(b)

	S1	S2	S3	S4	S5	S6	S7	S8	S9	S10
S5, i.e., C1	7*	13	25**	39	0	8	5	13	43	26
S9, i.e., C2	36	30	18	6	43	37	40	30	0	17
Assigned Cluster	C1	C1	C2	C2	C1	C1	C1	C1	C2	C2

Figure 7.18 (a) Distance matrix at m: 0 (b) Data objects split after two clusters

In Figure 7.18 (b), the instances with minimum distance from cluster C1 and C2 are assigned to that cluster, For example,

*d(S1, C1) = 7 and d(S1, C2) = 36, so, min(7, 36) = 7, i.e., C1

**Similarly, d(S3, C1) = 25 and d(S3, C2) = 18, so, min(25, 18) = 18, i.e., C2

From the figure, it has been observed that

Cluster C1 includes – S1, S2, S5, S6, S7, S8, and

Cluster C2 includes – S3, S4, S9, S10

Since the stopping criterion hasn't been met, we will split up the largest cluster, i.e., C1. For this distance matrix will be computed for C1 as given in Table 7.46.

Table 7.46 Distance matrix for cluster C1

	S1	S2	S5	S6	S7	S8
S1	0					
S2	8	0				
S5	7	13	0			
S6	5	7	8	0		
S7	10	12	5	11	0	
S8	8	6	13	9	14	0

Since, the largest distance is 14, so C1 is split with S7 and S8 as seeds. They become the seeds of two new clusters. Splitting the entire group into these two clusters based on the distances in the distance matrix is shown in Table 7.47.

Table 7.47 Splitting of cluster C1 into two new clusters of S7 and S8

	S1	S2	S5	S6	S7	S8
S7,i.e, C3	10	12	5	11	0	14
S8, i.e., C4	8	6	13	9	14	0
Assigned Cluster	C4	C4	C3	C4	C3	C4

Here, Cluster C3 includes S5, S7 and cluster C4 includes S1, S2, S6, S8.

We already have another cluster as C2 (as described in Figure 7.18 (b)) which includes S3, S4, S9, S10. We can divide the cluster C3 further into two elementary clusters.

Now, the largest cluster, in this case is either C2 or C4 (both have the same number of objects). Here, we are considering cluster C2 as a candidate for a further split. For this the distance matrix is computed for cluster C2 as given in Table 7.48.

Table 7.48 Distance matrix for cluster C2

	S3	S4	S9	S10
S3	0			
S4	14	0		
S9	18	6	0	
S10	5	13	17	0

The largest distance is 18, so C2 has S3 and S9 as seeds for a further split. The result of splitting the entire group into these two clusters based on the distance in the distance matrix is given in Table 7.49.

Table 7.49 Splitting of cluster C2 into two new clusters of S3 and S9

	S3	S4	S9	S10
S3, i.e., C5	0	14	18	5
S9, i.e., C6	18	6	0	17
Assigned Cluster	C5	C6	C6	C5

Here, cluster C5 includes S3, S10 and cluster C6 includes S4, S9.

Both clusters C5 and C6 can be divided into two more elementary clusters. We already have other clusters namely cluster C3 that includes S5, S7 and cluster C4 that includes S1, S2, S6, S8. Now, the largest cluster is C4 thus, C4 is the candidate for the further split. For this the distance matrix is computed for C4 as given in Table 7.50.

Table 7.50 Distance matrix for cluster C4

	S1	S2	S6	S8
S1	0			
S2	8	0		
S6	5	7	0	
S8	8	6	9	0

The largest distance is 9, so C4 has S6 and S8 as seeds for a further split. The result of splitting the entire group into these two clusters based on the distance in the distance matrix is given in Table 7.51.

Table 7.51 Splitting of cluster C4 into two new clusters of S6 and S8

	S1	S2	S6	S8
S6, i.e., C7	5	7	0	9
S8, i.e., C8	8	6	9	0
Assigned Cluster	C7	C8	C7	C8

Here, Cluster C7 includes S1, S6 and cluster C8 includes S2, S8.

We already have other clusters as cluster C5 includes S3, S10 and cluster C6 includes S4, S9. At this stage each cluster can be divided into two clusters each of one object. Thus, the stopping criterion has been reached.

7.7.3 Density-based clustering

Density-based clustering algorithms perform the clustering of data by forming the cluster of nodes on the basis of the estimated density distribution of corresponding nodes in the region. In density-based clustering, clusters are dense regions in the data space. These clusters are separated by regions of lower object density. A cluster is defined as a maximal set of density-connected points.

In 1996, Martin Ester, Hans-Peter Kriegel, Jörg Sander and Xiaowei Xu proposed a Density-based clustering algorithm. The major strength of this approach is that it can identify clusters of arbitrary shapes. A Density-based clustering method is known as DBSCAN (Density-Based Spatial Clustering of Applications with Noise).

Familiarity with the following terms is a must in order to understand the workings of the DBSCAN algorithm.

Neighborhood (ε)

Neighborhood is an important term used in DBSCAN. It represents objects within a certain radius of from a centroid type object. The high-density neighborhood results if an object contains at least MinPts (minimum points) of objects in its neighborhood.

This concept is illustrated in Figure 7.19.

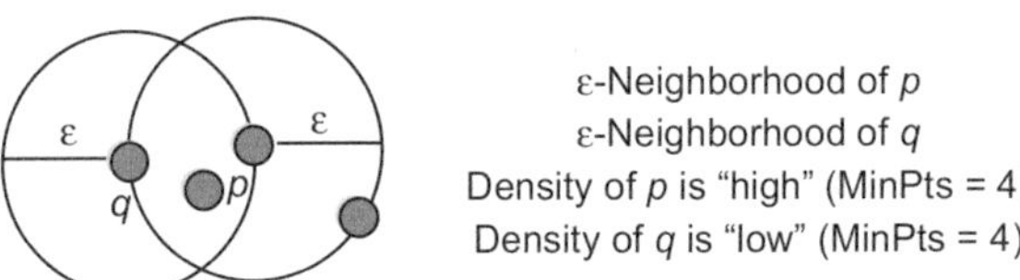

Figure 7.19 Concept of neighborhood and MinPts

Core, Border, and Outlier

A point is known as a core point if it has more than a specified number of points (MinPts) within neighborhood (ε). These points must lie at the interior of a cluster. A border point is a point if it has fewer than MinPts within neighborhood (ε), but it is in the neighborhood of a core point. A point is a noise or outlier point if it is neither a core point nor a border point. The concept of Core, Border, and Outlier is illustrated by considering Minpts = 4 in Figure 7.20.

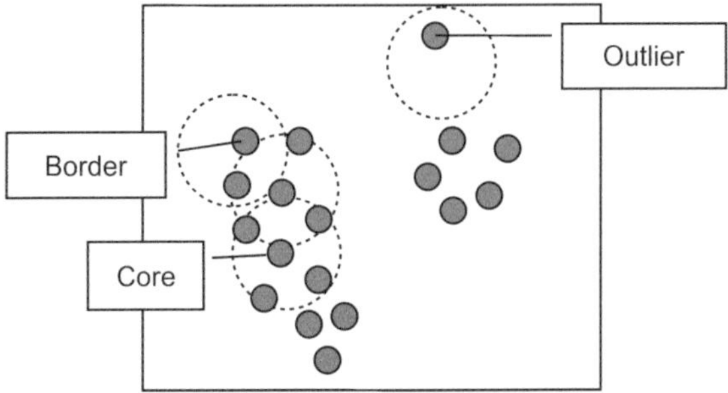

Figure 7.20 Concept of core, border and outlier

Density reachability; Directly and Indirectly density-reachable

DBSCAN's definition of a cluster is defined based on the concept of density reachability. Generally, a point q is directly density-reachable from a point p if it is not more distant than a given distance ε (i.e., is part of its ε-neighborhood). However, one may consider that p and q belong to the same cluster if point p is surrounded by necessarily many points.

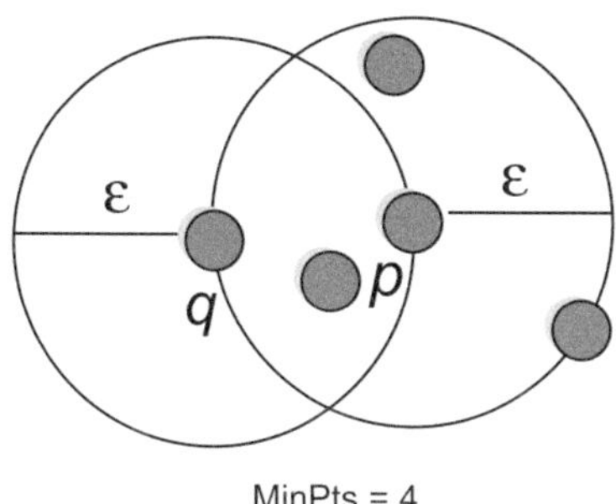

Figure 7.21 Concept of density reachability

As shown in Figure 7.21, if p is a core point and point q is in neighborhood ε of p then we can say that point q is directly density-reachable from point p.

Following are some important observations that can be drawn from data points given in Figure 7.21.

- Point q is directly density-reachable from point 'core point' p.
- Point q is not a core point as it has only 3 nodes in the neighborhood while MinPts is 4, therefore, p is not directly density-reachable from point q.
- Thus, Density-reachability is asymmetric

To further understand the concept of directly and indirectly density-reachable, let us consider Figure 7.22. Here, MinPts are 7.

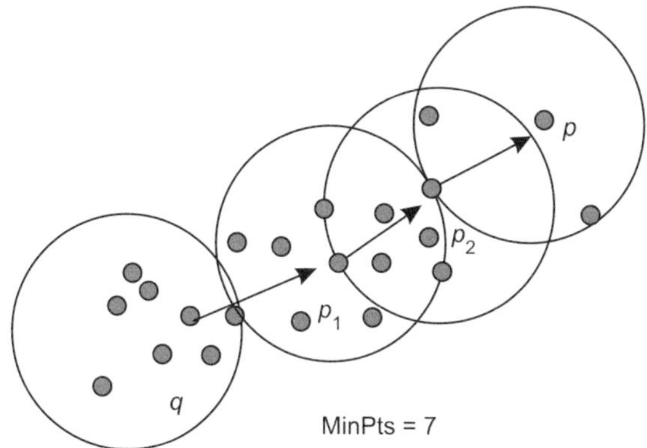

Figure 7.22 Concept of directly and indirectly density-reachable

As shown in Figure 7.22, following are some important observations:

- Point p_2 is a core point as it has more than 7 points within its neighborhood and point p is directly density-reachable from it.
- Point p_1 is also a core point and point p_2 is directly density-reachable from it.
- Point q is also a core point and point p_1 is directly density-reachable from it.
- Here, $p \rightarrow p_2 \rightarrow p_1 \rightarrow q$ form a chain.
- Point p is indirectly (through intermediate points p_1 and p_2) density-reachable from point q.
- Because p is not a core point as point q is not density-reachable from it. Point p has 6 nodes in the neighborhood while MinPts value is 7.

It is important to notice that the relation of density-reachable is not symmetric.

Let us consider another case given in Figure 7.23.

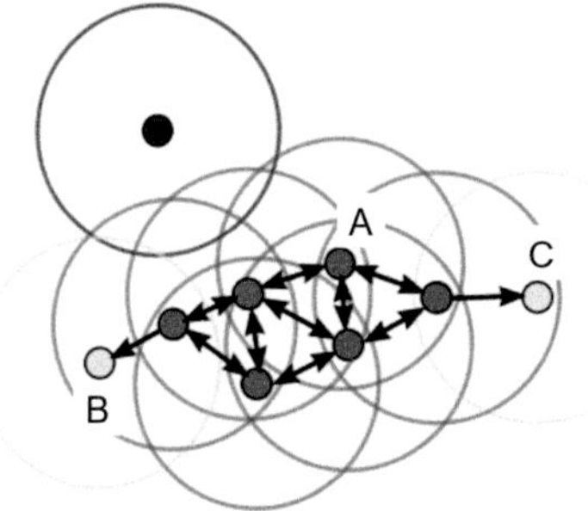

Figure 7.23 Another case of density reachability [see colour plate]

Here, in Figure 7.23, minPts = 4. Point A and the other red points are core points, because the area surrounding these points in an epsilon (ε) radius, contain at least 4 points (including the point itself). Because they are all reachable from one another, they form a single cluster. Points B and C are not core points, but are reachable from A (via other core points) and thus belong to the cluster as well. Point N is a noise point that is neither a core point nor directly-reachable.

Some more examples of DBSCAN are presented in Figure 7.24.

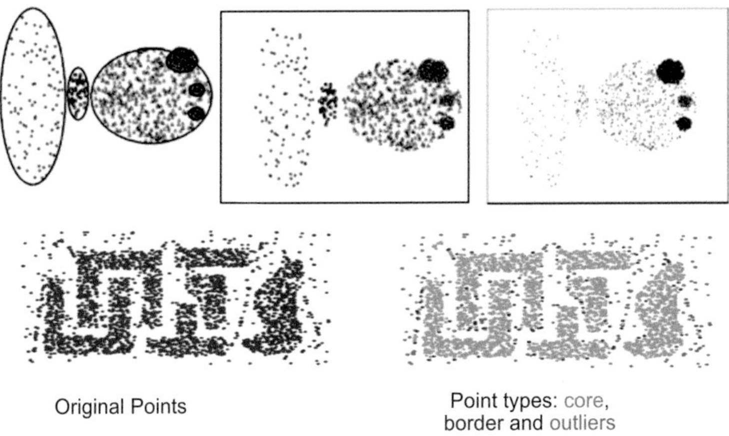

Figure 7.24 Some more examples of DBSCAN [see colour plate]

Thus, we can conclude that, a cluster then satisfies two properties:

- All points within the cluster are mutually density-connected.
- If a point is density-reachable from any point of the cluster, it is part of the cluster as well.

7.7.4 DBSCAN algorithm

After the understanding of concepts of neighborhood, core, border, outlier points and density reachability, DBSCAN algorithm can be summarized as given below.

Algorithm for DBSCAN

1. Find the ε (epsilon) neighbors of every point, and identify the core points with more than minPts neighbors.
2. Find the connected components of core points on the neighbourhood graph, ignoring all non-core points.
3. Assign each non-core point to a nearby cluster if the cluster is an ε (eps) neighbor, otherwise assign it to noise.

7.7.5 Strengths of DBSCAN algorithm

DBSCAN algorithm has following advantages.

- It is not required to specify the number of clusters in the data at the start in case of the DBSCAN algorithm.
- It requires only two parameters and does not depend on the ordering of the points in the database.
- It can identify clusters of arbitrary shape. It is also able to identify the clusters completely surrounded by a different cluster.
- DBSCAN is robust to outliers and has a notion of noise.

7.7.6 Weakness of DBSCAN algorithm

DBSCAN algorithm has following disadvantages.

- The DBSCAN algorithm is sensitive to the parameter, i.e., it is difficult to identify the correct set of parameters.
- The quality of the DBSCAN algorithm depends upon the distance measures like neighborhood (ε) and MinPts.
- The DBSCAN algorithm cannot cluster datasets accurately with varying densities or large differences in densities.

Remind Me

- Clustering is defined as grouping a set of similar objects into classes or clusters.
- A distance metric is a function d(x, y) that specifies the distance between elements of a set as a non-negative real number.
- Clustering methods/algorithms can be categorized into five categories. These are the: Partitioning method, Hierarchical method, Density-based method, Grid based method and Model based method.

- In k-means clustering algorithm, the objects are grouped into k number of clusters on the basis of attributes or features.
- Hierarchical clustering is a type of cluster analysis which seeks to generate a hierarchy of clusters. It is also called as Hierarchical Cluster Analysis (HCA).
- There are two types of Hierarchical clustering: agglomerative and divisive.
- Agglomerative is a 'bottom-up' approach. In this approach, each object is a cluster by itself at the start and its nearby clusters are repetitively combined resulting in larger and larger clusters until some stopping criterion is met.
- Divisive is a 'top-down' approach. In this approach, all objects start from one cluster, and partitions are performed repeatedly resulting in smaller and smaller clusters until some stopping criterion is met.
- The Density-based clustering algorithm performs the clustering of data by forming the cluster of nodes on the basis of the estimated density distribution of corresponding nodes in the region.
- Neighborhood represents objects within a radius from an object.
- Point is known as a core point if it has more than a specified number of points (MinPts) within neighborhood (ε). These points must lie at the interior of a cluster.
- A border point is a point if it has fewer than MinPts within neighborhood (ε), but it is in the neighborhood of a core point. Machine learning is a field that has grown out of AI.

Point Me (Books)

- Han, Jiawei, Micheline Kamber, and Jian Pei. 2011. *Data Mining: Concepts and Techniques*, 3rd ed. Amsterdam: Elsevier.
- Gupta, G. K. 2014. *Introduction to Data Mining with Case Studies*. Delhi: PHI Learning Pvt. Ltd.
- Mitchell, Tom M. 2017. *Machine Learning*. Chennai: McGraw Hill Education.
- Witten, Ian H., Eibe Frank, Mark A. Hall, and Christopher Pal. 2016. *Data Mining: Practical Machine Learning Tools and Techniques*, 4th ed. Burlington: Morgan Kaufmann.

Point Me (Video)

- K-Means Clustering Algorithm - Cluster Analysis | Machine Learning Algorithm | Data Science |Edureka, https://www.youtube.com/watch?v=4R8nWDh-wA0
- Hierarchical Clustering (Agglomerative and Divisive Clustering), https://www.youtube.com/watch?v=2z5wwyv0Zk4

Connect Me (Internet Resources)

- https://www.tutorialspoint.com/data_mining/dm_cluster_analysis.htm
- https://en.wikipedia.org/wiki/Hierarchical_clustering
- http://www.saedsayad.com/clustering.htm
- https://blogs.sas.com/content/subconsciousmusings/2016/05/26/data-mining-clustering/

Test Me

Answer these multiple choice questions based on your learning in this chapter.

1. Given two objects represented by the attribute values (1,6,2,5,3) and (3,5,2,6,6), compute the Manhattan distance between these two objects.
2. Given two objects represented by the attribute values (1,6,2,5,3) and (3,5,2,6,6), compute the Euclidean distance between these two objects.

3. Create four clusters for the given dataset using K-means algorithm, indicate all the intermediate steps.

Food item #	*Protein content, P*	*Fat content, F*
Food item #1	1.1	60
Food item #2	8.2	20
Food item #3	4.2	35
Food item #4	1.5	21
Food item #5	7.6	15
Food item #6	2.0	55
Food item #7	3.9	39

4. What is the importance of the sum of squared errors in a cluster?
5. The distances between some Indian cities are given below, Apply the clustering algorithm to make three clusters. Indicate intermediate steps.

	Bathinda	*Patiala*	*Delhi*	*Amritsar*	*Mathura*
Bathinda	0	190	400	250	460
Patiala	190	0	240	225	300
Delhi	400	240	0	450	60
Amritsar	250	225	450	0	510
Mathura	460	300	60	510	0

6. Use single link agglomerative clustering to group the data, describe by the following distance matrix.

	A	B	C	D
A	0	1	4	5
B		0	2	6
C			0	3
D				0

7. How do we decide which cluster to split next in case of divisive hierarchical method?
8. What are the strengths and weakness of DBSCAN? Why is it named DBSCAN?
9. Differentiate between border point and core point with an example.

8

Implementing Clustering with Weka and R

Chapter Objectives

- ✓ To apply the K-means algorithm in Weka and R language
- ✓ To interpret the results of clustering
- ✓ To identify the optimum number of clusters
- ✓ To apply classification on un-labeled data by using clustering as an intermediate step

8.1 Introduction

As discussed earlier, if data is not labeled then we can analyze this data by performing a clustering analysis, where clustering refers to the task of grouping a set of objects into classes of similar objects.

In this chapter, we will apply clustering on Fisher's Iris dataset. We will use clustering algorithms to group flower samples into clusters with similar flower dimensions. These clusters then become possible ways to group flowers samples into species. We will implement a simple k-means algorithm to cluster numerical attributes with the help of Weka and R.

In the case of classification, we know the attributes and classes of instances. For example, the flower dimensions and classes were already known to us for the Iris dataset. Our goal was to predict the class of an unknown sample as shown in Figure 8.1.

Earlier, we used the Weka J48 classification algorithm to build a decision tree on Fisher's Iris dataset using samples with known class, which helped in predicting the class of unknown samples. We used the flower's Sepal length and width, and the Petal length and width as the specific attributes for this. Based on flower dimensions and using this tree, we can identify an unknown Iris as one of three species, Setosa, Versicolor, and Virginica.

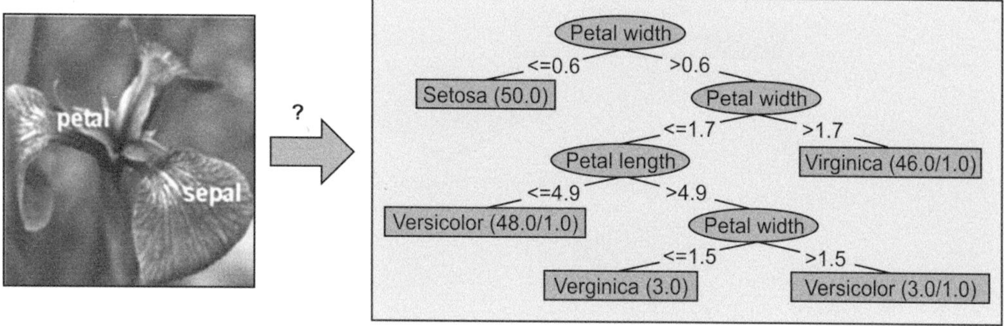

Figure 8.1 Classification of an unknown sample

In clustering, we know the attributes for the instances, but we don't know the classes. For example, we know the flower dimensions for samples of the Iris dataset but we don't know what classes exist as shown in Figure 8.2. Therefore, our goal is to group instances into clusters with similar attributes or dimensions and then identify the class.

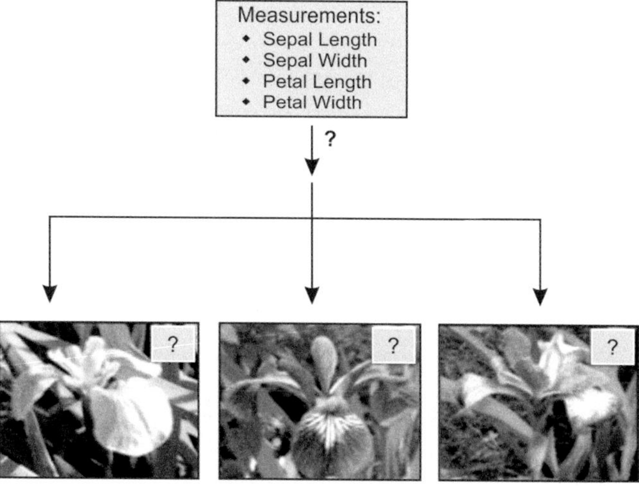

Figure 8.2 Clustering

In this chapter, we will learn what happens if we don't know what classes the samples belong to, or even how many classes there are, or even what defines a class? Since, Fisher's Iris dataset is already labeled, we will first make this dataset unlabeled by removing the class attribute, i.e., the species column. Then, we will apply clustering algorithms to cluster this data on the basis of its input attributes, i.e., Sepal length, Sepal width, Petal length, and Petal width. The advantage of using this dataset is that we can compare the results of our clustering algorithms with the labeled data to judge the accuracy of our clustering algorithms as depicted in Figure 8.3. For example, Anderson classified each of the samples, so after clustering the samples, we can compare the results of clustering with the assigned classes in the original dataset.

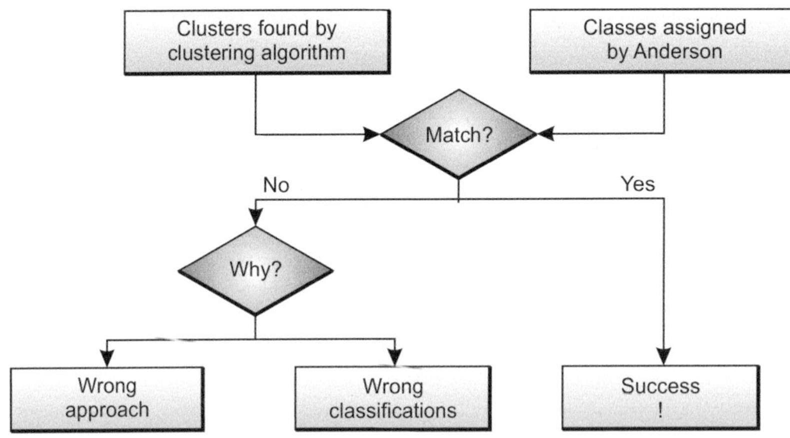

Figure 8.3 Clustering process

8.2 Clustering Fisher's Iris Dataset with the Simple k-Means Algorithm

Let's apply clustering on Fisher's Iris dataset using Weka's simple k-means algorithm. Since, Fisher's Iris dataset consists of samples belonging to three different species in the dataset, we will specify numClusters to be three. To help us interpret results, we'll set displayStdDevs to true so that we can see the standard deviations for the instance cluster assignments as shown in Figure 8.4.

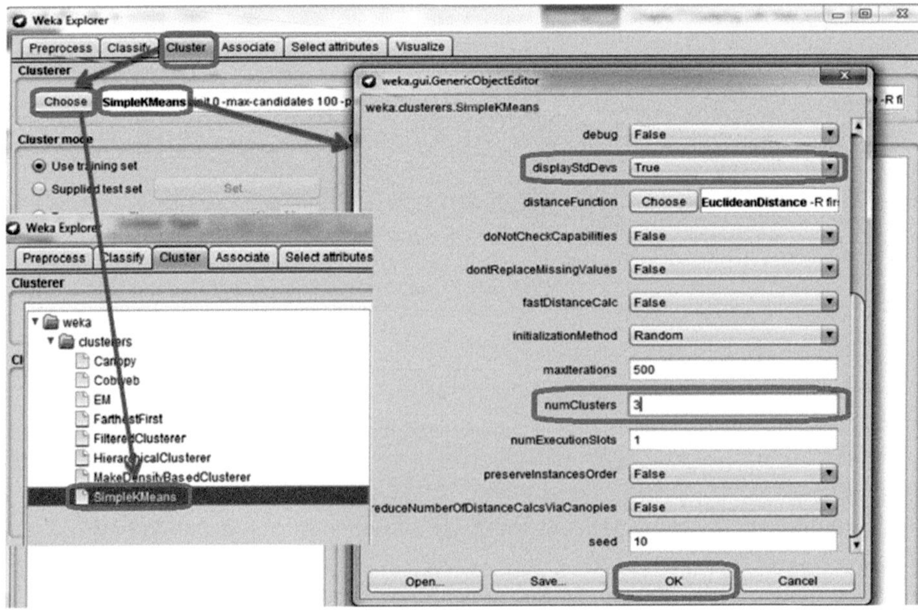

Figure 8.4 Applying the simple k-means algorithm in Weka

For clustering, as we are not doing any training or testing of dataset, so we will select ***Use training set*** in cluster mode. We also want to Store clusters for visualization.

As discussed earlier, for clustering, data should be unlabeled, so let us ignore the label attribute, i.e., the Species class attribute during application of the clustering algorithm, by using ***Ignore attributes*** and selecting ***Class*** in the ***Select items*** dialogue box as shown in Figure 8.5.

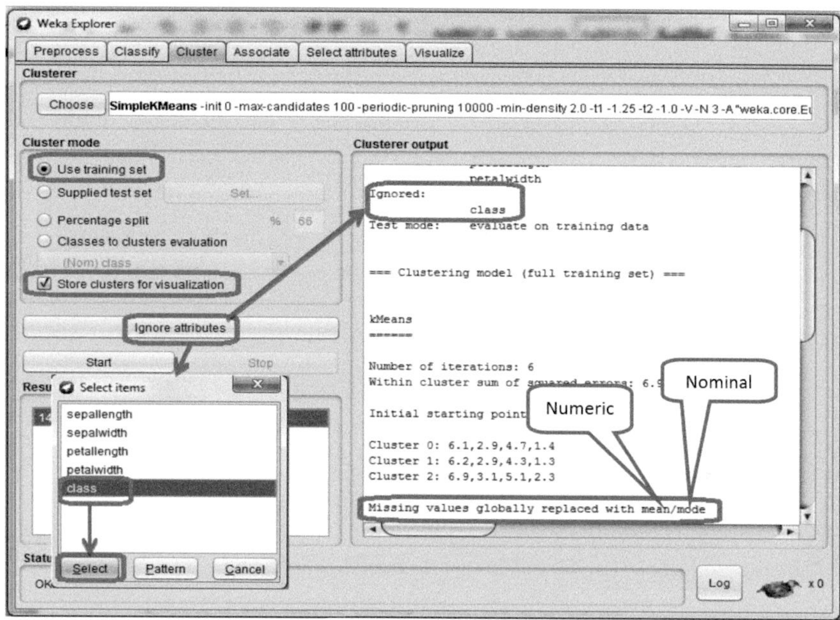

Figure 8.5 Applying the simple k-means algorithm in Weka: the next step

8.3 Handling Missing Values

In case, there exist any missing values in the dataset, it is handled by the simple k-Means clustering algorithm by itself. For missing numerical attributes, the missing value is filled in by the average value of all other values of the attribute. For nominal attributes, the missing value is replaced by the most commonly occurring nominal value for the attribute.

8.4 Results Analysis after Applying Clustering

After applying the simple k-means clustering algorithm, we see the centroids of the three clusters and standard deviations for the sample values in each cluster as shown in Figure 8.6. For the results, we can verify that the k-means clustering algorithm identifies three clusters of data having 61 instances in first cluster, 50 instances in second cluster and 39 instances in third cluster. Since, we are using the Iris dataset, we know that there are three clusters (Setosa, Versicolor and Verginica) having 50 instances each. Thus, out of three clusters, one cluster has been identified perfectly while there is shifting of 11 instances from one cluster to another, because identified count of clusters is 61, 50 and 39 as shown in Figure 8.6.

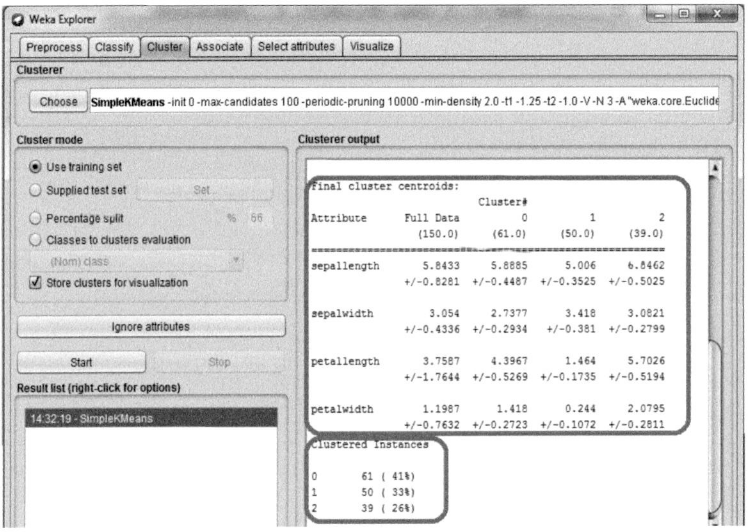

Figure 8.6 Clustering of Iris samples

To compare the results given by the clustering algorithm with the actual clusters, we select the ***Classes to cluster evaluation*** in cluster mode and re-run the clustering algorithm as shown in Figure 8.7. Using this, we can get more information on where Weka put each Iris sample.

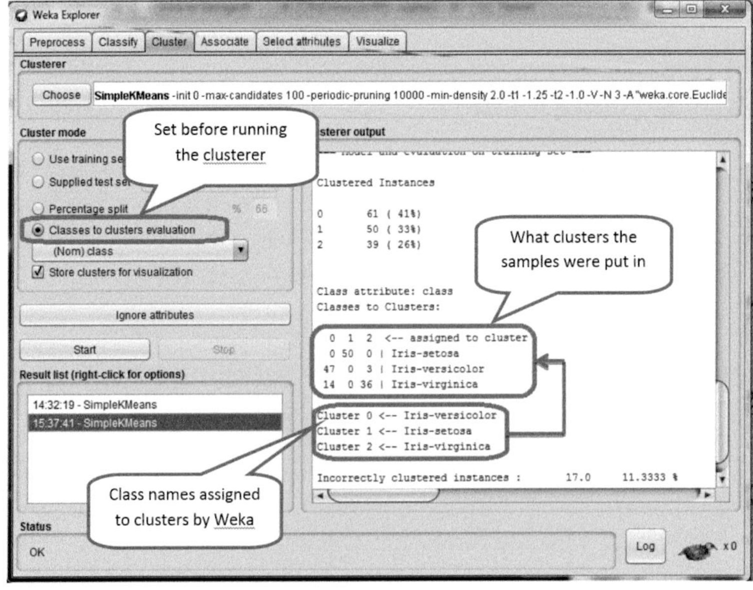

Figure 8.7 Class to cluster evaluation and confusion matrix

From the confusion matrix in Figure 8.7, it can be observed that all the Setosa fall into a distinct cluster, i.e., cluster 1. We also see that the algorithm got most of the Versicolor and Virginica right in cluster 0 and cluster 2, respectively. But some of the Versicolor and Virginica did get mixed up with each other, i.e., 3 Versicolor fall into the Virginica cluster and 14 Virginica fall into the Versicolor cluster. By specifying the ***numClusters*** to value 3, we can analyze that the simple k-means algorithm did a pretty good job of distinguishing between the different Iris species. We got 17 samples out of 150 samples that were classified wrongly according to Anderson's classification.

The clusters assigned by the clustering algorithm can be visualized across any of the input attributes. For example, Figure 8.8 shows the visualization of clusters along with the plot axis selected as Petal length and Petal width. Jitter may be increased to see all the samples.

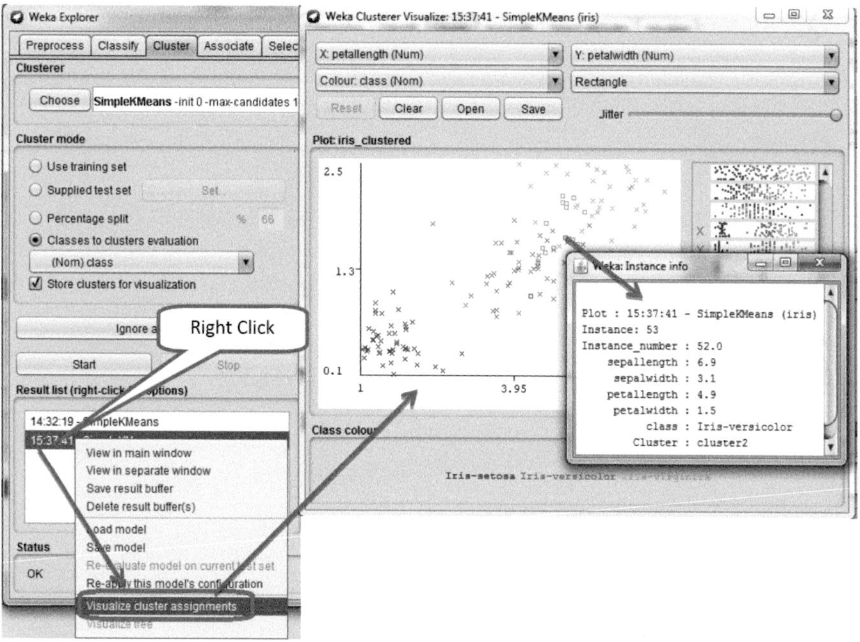

Figure 8.8 Cluster visualization [see colour plate]

The samples which are classified correctly are shown by cross symbols and wrongly classified samples are shown by squares in Figure 8.8. As we discussed earlier, Setosa got classified correctly and ended up in the right cluster. But we have some errors for Vrsicolor and Virginica, as indicated by the square boxes. If you right-click on any point on the plot, you can find out more about the associated sample.

Let us consider the plot of Petal length versus Petal width as shown in Figure 8.9. Through visual examination, it can be analyzed that some of the Versicolor instances that have been identified in the Virginica cluster, while it appears that on the basis of their Petal length vs. Petal width, they should be identified differently. And similarly, there are some Verginica instances identified as Versicolor while it appears that on the basis of the plot of Petal length vs. Petal width, they should be identified differently.

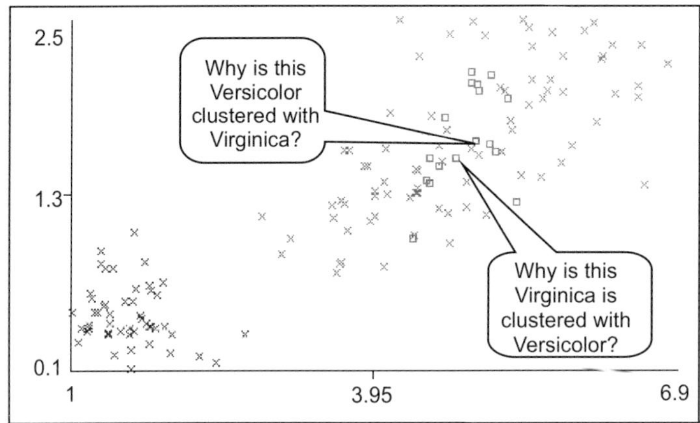

Figure 8.9 Cluster visualization for Petal length vs. Petal width [see colour plate]

Through visual examination shown in Figure 8.10, we have drawn boundaries which seems to separate the three species pretty reliably, based on just two of these attributes, i.e., Petal length and Petal width. Consider the example of sample 50 that is classed as Versicolor by Anderson, and lies on the Versicolor side of the species boundary. Therefore, the clustering algorithm should have put this sample in the Versicolor cluster. But the simple k-means put this sample in the Virginica cluster as shown in Figure 8.10.

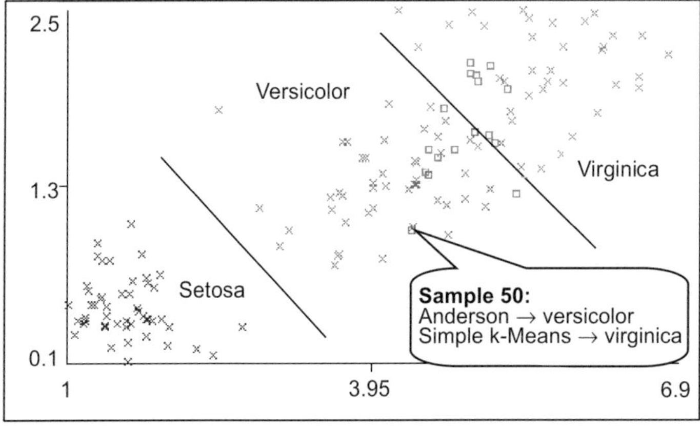

Figure 8.10 Cluster visualization with respect to Petal length vs. Petal width [see colour plate]

Now the question arises that why certain samples which clearly seem to belong to one cluster on this plot end up being put into a different cluster? The reason is that the clustering algorithm used information from all four flower dimensions to form the clusters, not just the two attributes shown in Figure 8.11, the plot of Sepal length vs. Sepal width. Again, species boundaries drawn by visual inspection are shown in Figure 8.11.

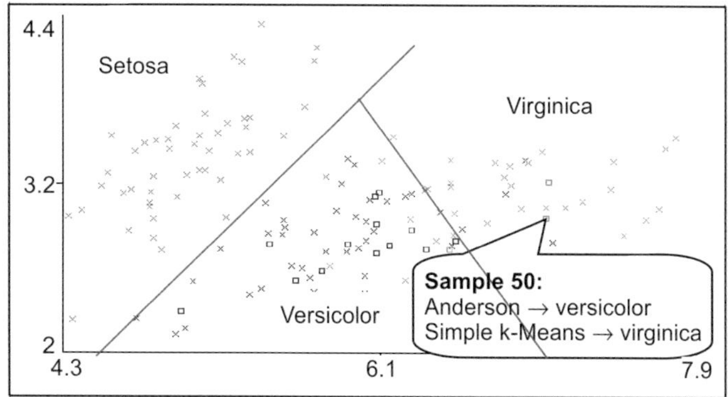

Figure 8.11 Cluster visualization with respect to Sepal length vs. Sepal width [see colour plate]

So, if we look at Petal length and Petal width, sample 50 looks like Versicolor, but if we look at Sepal length and Sepal width, it looks like Virginica. The point is that the clustering algorithm takes into account all attributes (except class attributes) when clustering samples. So, when all flower dimensions are taken into consideration, the simple k-means algorithm puts sample 50 in the Virginica cluster, not Versicolor.

In contrast, recall that for our decision tree classifier, it made decisions only on the basis of Petal length and Petal width measurements. It did not consider Sepal length and width in the classifier.

8.4.1 Identification of centroids for each cluster

The dimensions of the centroid of each of the clusters built by the clustering algorithm can be seen in the clustering output window along with standard deviation as shown in Figure 8.12. The centroid is the center of mass of the measurements for a particular attribute and particular cluster.

Final cluster centroids:

Attribute	Full Data (150.0)	Cluster# 0 (61.0)	1 (50.0)	2 (39.0)
sepallength	5.8433 +/-0.8281	5.8885 +/-0.4487	5.006 +/-0.3525	6.8462 +/-0.5025
sepalwidth	3.054 +/-0.4336	2.7377 +/-0.2934	3.418 +/-0.381	3.0821 +/-0.2799
petallength	3.7587 +/-1.7644	4.3967 +/-0.5269	1.464 +/-0.1735	5.7026 +/-0.5194
petalwidth	1.1987 +/-0.7632	1.418 +/-0.2723	0.244 +/-0.1072	2.0795 +/-0.2811

Figure 8.12 Cluster visualization with respect to Sepal length vs. Sepal width

Let us observe the plot of Sepal length vs. Sepal width, with the centroid and standard deviation statistics as shown in Figure 8.13. This information tells us something about the 'quality' of the clusters formed. First, the farther apart the centroids are, the less the clusters overlap, so, logically, the higher the quality of the clusters. Second, the lower the standard deviations, the more tightly the samples in a cluster are grouped around the centroid, which also means high quality clusters.

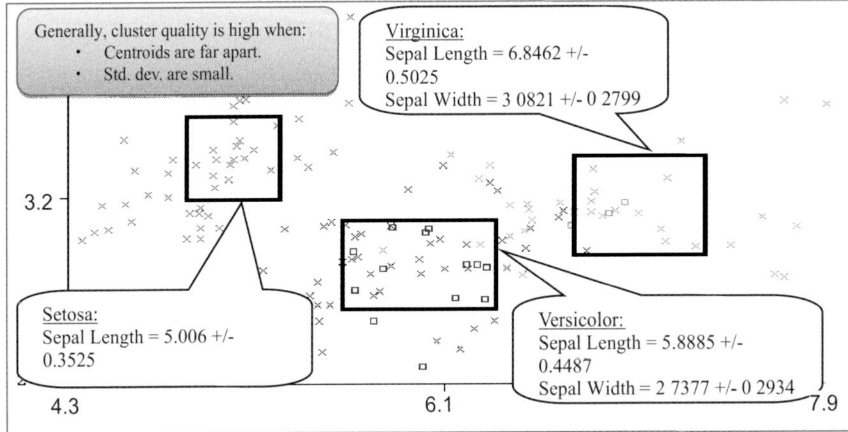

Figure 8.13 Cluster visualization with respect to Sepal length vs. Sepal width [see colour plate]

The simple k-means clustering algorithm provides another useful measure for assessing clustering results and it is the within cluster sum of squared errors.

8.4.2 Concept of within cluster sum of squared error

To understand the concept of within cluster sum of square error, let us consider the error for Petal width on sample 5 as shown in Figure 8.14. The Petal width for sample 5 is 3.6. The clustering algorithm put sample 5 in cluster 1. The Petal width centroid for cluster 1 is 3.418. The error is simply the difference between these two values, i.e, 3.6 - 3.418 = 0.182. We do the squaring to make sure all the errors are positive numbers.

```
Number of iterations: 6
Within cluster sum of squared errors: 6.998114004826762

Initial starting points (random):

Cluster 0: 6.1,2.9,4.7,1.4
Cluster 1: 6.2,2.9,4.3,1.3
Cluster 2: 6.9,3.1,5.1,2.3

Missing values globally repl

Final cluster centroids:
                                 Cluster#
Attribute        Full Data          0              2
                  (150.0)        (61.0)      (50.0        (39.0)
=====================================================================
sepallength         5.8433        5.8885        5.00         6.8462
                 +/-0.8281    +/-0.4487    +/-0.352      +/-0.5025

sepalwidth           3.054        2.7377       3.418         3.0821
                 +/-0.4336    +/-0.2934    +/-0.381      +/-0.2799

petallength         3.7587        4.3967       1.464         5.7026
                 +/-1.7644    +/-0.5269    +/-0.1735     +/-0.5194

petalwidth          1.1987         1.418       0.244         2.0795
                 +/-0.7632    +/-0.2723    +/-0.1072     +/-0.2811
```

The clusterer put sample 5 of the dataset into cluster 1.
Sepal width for sample 5 = 3.6
Error for sample 5 =
(3.6-3.418) = 0.182

Figure 8.14 Within cluster sum of squared error

If you square that error for each sample in the cluster and add this up for all the samples in the dataset, you get the within cluster sum of squared errors for that clustering run. Obviously, lower the error, the better the results of the run.

8.4.3 Identification of the optimum number of clusters using within cluster sum of squared error

In our example Iris database for clustering, we already know that there are three specifies of flowers so we have set number of the cluster to 3 for the application of the k-means clustering algorithm. But in case the dataset is unlabeled, how do we decide about the optimum number of clusters. To decide about an optimum number of clusters for unlabeled data, Within Cluster Sum of Squared Error plays a very important role.

To identify this optimum number, we first set k = 1 (number of clusters) and find corresponding within cluster sum of square error. Then we change k to 2 and find corresponding within cluster sum of square error. We repeat this step by increasing the value of k by 1 and plot a graph for the value of k and corresponding within cluster sum of square error as shown in Figure 8.15.

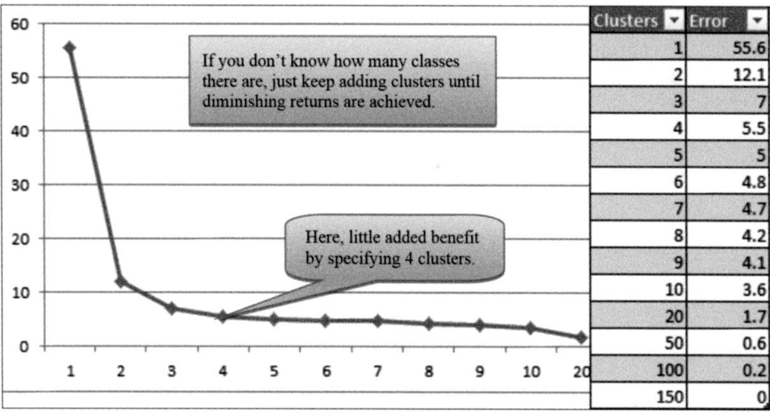

Clusters	Error
1	55.6
2	12.1
3	7
4	5.5
5	5
6	4.8
7	4.7
8	4.2
9	4.1
10	3.6
20	1.7
50	0.6
100	0.2
150	0

Figure 8.15 Error vs. number of clusters

In the graph, we have to identify the point where the improvement in within cluster sum of square error stops improving. In our example database, it appears that till 3 clusters, we see a significant reduction in error, with diminishing returns setting in at about the fourth cluster. So, it appears that perhaps 3 clusters would be a good conclusion, based on this dataset and clustering algorithm.

It is important to note that if we continue to increase the number of clusters then within cluster sum of square error further reduces and if we make the number of clusters equal to the number of instances in the dataset then within cluster sum of square error is reduced to zero. This case is another form of over-fitting of clusters. So, reducing the within cluster sum of square error should not be the only criteria to identify the number of clusters as it may result in over-fitting of clusters.

So, the number of clusters should be chosen at a point where the improvement of reduction in within cluster sums of square error is diminishing, i.e., where the slope appears to flatten out sharply.

8.5 Classification of Unlabeled Data

We have already discussed in previous chapters, that to apply classification on data to make a prediction, the important requirement is labeled data. In simple words, we can only apply classification if data is labeled. But in most of the cases, data may be unlabeled, as it is a very costly affair in terms of manpower hours to prepare labeled data.

Then the question arises, Is it possible to apply classification on unlabeled data?

Let us ponder on this question for a moment.

The answer to this question is Yes! It is possible to apply classification on unlabeled data by following some intermediate steps.

Of course, we cannot directly apply classification on unlabeled data, but we can apply the clustering algorithm on this data to make clusters or groups based on input attributes. Then these clusters can be added to the dataset and to set it as a class attribute, or, as an output attribute to make predictions by using classification algorithms.

Now, in the coming section, we will discuss this process of applying classification on unlabeled data. This process has been depicted in Figure 8.16 by considering the Iris dataset.

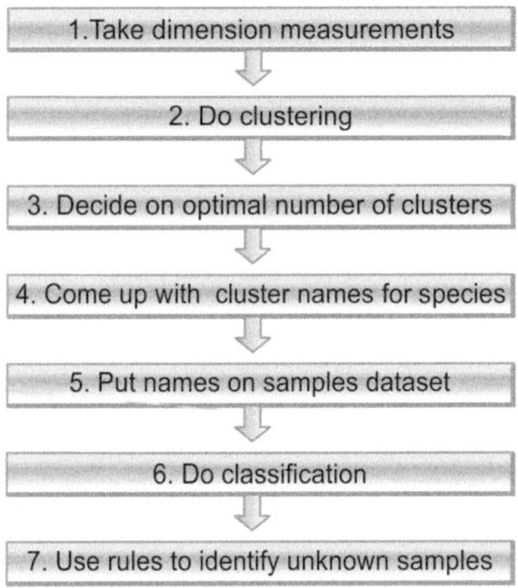

Figure 8.16 Classification process of unlabeled data

Till this point, we have completed the first three steps and successfully made three clusters of data by applying the simple k-means algorithm. Now, let us perform steps 4 and 5 as discussed below.

8.5.1 Adding clusters to dataset

Once we have determined the optimum number of clusters, we can group the samples into these clusters, and then we can come up with cluster names, like, say, Cluster1, Cluster2, Cluster3 and so on and can add it to our dataset.

In this section, we will discuss how we can add clusters found by a clustering algorithm to the dataset.

To add clusters to the dataset as one of the attributes, we have to use the ***Preprocess*** tab; upload the Iris dataset and then select ***No class***. We choose this option because we don't want Weka to assume any of the attributes as a class attribute. Now, we have to add an attribute to our dataset that will hold the name of the cluster that Weka will put each sample into. So, still on the ***Preprocess*** tab, we go to ***Choose***, and then select the ***AddCluster*** filter, but do not ***Apply*** the filter yet as shown in Figure 8.17.

Note: Make sure that ***No class*** is still selected, or you won't be able to select ***AddCluster***.

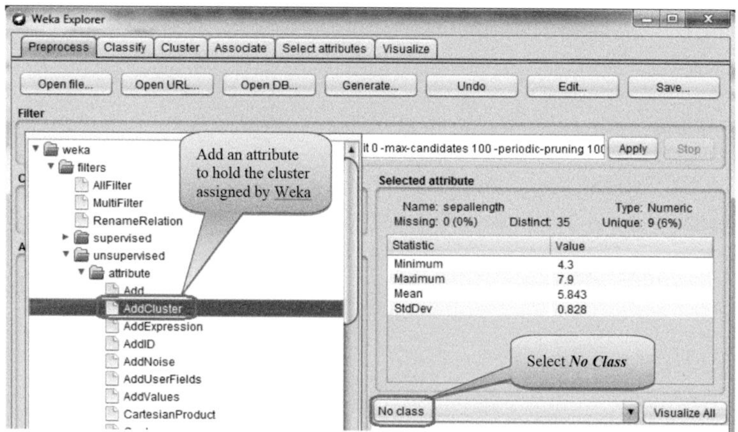

Figure 8.17 Choosing AddCluster filter

Before applying the ***AddCluster*** filter, we need to configure it. Here, we will ***Choose*** the ***SimpleKMeans*** clusterer, and specify ***numClusters*** as 3. Now, we still need to ignore the ***Species*** attribute, which we do by ***settingIgnoredAttributeIndices*** to 5, since ***Species*** is the 5th column in the dataset as shown in Figure 8.18.

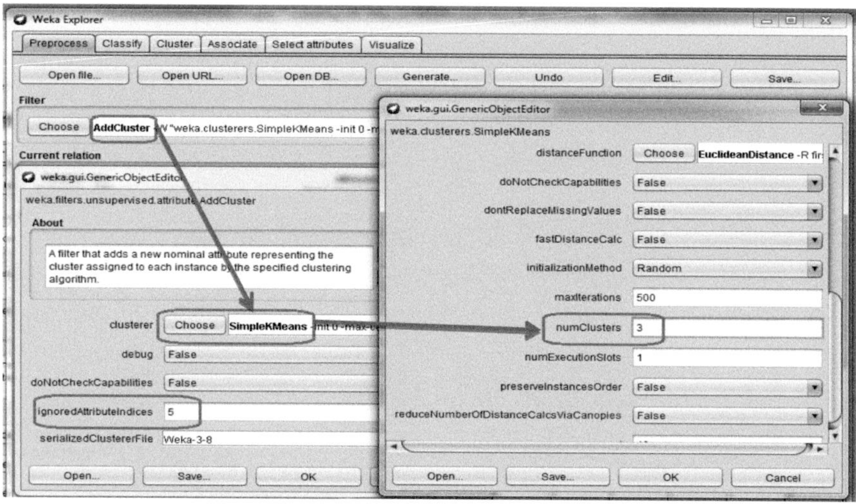

Figure 8.18 Configuration settings of AddCluster filter

Go ahead and ***Apply*** the ***AddCluster*** filter. Applying the ***AddCluster*** filter automatically runs the selected algorithm. In other words, we do not need to go to the ***Cluster*** tab and run ***SimpleKMeans***, since applying the filter does this automatically. When we ***Apply*** the filter, we do see a new attribute called ***cluster*** pop up in the ***Attributes*** box as shown in Figure 8.19.

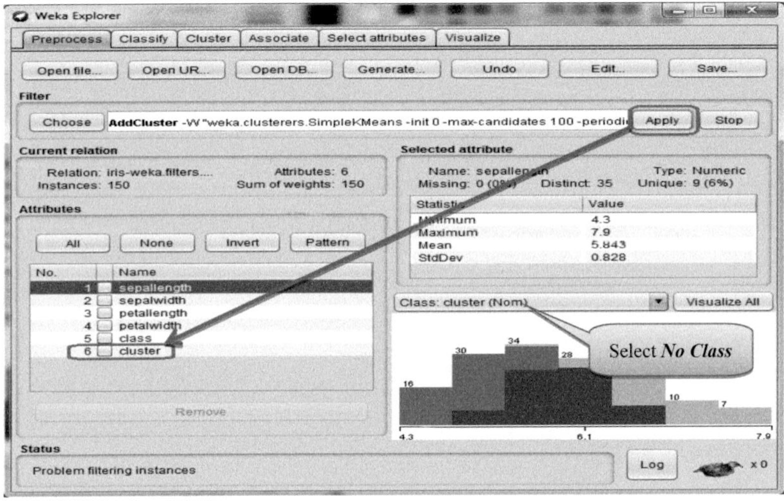

Figure 8.19 Application of AddCluster filter

To further analyze this clustering process, we can compare the values of cluster attribute (added by the clustering algorithm) with the already existing Species column, by clicking the ***Edit*** button. The label is highlighted, indicating that it is now the class attribute as shown in Figure 8.20. If you scroll around, you can find the 17 samples that Weka clustered differently than the species given in the original dataset. So, our results are the same regardless of which way we run ***SimpleKMeans***, except that now we have the cluster assignments added to the dataset.

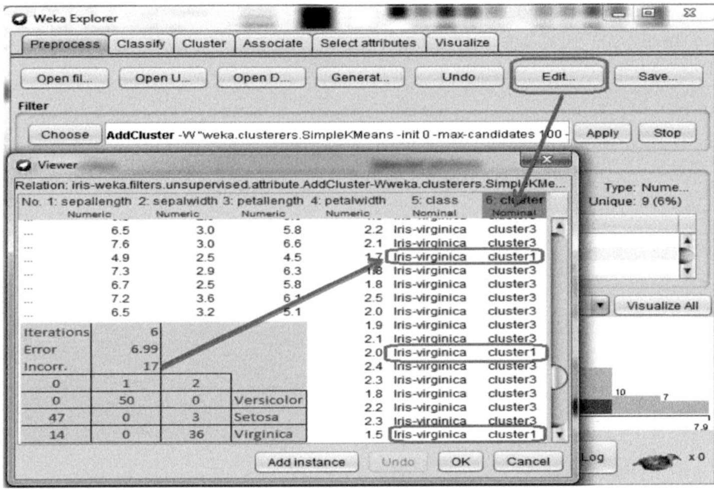

Figure 8.20 Comparison of values of the new added cluster attribute with the already existing class column

8.5.2 Applying the classification algorithm by using added cluster attribute as class attribute

We have a dataset where Weka has separated all the samples into three clusters, so what we will now do is build a J48 decision tree using the new cluster assignments as class values.

We start this by hopping over to the ***Preprocess*** tab and removing the ***Class*** attribute, which we do not want J48 to use when building its tree. Now we just go over to ***Classify***, choose ***J48*** with default settings, and run it.

Wow! J48 generates prediction rules as shown in Figure 8.21.

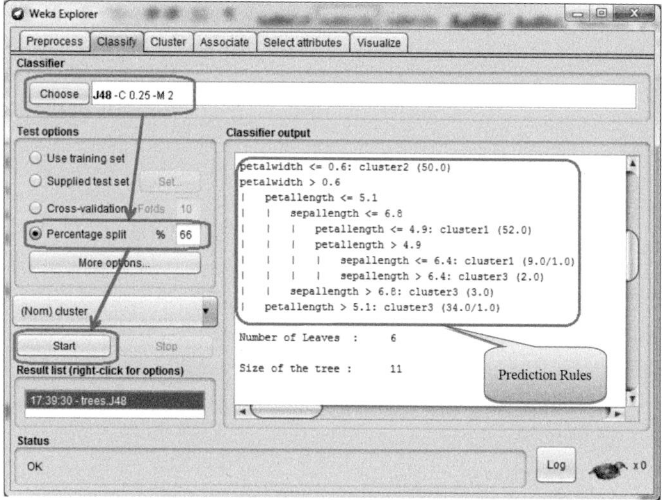

Figure 8.21 Prediction rules generated by J48

Now, by right clicking on the model, we get a visual depiction of the decision tree generated by the classifier as shown in Figure 8.22.

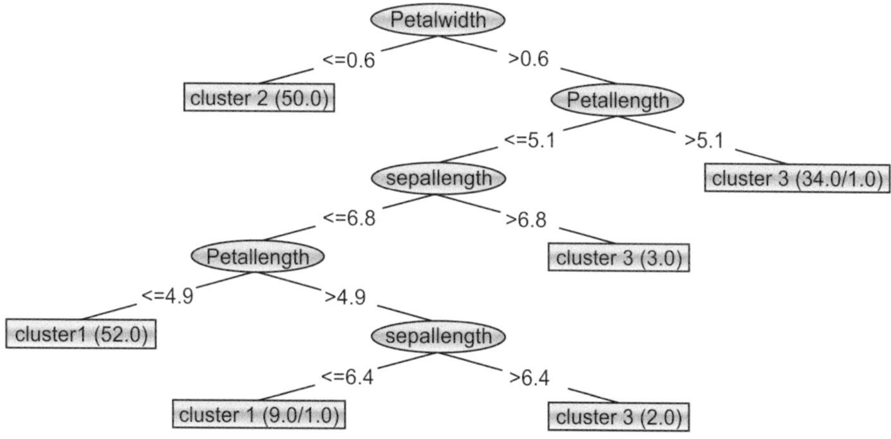

Figure 8.22 Decision tree

Now, let us compare the rules generated using clustering compared to the rules generated from the original dataset which contained Fisher's species attribute. It appears that when creating our decision tree from clustering results, Sepal length becomes important in distinguishing among species as shown in Figure 8.23 as clustering considers all four attributes to divide the instances into clusters and then these clusters are used to prepare the decision tree. Thus, all attributes appeared in the decision tree derived from clustering.

Derived from clustering

```
petalwidth <= 0.6: cluster2 (50.0)
petalwidth > 0.6
|   petallength <= 5.1
|   |   sepallength <= 6.8
|   |   |   petallength <= 4.9: cluster1 (52.0)
|   |   |   petallength > 4.9
|   |   |   |   sepallength <= 6.4: cluster1 (9.0/1.0)
|   |   |   |   sepallength > 6.4: cluster3 (2.0)
|   |   sepallength > 6.8: cluster3 (3.0)
|   petallength > 5.1: cluster3 (34.0/1.0)
```

Original

```
petalwidth <= 0.6: Iris-setosa (50.0)
petalwidth > 0.6
|   petalwidth <= 1.7
|   |   petallength <= 4.9: Iris-versicolor (48.0/1.0)
|   |   petallength > 4.9
|   |   |   petalwidth <= 1.5: Iris-virginica (3.0)
|   |   |   petalwidth > 1.5: Iris-versicolor (3.0/1.0)
|   petalwidth > 1.7: Iris-virginica (46.0/1.0)
```

Figure 8.23 Comparison of rules of clustering with rules of the decision tree

8.5.3 Pruning the decision tree

We can further simplify the generated decision tree by using the pruning property. Pruning is actually used to simplify the tree because normally J48 creates the branch of the tree if there are a minimum of two instances to follow the path. We can reduce the number of branches by increasing this number so that branch will be created only if more than *n* numbers of instances follow that path.

In the generic object editor for J48 (which will appear if we double click on the J48 classifier option as shown in Figure 8.24), increase ***minNumObj*** from the default value of **2** to a value of **10**. What this means is that J48 will prune the tree that it builds so that no leaf at the bottom of the tree will have any fewer than 10 iris samples in it as shown in Figure 8.24.

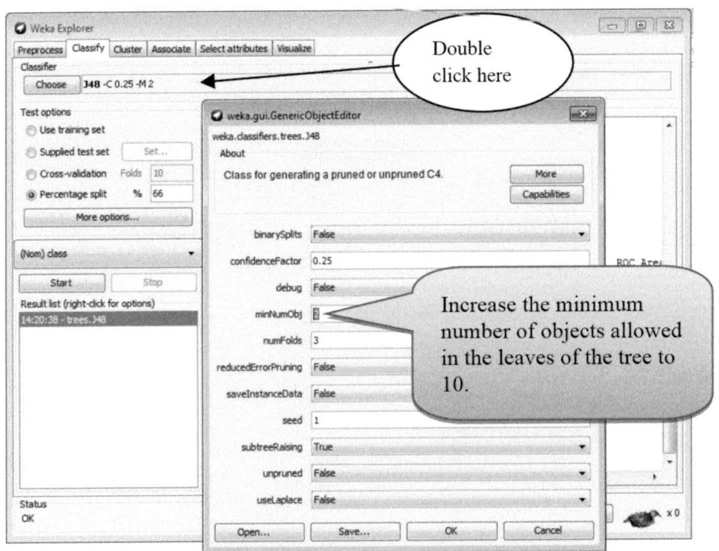

Figure 8.24 Pruning the decision tree

The result of increasing ***minNumObj*** from 2 to 10 is shown in Figure 8.25. Note that we do have a few additional misclassified samples, but we have also greatly simplified our rules.

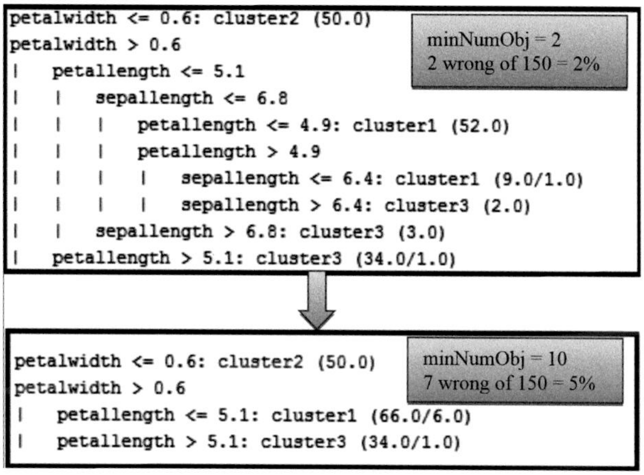

```
petalwidth <= 0.6: cluster2 (50.0)
petalwidth > 0.6
|   petallength <= 5.1
|   |   sepallength <= 6.8
|   |   |   petallength <= 4.9: cluster1 (52.0)
|   |   |   petallength > 4.9
|   |   |   |   sepallength <= 6.4: cluster1 (9.0/1.0)
|   |   |   |   sepallength > 6.4: cluster3 (2.0)
|   |   sepallength > 6.8: cluster3 (3.0)
|   petallength > 5.1: cluster3 (34.0/1.0)
```

minNumObj = 2
2 wrong of 150 = 2%

```
petalwidth <= 0.6: cluster2 (50.0)
petalwidth > 0.6
|   petallength <= 5.1: cluster1 (66.0/6.0)
|   petallength > 5.1: cluster3 (34.0/1.0)
```

minNumObj = 10
7 wrong of 150 = 5%

Figure 8.25 Analysis of rules after increasing ***minNumObj***

We have performed clustering on Fisher's Iris dataset using Weka and in the next section, we will implement the same concept using R language.

8.6 Clustering in R using Simple k-Means

The following steps are followed to perform k-means clustering in R.

Step1: Loading the dataset

We will first load the Iris dataset to perform clustering. Since the Iris dataset is widely used, the CRAN community has already provided the dataset in R's base data and we can immediately start using it in R.

The following command shows the Iris dataset statistics as shown in Figure 8.26.

```
> str(iris)
```

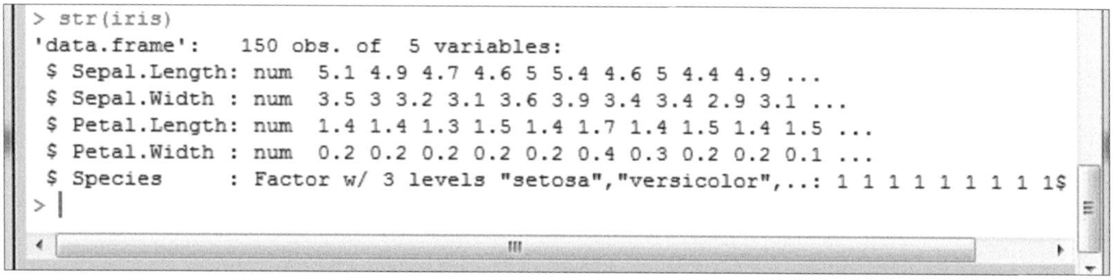

```
> str(iris)
'data.frame':   150 obs. of  5 variables:
 $ Sepal.Length: num  5.1 4.9 4.7 4.6 5 5.4 4.6 5 4.4 4.9 ...
 $ Sepal.Width : num  3.5 3 3.2 3.1 3.6 3.9 3.4 3.4 2.9 3.1 ...
 $ Petal.Length: num  1.4 1.4 1.3 1.5 1.4 1.7 1.4 1.5 1.4 1.5 ...
 $ Petal.Width : num  0.2 0.2 0.2 0.2 0.2 0.4 0.3 0.2 0.2 0.1 ...
 $ Species     : Factor w/ 3 levels "setosa","versicolor",..: 1 1 1 1 1 1 1 1 1$
>
```

Figure 8.26 Iris dataset statistics

Figure 8.26 shows that dataset contains 150 observations and five variables such as Sepal length, Sepal width, Petal length, Petal width, and species.

The following command converts the iris datset into dataframe and its output is shown in shown in Figure 8.27.

```
> iris _ df <- iris
> iris _ df
```

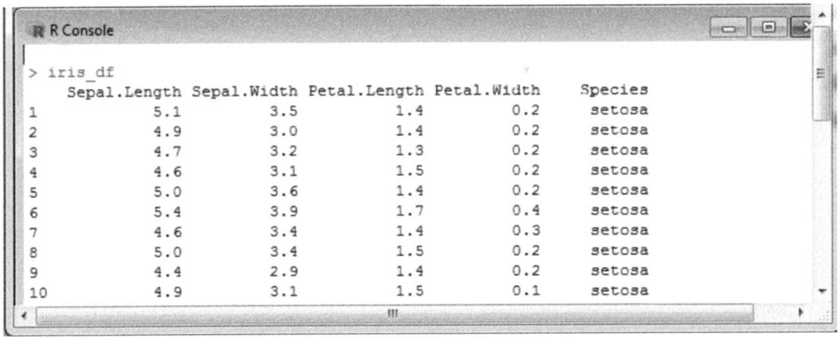

```
R Console
> iris_df
   Sepal.Length Sepal.Width Petal.Length Petal.Width    Species
1           5.1         3.5          1.4         0.2     setosa
2           4.9         3.0          1.4         0.2     setosa
3           4.7         3.2          1.3         0.2     setosa
4           4.6         3.1          1.5         0.2     setosa
5           5.0         3.6          1.4         0.2     setosa
6           5.4         3.9          1.7         0.4     setosa
7           4.6         3.4          1.4         0.3     setosa
8           5.0         3.4          1.5         0.2     setosa
9           4.4         2.9          1.4         0.2     setosa
10          4.9         3.1          1.5         0.1     setosa
```

Figure 8.27 Iris dataframe statistics

Step 2: Removal of the class variable from dataset

Out of these five attributes, four of our attributes are quantitative and one attributes (species) is categorical. Therfore, to perform clustering, we will remove the sepcies attribute from the dataset and save it in a different list for later use by using the following commands.

```
> species <  as.list(iris _ df$Species)
> species <- unlist(species)
> iris _ df <- iris _ df[1:4]
```

After running the above commmands, the fifth attribute (which is species) gets removed. Now the iris dataframe consists of four attributes as shown in Figure 8.28.

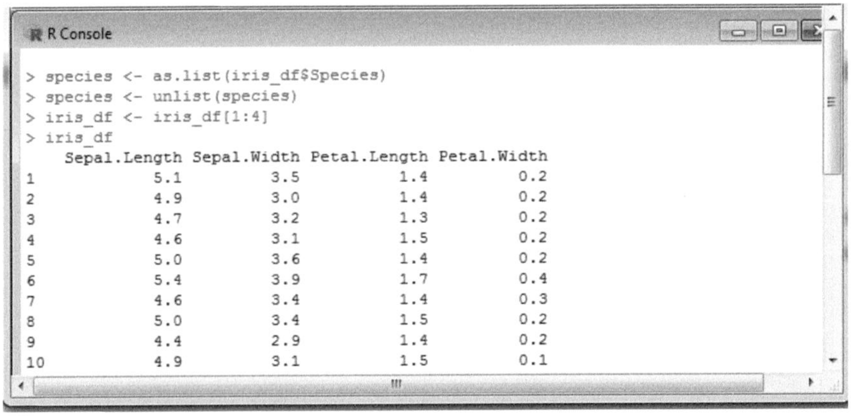

```
R Console
> species <- as.list(iris_df$Species)
> species <- unlist(species)
> iris_df <- iris_df[1:4]
> iris_df
   Sepal.Length Sepal.Width Petal.Length Petal.Width
1           5.1         3.5          1.4         0.2
2           4.9         3.0          1.4         0.2
3           4.7         3.2          1.3         0.2
4           4.6         3.1          1.5         0.2
5           5.0         3.6          1.4         0.2
6           5.4         3.9          1.7         0.4
7           4.6         3.4          1.4         0.3
8           5.0         3.4          1.5         0.2
9           4.4         2.9          1.4         0.2
10          4.9         3.1          1.5         0.1
```

Figure 8.28 Iris dataframe statistics after removal of species variable

Step 3: Apply k-means clustering

Now, we apply k-means clustering on the Iris data frame by specifying the number of clusters to 3 and number of iterations to 20 as given in following commands.

```
> irisCluster <- kmeans(iris_df, 3, nstart = 20)
> irisCluster
```

The output after running above commands is shown in Figure 8.29.

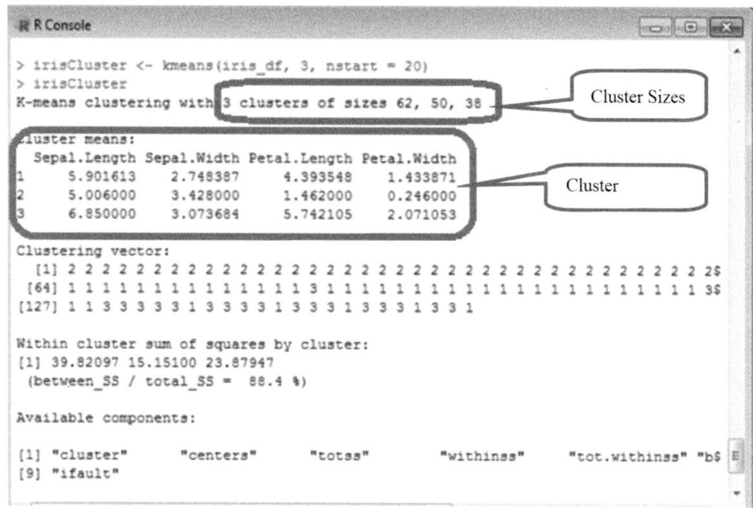

Figure 8.29 Results after applying k-means clustering

From Figure 8.29, it has been observed that clustering algorithm has identified 3 clusters such as 1, 2 and 3. The algorithm has put 62 samples in cluster 1, 50 samples in cluster 2 and 38 samples in cluster 3. We already know each class of Iris dataset consists of 50 samples. After analyzing the results shown in Figure 8.29, we can observe that 50 samples of one class has been identified correctly and 12 samples have been classified wrongly and assigned to a different class. The cluster size can also be identified using the following command and its output is shown in Figure 8.30.

```
> table(irisCluster$cluster)
```

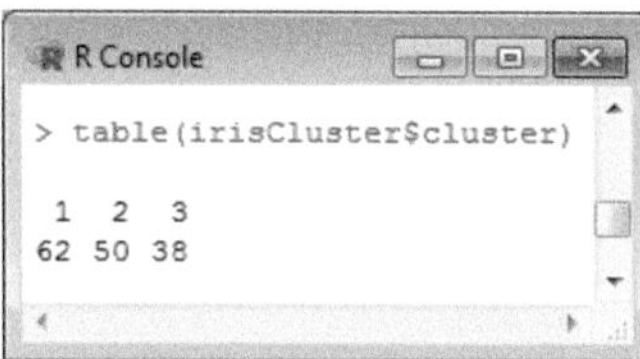

Figure 8.30 Cluster size

Similarly, the centroids of clusters are shown in Figure 8.29 and can also be identified using the following commands. The output of following command is shown in Figure 8.31.

```
> irisCluster$centers
```

```
R Console
> irisCluster$centers
  Sepal.Length Sepal.Width Petal.Length Petal.Width
1     5.901613    2.748387     4.393548    1.433871
2     5.006000    3.428000     1.462000    0.246000
3     6.850000    3.073684     5.742105    2.071053
> |
```

Figure 8.31 Cluster centroids

Figure 8.32 shows the plot between Petal Length and Petal Width after clustering using the following commnad.

```
> irisCluster$cluster <- as.factor(irisCluster$cluster)
> plot(iris _ df [, 3:4], col =(irisCluster$cluster) , main="K-Means result with 3
clusters", pch=20, cex=2)
```

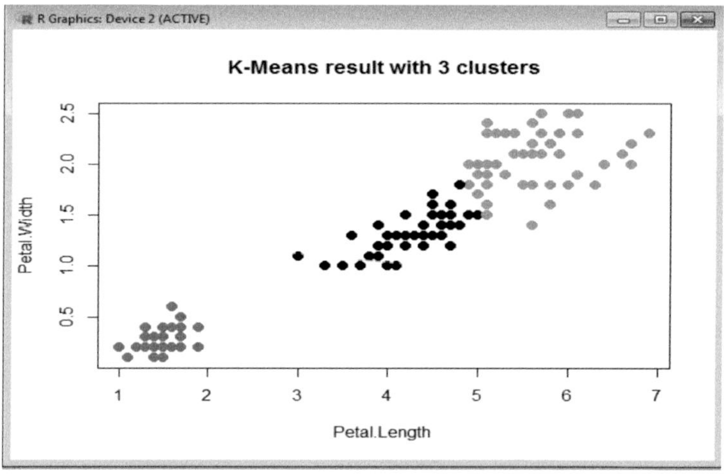

Figure 8.32 Plot of Petal length vs. Petal width after clustering [see colour plate]

8.6.1 Comparison of clustering results with the original dataset

Let's cross validate the results of clustering with original dataset. It can be done using the following command.

```
> table(irisCluster$cluster, iris$Species)
```

The output of this comparison is represented through a confusion matrix as shown in Figure 8.33.

```
> table(irisCluster$cluster, iris$Species)

    setosa versicolor virginica
  1      0          2        46
  2     50          0         0
  3      0         48         4
> |
```

Figure 8.33 Confusion matrix

As we can see, the data belonging to the Setosa species got grouped into cluster 2, Versicolor into cluster 3, and Virginica into cluster 1. The algorithm wrongly classified two samples belonging to Versicolor and four samples belonging to Virginica.

8.6.2 Adding generated clusters to the original dataset

The graphic expression of clusters can help us to evaluate whether the result makes sense. If we determine that it does, we can also include the results of cluster analysis in the original dataset. Thus, we bind the results of clustering analysis with the original dataset using the following command and its output is shown in Figure 8.34

```
# add cluster to original dataset
> iris.cluster = cbind(iris _ df, irisCluster[1])
> iris.cluster
```

```
R Console
> iris.cluster
   Sepal.Length Sepal.Width Petal.Length Petal.Width cluster
1           5.1         3.5          1.4         0.2       2
2           4.9         3.0          1.4         0.2       2
3           4.7         3.2          1.3         0.2       2
4           4.6         3.1          1.5         0.2       2
5           5.0         3.6          1.4         0.2       2
6           5.4         3.9          1.7         0.4       2
7           4.6         3.4          1.4         0.3       2
8           5.0         3.4          1.5         0.2       2
9           4.4         2.9          1.4         0.2       2
10          4.9         3.1          1.5         0.1       2
11          5.4         3.7          1.5         0.2       2
12          4.8         3.4          1.6         0.2       2
13          4.8         3.0          1.4         0.1       2
14          4.3         3.0          1.1         0.1       2
15|         5.8         4.0          1.2         0.2       2
```

Figure 8.34 Iris dataset after adding results of the clustering analysis

8.6.3 Apply J48 on the clustered dataset

The following commands are run to apply the decision tree and the classes predicted by its application are shown in Figure 8.35.

```
> library(party)
>
```

```
> iris.cluster$cluster <- as.factor(iris.cluster$cluster) # Convert "integer"
 data type to "factor" datatype
>
> target = cluster ~ Sepal.Length + Sepal.Width + Petal.Length + Petal.Width
>
> cdt <- ctree(target, iris.cluster) #Application of decision tree
>
> table(predict(cdt), iris.cluster$cluster) # Prediction of class
```

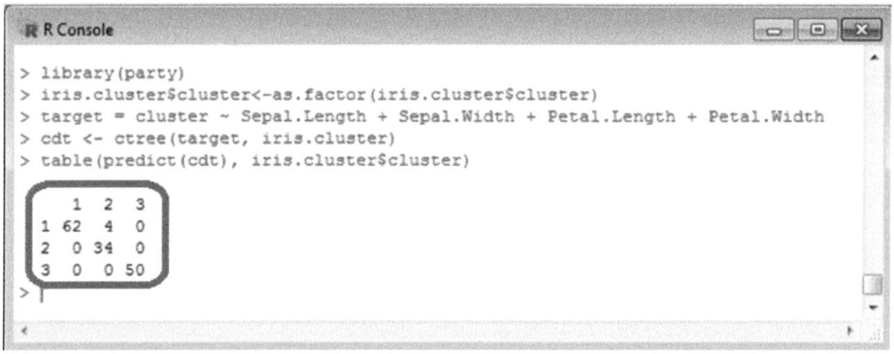

```
R Console
> library(party)
> iris.cluster$cluster<-as.factor(iris.cluster$cluster)
> target = cluster ~ Sepal.Length + Sepal.Width + Petal.Length + Petal.Width
> cdt <- ctree(target, iris.cluster)
> table(predict(cdt), iris.cluster$cluster)

   1  2  3
1 62  4  0
2  0 34  0
3  0  0 50
>
```

Figure 8.35 Apply decision tree on clustered results by simple k-means algorithm

The confusion matrix in Figure 8.35 shows that 50 instances of Setosa are classified correctly and 16 other instances are classified incorrectly.

Acknowledgement

We acknowledge the consent of Mr Mark Polczynski to use the ideas and illustrations given at Mark Polczynski in his Weka Tutorial 4 - Clustering.

Remind Me

- The simple k-means algorithm can be applied by selecting this algorithm in the clustering tab after loading the dataset.
- User can set the value of k, i.e, number of clusters by changing its settings.
- In k-means algorithm at Weka, the missing numeric value is filled by the average value of all other values of the attribute. For nominal attributes, the missing value is replaced by the most commonly occurring nominal value for the attribute.
- Optimum number of clusters can be selected by analyzing within cluster sum of squared error.
- Adding clusters to dataset is used to apply classification on un-labeled data.
- To prune the decision tree minNumObj value can be increased in the setting of the J48 algorithm.
- To apply k-means algorithm in R language ***kmeans()*** is used.
- The Table function is used in R to cross-validate the results of clustering with the original dataset.
- In R ***cbind()*** can be used to save all results of clustering to the original dataset.

Point Me (Books)

- Witten, Ian H., Eibe Frank, and Mark A. Hall. 2010. *Data Mining: Practical Machine Learning Tools and Techniques*, 3rd ed. Amsterdam: Elsevier.
- Bouckaert, Remco R., Eibe Frank, Mark Hall, Richard Kirkby, Peter Reutemann, Alex Seewald, and David Scuse. 2008. *WEKA Manual for Version 3-6-0*. Hamilton: University of Waikato.
- Lesmeister, Cory. 2015. *Mastering Machine Learning with R*. Birmingham: Packt Publishing Ltd.

Connect Me (Internet Resources)

- https://www.ibm.com/developerworks/library/os-weka2/index.html
- http://facweb.cs.depaul.edu/mobasher/classes/ect584/WEKA/k-means.html
- http://www.cs.ccsu.edu/~markov/ccsu_courses/datamining-ex3.html
- http://modelai.gettysburg.edu/2016/kmeans/assets/iris/Clustering_Iris_Data_with_Weka.pdf

Test Me

The purpose of this assignment is to verify that you have learnt the concepts of clustering. Carry out this assignment in both Weka and R to check your learning.

Task 1

Consider the dataset given below. It has 4 input attributes outlook, temperature, humidity and windy. Here, 'play' is the output attribute and these 14 records contain the information about weather conditions based on which it decides whether play took place or not.

Instance Number	*Outlook*	*Temperature*	*Humidity*	*Windy*	*Play*
1	sunny	hot	High	false	No
2	sunny	hot	High	true	No
3	overcast	hot	High	false	Yes
4	rainy	mild	High	false	Yes
5	rainy	cool	Normal	false	Yes
6	rainy	cool	Normal	true	No
7	overcast	cool	Normal	true	Yes
8	sunny	mild	High	false	No
9	sunny	cool	Normal	false	Yes
10	rainy	mild	Normal	false	Yes
11	sunny	mild	Normal	true	Yes
12	overcast	mild	High	true	Yes
13	overcast	hot	Normal	false	Yes
14	rainy	mild	High	true	No

- Apply classification on given data.
- Remove label and then apply clustering.
- Perform class to cluster evaluation.
- Apply classification on un-labeled dataset by removing play attribute.
- Compare the results of classification obtained in step 1 and step 4.
- Perform same operations in Weka and R.
- Prepare an analysis report for the same.

Task 2

- Consider the student performance of your class having following attributes.
  Rno, Name, Quiz1, MSE, Quiz2, Lab, ESE, Total
  Insert 30 dummy records in this excel file.
- Perform clustering on this dataset.
- Identify optimum number of clusters.
- After identification of optimum number of clusters, prepare clustering on this number.
- Perform same operations in Weka and R.
- Perform data analysis on the result obtained and prepare an analysis report for the same.

9

Association Mining

Chapter Objectives

- ✓ To comprehend the concept of association mining and its applications
- ✓ To understand the role of support, confidence and lift
- ✓ To comprehend the Naïve algorithm, Its limitations and improvements
- ✓ To learn about approaches for transaction database storage
- ✓ To understand and demonstrate the use of the apriori algorithm and the direct hashing and pruning algorithm
- ✓ To use dynamic Itemset counting to identify association rules
- ✓ To use FP growth for mining frequent patterns without candidate generation

9.1 Introduction to Association Rule Mining

Association rule mining often known as 'market basket' analysis is very effective technique to find the association of sale of item X with item Y. In simple words, market basket analysis consists of examining the items in the baskets of shoppers checking out at a market to see what types of items 'go together' as illustrated in Figure 9.1.

It would be useful to know, when people make a trip to the store, what kind of items do they tend to buy during that same shopping trip? For example, as shown in Figure 9.1, a database of customer transactions (i.e., shopping baskets) is given where each transaction consists of a set of items (i.e., products purchased during a visit). Association rule mining is used to identify groups of items which are frequently purchased together (customers' purchasing behavior). For example, 'IF one buys bread and milk, THEN he/she also buys eggs with high probability.' This information is useful for the store manager for better planning of stocking items in the store to improve its sale and efficiency.

Let us suppose that the store manager, receives customer complaints about heavy rush in his store and its consequent slow working. He may then decide to place associated items such as bread and milk together, so that customers can buy the items easier and faster than if these were at a distance. It also improves the sale of each product. In another scenario, let us suppose his store is new and the store manager wishes to display all its range of products to prospective customers. He may then decide to put the associated items, i.e., bread and milk, at opposite ends of the store and would place other new items and items being promoted in between them, thereby ensuring that many customers, on the way from bread to milk, would take notice of these and some would end up buying them.

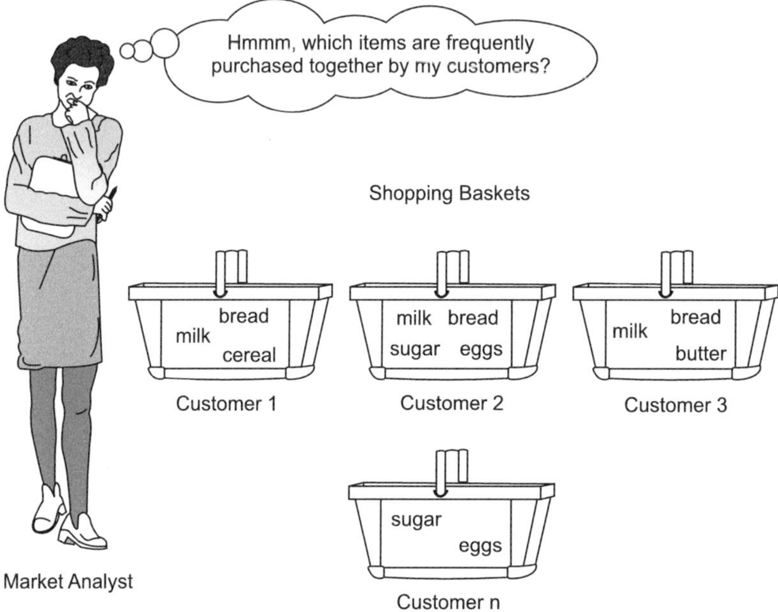

Figure 9.1 Need for association mining

Sometimes analysis of sale records leads to very interesting and unexpected results. In one very popular case study by Walmart USA, they had identified that people buying diapers often also bought beer. By putting the beer next to the diapers in their stores, it was found that the sales of each skyrocketed as depicted in Figures 9.2, 9.3 and 9.4.

Figure 9.2 Association of sale of beer and diapers

One may make multiple conclusions about the association of bear and diapers. It may be funny to assume that 'A beer before bed means a better night's sleep for the whole family.' But serious analysis could lead to 'Young couples prepare for the weekend by stocking up on diapers for the infants and beer for dad'.

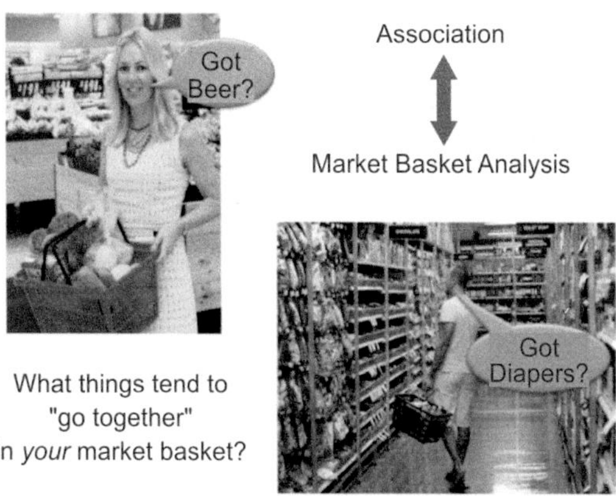

Figure 9.3 Association of sale of beer and diapers

Nevertheless, this story aptly illustrates the market basket concept of things 'going together', which is the basis of the data mining association function.

Figure 9.4 Association of sale of beer and diapers

Some other interesting findings of association mining may be trivial, for example, 'Customers who purchase maintenance agreements are very likely to purchase large appliances.' Or it may be unexplicable and unexpected, as in 'When a new restaurant opens, one of the most sold items is coffee'. This may be due to the reason that coffee is the cheapest item in the menu. So, to get the feel of the restaurant, people only order coffee. This type of finding suggests to the manager to increase the cost of coffee. It happens to be the reason why in many good restaurants, the price of coffee is alarming high.

Often, while conducting market basket analysis or association rule mining, the only source of data available on customers is the bills of purchase, which tells what items go together in a shopping cart, and can also show what items 'go together' at certain times of the day, days of the week, seasons of the year, credit versus cash versus check payment, geographical locations of stores, and so on. Discovering associations among these attributes can lead to fact-based marketing strategies for things like store floor plans, special discounts, coupon offerings, product clustering, catalog design, identifying items that need to be put in combo packs and can be used to compare stores as shown in Figure 9.5.

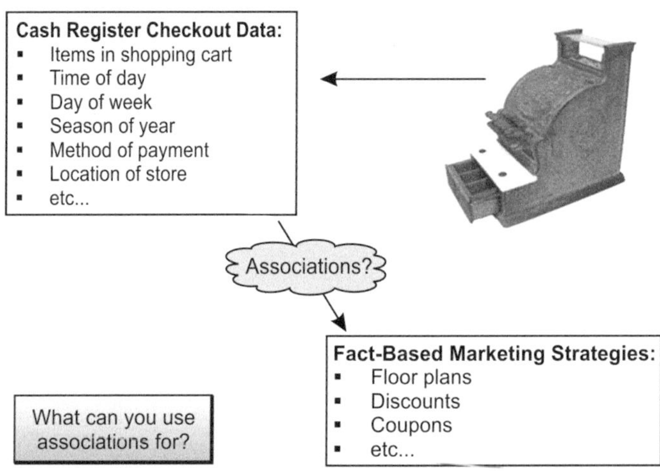

Figure 9.5 Association and customer purchase bills

Nowadays, recommendations given by online stores like Amazon and Flipkart also make use of association mining to recommend products related with your purchase and the system offers the list of products that others often buy together with the product you have just purchased. Besides the examples from market basket analysis given above, association rules are used today in many application areas such as intrusion detection, Web usage mining, bioinformatics and continuous production. Programmers use association rules to build programs capable of machine learning.

This is commonly known as market basket data analysis.

Association rule mining can also be used in applications like marketing, customer segmentation, web mining, medicine, adaptive learning, finance and bioinformatics, etc.

9.2 Defining Association Rule Mining

Association rule mining can be defined as identification of frequent patterns, correlations, associations, or causal structures among sets of objects or items in transactional databases, relational databases, and other information repositories.

Association rules are generally ***if/then*** statements that help in discovering relationships between seemingly unrelated data in a relational database or other information repository. For example, 'If a customer buys a dozen eggs, he is 80% likely to also purchase milk.'

An association rule consists of two parts, i.e., an antecedent (if) and a consequent (then). An antecedent is an object or item found in the data while a consequent is an object or item found in the combination with the antecedent.

Association rules are often written as $X \rightarrow Y$ meaning that whenever X appears Y also tends to appear. X and Y may be single items or sets of items. Here, X is referred to as the rule's antecedent and Y as its consequent.

For example, the rule found in the sales data of a supermarket could specify that if a customer buys onions and potatoes together, he or she will also like to buy burgers. This rule will be represented as onions, potatoes $\rightarrow$ burger.

The concept of association rules was formulated by two Indian scientists Dr Rakesh Agrawal and Dr R. Srikant. The detail about their brief profile is given in Section 9.7.1.

9.3 Representations of Items for Association Mining

Let us assume that the number of items in the shop stocks is n. In Table 9.1, there are 6 items in stock, namely, bread, milk, diapers, beer, eggs, cola, thus n = 6 for this shop.

The item list is represented by I and its items are represented by {i1,i2,...in}.

The number of transactions are represented by N transactions, i.e., N = 5 for the shop data as given in Table 9.1.

Table 9.1 Sale database

TID	*Items*
1	{Bread, Milk}
2	{Bread, Diapers, Beer, Eggs}
3	{Milk, Diapers, Beer, Cola}
4	{Bread, Milk, Diapers, Beer}
5	{Bread, Milk, Diapers, Cola}

Each transaction is denoted by T {t1, t2, ...,tN} each with a unique identifier (TID) and each transaction consists of a subset of items (possibly a small subset) purchased by one customer.

Let each transaction of m items be {i1,i2, ..., im}, where m <= n [number of items in a transaction should be less than or equal to total items in the shop]. Typically, transactions differ in the number of items.

As shown in Table 9.1, the first transaction is represented as T1 and it has two items, i.e., m = 2, with i1 = Bread and i2 = Milk. Similarly transaction T4, has four items, having m = 4, with i1 = Bread, i2 = Milk, i3 = Diapers and i4 = Beer.

Our task will be to find association relationships, given a large number of transactions, such that items that tend to occur together are identified. It is important to note that association rules mining does not take into account the quantities of items bought.

9.4 The Metrics to Evaluate the Strength of Association Rules

The metrics to judge the strength and accuracy of the rule are as follows:

- Support
- Confidence
- Lift

9.4.1 Support

Let N is the total number of transactions. Support of X is represented as the number of times X appears in the database divided by N, while the support for X and Y together is represented as the number of times they appear together divided by N as given below.

Support(X) = (Number of times X appears) / N = P(X)

Support(XY) = (Number of times X and Y appear together) / N = P(X $\cap$ Y)

Thus, Support of X is the probability of X while the support of XY is the probability of X $\cap$ Y.

Table 9.1, has been reproduced as Table 9.2 to calculate the supports for each item as given below:

Table 9.2 Sale database

TID	Items
1	{Bread, Milk}
2	{Bread, Diapers, Beer, Eggs}
3	{Milk, Diapers, Beer, Cola}
4	{Bread, Milk, Diapers, Beer}
5	{Bread, Milk, Diapers, Cola}

Support(Bread) = Number of times Bread appears / total number of translations = 4/5 = P(Bread)

Support(Milk) = Number of times Milk appears / total number of translations = 4/5 = P(Milk)

Support(Diapers) = Number of times Diapers appears / total number of translations = 4/5 = P(Diapers)

Support(Beer) = Number of times Beer appears / total number of translations =3/5 = P(Beer)

Support(Eggs) = Number of times Eggs appears / total number of translations =1/5 = P(Eggs)

Support(Cola) = Number of times Cola appears / total number of translations = 2/5 = P(Cola)

Support(Bread, Milk) = Number of times Bread, Milk appear together / total number of translations = 3/5 = P(Bread $\cap$ Milk)

Support(Diapers, Beer) = Number of times Diapers, Beer appears together / total number of translations = 3/5 = P(Diapers ∩ Beer)

A high level of support indicates that the rule is frequent enough for the business to take interest in it.

Support is very important metric because if a rule has low support then it may be the case that the rule occurs by chance and it will not be logical to promote items that customers seldom buy together. But if a rule has high support then that association becomes very important and if implemented properly will result in increase in revenue, efficiency and customer satisfaction.

9.4.2 Confidence

To understand the concept of confidence, let us suppose that support for X→Y is 80%, then it means that X→Y is very frequent and there are 80% chances that X and Y will appear together in a transaction. This would be of interest to the sales manager.

Let us suppose we have another pairs of items (A and B) and support for A→B is 50%.

Of course it is not as frequent as X→Y, but if this was higher, such as whenever A appears there is 90% chance that B also appears, then of course it would be of great interest.

Thus, not only the probability that A and B appear together matters, but also the conditional probability of B when A has already occurred plays a significant role. This conditional probability that B will follow when A has already been occurred is considered during determining the confidence of the rule.

Thus, Support and Confidence are important metrics to judge the quality of the association mining rule.

A high level of confidence shows that the rule is true often enough to justify a decision based on it.

Confidence for X→Y is defined as the ratio of the support for X and Y together to the support for X (which is same as the conditional probability of Y when X has already been occurred). Therefore if X appears much more frequently than X and Y appearing together, the confidence will be low.

Confidence of (X→Y) = Support(XY) / Support(X) = P(X ∩ Y) / P(X) = P(Y|X)

P(Y|X) is the probability of Y once X has taken place, also called the conditional probability of Y.

Let us consider Table 9.3 and Ttable 9.4 to further understand the concept of support and confidence.

Table 9.3 Example of the support measure

TID	Items	Support = Occurence / Total Support
1	ABC	Total Support = 5 Support {AB} = 2/5 = 40% Support {BC} = 3/5 = 60% Support {ABC} = 1/5 = 20%
2	ABD	
3	BC	
4	AC	
5	BCD	

Table 9.4 Example of the confidence measure

TID	Items	Given $X \Rightarrow Y$ Confidence = Occurence {X and Y}/ Occurence of (X)
1	ABC	Confidence $\{A \Rightarrow B\} = 2/3 = 66\%$ Confidence $\{B \Rightarrow C\} = 3/4 = 75\%$ Confidence $\{AB \Rightarrow C\} = 1/2 = 50\%$
2	ABD	
3	BC	
4	AC	
5	BCD	

Let us consider the database given in Table 9.5 for further understanding support and confidence.

Table 9.5 Database for identification of association rules

Antecedent	*Consequent*
A	0
A	0
A	1
A	0
B	1
B	0
B	1

There are two rules derived from the association of these combinations:

Rule 1: A implies 0, i.e., A→0

Rule 2: B implies 1, i.e., B→1

The support for Rule 1 is the Number of times A and 0 appear together / Total Number of transactions.

Thus, Support of Rule 1 = 3/7

The Support for Rule 2 is the Number of times B and 1 appear together / Total Number of transactions.

Support of Rule 2 = 2/7

The Confidence for Rule 1 is Support of (A,0) / Support A, i.e.,

(Number of times A and 0 appear together / Total number of items) DIVIDED BY

(Number of times A appears / Total number of items)

Here, total number of items get cancelled.

Thus, the Confidence for Rule 1 is the Number of times A and 0 appear together / Number of times A appears.

So the Confidence for Rule 1 is 3/4

Similarly, the Confidence for Rule 2 is 2/3

Going back to our general example involving 'X' (the Antecedent) and 'Y' (the Consequence), the Confidence of the rule does not depend on the frequency of 'Y' appearing. But in order to identify the strength of the rule it is important to consider the frequency of X and Y; X only; and Y only. In simple words, it is important to consider the whole dataset.

TheLift of the rule however considers the whole dataset, by taking into account the probability of Y also, in deciding the strength of the rule. So, Lift is the third important metric to check the strength or power of the rule.

9.4.3 Lift

It is very important to consider the frequency of Y or probability of Y for the effectiveness of the association mining rule X→Y.

As already explained, Confidence is the conditional probability of Y when X has already occurred. It is very important to consider how frequent Y is to guage the effectiveness of the confidence.

Thus, Lift is the ratio of conditional probability of Y when X is given to the unconditional probability of Y in the dataset. In simple words, it is Confidence of X→Y divided by the probability of Y.

Lift = P(Y|X) / P(Y)

Or

Lift = Confidence of (X→Y) / P(Y)

Or

Lift = $(P(X \cap Y) / P(X))/P(Y)$

Thus, lift can be computed by dividing the confidence by the unconditional probability of consequent Y.

Let us suppose that Coke is a very common sales item in a store and that it usually appears in most of the transactions. Let us suppose that we have a rule of Candle→Coke which has a support of 20% and has a confidence of 90%. It is very logical to think that if coke is very popular and it appears in 95% of transactions, then obviously it also appears quite often with the candle as well. So, the rule for association of candle and coke will not be all that useful. But if we find that Candle→ Matchbox also has a support of 20% and a confidence of 90% then it is logical to suppose that the frequency of matchbox sales is very little as compared to the sale of coke. And the rule suggests that when we make a sale of candles, 90% chance indicates that a matchbox will also be sold in the same transaction. It is more effective and logical to conclude that when we sell a candle then we also sell a coke (coke is popular and will appear with every item not just with candle). As support and confidence are unable to handle this case, it is handled by the lift of the rule.

In this case, the probability of Y is very low in case of Candle→ Matchbox (Here, Y is matchbox) and will be very high in case of Candle→Coke (Here, Y is coke).

One can note that the low probability of Y, makes the X→Y rule more effective as compared to high probability of Y. Lift takes the note of this, and is defined as follows.

Lift = P(Y|X) / P(Y)

Or

Lift = Confidence of (X→Y) / P(Y)

Or

Lift = (P(X ∩ Y) / P(X)) / P(Y)

Thus, the high probability of Y, i.e., P(Y) makes lift less effective and its low value makes it more effective.

Let us again consider the data given in Table 9.5, which has been reproduced in Table 9.6 for quick reference to calculate the lift of Rule 1 and Rule 2 as discussed earlier.

Table 9.6 Dataset

Antecedent	*Consequent*
A	0
A	0
A	1
A	0
B	1
B	0
B	1

Lift for Rule1, i.e., A→0 = P (0 | A) / P(0) = (P (A ∩ 0) / P(A))/ P(0) = (3/4) / (4/7)=1.3125

Lift for Rule2, i.e., B→1= P (1|B) / P(1) = (P (B ∩ 1) / P (B))/ P(1) = (2/3) / (3/7) =1.55

As discussed earlier, the confidence for Rule 1 is 3/4=0.75 and confidence for Rule 2 is 0.66.

It should be observed that although the Rule 1 has higher confidence as compared to Rule 2, but it has lower lift as compared to Rule 2.

Naturally, it would appear that Rule1 is more valuable because of having higher confidence; it appears more accurate (better supported). But, the accuracy of the rule can be misleading if it is independent of the dataset. Lift, as a metric is important because it considers both the confidence of the rule and the overall dataset.

In order to understand the importance of lift let us consider modified dataset given in Table 9.7.

In this modified database another five records have been added to the existing database (the five at the bottom). In these five records 0 appears four times, i.e., in the modified database 0 becomes more frequent; so, its probability has been increased, while the probability of 1 has been reduced.

Thus for first rule, i.e., A→0 the lift of the rule has been reduced in the modified database while it has same value of confidence as calculated below.

Support of A→0 = 3/12

Confidence of A→0 = Support(A,0) / Support(A) = 3/4 = 0.75

Lift = Confidence (A,0) / Support(0) = (3/4) / (8/12) = 36/32 = 1.125

Here, the lift of rule 1 has been reduced from 1.312 in the original dataset to 1.125 in the modified dataset, so the strength of rule 1 has been decreased in the modified dataset.

For Rule 2, i.e., B→1, the lift rule has been improved in the modified database while it has same value of confidence as calculated below.

Support of B→1 = 2/12

Confidence of B→1 = Support(B,1) / Support(B) = 2/3 = 0.66

Lift = Confidence / Support(1) = (2/3) / (4/12) =2

Here, the lift of Rule 2 has been increased from 1.555 in the original dataset to 2 in the modified dataset, so the strength of Rule 2 has been improved in the modified dataset. Thus, lift considers both the confidence of the rule and the overall dataset.

Table 9.7 Modified dataset

Antecedent	Consequent
A	0
A	0
A	1
A	0
B	1
B	0
B	1
C	0
D	0
C	0
C	1
E	0

Five new records inserted into the database (last five rows)

Another representation of association rules

Sometimes, the representation of association rules also includes support and confidence as shown in Figure 9.6.

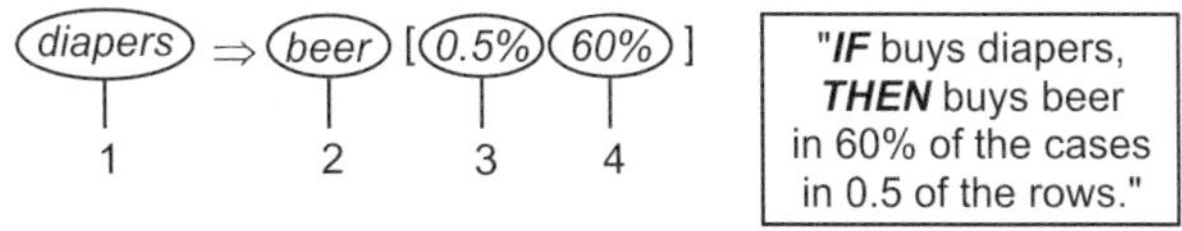

Figure 9.6 Representation of association rules

diapers ⇒ beer [0.5%, 60%]

Here,

1. Antecedent, left-hand side (LHS), body
2. Consequent, right-hand side (RHS), head
3. Support, frequency
4. Confidence, strength

9.5 The Naïve Algorithm for Finding Association Rules

To understand the Naïve Algorithm, let us consider the sales record of a grocery store. For simplicity, only four sale transactions of it are considered which deal with only four items for sale (Bread, Cornflakes, Jam and Milk) as shown in Table 9.8 and a naïve brute force algorithm is used to perform the task to identify the association of items in this sale record.

Let us find the association rules having minimum 'support' of 50% and minimum 'confidence' of 75%.

Table 9.8 Sale record of grocery store

Transaction ID	*Items*
100	Bread, Cornflakes
101	Bread, Cornflakes, Jam
102	Bread, Milk
103	Cornflakes, Jam, Milk

9.5.1 Working of the Naïve algorithm

In order to find association rules, the first step of the naïve algorithm is to list all the combinations of the items that are in stock and then identify the frequent combinations or combinations having frequency more than or equal to a specified support limit. Using this approach, the association rules that have the 'confidence' more than the threshold limit are identified.

Here, we have four items in stock, thus there are 2^4 possible combinations that we can create by considering null as one combination and if we ignore null then the following 15 combinations are possible as given in Table 9.9 along with their frequencies of occurrence in the transaction database.

Table 9.9 List of all itemsets and their frequencies

Itemsets	*Frequency*
Bread	**3**
Cornflakes	**3**
Jam	**2**
Milk	**2**
(Bread, Cornflakes)	**2**
(Bread, Jam)	1
(Bread, Milk)	1
(Cornflakes, Jam)	**2**

Contd.

Itemsets	Frequency
(Cornflakes, Milk)	1
(Jam, Milk)	1
(Bread, Cornflakes, Jam)	1
(Bread, Cornflakes, Milk)	0
(Bread, Jam, Milk)	0
(Cornflakes, Jam, Milk)	1
(Bread, Cornflakes, Jam, Milk)	0

Here, the minimum required support is 50% and we have to identify the frequent itemsets that appear in at least two transactions. The list of frequencies shows that all four items Bread, Cornflakes, Jam and Milk are frequent. It has been observed that the frequency goes down when we look at 2-itemsets and only two 2-itemsets such as (Bread, Cornflakes) and (Cornflakes, Jam) are frequent. All the frequent itemsets has been shown in bold in Table 9.8. There are no three or four itemsets that are frequent. The frequent itemsets are provided in Table 9.10.

Table 9.10 The set of all frequent items

Itemsets	Frequency
Bread	3
Cornflakes	3
Jam	2
Milk	2
(Bread, Cornflakes)	2
(Cornflakes, Jam)	2

As we are interested in association rules that can only occur with item pairs, thus individual frequent items Bread, Cornflakes, Jam and Milk are ignored, and item pairs (Bread, Cornflakes) and (Cornflakes, Jam) are considered for association rule mining.

Now, the association rules for the two 2-itemsets (Bread, Cornflakes) and (Cornflakes, Jam) are determined with a required confidence of 75%.

It is important to note that every 2-itemset (A, B) can lead to two rules A→B and B→A if both satisfy the required confidence. As stated earlier, confidence of A→B is given by dividing the support for A and B together, by the support for A.

Therefore, we have four possible rules which are given as follows along with their confidence:

Bread→Cornflakes

Confidence = Support of (Bread, Cornflakes) / Support of (Bread) = 2/3 = 67%

Cornflakes→Bread

Confidence = Support of (Cornflakes, Bread) / Support of (Cornflakes) = 2/3 = 67%
Cornflakes→Jam
Confidence = Support of (Cornflakes, Jam) / Support of (Cornflakes) = 2/3 = 67%
Jam→Cornflakes
Confidence = Support of (Jam, Cornflakes) / Support of (Jam) = 2/2 = 100%

Therefore, only the last rule Jam→Cornflakes has more than the minimum required confidence, *i.e.*, 75% and it qualifies. The rules having more than the user-specified minimum confidence are known as confident.

9.5.2 Limitations of the Naïve algorithm

We can observe that in Table 9.7, we had a small number of items. However, the number of all possible combinations for which we have to calculate the frequency grows enormously as the number of items increase in the dataset. When dealing with 4 itemsets, it produces 15 different combinations in Table 9.8 and if we include a null combination (a combination with no items) as well, we would obtain 16. If there are six items it would have produced 64 combinations and if the number of items were 10 then we would have a table with 1024 combinations.

This simple algorithm works well with four items but if the number of items is say 100, the number of combinations is much larger, in billions. The number of combinations becomes about a million with 20 items since the number of combinations is 2^n with n items. The naive algorithm can be improved to deal more effectively with larger datasets.

9.5.3 Improved Naïve algorithm to deal with larger datasets

Rather than counting all the possible item combinations in the stock it will be better to focus only on the items that are sold in transactions. Because, we may have hundreds of items in stock but we are concerned with finding associations only for the items that are being sold together. Thus, it is natural to to focus only on the items that are sold in transactions instead of all the items available in stock.

We can look at each transaction and count only the combinations that actually occur; with this approach we do not count itemsets with zero frequency. And that will be an improvement.

As an example, Table 9.11 lists all the actual combinations occurring within the transactions given in Table 9.8.

Table 9.11 All possible combinations with nonzero frequencies

Transaction ID	*Items*	*Combinations*
100	Bread, Cornflakes	(Bread, Cornflakes)
200	Bread, Cornflakes, Jam	(Bread, Cornflakes), (Bread, Jam), (Cornflakes, Jam), (Bread, Cornflakes, Jam)
300	Bread, Milk	(Bread, Milk)
400	Cornflakes, Jam, Milk	(Cornflakes, Jam), (Cornflakes, Milk), (Jam, Milk), (Cornflakes, Jam, Milk)

We therefore only need to look at the following combinations and their frequencies are given in Table 9.12.

Table 9.12 Frequencies of all itemsets with nonzero frequencies

Itemsets	*Frequency*
Bread	3
Cornflakes	3
Jam	2
Milk	2
(Bread, Cornflakes)	2
(Bread, Jam)	1
(Cornflakes, Jam)	2
(Bread, Cornflakes, Jam)	1
(Bread, Milk)	1
(Cornflakes, Milk)	1
(Jam, Milk)	1
(Cornflakes, Jam, Milk)	1

We can now proceed as before. This would work better since the list of item combinations is significantly reduced from 15 (as given in Table 9.8) to 12 (as given in Table 9.11) and this reduction is likely to be much larger for bigger problems. Regardless of the extent of the reduction, this list will also become very large for, say, 1000 items since it includes all the nonzero itemsets that exist in the transactions database whether they have minimum support or not. Therefore, the naïve algorithm or any improvement of it is not suitable for large problems. We will discuss a number of algorithms for more efficiently solving the association rule problem starting with the classical ***Apriori algorithm***.

Before starting with the Apriori algorithm, it is important to discuss different ways to store our transaction database in computer memory because, it will have an impact on performance if we are processing a large number of transactions. In the next section, implementation issues of transition storage have been discussed.

9.6 Approaches for Transaction Database Storage

It is important to understand different ways to store a dataset of transactions before processing it using algorithms, as storage is an important issue for its performance.

There are three ways to store datasets of transactions. These are as follows.

- Simple Storage
- Horizontal Storage
- Vertical Storage

Let us suppose the number of items be five; to demonstrate the different options. Let them be {I1, I2, I3, I4, I5}. Let there be only seven transactions with transaction IDs {T1, T2, T3, T4, T5, T6, T7}. This set of seven transactions with five items can be stored using three different methods given as follows.

9.6.1 Simple transaction storage

The first representation is commonly used and known as Simple Transaction Storage. Each row of the table shows the transaction ID and the purchased items as given in Table 9.13.

Table 9.13 A simple representation of transactions as an item list

Transaction ID	*Items*
T1	I1, I2, I4
T2	I4, I5
T3	I1, I3
T4	I2, I4, I5
T5	I4, I5
T6	I2, I3, I5
T7	I1, I3, I4

9.6.2 Horizontal storage

In this representation, each row is still a transaction, but columns have been created for each item. In the cell, 1 is filled against the item that occurs in a transaction and 0 against the rest as shown in Table 9.14.

Table 9.14 Horizontal storage representation

TID	*I1*	*I2*	*I3*	*I4*	*I5*
T1	1	1	0	1	0
T2	0	0	0	1	1
T3	1	0	1	0	0
T4	0	1	0	1	1
T5	0	0	0	1	1
T6	0	1	1	0	1
T7	1	0	1	1	0

The advantage of this storage system is that we can count the frequency of each item by counting the '1's in the given column. As we can easily calculate the frequency of item I1 as 3 and item I4 as

5. We can also easily calculate the frequency of item pairs by counting the 1's that result after an 'AND' operation on corresponding columns. For example, the frequency of item pairs I1 and I2 is 1 (By AND operation on column of I1 and I2 we will get only one 1, i.e., T1).

9.6.3 Vertical representation

In this representation as given in Table 9.15, the transaction list is turned around. Rather than using each row to represent a transaction of the items purchased, each row now represents an item and it indicates transactions in which the item appears. The columns now represent the transactions. This representation is also called a TID-list since for each item it provides a list of TIDs (Transition Ids).

Table 9.15 Vertical storage representation

Item	*TID*						
	T1	T2	T3	T4	T5	T6	T7
I1	1	0	1	0	0	0	1
I2	1	0	0	1	0	1	0
I3	0	0	1	0	0	1	1
I4	1	1	0	1	1	0	1
I5	0	1	0	1	1	1	0

A vertical representation also facilitates counting of items by counting the number of 1s in each row and in case of 2-itemsets, where you want to find out the frequency of occurrences of 2 items together in a transaction, you have to refer to the intersection of 2 rows corresponding to the items, and inspect one column at a time.

Example: If you want to find out frequency of item pairs (I1,I2) just look at rows I1 and I2 for each column if values of both I1 and I2 is 1 then this means I1 and I2 are occurring together in a transaction hence write their count as 1, move further in some way for each transaction. Finally you will get Table 9.16.

From the table it can be seen that the count for item pair {I1,I2}is 1; similarly the count of item pair {I1, I4} is 2. (Table 9.16)

Table 9.16 Frequency of item pairs

	T1	T2	T3	T4	T5	T6	T7
I1, I2	1	0	0	0	0	0	0
I1, I4	1	0	0	0	0	0	1

The vertical representation is not storage efficient in case of very large number of transactions. Also, if an algorithm needs data in the vertical representation then there would be a cost in transforming data from the horizontal representation to the vertical one.

With this we can move on to the concept of the Apriori algorithm.

9.7 The Apriori Algorithm

The Apriori algorithm was developed by two Indians Rakesh Agrawal and Ramakrishnan Srikant in 1994, to mine frequent itemsets for identifying association rules.

It should be a matter of pride and motivation to have two Indians as inventors of association mining. Their work is the base for commonly used recommendation systems for modern applications such as product recommendations for online purchases and video recommendation and so on.

A brief profile of these two scientists, based on Wikipedia, has been presented below to motivate readers and in appreciation of their efforts.

9.7.1 About the inventors of Apriori

Rakesh Agrawal is the President and Founder of the Data Insights Laboratories. He is also the President of the Professor Ram Kumar Memorial Foundation.

Rakesh is an innovator and thought leader driven by the desire to make the world better through scientific breakthroughs and by building practical working systems. He is the recipient of the ACM-SIGKDD Inaugural Innovation Award, ACM-SIGMOD Edgar F. Codd Innovations Award, VLDB 10-Yr Most Influential Paper Award. Scientific American has included him in its first list of 50 top scientists and technologists.

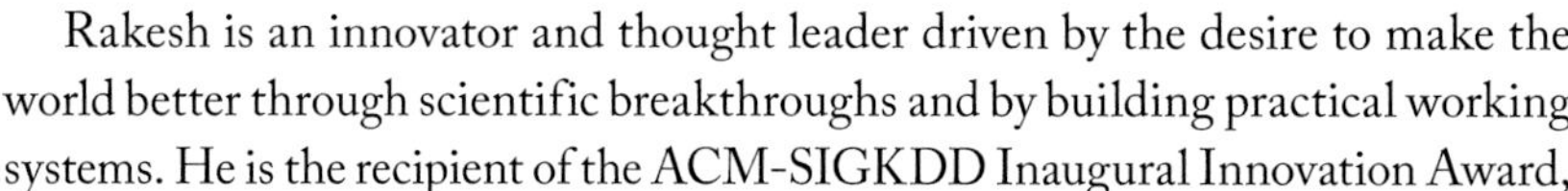

Until recently, Rakesh was a Microsoft Technical Fellow and headed the Search Labs in Microsoft Research. Prior to joining Microsoft in March 2006, Rakesh was an IBM Fellow and led the Quest group at the IBM Almaden Research Center. Earlier, he was with the Bell Laboratories, Murray Hill from 1983 to 1989. He also worked for three years at a leading Indian, namely Bharat Heavy Electricals Ltd. He received the M.S. and Ph.D. degrees in Computer Science from the University of Wisconsin-Madison in 1983. He also holds a B.E. degree in Electronics and Communication Engineering from IIT-Roorkee, and a two-year Post Graduate Diploma in Industrial Engineering from the National Institute of Industrial Engineering (NITIE), Bombay. Both IIT-Roorkee and NITIE have decorated him with their distinguished alumni awards.

Rakesh has been granted 83 patents. He has published more than 200 research papers, many of them considered seminal. He has written the 1st as well as the 2nd highest cited of all papers in the fields of databases and data mining (18th and 26th most cited across all computer science). Wikipedia lists one of his papers as one of the most influential database papers. His papers have been cited more than 80,000 times, with more than 25 of them receiving more than 500 citations each and three of them receiving 5,000 citations each (Google Scholar). He is the most cited author in the field of database systems and the 26th most cited author across all of Computer Science (Citeseer). His research has been featured in N.B.C., New York Times, and several other media channels.

It is rare that a researcher's work creates not only a product, but a whole new industry. IBM's data mining product, Intelligent Miner, grew straight out of Rakesh's research. IBM's introduction of Intelligent Miner and associated services created a new category of software and services. His research has been incorporated into many other commercial products, including DB2 Mining Extender, DB2 OLAP Server, WebSphere Commerce Server, and Microsoft Bing Search engine, as well as many research prototypes and applications.

To know more, please visit http://rakeshagrawal.org/

Ramakrishnan Srikant is a Distinguished Research Scientist at Google. His research interests include data mining, online advertising, and user modeling. He previously managed the Privacy Research group, part of the Intelligent Information Systems Research department at IBM's Almaden Research Center.

Srikant has published more than 30 research papers that have been extensively cited. He has been granted 25 patents. Dr Srikant was a key architect for the IBM Intelligent Miner, and contributed the association rules and sequential patterns modules to the product.

Srikant received the ACM SIGKDD Innovation Award (2006) for his seminal work on mining association rules and privacy preserving data mining, the 2002 ACM Grace Murray Hopper Award for his work on mining association rules, the VLDB 2004 Ten Year Best Paper Award, and the ICDE 2008 Influential Paper Award. He was named an IBM Research Division Master Inventor in 1999. He has received 2 Outstanding Technical Achievement Awards for his contributions to the Intelligent Miner, and an Outstanding Innovation Award for his work on Privacy in Data Systems.

Srikant received his M.S. and Ph.D. from the University of Wisconsin, Madison and his B. Tech. from the Indian Institute of Technology, Madras.

To know more, please visit http://www.rsrikant.com/index.html

9.7.2 Working of the Apriori algorithm

The Apriori algorithm has been named so on the basis that it uses prior knowledge of frequent itemset properties. This algorithm consists of two phases. In the first phase, the frequent itemsets, i.e., the itemsets that exceed the minimum required support are identified. In the second phase, the association rules meeting the minimum required confidence are identified from the frequent itemsets. The second phase is comparatively straight forward – therefore, the major focus of research in this field is to improve the first phase.

To understand the Apriori algorithm, let us follow the learn by example approach. We will first apply this algorithm on a simple database to illustrate its working and then we will go into detail to learn the concept more deeply.

Example: Let us consider an example of only five transactions and six items. We want to identify association rules with 50% support and 75% confidence with the Apriori algorithm. The transactions are given in Table 9.17.

Table 9.17 Transactions database

Transaction ID	Items
T1	Bread, Cornflakes, Eggs, Jam
T2	Bread, Cornflakes, Jam
T3	Bread, Milk, Tea
T4	Bread, Jam, Milk
T5	Cornflakes, Jam, Milk

For 50% support each frequent item must appear in at least three transactions. The first phase of the Apriori algorithm will be to find frequent itemsets.

Phase 1: Identification of frequent itemsets

It starts with the identification of candidate 1 itemsets, represented by C1 (one itemsets that may be frequent) and it is always the items in the stock which the store deals with, Here, we have six items, so C1 will be as shown below.

Table 9.18 Candidate one itemsets C1

Item
Bread
Cornflakes
Eggs
Milk
Jam
Tea

From Candidate 1 itemsets, frequent one-itemsets are represented by L1 and found by calculating the count of each candidate item and selecting only those counts which are equal to or more than the threshold limit of support, i.e., 3 in this case. Thus, frequent single itemsets, L1, will be as shown in Table 9.19.

Table 9.19 Frequent items L1

Item	*Frequency*
Bread	4
Cornflakes	3
Milk	3
Jam	4

Then, the candidate 2-itemsets or C2 are determined per the process illustrated below:
C2 = L1 JOIN L1.
The joining of L1 with itself has been illustrated below.

Bread		Bread
Cornflakes	JOIN	Cornflakes
Milk		Jam
Jam		Milk

In the Join operation the first step will be to perform a Cartesian product, i.e., to make all possible pairs between L1 and L1 as shown below.

Bread, Bread
Bread, Cornflakes
Bread, Milk
Bread, Jam
Cornflakes, Bread
Cornflakes, Cornflakes
Cornflakes, Milk
Cornflakes, Jam
Milk, Bread
Milk, Cornflakes
Milk, Milk
Milk, Jam
Jam, Bread
Jam, Cornflakes
Jam, Milk
Jam, Jam

Here, we have 16 possible pairs. In association mining, we are interested in item pairs, so the pairs having same itemsets (like Bread, Bread) need to be considered for removal from the list. Similarly, if we already have an item pair of Milk, Jam then there is no need to list item pair Jam, Milk so it will also be removed from the list.

Thus, to create C2 the following steps are applied:

- Perform Cartesian product of L1 with itself
- Some item pairs may have identical items. Keep just one. Remove the extras.
- Select only those item pairs in which items are in lexical order (so that if we have Milk, Jam then Jam, Milk should not appear).

Thus, the final C2 will be as shown below:

Bread, Cornflakes
Bread, Milk
Bread, Jam
Cornflakes, Milk
Cornflakes, Jam
Milk, Jam

The frequency of each of these item pairs will be found as shown in the table given below.

Table 9.20 Candidate item pairs C2

Item pairs	*Frequency*
(Bread, Cornflakes)	2
(Bread, Milk)	2
(Bread, Jam)	3

Contd.

Item pairs	*Frequency*
(Cornflakes, Milk)	1
(Cornflakes, Jam)	3
(Milk, Jam)	2

We therefore have only two frequent item pairs in L2 as shown in Table 9.21.

Table 9.21 Frequent two item pairs L2

Item pairs	*Frequency*
(Bread, Jam)	3
(Cornflakes, Jam)	3

Generation of C3 from L2

C3 is generated from L2 by carrying out a JOIN operation over L2 as shown below.

C3 = L2 JOIN L2

It will involve the same steps as performed for C2, but it has one important pre-requisite for Join, i.e., two items are joinable if their first item is common. In a generalized case:

Ck = Lk-1 JOIN Lk-1

And they are joinable if their first k-2 items are the same. So, in case of C3, the first item should be the same in L2, while in case of C2 there is no requirement of first item similarity because k-2 in the C2 case is 0.

From {Bread, Jam} and {Cornflakes, Jam} two frequent 2-itemsets, we do not obtain a candidate 3-itemset since we do not have two 2-itemsets that have the same first item. This completes the first phase of the Apriori algorithm.

Phase 2: Generation of rules

The two frequent 2-itemsets given above lead to the following possible rules.

Bread→Jam

Jam→Bread

Cornflakes→Jam

Jam→Cornflakes

The confidence of these rules is obtained by dividing the support for both items in the rule by the support for the item on the left-hand side of the rule. The confidence of the four rules therefore are 3/4 = 75%, 3/4 = 75%, 3/3 = 100%, and 3/4 = 75% respectively. Since all of them have a minimum 75% confidence, they all qualify.

In order to generalize the Apriori algorithm, let us define the representation of itemsets.

Representation of Itemsets

To generate C_k, let us first define L_{k-1}.

Let *l*1 and *l*2 be itemsets in list L_{k-1} and the notation *li*[*j*] refers to the *j*th item in *li*.

To generate C2 from L1, C2 is represented as C_k and L1 as L_{k-1}. Let us consider L1 as shown in Table 9.22, the description of each item list has been given below.

Table 9.22 L1 for generation of C2 having only one element in each list

L1	
1	represented as item list l1 and its item, i.e., 1 is represented as l1[1].
2	represented as item list l2 and its item, i.e., 2 is represented as l2[1].
3	represented as item list l3 and its item, i.e., 3 is represented as l3[1].
5	represented as item list l4 and its item, i.e., 5 is represented as l4[1].

Let us consider L2 given in Table 9.23.

Table 9.23 L2 for generation of C3 (i.e., K=3) having two elements in each list

L2	
1,2	represented as item list l1 and its item, 1 is represented as l1[1] or l1[k-2] and 2 is represented as l1[2] or l1[k-1]
4,5	represented as item list l2 and its item, 4 is represented as l2[1] or l2[k-2] and 5 is represented as l2[2] or l2[k-1]
2,6	represented as item list l3 and its item, 2 is represented as l3[1] or l3[k-2] and 6 is represented as l3[2] or l3[k-1]

Let us consider L3 given in Table 9.24.

Table 9.24 L3 for generation of C4 (i.e., K = 4) having three elements in each list

L3	
1,2,3	represented as item list l1 and its item, 1 is represented as l1[1] or l1[k-3] and 2 is represented as l1[2] or l1[k-2] and 3 is represented as l1[3] or l1[k-1]
1,2,5	represented as item list l2 and its item, 1 is represented as l2[1] or l2[k-3] and 2 is represented as l2[2] or l2[k-2] and 5 is represented as l2[3] or l2[k-1]
2,3,6	represented as item list l3 and its item, 2 is represented as l3[1] or l3[k-3] and 3 is represented as l3[2] or l3[k-2] and 6 is represented as l1[3] or l1[k-1]

Defining Phase 1: Identification of frequent itemsets

The Apriori algorithm uses an iterative approach and is also known as a level-wise search where k-itemsets are used to search (k+1) itemsets. First, the database is scanned to find the set of frequent 1-itemsets to accumulate the count for each item denoted as C1, known as candidate 1-itemset, and gathering those items satisfying minimum required support denoted as L1, frequent 1-itemset.

Next, L1 is used to find C2, candidate 2-itemsets and collecting those items that satisfy minimum support denoted as L2, frequent 2-itemsets; which is used to find C3, candidate 3-itemsets; which is used further to identify L3, frequent 3-itemsets and so on, until no more frequent k-itemsets can be found. This process has been illustrated in Figure 9.7. The finding of each L_k requires one full scan of the database.

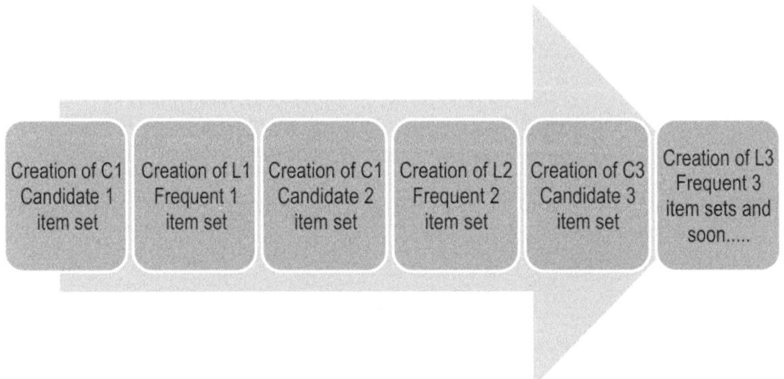

Figure 9.7 Process for identification of frequent itemsets

To proceed further, we have to generate C2 based on L1. To understand the generation of candidate itemsets, it is important to understand the representation of items in the item lists.

Step 3: Form candidate 2 itemset pair, i.e., C2.

C2 is created by joining L1 with itself by using following joining rule.

The join step

To find C_k, a set of candidate k-itemsets denoted as C_k is generated by joining L_{k-1} with itself. Let $l1$ and $l2$ be itemsets in L_{k-1}, the notation $li[j]$ refers to the jth item in li, e.g., $l1[k-2]$ refers to the second last item in $l1$. By convention, the prior assumption is that items within a transaction or itemset are sorted in lexicographic order. For the (k-1) itemset, li, this means that the items are sorted such that $li[1] < li[2] < : : : < li[k-1]$.

The join, L_{k-1} on L_{k-1}, is performed, where members of L_{k-1} are joinable if their first (k-2) items are in common.

That is, members $l1$ and $l2$ of L_{k-1} are joined if $(l1[1] = l2[1]) \wedge (l1[2] = l2[2]) \wedge : : : \wedge (l1[k-2] = l2[k-2]) \wedge (l1[k-1] < l2[k-1])$. The condition $l1[k-1] < l2[k-1]$ simply ensures that no duplicates are generated.

The resulting itemset formed by joining $l1$ and $l2$ is $l1[1], l1[2], : : : , l1[k-2], l1[k-1], l2[k-1]$.

Thus, there are three important points that make items of L_{k-1} joinable and these are as follows.

Point 1: The members of L_{k-1} *are joinable if their first (k-2) items are in common*

It means for C2 = L1 JOIN L1, with k = 2, there is no requirement for having the first common data item, because k-2 = 0.

For C3 = L2 JOIN L2, with k = 3, the first k-2, i.e., first 1 item should be the same in the itemset.

For C4 = L3 JOIN L3, having k = 4, the first k-2, i.e., first 2 items should be the same in the itemset.

For example, Let us verify whether L1 given in Table 9.25 is joinable or not, to create C2.

Table 9.25 L1

L1
1
2
3

C2 = L1 JOIN L1

*There is no requirement for first common item because k-2 = 0 in this case and all itemsets, i.e., 1, 2 and 3 are joinable.

Now, let us verify whether L2 given in Table 9.26 is joinable or not to create C3.

Table 9.26 L2

L2	
1,2	represented as item list l1 and its item, i.e.,1 is represented as l1[1] or l1[k-2] and 2 is represented as l1[2] or l1[k-1]
1,3	represented as item list l2 and its item, i.e.,1 is represented as l2[1] or l2[k-2] and 3 is represented as l2[2] or l2[k-1]
2,5	represented as item list l3 and its item, 2 is represented as l3[1] or l3[k-2] and 5 is represented as l3[2] or l3[k-1]

C3 = L2 JOIN L2 [Here, k = 3]

Itemsets are joinable only if their first k-2 itemsets, i.e., first 1 item is common. Thus, itemsets 1, 2 and 1, 3 are joinable as their first element is 1 in both the itemsets.

Now, let us identify that L3 given in Table 9.27 is joinable or not to create C4.

Table 9.27 L3

L3	
1,2,3	represented as item list l1 and its item, i.e.,1 is represented as l1[1] or l1[k-3] and 2 is represented as l1[2] or l1[k-2] and 3 is represented as l1[3] or l1[k-1]
1,2,5	represented as item list l2 and its item, i.e.,1 is represented as l2[1] or l2[k-3] and 2 is represented as l2[2] or l2[k-2] and 5 is represented as l2[5] or l2[k-1]
1,3,5	represented as item list l3 and its item, 1 is represented as l3[1] or l3[k-3] and 3 is represented as l3[2] or l3[k-2] and 5 is represented as l1[3] or l1[k-1]

C4 = L3 JOIN L3 [Here, k = 4]

Itemsets are joinable only if their first k-2 itemsets, i.e., first 2 items are common in this case. Thus, itemsets 1, 2, 3 and 1, 2, 5 are joinable as their first two elements, i.e., 1 and 2 are common in both the itemsets.

Point 2

In joinable item lists l1(k-1) should be less than l2(k-1), i.e., l1(k-1)<l2(k-1): this rule ensures that items in the itemset should be in lexicographic order and there is no repetition.

To understand this condition, let us find C2 for given L1 in Table 9.28.

Table 9.28 L1

L1
1
2
3
5

As discussed earlier, there is no requirement for the first common item, because k-2 = 0 in this case and all itemsets, i.e., 1, 2, 3 and 5 are joinable.

Thus, C2 = L1 JOIN L1 (the base for join is the Cartesian product of two itemsets) as illustrated in Table 9.29.

Table 9.29 Generation of C2

1		1
2	JOIN	2
3		3
5		5

Possible pairs for 1 are 11*, 12, 13&15

*11 will not appear in the final list because, here l1(1) = l2(1) and according to the joining rule l1(1) should be less than l2(1) [1 is not less than 1].

Thus, selected pairs for 1 are 12, 13 & 15

Possible pairs for 2 are 21*, 22*, 23 & 25

21 and 22 will not be selected because, l1(1) is not less than l2(1) [2 is not less than 1 and 2 is not less than 2].

Thus, selected pairs for 2 are 23 & 25

Possible pairs for 3 are 31*, 32*, 33* & 35

31, 32 and 33 will not be selected because , l1(1) is not less than l2(1) [3 is not less than 1; 3 is not less than 2; and 3 is not less than 3].

Thus, the selected pair for 3 is 35
Possible pairs for 5 are 51*, 52*, 53* & 55*
*No item will be selected because, l1(1) in not less than l2(1) [5 is not less than 1,2,3 and 5].
Thus, C2 will be as shown in Table 9.30.

Table 9.30 Generated C2

C2
12
13
15
23
25
35

Point 3

The resulting itemset formed by joining *l*1 and *l*2 is *l*1[1], *l*1[2], : : : , *l*1[*k*-2], *l*1[*k*-1], *l*2[*k*-1].

It means that, resulting itemset will contain all the items of the first item list, i.e., from item 1 to k-1 and last item of the second item list, i.e., k-1 item of second list, because other k-2 items of second list are already there, as they are common with first list.

To illustrate this point, let us identify C3 for given L2 in Table 9.31.

Table 9.31 L2

L2
1,2
1,3
2,3

Here, itemsets 1, 2 (first list) and 1, 3 (second list) are joinable. The final item list for C3 will be all items of first list and last item of second list.

Thus, C3 will be as shown in Table 9.32.

Table 9.32 C3

C3
1, 2, 3

Let us identify C4 for the given L3 in Table 9.33.

Table 9.33 L3

L3
1, 2, 4
1, 2, 5
1, 2, 7
1, 3, 6

Here, itemsets (1, 2, 4), (1, 2, 5) and (1, 2, 7) are joinable. The resultant C4 will be as shown in Table 9.34.

Table 9.34 C4

C4	
1, 2, 4, 5	Considering (1, 2, 4) as first list and (1, 2, 5) second list
1, 2, 4, 7	Considering (1, 2, 4) as first list and (1, 2, 7) second list
1, 2, 5, 7	Considering (1, 2, 5) as first list and (1, 2, 7) second list

Example

Let us understand the process for identification of frequent itemsets for the given transaction database of Table 9.35. The threshold value of support is 50% and confidence is 70%,

Table 9.35 Transaction database

T1	1,3,4
T2	2,3,5
T3	1,2,3,5
T4	2,5

Step 1

Create C1 candidate 1-itemsets. It is all the items in the transaction database as shown in Figure 9.11. Figure 9.8 also contains the frequency of each item.

Scan D → Count C_1

C_1	Count
1	2
2	3
3	3
4	1
5	3

Figure 9.8 C1, candidate 1-itemset and their count

Step 2

Create frequent 1-itemset, i.e., list of 1-itemsets whose frequency is more than the threshold value of support, i.e., 2 as shown in Figure 9.9.

C_1	Count		L_1
1	2		1
2	3	generate L_1	2
3	3	→	3
4	1		5
5	3		

Figure 9.9 L1, frequent 1-itemset

Candidate two itemsets, C2 with its frequency count as given in Table 9.36.

Table 9.36 Generation of C2

C2	Count
1, 2	1
1, 3	2
1, 5	1
2, 3	2
2, 5	3
3, 5	2

L2 is created by selecting those candidate pairs having support of 2 or more as shown in Table 9.37.

Table 9.37 Generation L2

L2
1, 3
2, 3
2, 5
3, 5

From the given L2, the next step will be to generate C3 by using L2 JOIN L2
Thus, C3 will be as shown in Table 9.38.

Table 9.38 Generation of C3

C3
2, 3, 5

The frequency of candidate three itemset 2, 3, 5 is 2, so C3 is qualified as L3. Thus, frequent three itemset is 2, 3, 5 for given dataset.

This is the final frequent item list and it completes the first phase of the Aproiri algorithm to find the frequent itemsets.

Phase 2: Generating association rules from frequent itemsets

To understand the process of generation of association rules from the frequent itemset, let us consider frequent itemset *l*.

- For each frequent itemset *l* generates all non-empty subsets of *l*.
- For every non-empty subset *s* of *l*, output the rule *s*→*l*-*s* and if the confidence of the rule is more than the threshold value of the confidence, then, this rule will be selected as the final association rule.

Let us generate the rules for the frequent itemset (2, 3, 5) represented as *l*. Here, non-empty subsets are {{2},{3},{5},{(2, 3)}, {(2, 5)},{(3, 5)}.

For every non-empty subset, the rule will be generated as follows.

2→3, 5 [Here, (2) is *s* and (3, 5) is *l*-*s*]
3→2, 5
5→2, 3
2, 3→5
2, 5→3
3, 5→2

The next step will be to calculate the confidence for each rule as shown below.

2→3, 5; Confidence = S(2∩3∩5) / S(2) = 2/3 = 0.67
3→2, 5; Confidence = S(2∩3∩5) / S(3) = 2/3 = 0.67
5→2, 3; Confidence = S(2∩3∩5) / S(5) = 2/3 = 0.67
2, 3→5; Confidence = S(2∩3∩5) / S(2∩3) = 2/2 = 1.0
2, 5→3; Confidence = S(2∩3∩5) / S(2∩5) = 2/3 = 0.67
3, 5→2; Confidence = S(2∩3∩5) / S(3∩5) = 2/2 = 1.0

Here, the minimum threshold for confidence is 70%, thus selected association rules are as follows.

2, 3→5;
3, 5→2;

The possible rules from 2, 3→5

It is intuitive to create two new rules as 2→5 and 3→5 from the given rule. Since 2, 3→5 has confidence more than the threshold limit, in this case, it is not implicit or guaranteed that 2→3 and 3→5 will have confidence more than the threshold limit as there is no correlation between denominator and quotient of both the rules as shown below.

Confidence of 2, 3→5 = S(2∩3∩5) / S(2∩3)
Confidence of 2→5 = S(2∩5) / S(2)

Same is the case for 3→5 as shown below.

Confidence of 3→5 = S(3∩5) / S(3)

Thus, the given high confidence rule 2, 3→5 does not implicitly state that 2→5 and 3→5 will have its confidence more than the threshold limit. Thus, there is a need to calculate the confidence of these rules as shown in Table 9.39.

Similarly, the given high confidence rule 3, 5→2 does not implicitly state that 3→2 and 5→2 will have its confidence more than the threshold limit. Thus, again there is a need to calculate the confidence of these rules as shown in Table 9.39.

Table 9.39 Calculation of confidence

Rule	*Confidence*
2, 3→5	1.0
2→5	S(2∩5) / S(2) = 3/3 = 1.0
3→5	S(2∩5) / S(3) = 3/3 = 1.0
3, 5→2	1.0
3→2	S(3∩2) / S(3) = 2/3 = 0.67
5→2	S(5∩2) / S(5) = 3/3 = 1.0

Thus, final rules having confidence more than the threshold limit, i.e., 75% are as follows.

Selected Association rules are
2, 3→5
2→5
3→5
3, 5→2
5→2

Apriori property

Apriori property states that all nonempty subsets of a frequent itemset must also be frequent.

It means all the subsets of the candidate itemset should be frequent otherwise that itemset will be removed from the candidate itemset. This step is called pruning of the candidate itemset and it will help to reduce the search space and to improve the performance of the algorithm because now the frequency of fewer item pairs need to be computed.

Lattice structure of frequent itemsets

The Apriori property that defines an itemset can be frequent only if all the subsets of the itemset are frequent. This can be illustrated by a lattice structure. Let us suppose there are four items A, B, C and D in the dataset. Then, the four-itemset ABCD will be frequent only if three itemsets

ABC, ABD, ACD and BCD are frequent. These three itemsets are frequent only if their subsets, i.e., AB, AC, BC, BD, AD and CD are frequent. And these two itemsets are frequent only if their subsets, i.e., A, B, C and D items are also frequent as shown in Figure 9.10.

From the lattice structure we can conclude that the Apriori algorithm works bottom up one level at a time, i.e., it first computes frequent 1-itemsets, the candidate 2-itemsets and then frequent 2-temsets and so on. The number of scans of the transaction database is equal to the maximum number of items in the candidate itemsets.

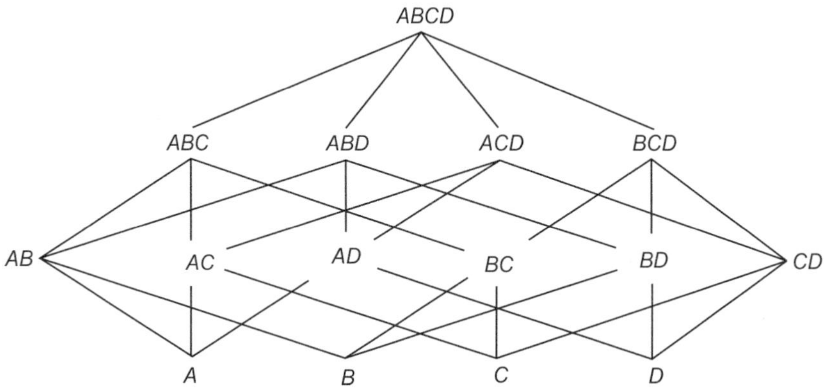

Figure 9.10 Lattice structure of frequent itemsets

For example, Apriori property states that for a frequent three itemset (1, 2, 3) all of its non empty subsets, i.e., (1, 2), (2, 3) and (1, 3) must be frequent, because, support of a superset is always less than or equal to support of its subset. It means that if (1, 3) is not frequent then (1, 2, 3) will also not be frequent.

This Apriori property also explains the significance of having first k-2 items common in a joining principle.

Let us suppose, we have L2 that is (1, 2) and (2, 3), then, one may suppose that it could produce a set (1,2,3) as C3. But as discussed earlier, (1, 2, 3) should be frequent only if all of its nonempty subsets, i.e., (1, 2), (2, 3) and (1, 3) are frequent. Here, as given in L2 (1, 3) is not frequent. So, itemsets given in L2 are considered as non joinable and the condition of having first k-2 items common is enforced to ensure it.

Now, what would happen if L2 has (1, 2) and (1, 3) but not (2, 3)? Then, according to the joining principle C3 will be generated as (1, 2, 3), but it will be discarded by the Apriori property because one of its nonempty subset, i.e., (2, 3) is not frequent. Thus, the combination of joining principle and apriori property make the whole process complete.

In conclusion, it is not the only joining principle that decides about the candidate itemsets, the joining principle can produce some extra items sets that can be removed further by the pruning or apriori property.

Example: Find association rules for the transaction data given in Table 9.40 for having support 15% and confidence 70%.

Table 9.40 Transaction database for identification of association rules

TID	*List of Items*
10	I1, I2, I5
20	I2, I4
30	I2, I3
40	I1, I2, I4
50	I1, I3
60	I2, I3
70	I1, I3
80	I1, I2, I3, I5
90	I1, I2, I4

The frequency count for each item, C1 is given in Table 9.41.

Table 9.41 C1

C1	*Count*
I1	6
I2	7
I3	5
I4	3
I5	2

All the items have frequency more than the specified support limit, thus all 1-item candidate sets given as C1 qualify as 1-item frequent itemset L1. The next step will be to generate C2.

C2 = L1 JOIN L1

The process of creation of C2 and L2 is illustrated in Figure 9.11.

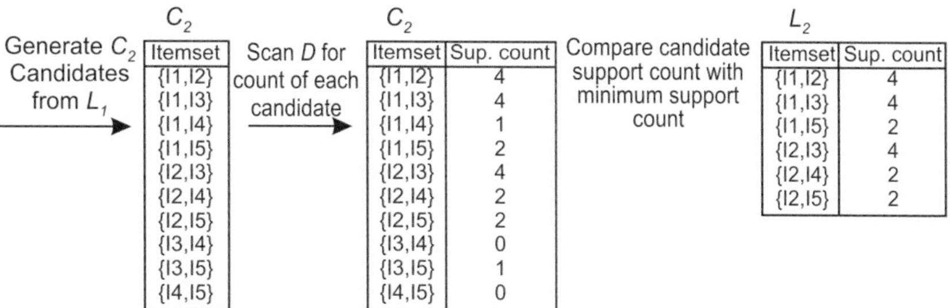

Figure 9.11 Generation of C2 and L2

From the given L2, C3 is generated by considering those item pairs whose first k-2 items, i.e. first 1 item is common as shown in Table 9.42.

Table 9.42 Generation of C3

C3
I1, I2, I3
I1, I2, I5
I1, I3, I5
I2, I3, I4
I2, I3, I5
I2, I4, I5

Before finding the frequency of each candidate item pair, the Apriori property will be applied to prune the candidate list.

Prune using the Apriori property: All nonempty subsets of a frequent itemset must also be frequent. Do any of the candidates have a subset that is not frequent? Let us check that as shown in Table 9.43.

Table 9.43 Pruning of candidate itemset C3

I1, I2, I3	The 2-item subsets of I1, I2 and I3 are (I1, I2), (I1, I3), and (I2, I3). All 2-item subsets are members of L2. Therefore, keep I1, I2 and I3 in C3.	Qualify
I1, I2, I5	The 2-item subsets of I1, I2 and I5 are (I1, I2), (I1, I5), and (I2, I5). All 2-item subsets are members of L2. Therefore, keep I1, I2 and I5 in C3.	Qualify
I1, I3, I5	The 2-item subsets of I1, I3 and I5 are (I1, I3), (I1, I5), and (I3, I5). Since, (I3, I5) is not a member of L2, and so it is not frequent. Therefore, remove I1, I3 and I5 from C3.	Does not qualify
I2, I3, I4	The 2-item subsets of I2, I3 and I4 are (I2, I3), (I2, I4), and (I3, I4). Since, (I3, I4) is not a member of L2, and so it is not frequent. Therefore, remove I2, I3 and I4 from C3.	Does not qualify
I2, I3, I5	The 2-item subsets of I2, I3 and I5 are (I2, I3), (I2, I5), and (I3, I5). Since, (I3, I5) is not a member of L2, so it is not frequent. Therefore, remove I2, I3 and I5 from C3.	Does not qualify
I2, I4, I5	The 2-item subsets of I2, I4 and I5 are (I2, I4), (I2, I5), and (I4, I5). Since, (I4, I5) is not a member of L2, it is not frequent. Therefore, remove I2, I4 and I5 from C3.	Does not qualify

Thus pruned C3 will be as shown in Table 9.44.

Table 9.44 Pruned C3

Pruned C3
I1, I2, I3
I1, I2, I5

It is important to note that pruning results into improving the efficiency of the algorithm, as in this case instead of finding the count of six three item pairs, there is a need to find the count for only 2 three item pairs (pruned list) which is a significant improvement in the efficiency of the system.

The process of creation of L3 from C3 by identifying those 3 itemsets that has a frequency more than or equal to the given value of threshold value of support, i.e., 2 has been shown below in Figure 9.12.

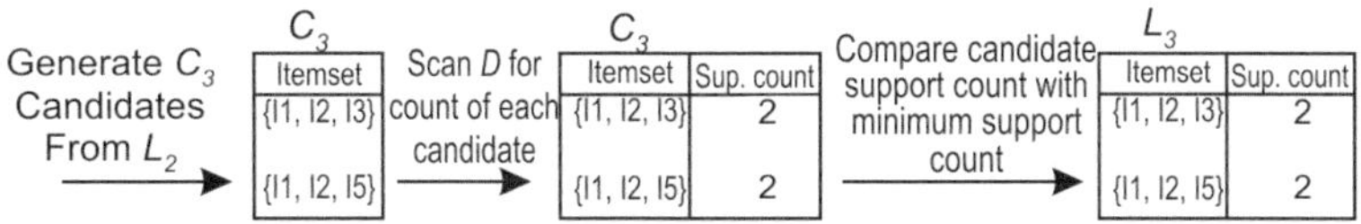

Figure 9.12 Generation of C3 and L3

The next step will be to generate C4 as shown below.

C4 = L3 JOIN L3

C4 will be I1, I2, I3 & I5, because 2 items are common as shown in Table 9.45.

Table 9.45 C4

C4
I1, I2, I3, I5

But this itemset is pruned by the Apriori property because its subset (I2, I3, I5) is not frequent as it is not present in L3. Thus, C4 is null and the algorithm terminates at this point, having found all of frequent itemsets as shown in Table 9.46.

Table 9.46 Pruned C4

C4
NULL

In this case, instead of finding the count of 1 four-item pair, pruning indicates that there is no need to find its count as all its subsets are not frequent.

With this, the first phase of the Apriori algorithm has been completed. Now the next phase to generate association rules from frequent itemsets will be performed.

Phase 2: Generating association rules from frequent itemsets

Let us apply this rule to frequent 3-itemsets (I1, I2, I3) and (I1, I2, I5) found in case of example given in Table 9.40.

For first frequent itemset (I1, I2, I3), non-empty subsets are {{I1},{I2},{I3},{(I1, I2)}, {(I1, I3)},{(I2, I3)}.

For every non-empty set, the rule will be generated as follows:

I1→I2, I3 [Here, (I1) is *s* and I2 and I3 are *l-s*]

I2→I1, I3

I3→I1, I2

I1, I2→I3

I1, I3→I2

I2, I3→I1

The next will be to calculate the confidence for each rule as shown below.

I1→I2, I3; Confidence = S(I1∩I2∩I3) / S(I1) = 2/6 = 0.3

I2→I1, I3; Confidence = S(I1∩I2∩I3) / S(I2) = 2/7 = 0.28

I3→I1, I2; Confidence = S(I1∩I2∩I3) / S(I3) = 2/5 = 0.4

I1, I2→I3; Confidence = S(I1∩I2∩I3) / S(I1∩I2) = 2/4 = 0.5

I1, I3→I2; Confidence = S(I1∩I2∩I3) / S(I1∩I3) = 2/4 = 0.5

I2, I3→I1; Confidence = S(I1∩I2∩I3) / S(I2∩I3) = 2/4 = 0.5

Since, the minimum threshold is 70%, there are no rules that qualify from the frequent itemset {1, 2, 3}.

Now, let us apply this rule to second frequent 3-itemset (I1, I2, I5). For this frequent itemset, non-empty subsets are {I1}, {I2}, {I5}, {(I1, I2)}, {(I1, I5)}, {(I2, I5)}.

For every non-empty set the rule will be generated as follows:

I1→I2, I5 (Here, (I1) is *s* and I2 and I5 are *l-s*]

I2→I1, I5

I5→I1, I2

I1, I2→I5

I1, I5→I2

I2, I5→I1

The next step will be to calculate the confidence for each rule as shown below.

I1→I2, I5; Confidence = S(I1∩I2∩I5) / S(I1) = 2/6 = 0.3

I2→I1, I5; Confidence = S(I1∩I2∩I5) / S(I2) = 2/7 = 0.28

I5→I1, I2; Confidence = S(I1∩I2∩I5) / S(I5) = 2/2 = 1

I1, I2→I5; Confidence = S(I1∩I2∩I5) / S(I1∩I2) = 2/4 = 0.5

I1, I5→I2; Confidence = S(I1∩I2∩I5) / S(I1∩I5) = 2/2 = 1

I2, I5→I1; Confidence = S(I1∩I2∩I5) / S(I2∩I5) = 2/2 = 1

Now, there are three rules whose confidence is more than minimum threshold value of 70%, and these rules are as follows:

I5→I1, I2

I1, I5→I2

I2, I5→I1

The possible rules from I5→I1, I2

It is intuitive to create two new rules as I5→I1 and I5→I2 from the given rule.

Since, I5→I1, I2 has confidence more than threshold limit, so it is implicit that I5→I1 and I5→I2 will also have their confidence more than the threshold limit as justified below.

Confidence of I5→I1,I2 = S(I5∩I1∩I2) / S(I5)

Confidence of I5→I1 = S(I5∩I1) / S(I5)

Since, Support of subset (I5, I1) will be more than or equal to Support of superset (I5, I1, I2), it is implicit that Confidence of I5→I1 will be more than equal to Confidence of I5→I1, I2.

Similarly, Confidence of I5→I2 = S(I5∩I2) / S(I5) will be more than equal to Confidence of I5→I1,I2.

Thus, I5→I1 and I5→I2 will also have their confidence more than the threshold limit.

Discussing possible rules from I2, I5→I1

It is intuitive to create two new rules as I2→I1 and I5→I1 from the given rule. I2, I5→I1 has confidence more than the threshold limit, but it is not implicit or guaranteed that I2→I1 and I5→I1 will have their confidence more than the threshold limit as explained below.

Confidence of I2, I5→I1 = S(I2∩I5∩I1) / S(I2∩I5)

Confidence of I2→I1 = S(I2∩I1) / S(I2)

Here, there is no correlation between denominator and quotient of both the rules, so it is not implicit that this rule will also have its confidence more than the threshold.

Similarly, the Confidence of I5→I1 = S(I5∩I1) / S(I5)

Again, there is no correlation between denominator and quotient of this rule with I2, I5→I1 rules, so it is not implicit that this rule will also have its confidence more than the threshold.

The given high confidence rule I2, I5→I1 does not implicitly state that I2→I1 and I5→I1 will have their confidence more than the threshold limit. Thus, there is a need to calculate the confidence of these rules.

Similarly, the given high confidence rule I1, I5→I2 does not implicitly state that I1→I2 and I5→I2 will have their confidence more than the threshold limit. Thus, again there is a need to calculate the confidence of these rules.

The process of generation of all association rules from I5→I1, I2; I2, I5→I1 and I1, I5→I2 rules has been illustrated in Table 9.47.

Table 9.47 Generation of association rules

Association Rule	*Discussion*	*Confidence*	*More than threshold limit Or Not*
I5→I1, I2	Already identified	1.0	Yes
I5→I1	Implicit	No need to calculate it will be more than or equal to I5→I1, I2	Yes
I5→I2	Implicit	No need to calculate it will be more than or equal to I5→I1, I2	Yes

Contd.

Association Rule	Discussion	*Confidence*	*More than threshold limit Or Not*
I2, I5→I1	Already identified	1.0	Yes
I2→I1	Not found earlier, confidence need to be calculated	Confidence of I2→I1 = S(I2∩I1) / S(I1) = 4/6 = 67%	No
I5→I1	Already found from I5→I1, I2 given in row 2	No need to calculate it will be more than or equal to I5→I1, I2	Yes (Already listed)
I1, I5→I2	Already identified	1.0	Yes
I1→I2	Not found earlier, so confidence needs to be calculated	Confidence of I1→I2 = S(I2∩I1) / S(I2) = 4/7 = 57%	No
I5→I2	Already found from I5→I1, I2 given in row 3		Yes (Already listed)

During generation of the final rules, it is important to look at L2 because there may be some frequent 2-itemsets that have not appeared in three itemsets and may be left out. The frequent 2 itemsets generated earlier have been reproduced in Table 9.48 from Figure 9.10.

Table 9.48 Frequent 2-itemsets, i.e., L2

L2	Discussion	*New Rules Identified*
I1, I2	This item pair has already been covered as it is a sub set of I5 ›I1, I2; I2, I5→I1 and I1, I5→I2 rules discussed in Table 9.47.	NIL
I1, I3	This item pair has not already been covered. So, confidence needs to be calculated for possible rules of this item pair I1, I3. I1→I3, Confidence = S(I1∩I3) / S(I1) = 4/6 = 66% I3→I1, Confidence = S(I3∩I1) / S(I3) = 4/5 = 80%	Since, I3→I1 has confidence more than the threshold limit. So, the new rule identified is I3→I1.
I1, I5	This item pair has already been covered as it is a sub set of I5→I1, I2; I2, I5→I1 and I1, I5→I2 rules.	NIL
I2, I3	This item pair has not already been covered. So, confidence needs to be calculated for possible rules of this item pair I2, I3. I2→I3, Confidence = S(I2∩I3) / S(I2) = 4/7 = 57% I3→I2, Confidence = S(I2∩I3) / S(I3) = 4/5 = 80%	I3→I2
I2, I4	This item pair has not already been covered. So, confidence needs to be calculated for possible rules of this item pair I2, I4. I2→I4, Confidence = S(I2 I4) / S(I2) = 2/7 = 28% I4→I2, Confidence = S(I4 I2) / S(I4) = 2/3 = 66%	NIL, because the confidence of both the rules is less than threshold limit; so, no new rule has been found.
I2, I5	This item pair has already been covered as it is a sub set of I5→I1, I2; I2, I5→I1 and I1, I5→I2 rules.	NIL

Here, we have identified two new rules by considering L2 and these are I3→I1 and I3→I2, both of which has its confidence more than threshold limit of 70%.

The final association rules having support more than 20% and confidence more than 70% are given below.

I5→I1, I2

I2, I5→I1

I1, I5→I2

I5→I1

I5→I2

I3→I1

I3→I2.

Example: Consider a store having 16 items for sale as listed in Table 9.49. Now consider the 25 transactions on the sale of these items as given in Table 9.50. As usual, each row in the table represents one transaction, that is, the items bought by one customer. In this example, we want to find association rules that satisfy the requirement of 25% support and 70% confidence.

Table 9.49 List of grocery items

Item number	Item name
1	Biscuit
2	Bournvita
3	Bread
4	Butter
5	Coffee
6	Cornflakes
7	Chocolate
8	Curd
9	Eggs
10	Jam
11	Juice
12	Milk
13	Rice
14	Soap
15	Sugar
16	Tape

In Table 9.50 showing 25 transactions, we list the names of items of interest but it would be more storage efficient to use item numbers.

Table 9.50 Transaction data

TID	Items
1	Biscuit, Bournvita, Butter, Cornflakes, Tape
2	Bournvita, Bread, Butter, Cornflakes
3	Butter, Coffee, Chocolate, Eggs, Jam
4	Bournvita, Butter, Cornflakes, Bread, Eggs
5	Bournvita, Bread, Coffee, Chocolate, Eggs
6	Jam, Sugar
7	Biscuit, Bournvita, Butter, Cornflakes, Jam
8	Curd, Jam, Sugar
9	Bournvita, Bread, Butter, Coffee, Cornflakes
10	Bournvita, Bread, Coffee, Chocolate, Eggs
11	Bournvita, Butter, Eggs
12	Bournvita, Butter, Cornflakes, Chocolate, Eggs
13	Biscuit, Bournvita, Bread
14	Bread, Butter, Coffee, Chocolate, Eggs
15	Coffee, Cornflakes
16	Chocolate
17	Chocolate, Curd, Eggs
18	Biscuit, Bournvita, Butter, Cornflakes
19	Bournvita, Bread, Coffee, Chocolate, Eggs
20	Butter, Coffee, Chocolate, Eggs
21	Jam, Sugar, Tape
22	Bournvita, Bread, Butter, Cornflakes
23	Coffee, Chocolate, Eggs, Jam, Juice
24	Juice, Milk, Rice
25	Rice, Soap, Sugar

Computing C1

All 16 items are candidate items for a frequent single-itemset. So, all the items listed in Table 9.49 will act as C1.

Computing L1

To find the frequent single itemset, we have to scan the whole database to count the number of times each of the 16 items has been sold. Scanning transaction database only once, we first set up the list of items and one transaction at a time, update the count of every item that appears in that transaction as shown in Table 9.51.

Table 9.51 Frequency count for all items

Item no.	*Item name*	*Frequency*
1	Biscuit	4
2	Bournvita	13
3	Bread	9
4	Butter	12
5	Coffee	9
6	Cornflakes	9
7	Chocolate	10
8	Curd	2
9	Eggs	11
10	Jam	6
11	Juice	2
12	Milk	1
13	Rice	2
14	Soap	1
15	Sugar	4
16	Tape	2

The items that have the necessary support (25% support in 25 transactions) must occur in at least 7 transactions. The frequent 1-itemset or L1 is now given in Table 9.52.

Table 9.52 The frequent 1-itemset or L1

Item	*Frequency*
Bournvita	13
Bread	9
Butter	12

Contd.

Item	Frequency
Coffee	9
Cornflakes	9
Chocolate	10
Eggs	11

Computing C2

C2 = L1 JOIN L1

This will produce 21 pairs as listed in Table 9.53. These 21 pairs are the only ones worth investigating since they are the only ones that could be frequent.

Table 9.53 The 21 candidate 2-itemsets or C2

{Bournvita, Bread}
{Bournvita, Butter}
{Bournvita, Coffee}
{Bournvita, Cornflakes}
{Bournvita, Chocolate}
{Bournvita, Eggs}
{Bread, Butter}
{Bread, Coffee}
{Bread, Cornflakes}
{Bread, Chocolate}
{Bread, Eggs}
{Butter, Coffee}
{Butter, Cornflakes}
{Butter, Chocolate}
{Butter, Eggs}
{Coffee, Cornflakes}
{Coffee, Chocolate}
{Coffee, Eggs}
{Cornflakes, Chocolate}
{Cornflakes, Eggs}
{Chocolate, Eggs}

Computing L2

This step is the most resource intensive step. We scan the transaction database once and look at each transaction and find out which of the candidate pairs occur in that transaction. This then requires scanning the list C2 for every pair of items that appears in the transaction that is being scanned. Table 9.54 presents the number of times each candidate 2-itemset appears in the transaction database example given in Table 9.50.

Table 9.54 Frequency count of candidate 2-itemsets

Candidate 2-itemset	*Frequency*
{Bournvita, Bread}	8
{Bournvita, Butter}	9
{Bournvita, Coffee}	4
{Bournvita, Cornflakes}	8
{Bournvita, Chocolate}	4
{Bournvita, Eggs}	6
{Bread, Butter}	5
{Bread, Coffee}	5
{Bread, Cornflakes}	3
{Bread, Chocolate}	4
{Bread, Eggs}	5
{Butter, Coffee}	4
{Butter, Cornflakes}	8
{Butter, Chocolate}	4
{Butter, Eggs}	6
{Coffee, Cornflakes}	2
{Coffee, Chocolate}	7
{Coffee, Eggs}	7
{Cornflakes, Chocolate}	1
{Cornflakes, Eggs}	2
{Chocolate, Eggs}	9

From this list we can find the frequent 2-itemsets or the set L2 by selecting only those item pairs from Table 9.54 given above, having a frequency equal to or more than 7. Therefore the list of frequent-2 itemsets or L2 is given in Table 9.55. Usually L2 is smaller than L1 but in this example they both have seven itemsets and each member of L1 appears as a subset of some member of L2. This is unlikely to be true when the number of items is large.

Table 9.55 The frequent 2-itemsets or L2

Frequent 2-itemset	Frequency
{Bournvita, Bread}	8
{Bournvita, Butter}	9
{Bournvita, Cornflakes}	8
{Butter, Cornflakes}	8
{Coffee, Chocolate}	7
{Coffee, Eggs}	7
{Chocolate, Eggs}	9

Computing C3

C3 = L2 JOIN L2 (First item should be common)

To find the candidate 3-itemsets or C3, we combine the appropriate frequent 2-itemsets from L2 (these must have the same first item) and obtain four such itemsets as given in Table 9.56.

Table 9.56 Candidate 3-itemsets or C3

Candidate 3-itemset
{Bournvita, Bread, Butter}
{Bournvita, Bread, Cornflakes}
{Bournvita, Butter, Cornflakes}
{Coffee, Chocolate, Eggs}

Pruning C3

Before processing further to calculate the frequency of each 3-item pairs, it is important to apply the Apriori property to prune the candidate 3-itemsets as shown in Table 9.57.

Table 9.57 Pruning of candidate itemset C3

Candidate Item Pair	*Discussion*	*Qualify or Not*
{Bournvita, Bread, Butter}	Its subsets are (Bournvita, Bread), (Bournvita, Butter) and (Bread, Butter). Out of these subsets (Bread, Butter) is not frequent as it is not in L2 given in Table 9.55. Thus, {Bournvita, Bread, Butter} will be removed from C3.	Not Qualified, so will be pruned
{Bournvita, Bread, Cornflakes}	Its subsets are (Bournvita, Bread), (Bournvita, Cornflakes) and (Bread, Cornflakes). Out of these subsets, (Bread, Cornflakes) is not frequent as it is not in L2. Thus, {Bournvita, Bread, Cornflakes} will be removed from C3.	Not Qualified, so will be pruned
{Bournvita, Butter, Cornflakes}	Its subsets are (Bournvita, Butter), (Bournvita, Cornflakes) and (Butter, Cornflakes). Here all subsets are frequent as they are in L2. Thus, {Bournvita, Butter, Cornflakes} will be retained in C3.	Qualified
{Coffee, Chocolate, Eggs}	Its subsets are (Coffee, Chocolate), (Coffee, Eggs) and (Chocolate, Eggs). Here, all subsets are frequent as they are in L2. Thus, {Coffee, Chocolate, Eggs} will be retained in C3.	Qualified

Thus, pruned C3 will be as shown in Table 9.58.

Table 9.58 Pruned candidate itemset C3

{Bournvita, Butter, Cornflakes}
{Coffee, Chocolate, Eggs}

As observed, this pruning step has reduced the candidate items from 4 to 2 and it improves the performance of the algorithm. Table 9.59 shows candidate 3-itemsets or C3 and their frequencies.

Table 9.59 Candidate 3-itemsets or C3 and their frequencies

Candidate 3-itemset	*Frequency*
{Bournvita, Butter, Cornflakes}	8
{Coffee, Chocolate, Eggs}	7

Computing L3

Table 9.60 now presents the frequent 3-itemsets or L3. Note that only one member of L2 is not a subset of any itemset in L3. That 2-itemset is {Bournvita, Bread}.

Table 9.60 The frequent 3-itemsets or L3

Frequent 3-itemset	*Frequency*
{Bournvita, Butter, Cornflakes}	8
{Coffee, Chocolate, Eggs}	7

Computing C4

C4 = L3 JOIN L3 (First two items should be common)

Since, no first two items are common, thus, C4 is null.

This is the end of frequent itemset generation since there cannot be any candidate 4-itemsets.

Finding the rules

The rules obtained from frequent 3-itemsets would always include some rules that we could obtain from L2 embedded in them, but some additional rules will be obtainable from itemsets in L2 which are not subsets of itemsets in L3, for example, {Bournvita, Bread} in this case.

Here, the frequent itemset is {Bournvita, Butter, Cornflakes} whose resulting subsets are as followed:

{Bournvita},{Butter},{Cornflakes},{Bournvita, Butter},{Butter, Cornflakes},{Bournvita, Cornflakes} [represented by *s*, and the superset or whole list {Bournvita, Butter, Cornflakes} is represented as *l*, and the rules will be generated in the form of *s*→*l*-*s*].

The rules generated from {Bournvita, Butter, Cornflakes} are as follows.

Bournvita→Butter, Cornflakes
Butter→Bournvita, Cornflakes
Cornflakes→Bournvita, Butter
Bournvita, Butter→Cornflakes
Bournvita, Cornflakes→Butter
Butter, Cornflakes→Bournvita

Now, let us calculate the confidence of these rules as shown in Table 9.61.

Table 9.61 Confidence of association rules from {Bournvita, Butter, Cornflakes}

Rule	*Support of Both together*	*Frequency of Antecedent LHS (Refer to Table 9.52 and 9.55)*	*Confidence*	*Whether Confidence is more than threshold limit or not*
Bournvita→Butter, Cornflakes	8	13	8/13 = 0.61	No
Butter→Bournvita, Cornflakes	8	12	8/12 = 0.67	No
Cornflakes→Bournvita, Butter	8	9	8/9 = 0.89	Yes
Bournvita, Butter→Cornflakes	8	9	8/9 = 0.89	Yes
Bournvita, Cornflakes→Butter	8	8	8/8 = 1.0	Yes
Butter, Cornflakes→Bournvita	8	8	8/8 = 1.0	Yes

We also have two rules from L2 for a frequent item pair {Bournvita, Bread} let us calculate its confidence as shown in Table 9.62.

Table 9.62 Confidence of association rules from {Bournvita, Bread}

Rule	*Support of Both together*	*Frequency of Antecedent LHS (Refer to Tables 9.52 and 9.55)*	*Confidence*	*Whether Confidence is more than threshold limit or not*
Bournvita →Bread	8	13	8/13 = 0.61	No
Bread→Bournvita	8	9	8/9 = 0.89	Yes

Thus, from this discussion we have found out five rules having confidence more than 70% as shown below in Table 9.63.

Table 9.63 Identified rules from {Bournvita, Butter, Cornflakes} having confidence more than 70%

Cornflakes→Bournvita, Butter
Bournvita, Butter→Cornflakes
Bournvita, Cornflakes→Butter
Butter, Cornflakes→Bournvita
Bread→Bournvita

Now, let us find all possible rules from these identified rules as shown in Table 9.64.

Table 9.64 List of all possible rules from rules given in Table 9.61

Rules	*Discussion*	*Rules having confidence more than the threshold value*
Cornflakes→ Bournvita, Butter	It has confidence 0.89 as discussed in Table 9.61. [Formula = S (Cornflakes, Bournvita, Butter) / S(Cornflakes)]	Cornflakes→ Bournvita, Butter
Cornflakes→ Bournvita	It is intuitive that this rule will have confidence greater than the threshold limit as its formula is S (Cornflakes, Bournvita) / S(Cornflakes). Since, support of subset, i.e, Cornflakes, Bournvita, should be equal to or more than superset, Cornflakes, Bournvita, Butter so this rule qualifies. (Resulting confidence = 0.89)	Cornflakes→ Bournvita

Contd.

Rules	*Discussion*	*Rules having confidence more than the threshold value*
Cornflakes→Butter	It is also intuitive that this rule will have confidence greater than the threshold limit as its formula is S (Cornflakes, Butter) / S(Cornflakes). Since, support of subset, i.e, Cornflakes, Butter should be equal to or more than superset, Cornflakes, Bournvita, Butter so this rule qualifies. (Resulting confidence = 0.89)	Cornflakes→ Butter
Bournvita, Butter→ Cornflakes	It has confidence 0.89 as shown in Table 9.61. [Formula = S (Bournvita, Butter, Cornflakes) / S(Bournvita, Butter)]	Bournvita, Butter→ Cornflakes
Bournvita→ Cornflakes	It is not intuitive that this rule will have confidence more than the threshold limit as its formula is S (Bournvita, Cornflakes) / S(Bournvita). So, let us calculate its confidence. Confidence= S (Bournvita, Cornflakes) / S(Bournvita) = 8/13 = 0.61. This rule has confidence less than threshold limit, so it will be discarded.	Discarded
Butter→ Cornflakes	It is not intuitive that this rule will have confidence more than the threshold limit as its formula is S (Butter, Cornflakes)/S(Butter). So, let us calculate its confidence. Confidence = S (Butter, Cornflakes) / S(Butter) = 8/12 = 0.67 This rule has confidence less than threshold limit, so it will be discarded.	Discarded
Bournvita, Cornflakes→Butter	It has confidence 1.0 as shown in Table 9.61.	Bournvita, Cornflakes→ Butter
Bournvita→Butter	It is not intuitive that this rule will have confidence more than the threshold limit. So, let us calculate its confidence. Confidence = S (Bournvita, Butter) / S(Bournvita) = 9/13 = 0.69 This rule has confidence less than threshold limit, so it will be discarded.	Discarded
Cornflakes→Butter	It is not intuitive that this rule will have confidence more than the threshold limit. So, let us calculate its confidence. Confidence = S (Cornflakes, Butter) / S(Cornflakes) = 8/9 = 0.88 This rule has confidence more than threshold limit, so it will be selected.	Cornflakes→ Butter

Contd.

Rules	*Discussion*	*Rules having confidence more than the threshold value*
Butter, Cornflakes→ Bournvita	It has confidence 1.0 as shown in Table 9.61.	Butter, Cornflakes→ Bournvita
Butter→ Bournvita	It is not intuitive that this rule will have confidence more than the threshold limit. So, let us calculate its confidence. Confidence = S (Butter, Bournvita) / S(Butter) = 8/12 = 0.67 This rule has confidence less than threshold limit, so it will be discarded.	Discarded
Cornflakes→ Bournvita	It is not intuitive that this rule will have confidence more than the threshold limit. So, let us calculate its confidence. Confidence = S (Cornflakes, Bournvita) / S(Cornflakes) = 8/9 = 0.89 This rule has confidence more than threshold limit, so it will be selected.	Cornflakes→ Bournvita

Similarly, we will examine the other 3-itemset {Coffee, Chocolate, Eggs}.

Table 9.65 Confidence of association rules from {Coffee, Chocolate, Eggs}

Rule	*Support*	*Frequency of LHS (Antecedent)*	*Confidence*
Coffee→Chocolate, Eggs	7	9	0.78
Chocolate→Coffee, Eggs	7	10	0.70
Eggs→Coffee, Chocolate	7	11	0.64
Chocolate, Eggs→Coffee	7	9	0.78
Coffee, Eggs→Chocolate	7	7	1.0
Coffee, Chocolate→Eggs	7	7	1.0

Again, the confidence of all these rules, except the third, is higher than 70%, and so five of them also qualify.

List of all possible rules for three item pairs {Coffee, Chocolate, Eggs} has been explained in Table 9.66, given below.

Table 9.66 List of all possible rules from rules given in Table 9.65

Rules	*Discussion*	*Rules having confidence more than the threshold value*
Coffee→Chocolate, Eggs	It has confidence of 0.78 as shown in Table 9.65.	Coffee→Chocolate, Eggs
Coffee→Eggs	It is intuitive from rule Coffee→Chocolate, Eggs	Coffee→Eggs
Chocolate→Coffee, Eggs	It has confidence of 0.70 as shown in Table 9.65.	Chocolate→Coffee, Eggs
Chocolate→Coffee	It is intuitive from rule Chocolate→Coffee, Eggs	Chocolate→Coffee
Chocolate→Eggs	It is intuitive from rule Chocolate→Coffee, Eggs	Chocolate→Eggs
Chocolate, Eggs→Coffee	It has confidence of 0.78 as shown in Table 9.65.	Chocolate, Eggs→Coffee
Chocolate→Coffee	It is non intuitive, so let us calculate its confidence. Confidence = S(Chocolate, Coffee) / S(Coffee) = 7/9 = 0.77 Since, confidence is more than the threshold so this rule will be selected.	Chocolate→Coffee
Eggs→Coffee	It is non intuitive, so let us calculate its confidence. Confidence = S(Eggs, Coffee) / S(Eggs) = 7/11 = 0.64 Since, confidence is less than the threshold so this rule will be discarded.	Discarded
Coffee, Eggs→Chocolate	It has confidence 1.0 as discussed in Table 9.65.	Coffee, Eggs→Chocolate
Coffee→Chocolate	It is non intuitive, so let us calculate its confidence. Confidence = S(Coffee, Chocolate) / S(Coffee) =7/9 = 0.77 Since, confidence is more than the threshold so this rule will be selected.	Coffee→Chocolate
Eggs→Chocolate	It is non intuitive, so let us calculate its confidence. Confidence = S(Eggs, Chocolate) / S(Eggs) = 9/11= 0.81 Since, confidence is more than the threshold so this rule will be selected.	Eggs→Chocolate

Contd.

Rules	*Discussion*	*Rules having confidence more than the threshold value*
Coffee, Chocolate→Eggs	It has confidence 1.0 as shown in Table 9.65.	Coffee, Chocolate→Eggs
Coffee→Eggs	This rule is non intuitive, but it is already selected as given in row 2 from rule Coffee→Chocolate, Eggs	Coffee→Eggs
Chocolate→Eggs	This rule is non intuitive, but it is already selected as given in row 5 from rule Chocolate→Coffee, Eggs	Chocolate→Eggs

Thus, all association mining rules for the given database and having confidence of more than 70% are listed in Table 9.67.

Table 9.67 All association rules for the given database

Rule No.	*Rule*	*Confidence*
1	Bread→Bournvita	0.89
2	Cornflakes→ Bournvita, Butter	0.89
3	Cornflakes→ Bournvita	0.89
4	Cornflakes→ Butter	0.89
5	Bournvita, Butter→ Cornflakes	0.89
6	Bournvita, Cornflakes→ Butter	1
7	Cornflakes→ Butter	0.89
8	Butter, Cornflakes→ Bournvita	1
9	Coffee→Chocolate, Eggs	0.78
10	Coffee→Chocolate	0.78
11	Coffee→Eggs	0.78
12	Chocolate→Coffee, Eggs	0.7
13	Chocolate→Coffee	0.7
14	Chocolate→Eggs	0.9
15	Chocolate, Eggs→Coffee	1
16	Coffee, Eggs→Chocolate	1
17	Eggs→Chocolate	0.82
18	Coffee, Chocolate→Eggs	1

9.8 Closed and Maximal Itemsets

To further improve the efficiency of the association mining process, frequent itemsets can be divided into closed and maximal itemsets.

A frequent closed itemset is a frequent itemset X such that there exists no superset of X with the same support count as X.

A frequent itemset Y is maximal if it is not a proper subset of any other frequent itemset. Therefore a maximal itemset is a closed itemset, but a closed itemset is not necessarily a maximal itemset as shown in Figure 9.13.

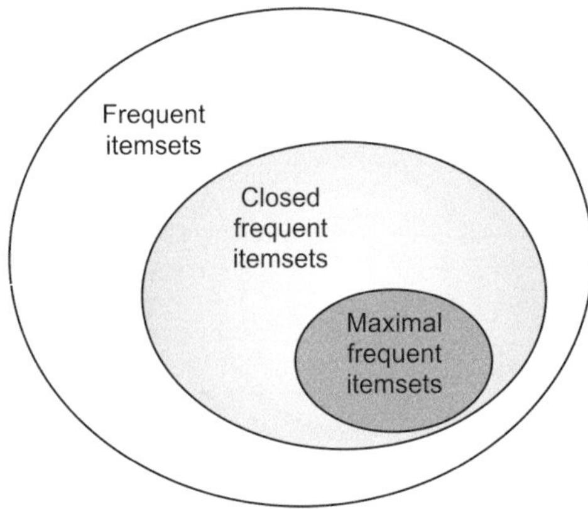

Figure 9.13 Illustration of closed and maximal frequent itemsets

The concept of Closed and maximal itemsets have been explained with an example database.

Example: Consider the transaction database in Table 9.68 with minimum support required to be 40%.

Table 9.68 A transaction database to illustrate closed and maximal itemsets

100	Butter, Curd, Jam
200	Butter, Curd, Jam, Muffin
300	Curd, Jam, Nuts
400	Butter, Jam, Muffin, Nuts
500	Muffin, Nuts

There are a total of 14 frequent itemsets as shown in Table 9.69 and the closed and maximal itemsets for the given database have also been presented there.

Table 9.69 Frequent itemsets for the database in Table 9.68

Itemset	*Support*	*Closed?*	*Maximal?*	*Both?*
{Butter}	3	No, there exists a superset of Butter with the same support 3, i.e., {Butter, Jam}	No, it is a proper subset of another frequent itemset, i.e, {Butter, Curd, Jam}	No
{Curd}	3	No, there exists a superset of Curd with the same support 3, {Curd, Jam}	No, it is a proper subset of another frequent itemset, i.e, {Butter, Curd, Jam}	No
{Jam}	4	Yes, there exists no superset of Jam with the same support 4	No, it is a proper subset of another frequent itemset, i.e, {Butter, Curd, Jam}	No
{Muffin}	3	Yes, there exists no superset of Muffin with the same support 3	No, it is a proper subset of another frequent itemset, i.e, {Muffin, Nuts}	No
{Nuts}	3	Yes, there exists no superset of Nuts with the same support 3	No, it is a proper subset of another frequent itemset, i.e, {Muffin, Nuts}	No
{Butter, Curd}	2	No, there exists a superset of Butter, Jam with the same support 2, i.e., {Butter, Curd, Jam}	No, it is a proper subset of another frequent itemset, i.e, {Butter, Curd, Jam}	No
{Butter, Jam}	3	Yes, there exists no superset of Butter, Jam with the same support 3	No, it is a proper subset of another frequent itemset, i.e, {Butter, Curd, Jam}	No
{Butter, Muffin}	2	No, there exists a superset of Butter, Muffin with the same support 2, i.e., {Butter, Jam, Muffin}	No, it is a proper subset of another frequent itemset, i.e, {Butter, Jam, Muffin}	No
{Curd, Jam}	3	Yes, there exists no superset of Curd, Jam with the same support 3	No, it is a proper subset of another frequent itemset, i.e, {Butter, Curd, Jam}	No
{Jam, Muffin}	2	No, there exists a superset of Jam, Muffin with the same support 2, i.e., {Butter, Jam, Muffin}	No, it is a proper subset of another frequent itemset, i.e, {Butter, Jam, Muffin}	No
{Jam, Nuts}	2	Yes, there exists no superset of Jam, Nuts with the same support 2	Yes, it is not proper subset of any other frequent itemset	Yes

Contd.

Itemset	Support	Closed?	Maximal?	Both?
{Muffin, Nuts}	2	Yes, there exists no superset of Muffin, Nuts with the same support 2	Yes, it is not proper subset of any other frequent itemset	Yes
{Butter, Curd, Jam}	2	Yes, there exists no superset of Butter, Curd, Jam with the same support 2	Yes, it is not proper subset of any other frequent itemset	Yes
{Butter, Jam, Muffin}	2	Yes, there exists no superset of Butter, Jam, Muffin with the same support 2	Yes, it is not proper subset of any other frequent itemset	Yes

One can observe that there are 9 closed frequent itemsets and 4 maximal frequent itemsets as shown in Table 9.69.

It is important to note that closed and maximal frequent itemsets are often smaller than all frequent itemsets and association rules can be generated directly from them. Thus, it is desirable that instead of mining every frequent itemset, an efficient algorithm should mine only maximal frequent itemsets. The association of frequent itemsets, closed frequent itemsets and maximal frequent itemsets has been illustrated in Figure 9.16 for better understanding. From this one can observe that a maximal itemset is a closed itemset, but a closed itemset is not necessarily a maximal itemset.

9.9 The Apriori–TID Algorithm for Generating Association Mining Rules

Apriori–TID uses the Apriori algorithm to generate the candidate and frequent itemsets, but the difference is that it uses the TID or vertical storage approach (discussed in Section 9.6.3) for its implementation.

The working of the Apriori–TID algorithm is given as follows.

1. Scan the whole transaction database to convert it into TID storage and represent it as T1 (i.e., each entry of T1 consists of all items in the transaction along with the corresponding TID).
2. Calculate the frequent 1-itemset L1 using T1.
3. Obtain C2 by applying the joining principle discussed under the Apriori algorithm.
4. Calculate the support for the candidates in C2 with the help of T1 by intersecting corresponding rows and a new TID dataset is created and represent it as T2 containing two item pairs.
5. Generate L2 from C2 by the usual means and then generate C3 from L2, again by using the joining principle.
6. Generate T3 using T2 and C3. This process is repeated until the set of candidate k-itemsets is an empty set.

Example of Apriori–TID: Let us understand this concept with an example database of transactions given in Table 9.70 for finding frequent itemsets with the Apriori–TID algorithm. Here, minimum support is 50% and minimum confidence is 75%.

Table 9.70 Transaction database

100	Butter, Curd, Eggs, Jam
200	Butter, Curd, Jam
300	Butter, Muffin, Nuts
400	Butter, Jam, Muffin
500	Curd, Jam, Muffin

Step 1:

Scan the entire transaction database to convert it into TID storage represented as T1 as given in Table 9.71.

Table 9.71 Transaction database T1

	100	*200*	*300*	*400*	*500*
Butter	1	1	1	1	0
Curd	1	1	0	0	1
Eggs	1	0	0	0	0
Jam	1	1	0	1	1
Muffin	0	0	1	1	1
Nut	0	0	1	0	0

Step 2:

Frequent 1-itemset L1 is calculated using T1.

Since, the minimum support is 3, all items have been selected as frequent items having support equal or more than threshold limit of support, i.e., 3 with the help of T1.

Thus, L1 is as shown in Table 9.72.

Table 9.72 L1

Itemset	Support
Butter	4
Curd	3
Jam	4
Muffin	3

Step 3:

C2 is obtained by applying the joining principle, i.e., L1 JOIN L1

Thus, C2 will be as given in Table 9.73.

Table 9.73 C2

Itemsets
Butter, Curd
Butter, Jam
Butter, Muffin
Curd, Jam
Curd, Muffin
Jam, Muffin

Step 4:

Support for the candidates in C2 is then calculated with the help of T1 by intersecting corresponding rows and a new TID dataset is created represented as T2 containing two item pairs as illustrated in Table 9.74.

Table 9.74 Transaction database T2

	100	200	300	400	500
Butter, Curd	1	1	0	0	0
Butter, Jam	1	1	0	1	0
Butter, Muffin	0	0	1	1	0
Curd, Jam	1	1	0	0	1
Curd, Muffin	0	0	0	0	1
Jam, Muffin	0	0	0	1	1

Thus, support for C2 is given in Table 9.75.

Table 9.75 Support for C2

Itemsets	*Support*
Butter, Curd	2
Butter, Jam	3
Butter, Muffin	2
Curd, Jam	3
Curd, Muffin	1
Jam, Muffin	2

Step 5:

L2 is then generated from C2 as shown in Table 9.76.

Table 9.76 L2

Itemsets	*Support*
Butter, Jam	3
Curd, Jam	3

Thus, {Butter, Jam} and {Curd, Jam} are the frequent pairs and they generate L2. C3 may also be generated but it is observed that C3 is empty because the first item is not common in the L2 item .pairs. If C3 was not empty then it would be used to identify T3 using the transaction set T2. That would result in a smaller T3 and it might have resulted in the removal of a transaction or two. In the example database, all the records of T2 have been removed and T3 is null.

The generation of association rules from the derived frequent set can be done in the usual way.

Advantages of the Apriori–TID algorithm

The advantage of Apriori–TID algorithm is in the storage structure because it facilitates counting of items by counting the number of 1s in each row and the number of 2-itemsets can be counted by finding the intersection of the two rows.

The other main advantage of the Apriori–TID algorithm is that the size of T_k is generally smaller than the transaction database.

Because the support for each candidate k-itemset is counted using the corresponding T_k, therefore this algorithm runs faster than the basic Apriori algorithm. It is important to note that both Apriori and Apriori–TID use the same candidate generation algorithm, and therefore they count the same itemsets.

9.10 Direct Hashing and Pruning (DHP)

A major shortcoming of the Apriori algorithm is that it cannot prune 2 itemset candidate items. As C2 is derived from L1 by using following formula:

C2 = L1 Join L1.

Since, every subset of C2 is a member of L1, C2 cannot be pruned by the Apriori property, i.e., subset of frequent itemsets should also be frequent. In case of C2, all the subsets are frequent, i.e., member of L1, so it cannot be pruned. However, Apriori property is very helpful in pruning higher order candidate itemsets like C3 or C4.

The DHP algorithm is useful as it overcomes this limitation since it has the capability to prune C2; this is important to improve performance.

Working of the DHP algorithm

This algorithm employs a hash-based technique for reducing the count of candidate itemsets generated in the first pass (i.e., a significantly smaller C2 is generated). The number of itemsets in C2 generated using DHP can be smaller in magnitude; therefore the scan to identify L2 is more efficient.

The steps to be taken to operate DHP are:

1. Find all frequent 1-itemsets and all the candidate 2-itemsets by using the same steps as the Apriori algorithm, i.e., C2 is generated by L1 JOIN L1.
2. Generate all possible 2-itemsets in each transaction and assign a code to each item and itemsets.
3. All the possible 2-itemsets are hashed to a hash table by using the code of each itemset. For hashing, a hash function is applied on each code and a bucket is assigned to each itemset based on the output of the hash function. The count of each bucket in the hash table is increased by one, each time when an itemset is hashed to that bucket. When different itemsets are hashed to the same bucket then collisions can occur. To assign a flag for each bucket, a bit vector is associated with the hash table. If the bucket count is equal or above the minimum required support count, then accordingly flag in the bit vector is set to 1, otherwise it is set to 0.
4. In this step C2 is pruned. Each item pair of C2 generated in step 1 is checked for the bit vector of its corresponding bucket to which it was assigned in step 3. If its bit vector is 0, then the item pair will be pruned and removed from C2, while all those item pairs having a bit vector of 1 are retained in C2. This step helps to prune C2 and this pruning of C2 is the major objective of the DHP algorithm.
   It is important to note that, having the corresponding bit vector or bit set does not guarantee that the itemset is frequent; this is due to collisions. The hash table filtering does reduce C2, significantly.
5. Then, from the pruned C2, frequent item pairs, L2 is generated and process continues as in Aproiroi property.
6. In this step, the hash table for the next step is generated. Only those itemsets that are frequent, i.e. in L2, are kept in the database. The pruning not only trims each transaction by removing the unwanted itemsets but also removes transactions that have no itemsets that could be frequent.
7. The algorithm is continued till no more candidate itemsets are identified. The whole transaction database is scanned to identify the support count for each itemset despite using a hash table to identify the frequent itemsets. Now, the database seems relatively smaller because of the pruning. The algorithm identifies the frequent itemsets as earlier by checking against the minimum support when the support count is calculated. The algorithm then produces candidate itemsets similar to what the Apriori algorithm does.

To get a clear idea about the working of DHP algorithm, let us consider some case studies by way of examples. After going through these examples, this algorithm will become clear to you.

Example: Using the DHP algorithm

To understand this concept, let us identify the association rules satisfying 50% support and 75% confidence for the transaction database given in Table 9.77 with the DHP algorithm.

Table 9.77 Transaction database

100	Butter, Curd, Eggs, Jam
200	Butter, Curd, Jam
300	Butter, Muffin, Nuts
400	Butter, Jam, Muffin
500	Curd, Jam, Muffin

Let us first find all frequent 1-itemsets and in this case it will all those items that appear 3 or more times in the database. The L1 is given in Table 9.78.

Table 9.78 Frequent 1-itemset L1

Butter
Curd
Jam
Muffin

Then, generate C2 from L1, i.e., L1 JOIN L1. This is given in Table 9.78. Here, for simplicity we are representing each item by its first alphabet.

Table 9.79 Candidate 2 itemsets C2

BC ('B' for Butter and 'C' for Curd)
BJ
BM
CJ
CM
JM

Since, the size of C2 is 6 and the major advantage of DHP is to prune C2 so hashing is applied on each item pair as discussed below.

To apply hashing, the next step is to generate all possible 2-itemsets for each transaction as shown in Table 9.80.

Table 9.80 Possible 2-itemsets for each transaction

100	(Butter, Curd), (Butter, Eggs), (Butter, Jam), (Curd, Eggs), (Curd, Jam), (Eggs, Jam)
200	(Butter, Curd), (Butter, Jam), (Curd, Jam)
300	(Butter, Muffin), (Butter, Nuts), (Muffin, Nuts)
400	(Butter, Jam), (Butter, Muffin), (Jam, Muffin)
500	(Curd, Jam), (Curd, Muffin), (Jam, Muffin)

For a support of 50%, the frequent items are Butter, Curd, Jam, and Muffin as shown in Table 9.81. Now, to hash the possible 2-itemsets, a code is assigned to each item as given in Table 9.82.

Table 9.81 Frequent itemsets for a support of 50%

Bread
Curd
Jam
Muffin

Table 9.82 Code for each item

Code	*Item Name*
1	Butter
2	Curd
3	Eggs
4	Jam
5	Muffin
6	Nuts

For each pair, a numeric value is obtained by representing Butter by 1, Curd by 2 and so on as shown in the above table. Then, each pair is represented by a two-digit number, for example, (Butter, Curd) is represented by 12; (Curd, Jam) is represented by 24 and so on.

The coded value for each item pair is given in Table 9.83.

Table 9.83 Coded representation for each item pair

100	12, 13, 14, 23, 24, 34
200	12, 14, 24
300	15, 16, 56
400	14, 15, 45
500	24, 25, 45

Now, the hash function is applied on coded values so that these items can be assigned to different buckets. Here, we are using modulo 8 number, i.e., dividing the code by 8 and using the remainder as hash function for the given dataset.

Hash function: Modulo 8, i.e., divide the concerned item pair code by 8 and use the remainder as its bucket number.

The guidelines to decide about hash function have been discussed later. For the moment, let's apply hash function to each item pair and assign the item pairs to each bucket on the basis of modulo 8 as shown in Table 9.60.

Applying the hash function to each item pair in transaction 100, the first item pair is 12, and when modulo 8 hash function is applied on 12, it gives a remainder of 4, so 12 is assigned to bucket 4. The next item pair in transaction 100 is 13, and gives a remainder of 5 after dividing it by 8, so 13 is assigned to bucket 5. Similarly, 14 has a remainder of 6, 23 has a remainder of 7, 24 has the remainder 0 and 34 has a remainder of 2, so these item pairs are assigned corresponding bucket numbers as shown in Table 9.84. This process is repeated for each transaction and every item pair is assigned to its corresponding bucket.

Table 9.84 Assigning item pairs to buckets based on hash function modulo 8

0	1	2	3	4	5	6	7	*Bucket address*
24 24 16 56 24	25	34		12 12	13 45 45	14 14 14	23 15 15	Item pairs
5	1	1	0	2	3	3	3	Support of bucket
1	0	0	0	0	1	1	1	Bit Vector (it refers to a sequence of numbers which are either 0 or 1 and stored contiguously in memory)

After assigning every item pair to its corresponding bucket, the support or count for each bucket has been calculated and if its support is equal to the threshold value then the corresponding bit vector is set 1 as shown in Table 9.84.

Now, C2 is pruned by checking the bit vector of the corresponding bucket for each candidate item pair. And only those item pairs are retained in C2 which have the corresponding bit vector as 1. The process of pruning of C2 has been illustrated in Table 9.85.

It has been noted that pair BC, i.e, 12 belong to the bucket with support of 2, since its support is less than threshold value of support so its corresponding bit vector is 0 and this item pair has been removed from C2; in other words, C2 has been pruned.

Similarly, this analysis is performed for each item pair of C2 as shown in Table 9.85.

Table 9.85 Pruning of C2

Item Pairs in C2	*Bucket*	*Bit Vector*	*Remarks*	*Pruned C2*
BC, i.e., 12	4	0	Removed from C2	
BJ, i.e., 14	6	1	Will be retained	BJ
BM, i.e., 15	7	1	Will be retained	BM
CJ, i.e., 24	0	1	Will be retained	CJ
CM, i.e., 25	1	0	Removed from C2	
JM, i.e., 45	5	1	Will be retained	JM

These candidate pairs are then hashed to the hash table and those candidate pairs are removed that are hashed to locations where the bit vector bit is not set. Table 9.85 illustrates that (B, C) and (C, M) have been eliminated from C2. Now, only four candidate item pairs are left instead of six item pairs in C2 and thus, C2 has been pruned as given in the last column of Table 9.85. After that, analyze the transaction database and modify it to include only these candidate pairs as given in Table 9.86.

Now, from the pruned C2, let us find L2 as shown in Table 9.86.

Table 9.86 Finding L2

Itemset	*Count*
BJ	3
BM	2
CJ	3
JM	2

Thus, L2 has two item pairs, i.e, BJ and CJ. Now, let us use L2 by selecting only those item pairs of the transaction database that qualify by being above the threshold value of support. The method of finding three itemsets is shown in Table 9.87.

Table 9.87 Finding three itemsets

TID	*Original Item groups*	*Selected Item pairs according to L2*	*Three Item groupings (sets)*
100	(Butter, Curd), (Butter, Eggs), (Butter, Jam), (Curd, Eggs), (Curd, Jam), (Eggs, Jam)	(Butter, Jam), (Curd, Jam)	NIL
200	(Butter, Curd), (Butter, Jam), (Curd, Jam)	(Butter, Jam), (Curd, Jam)	NIL
300	(Butter, Muffin), (Butter, Nuts), (Muffin, Nuts)	NIL	NIL
400	(Butter, Jam), (Butter, Muffin), (Jam, Muffin)	(Butter, Jam)	NIL
500	(Curd, Jam), (Curd, Muffin), (Jam, Muffin)	(Curd, Jam)	NIL

As shown above in Table 9.87, there are no 3-Item groups, and this complete the process of identifying frequent item pairs .So, in this case, there are two item pairs (Butter, Jam) and (Curd, Jam).We will find out the rules for selected item pairs in the same way as we did in the Apriori algorithm, previously. Proceed as follow:

These item pairs produce four rules as shown below.

Butter → Jam
Jam → Butter
Curd → Jam
Jam → Curd
Now, let us calculate their confidence as shown below.
Confidence of Butter → Jam = S (Butter, Jam) / S(Butter) = 3/4 = 0.75
Jam → Butter = S (Jam, Butter) / S(Jam) = 3/4 = 0.75
Curd → Jam = S (Curd, Jam) / S(Curd) = 3/3 = 1.0
Jam → Curd = S (Jam, Curd) / S(Jam) = 3/4 =1.0
Based on given threshold value of confidence we can select the qualified rules.

It is important to note that, the DHP algorithm usually performs better than the Apriori algorithm during the initial stages, especially during L2 generation. Added to this improvement is also the feature that trims and prunes the transaction set progressively, thereby improving the overall efficiency of the algorithm. The startup phase of DHP does consume some extra resources when the hash table is constructed but this is outweighed by the advantages gained during the later phases when both the number of candidate itemsets and the transaction set are reduced (pruned better).

Guidelines for selection of the hash function

As one of the major objectives of the DHP algorithm is to reduce the size of C2, it is essential that the hash table is large enough so that the collisions are low, i.e., different item pairs should not be hashed into the same bucket. In case of collisions, the bit vector is not very effective because in this case more than one item pair is contributing to support for the bucket and in ideal case it should be the support of only one item pair that should contribute, so that candidate item pairs are close to frequent item pairs.

If the hash table is too small and the collisions are high then more than one itemset will hash to most of the buckets. It will result into loss of effectiveness of the hash table in reducing the number of candidate itemsets C2. This is what happened in the example above in which we had collisions in three of the eight buckets. If the minimum support count is low, it is even more important that all collisions should be avoided.

If the hash table is too large then calculation will increase as we have to calculate the values for each bucket. Thus, the hash function should be selected in such a manner that it results in the least collisions.

Increasing the efficiency of the DHP algorithm

For efficient working of DHP, it is best to ensure that the hash table resides in the main memory. If the hash table does not fit in the main memory, additional disk I/O costs will apply which may again reduce the efficiency. This algorithm is most efficient when the number of itemsets in L2 is lot smaller than C2. This reduction in database size will have a positive impact on the efficiency of the algorithm.

The efficient pruning of the database, particularly C2, helps DHP to achieve a significantly shorter execution time than the Apriori algorithm.

Some more examples of DHP and Apriori algorithms

Another example will help in comparing Apriori with the DHP algorithm. In this example, we will first apply the Apriori algorithm to identify frequent item pairs; then we will apply the DHP algorithm for the same identification to illustrate differences in the process. Here, we have to find frequent item pairs with support more than 40% for the database given in Table 9.88.

By applying both the algorithms on the same database, comparison of the workings of both algorithms will be easy.

Table 9.88 Transaction database for Apriori and DHP

TID	*Items*
100	A C D
200	B C E
300	A B C E
400	B E

The process to identify frequent item pairs through the Apriori algorithm has been illustrated in Figure 9.14.

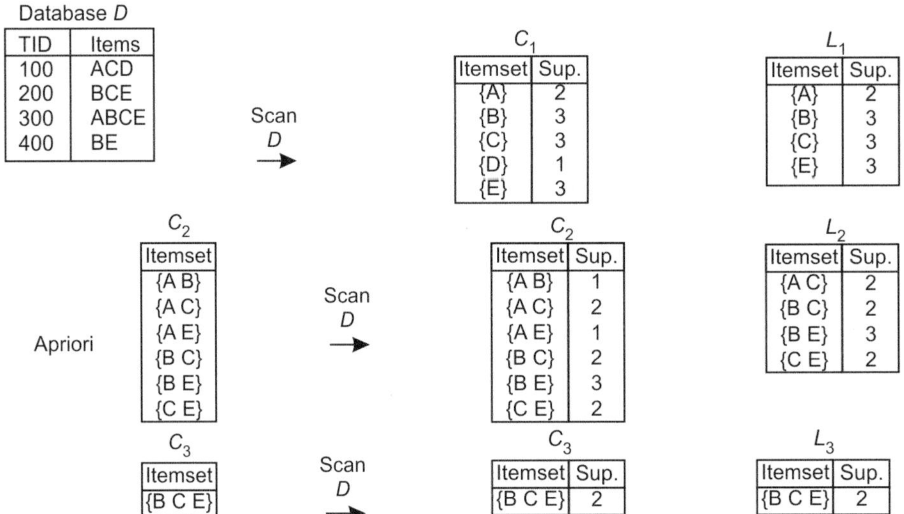

Figure 9.14 Process by the Aprioiri algorithm method

The process to identify frequent item pairs through DHP algorithm has been illustrated in Figure 9.15.

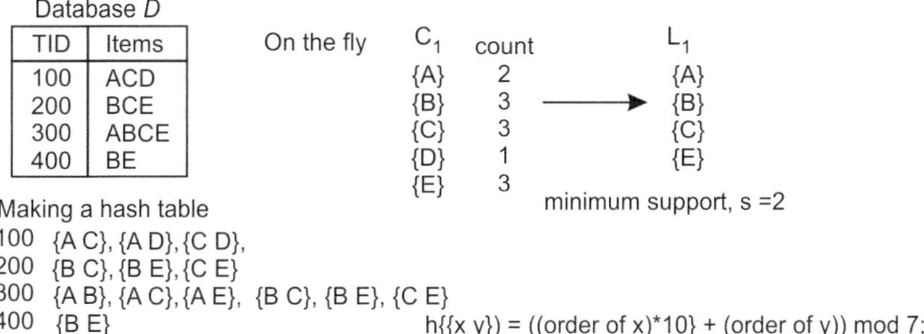

Figure 9.15 Process by the DHP algorithm method

Now, to hash the possible 2-itemsets, the code is assigned to each item. Let us assign code to each item as given in Table 9.89.

Table 9.89 Code for each item

Item	*Code*
A	1
B	2
C	3
D	4
E	5
F	6

A numeric value is attained for each pair by representing A by 1, B by 2 and so on as given in above table. Then each pair is represented by a two-digit number, for example, AC by 13 and AD by 14. The coded value for each item pair is given in Table 9.90.

Table 9.90 Coded representation for each item pair

TID	*Item pairs code*
100	13 (AC), 14(AD), 34 (CD)
200	23 (BC), 25 (BE), 35 (CE)
300	12 (AB), 13 (AC), 15 (AE), 23 (BC), 25 (BE), 35 (CE)
400	25 (BE)

Now, hash function is applied on the coded values so that these items can be assigned to different buckets. Here, we are using modulo 7 number, i.e., dividing by 7 and using the remainder as hash function for the given dataset as given in Table 9.91.

Table 9.91 Assigning of item pairs to buckets based on hash function modulo 7

0	1	2	3	4	5	6	Bucket address
14 35 35	15	23 23		25 25 25	12	13 34 13	Item pairs
3	1	2	0	3	1	3	Support of bucket
1	0	1	0	1	0	1	Bit Vector

The process of pruning C2 based on bit vector has been shown in Table 9.92.

Table 9.92 Pruning of C2

Item Pairs in C2	*Bucket*	*Bit Vector*	*Remarks*	*Pruned C2*
AB, i.e., 12	5	0	Removed from C2	
AC, i.e., 13	6	1	Will be retained	AC
AE, i.e., 15	1	0	Removed from C2	
BC, i.e., 23	2	1	Will be retained	BC
BE, i.e., 25	4	1	Will be retained	BE
CE, i.e., 35	0	1	Will be retained	CE

This pruned C2 is used to find L2 as shown in Table 9.93.

Table 9.93 Finding L2

Item pairs	*Count*
AC	2
BC	2
BE	3
CE	2

All these item pairs have support more than threshold limit. This L2 will be used for identifying three item pairs by selecting only those item pairs from Table 9.90 which are having support more than the threshold limit, as shown below in Table 9.94

Table 9.94 Identifying three itemsets

TID	Original Item Pairs	Selected Item Pairs according to L2	Three Itemsets
100	AC, AD, CD	AC	NIL
200	BC, BE, CE	BC, BE, CE	BCE
300	AB, AC, AE, BC, BE, CE	AC, BC, BE, CE	BCE
400	BE	BE	NIL

Here, BCE has a support of 2; thus, the frequent item group is BCE.

In next phase, association rules for three item group BCE can be found by using the same approach as discussed in the Apriori algorithm.

Example: Let us consider, the database given in Table 9.95 for identification of frequent item pairs with the Apriori algorithm and the DHP algorithm for minimum support of 50%.

Table 9.95 Transaction database

TID	Item Bought
100	1, 2, 3, 4
200	5, 6, 7, 8, 9
300	6, 8, 9, 10
400	2, 3, 9

The process to identify frequent item pairs through Apriori algorithm has been illustrated in Figure 9.16.

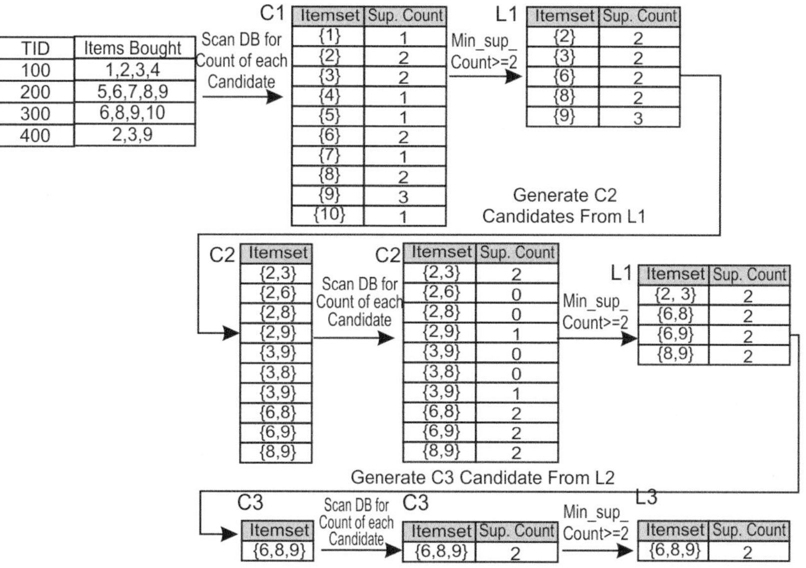

Figure 9.16 Identifying frequent item pairs and groups by Apriori algorithm

Thus, the process of the Apriori algorithm has produced a frequent three item group {6, 8, 9}.

The process to identify frequent item pairs and groups through the DHP algorithm has been illustrated in Table 9.96.

Table 9.96 Coded item pairs for DHP

TID	*Items bought*	*Item pairs code*
100	1,2,3,4	12,13,14,23,24,34
200	5,6,7,8,9	56,57,58,59,67,68,69,78,79,89
300	6,8,9,10	68,69,610,89,810,910
400	2,3,9	23,29,39

Now, the hash function is applied on coded values so that these items can be assigned to different buckets. Here, we are going to use Modulo 11 number, i.e., dividing by 11 and using the remainder as hash function to assign buckets for the given dataset.

Let's apply hash function to each item pair and assign the item pairs to each bucket on the basis of modulo 11 as shown in Table 9.97.

Table 9.97 Assigning of item pairs to buckets based on hash function modulo 11

0	1	2	3	4	5	6	7	8	9	10	Bucket address
	12 23 34 56 67 89 23	13 24 57 68 68	14 58 69 69	59	610	39	29 810	910			Item pairs
0	7	5	4	1	1	1	2	1	0	0	Support of bucket
0	1	1	1	0	0	0	1	0	0	0	Bit Vector

The pruning of C2 has been illustrated in Table 9.98.

Table 9.98 Pruning of C2

Item Pairs in C2	*Bucket*	*Bit Vector*	*Remarks*	*Pruned C2*
23	1	1	Will be retained	23
26	-	-	Removed from C2	
28	-	-	Removed from C2	
29	7	1	Will be retained	29
36	-	-	Removed from C2	

Contd.

Item Pairs in C2	Bucket	Bit Vector	Remarks	Pruned C2
38	-	-	Removed from C2	
39	6	0	Removed from C2	
68	2	1	Will be retained	68
69	3	1	Will be retained	69
89	1	1	Will be retained	89

This pruned C2 is used to find L2 as shown in Table 9.99.

Table 9.99 Finding L2

Item pair	Count
23	2
29	1
68	2
69	2
89	2

Thus, L2 is 23, 68, 69 and 89, which is used to find three item groups as shown in Table 9.100.

Table 9.100 Finding three itemsets

TID	Original Item pairs	Selected Item pairs according to L2	Three Itemsets
100	12,13,14,23,24,34	23	NIL
200	56,57,58,59,67,68,69,78,79,89	68,69,89	689
300	68,69,610,89,810,910	68,69,89	689
400	23,39	23	NIL

Here, 689 has a support of 2 and so the frequent item grouping is 689.

We have found the identical three item grouping by using both the Apriori and the DHP algorithms. Now, the same procedure that was discussed in the section on the Apriori algorithm can be applied to determine rules for the three item group {6, 8, 9}.

9.11 Dynamic Itemset Counting (DIC)

The major issue with the Apriori algorithm is that it requires multiple scans of the transaction database which is equal to the number of items in the last candidate itemset that was checked for its support.

For example, to identify candidate 3-itemset groupings, it will require a minimum of 3 scans of the database and to identify candidate 4-itemset groupings, it will require four scans of the database.

The major advantage of the Dynamic Itemset Counting (DIC) algorithm is that it requires only 2 scans of the database to identify frequent item pairs in the whole database. It reduces the number of scans required by not just doing one scan for the frequent 1-itemset and another for the frequent 2-itemset but combining the counting for a number of itemsets as soon as it appears that it might be necessary to count it.

The basic algorithm is as follows.

1. Divide the transaction database into *n* number of partitions.
2. In the first partition of the transaction database, count the 1-itemsets.
3. Count the 1-itemsets at the beginning of the second partition of the transaction database and also start counting the 2-itemsets using the frequent 1-itemsets from the first partition.
4. Count the 1-itemsets and the 2-itemsets at the beginning of the third partition and also start counting the 3-itemsets using results from the first two partitions.
5. Continue this process until the whole database is scanned once. There will be final set of frequent 1-itemsets once you scan the database fully.
6. Go back to the starting of the transaction database and continue counting the 2-itemsets and the 3-itemsets, etc.
7. After the end of the first partition in the second scan of the database, the whole database has been scanned for 2-itemsets. Therefore, we have the final set of frequent 2-itemsets.
8. After the end of the second partition in the second scan of the database, the whole database has been scanned for 3-itemsets. Therefore, we have the final set of frequent 3-itemsets.
9. This process is continued in a similar manner until no frequent k-itemsets are identified.

Illustration on working of the DIC algorithm

Let us consider, a dataset having 100 records which is divided into a number of, say 5 equal partitions. Now, the major assumption in DIC is that the data should be homogeneous throughout the file. This means that all the items should appear in partitions and the percentage of each item in the partition should be same as percentage of each item in whole dataset. In simple words, if there are 5 items A, B, C, D and E in the dataset then each of these items should appear in the each partition and if the percentage of item A in the whole transaction dataset is 60%, then it should be the same in each partition, i.e, if the count of data item A is 50 in whole dataset of 100 transactions, then the item should have the count of 10 in each partition of 20 records i.e. 50% both ways.

On the assumption that data is homogenous throughout in each partition, data is processed for the DIC algorithm.

Here, we have a database of 100 transactions which is divided into five equal partitions of 20 records each. During counting of the 1-itemsets in the first partition of the transaction database, we have identified data items A, B, C and D in the first partition. The count of these items is indicated as C_A, C_B and so on. Count the 1-itemsets at the beginning of the second partition, and also starts counting the 2-itemsets using the frequent 1-itemsets from the first partition, i.e. we also start counting two item pairs, i.e., AB, AC, AD, BC, BD and CD. The working of the DIC algorithm has been illustrated in Table 9.101.

It has been observed the counting of 1-itemsets, i.e., A, B, C and D has been completed after

Table 9.101 Working of the DIC algorithm for the example database

Total dataset of 100 records	Partition-1 20 records	PHASE-1 1-iemsets A-C_A B-C_B C-C_C D-C_D				PHASE-2 2-itemsets AB-C_{AB} AC-C_{AC} AD-C_{AD} BC-C_{BC} BD-C_{BD} CD-C_{CD}	PHASE-2 3-itemsets ABC-C_{ABC} ABD-C_{ABD} ACD-C_{ACD} BCD-C_{BCD}	PHASE-2 4-itemsets ABCD- C_{ABCD}	**Count of 2-itemset has been completed after first partition of second pass**
	Partition-2 20 records	1-iemsets A-C_A B-C_B C-C_C D-C_D	2-itemsets AB-C_{AB} AC-C_{AC} AD-C_{AD} BC-C_{BC} BD-C_{BD} CD-C_{CD}			PHASE-2 3-itemsets ABC-C_{ABC} ABD-C_{ABD} ACD-C_{ACD} BCD-C_{BCD}	PHASE-2 4-itemsets ABCD-C_{ABCD}	**Count of 3-itemset has been completed after second partition of second pass**	
	Partition-3 20 records	1-iemsets A-C_A B-C_B C-C_C D-C_D	2-itemsets AB-C_{AB} AC-C_{AC} AD-C_{AD} BC-C_{BC} BD-C_{BD} CD-C_{CD}	3-itemsets ABC-C_{ABC} ABD-C_{ABD} ACD-C_{ACD} BCD-C_{BCD}		PHASE-2 4-itemsets ABCD-C_{ABCD}	Count of 4-itemsets has been completed after third partition of second pass		

Contd.

	Partition-4 20 records	1-iemsets A-C_A B-C_B C-C_C D-C_D	2-itemsets AB-C_{AB} AC-C_{AC} AD-C_{AD} BC-C_{BC} BD-C_{BD} CD-C_{CD}	3-itemsets ABC-C_{ABC} ABD-C_{ABD} ACD-C_{ACD} BCD-C_{BCD}	4-itemsets ABCD-C_{ABCD}		
	Partition-5 20 records	1-iemsets A-C_A B-C_B C-C_C D-C_D	2-itemsets AB-C_{AB} AC-C_{AC} AD-C_{AD} BC-C_{BC} BD-C_{BD} CD-C_{CD}	3-itemsets ABC-C_{ABC} ABD-C_{ABD} ACD-C_{ACD} BCD-C_{BCD}	4-itemsets ABCD-C_{ABCD}	Count of 1-itemset has been completed after one pass	

one pass, the counting of 2-itemset has been completed after the first partition of the second pass, counting of 3-itemsets has been completed after the second partition of the second pass and counting of 4-itemsets has been completed after the third partition of the second pass. It is clear from above illustration that DIC will require only two scans of database while Apriori will require 4 scans for the identification of frequent 4-itemsets.

Major condition to make DIC effective

The DIC algorithm works well when the data throughout the file is relatively homogeneous as it starts counting of the 2-itemset before having a count of final 1-itemset. The algorithm is not able to identify the large itemset till the whole database is scanned if the data distribution is not homogeneous. The major benefit of DIC is that it finishes the counting of the itemset in two scans of the database while Apriori often takes three or more scans.

9.12 Mining Frequent Patterns without Candidate Generation (FP Growth)

As only frequent items are required for identifying the association rules, so it is best to identify the frequent items in the dataset and ignore all others. The FP growth works on the same principle and instead of generating candidate itemsets as in the case of the Aprioiri algorithm, frequent pattern-growth (FP growth) only tests and generates frequent itemsets. Thus, the major difference between the Apriori algorithm and FP growth is that FP growth does not generate candidate itemsets, it only tests, whereas the Apriori algorithm generates candidate itemsets and then tests them.

To improve the performance of the algorithm, it uses the principle to store frequent items in a compact structure which does not require the need to use the original transaction database repeatedly.

The working of the FP growth algorithm is as follows:

1. Like the Apriori algorithm, the transaction database is scanned once to identify all the 1-itemset frequent items and their supports are noted down.
2. Then 1-itemset frequent items are sorted in descending order of their support.
3. After that the FP-tree is created with a 'NULL' root.
4. Then the first transaction is obtained from the transaction database and all the non-frequent items are removed. And the remaining items are listed according to the order in the sorted frequent items.
5. After this, the first branch of the tree is constructed using the transaction with each node corresponding to a frequent item and by setting the frequency of each item as 1 for the first transaction.
6. Then the next transaction is retrieved from the transaction database and all the non-frequent items are removed. And the remaining items are listed according to the order in the sorted frequent items as done in step 4.
7. Now, the transaction is inserted in the tree using any common prefix that may appear and

count of items is increased by 1. If no common prefix is found then the branch of the tree is constructed using the transaction; with each node corresponding to a frequent item and by setting the frequency of each item as 1.

8. Step 6 is repeated until all transactions in the database have been processed.

To understand this algorithm let us find frequent item pairs by building FP-trees for the following database.

Example: Let us consider a transaction database shown in Table 9.102. The minimum support required is 50% and confidence is 75%.

Table 9.102 Transaction database

100	Butter, Curd, Eggs, Jam
200	Butter, Curd, Jam
300	Butter, Eggs, Muffin, Nuts
400	Butter, Eggs, Jam, Muffin
500	Curd, Jam, Muffin

According to the algorithm, the first step will be to scan the transaction database to identify all the frequent items in the 1-itemsets and sort them in descending order of their support.

The frequent 1-itemset database sorted on the basis of frequency is shown in Table 9.103.

Table 9.103 Frequency of each item in sorted order

Item	*Frequency*
Butter	4
Jam	4
Curd	3
Eggs	3
Muffin	3

Here, Nuts has been removed as it has a support of 1 only, which is less than the threshold limit of support (which is 3 in our case).

To create the FP-tree, the next step will be to exclude all the items that are not frequent from the transactions and sort the remaining frequent items in descending order of their frequency count. The example transaction database will be processed accordingly. The updated database after eliminating the non-frequent items and reorganising the frequent items on the basis of frequency, is shown in Table 9.104.

Table 9.104 Updated database after eliminating the non-frequent items and reorganising it according to support

Transaction ID	*Items*
100	Butter, Jam, Curd, Eggs
200	Butter, Jam, Curd
300	Butter, Eggs, Muffin
400	Butter, Jam, Eggs, Muffin
500	Jam, Curd, Muffin

It is important to note that in case of identical support, items are arranged according to lexicographic or sorted order. Now, we create the FP-tree by using the algorithm discussed above. For simplicity of discussion, we are referencing items with their first letter, i.e, Butter by B, Jam by J and so on.

An FP-tree consists of nodes. Here, each node contains three fields, i.e, an item name, a count, and a node link as given in Figure 9.17. To built the FP-tree let us consider first transaction, i.e., 100 having Butter, Jam, Curd, Eggs as items. Each item node will be created from the root node, i.e., NULL as shown in Figure 9.17. The tree is built by making a root node labeled NULL. A node is made for each frequent item in the first transaction and the count is set to 1. For example, to build the FP-tree of Figure 9.17, the first transaction {B, J, C, E} is inserted in the empty tree with the root node labeled NULL. Each of these items is given a frequency count of 1.

Next, the tree is traversed for the next transaction, i.e., 200. If a path already exists then it will follow the same path and corresponding count of item is increased by 1. If a path does not exist then a new path will be created. Next the second transaction, which is {B, J, C} having all the items common with first, is inserted. It changes the frequency of each item, i.e., {B, J, C} to 2. The FP for first two transactions is shown in Figure 9.18.

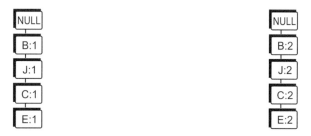

Figure 9.17 FP-tree for first transaction, i.e., 100 only

Figure 9.18 FP-tree for the first two transactions

Similarly, third transaction is considered and {B, E, M} is inserted. This requires that nodes for E and M be created. The counter for B goes to 3 and the counter for E and M is set to 1.The FP-tree for first three transactions is shown in Figure 9.19.

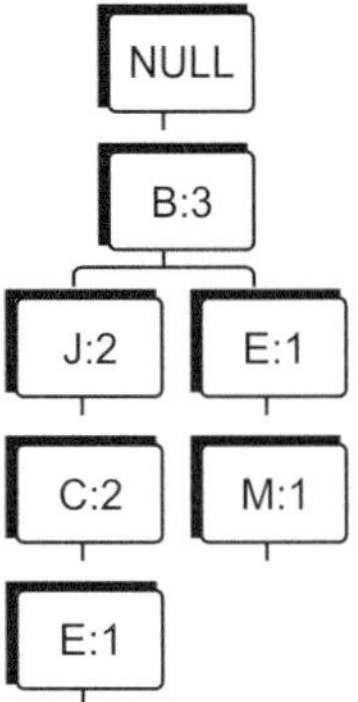

Figure 9.19 FP-tree for first three transactions

The next transaction {B, J, E, M} results in counters for B and J going up to 4 and 3 respectively and a new nodes for E and M have been inserted with count of 1 under node J as shown in Figure 9.20.

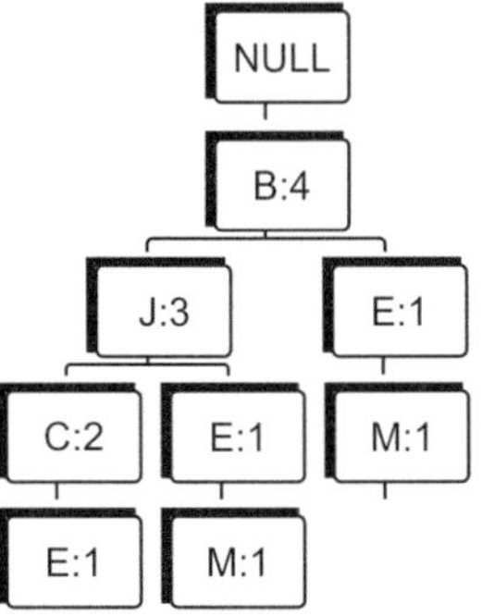

Figure 9.20 FP-tree for first four transactions

The last transaction {J, C, M} results in a brand new branch for the tree which is shown on the right-hand side in Figure 9.21 with a counter of 1 for each item.

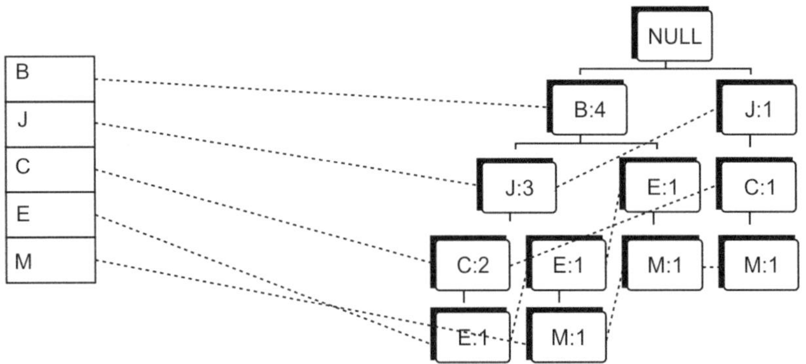

Figure 9.21 The final FP-tree for the example database after five transactions

The count tells the number of occurrences the path (constructed from the root node to this node) has in the transaction database. The node link is a link to the next node in the FP-tree containing the same item name or a null pointer if this node is the last one with this name. The FP-tree also consists of a header table with an entry for each itemset and a link to the first item in the tree with the same name. This linking is done to make traversal of the tree more efficient. Nodes with the same item name in the tree are linked via the dotted node-links.

The nodes near the root in the tree are more frequent than those further down the tree. Each identical path is only stored in the FP-tree once, which often makes the size of an FP-tree smaller than the corresponding transactional database. The height of an FP-tree is always equal to the maximum number of itemsets in a transaction excluding the root node. The FP-tree is compact and often orders of magnitude smaller than the transaction database. Once the FP-tree is constructed, the transaction database is not required.

Identification of frequent itemsets from FP-tree

The mining on the FP-tree structure is performed using the Frequent Pattern growth (FP growth) algorithm. This algorithm starts with the least frequent item, *i.e.*, the last item in the header table. Then the algorithm identifies all the paths from the root to this least frequent item and adjusts the count on the basis of the item's support count.

First, look at Figure 9.21 built using the FP-tree to identify the frequent itemsets in the example.

Start with the item M and identify the patterns given as follows:

Identification of patterns for item M

BEM(1)
BJEM(1)
JCM(1)

From this we can identify that, the support for BM is 2 (1 from BEM and 1 from BJEM), but its support is less than the threshold limit of 3, so this item pair will be discarded and we have identified no frequent item pairs by using item M.

Next consider the item E and identify the patterns given as follows:

Identification of patterns for item E

BJCE(1)
BJE(1)
BE(1)

From this we can identify that the support for BE is 3 (1 from BJCE, 1 from BJE and 1 from BE). However there is also a three item pair BJE having a support of 2 (1 from BJCE and 1 BJE), but its support is less than threshold value so will be discarded.

So, we have identified BE has two item pairs having support more than the threshold limit.

Next consider the item C and identify the following patterns:

Identification of patterns for item C

BJC(2)
JC(1)

From this we can identify that, the support for JC is 3 (2 from BJC and 1 from JC). There is no other item pair having support equal to or more than 3.

So, we have identified JC has two item pairs having supports more than the threshold limit.

Next consider the item J to identify its patterns.

Identification of patterns for item J

BJ(3)
J(1)

From this we can identify that, the support for BJ is 3. There is no other item pair having support equal to or more than 3.

So, we have identified that BJ has two item pairs having support more than the threshold limit.

Since, B is at top of the tree and cannot have any item prior to it to make a pair, so there is no need to follow links for item B. Thus, when the tree only contains one path, the algorithm will find all the possible combinations of the items in the itemset that support the minimum support count. It is therefore important to start with the least frequent item the first time, otherwise the items with the higher frequency will not be considered.

Thus, the final list of frequent item pairs for the given database of transactions is shown in Table 9.105.

Table 9.105 Frequent item pairs for database example given in table

Frequent Item pairs	*Count*
BE	3
JC	3
BJ	3

Finding association rules

To find the association mining rules, the same approach is followed as in Apriori algorithm.

For item pair BE, the possible rules are B→E and E→B. The confidence for each rule will be calculated and if its value is more than given threshold value of confidence then corresponding rule will be selected otherwise it will be discarded. The same approach will be followed for other frequent item pairs JC and BJ to find association rules for the given dataset.

The readers are advised to identify association mining rules that have confidence of more than 80%.

I hope that, you have identified it correctly and answer is E→B and C→J as explained below.

Confidence of (B→E) = S(B∩E) / S(B) = 3/4 =0.75 [support of individual items is given in Table 9.101]

Confidence of (E→B) = S(E∩B) / S(E) = 3/3 =1.0

Confidence of (J→C) = S(J∩C) / S(J) = 3/4 = 0.75

Confidence of (C→J) = S(C∩J) / S(C) = 3/3 =1

Confidence of (B→J) = S(B∩J) / S(B) =3/4 = 0.75

Confidence of (J→B) = S(J∩B) / S(J) = 3/4 = 0.75

Example: Let us consider another database given in Table 9.106, to identify frequent item pairs having support more than 50%.

Table 9.106 Transaction database

TID	Items
100	A C D
200	B C E
300	A B C E
400	B E

The count for each item is given in Table 9.107.

Table 9.107 Count for each data item

Item	Count
A	2
B	3
C	3
D	1
E	3

On the basis of the frequent items given in Table 9.108, those items are selected that have support equal to or more than 2 and these frequent items are sorted on the basis of their frequency as shown in Table 9.108.

Table 9.108 Frequency of each item in sorted order

Item	Count
B	3
C	3
E	3
A	2

Now, the non-frequent items are removed from the transaction database and items are ordered on the basis of their frequency as given in the above table. The database after eliminating the items that are not frequent and reorganising them on the basis of their frequency is shown in Table 9.109.

Table 9.109 Modified database after eliminating the non-frequent items and reorganising

TID	Items
100	C A
200	B C E
300	B C E A
400	B E

The process of creating the FP-tree for the database given above has been shown in Figure 9.22 on a step-by-step basis.

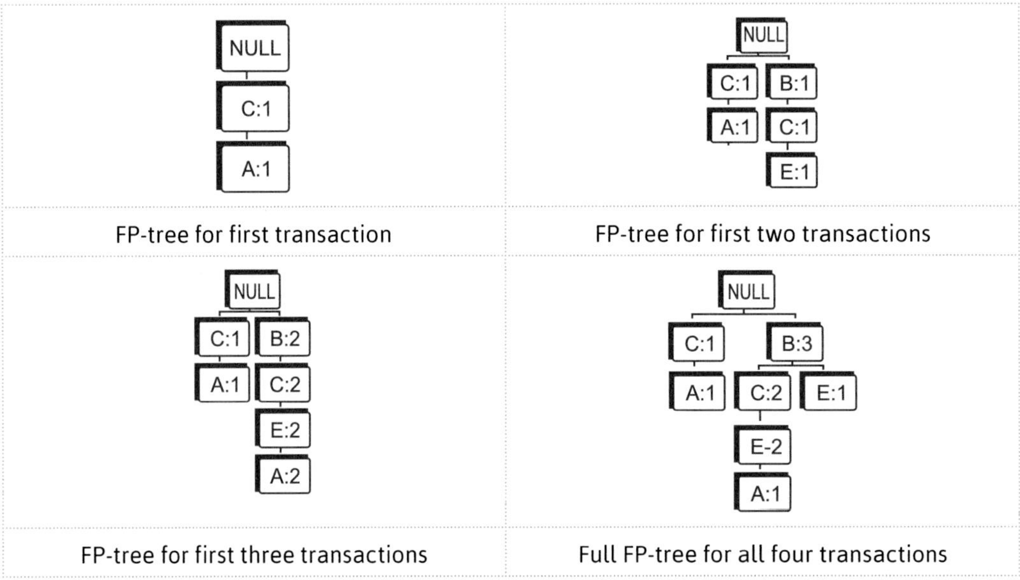

Figure 9.22 Illustrating the step-by-step creation of the FP-tree

Thus, the final FP-tree with nodes will be as shown in Figure 9.23.

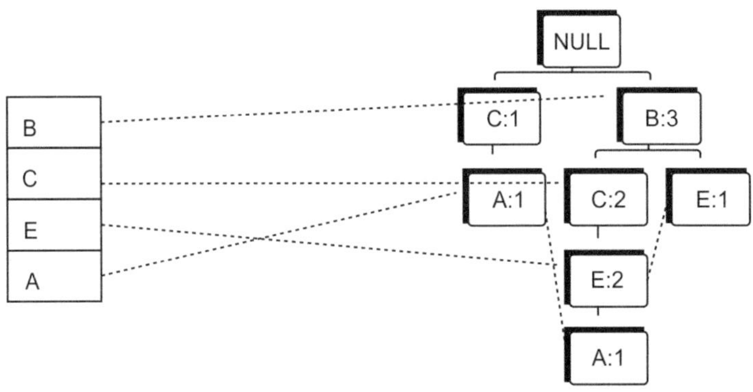

Figure 9.23 Final FP-tree for database given in Table 9.105

Identification of Frequent Itemsets from the FP-tree

Start with the item A and identify the patterns given as follows:

Identification of patterns for item A

CA(1),
BCEA(1),

The support for CA is 2 (1 from CA and 1 from BCEA) and it is equal to the threshold limit thus CA is identified as a frequent item pair.

Next consider the item E and identify the following patterns:

Identification of patterns for item E

BCE(2)
BE(1)

The support for BCE is 2 and it is equal to the threshold limit thus BCE is identified as a frequent 3-itemset.

Also from E, BE is identified as a frequent 2-item pair, since it has a support of 3 (2 from BCE and 1 from BE).

Thus, we have selected two frequent item pairs from E, i.e., BCE and BE.

Next consider the item C and examine the following patterns:

Identification of patterns for item C

BC(2)

The support for BC is 2 and it is equal to the threshold limit thus BC is identified as a frequent item pair.

Since, B is at top of the tree and cannot have any item prior to it to make a pair, so there is no need to follow links for item B.

The final list of frequent item pairs for the given database of transactions is as shown in Table 9.110.

Table 9.110 Frequent item pairs for the example database

Frequent Item pairs	*Count*
CA	2
BCE	2
BE	2
BC	2

Finding association rules

The identification process of association rules having confidence more than 70% has been shown in Table 9.111.

Table 9.111 Calculation of confidence for identification of association rules

CA	C→A = S(C∩A) / S(C) = 2/3 = 0.67 A→C = S(A∩C) / S(A) = 2/2 = 1.0	Selected rule is A→C
BCE	B→CE = S(B∩C∩E) / S(B) = 2/3 = 0.67	Confidence is less then threshold value, so it will be discarded.
	CE→B = S(B∩C∩E) / S(CE) = 2/2 = 1.0 Possible other non-implied rules are: C→E, E→B C→E = S(C∩E) / S(C) = 2/3 = 0.67 E→B = S(E∩B) / S(E) = 2/3 = 0.67	Selected rule is CE→B. Others are discarded
BE	B→E = S(B∩E) / S(B) =2/3 = 0.67 E→B = S(E∩B) / S(E) =2/3 = 0.67	Both the rules are discarded.
BC	B→C = S(B∩C) / S(B) = 2/3 = 0.67 C→B = S(C∩B) / S(C) = 2/3 = 0.67	Both the rules are discarded.

Thus, final association rules having confidence more than 70% are CE→B and A→C.

Example: Let us consider another database given in Table 9.112, to identify frequent item pairs having support more than 50%.

Table 9.112 Transaction database

Tr.	Itemsets
T1	{1,2,3,4}
T2	{1,2,4}
T3	{1,2}
T4	{2,3,4}
T5	{2,3}
T6	{3,4}
T7	{2,4}

The count for each item is given in Table 9.113.

Table 9.113 Frequency of each item

Item	Support
{1}	3
{2}	6
{3}	4
{4}	5

On the basis of the frequent items given in Table 9.114, those items are selected that have support equal to or more than 2 and these frequent items are sorted on the basis of their frequency as shown in Table 9.114.

Table 9.114 Frequency of each item in sorted order

Item	Support
{2}	6
{4}	5
{3}	4
{1}	3

Now, the non-frequent items are removed from the transactions and items are organized according to their frequency as given in the above Table 9.114. Since, all items are frequent, transaction items are reorganized according to their support as shown in Table 9.115.

Table 9.115 Modified database after eliminating the non-frequent items and reorganizing

T1	2 4 3 1
T2	2 4 1
T3	2 1
T4	2 4 3
T5	2 3
T6	4 3
T7	2 4

The process of creating the FP-tree for this database has been shown in Figure 9.24 on a step-by-step basis.

FP-tree for first transaction: {2 4 3 1}

FP for first and second transaction {2 4 1}

Contd.

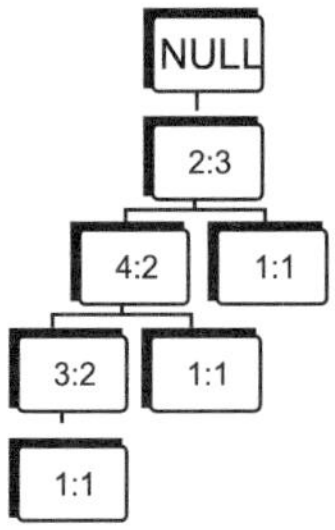

FP for first, second and third transaction {2 1}	FP for first, second, third and fourth transaction {2 4 3}
FP for first, second, third, fourth and fifth transaction {2 3}	FP for first, second, third, fourth, fifth and sixth transaction {4 3}
FP for first, second, third, fourth, fifth, sixth and seventh transaction {2 4}	

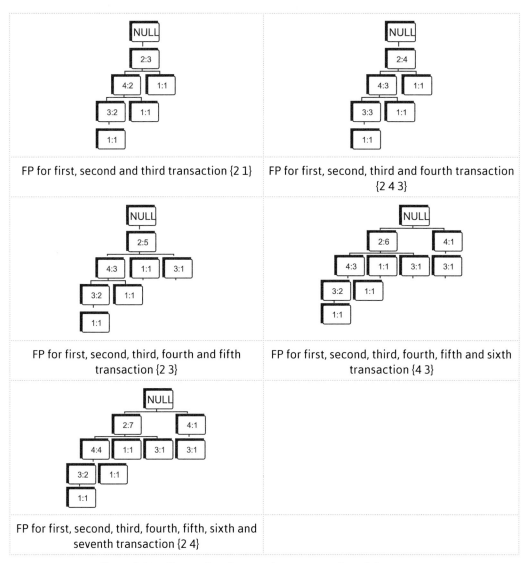

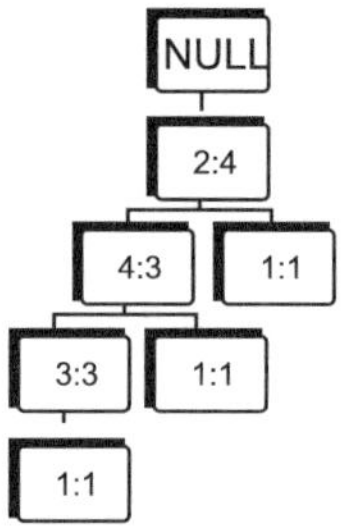

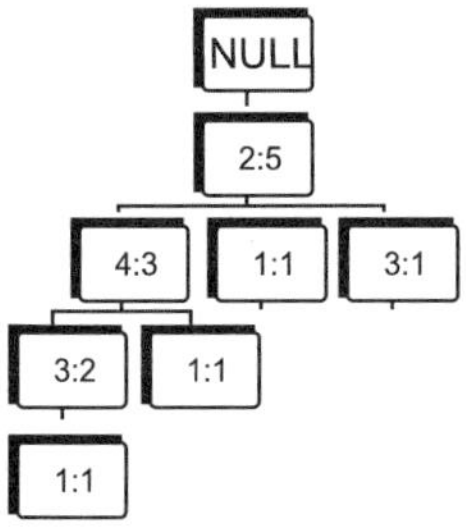

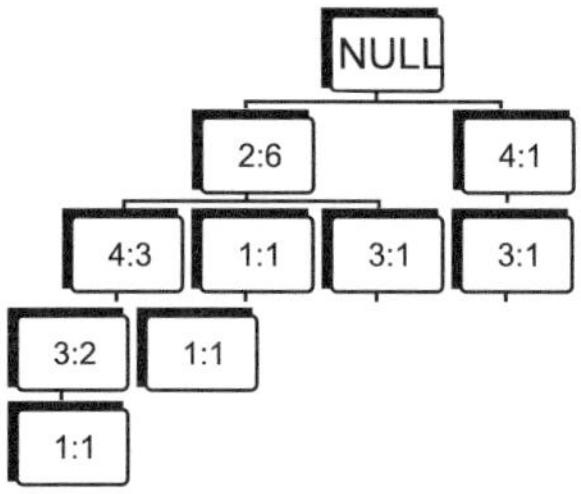

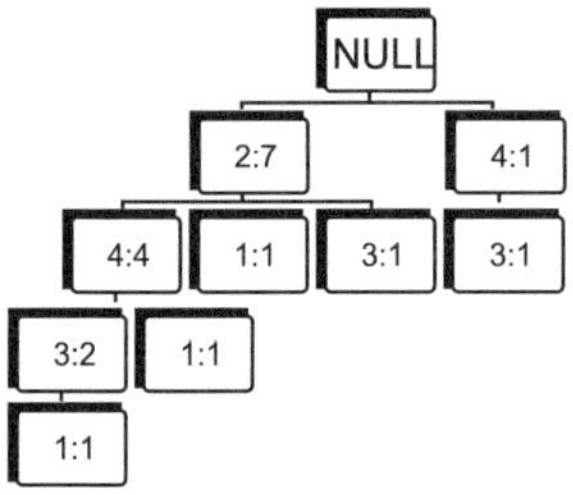

Figure 9.24 Illustrating the step-by-step creation of the FP-tree

Thus, the final FP-tree with nodes will be as shown in Figure 9.25.

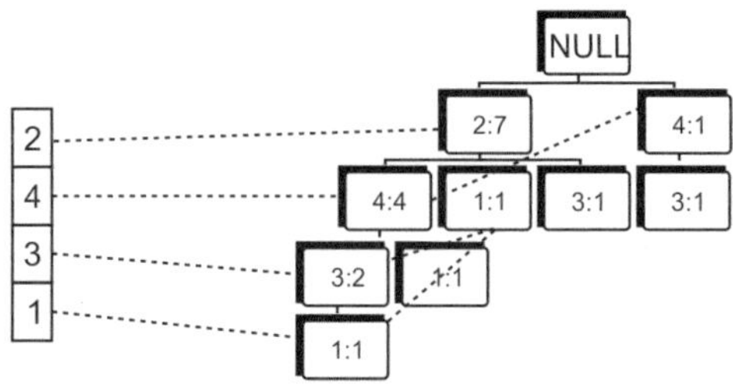

Figure 9.25 FP-tree for the example database

Identification of frequent itemsets from the FP-tree

Start with the item 1 and identify the patterns given as follows.

Identification of patterns for item 1

2431(1)
241(1)
21 (1)

The support for 21 is 3 (1 from 2431, 1 from 241 and 1 from 21) and it is equal to the threshold limit thus 21 is a identified as frequent item pair.

Next consider the item 3 and identify its patterns.

Identification of patterns for item 3

243(2)
23(1)
43(1)

The support for 43 is 3 (2 from 243 and 1 from 43) and it is equal to the threshold limit thus 43 is identified as a frequent item pair.

The support for 23 is also 3 (2 from 243 and 1 from 23) and it is equal to the threshold limit thus 23 is also identified as a frequent item pair.

Next consider the item 4 and identify its patterns.

Identifications of patterns for item 4

24(4)

The support for 24 is 4 and it is more than threshold limit, thus 24 is identified as a frequent item pair.

The final list of frequent item pairs for given database of transactions is shown in Table 9.116.

Table 9.116 Frequent item pairs for example database

Item	Support
{1,2}	3
{3,4}	3
{2,3}	3
{2,4}	4

It is important to note that the order of data items does not matter in listing frequent item pairs.

Finding association rules

The identification process of association rules having confidence more than 70% has been shown in Table 9.117.

Table 9.117 Association rules for database given in Table 9.76

{1, 2}	1→2 = S(1∩2) / S(1) = 3/3 =1.0 2→1 = S(2∩1) / S(1) = 3/3 = 1.0	Both the rules, i.e., 1→2 and 2→1 are selected
{3, 4}	3→4 = S(3∩4) / S(3) = 3/4 = 0.75 4→3 = S(4∩3) / S(3) = 3/4 = 0.75	Both the rules, i.e., 3→4 and 4→3 are selected
{2, 3}	2→3 = S(2∩3) / S(2) = 3/6 = 0.50 3→2 = S(3∩2) / S(3) = 3/4 = 0.75	3→2 rule has been selected
{2, 4}	2→4 = S(2∩4) / S(2) = 4/6 = 0.67 4→2 = S(4∩2) / S(4) = 4/5 = 0.80	4→2 rule has been selected

Thus, final association rules having confidence more than 70% are 1→2, 2→1, 3→4, 4→3, 3→2 and 4→2.

9.12.1 Advantages of the FP-tree approach

The advantages of the FP-tree algorithm over the Apriori algorithm are as follows:

- The FP-tree algorithm avoids the need to scan the database more than twice to identify the counts of support.
- The FP-tree completely eliminates the requirement of costly candidate generation, which can be expensive in case of the Apriori algorithm for the candidate set C2.
- The FP growth algorithm is better than the Apriori algorithm when the transaction database is huge and the minimum support count is low. Because in case of low minimum support count, there will be more items that will satisfy the support count and hence the size of the candidate sets for Apriori will be large. As the database grows, FP growth uses an efficient structure to mine patterns.

9.12.2 Further improvements of FP growth

In spite of the advantages there are possibilities to make the algorithm even more efficient and scalable. Important observations to further improve the performance of FP growth are as follows:

- It works best if the FP-tree fits in the main memory. However, in large databases this will not always be possible, and then it is better to first divide the database and then constructs FP-trees for each of the databases.
- Use ***B+-tree*** to index the FP-tree for faster access to items in the FP-tree.
- If the same data is used multiple times with different minimum confidence thresholds in order to yield different association rule mining then, it could be useful to use the same FP-tree results. This will save the initial cost of generating the FP-tree and make the algorithm overall more efficient.
- Sometimes the minimum support count will be different in different tasks, so to overcome this problem, the lowest minimum support count is used in the materialization of the FP-tree. When a higher support count is wanted, only the top of the FP-tree is used. Because of the structure of the FP-tree, it is easy to have different support counts.

Remind Me

- Association rule mining can be defined as identification of frequent patterns, correlations, associations, or causal structures among sets of objects or items in transactional databases, relational databases, and other information repositories.
- Association rule mining often known as 'market basket' analysis is a very effective technique to find the association of sale of item X with item Y.
- Association rules are often written as X→Y meaning that whenever X appears Y also tends to appear.
- The metrics to evaluate the strength of association rules are support, confidence and lift.
- Let N is the total number of transactions. Support of X is represented as the number of times X appears in the database divided by N.
- Confidence for X→Y is defined as the ratio of the support for X and Y together to the support for X (which is same as the conditional probability of Y when X has already occurred).
- Lift is the ratio of conditional probability of Y when X is given to the unconditional probability of Y in the dataset.
- Rather than counting all the possible item combinations in the stock, the improved Naïve algorithm focuses only on the items that are sold in transactions.
- There are three ways to store datasets of transactions, i.e., simple storage, horizontal storage and vertical storage.
- The name of the Apriori algorithm is assigned on the basis of the fact that it uses prior knowledge of frequent itemset properties.
- The Apriori algorithm consists of two phases. In the first phase, the frequent itemsets, i.e., the itemsets that exceed the minimum required support are identified. In the second phase, the association rules meeting the minimum required confidence are identified from the frequent itemsets.
- Apriori property states that all nonempty subsets of a frequent itemset must also be frequent.
- Association rules for frequent itemset l generate all non-empty subsets of l and for every non-empty subset s of l, the output rule is s→l-s and if the confidence of the rule is more than the threshold value of the confidence then, this rule will be selected in the final association rules.
- Apriori–TID uses the Apriori algorithm to generate the candidate and frequent itemsets. The only difference is that it uses TID or vertical storage approach for its implementation.
- The DHP algorithm is useful to improve the pruning of C2.This algorithm employs a hash-based technique for reducing the count of candidate itemsets generated in the first pass.

Point Me (Books)

- Han, Jiawei, Micheline Kamber, and Jian Pei. 2011. *Data Mining: Concepts and Techniques*, 3rd ed. Amsterdam: Elsevier.
- Gupta, G. K. 2014. *Introduction to Data Mining with Case Studies*. Delhi: PHI Learning Pvt. Ltd.
- Mitchell, Tom M. 2017. *Machine Learning*. Chennai: McGraw Hill Education.
- Witten, Ian H., Eibe Frank, Mark A. Hall, and Christopher Pal. 2016. *Data Mining: Practical Machine Learning Tools and Techniques*, 4th ed. Burlington: Morgan Kaufmann.

Point Me (Video)

- https://www.coursera.org/lecture/text-mining/1-7-word-association-mining-and-analysis-Uufkz

Connect Me (Internet Resources)

- https://en.wikipedia.org/wiki/Association_rule_learning
- https://www.hackerearth.com/blog/machine-learning/beginners-tutorial-apriori-algorithm-data-mining-r-implementation/

Test Me

Answer these questions based on your learning in this chapter.

1. Apply the Apriori and DHP algorithms to find frequent itemsets for the following dataset, Minimum support is 50%.

TID	*List of Items*
100	I1, I2, I5
200	I2, I4
300	I2, I3
400	I1, I2, I4
500	I1, I3
600	I2, I3
700	I1, I3
800	I1, I2, I3, I5
900	I1, I2, I3

2. Identify C4 after pruning the following frequent three itemsets as L3. Justify your answer. {3,4,5}, {3,4,7}, {3,5,6}, {3,5,7}, {3,5,8}, {4,5,6}, {4,5,7}
3. Show that if the rule ABC→ D does not have the minimum confidence required, then the rules like AB→CD, A→BCD and C→ABD will also not have the minimum confidence.
4. Compute the support for itemsets *{e}*, *{b, d}*, and *{b, d, e}* by treating each transaction ID as a market basket.

Customer ID	*Transaction ID*	*Items Bought*
1	0001	{a, d, e}
1	0024	{a, b, c, e}
2	0012	{a, b, d, e}
2	0031	{a, c, d, e}
3	0015	{b, c, e}
3	0022	{b, d, e}
4	0029	{c, d}
4	0040	{a, b, c}
5	0033	{a, d, e}
'5	0038	{a, b, e}

Also compute the confidence and lift for the association rules
{b, d} → {e} and {e} → {b, d}.

5. Consider the following group of frequent 3-itemsets and hence, identify C4 after pruning the following frequent three itemsets as L3. Justify your answer.
{1, 2, 3}, {1, 2, 4}, {1, 2, 5}, {1, 3, 4}, {1, 3, 5}, {2, 3, 4}, {2, 3, 5}, {3, 4, 5}.
6. Apply the Apriori algorithm and the FP-tree growth approach for the following database to identify frequent itemsets with minimum support of 50%. Also find association rules having confidence of more than 75%.

Transaction ID	*Items Bought*
1	{Milk, Beer, Diapers}
2	{Bread, Butter, Milk}
3	{Milk, Diapers, Cookies}
4	{Bread, Butter, Cookies}
5	{Beer, Cookies, Diapers}
6	{Milk, Diapers, Bread, Butter}
7	{Bread, Butter, Diapers}
8	{Beer, Diapers}
9	{Milk, Diapers, Bread, Butter}
10	{Beer, Cookies}

7. For an Apriori algorithm the L2 is given below:

L_2	
Itemset	*Sup. count*
{I1, I2}	4
{I1, I3}	4
{I1, I5}	2
{I2, I3}	4
{I2, I4}	2
{I2, I5}	2

What will be C3 after pruning? Justify your answer.

8. Apply the DHP algorithm to find association mining rules for the following dataset with minimum support 50% and confidence 75%.

TID	*Items Bought*
100	1, 2, 3, 4
200	5, 6, 7, 8, 9
300	6, 8, 9, 10
400	2, 3, 9

Also apply the FP growth algorithm to find the most frequent items pair(s).

9. What is wrong in the following L3:

   L2
   XY
   XZ

   L3
   XYZ
10. What are rules that can be generated from the three itemset {1,2,3}?
11. How is lift calculated in case of A->B
12. Convert the given transaction database to TID-list representation.

Transaction ID	*Items Bought*
100	Bread, Cheese
200	Bread, Cheese, Juice
300	Bread, Milk
400	Cheese, Juice, Milk

13. Frequent 2-itemsets are: {1,2}, {1,3}, {1,5}, {2,3}, {2,4}, {2,5}. What will be a pruned candidate 3-itemset?
14. Given a set of transactions, find rules to predict the occurrence of an item on the basis of the occurrences of other items in the transaction. The value of support is 40% and confidence is 70%.

TID	*Items Bought*
1	Bread, Milk
2	Bread, Diaper, Beer, Eggs
3	Milk, Diaper, Beer, Coke
4	Bread, Milk, Diaper, Beer
5	Bread, Milk, Diaper, Coke

Also apply the FP growth algorithm to find frequent item pairs.

10

Implementing Association Mining with Weka and R

Chapter Objectives

- ✓ To demonstrate the use of the association mining algorithm.
- ✓ To apply association mining on numeric data
- ✓ To comprehend the use of class association rules
- ✓ To compare the decision tree classifier with association mining
- ✓ To conduct association mining with R language

10.1 Association Mining with Weka

Let us consider the 'to-play-or-not-to-play' dataset given in Figure 10.1 for getting hands on experience with association mining in Weka. This dataset is available as default dataset in the ***data*** folder of Weka with the file name ***weather.nominal.arff.***

weather.nominal.arff *

Relation: weather.symbolic

No.	outlook Nominal	temperature Nominal	humidity Nominal	windy Nominal	play Nominal
1	sunny	hot	high	FALSE	no
2	sunny	hot	high	TRUE	no
3	overcast	hot	high	FALSE	yes
4	rainy	mild	high	FALSE	yes
5	rainy	cool	normal	FALSE	yes
6	rainy	cool	normal	TRUE	no
7	overcast	cool	normal	TRUE	yes
8	sunny	mild	high	FALSE	no
9	sunny	cool	normal	FALSE	yes
10	rainy	mild	normal	FALSE	yes
11	sunny	mild	normal	TRUE	no
12	overcast	mild	high	TRUE	yes
13	overcast	hot	normal	FALSE	yes
14	rainy	mild	high	TRUE	no

Figure 10.1 Snapshot of the 'play-or-no-play' dataset

This dataset has four attributes describing weather conditions and a fifth attribute is a class attribute that indicates based on the weather conditions of the day, whether Play was held or not. There are 14 instances, or samples in this dataset.

It is important to note that in classification, we are interested in assigning the output attribute to play or no play. But in Association mining we are interested in finding association rules based on the associations between all the attributes that came together. Thus, in association we do not take class attributes into consideration.

If we compare this dataset with the ***transactions*** dataset discussed in the last chapter for market basket analysis, you can find equivalence between transaction id and data items purchased in that transaction.

Here, No. 1 to 14, i.e. the instances act as transaction ids and the values of attributes given in the row corresponding to the given instance are acting as data items for that instance. Here we are interested in finding associations by observing the facts like **Outlook = sunny AND Temperature = hot is more common than the association of Outlook = sunny AND Temperature = cool** occurring together as shown in Figure 10.2.

Outlook	Temp.	Humidity	Windy	Play
sunny	hot	high	false	no
sunny	hot	high	true	no
overcast	hot	high	false	yes
rainy	mild	high	false	
rainy	cool	normal	false	
rainy	cool	normal	true	
overcast	cool	normal	true	
sunny	mild	high	false	no
sunny	cool	normal	false	yes
rainy	mild	normal	false	yes
sunny	mild	normal	true	yes
overcast	mild	high	true	yes
overcast	hot	normal	false	yes
rainy	mild	high	true	no

For association, we look for things that "go together"

Figure 10.2 Associations between items

Weka contains an ***Associate*** tab which aids in applying different association algorithms in order to find association rules from datasets. One such algorithm is the ***Predictive Apriori*** association algorithm that optimally combines support and confidence to calculate a value called ***predictive accuracy*** as depicted in Figure 10.3.

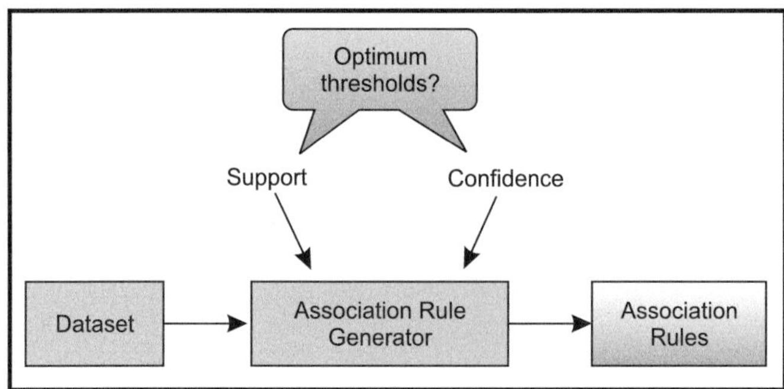

Figure 10.3 Working of Predictive Apriori

The user only needs to specify how many rules they would like the algorithm to generate, and the algorithm takes care of optimizing support and confidence to find the best rules.

10.2 Applying Predictive Apriori in Weka

Objective:

To Apply the Predictive Apriori algorithm and find associations rules for the dataset given in Figure 10.1

Steps:

1. *Dataset loading:*

Step 1 : Open Weka to get the ***Weka GUI Chooser Panel,*** then click on the ***Explorer*** option out of the 4 offered options.

Step 2 : Now in the ***Preprocess*** tab click on the ***Open file*** button and choose the **weather.nominal. arff** as shown in Figure 10.4.

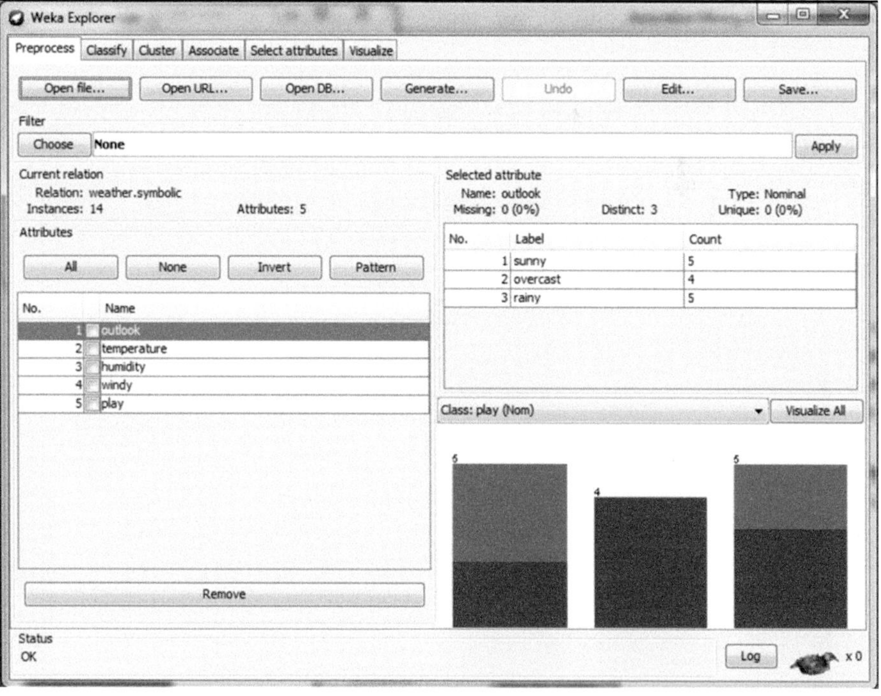

Figure 10.4 Loading the weather.nominal.arff

Step 3 : Click on the ***Associate*** Tab inside the Weka window (top). Now click on ***Choose*** button and select ***Apriori*** under ***association*** as shown in Figure 10.5.

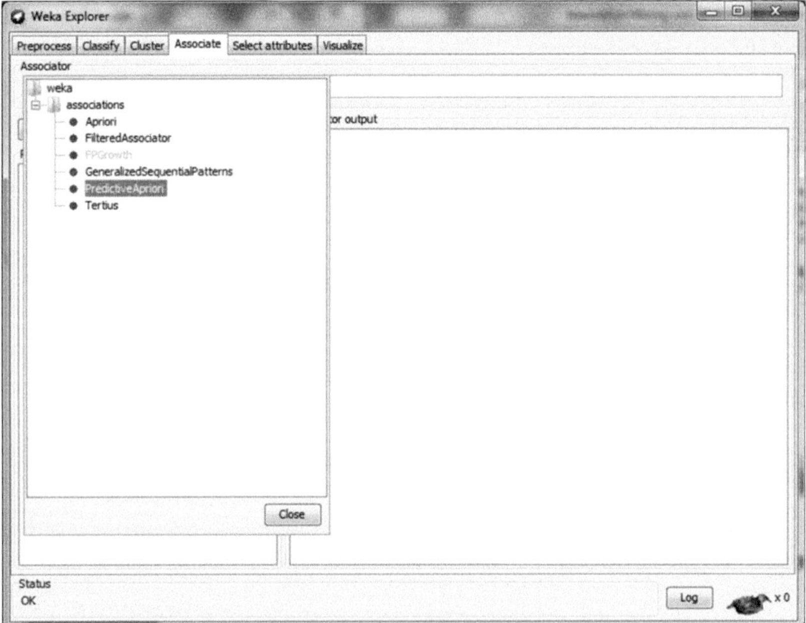

Figure 10.5 Selecting the Predictive Apriori algorithm for association mining

Step 4: Now, Left click on the ***Associator*** field where ***Predictive Apriori*** is written. This will open the property window for Apriori; and open ***Generic Object Editor*** as shown in Figure 10.6.

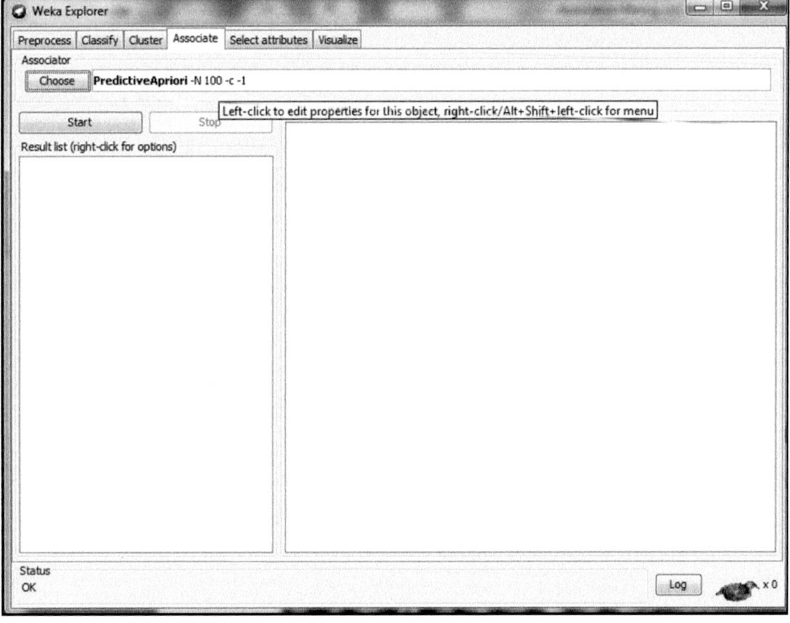

Figure 10.6 Changing parameters for Predictive Apriori

It has three parameters options as shown in Figure 10.7 and description of each parameter (user can click on the ***More*** button to view these details) is given in Table 10.1.

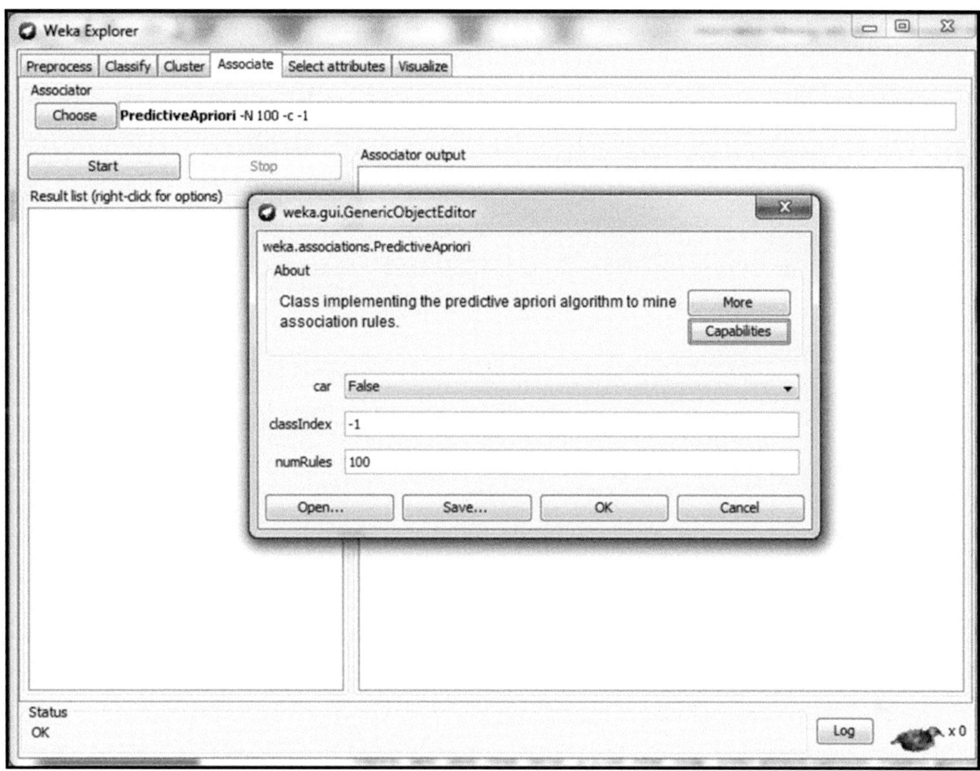

Figure 10.7 Parameters of the Predictive Apriori algorithm

Table 10.1 Description of parameters

car	Stands for class association rules. If enabled, class association rules are mined instead of (general) association rules.
classIndex	It is the index of the class attribute. If set to -1, the last attribute will be taken as the class attribute.
numRules	It is number of rules to find. The default value of number of rules generated is 100.

Let us go with default value and keep the values same for now, press the cancel button to exit out of this window.

Step 5 : Finally click on the ***Start*** button to start the Predictive Apriori Algorithm on our uploaded database. The output for the algorithm results will be shown on the right hand side of Weka window under the ***Associator Output*** as shown in Figure 10.8.

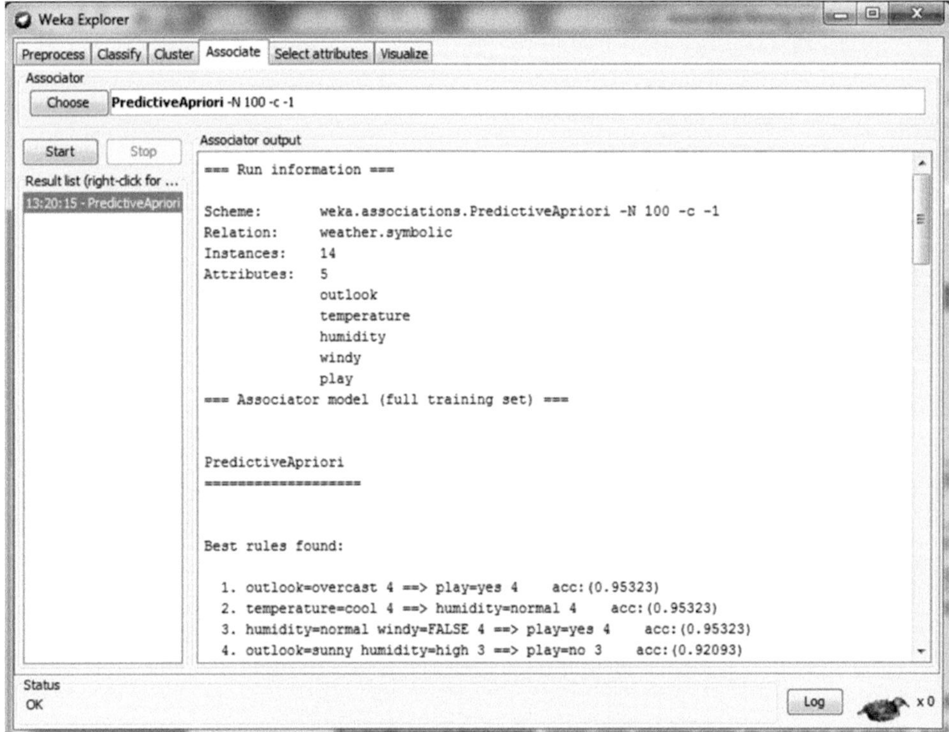

Figure 10.8 Association mining rules

Result interpretation:

The list of top 20 rules out of 100 association rules generated by Predictive Apriori, with their corresponding predictive accuracy is given below. It is important to note that predictive accuracy combines support and confidence into a single value and it indicates the strength of the rule.

Best rules found have been indicated in bold-face:

1. **outlook = overcast 4 ==> play = yes 4 acc:(0.95323)**
2. **temperature = cool 4 ==> humidity = normal 4 acc:(0.95323)**
3. humidity = normal windy = FALSE 4 ==> play = yes 4 acc:(0.95323)
4. outlook = sunny humidity = high 3 ==> play = no 3 acc:(0.92093)
5. outlook = sunny play= no 3 ==> humidity = high 3 acc:(0.92093)
6. outlook = rainy windy = FALSE 3 ==> play = yes 3 acc:(0.92093)
7. outlook = rainy play = yes 3 ==> windy = FALSE 3 acc:(0.92093) 8. outlook = sunny temperature = hot 2 ==> humidity = high play = no 2 acc:(0.86233)
9. outlook = sunny humidity=normal 2 ==> play=yes 2 acc:(0.86233)
10. outlook = sunny play = yes 2 ==> humidity = normal 2 acc:(0.86233)
11. outlook = overcast temperature = hot 2 ==> windy = FALSE play = yes 2 acc:(0.86233)
12. outlook = overcast windy = FALSE 2 ==> temperature = hot play = yes 2 acc:(0.86233)
13. outlook = rainy humidity = high 2 ==> temperature = mild 2 acc:(0.86233)

14. outlook = rainy windy = TRUE 2 ==> play = no 2 acc:(0.86233)
15. outlook = rainy play = no 2 ==> windy = TRUE 2 acc:(0.86233)
16. temperature = hot play =yes 2 ==> outlook = overcast windy = FALSE 2 acc:(0.86233)
17. temperature = hot play = no 2 ==> outlook = sunny humidity = high 2 acc:(0.86233)
18. temperature = mild humidity =normal 2 ==> play = yes 2 acc:(0.86233)
19. temperature = mild play=no 2 ==> humidity = high 2 acc:(0.86233)
20. temperature = cool windy = FALSE 2 ==> humidity = normal play = yes 2 acc:(0.86233)

The relation for support, confidence and predictive accuracy for rule 2 is shown in Figure 10.9.

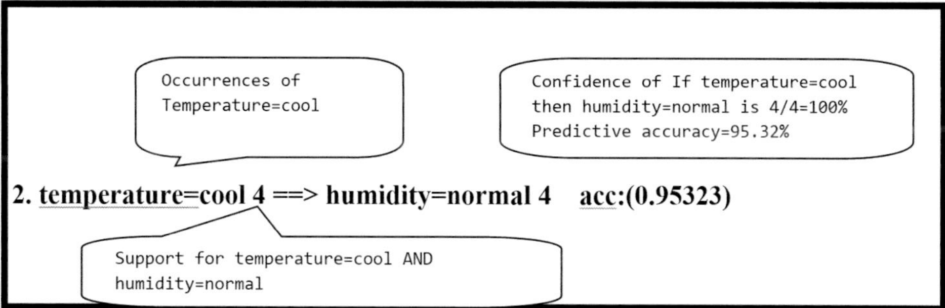

Figure 10.9 Analysis of rule 2

By observing these rules, one can appreciate that Weka generates a vast number of association rules by using various attributes in the dataset and some rules have multiple precedent terms or multiple antecedent terms or both as given in rule number 5 and 8 as shown below.

5. outlook = sunny play = no 3 ==> humidity = high 3 acc:(0.92093)
8. outlook = sunny temperature = hot 2 ==> humidity = high play = no 2 acc:(0.86233)

10.3 Rules Generation Similar to Classifier Using Predictive Apriori

We have already discussed that association mining treats all attributes in a dataset like items in a market basket, and so the **class attribute** Play in this dataset is treated like any normal data item. But we can configure the algorithm such that it will treat the last column of the dataset, i.e., Play (or No Play) in this case, as a class attributes and will generate rules only pertaining to this class attribute, by keeping it as the antecedent of the rule.

In other words, association mining can also predict whether or not the Play will happen based on weather conditions, by generating the rules like (Rule 6) as presented below.

6. outlook = rainy windy = FALSE 3 ==> play = yes 3 acc:(0.92093)

Thus, there is a linkage between classification and association. The ***PredictiveApriori*** algorithm as implemented in Weka takes advantage of this linkage, by setting the ***car*** (class association rules) property to ***true***. In Weka, open up the ***Generic Object Editor*** for Predictive Apriori and set ***car*** to ***true*** as shown in Figure 10.10.

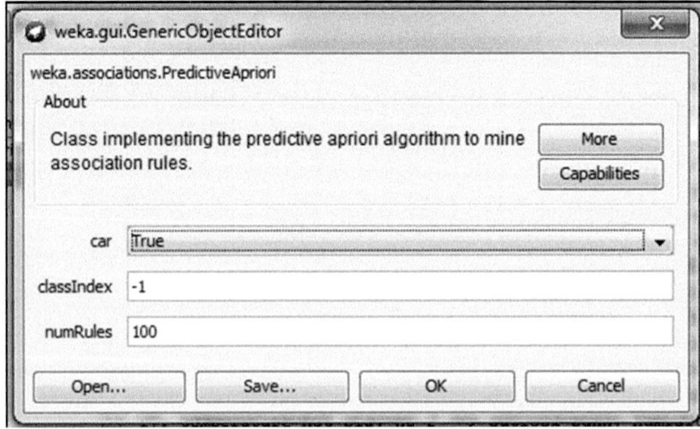

Figure 10.10 Setting CAR to true for getting class association rules

Click ***Start*** to generate the rules and the rules will be generated in the output of Associator and one finds that it only produces the rules having the Play attribute as antecedent.

The top 20 rules produced by Associator are shown below.

Best rules found:

1. outlook = overcast 4 ==> play = yes 4 acc:(0.97594)
2. humidity = normal windy = FALSE 4 ==> play = yes 4 acc:(0.97594)
3. outlook = sunny humidity = high 3 ==> play = no 3 acc:(0.96426)
4. outlook = rainy windy = FALSE 3 ==> play = yes 3 acc:(0.96426)
5. outlook = sunny temperature = hot 2 ==> play = no 2 acc:(0.94406)
6. outlook = sunny humidity = normal 2 ==> play = yes 2 acc:(0.94406)
7. outlook = rainy windy = TRUE 2 ==> play = no 2 acc:(0.94406)
8. temperature = mild humidity = normal 2 ==> play = yes 2 acc:(0.94406)
9. temperature = cool windy = FALSE 2 ==> play = yes 2 acc:(0.94406)
10. humidity = normal 7 ==> play = yes 6 acc:(0.79098)
11. temperature = cool 4 ==> play = yes 3 acc:(0.64898)
12. windy = FALSE 8 ==> play = yes 6 acc:(0.6316)
13. outlook = sunny windy = FALSE 3 ==> play = no 2 acc:(0.60315)
14. outlook = rainy temperature = mild 3 ==> play = yes 2 acc:(0.60315)
15. temperature = hot humidity = high 3 ==> play = no 2 acc:(0.60315)
16. temperature = mild windy = TRUE 3 ==> play = yes 2 acc:(0.60315)
17. humidity = high windy = TRUE 3 ==> play = no 2 acc:(0.60315)
18. temperature = mild 6 ==> play = yes 4 acc:(0.58611)
19. outlook = sunny 5 ==> play = no 3 acc:(0.56112)
20. outlook = rainy 5 ==> play = yes 3 acc:(0.56112)

10.4 Comparison of Association Mining CAR Rules with J48 Classifier Rules

Objective:

To compare the output of CAR (class association rules) with the J48 classifier rules (as both of them generate rules corresponding to the class attribute.)

Steps:

Let us apply the J48 Classifier on the same dataset by following steps given below:

Step 1 : Click on ***Classifier tab*** and select *J48* under trees as shown in Figure 10.11.

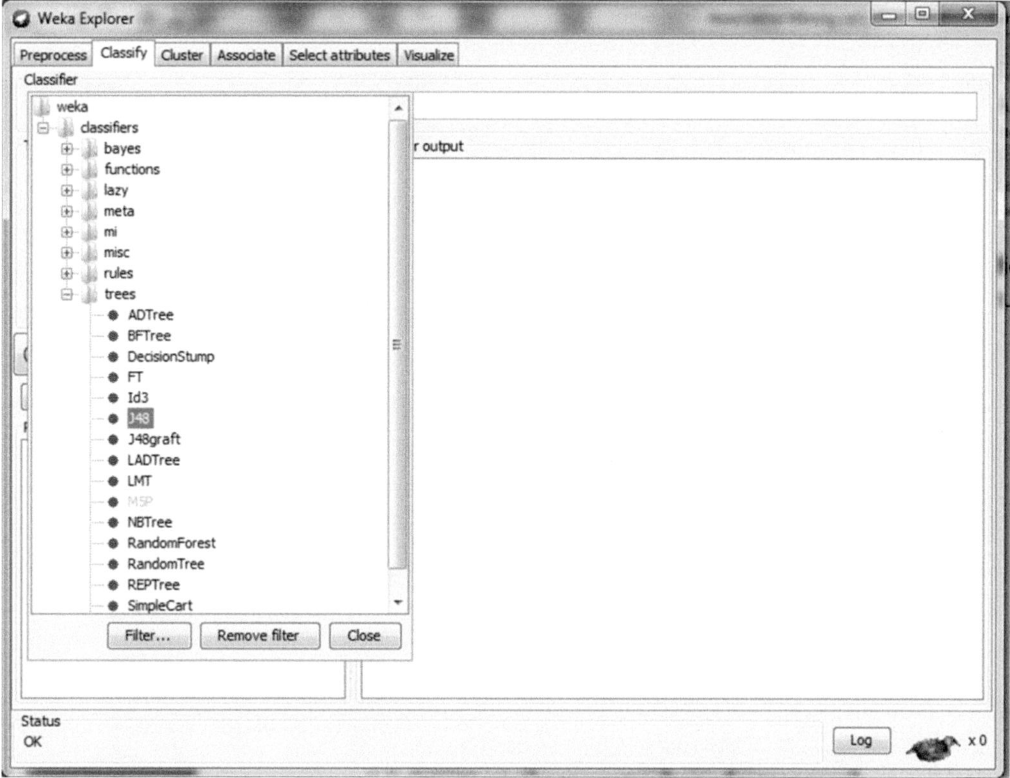

Figure 10.11 Application of the J48 algorithm on dataset 'play-or-no-play'

Step 2 : Now, Select the ***Use training set*** option under ***Test Options***. Since the dataset contains just 14 records it is important to select the whole dataset for building the classifier.

Next, Click on the ***Start*** button to get the output of the classifier as shown in Figure 10.12.

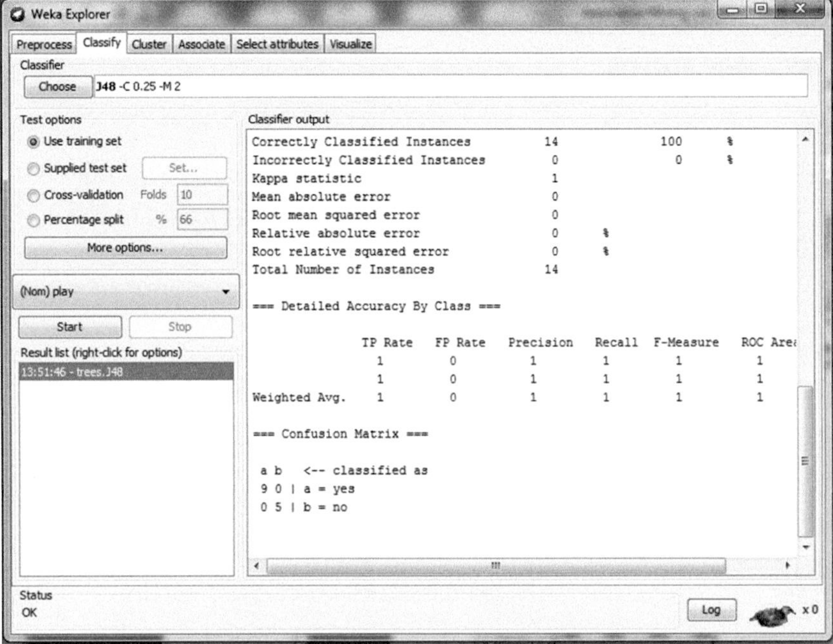

Figure 10.12 Selection of use training set to build the model

Step 3 : Right click on the ***Result list*** of the classifier and select ***visualize tree*** as shown in Figure 10.13.

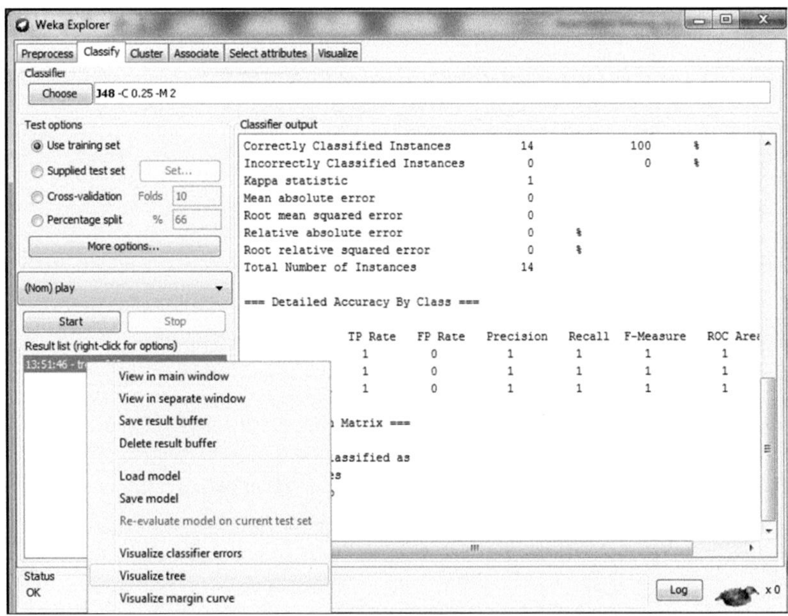

Figure 10.13 Select the 'Visualize tree' to get a decision tree

The decision tree will be generated as shown in Figure 10.14.

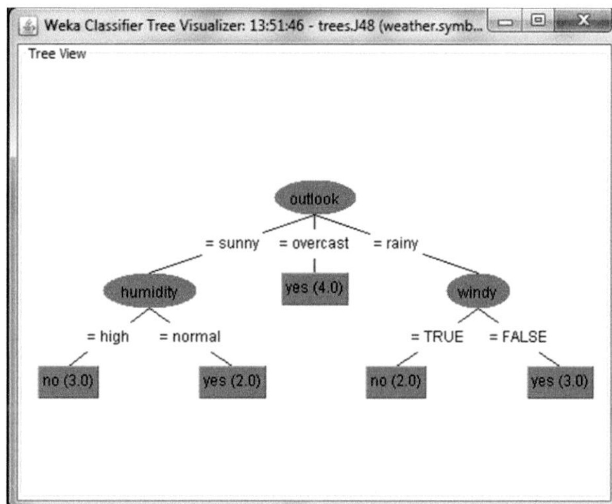

Figure 10.14 Decision tree for dataset 'play-or-no-play'

The user can enlarge this window and right click on the empty area of the tree and select option **Fit to Screen** to resize the size of the tree.

Result interpretation

Now, let us compare the rules given by this decision tree with the class association rules generated by the Predictive Apriori algorithm (which was discussed earlier in ***Section 10.3***).

One can analyze that - the rules of decision tree such as, **if outlook is overcast then play is yes,** is also produced by class association rules and it is ranked as one of the best rules at **rule 1.**

Similarly, the rule of decision tree - **if outlook = sunny and humidity = high then play is no,** is also produced by class association rules and it is given as one of the best rules being ranked at **rule 3.**

The rule of **outlook = sunny and humidity = normal 2, then play is yes 2,** is allotted to position 6 by **car.**

The readers are advised to look for the other two rules given by the decision tree that are also in the rules generated by **car** (class association rules). Hopefully you would have identified them correctly at positions 4 and 7. For clarity, **car** rules are reproduced again and out of these rules, the rules given by the decision tree have been shown in bold.

1. **outlook = overcast 4 ==> play = yes 4 acc:(0.97594)**
2. humidity = normal windy = FALSE 4 ==> play = yes 4 acc:(0.97594)
3. **outlook = sunny humidity = high 3 ==> play = no 3 acc:(0.96426)**
4. **outlook = rainy windy = FALSE 3 ==> play = yes 3 acc:(0.96426)**
5. **outlook = sunny temperature = hot 2 ==> play = no 2 acc:(0.94406)**
6. **outlook = sunny humidity = normal 2 ==> play = yes 2 acc:(0.94406)**
7. **outlook = rainy windy = TRUE 2 ==> play = no 2 acc:(0.94406)**
8. temperature = mild humidity = normal 2 ==> play = yes 2 acc:(0.94406)

9. temperature = cool windy = FALSE 2 ==> play = yes 2 acc:(0.94406)
10. humidity = normal 7 ==> play = yes 6 acc:(0.79098)
11. temperature = cool 4 ==> play = yes 3 acc:(0.64898)
12. windy = FALSE 8 ==> play = yes 6 acc:(0.6316)
13. outlook = sunny windy = FALSE 3 ==> play = no 2 acc:(0.60315)
14. outlook = rainy temperature = mild 3 ==> play = yes 2 acc:(0.60315)
15. temperature = hot humidity = high 3 ==> play = no 2 acc:(0.60315)
16. temperature = mild windy = TRUE 3 ==> play = yes 2 acc:(0.60315)
17. humidity = high windy = TRUE 3 ==> play = no 2 acc:(0.60315)
18. temperature = mild 6 ==> play = yes 4 acc:(0.58611)
19. outlook = sunny 5 ==> play = no 3 acc:(0.56112)
20. outlook = rainy 5 ==> play = yes 3 acc:(0.56112)

One can easily conclude that the association mining rules are more exhaustive than rules produced by J48 classifier. And ***car*** not only produces the rules involving outlook (root attribute of the decision tree) with other attributes but it also produce rules involving the other possible input attributes for output attribute (play) as shown below in case of **rule number 17** and **rule number 18.**

17. humidity = high windy = TRUE 3 ==> play = no 2 acc:(0.60315)
18. temperature = mild 6 ==> play = yes 4 acc:(0.58611)

10.5 Applying the Apriori Algorithm in Weka

To apply the Apriori algorithm on the given dataset of '***play-or-no-play***' the user needs to select ***Apriori*** algorithm under the ***Associate*** tab in Weka as shown in Figure 10.15.

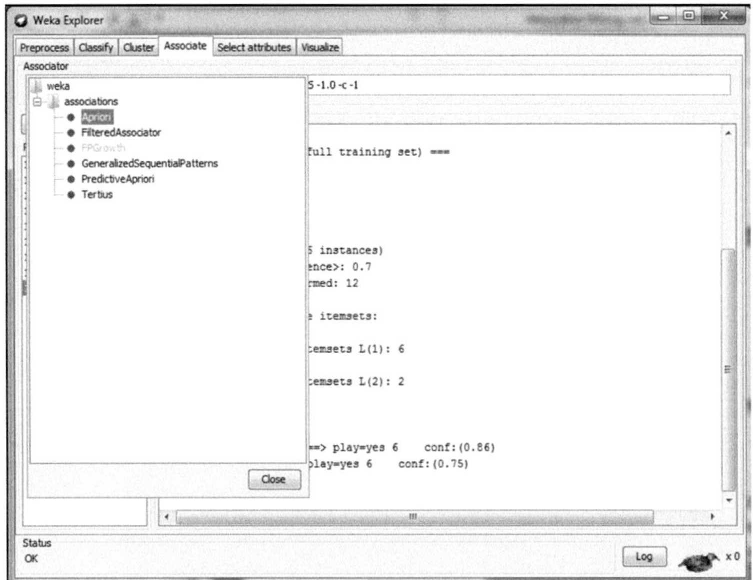

Figure 10.15 Selection of the Apriori algorithm

To change the parameters or to configure the default values for this algorithm, left click on the name of algorithm in the ***Associator*** pane (on left) and it will open ***Generic Object Editor*** of Apriori algorithm as shown in Figure 10.16.

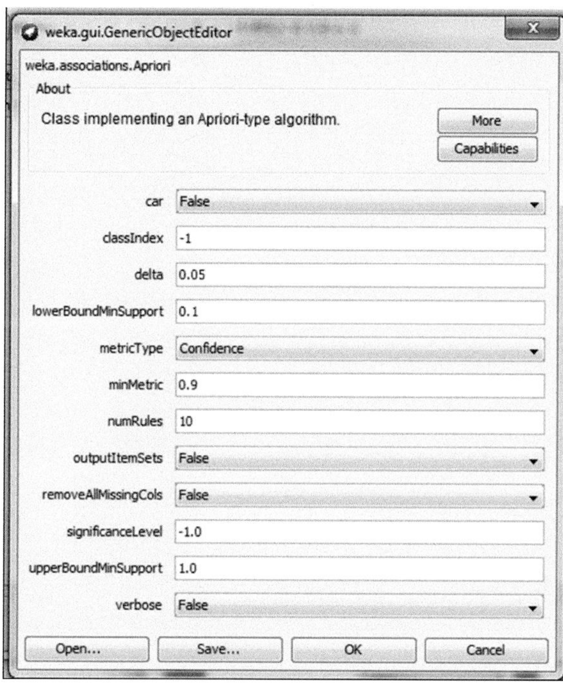

Figure 10.16 Generic Object Editor to change the default values of the Apriori algorithm

One can use this option to specify the threshold values of ***Support, Confidence, Lift and car*** etc. The description of important options is given in Table 10.2.

Table 10.2 Description of available property options of the Apriori algorithm

lowerBoundMinSupport	Lower boundary for minimum support. It is used to set the threshold value of the support in the range of 0 to 1.
metricType – Conviction	Set the type of metric by which to rank rules. Options are Confidence, Lift. User can select the desired metric and set its value in the **minMetric** field discussed below. By default, it is Confidence.
minMetric -- Minimum metric score	Considers only those rules with scores higher than this value. If selected metric is confidence or lift then the value of the selected metric can be changed through this parameter.
numRules	Number of rules to find.
removeAllMissingCols	Remove columns with all missing values.

The default values of these properties are shown in Figure 10.17.

Figure 10.17 Default values of the properties of the Apriori algorithm

One can appreciate that the default minimum support (***lowerBoundMinSupport: 0.1***) is 10% and confidence (***metricType:*** Confidence and ***minMtric***:0.9) is 90%. Users can change the threshold values of Support and Confidence by changing these values. To find association rules with these default values, save all the changes you made by clicking OK in the ***Generic Object Editor*** Window. Finally, click ***Start*** to generate the rules. The association mining rules will appear in ***Associator output***. Some of best rules which are found have been reproduced below.

Best rules found:

1. outlook = overcast 4 ==> play = yes 4 conf:(1)
2. temperature = cool 4 ==> humidity = normal 4 conf:(1)
3. humidity = normal windy = FALSE 4 ==> play = yes 4 conf:(1)
4. outlook = sunny play = no 3 ==> humidity = high 3 conf:(1)
5. outlook = sunny humidity = high 3 ==> play = no 3 conf:(1)
6. outlook = rainy play = yes 3 ==> windy = FALSE 3 conf:(1)
7. outlook=rainy windy=FALSE 3 ==> play=yes 3 conf:(1)
8. temperature = cool play = yes 3 ==> humidity = normal 3 conf:(1)
9. outlook = sunny temperature = hot 2 ==> humidity = high 2 conf:(1)
10. temperature = hot play = no 2 ==> outlook = sunny 2 conf:(1)

Users are now advised to find the association mining rules having support of 40% and confidence of 70%.

The best found association rules for above threshold values are reproduced below for verification of with your results.

With the Apriori

=======

Minimum support: 0.4 (6 instances)
Minimum metric <confidence>: 0.7
Number of cycles performed: 12
Generated sets of large itemsets:
Size of set of large itemsets L(1): 6
Size of set of large itemsets L(2): 2

Best rules found:

1. humidity = normal 7 ==> play = yes 6 conf:(0.86)
2. windy = FALSE 8 ==> play = yes 6 conf:(0.75)

Similarly, readers can try several different threshold values to find a variety of association rules. For example, find association rules for support of 30% and confidence of 80%.

10.6 Applying the Apriori Algorithm in Weka on a Real World Dataset

Objective:

To run the Apriori algorithm on a given dataset (Table 10.3) and hence choose the best Association Rule using Weka.

This is same dataset regarding the store which we have discussed while applying the Apriori algorithm.Now we will apply the same algorithm in Weka and will compare the results of Weka with the Apriori rules which we generated in the previous chapter.

Table 10.3 Transaction database of a store

Transaction ID	*Items*
100	Bread, Cornflakes
101	Bread, Cornflakes, Jam
102	Bread, Milk
103	Cornflakes, Jam, Milk

Steps:

Dataset creation:

Step 1 : Open MS Excel and tabulate the data as shown in Figure 10.18.

	A	B	C	D	E
1	Transaction	Bread	Cornflake	Jam	Milk
2	100	1	1		
3	200	1	1	1	
4	300	1			1
5	400		1	1	1

Figure 10.18 Daily item dataset

Step 2 : Next, save the file as a **CSV** file. For saving a file in CSV format, switch to the ***File*** tab in MS Excel and then click on ***Save As.*** A dialog box will pop-up, give ***File name*** as **DailyItem Dataset** and choose ***Save as Type*** as CSV (Comma delimited). Finally click on ***Save*** button to save the file on ***Desktop*** as shown in Figure 10.19.

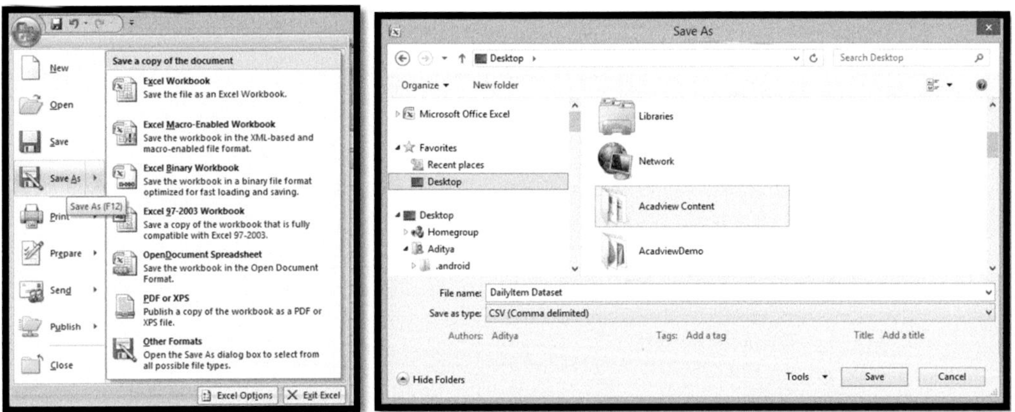

Figure 10.19 Saving the file in CSV format

2. *Running the Apriori algorithm:*

Step 1 : Open Weka to get the ***Weka GUI Chooser Panel,*** now click on the ***Explorer*** option out of the 4 offered options as shown in Figure 10.20.

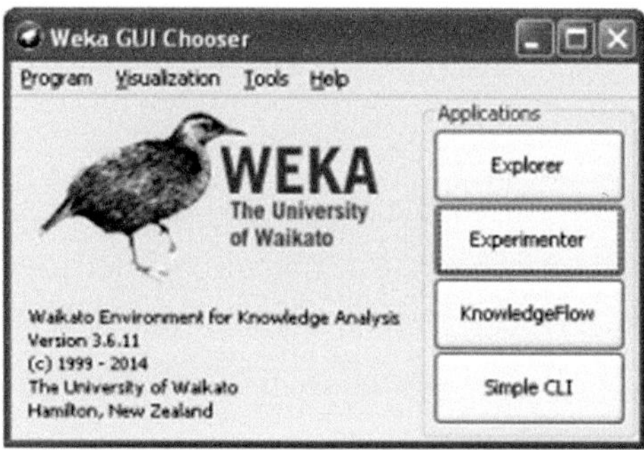

Figure 10.20 Weka GUI Chooser Panel

Step 2 : Now in the ***Preprocess*** tab click on ***Open file*** button and choose the **DailyItem Dataset (.csv)** we created in previous steps from ***Desktop.*** Once the dataset gets loaded into Weka you will see the names of all the Attributes as shown in Figure 10.21.

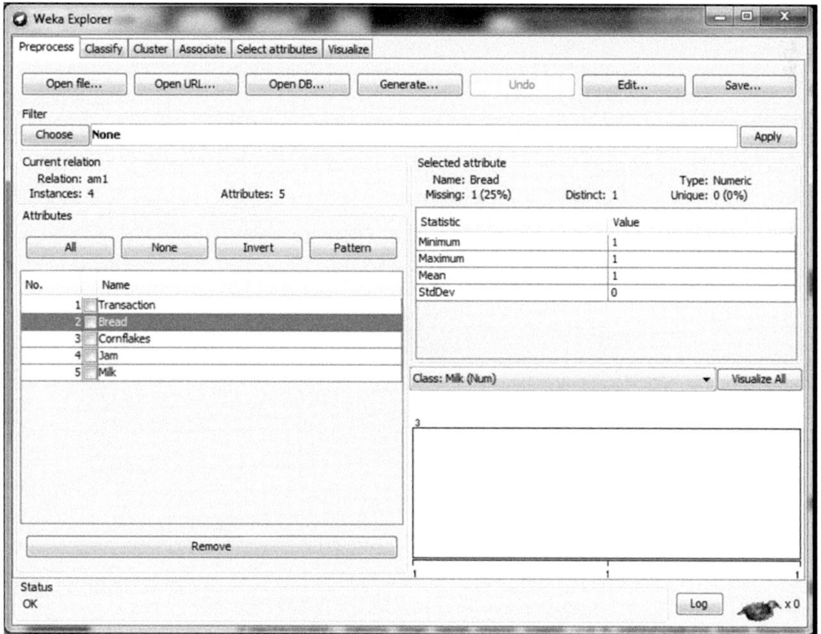

Figure 10.21 Dataset uploaded in Weka

Step 3 : Once data is loaded, Weka will consider all columns as numeric but association mining cannot be directly applied on numeric data, so it is required to convert this numeric data to nominal form before running the programme. For this, just under the ***Open file*** button you will see a ***Choose*** button which will help in choosing a filter to be applied on our dataset.

Select ***filters -> unsupervised ->Numeric to Nominal filter***

Finally click on the ***Choose*** button as shown in Figure 10.22.

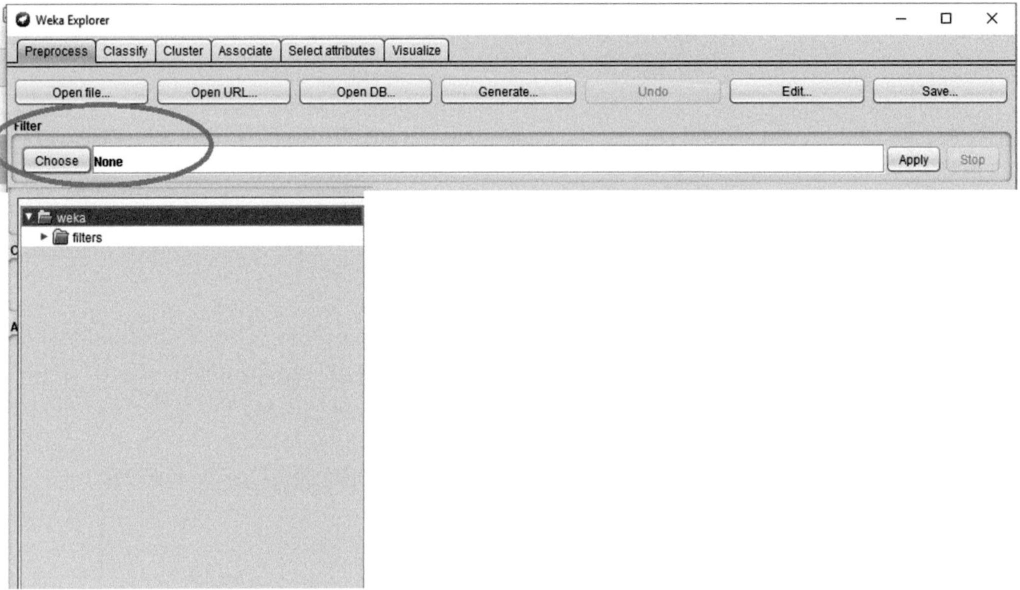

Figure 10.22 Choosing numeric to nominal filter in Weka

Step 4 : After selecting the Numeric to Nominal filter we have to apply it on our dataset. To do this, click on the ***Apply*** button as shown in Figure 10.23.

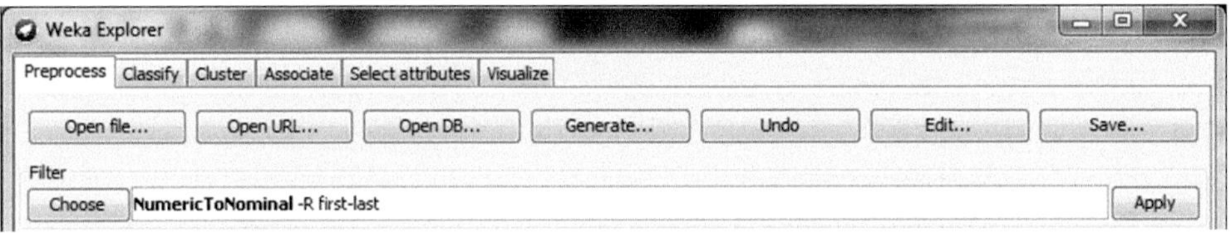

Figure 10.23 Changing from numeric to nominal filter

Step 5 : After inserting a Dataset into Weka and applying the Filter on your dataset, you can remove undesirable attributes before running the Apriori Algorithm. Since the transaction attribute does not play any role in association mining, it is better to remove it before applying association mining.

For doing so, just select the ***Transaction*** attribute from the left pane and correspondingly click on ***Remove*** button to delete the attribute as shown in Figure 10.24.

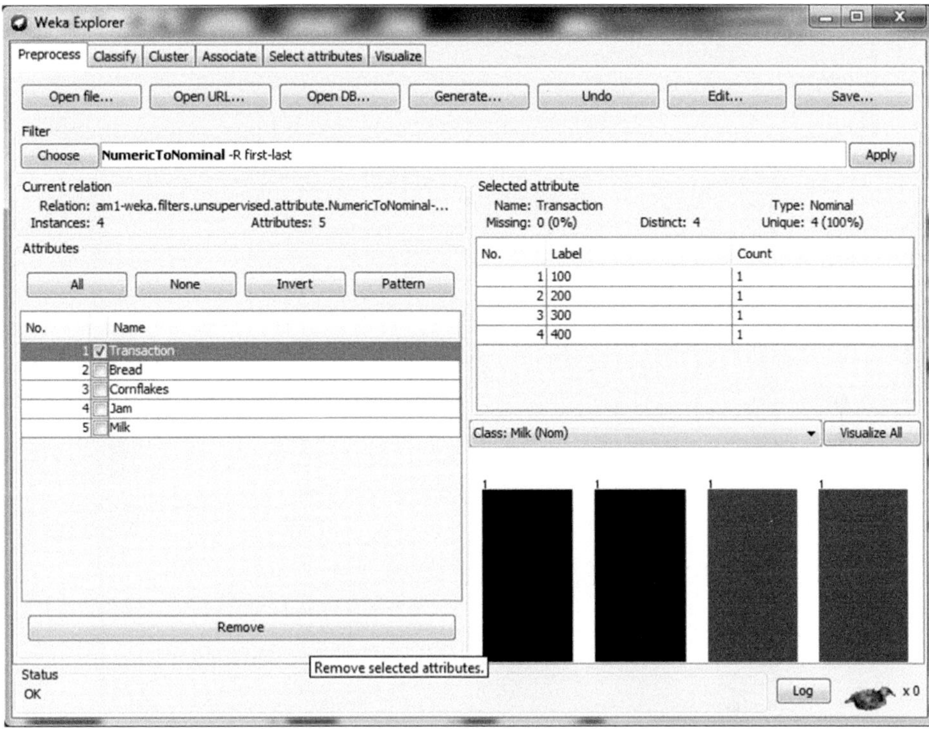

Figure 10.24 Removing the Transaction attribute

Step 6 : Click on the ***Associate*** Tab inside the Weka window (top). Now click on the ***Choose*** button and select ***Apriori*** under ***association*** as shown in Figure 10.25.

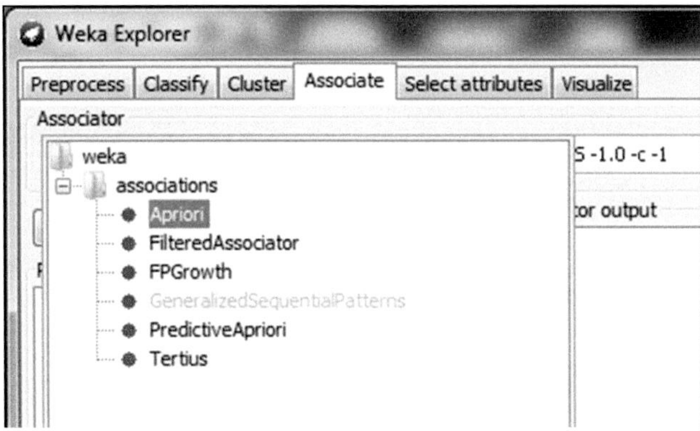

Figure 10.25 Applying the Apriori algorithm

Step 7 : Now, Left click on the ***Associator*** field where ***Apriori*** is written. This will open the property window for Apriori; i.e. it opens the ***Generic Object Editor*** as shown in Figure 10.26.

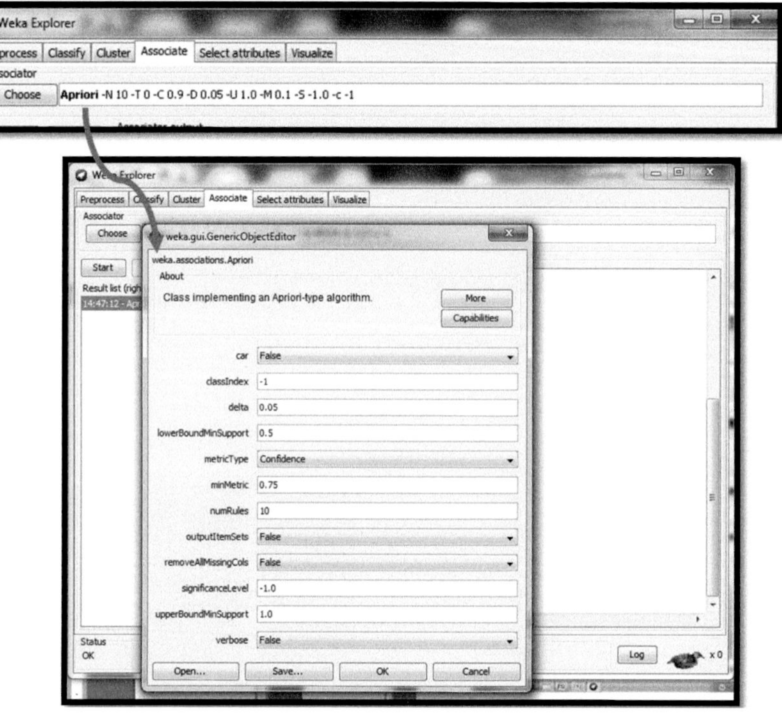

Figure 10.26 Opening the Generic Object Editor

Step 8 : Now the values fed in ***Generic Object Editor*** will decide what rules are yielded by Apriori. So fill the following values :

- In the ***lowerBoundMinSupport***, supply the minimum threshold of support, i.e., which in this case is **0.5.**
- In the ***metricType***, select ***Confidence.***
- In the ***minMetric***, enterly the minimum threshold of confidence, which in this case is **0.75.**
- In the ***numRules***, enter the number of rules you want Apriori to find, which in our case is **10.**

Click on the ***OK*** button to save the configuration for Apriori.

Step 9 : Finally click on the ***Start*** button to start the Apriori Algorithm to run on our **DailyItem dataset**. The output for the algorithm results will be shown on the right hand side of the Weka window. (as shown in Figure 10.27)

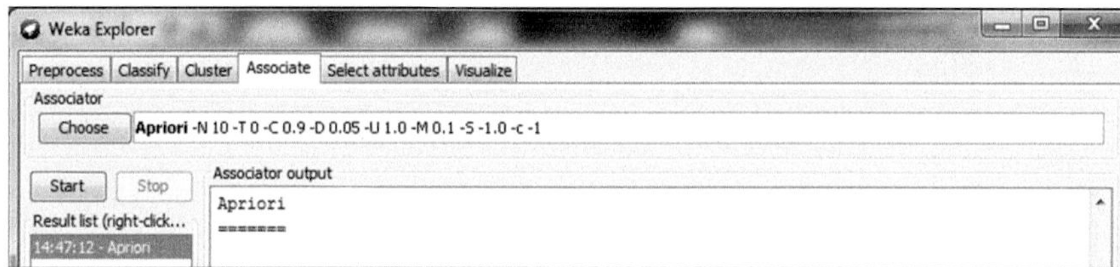

Figure 10.27 Starting the Apriori algorithm

Step 10 : Interpret the Results which have been generated as shown in Figure 10.28.

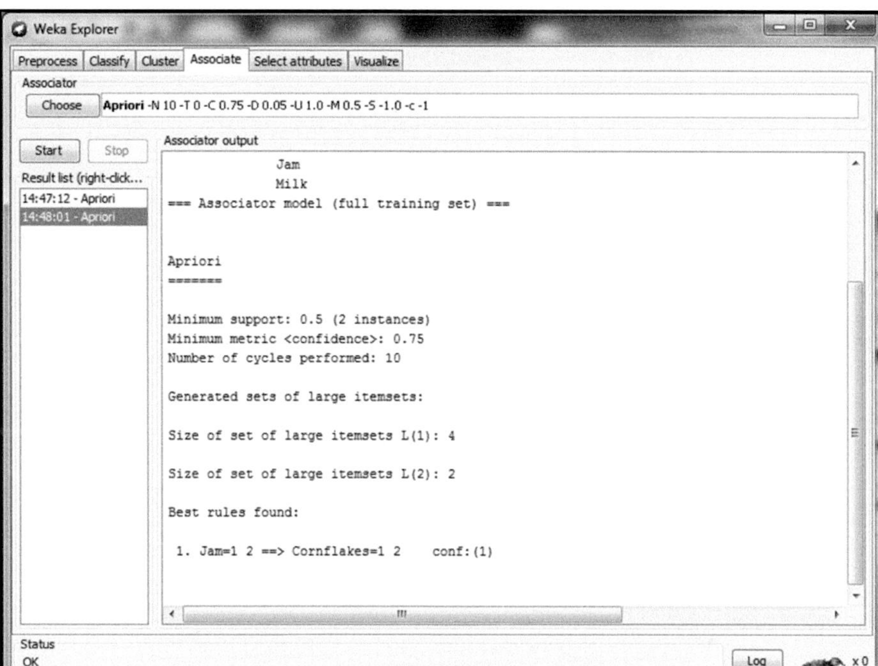

Figure 10.28 Results after running the Apriori algorithm

Result interpretation:

The best Association Rule which we obtained after running the Predictive Apriori Algorithm on the given **DailyItem Dataset** is, ***Jam → Cornflakes*** as we got 100% Predictive accuracy (confidence =1) for this combination. This result is the same as discussed in the previous chapter under Section 9.5.1.

10.7 Applying the Apriori Algorithm in Weka on a Real World Larger Dataset

Objective:

To run the Apriori algorithm on a given dataset with pre-defined support and confidence, and then interpret the output.

Let us consider as an example, the dataset given in Table 10.4, consisting of only five transactions and six items. We want to identify association rules with 50% support and 75% confidence using the Apriori algorithm. This is the same dataset on which we have previously applied Apriori algorithm. Now we will apply the same algorithm in Weka and will compare the results of Weka with the Apriori rules which we found on the same dataset in the previous chapter.

Table 10.4 Sample dataset of a store

Transaction ID	*Items*
T1	Bread, Cornflakes, Eggs, Jam
T2	Bread, Cornflakes, Jam
T3	Bread, Milk, Tea
T4	Bread, Jam, Milk
T5	Cornflakes, Jam, Milk

Steps: Dataset creation

Step 1 : Open MS Excel and tabulate the data as shown in Figure 10.29.

Next, save the file as a **CSV** file. For saving a file in CSV format, switch to the ***File*** tab in MS Excel and then click on ***Save As.***

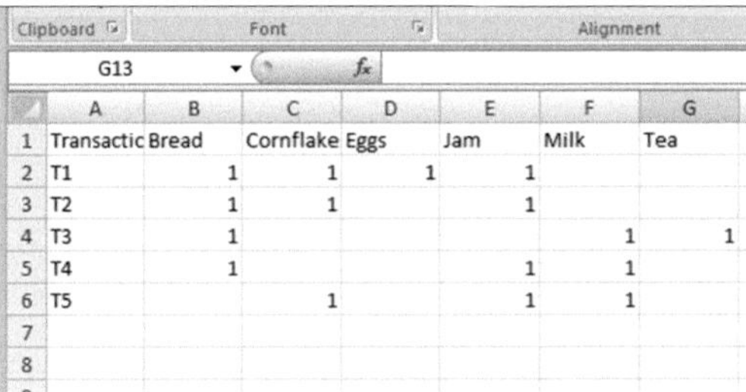

	A	B	C	D	E	F	G
1	Transactic	Bread	Cornflake	Eggs	Jam	Milk	Tea
2	T1	1	1	1	1		
3	T2	1	1		1		
4	T3	1				1	1
5	T4	1			1	1	
6	T5		1		1	1	

Figure 10.29 Saving the file in CSV format

A dialog box will pop-up, enter the ***File name*** as **DailyItem2 Dataset** and choose ***Save as Type*** as CSV (Comma delimited) . Finally click on the ***Save*** button to save the file on Desktop as shown in Figure 10.30.

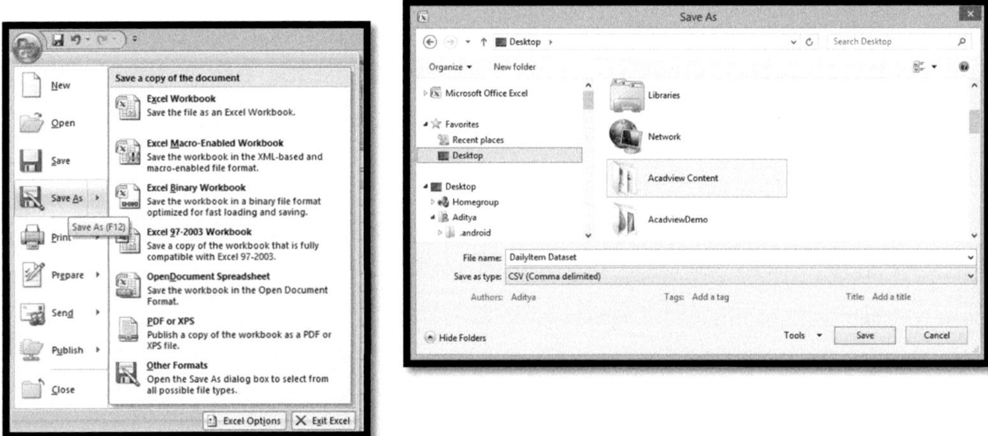

Figure 10.30 Saving the file in CSV format

Running the Apriori algorithm:

Step 1 : Open Weka to get the ***Weka GUI Chooser Panel,*** now click on the ***Explorer*** option out of the 4 offered options as shown in the Figure 10.31.

Figure 10.31 Weka GUI Chooser Panel

Step 2 : Now in the ***Preprocess*** tab click on the ***Open file*** button and choose the **DailyItem2 Dataset(.CSV)** we created in previous steps from ***Desktop.*** Once the dataset gets loaded into Weka you will see the names of all the Attributes as shown in Figure 10.32.

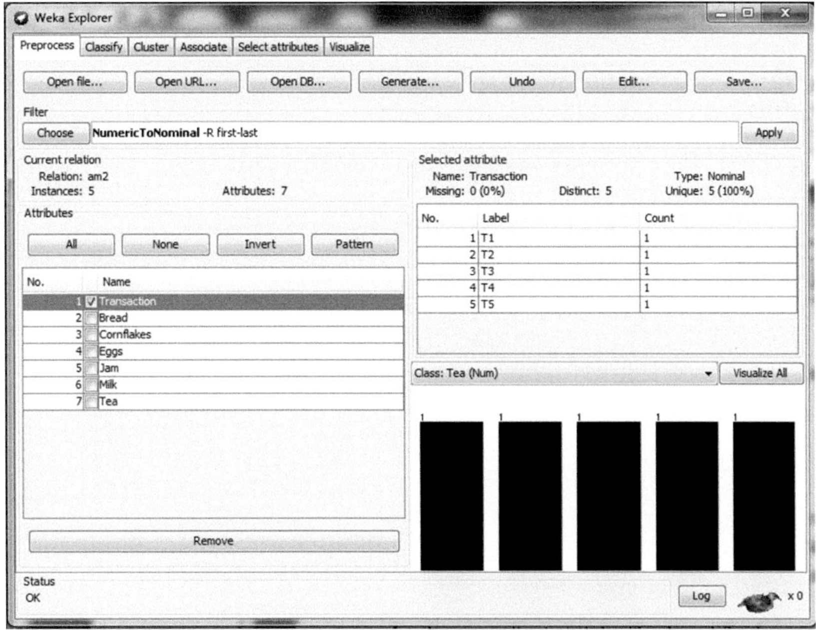

Figure 10.32 Dataset uploaded in Weka

Step 3 : Once data is loaded, Weka will consider all columns as numeric and since association mining cannot be directly applied on numeric data, it is required to convert this numeric data to nominal before running the programme. For this, just under the ***Open file*** button you will see a

Choose button which will help us in choosing a filter to be applied on our dataset. Select ***filters -> unsupervised ->Numeric to Nominal filter***

and finally click on the ***Choose*** button.

Step 4 : After selecting the Numeric to Nominal filter we have to apply it on our dataset. To do this, click on the ***Apply*** button. After this you will have something like Figure 10.33.

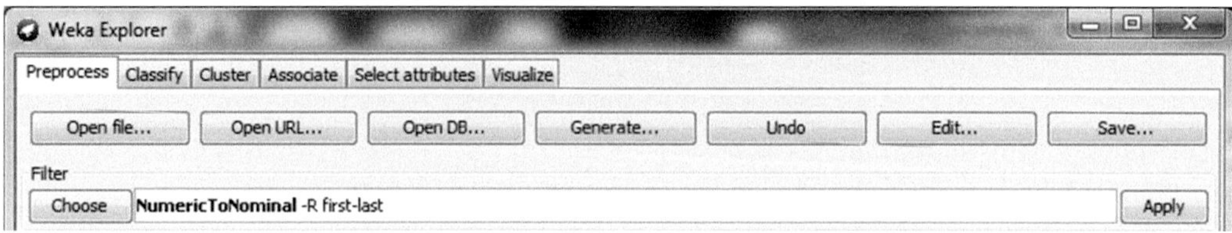

Figure 10.33 Weka numeric to nominal filter applied

Step 5 : After inserting a Dataset into Weka and applying the Filter on your dataset, you can remove attributes before we run the Apriori Algorithm. For doing so, just select the ***Transaction*** attribute from the left pane and correspondingly click on ***Remove*** button to delete the attribute as shown in Figure 10.34.

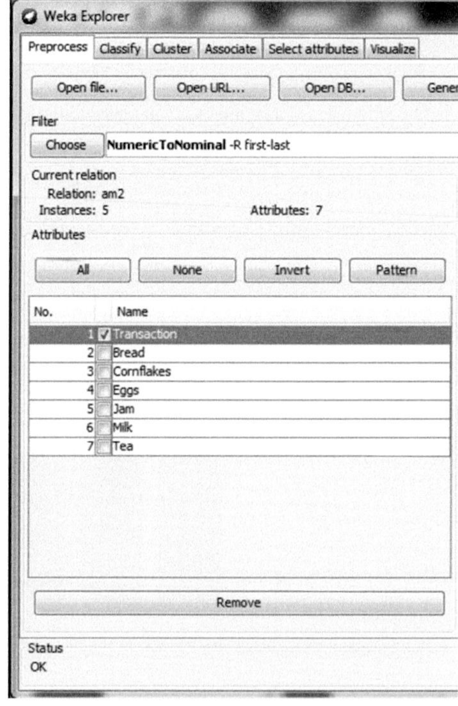

Figure 10.34 Removing the Transaction attribute

Step 6 : Click on the ***Associate*** Tab inside the Weka window (top). Now click on the ***Choose*** button and select ***Apriori*** under ***association*** as shown in Figure 10.35.

Figure 10.35 Choosing the Apriori algorithm

Step 7 : Now, Left click on the ***Associator*** field where ***Apriori*** is written. This will open the property window for Apriori i.e. it opens the ***Generic Object Editor*** .

Step 8 : Now the values which are fed into the Generic Object Editor will be processed leading to rules being yielded by Apriori. So fill the following values :

- In the ***lowerBoundMinSupport,*** supply the minimum threshold of support, i.e., which in this case is **0.5.**
- In the ***metricType*** , select ***Confidence.***
- In the ***minMetric,*** supply the minimum threshold of confidence, in our case it is **0.75.**

Click on the ***OK*** button to save the configuration for Apriori.

Step 9 : Finally click on the ***Start*** button to start the Apriori Algorithm to run on our **DailyItem2 dataset**. The output for the algorithm results will be shown on the right hand side of Weka window as shown in Figure 10.36.

Step 10 : Interpret the Results.

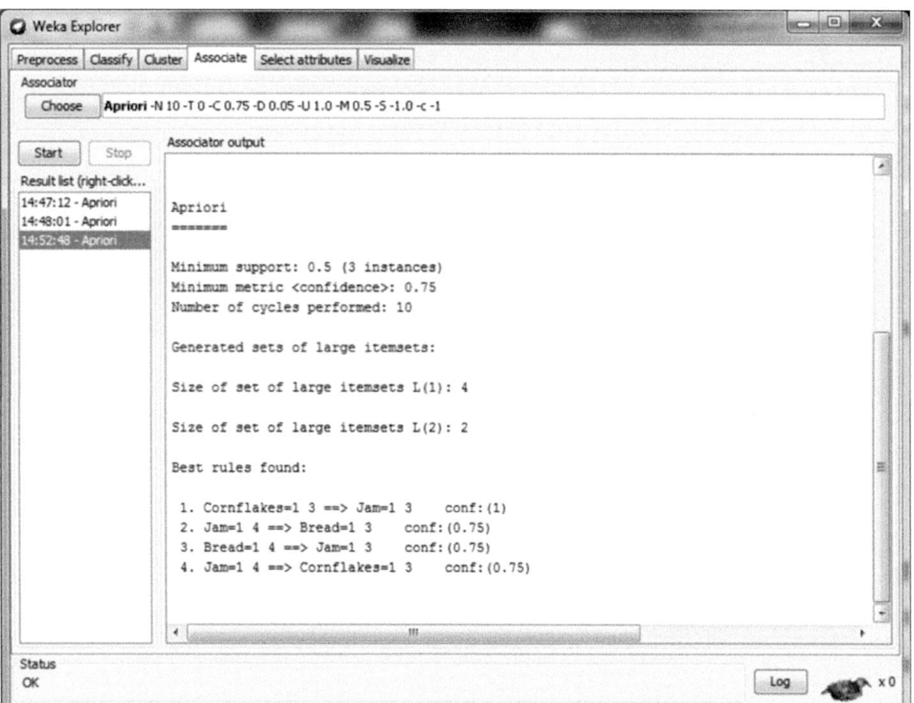

Figure 10.36 Results after running the Apriori algorithm on DailyDataset2

Result interpretation:

The best Association Rules which we obtained after running the Apriori Algorithm on the given **DailyItem Dataset** can be seen in the screenshot shown above.

Some of the best rules provided out by Apriori Algorithm are as followes:

Bread→Jam

Jam→Bread

Cornflakes→Jam

Jam→Cornflakes

The confidence of these rules is obtained by dividing the support for both items in the rule by the support for the item on the left-hand side of the rule. The confidence of the four rules therefore are 3/4 = 75%, 3/4 = 75%, 3/3 = 100%, and 3/4 = 75% respectively. Since all of them have a minimum 75% confidence, they all qualify.

One can verify that Weka has produced the same association rules that we had obtained in the last chapter by applying the Apriori algorithm on the same dataset in Section 9.7.2.

10.8 Applying the Apriori Algorithm on a Numeric Dataset

The performance records of students in a subject can be analyzed to find interesting associations between different attributes such as the association of MST marks with the final grade of the student; or, the association of lab marks with ESE marks and so on.

In order to apply association mining on student performance records for a particular subject. Let us consider the result of the data warehouse and data mining course of last semester. The attributes, designated from A to E are: Roll Number, Name, MST (Maximum Marks 20), Quiz (Maximum Marks 15), Lab (Maximum Marks 20), ENDSEM (Maximum Marks 45), Total (Maximum Marks 100) and Final Grade.These are given in Table 10.5. Now, the instructor wishes to find associations between different attributes to analyze the performance of students.

Table 10.5 Performance record of students in a data warehouse and data mining course

Roll No.	*Name*	*MST(20.0)*	*Quiz (15)*	*Lab (20.0)*	*ENDSEM (45.0)*	*Total (100.0)*	*Grade*
1	*******	6	4	12	8.5	30.5	E
2	*******	8.5	7	15	16	46.5	D
3	*******	2.5	6.5	14	1.5	24.5	E
4	*******	14.5	8.5	17	18	58	C
5	*******	16	5	18	20.5	59.5	B
6	*******	17	7.5	19	37	80.5	A

Contd.

Roll No.	Name	MST(20.0)	Quiz (15)	Lab (20.0)	ENDSEM (45.0)	Total (100.0)	Grade
7	*******	16	7	16	25.5	64.5	B
8	*******	16	6.5	17	18	57.5	B
....							
....							
9	*******	20	8	19	30.5	77.5	A

Steps :

Step 1 : Open ***MS Excel*** and tabulate the data. Next, save the file as a CSV file. For saving a file in the CSV format, switch to the ***File*** tab in MS Excel and then click on ***Save As***. A dialog box will pop up;, enter File name as DailyItem Dataset and choose as ***CSV (Comma delimited)*** in the ***Save as Type*** space. Finally click on the ***Save*** button to save the file on Desktop as shown in Figure 10.37.

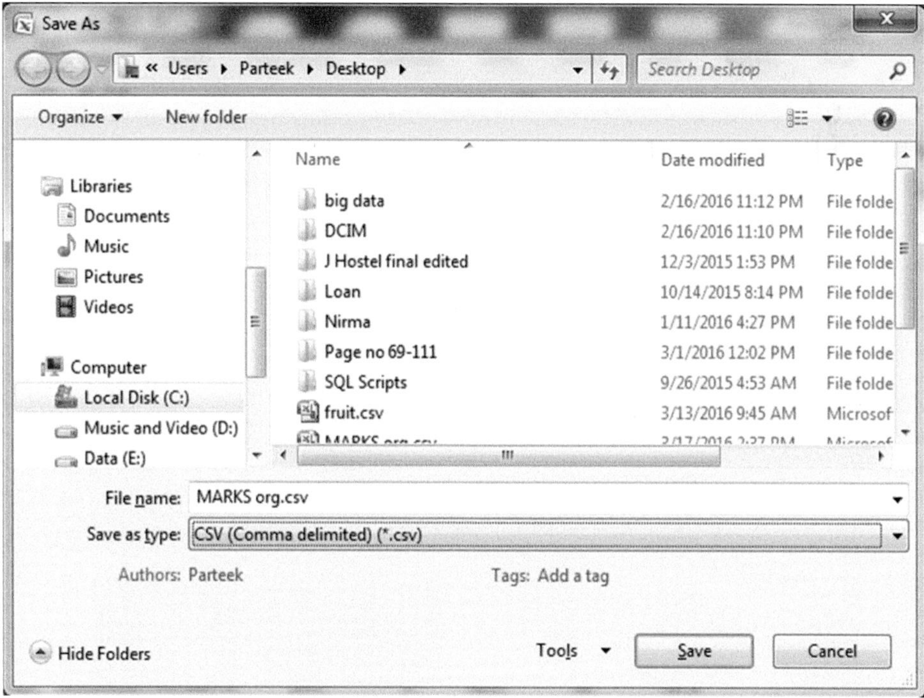

Figure 10.37 Saving in CSV format

Step 2 : Next, Load the CSV file created in the previous step to Weka by selecting the ***Open*** file button in the ***Preprocess*** tab of Weka. The loaded file in Weka is shown in Figure 10.38.

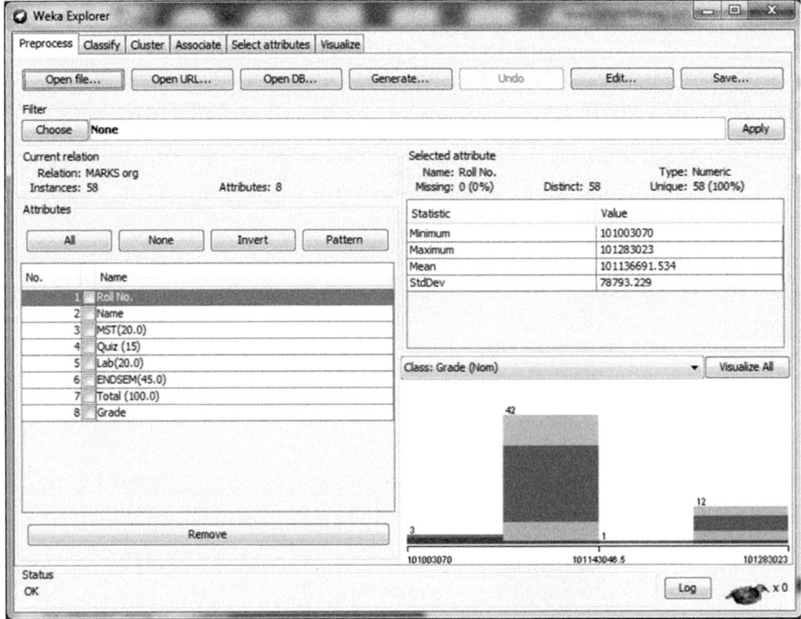

Figure 10.38 Loading the student performance dataset

Step 3: Since Roll No. and Name columns do not play any role in association mining so remove them. To do so, select them and press the button ***Remove*** as shown in Figure 10.39.

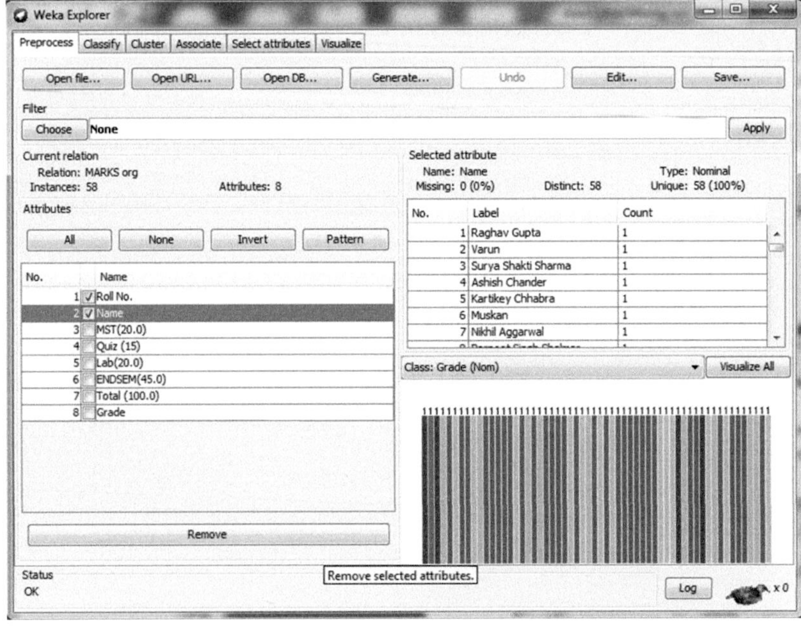

Figure 10.39 Removal of Roll No. and Name columns

But the data is ***numeric*** in nature and association mining cannot be applied on numeric data, as association rule mining works only on nominal values. So, it is necessary to convert the numeric data into nominal values by the conversion process called ***discretizing.***

Here, we are not using the filter ***NumerictoNominal*** but we still want to convert marks into nominal values like Poor, Average, Good and such, for better analysis.

If the user tries to apply association mining on numeric dataset (as in our case), then the user won't be able to use the association mining algorithm option as it is disabled for numeric data as shown in Figure 10.40.

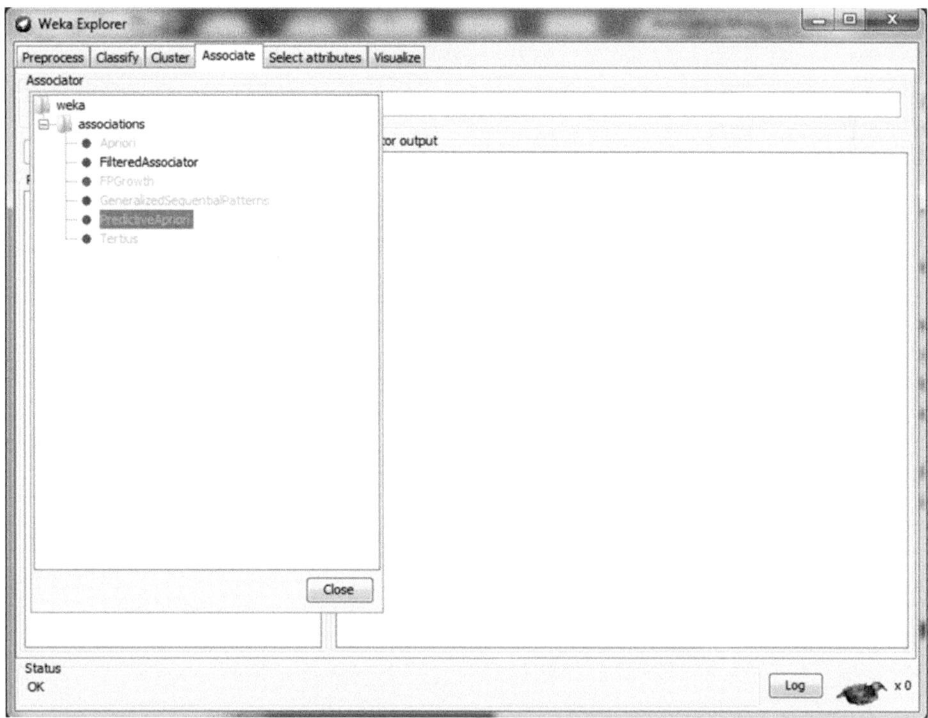

Figure 10.40 Association mining algorithms are disabled for numeric data

Step 4 : Thus, to perform the Discretizing operation of converting numeric values to nominal, the user can apply one of the Weka filters which discretizes the data values. There are **two types of discretization,** namely, **equal interval** and **equal frequency**. Both are similar to binning (discussed earlier). Accordingly we will use the term 'bin' for each different group. In equal interval discretization, we calculate a bin size and then put the samples into the appropriate bin. In equal frequency discretization, we allow the bin sizes to vary, where our goal is to choose bin sizes so that every bin has about the same number of samples in it. The idea is that if each bin has the same number of samples, no bin, or group, will have greater or lesser impact on the results of data mining. To apply the discretization filter, click on the ***Choose*** button for selecting the filter. This brings up a folder tree.

Follow the path: ***Weka→filters→unsupervised→attribute→Discretize*** as shown in Figure 10.41.

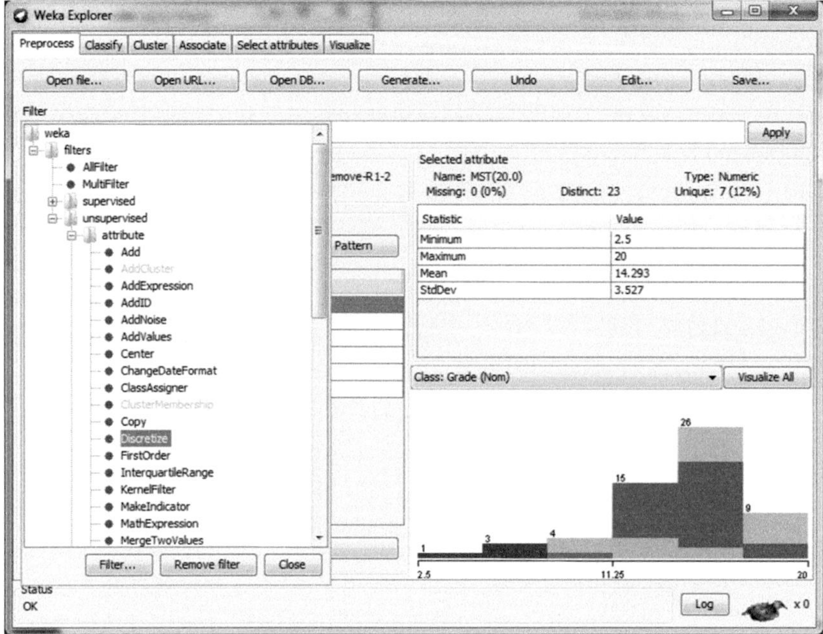

Figure 10.41 Selection of the Discretize filter

When the user clicks on ***Discretize***, he or she will be returned to the ***Preprocess*** tab, as shown in Figure 10.42.

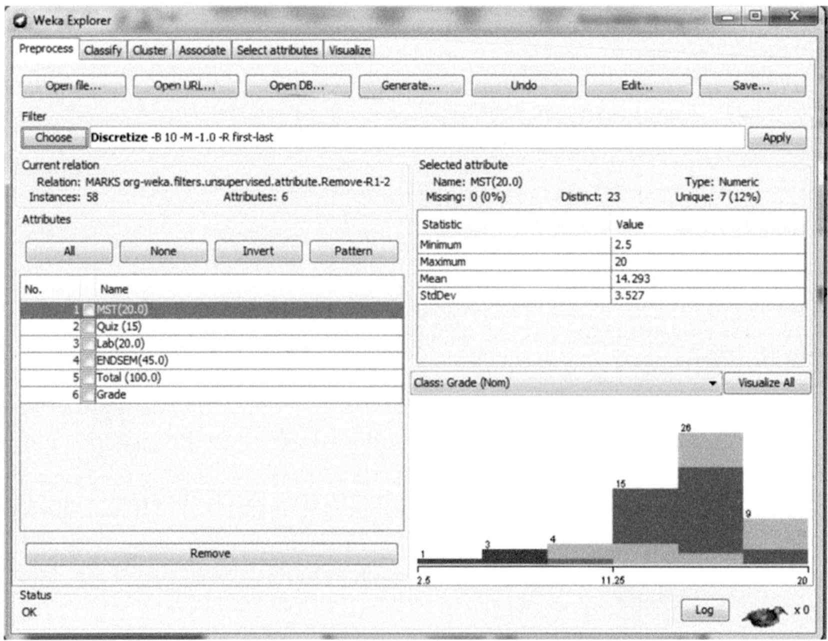

Figure 10.42 Discretization of numeric data

Step 5 : Click on ***Discretize*** to open the ***Generic Object Editor*** in order to change the properties of the ***Discretize*** filter as shown in Figure 10.43.

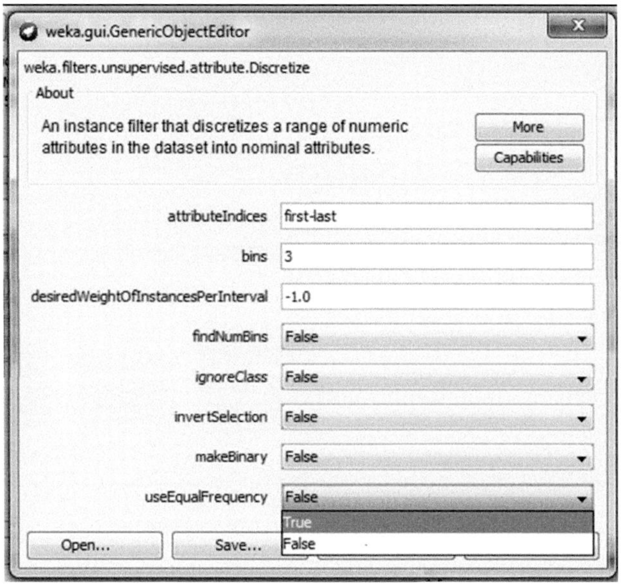

Figure 10.43 Generic Object Editor for changing properties of the Discretize filter

For the analysis of marks, we will be interested in Low, Medium and High values for each column so carry out the following changes:

- Set the number of ***bins*** to **3** from the default value of 10
- Set the ***useEqualFrequency*** attribute to ***True*** so that 1/3 of students are put into each bin of High, Medium and Low on the basis of their marks as shown in Figure 10.44

Step 6 : Now click on ***apply*** as shown in Figure 10.44 to apply the Discretize filter.

It will convert all values of attributes to nominal and the reader can cross check these values by selecting each column one by one and by checking its statistical values one can find that each column has been converted to nominal as shown in case of MST column given in Figure 10.44. One can also confirm that each column has been converted to three bins with numbers 1, 2 and 3 and the range of marks for that bin become the **label** of that field. In case of MST, the label of the first bin is '(-inf-13.75)' [marks from 0 to 13.75], for the second bin it is '(-13.75-15.75)' [marks from 13.75 to 15.75] and for the third bin it is '(15.75-inf)' [marks from 15.75 to 20]. The number of students in each range has been specified in the count column as shown in Figure 10.44

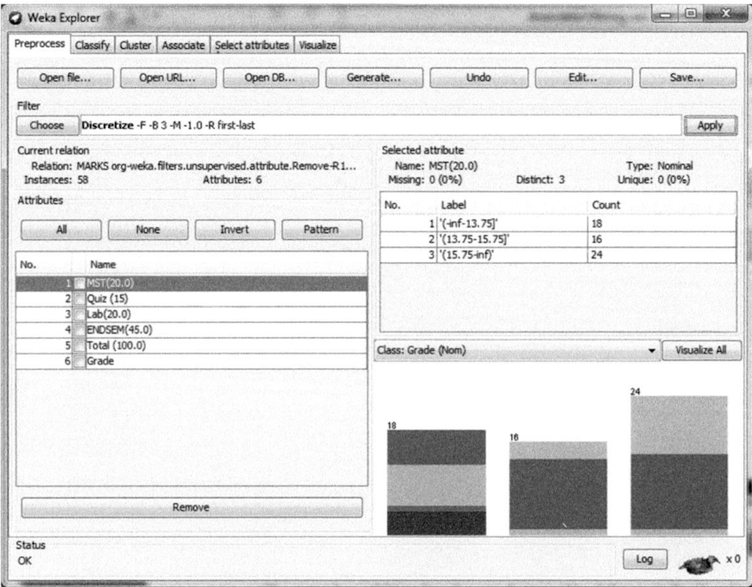

Figure 10.44 Discretization of data

Now that each column has been converted to nominal values, we can apply association mining on our dataset. So, select the ***associate*** tab and select ***PredictiveApriori*** as shown in Figure 10.45.

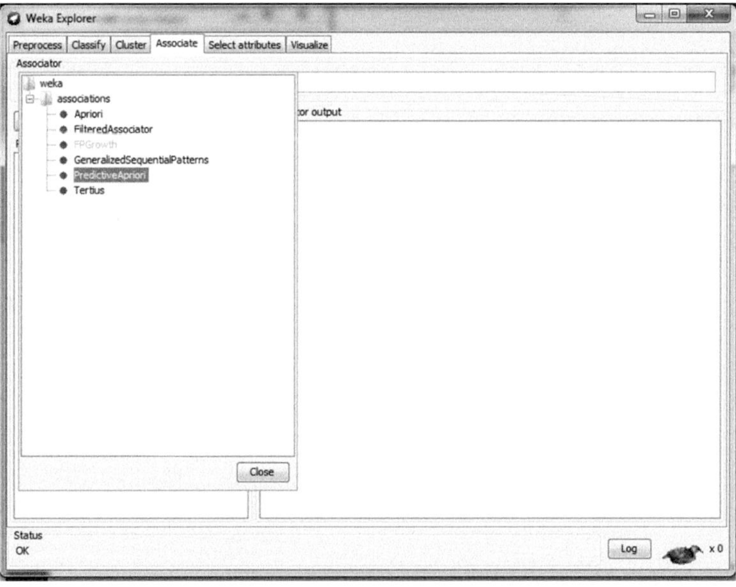

Figure 10.45 Application of the Predictive Apriori algorithm on nominal data

Step 7: Now, press the button ***Start*** and run the algorithm to find association mining rules for the given dataset. Some of best rules are shown below:

Best rules found:

1. Total (100.0) ='(58.25-69.25]' 20 ==> Grade = B 20 acc:(0.99441)
2. Grade = A 13 ==> Total (100.0) = '(69.25-inf)' 13 acc:(0.99297)
3. MST(20.0) = '(-inf-13.75]' ENDSEM(45.0) = '(-inf-21.5]' 12 ==> Total (100.0) = '(-inf-58.25]' 12 acc:(0.99247)
4. MST(20.0) = '(-inf-13.75]' Lab(20.0) = '(-inf-15.75]' 11 ==> Total (100.0) = '(-inf-58.25]' 11 acc:(0.99182)
5. Lab(20.0) = '(17.25-inf)' Total (100.0) = '(69.25-inf)' 11 ==> Grade = A 11 acc:(0.99182)
6. Grade = C 9 ==> Total (100.0) = '(-inf-58.25]' 9 acc:(0.98968)
7. Lab(20.0) = '(-inf-15.75]' ENDSEM(45.0) = '(-inf-21.5]' 9 ==> Total (100.0) = '(-inf-58.25]' 9 acc:(0.98968)
8. Quiz (15) = '(6.75-7.75]' ENDSEM(45.0) = '(21.5-27.75]' Grade = B 9 ==> Total (100.0) = '(58.25-69.25]' 9 acc:(0.98968)
9. Lab(20.0) = '(17.25-inf)' ENDSEM(45.0) = '(21.5-27.75]' Grade = B 8 ==> Total (100.0) = '(58.25-69.25]' 8 acc:(0.98791)
10. MST(20.0) = '(13.75-15.75]' ENDSEM(45.0) = '(21.5-27.75]' 7 ==> Total (100.0) = '(58.25-69.25]' Grade = B 7 acc:(0.98532)

Some important observations are:

1. Total (100.0) = '(58.25-69.25]' 20 ==> Grade = B 20 acc:(0.99441)
   If the total marks secured by a student, is between 58.25 and 69.25, then hisor her grade is 'B'.
2. Grade = A 13 ==> Total (100.0) = '(69.25-inf)' 13 acc:(0.99297)
   If the Grade is 'A', then the total marks secured by that student is more than 69.25.
6. Grade = C 9 ==> Total (100.0) = '(-inf-58.25]' 9 acc:(0.98968)
   If the Grade is 'C', then the total marks secured by that student is less than or equal to 58.25.

These rules can be made more informative and if instead of distributing the students into three bins so that 1/3 of students put in to each bin of High, Medium and Low on the basis of their marks in that column, it will be better to consider the top 20% students as High, the bottom 20% students as low and the remaining 60% students as Medium based on their performance in a particular test (a column in the case of the dataset). This can be done by **performing Discretization manually.** This 20% boundary for extremely high and low values is arbitrary. We have chosen it here just to illustrate a possible approach to applying association to this dataset.

10.9 Process of Performing Manual Discretization

First open the excel file of student performance and delete Roll No. and Name columns as they will not play any role in association mining. Let us start with MST marks first. carry out sorting (high to low) on the MST attribute. Since we have a total of 60 records, select the first 12 records (20% records) and replace their MST marks with H. Next, select records from record number 49 to 60 (the last 12 records) and mark them with L. The MST marks of remaining 36 records (60% records) will be replaced with M as shown in Figure 10.46 (a), (b) and (c).

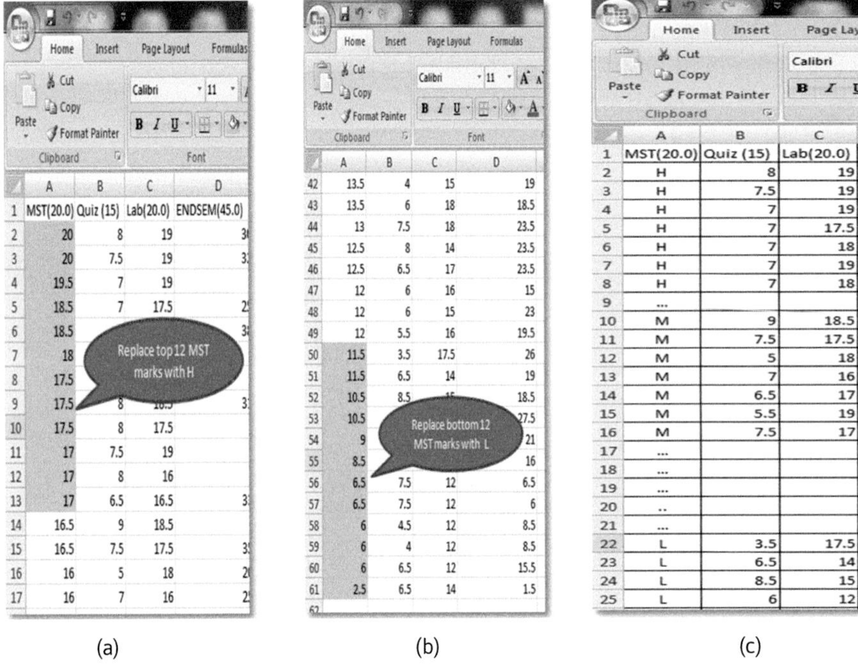

(a) (b) (c)

Figure 10.46 Manual Discretization

In case the value at the cutoff point is the same for two or more students, then we have to shift the cut off either up or down, to a point where change in the value occurs. We cannot set the same values in two different classes. For example, if the marks of the 11th, 12th and 13th students are same, then the cutoff for L for the MST column will need to be raised to the 10th record, i.e. 11.5 marks as shown in Figure 10.47.

	MST(20.0)	Quiz (15)	Lab(20.0)	ENDSEM(45.0)	Total (100.0)	Grade
1	2.5	6.5	14	1.5	24.5	E
2	6	4	12	8.5	30.5	E
3	6	6.5	12	15.5	40	E
4	6.5	7.5	12	6.5	32.5	E
5	8.5	7	15	16	46.5	D
6	9	7.5	17	21	54.5	C
7	10.5	8.5	15	18.5	52.5	C
8	10.5	6	12	27.5	56	C
9	11.5	3.5	17.5	26	58.5	B
10	11.5	6.5	14	19	51	C
11	12	6	16	15	49	C
12	12	6	15	23	56	B
13	12	5.5	16	19.5	53	C
14	12.5	8	14	23.5	58	B
15	12.5	6.5	17	23.5	59.5	B
16	13	7.5	18	23.5	62	B
17	13.5	4	15	19	51.5	C
18	13.5	6	18	18.5	56	B
19	14	9	18.5	22	63.5	B
20	14	5.5	15	27.5	62	B
21	14	7	16	32.5	69.5	B
22	14	4.5	14	26.5	59	B
23	14	7.5	16	23.5	61	B

Figure 10.47 Modified cut off when more than one student has the same marks at the cut

The process of manual Discretization will be followed for each column. Repeating this process for the Quiz column, we will sort it from smallest to highest; marking the first 12 records as L, the last 12 records as H and the remaining 36 records as M. If marks for the 12th and the next consequent records are the same, then the cutoff will be adjusted in such a way that same marks will not fall into separate categories of L and M.

Finally, the dataset will look like what is shown in Figure 10.48 and now it is ready for processing with Weka to find the association mining rules.

1	MST(20.0)	Quiz (15)	Lab(20.0)	ENDSEM(45.0)	Grade
2	L	M	L	L	E
3	L	M	L	L	E
4	L	L	L	L	E
5	M	M	M	L	C
6	M	M	M	L	C
7	M	H	H	L	B
8	L	M	L	L	E
9	L	M	L	L	D
10	M	M	M	L	B
11	M	M	M	L	B
12	M	H	M	L	C
13	L	H	L	M	C
14	M	M	M	M	B
15	M	M	M	M	B
16	L	M	L	M	C
17	M	L	L	M	C
18	M	L	M	M	C
19	M	L	M	M	B
20	L	M	M	M	C
21	M	H	M	M	B
22	M	H	H	M	B
23	M	M	L	M	B
24	M	H	L	M	B

Figure 10.48 Dataset with Manual Discretization

To apply association mining on the given dataset, save it in *csv* file format and load this csv file into Weka as shown in Figure 10.49.

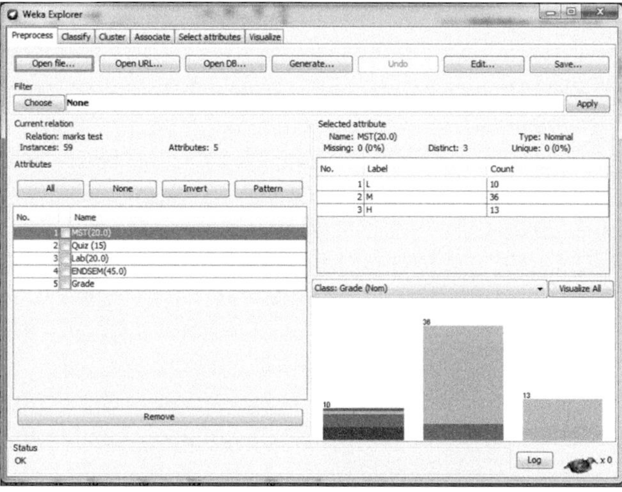

Figure 10.49 Loading the marks file

Now apply the ***Predictive Apriori*** algorithm from the ***Associate*** tab in Weka. Some of the best rules identified by the system are given below:

Best rules found:

1. MST(20.0) = H ENDSEM(45.0) = H 7 ==> Grade = A 7 acc:(0.97376)
2. MST(20.0) = M Quiz (15) = L 6 ==> ENDSEM(45.0) = M 6 acc:(0.96551)
3. MST(20.0) = M Lab(20.0) = L 6 ==> ENDSEM(45.0) = M 6 acc:(0.96551)
4. MST(20.0) = L ENDSEM(45.0) = L 5 ==> Lab(20.0) = L 5 acc:(0.95318)
5. Quiz (15) = M Lab(20.0) = H 5 ==> MST(20.0) = H 5 acc:(0.95318)
6. Quiz (15) = L Grade = B 5 ==> ENDSEM(45.0) = M 5 acc:(0.95318)
7. Lab(20.0) = L ENDSEM(45.0) = L 5 ==> MST(20.0) = L 5 acc:(0.95318)
8. Lab(20.0) = L Grade = B 5 ==> MST(20.0) = M ENDSEM(45.0) = M 5 acc:(0.95318)
9. Lab(20.0) = M ENDSEM(45.0) = L 5 ==> MST(20.0) = M 5 acc:(0.95318)
10. Lab(20.0) = H ENDSEM(45.0) = H 5 ==> Grade = A 5 acc:(0.95318)
11. MST(20.0) = M Quiz (15) = H ENDSEM(45.0) = M 5 ==> Grade = B 5 acc:(0.95318)
12. Grade = E 4 ==> MST(20.0) = L Lab(20.0) = L 4 acc:(0.93429)
13. Grade = E 4 ==> MST(20.0) = L ENDSEM(45.0) = L 4 acc:(0.93429)
14. MST(20.0) = L Grade = E 4 ==> Lab(20.0) = L ENDSEM(45.0) = L 4 acc:(0.93429)
15. MST(20.0) = L Grade = C 4 ==> ENDSEM(45.0) = M 4 acc:(0.93429)
16. MST(20.0) = H Grade = B 4 ==> ENDSEM(45.0) = M 4 acc:(0.93429)
17. Quiz (15) = H ENDSEM(45.0) = H 4 ==> Grade = A 4 acc:(0.93429)
18. Lab(20.0) = L Grade = C 4 ==> ENDSEM(45.0) = M 4 acc:(0.93429)
19. MST(20.0) = M Quiz (15) = M ENDSEM(45.0) = L 4 ==> Lab(20.0) = M 4 acc:(0.93429)
20. MST(20.0) = M Quiz (15) = M ENDSEM(45.0) = H 4 ==> Lab(20.0) = M 4 acc:(0.93429)

Now let us find the rules for grade only by enabling ***car*** to ***true.***

The best 20 rules are given below:

Best rules found:

1. MST(20.0) = H ENDSEM(45.0) = H 7 ==> Grade = A 7 acc:(0.97316)
2. Lab(20.0) = H ENDSEM(45.0) = H 5 ==> Grade = A 5 acc:(0.95636)
3. MST(20.0) = M Quiz (15) = H ENDSEM(45.0) = M 5 ==> Grade = B 5 acc:(0.95636)
4. Quiz (15) = H ENDSEM(45.0) = H 4 ==> Grade = A 4 acc:(0.94162)
5. Quiz (15) = H Lab(20.0) = M ENDSEM(45.0) = M 4 ==> Grade = B 4 acc:(0.94162)
6. MST(20.0) = L Quiz (15) = M ENDSEM(45.0) = M 3 ==> Grade = C 3 acc:(0.91904)
7. MST(20.0) = L Lab(20.0) = L ENDSEM(45.0) = M 3 ==> Grade = C 3 acc:(0.91904)
8. MST(20.0) = H Lab(20.0) = M ENDSEM(45.0) = M 3 ==> Grade = B 3 acc:(0.91904)
9. MST(20.0) = M Quiz (15) = M ENDSEM(45.0) = M 13 ==> Grade = B 12 acc:(0.88767)
10. MST(20.0) = M Quiz (15) = M Lab(20.0) = L 2 ==> Grade = B 2 acc:(0.88325)
11. MST(20.0) = M Lab(20.0) = H ENDSEM(45.0) = M 2 ==> Grade = B 2 acc:(0.88325)
12. MST(20.0) = H Quiz (15) = H Lab(20.0) = H 2 ==> Grade = A 2 acc:(0.88325)
13. MST(20.0) = M ENDSEM(45.0) = M 24 ==> Grade = B 21 acc:(0.82198)

14. Lab(20.0) = M ENDSEM(45.0) = M 21 ==> Grade = B 18 acc:(0.80371)
15. ENDSEM(45.0) = H 13 ==> Grade = A 11 acc:(0.77475)
16. MST(20.0) = H Lab(20.0) = H 7 ==> Grade = A 6 acc:(0.76918)
17. MST(20.0) = M Lab(20.0) = L 6 ==> Grade = B 5 acc:(0.73884)
18. MST(20.0) = M Quiz (15) = M 21 ==> Grade = B 16 acc:(0.7304)
19. ENDSEM(45.0) = M 35 ==> Grade = B 26 acc:(0.72725)
20. MST(20.0) = M 36 ==> Grade = B 26 acc:(0.70941)

Now, if the user is not interested with those rules which have M values, then we can reprocess our excel data by replacing M with '**?**' in the excel file as shown in Figure 10.50, then the records containing ? will be ignored during generation of association rules, because ? indicates missing values in Weka and all the records containing missing values will be ignored during generation of association mining rules.

	A	B	C	D	E
1	MST(20.0)	Quiz (15)	Lab(20.0)	ENDSE?(45.0)	Grade
2	L	?	L	L	E
3	L	?	L	L	E
4	L	L	L	L	E
5	?	?	?	L	C
6	?	?	?	L	C
7	?	H	H	L	B
8	L	?	L	L	E
9	L	?	L	L	D
10	?	?	?	L	B
11	?	?	?	L	B
12	?	H	?	L	C
13	L	H	L	?	C
14	?	?	?	?	B
15	?	?	?	?	B
16	L	?	L	?	C
17	?	L	L	?	C
18	?	L	?	?	C
19	?	L	?	?	B
20	L	?	?	?	C
21	?	H	?	?	B
22	?	H	H	?	B
23	?	?	L	?	B
24	?	H	L	?	B
25	?	?	?	?	B

Figure 10.50 Replacing M with '?'

Save this file in ***csv*** with a different name and load it on Weka to generate association mining rules. Some of best rules found are:

Best rules found:

1. MST(20.0) = H ENDSEM(45.0) = H 7 ==> Grade = A 7 acc:(0.9856)
2. MST(20.0) = L ENDSEM(45.0) = L 5 ==> Lab(20.0) = L 5 acc:(0.97495)
3. Lab(20.0) = L ENDSEM(45.0) = L 5 ==> MST(20.0) = L 5 acc:(0.97495)
4. Lab(20.0) = H ENDSEM(45.0) = H 5 ==> Grade = A 5 acc:(0.97495)
5. Grade = E 4 ==> MST(20.0) = L Lab(20.0) = L 4 acc:(0.96357)
6. Grade = E 4 ==> MST(20.0) = L ENDSEM(45.0) = L 4 acc:(0.96357)
7. MST(20.0) = L Grade = E 4 ==> Lab(20.0) = L ENDSEM(45.0) = L 4 acc:(0.96357)
8. Quiz (15) = H ENDSEM(45.0) = H 4 ==> Grade = A 4 acc:(0.96357)
9. MST(20.0) = H Quiz (15) = H Lab(20.0) = H 2 ==> Grade = A 2 acc:(0.90132)
10. MST(20.0) = H Lab(20.0) = H 7 ==> Grade = A 6 acc:(0.76649)
11. Lab(20.0) = H Grade = A 7 ==> MST(20.0) = H 6 acc:(0.76649)
12. ENDSEM(45.0) = H 13 ==> Grade = A 11 acc:(0.75458)
13. Grade = A 14 ==> ENDSEM(45.0) = H 11 acc:(0.70253)
14. MST(20.0) = L 10 ==> Lab(20.0) = L 8 acc:(0.68744)
15. MST(20.0) = L ENDSEM(45.0) = L 5 ==> Lab(20.0) = L Grade = E 4 acc:(0.66253)
16. Lab(20.0) = L ENDSEM(45.0) = L 5 ==> MST(20.0) = L Grade = E 4 acc:(0.66253)
17. Lab(20.0) = H ENDSEM(45.0) = H 5 ==> MST(20.0) = H Grade = A 4 acc:(0.66253)
18. MST(20.0) = H 13 ==> Grade = A 9 acc:(0.61176)
19. Lab(20.0) = L Grade = C 4 ==> MST(20.0) = L 3 acc:(0.59941)
20. MST(20.0) = H Grade = A 9 ==> Lab(20.0) = H 6 acc:(0.57572)

And by enabling ***car*** rules to be ***true*** we get rules which are given below:

Best rules found:

1. MST(20.0) = H ENDSEM(45.0) = H 7 ==> Grade = A 7 acc:(0.9866)
2. Lab(20.0) = H ENDSEM(45.0) = H 5 ==> Grade = A 5 acc:(0.98035)
3. Quiz (15) = H ENDSEM(45.0) = H 4 ==> Grade = A 4 acc:(0.97464)
4. MST(20.0) = H Quiz (15) = H Lab(20.0) = H 2 ==> Grade = A 2 acc:(0.94776)
5. MST(20.0) = H Lab(20.0) = H 7 ==> Grade = A 6 acc:(0.82715)
6. ENDSEM(45.0) = H 13 ==> Grade = A 11 acc:(0.79515)
7. MST(20.0) = L ENDSEM(45.0) = L 5 ==> Grade = E 4 acc:(0.75507)
8. Lab(20.0) = L ENDSEM(45.0) = L 5 ==> Grade = E 4 acc:(0.75507)
9. MST(20.0) = H Quiz (15) = H 4 ==> Grade = A 3 acc:(0.70206)
10. MST(20.0) = H 13 ==> Grade = A 9 acc:(0.6782)

10.10 Applying Association Mining in R

Installing arules

For association mining, there is a need to install the library ***'arules'***. If the library is not installed then first install the package *'arules'* otherwise the R console will print the message 'there is no package called *'arules'* as shown in Figure 10.51.

```
> install.packages ("arules") # Install the package for association mining
>
> library(arules) # load the "arules" library
```

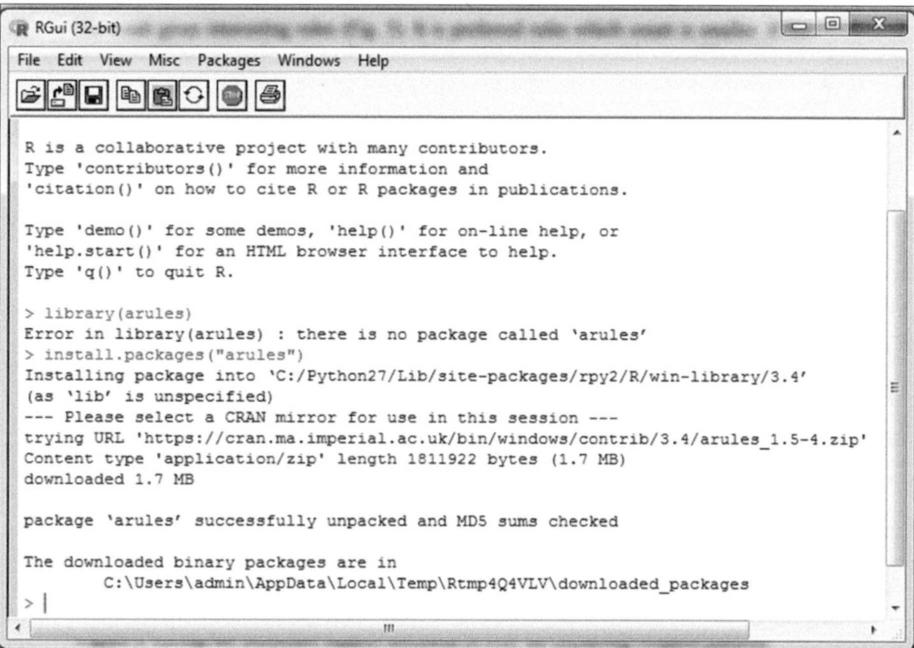

Figure 10.51 Installation of the 'arules' library

10.11 Implementing Apriori Algorithm

Step 1: Loading the dataset

Read the ***weather_nominal.csv*** file using the ***read.csv*** function as shown in Figure 10.52. The ***summary ()*** function can be used to see instances of the loaded dataset.

```
> data <- read.csv("D://weather _ nominal.csv", header = TRUE) # Reading of weather data
>
> summary (data) # Print summary of dataset
>
> names(data) # Display column names of dataset
```

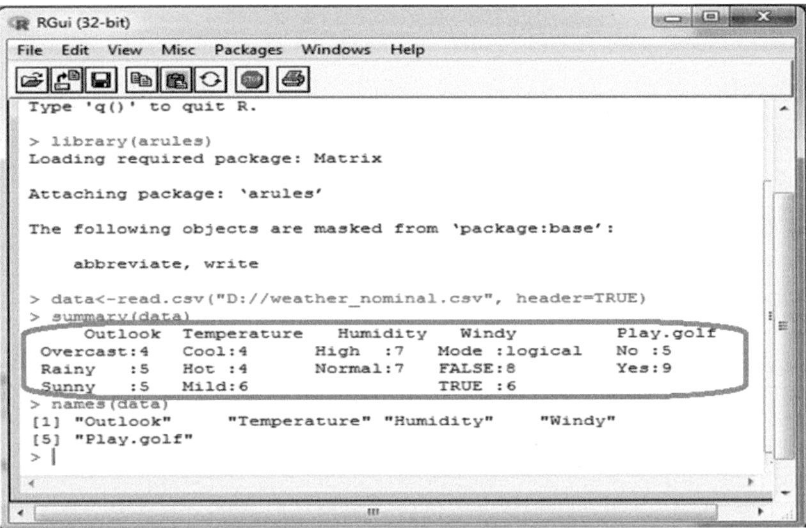

Figure 10.52 Loading the dataset

Step 2: Apply the Apriori algorithm

Run the Apriori algorithm on the dataset given; as follows. We can also set the parameters by specifying minimum values for support and confidence as shown in Figure 10.53.

```
> rules<-apriori(dataset, parameter=list(target="rules"))
```

OR

```
> rules <-apriori(dataset, parameter=list(sup=0.01, conf=0.5, target="rules"))
```

```
R Console

> data<-read.csv("D://weather_nominal.csv", header=TRUE)
> rules<-apriori(data, parameter=list(target="rules"))
Apriori

Parameter specification:
 confidence minval smax arem  aval originalSupport maxtime support minlen
        0.8    0.1    1 none FALSE            TRUE       5     0.1      1
 maxlen target   ext
     10  rules FALSE

Algorithmic control:
 filter tree heap memopt load sort verbose
    0.1 TRUE TRUE  FALSE TRUE    2    TRUE

Absolute minimum support count: 1

set item appearances ...[0 item(s)] done [0.00s].
set transactions ...[11 item(s), 14 transaction(s)] done [0.00s].
sorting and recoding items ... [11 item(s)] done [0.00s].
creating transaction tree ... done [0.00s].
checking subsets of size 1 2 3 4 done [0.00s].
writing ... [28 rule(s)] done [0.00s].
creating S4 object  ... done [0.00s].
>
```

Figure 10.53 Loading the dataset and running Apriori

We can also print the association rules generated by Apriori using a function called ***inspect ()*** as shown in Figure 10.54 which shows the first 20 rules.

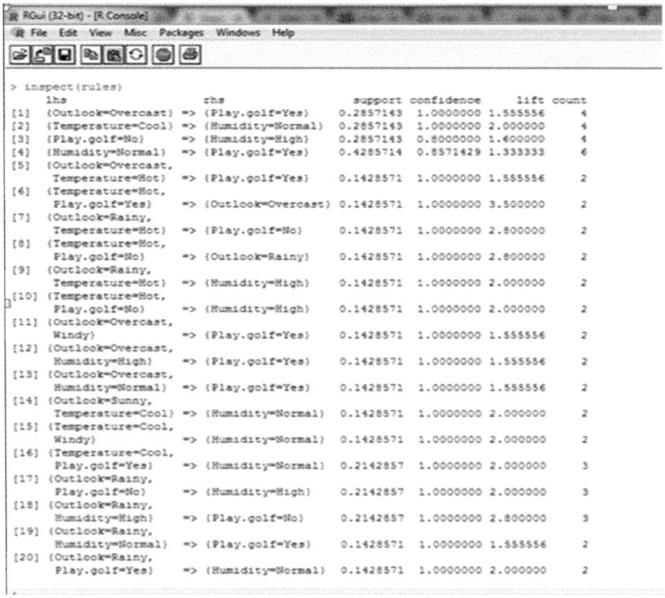

```
RGui (32-bit) - [R Console]
File Edit View Misc Packages Windows Help

> inspect(rules)
     lhs                        rhs                   support   confidence     lift count
[1]  {Outlook=Overcast}     => {Play.golf=Yes}        0.2857143  1.0000000 1.555556     4
[2]  {Temperature=Cool}     => {Humidity=Normal}      0.2857143  1.0000000 2.000000     4
[3]  {Play.golf=No}         => {Humidity=High}        0.2857143  0.8000000 1.600000     4
[4]  {Humidity=Normal}      => {Play.golf=Yes}        0.4285714  0.8571429 1.333333     6
[5]  {Outlook=Overcast,
      Temperature=Hot}      => {Play.golf=Yes}        0.1428571  1.0000000 1.555556     2
[6]  {Temperature=Hot,
      Play.golf=Yes}        => {Outlook=Overcast}     0.1428571  1.0000000 3.500000     2
[7]  {Outlook=Rainy,
      Temperature=Hot}      => {Play.golf=No}         0.1428571  1.0000000 2.800000     2
[8]  {Temperature=Hot,
      Play.golf=No}         => {Outlook=Rainy}        0.1428571  1.0000000 2.800000     2
[9]  {Outlook=Rainy,
      Temperature=Hot}      => {Humidity=High}        0.1428571  1.0000000 2.000000     2
[10] {Temperature=Hot,
      Play.golf=No}         => {Humidity=High}        0.1428571  1.0000000 2.000000     2
[11] {Outlook=Overcast,
      Windy}                => {Play.golf=Yes}        0.1428571  1.0000000 1.555556     2
[12] {Outlook=Overcast,
      Humidity=High}        => {Play.golf=Yes}        0.1428571  1.0000000 1.555556     2
[13] {Outlook=Overcast,
      Humidity=Normal}      => {Play.golf=Yes}        0.1428571  1.0000000 1.555556     2
[14] {Outlook=Sunny,
      Temperature=Cool}     => {Humidity=Normal}      0.1428571  1.0000000 2.000000     2
[15] {Temperature=Cool,
      Windy}                => {Humidity=Normal}      0.1428571  1.0000000 2.000000     2
[16] {Temperature=Cool,
      Play.golf=Yes}        => {Humidity=Normal}      0.2142857  1.0000000 2.000000     3
[17] {Outlook=Rainy,
      Play.golf=No}         => {Humidity=High}        0.2142857  1.0000000 2.000000     3
[18] {Outlook=Rainy,
      Humidity=High}        => {Play.golf=No}         0.2142857  1.0000000 2.800000     3
[19] {Outlook=Rainy,
      Humidity=Normal}      => {Play.golf=Yes}        0.1428571  1.0000000 1.555556     2
[20] {Outlook=Rainy,
      Play.golf=Yes}        => {Humidity=Normal}      0.1428571  1.0000000 2.000000     2
```

Figure 10.54 First 20 Association Rules

10.12 Generation of Rules Similar to Classifier

If we set the right hand side in the 'appearance'parameter of the Apriori function to display class only, then we can get the rules to predict the class of an unknown sample as shown in Figure 10.55.

```
> rules<- apriori(data, parameter = list(supp=0.005, conf=0.8), appearance = list(rhs=c("Play.golf=Yes", "Play.golf=No")))
>
> rules.sorted <- sort(rules, by="lift")
>
>inspect(rules)
```

The Figure 10.55 shows the 20 rules out of 45 rules identified. Sorting is on the basis of lift.

	lhs		rhs	support	confidence	lift	count
[1]	{Outlook=Rainy,Temperature=Hot}	=>	{Play.golf=No}	0.14285714	1.0000000	2.800000	2
[2]	{Temperature=Hot,Windy}	=>	{Play.golf=No}	0.07142857	1.0000000	2.800000	1
[3]	{Outlook=Rainy,Humidity=High}	=>	{Play.golf=No}	0.21428571	1.0000000	2.800000	3
[4]	{Outlook=Sunny,Windy}	=>	{Play.golf=No}	0.14285714	1.0000000	2.800000	2
[5]	{Outlook=Rainy,Temperature=Hot,Windy}	=>	{Play.golf=No}	0.07142857	1.0000000	2.800000	1
[6]	{Outlook=Rainy,Temperature=Hot,Humidity=High}	=>	{Play.golf=No}	0.14285714	1.0000000	2.800000	2
[7]	{Temperature=Hot,Humidity=High,Windy}	=>	{Play.golf=No}	0.07142857	1.0000000	2.800000	1
[8]	{Outlook=Sunny,Temperature=Cool,Windy}	=>	{Play.golf=No}	0.07142857	1.0000000	2.800000	1
[9]	{Outlook=Rainy,Temperature=Mild,Humidity=High}	=>	{Play.golf=No}	0.07142857	1.0000000	2.800000	1
[10]	{Outlook=Rainy,Humidity=High,Windy}	=>	{Play.golf=No}	0.07142857	1.0000000	2.800000	1
[11]	{Outlook=Sunny,Temperature=Mild,Windy}	=>	{Play.golf=No}	0.07142857	1.0000000	2.800000	1
[12]	{Outlook=Sunny,Humidity=High,Windy}	=>	{Play.golf=No}	0.07142857	1.0000000	2.800000	1
[13]	{Outlook=Sunny,Humidity=Normal,Windy}	=>	{Play.golf=No}	0.07142857	1.0000000	2.800000	1
[14]	{Outlook=Rainy,Temperature=Hot,Humidity=High,Windy}	=>	{Play.golf=No}	0.07142857	1.0000000	2.800000	1
[15]	{Outlook=Sunny,Temperature=Cool,Humidity=Normal,Windy}	=>	{Play.golf=No}	0.07142857	1.0000000	2.800000	1
[16]	{Outlook=Sunny,Temperature=Mild,Humidity=High,Windy}	=>	{Play.golf=No}	0.07142857	1.0000000	2.800000	1
[17]	{Outlook=Overcast}	=>	{Play.golf=Yes}	0.28571429	1.0000000	1.555556	4
[18]	{Outlook=Overcast,Temperature=Hot}	=>	{Play.golf=Yes}	0.14285714	1.0000000	1.555556	2
[19]	{Temperature=Hot,Humidity=Normal}	=>	{Play.golf=Yes}	0.07142857	1.0000000	1.555556	1
[20]	{Outlook=Overcast,Temperature=Cool}	=>	{Play.golf=Yes}	0.07142857	1.0000000	1.555556	1

Figure 10.55 Best 20 rules sorted according to lift

10.13 Comparison of Association Mining CAR Rules with J48 Classifier Rules

First of all, install the *'rpart'* package to implement decision tree. Then, the *rpart( )* function is applied on the loaded weather dataset to build the decision tree.

```
>library(rpart) ## Loading of packages
>
> data<-read.csv("D://weather _ nominal.csv", header=TRUE) ## Reading of Data
> fit <- rpart(Play.golf ~ Outlook + Temperature + Humidity + Windy, method="class",
data=data, control=rpart.control(minsplit=1))
> print(fit)
```

The classification performed by the decision tree is shown in Figure 10.56.

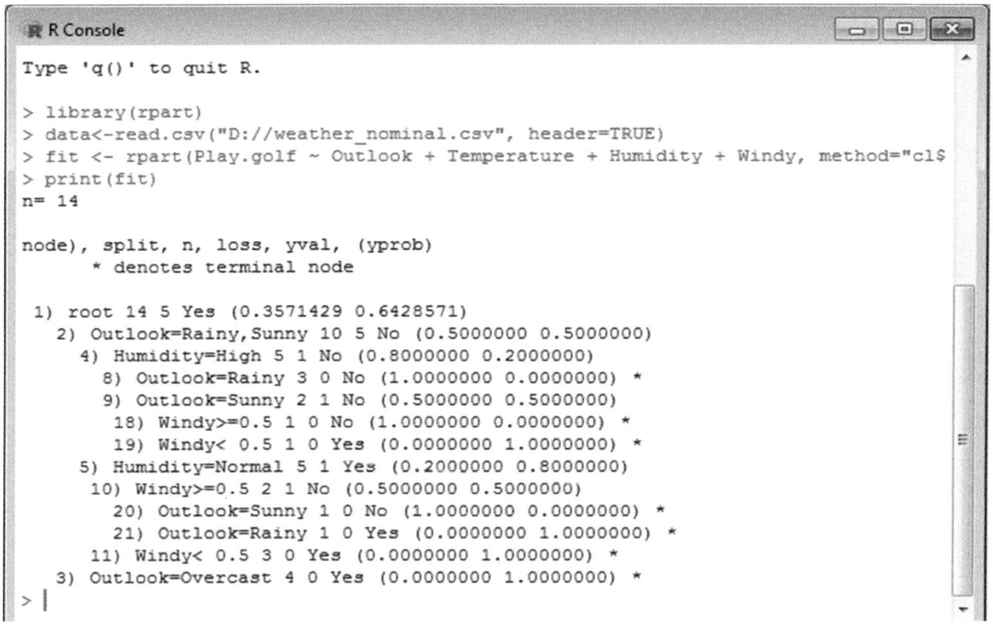

```
R Console
Type 'q()' to quit R.

> library(rpart)
> data<-read.csv("D://weather_nominal.csv", header=TRUE)
> fit <- rpart(Play.golf ~ Outlook + Temperature + Humidity + Windy, method="cl$
> print(fit)
n= 14

node), split, n, loss, yval, (yprob)
      * denotes terminal node

 1) root 14 5 Yes (0.3571429 0.6428571)
   2) Outlook=Rainy,Sunny 10 5 No (0.5000000 0.5000000)
     4) Humidity=High 5 1 No (0.8000000 0.2000000)
       8) Outlook=Rainy 3 0 No (1.0000000 0.0000000) *
       9) Outlook=Sunny 2 1 No (0.5000000 0.5000000)
        18) Windy>=0.5 1 0 No (1.0000000 0.0000000) *
        19) Windy< 0.5 1 0 Yes (0.0000000 1.0000000) *
     5) Humidity=Normal 5 1 Yes (0.2000000 0.8000000)
      10) Windy>=0.5 2 1 No (0.5000000 0.5000000)
        20) Outlook=Sunny 1 0 No (1.0000000 0.0000000) *
        21) Outlook=Rainy 1 0 Yes (0.0000000 1.0000000) *
      11) Windy< 0.5 3 0 Yes (0.0000000 1.0000000) *
   3) Outlook=Overcast 4 0 Yes (0.0000000 1.0000000) *
> |
```

Figure 10.56 Decision tree rules

The complete summary about each node of the decision tree can be visualized using the ***summary()*** function as shown in Figure 10.57.

```
R Console
> summary(fit)
Call:
rpart(formula = Play.golf ~ Outlook + Temperature + Humidity +
    Windy, data = data, method = "class", control = rpart.control(minsplit = 1))
  n= 14

    CP nsplit rel error xerror      xstd
1 0.30      0       1.0    1.0 0.3585686
2 0.10      2       0.4    1.2 0.3703280
3 0.01      6       0.0    1.4 0.3741657

Variable importance
    Outlook    Humidity       Windy Temperature
         43          23          20          14

Node number 1: 14 observations,    complexity param=0.3
  predicted class=Yes  expected loss=0.3571429  P(node) =1
    class counts:     5     9
   probabilities: 0.357 0.643
  left son=2 (10 obs) right son=3 (4 obs)
  Primary splits:
      Outlook     splits as  RLL,        improve=1.4285710, (0 missing)
      Humidity    splits as  LR,         improve=1.2857140, (0 missing)
      Windy       < 0.5 to the right,    improve=0.4285714, (0 missing)
      Temperature splits as  RLR,        improve=0.2285714, (0 missing)

Node number 2: 10 observations,    complexity param=0.3
  predicted class=No   expected loss=0.5  P(node) =0.7142857
    class counts:     5     5
   probabilities: 0.500 0.500
  left son=4 (5 obs) right son=5 (5 obs)
  Primary splits:
      Humidity    splits as  LR,         improve=1.8000000, (0 missing)
      Temperature splits as  RLR,        improve=1.2500000, (0 missing)
      Windy       < 0.5 to the right,    improve=0.8333333, (0 missing)
```

Figure 10.57 Summary of decision tree nodes

The decision tree can be plotted using the ***plot()*** function and then the *text( )* function is used to label the nodes of decision tree as shown in Figure 10.58.

```
> plot(fit, uniform=TRUE, main="Decision Tree - Play?")
> text(fit, use.n=TRUE, all=TRUE, cex=.8)
```

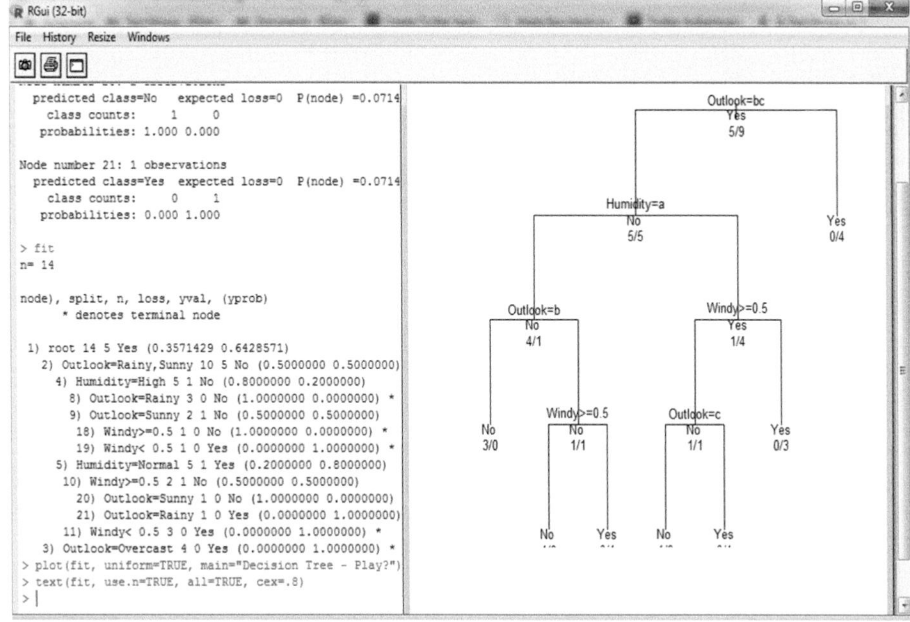

Figure 10.58 Plotting the decision tree

From the decision tree one can perform analysis to find similarities between rules produced by decision tree and CAR options of association mining.

10.14 Application of Association Mining on Numeric Data in R

Figure 10.59 shows the loading of the marks dataset. It shows the summary about each attribute of the dataset. From the Figure, it has been observed that there are 8 attributes such as Roll No., Name, MST, Quiz, Lab, ENDSEM, Total and Grade. The Figure also shows that there are total 69 students out of which 9 students got grade A, 29 got B, 28 got C, 2 got D and 1 got E.

```
> library(arules)
> data<- read.csv("D://marks.csv", header=TRUE)
> summary(data)
```

```
RGui (32-bit)
File  Edit  View  Misc  Packages  Windows  Help

> library(arules)
> data<- read.csv("D://marks.csv", header=TRUE)
> summary(data)
     Rollno                          Name           MST              Quiz
 Min.   :101103002   Abhay Singh     : 1   Min.   : 7.00   Min.   : 5.00
 1st Qu.:101103101   Abhinav Acharya: 1   1st Qu.:13.50   1st Qu.: 9.25
 Median :101113024   Akshit Khajuria: 1   Median :17.00   Median :11.00
 Mean   :101146379   Ankit Madan     : 1   Mean   :16.17   Mean   :10.45
 3rd Qu.:101153009   Anmol Trivedi   : 1   3rd Qu.:19.50   3rd Qu.:12.00
 Max.   :101293011   Anmol Verma     : 1   Max.   :23.50   Max.   :13.75
                     (Other)         :63
      Lab             EST             Total           Grade
 Min.   : 8.0   Min.   :13.50   Min.   :36.75   A: 9
 1st Qu.:14.0   1st Qu.:25.50   1st Qu.:64.25   B:29
 Median :15.0   Median :29.00   Median :70.50   C:28
 Mean   :15.2   Mean   :28.52   Mean   :70.34   D: 2
 3rd Qu.:17.0   3rd Qu.:32.00   3rd Qu.:79.00   E: 1
 Max.   :19.0   Max.   :36.50   Max.   :89.75

> names(data)
[1] "Rollno" "Name"   "MST"    "Quiz"   "Lab"    "EST"    "Total"  "Grade"
>
```

Total=69 students

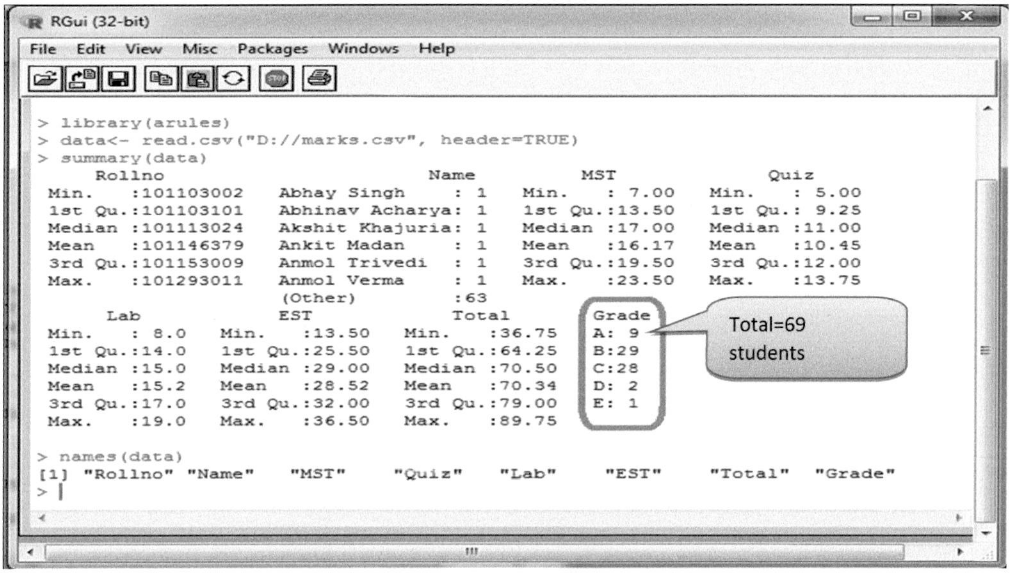

Figure 10.59 Summary of the marks dataset

Since, Roll No. and Name columns do not play any role in association mining so these columns can be removed using the slicing in R as shown in Figure 10.60.

```
> data<- data [-1 : -2]
> data
```

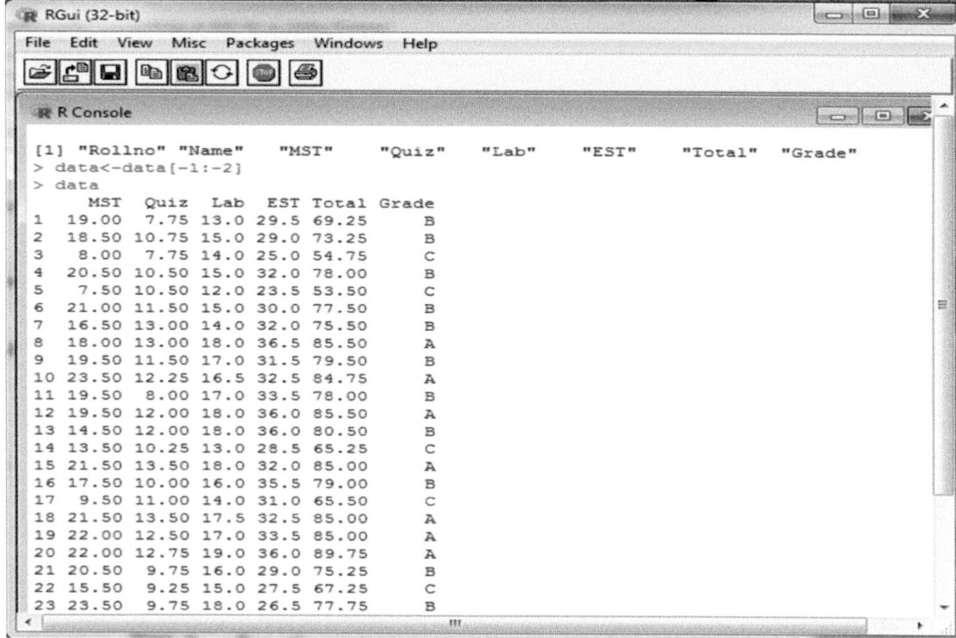

Figure 10.60 Removal of columns

Since this data is numeric in nature and association mining cannot be applied on numeric data we need to convert it into nominal by discretizing. For discretization, we first have to convert the dataset into a data frame as shown in Figure 10.61.

```
> y<-data.frame(lapply(data, as.integer))
```

```
R Console
> y<-data.frame(lapply(data, as.integer))
> y
   MST Quiz Lab EST Total Grade
1   19    7  13  29    69     2
2   18   10  15  29    73     2
3    8    7  14  25    54     3
4   20   10  15  32    78     2
5    7   10  12  23    53     3
6   21   11  15  30    77     2
7   16   13  14  32    75     2
8   18   13  18  36    85     1
9   19   11  17  31    79     2
10  23   12  16  32    84     1
11  19    8  17  33    78     2
12  19   12  18  36    85     1
13  14   12  18  36    80     2
14  13   10  13  28    65     3
15  21   13  18  32    85     1
16  17   10  16  35    79     2
17   9   11  14  31    65     3
18  21   13  17  32    85     1
19  22   12  17  33    85     1
20  22   12  19  36    89     1
```

Figure 10.61 Converting the dataset into a data frame

And then use the ***discretize ()*** function to discretize all the columns of the dataset as shown in Figure 10.62.

```
> for (i in 1:6){y[,i]<-discretize(y[,i])}
```

```
RGui (32-bit)
File Edit View Misc Packages Windows Help
> for (i in 1:6){y[,i]<-discretize(y[,i])}
> y
           MST          Quiz         Lab         EST       Total       Grade
1  [17.7,23.0] [ 5.00, 7.67) [11.7,15.3) [28.3,36.0] [53.7,71.3) [1.00,2.33)
2  [17.7,23.0] [ 7.67,10.33) [11.7,15.3) [28.3,36.0] [71.3,89.0] [1.00,2.33)
3  [ 7.0,12.3) [ 5.00, 7.67) [11.7,15.3) [20.7,28.3) [53.7,71.3) [2.33,3.67)
4  [17.7,23.0] [ 7.67,10.33) [11.7,15.3) [28.3,36.0] [71.3,89.0] [1.00,2.33)
5  [ 7.0,12.3) [ 7.67,10.33) [11.7,15.3) [20.7,28.3) [36.0,53.7) [2.33,3.67)
6  [17.7,23.0] [10.33,13.00] [11.7,15.3) [28.3,36.0] [71.3,89.0] [1.00,2.33)
7  [12.3,17.7) [10.33,13.00] [11.7,15.3) [28.3,36.0] [71.3,89.0] [1.00,2.33)
8  [17.7,23.0] [10.33,13.00] [15.3,19.0] [28.3,36.0] [71.3,89.0] [1.00,2.33)
9  [17.7,23.0] [10.33,13.00] [15.3,19.0] [28.3,36.0] [71.3,89.0] [1.00,2.33)
10 [17.7,23.0] [10.33,13.00] [15.3,19.0] [28.3,36.0] [71.3,89.0] [1.00,2.33)
11 [17.7,23.0] [ 7.67,10.33) [15.3,19.0] [28.3,36.0] [71.3,89.0] [1.00,2.33)
12 [17.7,23.0] [10.33,13.00] [15.3,19.0] [28.3,36.0] [71.3,89.0] [1.00,2.33)
13 [12.3,17.7) [10.33,13.00] [15.3,19.0] [28.3,36.0] [71.3,89.0] [1.00,2.33)
14 [12.3,17.7) [ 7.67,10.33) [11.7,15.3) [20.7,28.3) [53.7,71.3) [2.33,3.67)
15 [17.7,23.0] [10.33,13.00] [15.3,19.0] [28.3,36.0] [71.3,89.0] [1.00,2.33)
16 [12.3,17.7) [ 7.67,10.33) [15.3,19.0] [28.3,36.0] [71.3,89.0] [1.00,2.33)
17 [ 7.0,12.3) [10.33,13.00] [11.7,15.3) [28.3,36.0] [53.7,71.3) [2.33,3.67)
18 [17.7,23.0] [10.33,13.00] [15.3,19.0] [28.3,36.0] [71.3,89.0] [1.00,2.33)
19 [17.7,23.0] [10.33,13.00] [15.3,19.0] [28.3,36.0] [71.3,89.0] [1.00,2.33)
20 [17.7,23.0] [10.33,13.00] [15.3,19.0] [28.3,36.0] [71.3,89.0] [1.00,2.33)
```

Figure 10.62 Discretization of data

Now, apply the ***apriori ()*** function to perform association mining as shown in Figure 10.63.

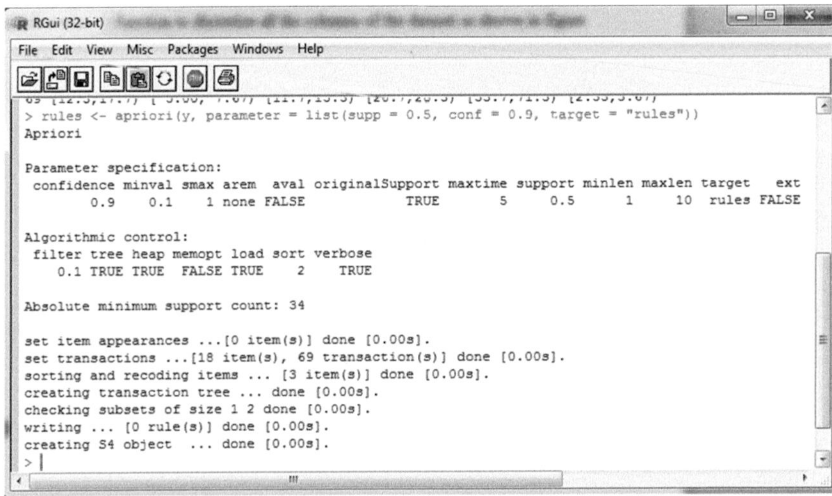

Figure 10.63 Applying Apriori

This illustrates the steps that need to be followed to apply association mining in R.

Remind Me

- Weka contains an Associate tab which aids in applying different association algorithms in order to find association rules from datasets.
- One such algorithm is the Predictive Apriori association algorithm that optimally combines support and confidence to calculate a value termed predictive accuracy
- We can set the value of support, confidence and number of rules using the General Object Editor of the Apriori algorithm.
- CAR can be enabled to find the rules by considering the class attribute or the last attribute of the dataset as a consequent of the rule.
- To apply association mining in R, there it is required to install the library 'arules'.
- We can use apriori( ) in R to find association mining rules for the given dataset.

Point Me (Books)

- Witten, Ian H., Eibe Frank, and Mark A. Hall. 2010. *Data Mining: Practical Machine Learning Tools and Techniques*, 3rd ed. Amsterdam: Elsevier.
- Lesmeister, Cory. 2015. *Mastering Machine Learning with R*. Birmingham: Packt Publishing Ltd.

Connect Me (Internet Resources)

- https://machinelearningmastery.com/market-basket-analysis-with-association-rule-learning/
- http://facweb.cs.depaul.edu/mobasher/classes/ect584/Weka/associate.html
- https://www.r-bloggers.com/association-rule-learning-and-the-apriori-algorithm/
- http://mhahsler.github.io/arules/

Do It Yourself

The purpose of this assignment is to verify that you have learnt the concepts of association mining. Carry out this assignment in both Weka and R to check your learning.

1. Apply association mining with the Apriori algorithm on the following dataset with Weka and R to find the best rules with threshold value of support of 50% and confidence of 70%,

   Transaction database

T1	1,3,4
T2	2,3,5
T3	1,2,3,5
T4	2,5

   Compare your findings with the discussion given in the previous chapter under Section 9.7.2.
2. Find association rules with the Apriori algorithm for the transaction data base given below for having support of more than 20% and confidence more than 70%.

Transaction database for identification of association rules

TID	List of Items
10	I1, I2, I5
20	I2, I4
30	I2, I3
40	I1, I2, I4
50	I1, I3
60	I2, I3
70	I1, I3
80	I1, I2, I3, I5
90	I1, I2, I4

Compare your findings with the discussion given in the previous chapter under Section 9.7.2.

3. Find association rules with the Apriori algorithm for the transaction data base given below for support more than 25% and confidence 70%.

Transaction database for identification of association rules

TID	Items
1	Biscuit, Bournvita, Butter, Cornflakes, Tape
2	Bournvita, Bread, Butter, Cornflakes
3	Butter, Coffee, Chocolate, Eggs, Jam
4	Bournvita, Butter, Cornflakes, Bread, Eggs
5	Bournvita, Bread, Coffee, Chocolate, Eggs
6	Jam, Sugar
7	Biscuit, Bournvita, Butter, Cornflakes, Jam
8	Curd, Jam, Sugar
9	Bournvita, Bread, Butter, Coffee, Cornflakes
10	Bournvita, Bread, Coffee, Chocolate, Eggs
11	Bournvita, Butter, Eggs
12	Bournvita, Butter, Cornflakes, Chocolate, Eggs
13	Biscuit, Bournvita, Bread
14	Bread, Butter, Coffee, Chocolate, Eggs
15	Coffee, Cornflakes

TID	*Items*
16	Chocolate
17	Chocolate, Curd, Eggs
18	Biscuit, Bournvita, Butter, Cornflakes
19	Bournvita, Bread, Coffee, Chocolate, Eggs
20	Butter, Coffee, Chocolate, Eggs
21	Jam, Sugar, Tape
22	Bournvita, Bread, Butter, Cornflakes
23	Coffee, Chocolate, Eggs, Jam, Juice
24	Juice, Milk, Rice
25	Rice, Soap, Sugar

Compare your findings with the discussion given in the previous chapter under Section 9.7.2.

4. Find association rules with FP growth and Apriori algorithm for the transaction data base given below for support more than 40% and confidence 70%.

Transaction database for identification of association rules

TID	*Items*
100	A C D
200	B C E
300	A B C E
400	B E

Compare your findings with the discussion given in the previous chapter under Section 9.11.

5. Find association rules with FP growth and Apriori algorithm for the transaction data base given below for support more than 50% and confidence 70%.

Transaction database for identification of association rules

TID	*Items*
100	1, 2, 3, 4
200	5, 6, 7, 8, 9
300	6, 8, 9, 10
400	2, 3, 9

Compare your findings with the discussion given in the previous chapter under Section 9.11.

11

Web Mining and Search Engines

Chapter Objectives

- ✓ To understand what is meant by web mining and its types
- ✓ To understand the working of the HITS algorithm
- ✓ To know the brief history of search engines
- ✓ To understand a search engine's architecture and its working
- ✓ To understand the PageRank algorithm and its working
- ✓ To understand the concepts of precision and recall

11.1 Introduction

Since Berners-Lee (inventor of the World Wide Web) created the first web page in 1991, there has been an exponential growth in the number of websites worldwide. As of 2018, there were 1.8 billion websites in the world. This growth has been accompanied with another exponential increase in the amount of data available and the need to organize this data in order to extract useful information from it.

Early attempts to organize such data included creation of web directories to group together similar web pages. The web pages in these directories were often manually reviewed and tagged based on keywords. As time passed by, search engines became available which employed a variety of techniques in order to extract the required information from the web pages. These techniques are called web mining. Formally, web mining is the application of data mining techniques and machine learning to find useful information from the data present in web pages.

Web mining is divided into three parts, i.e. web content mining, structure mining, and usage mining as shown in Figure 11.1.

We will discuss each type of web mining in brief.

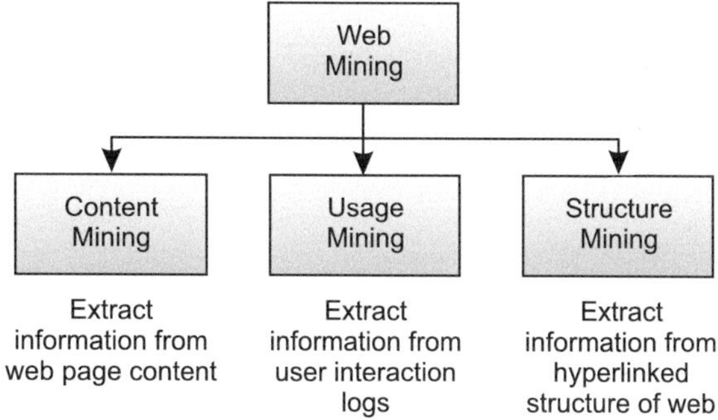

Figure 11.1 Categories of web mining

11.2 Web Content Mining

Web content mining deals with extracting relevant knowledge from the contents of a web page. During content mining, we totally ignore how other web pages link to a given web page or how users interact with it. A trivial approach to web content mining is based on location and frequency of keywords. But this gives rise to two problems: first, the problem of scarcity and second, the problem of abundance. The problem of scarcity occurs with those queries that either generate a few results or no results at all. The problem of abundance occurs with the queries that generate too many search results. The root cause of both the problems is the nature of data present on the web. The data is usually present in the form of HTML which is semi-structured and useful information is generally scattered across multiple web pages.

11.2.1 Web document clustering

Web document clustering is an approach to manage large number of documents based on keywords. The core idea is to form meaningful clusters of the web pages instead of returning a list of web pages arranged by their rank. Cluster analysis techniques, namely K-mean and agglomerative clustering, can be used to achieve this goal. The input attribute set for applying clustering techniques is generally vector of words and their frequency in a given web page. But, such clustering techniques don't give adequate results.

Another approach to web document clustering is based on Suffix Tree Clustering.

11.2.2 Suffix Tree Clustering (STC)

STC does clustering based upon phrases rather than frequency of keywords. STC works as follows:

Step 1: Obtain text from the web page. For every sentence in the text, filter out common words and punctuations. Convert the remaining words into their root form.

Step 2: Make a tree based on the list of words obtained in step 1.

Step 3: Compare trees obtained from various documents. Tree having same root to leaf node sequence of words are grouped into same cluster.

As shown in the Figure 11.2 below, STC considers the sequence of phrases in the document and thus tries to cluster the document in a more meaningful manner.

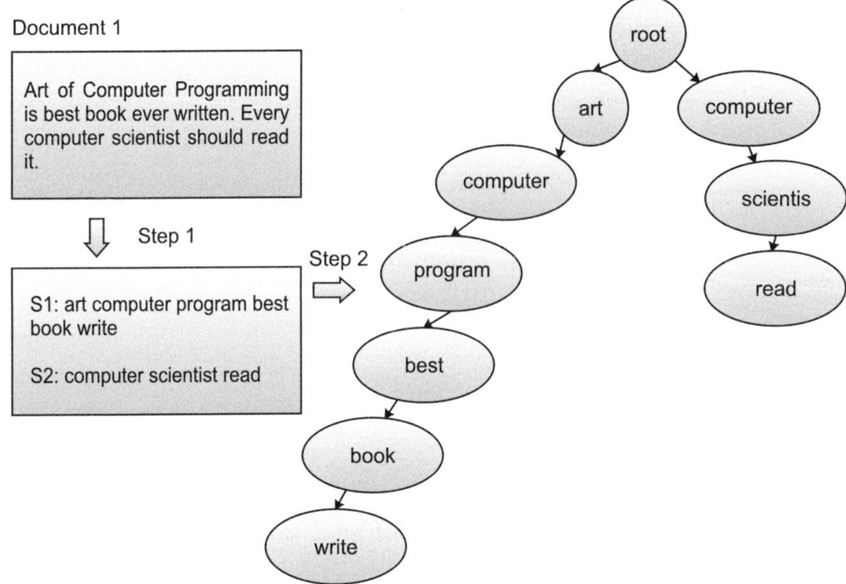

Figure 11.2 Suffix tree clustering example

11.2.3 Resemblance and containment

Further, in order to improve query results, there is a need to remove duplicate web pages or pages which are almost identical from the search results. The concepts of resemblance and containment help to accomplish this purpose. Resemblance is the term for how similar two documents are to each other. It has a value between 0 and 1 (both inclusive). A value of 1 represents the same document. A value close to 1 represents an almost similar document and a value close to 0 represents a completely different document. Containment is the term for the existence of one document inside another. It also has value between 0 and 1 with value of 1 representing that the first document is present inside the second and value of 0 stating otherwise.

To define resemblance and containment mathematically, the concept of shingles is used. The document is divided into sets with continuous sequence of words of length L. These sequences are called ***shingles***. So, for given two documents X and Y, resemblance R(X, Y) and containment C(X, Y) is defined as:

$$R(X, Y) = \{S(X) \cap S(Y)\} / \{S(X) \cup S(Y)\}$$

$$C(X, Y) = \{S(X) \cap S(Y)\} / \{S(X)\}$$

Where, S(X) and S(Y) are sets of shingles for document X and Y respectively.

From the formulas one can understand that Resemblance is equal to the total number of shingles that are common between two documents X and Y, divided by the total number of shingles in both the documents.

Containment is equal to the total number of shingles that are common between two documents X and Y, divided by the total number of shingles in original document X.

There are various ways to find similar web pages. One approach is to use the Linux ***diff*** tool to compare every pair of document. Another approach is based on the concept of fingerprinting.

11.2.4 Fingerprinting

Fingerprinting works by dividing a document into a continuous sequence of words (shingles) of every possible length. For instance, consider two documents with the respective content given below.

Document 1: I love machine learning.

Document 2: I love artificial intelligence.

For the above two documents, let us consider every sequence for the shingle length two.

Table 11.1 Sequences of length two

Document 1	*Document 2*
I love love machine machine learning	I love love artificial artificial intelligence

Using sequences enumerated in Table 11.1, we can clearly see that only 1 out of 3 sequences match. This is used to find similarity between two documents. Despite being very accurate this method is seldom used because it is very inefficient for documents with large numbers of words.

11.3 Web Usage Mining

Web usage mining deals with extracting useful information from log data about a user's interaction with the web pages. The main aim of web usage mining is to predict user behaviour while interacting with a web page in order to make the web page more customer centric and for better monetization or business strategies. For example, if the majority of visitors to a specific web page are coming from Facebook pages as compared to Twitter, then it would be much more profitable to invest in Facebook ads rather than investing in Twitter ads. In order to perform web usage mining, information as listed below in Table 11.2 is usually collected.

The data collected above is analyzed either using association mining or clustering in order to obtain hidden knowledge. Association mining can be used in discovering affinity between pages on a website. Log data may be converted into transactions like those used in market basket analysis with each node visited being treated like an item that is bought, but problems arise since in web traversing it is not uncommon for a user to return to a node while in market basket there is no equivalent structure possible.

Such analysis can reveal hidden knowledge. For instance, after analyzing data we may come to know that whenever a user visits page A then he/she also visits page B with 75% confidence or more. These types of associations are useful since it may be that pages A and B can be restructured so that the information that the user is seeking from page B could even be made available on page A; making the page A more customer centric.

Table 11.2 Important parameters for web usage mining

Important Parameters	*Description*
Number of hits	Total number of times a web page has been requested within a specific time duration
Number of visitors	Total number of visitors of the website within a specific time duration
Referer	The website from which the user came to the current web page
Landing page	The web page which served as entry point for the user
Session duration	Time spent by the user on the website
Path analysis	Pages that the user visited on the website
Browser type	Browser being used by the user
Device type	Type of devices being used by the user (desktop/mobile/tablet)
Operating system	Operating system being used by the user (Linux/iOS/Windows/Android)
Cookies	Cookie is the term for a small amount of data that can be stored within user's browser. It is generally used to identify user, save authentication tokens and so on.

11.4 Web Structure Mining

Web structure mining aims at obtaining information from the hyperlinked structure of the web. The web structure plays an important role in ranking of web pages and identifying the pages which act as authority on certain types of information. Apart from discovering authority sites, web structure is also used to identify hubs, i.e., the websites which link to many authority websites.

In the next section, the HITS algorithm is presented which uses web structure in order to identify hubs and authorities. Later, the PageRank algorithm will be presented which also uses web structure in order to rank web pages.

11.4.1 Hyperlink Induced Topic Search (HITS) algorithm

HITS algorithm (also known as hubs and authorities) is an algorithm that analyzes hyperlinked structure of the web in order to rank web pages. It was developed by Jon Kleinberg in 1999. It was used when the Internet was still in its nascency and web page directories were used widely.

HITS works on the basis of the concept of hubs and authority. HITS is based on the assumption that web pages which act as directories are not themselves authority on any information but act as a hub pointing out various web pages which may be the authority on the required information.

Let's understand the meaning of these two terms with the help of an example. Figure 11.3 shows a hyperlinked web structure where H1, H2 and H3 are search directories pages and A, B, C and D are web pages to which the directory pages have an outgoing hyperlink. Here, pages like H1, H2 and H3 act as hubs of information. They do not hold any information by themselves but they point out to other pages which according to them have the required information. In order words, the outgoing hyperlinks from hubs certify that the page they are pointing to have some authority on the required information. So, a good hub represents a page that points to many other pages, and a good authority represents a page that is linked by many different hubs. Formally, if the page *H1* provides a link to web page *A*, then *H1* confers some authority on page *A*.

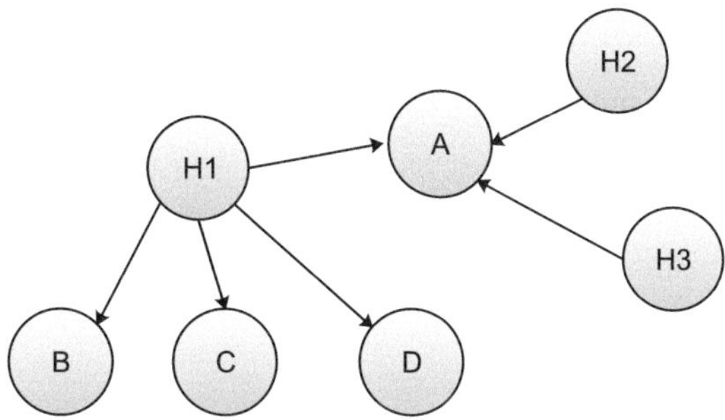

Figure 11.3 Hubs and Authority

Let us consider an example in order to understand the working of the HITS algorithm. The Figure 11.4 below shows a web page structure where each node represents a web page and arrows show the hyperlinks between the vertices.

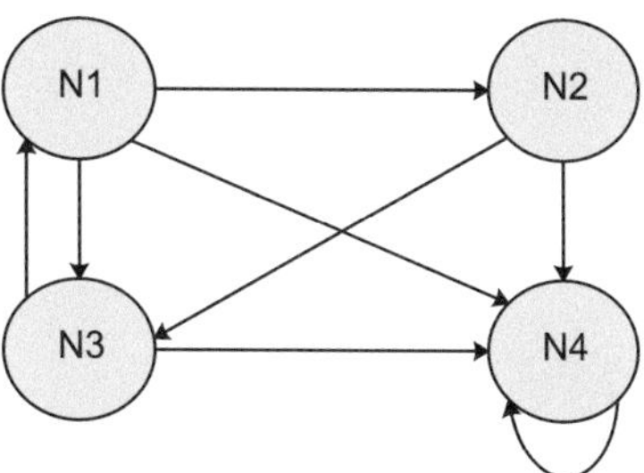

Figure 11.4 Example of a Web Page Structure

Step 1: Present the given web structure as an adjacency matrix in order to perform further calculations. Let the required adjacency matrix be A as shown in Figure 11.5.

	N1	N2	N3	N4
N1	0	1	1	1
N2	0	0	1	1
N3	1	0	0	1
N4	0	0	0	1

Figure 11.5 Adjacency matrix representing web structure shown in Figure 11.4

Step 2: Prepare the transpose of matrix A. It is given in Figure 11.6.

	N1	N2	N3	N4
N1	0	0	1	0
N2	1	0	0	0
N3	1	1	0	0
N4	1	1	1	1

Figure 11.6 Transpose Matrix of A

Step 3: Assume initial hub weight vector to be 1 and calculate authority weight vector by multiplying the transpose of matrix A with the initial hub weight vector as shown in Figure 11.7 below.

$$\begin{pmatrix} 0 & 0 & 1 & 0 \\ 1 & 0 & 0 & 0 \\ 1 & 1 & 0 & 0 \\ 1 & 1 & 1 & 1 \end{pmatrix} * \begin{pmatrix} 1 \\ 1 \\ 1 \\ 1 \end{pmatrix} = \begin{pmatrix} 1 \\ 1 \\ 2 \\ 4 \end{pmatrix}$$

Figure 11.7 Obtaining the Authority Weight Matrix

Step 4: Calculate the updated hub weight vector by multiplying the adjacency matrix A with authority weight matrix obtained in step 3.

$$\begin{pmatrix} 0 & 1 & 1 & 1 \\ 0 & 0 & 1 & 1 \\ 1 & 0 & 0 & 1 \\ 0 & 0 & 0 & 1 \end{pmatrix} * \begin{pmatrix} 1 \\ 1 \\ 2 \\ 4 \end{pmatrix} = \begin{pmatrix} 7 \\ 6 \\ 5 \\ 4 \end{pmatrix}$$

Figure 11.8 Updated Hub Weight Vector

As per the calculations done above, the graph shown in Figure 11.4 can be updated with hub and authority weights and can be represented as shown below in Figure 11.9.

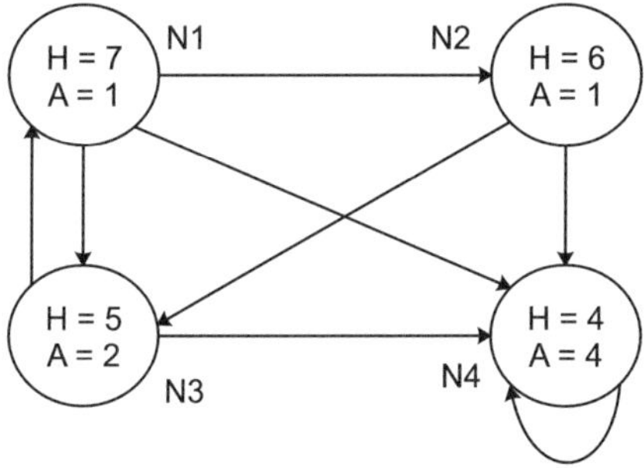

Figure 11.9 Web page structure with Hub and Authority Weights

This completes a single iteration of the HITS algorithm. In order to obtain much more accurate results, steps 3 and 4 can be repeated to obtain updated authority weight vectors and updated hub vector values.

From the above calculations, we can rank hubs and authorities and display authorities in search results in order of decreasing authority weight value. For instance, as per Figure 11.9, we can say that web page N4 has the highest authority for some keyword as it is hyperlinked to most high ranking hubs.

Over the years the Internet has become increasingly sophisticated and so has the World Wide Web with it. In the sections that fokkow, we will look at working and architecture of modern search engines and how they go about ranking search results.

11.5 Introduction to Modern Search Engines

The human urge to seek easy ways to find new information existenced long before the age of the computers. Libraries maintain catalogues and books come with indexes in order to facilitate easy searching. Search engines are software that allow us to search information based on some input. The first search engine was created in the year 1990 by Alan Emtage, a student at McGill University in Montreal. Its name was Archie. It searches were based on keywords and it showed all the web pages containing keywords that were given to it as input. It worked exactly like the search feature in any modern document editor. As years passed, many new search engines such as AltaVista and Lycos came into existence but no major improvements were made in how information was being searched and ranked. These historical search engines did something known as directory based search. A web directory is just a list of websites on similar topics. For instance, all websites related to food will be in one directory whereas websites dealing with games will be in another directory. So, when a user would enter a keyword, a list of websites from related directories would be shown.

In 1996 everything changed when two PhD students Larry Page and Sergey Brin from Stanford University started a research project named 'BackRub' based on a web page ranking algorithm developed by them. Eventually, they changed the name to Google. The name of the search engine originated from a misspelling of the word 'googol' which is the number 1 followed by 100 zeros. The algorithm used by Google to rank its search results is called PageRank. Fast forward to present day: modern search engines such as Google or Bing use complex algorithms based on machine learning in order to deliver the most relevant, and often personalized, content in response to a search query.

In the year 2000, Robin Li, a software developer, launched another search engine named Baidu from a hotel room in Beijing (China). It used a RankDex site-scoring algorithm for ranking web pages. The algorithm was itself developed and patented by Robin Li. The name Baidu means countless times and has been taken from a classical romantic Chinese poem. By year 2007, Baidu became the second largest search engine in the world.

In the year 2009, Microsoft, not wanting to be left behind in the race, launched Bing. Bing became the third largest search engine in just two years because of Microsoft's huge share of the personal computer's operating system market, with Bing as default search engine on all Microsoft's products.

Figure 11.10 below shows top search engines according to the market size they serve.

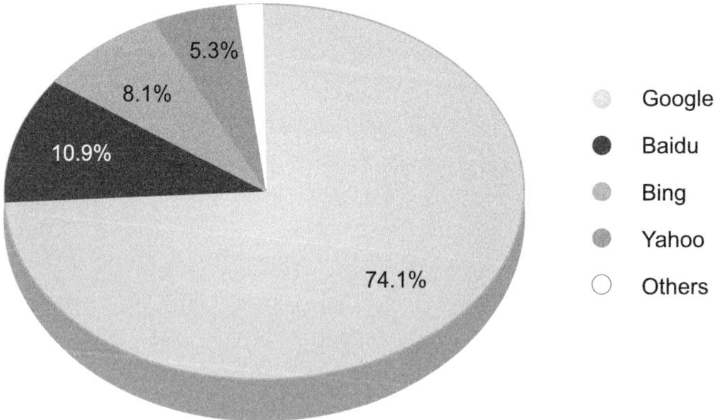

Figure 11.10 Search engines market share

In this chapter, we will examine how a modern search engine works. We will discuss the workings of the PageRank algorithm in detail and understand the concepts of precision and recall that are often used to evaluate the quality of search results.

11.6 Working of a Search Engine

Figure 11.11 below shows architecture of a modern search engine. Generally every search engine consists of the following modules: a web crawler, an indexer and a query processor. In this section, we will examine the working of each module in detail.

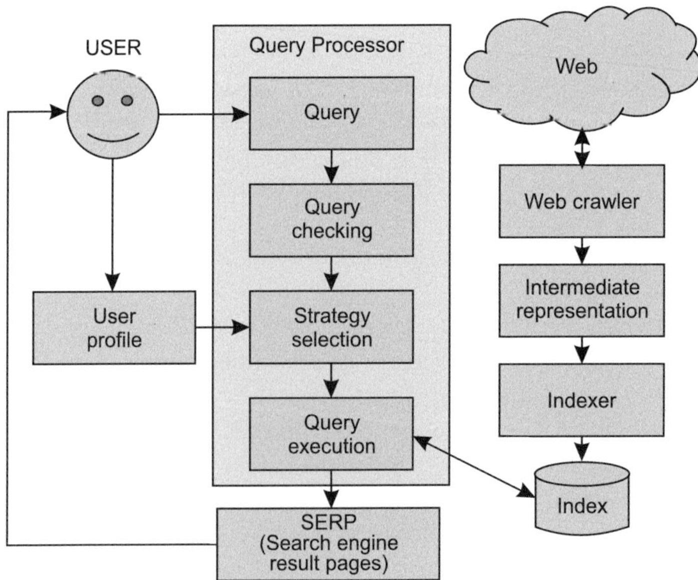

Figure 11.11 Architecture of a search engine

11.6.1 Web crawler

A web crawler is a simple piece of software whose responsibility is to visit every web page available on the World Wide Web (WWW) and fetch data from those web pages. The data fetched is stored to be processed later to create an index. Whenever you search anything on Google, you can click the arrow besides the link in the search result pages to see the data that Google has stored for the particular web page. A crawler is sometimes also called a spider, robot or a bot.

As there are billions of web pages online, a crawler generally runs parallel on a computer cluster. If a website does not want a search engine to crawl through its data or any particular web page then they can setup rules regarding it in the **robots.txt** file in the root directory of the web server. Developing a scalable crawler is a complex job as a crawler has to consider many variables such as how often a web page is updated. A simple web crawler follows the following algorithm.

Algorithm 11.1 General web crawling

1. Initialize list L1 of web pages to visit
2. Initialize empty list L2 to store web pages which have already been visited
3. For every web page P in L1
    a. If link is not in L2
        i. Visit P
        ii. Save data fetched from P
        iii. Extract all the links present in P and add them to L1
        iv. Add P to L2
4. Exit

In order for the above algorithm to work we have to provide an initial list of web pages. These initial web pages are generally known as seed pages. From the above algorithm it is clear that a crawler follows a graph traversal algorithm. This pattern is obvious because the World Wide Web itself is a graph of interconnected documents. It should also be noted that per the above algorithm, if a webpage is not hyperlinked to any other web page then a crawler will never be able to reach it. Thus, search engines depend on hyperlinks or manual submission of links in order to find new web pages. The hyperlinks from other web pages to a given web page are known as backlinks. In Section 11.7, we will see that these backlinks play an important role in the PageRank algorithm which is used to rank web pages in search results.

11.6.2 Indexer

The responsibility of an indexer is to identify the keywords of a web page and index the web pages with their respective keywords. Keywords are the words which give us an idea about the content of a web page. Generally keywords are extracted from the web page title, meta tags or from heading tags present in the HTML of the web page.

Traditionally, an indexer works as follows. First, a list of words from the page title, heading tags and the meta tags is extracted. Next common words such as *the*, *it*, *and*, *that* and suchlike are removed from this list and stemming is conducted on the remaining words. Stemming converts a word into its root form. For instance, words such as *computers*, *computing* and *computation* are all converted into the word *computer* after stemming. These root words are used as keywords. Now-a-days, advanced techniques of natural language processing are used in order to understand the content and the context of a web page and the keywords are generated based upon this analysis.

After generating these keywords an index is created which is queried when a user performs a search. For instance let us consider the index shown in Table 11.3. The first column shows the keywords and second column contains web page IDs related to the corresponding keywords.

Table 11.3 Index showing keywords and related web pages

Keywords	Web Page IDs
Program	1, 5, 10
Data Structure	9, 8, 6, 4
Algorithm	5, 8, 2, 3

Suppose for instance, when a user queries *Algorithms* then the query is first filtered to remove any common words. Next, the remaining words are converted into their root form. In our case, this would result in word *Algorithm* which will be queried and the web pages 5, 8, 2, and 3 will be shown in the search results. In next section, we will discuss the exact working of a query processor.

11.6.3 Query processor

The query processor is the most important module in a search engine. Traditionally query processors used to return web pages based on the matching keywords found in the index as explained in the last section.

Nowadays, query processors have become very sophisticated and often provide personalized search results based on user's profile. Where, user's profile is set of variables that describe a user such as the user's current location, gender, age, type of device (mobile or desktop). User profiles can help in providing much relevant search results. For instance, if a user in city Delhi will query for hospitals, then hospitals that are in the neighborhood of the user will form the search result. It would be illogical to show hospitals in some other city to the user currently present in Delhi. User profiles can be used in many more sophisticated ways. For instance, if a child searches for movies online then his or her search results should contain the list of movies appropriate for his or her age group.

A query processor works in multiple stages. When a user enters a query it is first passed to a checking module in order to correct any mistakes. This behaviour can be noticed if you misspell a word while performing a query on any modern search engine such as Google or Bing. Once the query is checked, it is categorized based on its type. For instance, a user might be searching for a specific product or service or the user maybe searching for an important news event. This categorization allows a search engine to provide far more relevant results to the user. Based on user profiles and the categorization a strategy is selected in order to query from the index. After the web pages have been retrieved from the index they are arranged in order of their relevance decided by using algorithms such as PageRank.

11.7 PageRank Algorithm

After enrolling in PhD program in computer science at Stanford University, Larry Page was in search of a dissertation theme and considered exploring the mathematical properties of the World Wide Web (WWW). His supervisor, Terry Winograd, encouraged him to pursue the idea. Larry Page was inspired by the fact that the number of citations of a research paper was proof of how good the paper actually was. So, he focused on the problem of finding out which web pages were linked to a given web page, considering the number and nature of such backlinks as valuable information for that web page just like paper citations. Sergey Brin, a fellow Stanford PhD student, soon joined Page's research project. Together, the pair authored a research paper titled 'The Anatomy of a Large-Scale Hypertextual Web Search Engine,' which became one of the most downloaded scientific documents in the history of the Internet at the time. Page and Brin developed the PageRank algorithm as part of their research. This algorithm formed the base for the Google search engine. The PageRank algorithm works on the basis of backlinks. It can be understood well by considering the social behaviour of human beings. For instance, if person A is very important, then many people will know him. This notion of knowing someone is similar to a web page linking to some other web page (a backlink). If a web page A is very important then many other web pages will link back to it. This is accompanied by the fact that if very important web pages link back to a certain page then that web page itself must be very important. Just like if many famous people know about a certain person then that person itself must be very important or famous.

Let us look into the mathematics of the PageRank algorithm. The PageRank algorithm uses probability theory at its core. The probability of a user clicking on a link may be estimated based on the number of links present in that web page. The more links a web page has the less chance that a user will click on a particular link. In other words, the probability of a user clicking any link is inversely proportional to the number of links on a web page. This means that if a user is on webpage A which has two links, with the first leading to web page B and the second leading to web page C, then there is 50% chance of user visiting web page B from web page A. This 50% chance is multiplied by a damping factor in order to accommodate for circumstances such as user leaving the web page A or jumping to another tab in the browser.

Let us call this probability A_C that is the probability of visiting the web page C from web page A. So, if three other web pages P, Q and R link-back to web page C and P_C, Q_C, and R_C are probabilities of visiting web page C from respective web pages then total probability of visiting web page C can be defined as sum total of all these probabilities. This allows us to calculate how likely a user is to visit a certain web page. This idea is the very core of the PageRank algorithm. Mathematically, the PageRank of any webpage A is as follows:

$$PR(A) = (1 - d) + d\left(\frac{PR(T_1)}{L(T_1)} + \frac{PR(T_2)}{L(T_2)} + \frac{PR(T_3)}{L(T_3)} + \dots\right)$$

Here, PR(A) represents PageRank of web page A, L(T) represents number of outgoing links from web page T and d is the damping factor. Here, the term (1 - d) represents the scenario when the user leaves the web page A. In simple words, PageRank of a web page is the probability of a user staying on that web page combined with probabilities of reaching that particular web page by following any backlink.

Let us consider an example in order to understand the concept of the PageRank algorithm more thoroughly.

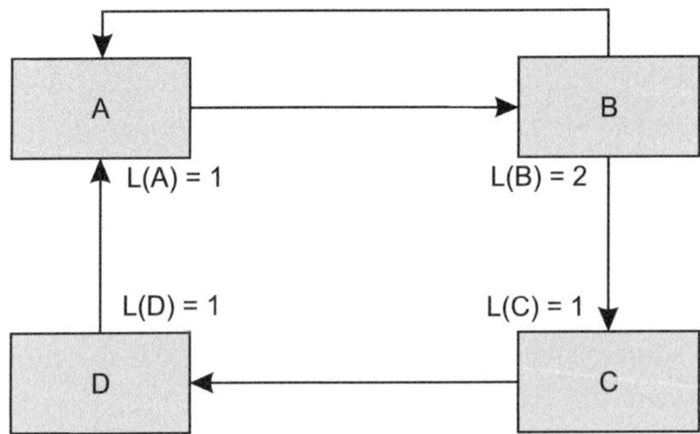

Figure 11.12 Four web pages with hyperlinks

Figure 11.12 shows a collection of four web pages where the arrow indicates the hyperlinks. For instance, an arrow goes from page B to page C indicates that page B has a link that will take the user to page C.

We know,

L(A) = 1 because web page A links to only one page, i.e., web page B,

L(B) = 2 because web page B links to two web pages A and C,

L(C) = 1 because web page C links to only one page, i.e., web page D and

L(D) = 1 because web page D links to only one page, i.e., web page A.

Let us assume that initial damping factor (d) is 0.7 then by applying the PageRank formula given above, we get following four linear equations:

$$PR(A) = (1-d) + d\left(\frac{PR(T_1)}{L(T_1)} + \frac{PR(T_2)}{L(T_2)} + \frac{PR(T_3)}{L(T_3)} + \ldots\right)$$

PR(A) = (1 - 0.7) + 0.7 (PR(B) / 2 + PR(D) / 1) = 0.3 + (0.7 / 2) (PR(B) + 2 PR(D)) ...1

As webpage A can be reached from webpage B and D only.

PR(B) = (1 - 0.7) + 0.7 (PR(A) / 1) = 0.3 + 0.7 (PR(A)) ...2

As webpage B can be reached from webpage A only.

PR(C) = (1 - 0.7) + 0.7 (PR(B) / 2) = 0.3 + (0.7 / 2) (PR(B)) ...3

As webpage C can be reached from webpage B only.

PR(D) = (1 - 0.7) + 0.7 (PR(C) / 1) = 0.3 + 0.7 (PR(C)) ...4

As webpage D can be reached from webpage C only.

Let's solve these Linear Equations:

Let's simplify the equations first, and for simplicity, let us assume

PR(A) = A , PR(B) = B, PR(C) = C and PR(D) = D.

From (...1): A = 0.3 + (0.7/2)(B + 2D)

Thus, $2A = 0.6 + 0.7(B + 2D)$ ...5

From (...2): $B = 0.3 + 0.7A$

From (...3): $2C = 0.6 + 0.7B$

From (...4): $D = 0.3 + 0.7C$

Let us eliminate B from equation 1, 3 and 4.

From (...2) we have $B = 0.3 + 0.7A$, multiply the equation by 0.7

We get $0.7\,B = 0.21 + 0.49A$ ...6

Now substitute value of 0.7B in equation 5 as shown below.

$2A = 0.6 + 0.7(B + 2D)$

$2A = 0.6 + (0.21 + 0.49A) + 1.4D$

$1.51A = 0.81 + 1.4D$ ...7

Similarly substitute value of 0.7B (given in equation 6) to equation 3 as shown below.

$C = 0.3 + (0.7 / 2)\,B$

$2C = 0.6 + 0.7B$

$2C = 0.6 + 0.21 + 0.49A$

$C = (0.81 + 0.49A) / 2$ ...8

Now, let us eliminate C from equation 4 by substituting the value of C obtained in equation 8 as shown below.

$D = 0.3 + 0.7\,C$

$D = 0.3 + 0.7\,((0.81 + 0.49A) / 2)$

$D = 0.5835 + 0.1715A$ ...9

Let us substitute the value of D given in equation 9 in equation 7.

$1.51A = 0.81 + 1.4D$

$1.51A = 0.81 + 1.4\,(0.5835 + 0.1715A)$

$1.2699A = 1.6269$

$A = 1.281$ ...10

Now substitute the value of A in equation 9 as shown below.

$D = 0.5835 + 0.1715\,(1.281)$

$D = 0.803$ ...11

Now, substitute the value of A in equation 8 as shown below.

$C = (0.81 + 0.49A) / 2$

$C = (0.81 + 0.49 * 1.281) / 2$

$C = 0.719$ ...12

Finally, substitute the value of C in equation 6.

0.7 B = 0.21 + 0.49A

B = 0.3 + 0.7A

B = 0.3 + 0.7(1.281)

B = 1.197 ...13

Therefore, the respective PageRanks are as follows:

PR(A) = 1.281 PR(B) = 1.197 PR(C) = 0.719 PR(D) = 0.803

We can conclude that web page A has the highest PageRank followed by web pages B, D and C. It should be noted that the damping factor is itself a probability of the user leaving a web page, hence the value of d itself will always lie between 0 and 1.

Let us consider another example, this time with five web pages. Figure 11.13 shows a collection of five web pages where the arrow indicates the hyperlinks.

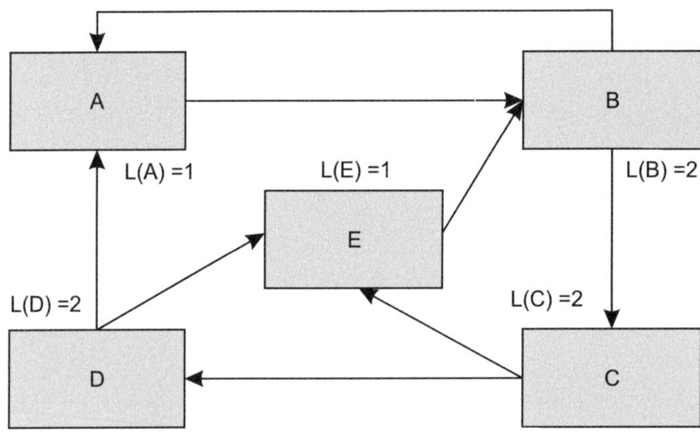

Figure 11.13 Five web pages with hyperlinks

We know,
L(A) = 1 because web page A links to only one page, i.e., web page B,
L(B) = 2 because web page B links to two web pages A and C,
L(C) = 2 because web page C links to two web pages D and E,
L(D) = 2 because web page D links to two web pages A and E and
L(E) = 1 because web page E links to only one page, i.e., web page B.

Let us assume that initial damping factor (d) is 0.6; then, by applying the PageRank formula, we get following five linear equations:

PR(A) = (1 - 0.6) + 0.6 (PR(B) / 2 + PR(D) / 2) = 0.4 + (0.6 / 2) (PR(B) + PR(D)) ...14

PR(B) = (1 - 0.6) + 0.6 (PR(A) / 1 + PR(E) / 1) = 0.4 + 0.6 (PR(A) + PR(E)) ...15

PR(C) = (1 - 0.6) + 0.6 (PR(B) / 2) = 0.4 + (0.6 / 2) (PR(B)) ...16

PR(D) = (1 - 0.6) + 0.6 (PR(C) / 1) = 0.4 + 0.6 (PR(C)) ...17

PR(E) = (1 - 0.6) + 0.6 (PR(C) / 2 + PR(D) / 2) = 0.4 + (0.6 / 2) (PR(C) + PR(D)) ...18

Let's solve these linear equations.

Let's simplify the equations first, and for simplicity, let us assume

PR(A) = A , PR(B) = B, PR(C) = C, PR(D) = D and PR(E) = E

From (…14): A = 0.4 + 0.3B + 0.3D …19

From (…15): B = 0.4 + 0.6A + 0.6E …20

From (…16): C = 0.4 + 0.3B …21

From (…17): D = 0.4 + 0.6C …22

From (...18): E = 0.4 + 0.3C + 0.3D …23

Let us eliminate C from equation 22 by substituting the value of C from equation 21.

C = 0.4 + 0.3 B

D = 0.4 + 0.6 C

D = 0.4 + 0.6(0.4 + 0.3B)

D = 0.64 + 0.18B …24

Let us eliminate C from equation 23 by substituting the value of C from equation 21.

C = 0.4 + 0.3 B

E = 0.4 + 0.3C + 0.3D

E = 0.4 + 0.3 (0.4 + 0.3B) + 0.3D

E = 0.52 +0.09B + 0.3D …25

Let us eliminate D from equation 23 by substituting the value of D from equation 24.

D = 0.64 + 0.18B

E = 0.52 +0.09B + 0.3D

E = 0.52 +0.09B + 0.3(0.64 + 0.18B)

E = 0.144B + 0.712 …26

Substitute the value of B from equation 20 in equation 26 as shown below.

B = 0.4 + 0.6A + 0.6E

E = 0.144B + 0.712

E = 0.144(0.4 + 0.6A + 0.6E) + 0.712

0.9136E = 0.7696 + 0.0864A …27

Let us eliminate D from equation 19 by substituting the value of D from equation 24.

D = 0.64 + 0.18B

A = 0.4 + 0.3B + 0.3D

A = 0.4 + 0.3B + 0.3(0.64 + 0.18B)

A = 0.592 + 0.354B …28

Substitute the value of B from equation 20 in equation 28 as shown below.

B = 0.4 + 0.6A + 0.6E

A = 0.592 + 0.354(0.4 + 0.6A + 0.6E)

0.0864A = 0.9136E - 0.7696

A = (0.9136E - 0.7696) / 0.0864 ...29

Substitute the value of A from equation 29 in equation 27 as shown below.

0.9136E = 0.7696 + 0.0864A

0.9136E = 0.7696 + 0.0864((0.9136E - 0.7696) / 0.0864)

E = 0.95

Put the value of E in equation 29, we get A = 1.19 as shown below.

A = (0.9136E - 0.7696) / 0.0864

A = 1.19

Put the value of E and A in equation 20,

B = 0.4 + 0.6A + 0.6E

B = 0.4 + 0.6*1.19 + 0.6*0.95

B = 1.69

Put the value of B in equation 21,

C = 0.4 + 0.3 B

C = 0.4 + 0.3 * 1.69

C= 0.91

Put the value of Bin equation 24,

D = 0.64 + 0.18B

D = 0.64 + 0.18*1.69

D = 0.94

Therefore the respective Page Ranks are as followed:

PR(A) = 1.19, PR(B) = 1.69, PR(C) = 0.91, PR(D) = 0.94 and PR(E) = 0.95.

We can conclude that web page B has the highest PageRank followed by web pages A, E, D and C; in that order.

The PageRank algorithm has certain drawbacks. From Figure 11.12, we can see that a backlink from web page B can be seen as a kind of vote that web page A receives from web page B and this vote enhances the PageRank of web page A.

The PageRank algorithm totally ignores the content of the webpage and considers backlink as the sole attribute for deciding a web page's rank. This has given rise to many problems namely - 'Google bomb' which is the practice of causing a website to rank highly in search engine results for irrelevant, unrelated or off-topic search terms by linking it heavily from other web pages. To overcome this drawback, Google has improved the PageRank algorithm by introducing many updates namely - Panda, Penguin and HummingBird.

11.8 Precision and Recall

Till now we have seen how a search engine works to generate a search engine result page (SERP) in response to a user query. We have also seen the PageRank algorithm which makes sure that good web pages must be ranked higher in the search results. Apart from being able to rank most relevant information much higher, there are two other parameters which are used to evaluate the quality of the search results of a search engine. These parameters are Precision and Recall. Let us understand these two concepts with the help of a Venn diagram.

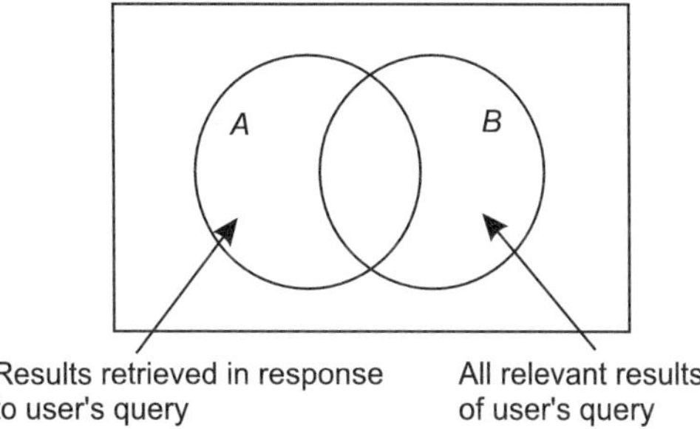

Figure 11.14 Venn diagram showing relevant and retrieved results

In the above Venn diagram, set A represents the results that were returned to a user in response to a query. Set B represents the results that are relevant to the query that the user performed. So, ($A \cap B$) represents the results that are both relevant and are shown to the user. Precision is defined as

Precision = Number of relevant items retrieved / Total retrieved items
= (Total retrieved $\cap$ Total relevant) / Total retrieved items

And Recall is defined as

Recall = Number of relevant retrieved / Total relevant items
= (Total retrieved $\cap$ Total relevant) / Total relevant items

We can clearly see that precision is defined as the proportion of search results that are relevant to the user's query whereas recall is the proportion of the relevant search results that are retrieved.

Although these two parameters are quite useful to evaluate the quality of search results but there is a major drawback. Set B shown in the above Venn diagram is impossible to measure. There is no way to formally define what is relevant to a user's query and what is not.

Example: Let us suppose that there are 200 pages available on Internet for machine learning. The search on this term returns total 210 pages, out of which 190 belongs to machine learning, calculate precision and recall for our algorithm.

Solution: Precision = Number of relevant items retrieved / Total retrieved items
= (Total retrieved $\cap$ Total relevant) / Total retrieved items
Precision = 190 / 210

Because, the Number of relevant items retrieved is 190 (belongs to machine learning) and the Total Number of retrieved items is 210 (these many pages were returned to user on his query).

Recall = Number of relevant retrieved / Total relevant items
= (Total retrieved $\cap$ Total relevant) / Total relevant items
Recall = 190 / 200

Because, the Number of relevant items retrieved (which are both relevant and retrieved) is 190 and the Total Number of relevant items is 200 (as only 200 pages of machine learning were there).

Nowadays modern search engines track users and collect vast amount of data such as what links did the user click, how much time was spent on which web page, how the user modified the query to improve his or her search results, and so on. This data is later analysed by machine learning algorithms in order to guess which web pages might have been relevant to the query made by the user.

Remind Me

- Web mining is the application of data mining techniques and machine learning to find useful information from data present in web pages.
- Web mining is divided into three parts, i.e, web content mining, structure mining and usage mining.
- Web content mining deals with extracting knowledge from the content of a web page.
- Web document clustering is an approach to manage the large number of documents based on keywords.
- Web document clustering is based on Suffix Tree Clustering.
- Resemblance indicates how similar two documents are to each other.
- It has a value between 0 and 1 (both inclusive). A value of 1 represents same document. Containment defines the existence of one document inside another. It also has value between 0 and 1 with value of 1 representing that first document is present inside the second and value of 0 stating otherwise.
- Web usage mining deals with extracting useful information from the log data about a user's interaction with the web pages.
- The web structure mining aims at obtaining information from the hyperlinked structure of the web.
- HITS algorithm (also known as hubs and authorities) is an algorithm that analyzes hyperlinked structure of the web in order to rank web pages. HITS works on the basis of the concept of hubs and authority.
- Generally every search engine consists of modules like a web crawler, an indexer and a query processor.
- The PageRank algorithm uses probability theory, at its core. The probability of a user clicking on a link may be estimated based on the number of links present in that web page. The more links a web page has the less chance that a user will click on a particular link.
- Precision is defined as Number of relevant items retrieved / Total retrieved items
- Recall is defined as Number of relevant retrieved / Total relevant items. Schema is logical description of database.

Point Me (Books)

- Conolly, Thomas, and Carolyn Begg. 2015. *Database Systems: A Practical Approach to Design, Implementation, and Management*, 6th ed. New York: Pearson Education.
- Thareja, Reema. 2009. *Data Warehousing*. Delhi: Oxford University Press.

Point Me (Video)

- Understanding Schemas in Datawarehousing | Edureka, https://www.youtube.com/watch?v=uigKK02XGxE

Connect Me (Internet Resources)

- https://searchengineland.com/new-google-ranking-study-shows-links-incredibly-important-ranking-algorithm-254188
- https://neilpatel.com/what-is-seo/
- http://www.cs.princeton.edu/~chazelle/courses/BIB/pagerank.htm

Test Me

Answer these questions based on your learning in this chapter.

1. What will be the page rank for each page in the following scenario? Here each page is not connected with any other page.

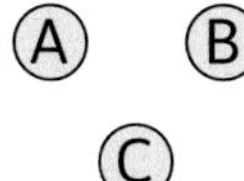

2. Write the formula to calculate page rank of page. Explain the meaning of each term used in this formula.
3. What is precision and recall? Why it is difficult to achieve precision and recall at the same time?
4. What is web mining? What are different categories of web content mining?
5. What is difference between resemblance and containment? Explain with examples.

12

Data Warehouse

Chapter Objectives

- ✓ To understand the need of an operational data store in OLTP and OLAP systems
- ✓ To understand data warehousing, its benefits and architecture
- ✓ To do a comparative study on OLAP, OLTP and ODS.
- ✓ To comprehend the concept of data mart.

In order to understand what an Operational Data Store is, it is very important to know what led to such Operational Data Stores and what the limitations were of OLTP systems to answer management queries.

12.1 The Need for an Operational Data Store (ODS)

Online Transaction Processing (OLTP) systems have become popular due to their versatility. Right from financial transactions to daily log operations, these are being used by myriad multinational companies and world level organizations to record transaction details.

In the present scenario, organizations and their branches operate in many locations across the world. Each, such, branch generates massive amounts of data. The management of a large retail chain operating from multiple locations, for example, will at the end of day, want to know about transactions done that day. One could take the case of a Dominos Pizza store, where the management needs to know the total sales for that day or other details such as the number and types of pizzas sold. Such companies rely on OLTP systems to get data from multiple stores spanning the world. On these OLTP systems, queries usually run on an indexed database, as this makes the searching fast and efficient. But unfortunately, data spread over multiple systems leads to a plethora of technical errors when carrying out the simple task of running queries on data stored on OLTP systems.

When dealing with corporate data it is also necessary to maintain correct and accurate information, in order to provide swift customer support services. This is possible if the data is acquired from all information sources.

It is very important for any organization's management to know the real state of affairs of their organization. However, OLTP systems fail badly, as they were not designed to support management queries. Management queries are very complex and require multiple joins and aggregations while being written. To overcome this limitation of OLTP systems some solutions were proposed, which are as follows.

I. On demand query

The On Demand query approach is also known as the lazy approach where management queries are run on OLTP systems in real-time. This means that as soon as data is received, the queries are run giving the management the advantage of up to date information. But due to the complex nature of queries, on demand query approach loads OLTP systems heavily and hence, is unacceptable in real life scenarios.

II. Eager approach

Another way to deal with OLTP systems is the Eager approach in which, all management queries are collected on a regular basis, and during non peak hours these queries are run on the OLTP systems. The results of these queries are stored separately, and whenever a request from management is found, the saved query results are provided.

The Eager approach is quite quick, giving it an advantage over the On Demand query approach. The limitation with the Eager approach is its inability to deliver up to date information. As queries are not run on real time data it carries data of some previous state.

III. Operational Data Store

Because both of these systems discussed above suffered from limitations, it led to the development of the Operational Data Store (ODS). This Operation Data Store is a special unified (separate) database that has been developed specifically to handle management queries. It is just like a short term (volatile) enterprise memory which contains recently stored organizational information. In the next few pages, we will discuss Operational Data Source in more detail.

12.2 Operational Data Store

Inmon and Imhoff (1996) defined ODS or Operational Data Store as 'A subject-oriented, integrated, volatile, current valued data store, containing only corporate detailed data.'

In order to understand ODS one needs to have a clear view of technical terms which Inmon and Imhoff used while defining an ODS. And so, we examine the ODS definition in detail.

Subject-Oriented

ODS is subject oriented, as it is built around the major data entity or subjects of an organization. For example, in a University, the data subject (entities under study) could be students, teachers, and various courses, whereas in a company the subjects might be workers, interns, services and items.

Integrated

ODS integrates (combines) data from multiple systems to provide a wide view of any enterprise's data, hence they are said to be 'integrated'.

Current valued

An ODS is always up to date as it doesn't contain obsolete data. Therefore, an ODS is always current valued due to its information nature (information is always up to date and shows the current state).

Volatile

ODS is described as a short term enterprise memory due to its volatile nature. ODS always updates its information, hence its data is volatile in nature (the older information is always replaced by the updated information).

Detailed

ODS is always detailed enough to cater to the needs of the operational management staff in an enterprise. Although it not as descriptive as its source OLTP is, it is still capable enough to highlight important organizational information.

ODS, may also be used as an interim database which could be used to build a data warehouse. Hence, ODS may also be considered as another type of data warehouse.

12.2.1 Types of ODS

An ODS could be classified into different types depending upon the needs of an organization as discussed below.

Type I: ODS as a reporting tool

This type of ODS is always up to date and is updated on a daily basis, making it the best tool for reporting any administrative process. For example, it could be used for providing total sales made per day, number of transactions done in a day and other logs.

Type II: ODS as a complex information tracker

Complex information such as locations, products, production duration can be easily derived using ODS. This kind of database is updated more frequently (perhaps hourly) to reflect changes.

Type III: ODS as customer relation management supporter

In order to support customer relationships, organizations use ODS as a tool for Customer Relationship Management. Such types of ODS are fed with synchronous or near-synchronous updates so as to provide customers with the most accurate and up to date information.

12.2.2 Architecture of ODS

A typical ODS architecture is illustrated in Figure 12.1. The very first step in loading ODS with information is the extraction of information from source databases, which needs to be done in an efficient way to ensure required quality of data. In the original source itself, the data is refreshed regularly and frequently and suitable checks are required to ensure the quality of data after each update.

Further, every ODS is required to satisfy normal integrity constraints such as existential integrity, referential integrity and appropriate ways to deal with null values. Preferably, the ODS should be a read-only database; a user must not be able to alter any ODS values.

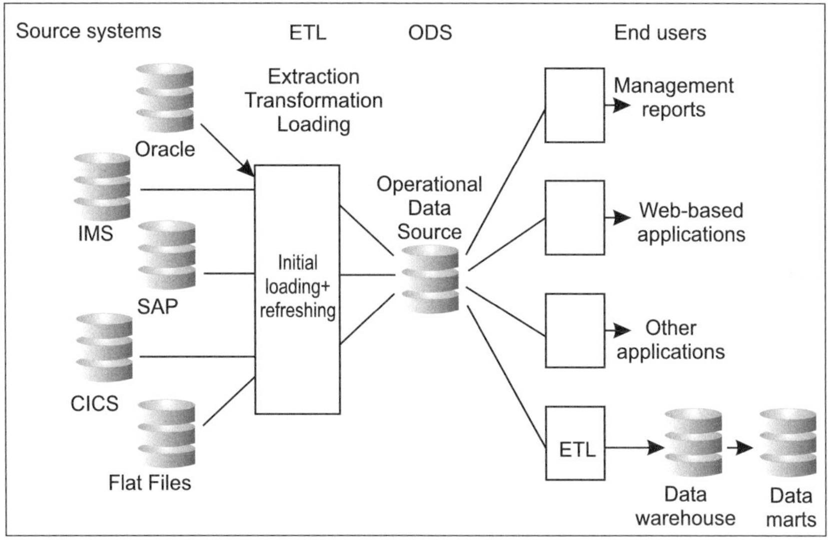

Figure 12.1 Architecture of an Operation Data Store

In order to build an ODS, the followings steps need to be performed.

Step 1 - The very first step is to populate ODS with apt information from some source OLTP. This step involves acquisition; the processes of extracting, transforming and loading (ETL) data from OLTP source systems.

Extraction, Transformation and Loading

The data in a ODS is typically loaded through an extraction, transformation, and loading (ETL) process from multiple data sources.

Consider a case of collecting information of Customers to prepare an ODS. Now, it is very important to always have up to date and accurate information of the customers, with whom the organization wants correspond. So, organizations are very careful about maintaining the correct data of their customer. But capturing correct details of millions of customers or suppliers is a very challenging task for any organization, as this data is entered by data entry operators, who usually make lots of mistakes while entering this data due to many factors. Hence, an ETL process involves identifying and correcting these hours of data entry in the best possible way. The different phases of an ETL process are as follows.

Extracting

The very first step is extraction of data, in which the source system's data is accessed first and is prepared further for processing and extracting required values. The whole process should be done with minimal resources. Apart from this, the best extraction strategy is one in which the source system's performance and response time remains un-altered.

There are multiple ways to perform extraction. One approach is ***Update Notification***. In this approach, whenever the data is changed or altered in the source system it will notify users about the change. This is the easiest way to extract data.

The other approach is ***Incremental Extract***. In this approach, many systems are incapable of providing notifications but are efficient enough to track down the changes that have been made to the source data.

The third approach is ***Full Extract***. It is used when the systems discussed above fail. When the system is neither able to notify nor able to track down the changes, the whole data is extracted and an old copy of data is maintained so as to identify what has been changed.

After extracting the data it is cleaned, to ensure its quality. Cleaning performed by following the rules of data unification, such as placing unique identifiers, e.g. phone numbers, Email conversion to standard form and validation of address fields.

Transforming

In the transform step, a set of rules are applied over the data, in order to transform it from source format to target format. These sometimes include dimension conversion as well. Aggregation, joining, derivation and calculation of new values are likely to happen in the Transform step.

Loading

The final step is loading in which it is ensured that processed data is loaded correctly into another database. All the indexes and constraints previously applied to the data needs to be disabled before the loading commences, and after successful loading one should ensure that these are put back in place.

This completes the first step in the process of constructing an ODS.

Step 2: After the database gets populated, next step is to build the ODS and check for anomalies. This also involves testing the ODS for performance before it can go online.

Step 3: To support end users requirements different web applications are developed on ODS. Sometimes reporting tools are also used to support management queries. The ODS can also be used to support other applications of the organization. Finally, the ODS can further be extended with ETL to build a larger data warehouse and data marts.

12.2.3 Advantages of the ODS

The advantages of building the ODS are:

- The ODS can be extended further to built a data warehouse which can store historical information as well (as shown in Figure 12.2). The data warehouse is considered as the long term memory of the organization as it stores the historical information of the organization.

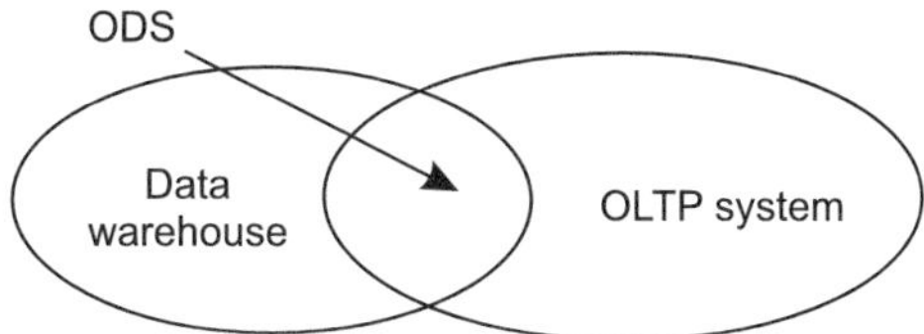

Figure 12.2 Relationship between OLTP, ODS and data warehouse systems

- Implementation of data warehouses by extending ODS consumes less time.
- ODS systems are more effective because they provide a holistic view of the enterprise's data.

12.3 Data Warehouse

A data warehouse is a historical database and should be considered as the long term memory of an organization. To understand this term better, let us consider the database of a University Management System. For the duration of study by a student at the university, his or her data will be retained in the main data store and all database operations such as insert, update, delete and retrieve will be performed on it. This database is usually called OLTP. But once a student has left, then his or her database is usually removed from OLTP because OLTP is meant to perform day-to-day operations. However, the management may be interested in retaining the data of old students. It can be used for later queries as well as for analysis purposes. Thus, all historical data can be vital for an organization for subsequent data analysis. All such historical records can be moved to a separate data store known as the data warehouse and may be called upon when required in the future.

Historical data is not to be tampered with; no insertion, up-dation and deletion are to be made. Usually, it is used only for retrieval such as verification and data analysis. Thus, when data is shifted from OLTP to the data warehouse it is de-normalized, because normalization was earlier conducted to remove insert, update and delete anomalies but now only retrieval is important. So, to improve the performance of retrieval, smaller tables are combined together to form larger tables under the de-normalization process to make retrieval or data analysis more efficient.

Data warehouses are typically used for Online Analytical Processing (OLAP) to support management queries.

They provide answers to common management queries like Who are our lowest/highest margin customers; What is the most effective distribution channel and a host of other questions. On a lighter note, without the support of data warehouse, the management has to rely on some sort of magician or astrologer to get answers to questions of the sort that have been illustrated in Figure 12.3.

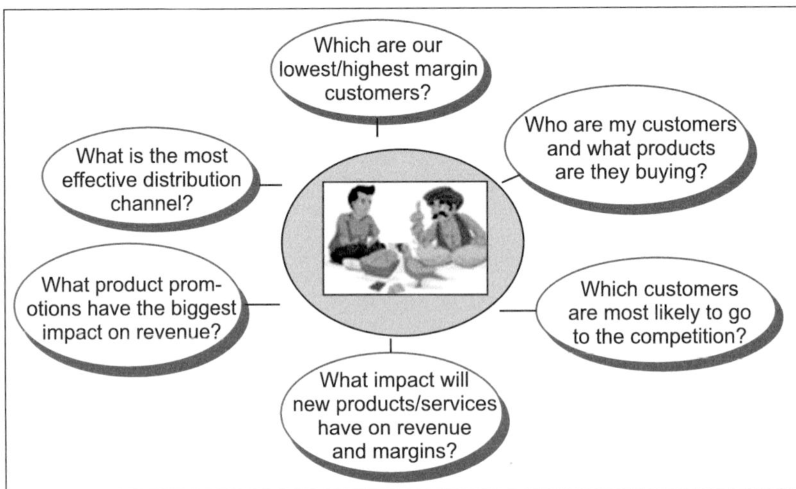

Figure 12.3 Answering management queries

Tech giant IBM, devised the concept of the data warehouse. They called them 'information warehouses'. Since then, Data warehousing systems have evolved as one of the principle technologies employed by modern enterprises for better profitability.

12.3.1 Historical developments in data warehousing

Figure 12.4 highlights the historical developments of data warehouse.

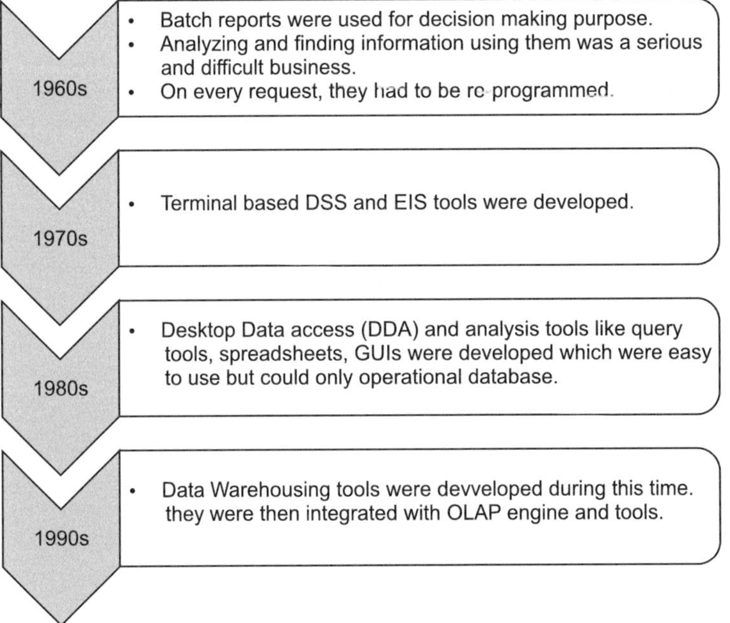

Figure 12.4 Historical developments of data warehouse

12.3.2 Defining data warehousing

The present concept of data warehousing owes much to American computer scientist, Bill Inmon, known as the 'father of data warehousing'.

According to Bill Inmon, a data warehouse could be defined as, 'A subject-oriented, integrated, time-variant, and non-volatile collection of data in support of management's decision-making process.'

Some terms used here are the same as those that appeared in the definition of ODS. Still, on examination: Subject-Oriented:

Data warehouses are subject oriented - they are built around the major data entity or subjects of an organization. For example, in a University, the data subject (entities under study) could be students, teachers, and various courses, whereas in a company the subjects might be workers, interns, services and items.

Integrated

A data warehouse integrates (combines) data from multiple systems to provide a wide view of any enterprise's data, hence they are said to be 'integrated'.

Time variant

Unlike ODS, in data warehouses data is not always up to date as it contains historical data which is valid or accurate till some point of time (or time interval).

Non-volatile

Data warehouse is described as a long term enterprise memory due to its non-volatile nature because the data is not updated in real time but is rather refreshed on a regular basis. Hence, the new data which is added goes in like a supplement to the database, rather than a replacement. The database continually absorbs this new data, incrementally integrating it with the previous data.

12.3.3 Data warehouse architecture

Every data warehouse has three fundamental components as shown in Figure 12.5. These are as follows.

- Load Manager
- Warehouse Manager
- Data Access Manager

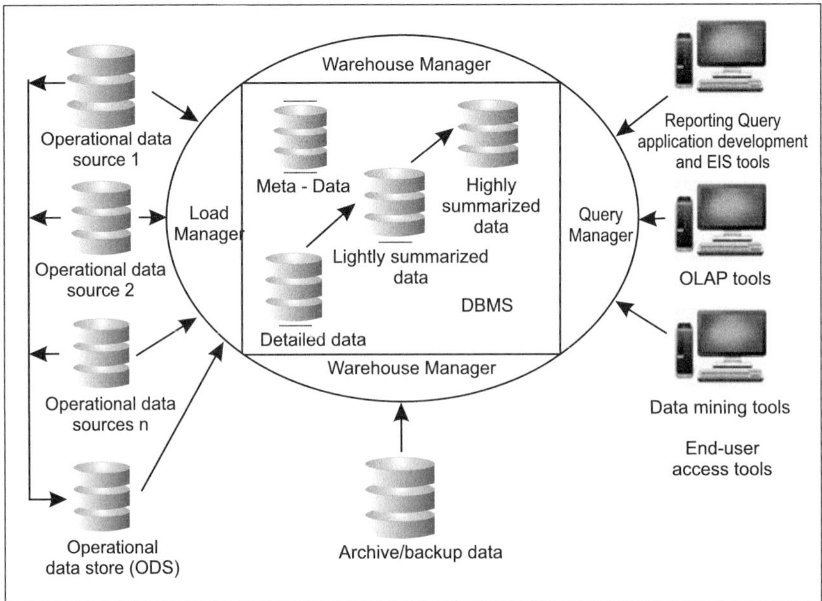

Figure 12.5 Architecture of a data warehouse

Load manager

The Load manager is responsible for Data collection from operational systems. It also performs data conversion into some usable form to be further utilized by the user. It includes all the programs and application interfaces which are required for extracting data from the operational systems, it's preparation and finally loading of data into the data warehouse itself.

It should perform the following tasks:

- Data Identification
- Data Validation for its accuracy
- Data Extraction from the original source
- Data Cleansing
- Data formatting
- Data standardization (i.e. bringing data into conformity with some standard format)
- Consolidates data from multiple sources to one place
- Establishment of Data Integrity using Integrity Constraints

Warehouse manager

The Warehouse manager is the main part of Data Warehousing system as it holds the massive amount of information from myriad sources. It organizes data in a way so it becomes easy for anyone to analyze or find the required information. It is the core of the data warehouse itself. It maintains three levels of information, i.e, detailed, lightly summarized and highly summarized. It also maintains mete data, i.e., data about data.

Query manager

Finally the Query manager is that interface which connects the end users with the information stored in data warehouse through the usage of specialized end-user tools. These tools are known as Data mining access tools. The market today is flooded with such tools which have common functionalities and a provision for customizing more features specific to an enterprise. These have various categories such as query and reporting, statistics, data discovery, etc.

12.3.4 Benefits of data warehousing

A data warehouse can do wonders if implemented successfully; some of its advantages and benefits are given below.

- ***Potential high ROI (Return on Investment)***
  Investing in Data Warehousing is itself a very big investment, but past reports suggest ROI growth up to 400% with Data Warehousing, making it valuable for business.
- ***Unbeatable competitive advantage***
  Implementation of Data Warehousing could give companies a competitive edge over their rivals. With Data Warehousing companies could discover previously unavailable facts and figures, trends and untapped information. Such new revelations would enhance the quality of decisions.
- ***High Productivity in corporate decision making and business intelligence***
  Data Warehousing combines data from multiple sources into meaningful information which could be analyzed and referred by managers to improve their decisions for organization.
- ***Cost effective***
  With Data Warehousing, it is possible to streamline the organization thereby reducing overheads and so reducing product costs.
- ***Enhanced customer service***
  Data Warehousing provides essential support when communicating with customers and so helps improve customer satisfaction and retain them.

Problems or limitations of data warehousing

The problems associated with developing and managing data warehousing are as follows.

- ***Underestimation of resources for data ETL***
  Quite often the user underestimates the total processing time required to perform extract, clean and load operations on data prior to warehousing. Thus, in real time implementation many other processes suffer and operations can suffer in the meanwhile.
- ***Erroneous source systems***
  There are many hidden problems associated with the source systems that are being used to feed data. These problems may remain unidentified for years, and after many years of lying undetected, they can suddenly emerge in embarrassing ways. For example, while entering details of brand new property, one finds that certain fields have allowed nulls. Often in such cases, the staff is found guilty of entering incomplete data.

- ***Required data not captured***
  Data warehouse stores detailed information, yet many times it intentionally misses few minor details which could later on be used for analysis or any other task. For example, the date of registration while adding details of a new property may not be used in source system but it might be very useful during analysis.
- ***Increased end user queries or demands***
  From the end user side queries never end. Even after initial queries have been satisfactorily addressed, a chain of further queries may follow.
- ***Loss of information during data homogenization***
  When data from multiple sources are combined, loss of information can occur while changing formats.
- ***High demand of resources***
  Resources such as large disk space are required for storing the huge quantity of data accumulated daily.
- ***Data ownership***
  Quite often when one department is asked for some data, it is reluctant or slow in processing the request. They may afraid of losing data ownership or control over data. This leads to lags and interruptions in the Data Warehousing process.
- ***Necessary maintenance***
  A data warehouse requires high maintenance. Any change in business process or reorganization of source systems may affect the data warehouse and all these things contribute to extremely high cost of maintenance.
- ***Long-duration projects***
  Right from planning to actual implementation data warehouses use up a lot of time and money; hence many organizations are reluctant initially.
- ***Complexity of integration***
  Data warehouse's performance could be determined based on its integration capabilities. Thus, an organization spends significantly large amount of time, in determining how well the multiple data warehousing tools can go together (or integrated) to chalk out a solution, which is a very difficult task as many tools are available.

The issues of data warehouse are summarized in Figure 12.6.

12.4 Data Marts

A department specific data warehouse is termed as 'data mart', which is a small localized data warehouse built for a single purpose. It is usually built to cater to the needs of a group of users or a department in an organization.

For example, an organization can have many departments, including finance, IT departments and others. Each of these departments can have their own data warehouses, which is nothing but the data mart of that particular department.

Thus, a data mart can be defined as 'a specialized, subject-oriented, integrated, time-variant, volatile data store in support of specific subset of management's decisions'.

In a simplified way we can define data marts as 'A subset of data warehouses that support the requirements of a particular department or business function'.

An organization could maintain both a data warehouse (representing data of all departments in a unified way) and individual departmental data marts. Hence, the data mart can be standalone (individual) or linked centrally to the corporate data warehouse as shown in Figure 12.7.

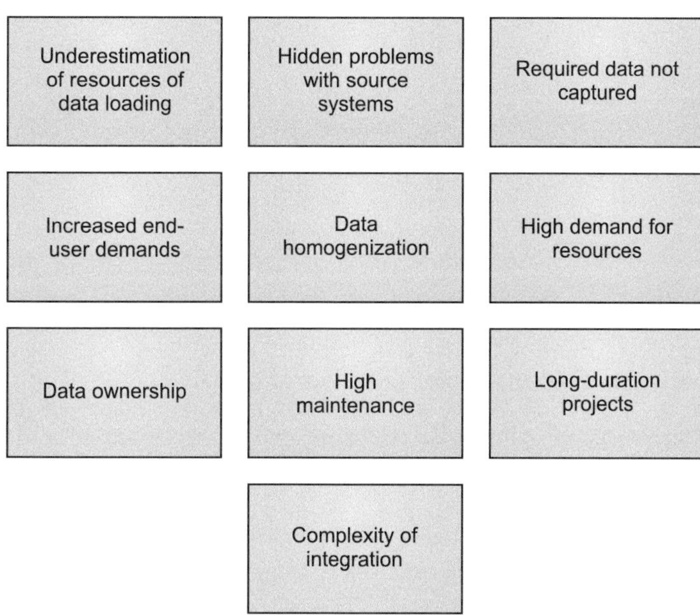

Figure 12.6 Limitations of data warehousing

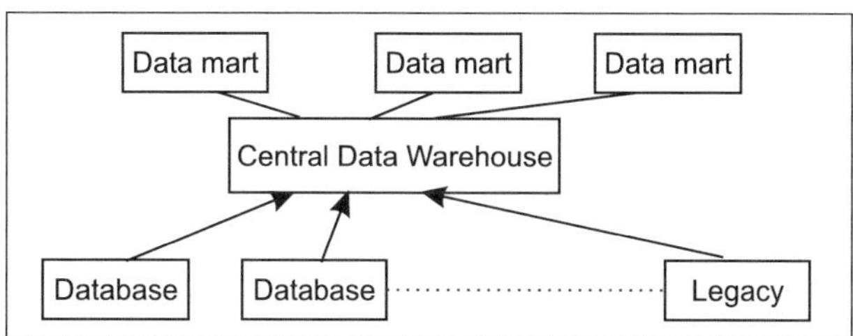

Figure 12.7 Data mart and data warehouse

It is often seen that as a data warehouse grows larger with more data, its ability to serve the different needs of any enterprise gets compromised. In such cases, data marts come to the rescue, as in a large enterprise, data marts tend to be a way to build a data warehouse in a sequential or a phased approach. A collection of data marts can constitute an enterprise-wide data warehouse. Conversely, a data warehouse may be visualized as a collection of subset of data marts as illustrated in Figure 12.8.

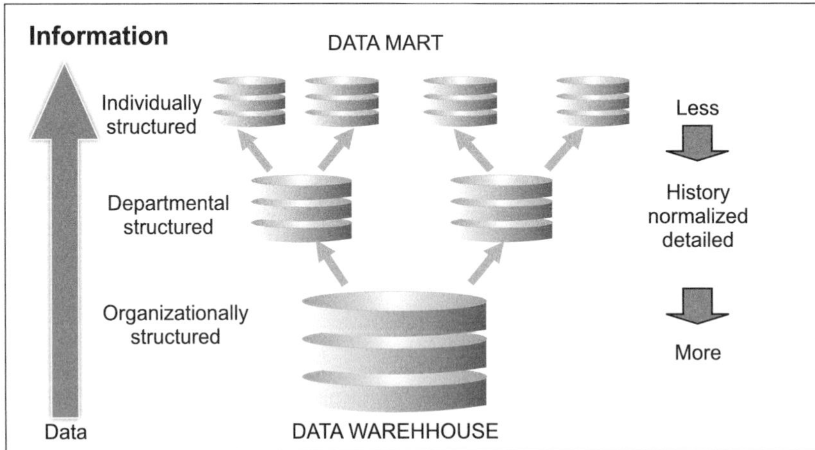

Figure 12.8 Relationship between data mart and data warehouse

Differences between data mart and data warehouse

Following are the characteristics that differentiate data marts and data warehouse.

- Data marts usually focus on the data requirements of some specific department rather than the whole organization.
- Detailed information is not contained by data marts (unlike data warehouses)
- They are easy to navigate, transfer and explore compared to data warehouses which workon large volumes of data.

Advantages of data marts

Following are the advantages of data marts.

- With data marts the user gets pertinent, to-the-point data. .
- Data marts respond quickly.
- Data operations such as data cleaning, loading, transformation, and integration are far easier and cheaper as data marts work with low volumes of data. Implementing and setting up a data mart is simpler than implementing a data warehouse for the whole enterprise.
- Compared to a data warehouse, implementing a data mart is a lot more economical.
- The potential users of a data mart can be grouped in a better way rather than involving large numbers of unnecessary members.
- Data marts are designed on the basis that there is no need to serve the entire enterprise. Therefore, the department can summarize, select and structure their own departments' data independently.
- Data marts can allow each department to work on a specific piece of historical data rather than the whole data.
- Departments can customize software for their data mart as per their needs.
- Data marts are cost efficient.

Limitations of data marts

The limitations of data marts are as follows:

- Once in operation, due to inherent limitations in design it becomes cumbersome to extend their scope to other departments.
- Data Integration problems are encountered often.
- When the data mart develops multiple dimensions then the scalability problem becomes common.

12.5 Comparative Study of Data Warehouse with OLTP and ODS

Finally to summarize the distinctions between OLTP, ODS and data warehouse as illustrated below in Table 12.1.

Table 12.1 Generalized distinction between ODS and data warehouse

ODS	*Data Warehouse*
High quality of data and easy availability of data is assured.	Imperfect Data which is sufficient for doing strategic analysis. Availability of data is not a primary concern.
Contains both Real Time and Current data.	Contains Historical data
Updated at the Data field level.	Normally, batch data loads. Data is appended, and not updated .
Typically detailed data only.	Contains summarized and detailed data.
Modeled to support rapid data updates (3NF).	Variety of modeling techniques used, typically multi-dimensional for data marts to optimize query performance.
Transactions resemble OLTP system transactions.	Queries are quite complex and even the data volumes are larger.
Aids in detailed decision making and operational reporting and hence it is used mostly at an operational level.	Aids in long term planning and decision making along with management reporting.

12.5.1 Data warehouses versus OLTP: similarities and distinction

OLTP or Online Transaction Processing systems are the traditional database systems which were designed to maximize the transaction processing capacity of organizational information. In contrast, data warehouses could hold data detailed and historical data which could be summarized to different levels and rarely subject to change. The comparison of OLTP and data warehousing usually used to perform OLAP (Online Analytical Processing) is shown in Table 12.2.

Table 12.2 Comparison of OLTP systems and data warehousing systems

OLTP System	*Data Warehousing System*
They hold Current data.	Designed to hold only Historical data.
Detailed data is stored.	It is flexible enough to store detailed, light or profoundly summarized data.
Nature of data is Dynamic.	Nature of data is Static.
Processing is recursive in nature.	Processing is rather unstructured and ad-hoc.
Transaction output is of high level.	Here, it is low or medium mostly.
Pattern of usage is predictable.	Pattern of usage is unpredictable.
Transaction-driven	Analysis driven
OLTP systems are application oriented.	They focus more on subject.
Day-to-day decisions are supported.	Long term or strategic decisions are taken through them.
Massive numbers of operational users are served.	Mostly for managerial users.

The comparison of OLTP and data warehouse with respect to their properties or characteristics is given in Table 12.3.

Table 12.3 Comparing OLTP and data warehouse system

Property	*OLTP System*	*Dulu Warehousing System*
Nature of the database	3NF	Multi-dimensional
Indexes	Few	Many
Joins	Many	Some
Duplicated data	Normalized data	De-normalized data
Derived data and aggregates	Rare	Common
Queries	Mostly predefined	Mostly ad-hoc
Nature of queries	Mostly simple	Mostly complex
Updates	All the time	Not allowed, only refreshed
Historical data	Often not available	Essential

Remind Me

- The operational data store is a special unified (separate) database that has been developed specifically to handle management queries.
- Inmon and Imhoff (1996) defined the operational data store as 'A subject-oriented, integrated, volatile, current valued data store, containing only corporate detailed data.'
- The data in an ODS is typically loaded through an extraction, transformation, and loading (ETL) process from multiple data sources.
- Data warehouse is defined as, 'A subject-oriented, integrated, time-variant, and non-volatile collection of data in support of management's decision-making process.'
- A data warehouse has three basic components - load manager, warehouse manager and data access manager.

Point Me (Books)

- Conolly, Thomas, and Carolyn Begg. 2015. *Database Systems: A Practical Approach to Design, Implementation, and Management*, 6th ed. New York: Pearson Education.
- Gupta, G. K. 2014. *Introduction to Data Mining with Case Studies*. Delhi: PHI Learning Pvt. Ltd.
- Kimball, Ralph, and Margy Ross. 2013. *The Data Warehouse Toolkit: the complete guide to dimensional modeling*, 3rd ed. Indianapolis: John Wiley & Sons.

Point Me (Video)

- Data Warehouse Tutorial For Beginners | Data Warehouse Concepts | Data Warehousing | Edureka, https://www.youtube.com/watch?v=J326LIUrZM8
- https://www.udemy.com/data-warehousing/

Connect Me (Internet Resources)

- https://www.tutorialspoint.com//cognos/data_warehouse_overview.htm
- https://www.guru99.com/data-warehousing-tutorial.html
- http://www.wideskills.com/data-warehousing-tutorial

Test Me

Answer these questions based on your learning in this chapter

1. Data warehouse contains .... that isn't seen in the operational environment.
   (a) Normalized data (b) Summary data
   (c) Both of these (d) None of these
2. The full form of ETL is ....
   (a) Execute transmit and load (b) Examine transform and load
   (c) Extract transform and load (d) None of these
3. Which of the following is also known as 'short term' memory of an enterprise'?
   (a) Data mart (b) Operational data store
   (c) Data warehouse (d) None of these
4. Which of the following is transaction driven?
   (a) Data mart (b) Operational data store
   (c) Data warehouse (d) OLTP

5. What is the need for ODS? What techniques are used to perform the tasks of ETL?
6. What is the advantage and disadvantage of eager approach to solve managerial queries?

Answer Keys:

1. (b)
2. (c)
3. (b)
4. (d)

13

Data Warehouse Schema

Chapter Objectives

- ✓ To understand the concept of dimension, measure and the fact table
- ✓ To able to apply different schema of data warehouse designs such as Star Schema, Snowflake Schema and Fact Constellation Schema on real world applications.
- ✓ To understand the differences between these schemas, their strengths and weakness.

13.1 Introduction to Data Warehouse Schema

Logical descriptions of database are known as Schema. It is the blueprint of the entire database. It defines how the data are organized and how the relations among them are associated. Data warehouse schema consists of the name and description of records including associated data items and aggregates. A database uses relational models whereas a data warehouse uses different types of schema, namely, Star, Snowflake, and Fact Constellation.

To start discussion on these schemas, it is important to understand the basic terminology used in this process, which is discussed below.

13.1.1 Dimension

The term 'dimension' in data warehousing is a collection of reference information about a measurable event. These events are stored in a fact table and are known as facts. The dimensions are generally the entities for which an organization wants to preserve records. The descriptive attributes are organized as columns in dimension tables by a data warehouse. For example, a student's dimension attributes could consist of first and last name, roll number, age, gender, or an address dimension that would include street name, state, and country attributes.

A dimension table consists of a primary key column that uniquely identifies each record (row) of dimension. A dimension is a framework that consists of one or more hierarchies that classify data. Usually dimensions are de-normalized tables and may have redundant data.

Let us take a quick recap of the concepts of normalization and de-normalization, as they will be used in this chapter. Normalization is a process of breaking up a larger table into smaller tables free of any possible insertion, updation or deletion anomalies. Normalized tables have reduced redundancy of data. In order to get full information, these tables are usually joined.

In de-normalization, smaller tables are merged to form larger tables to reduce joining operations. De-normalization is particularly performed in those cases where retrieval is a major requirement and insert, update, and delete operations are minimal, as in case of historical data or data warehouse. These de-normalized tables will have redundancy of data. For example, in case of EMP-DEPT database, there will be two normalized tables as EMP(eno, ename, job, sal, deptno) and DEPT(deptno, dname), while in case of de-normalization we will have single table EMP_DEPT with attributes eno, ename, job, sal, deptno, dname.

Let us consider Location and Item dimensions as shown in Figure 13.1. Here, in Location dimension location_id is the primary key with street_name, city, state_id and country_code as its attributes. Figure 13.1 (b) shows another dimension namely Item having item_code as primary key and item_name, item_type, brand_name, and supplier_id as other attributes.

Location Dimension
Locaton_id
Street_name
City
State_id
Country_code

(a)

Item Dimension
Item_code
Item_name
Item_type
Brand_name
Supplier_id

(b)

Figure 13.1 (a) location dimension, (b) item dimension

It is important to note that these dimensions may be de-normalized tables as the location dimension may be derived from location_detail (location_id, street_name, state_id) and state_detail (state_id, state_name, country_code) tables as shown in Figure 13.2.

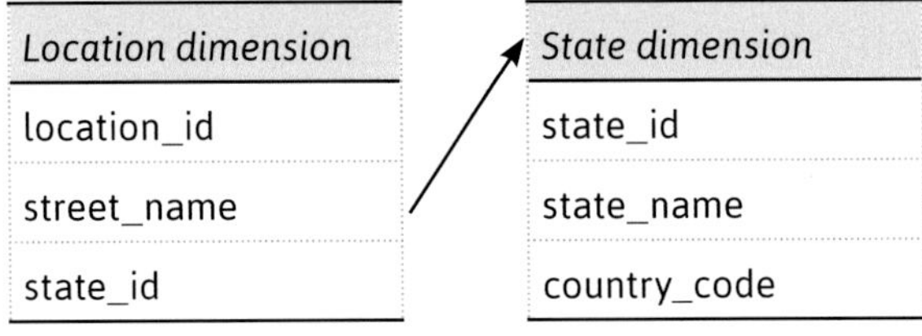

Figure 13.2 Normalized view

13.1.2 Measure

Measure is the term used for the values that rely on the dimensions. For example, amount sold, quantity sold, etc.

13.1.3 Fact Table

A 'fact table' is a group of associated data items. It consists of values of dimensions and measure. This means that a fact table can be defined from the given dimension and measure. A fact table typically consists of two types of columns such as foreign keys and measure. Foreign keys are linked to dimension tables and measures consist of numeric facts as shown in Figure 13.3. Fact tables are generally larger in size than dimension tables.

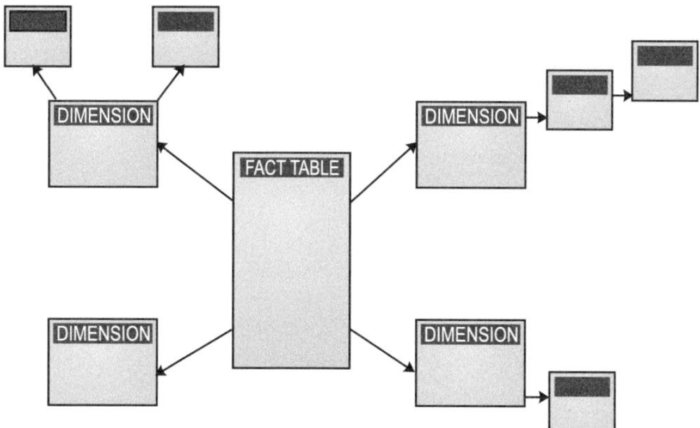

Figure 13.3 Representation of fact and dimension tables

A fact table can hold a dataset of facts at detailed or aggregated level. Let us consider a sales fact table as shown in Figure 13.4. It has time_key, item_code, branch_code and location_id as foreign keys of dimension tables and rupees_sold and units_sold as measure or aggregations. Here, FK indicates a foreign key.

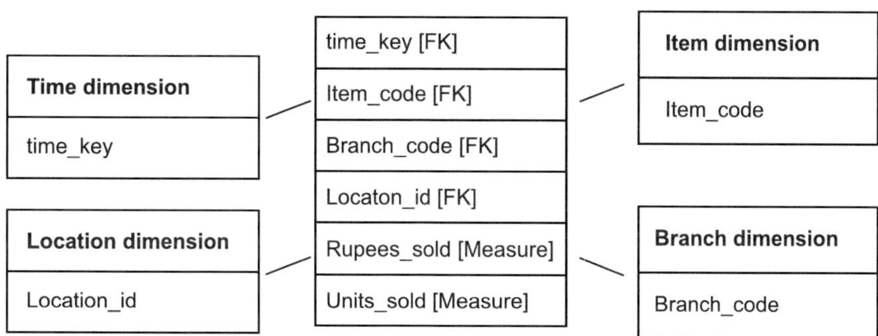

Figure 13.4 The sales fact table

13.1.4 Multi-dimensional view of data

Data consists of multiple dimensions. Dimensions often have hierarchies to show parent-child relationships.

13.2 Star Schema

The star schema is one of the simplest of data warehouse schemas. It is known as star because it appears like a star with points expanding from a center. Figure 13.3 represents the star schema in which the fact table is at the center and the dimension tables at the nodes of the star.

Each dimension in a star schema represents a one-dimensional table only and the dimension table consists of a set of attributes. Dimension tables comprise of relatively small numbers of records in comparison to fact tables, but each record may consist of a large number of attributes to describe the fact data. Fact tables usually consist of numeric facts and foreign keys to dimensional data.

Generally, fact tables are in third normal form (3NF) in the case of star schema while dimensional tables are in de-normalized form. Although the star schema is one of the simplest structures, it is still extensively used nowadays and recommended by Oracle. Figure 13.5 graphically presents a star schema.

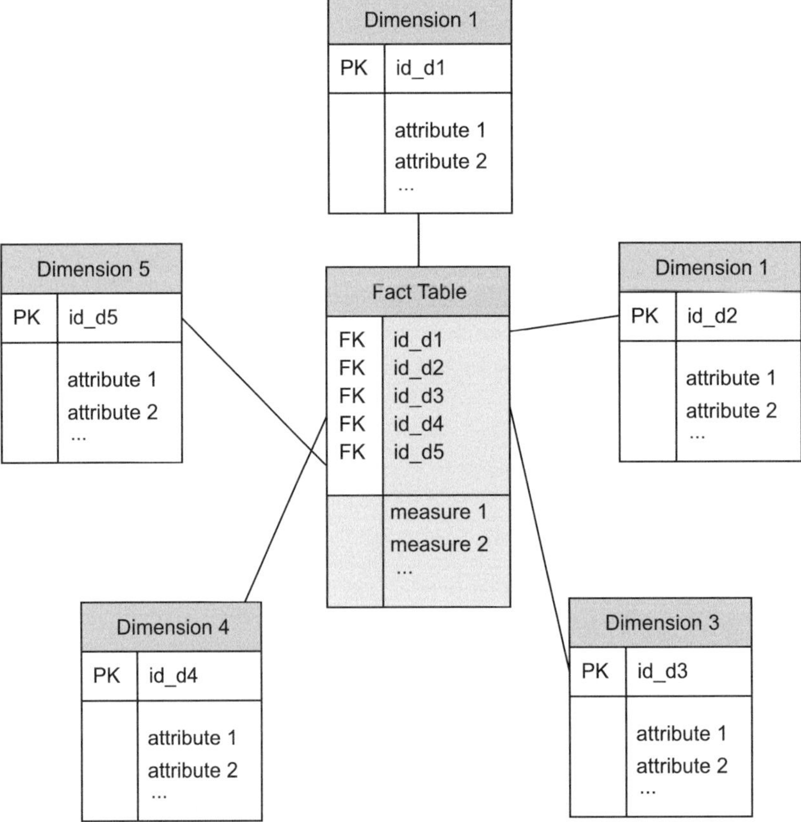

Figure 13.5 Graphical representation of Star schema

The star schema for analysis of sales of a company is shown in Figure 13.6. In this schema, sales fact are presented at the center of the star consisting of the foreign keys that are linked to each of the four corresponding dimension tables. The sales fact table also includes the measures such as rupees_sold and units_sold. It is important to note that here dimensions are de-normalized. For example, the location dimension table consists of attribute-sets such as {location_id, street_name, city, state_id, country_code} and it may have data redundancy due to its de-normalization. For example, both cities 'Patiala' and 'Amritsar' are located in the Punjab state of India. The records for these cities may result in data redundancy corresponding to the attributes country and state.

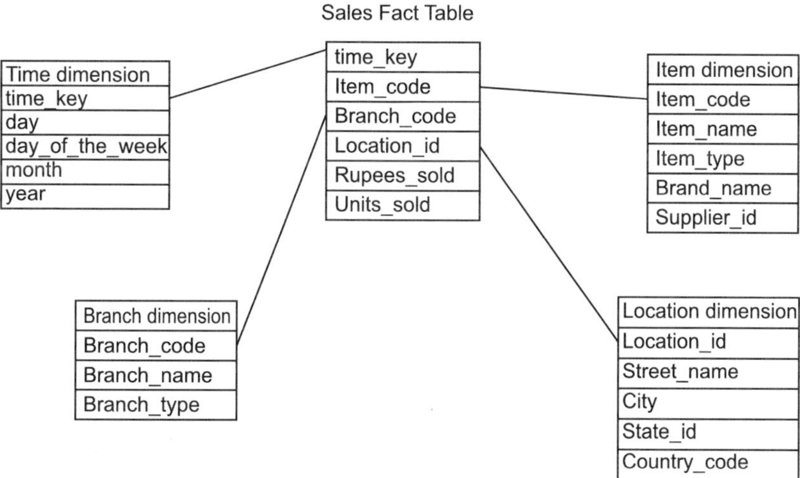

Figure 13.6 Star schema for analysis of sales

Main characteristics of star schema

The main characteristics of star schema are as follows:

- It has high query performance as it requires less join operations due to de-normalization of data.
- It has a simple structure which is easy to understand.
- It takes a relatively longer time to load the data into dimension tables due to de-normalization, that also causes data redundancy that may increase the size of table data.
- It is the most generally used and simplest structure in the data warehouse and supported by an enormous number of tools.

Advantages of star schema

The advantages of star schema are:

- It has simple queries as it will not require join operations due to de-normalization of data.
- In comparison to highly normalized schemas, star schema has basic business reporting logic.
- It has high query performance due to fewer join operations.
- It has fast aggregations due to its simpler queries.

Disadvantages of star schema

The disadvantages of star schema are:

- Data integrity cannot be applied in star schema because its database is de-normalized and contains redundant data.
- Inserts and updates in star schema can result in data anomalies due to data redundancy which normalized schemas are designed to avoid.
- It is not flexible in terms of analytical needs when compared to a normalized data model.
- It is too specific as it is designed for a fixed analysis of data and does not allow complex analytics.

13.3 Snowflake Schema

The major difference between star and snowflake schema is that the snowflake schema may consist of normalized dimensions while star schema always consists of de-normalized dimensions. Thus, snowflake schema is a modification of the star schema supporting normalization of dimension tables. Some dimension tables are normalized in snowflake schema which splits up the data into additional tables. Thus, 'Snowflaking' is a process of normalizing the dimension tables in a star schema. The resultant structure appears like a snowflake having a fact table at the center when all the dimension tables are completely normalized. For example, the item dimension table shown in Figure 13.7 is normalized by splitting it into two dimension tables such as item and supplier.

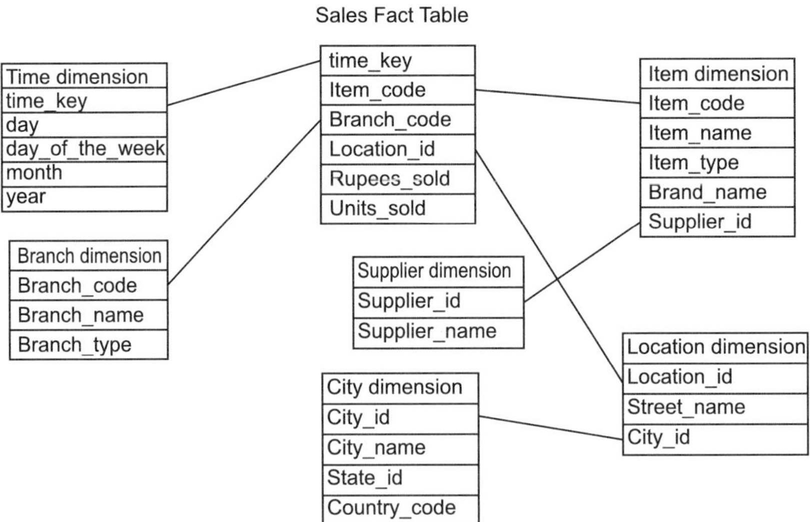

Figure 13.7 Snowflake schema for analysis of sales

Here, the item dimension table consists of the attributes set {item_code, item_name, item_type, brand_name, supplier_id}. Further, the supplier_id is associated to the supplier dimension table which consists of the attributes, namely, supplier_id and supplier_type.

Similarly, the location dimension table consists of the attributes set {location_id, street_name, city_id}. Further, the city_id is associated to the city dimension table which consists of the attributes, namely, city_id, city_name, state_id and country_code.

Another view of snowflake schema is illustrated in Figure 13.8. Here, shop dimension has been normalized into shop, city and region dimension. Similarly, time dimension has been normalized into time, month and quarter dimension. The client dimension has been normalized into client and client group dimension. And the product dimension has been normalized into product type, brand and supplier dimension as shown in Figure 13.8.

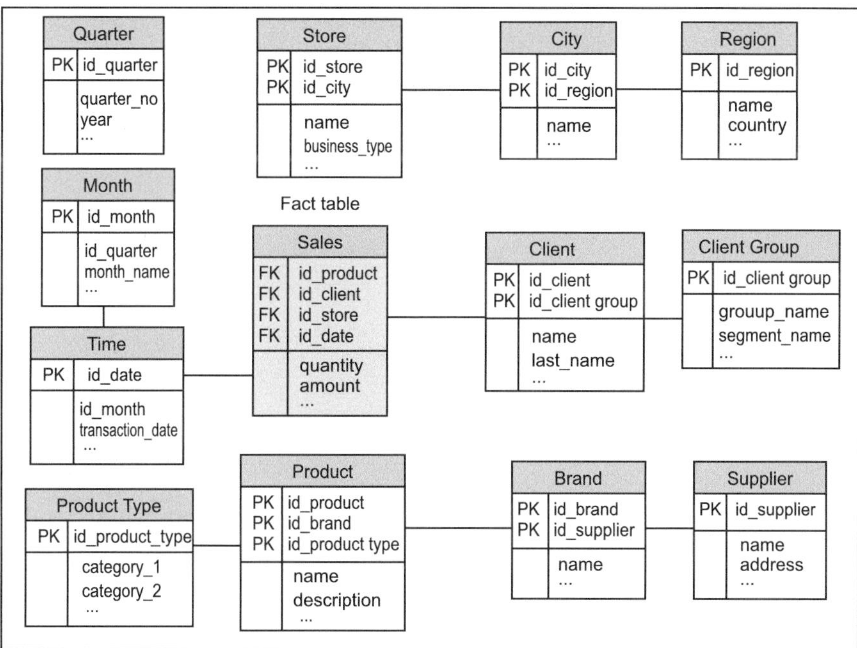

Figure 13.8 Snowflake schema

It is important to note that redundancy is reduced in snowflake schema due to normalization.

Advantages of snowflake schema

The advantages of snowflake schema are:

- The snowflake schema results in saving of storage space due to normalized attributes despite additional complexity in source query joins.
- Some OLAP multi-dimensional database modeling tools are optimized for snowflake schemas.

Disadvantages of snowflake schema

The disadvantages of snowflake schema are:

- It has complex queries due to join operations because dimensions are normalized.

- It has poor query performance due to joins required for normalized data.

In conclusion, the main goal of snowflake schema is to store the normalized data efficiently but it does so at the significant cost of query performance.

13.4 Fact Constellation Schema (Galaxy Schema)

The main difference between star/snowflake and fact constellation schema is that star/snowflake schema consist of only one fact table while fact constellation schema always consists of multiple fact tables. Therefore, fact constellation is also known as galaxy schema (multiple fact tables being viewed as a group of stars).

Fact constellation is a measure of online analytical processing, which is a collection of multiple fact tables sharing dimension tables. This is an improvement over Star schema.

Figure 13.9 shows an example of fact constellation schema as it has two fact tables, namely sales and shipping.

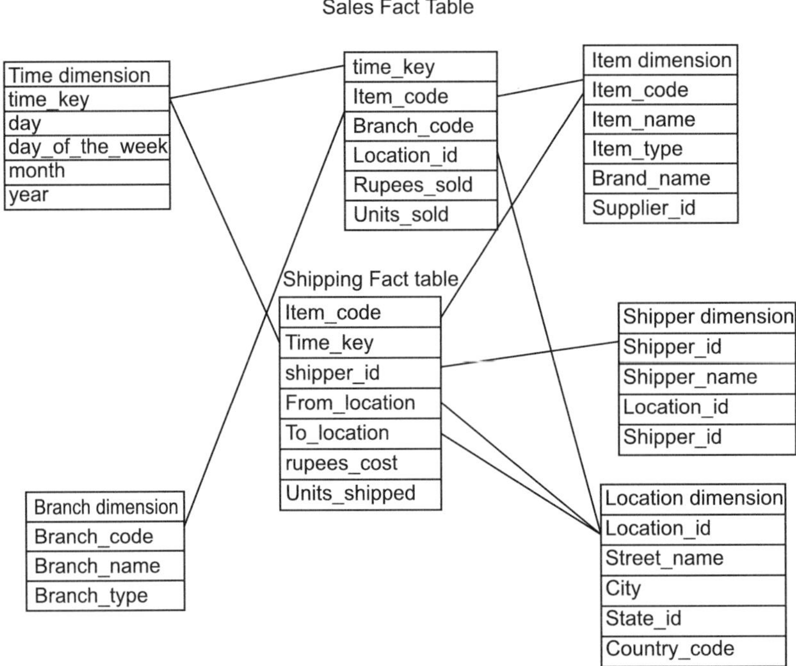

Figure 13.9 Fact constellation schema for analysis of sales

The sales fact table in the fact constellation schema is similar to the one in star schema. The sales fact table here, also consists of four attributes, namely, time_key, item_code, branch_code, location_id and two measures such as rupees_sold and units_sold as shown in Figure 13.9. And the shipping fact table consists of five attributes such as item_code, time_key, shipper_id, from_location, to_location and two measures such as rupees_cost and units_sold. In fact constellation schema, dimension tables can also be shared between fact tables. For example, the dimension tables, namely, location, item and time are shared between the fact tables shipping and sales as shown in Figure 13.9.

Advantages of fact constellation schema

The major advantage of this schema is that it provides better support to end user because it has multiple fact tables.

Disadvantages of fact constellation schema

The major disadvantage of this schema is its complicated design because of consideration of different variants of aggregation.

13.5 Comparison among Star, Snowflake and Fact Constellation Schema

The comparison among the data warehouse schemas on the basis of different parameters is given in Table 13.1.

Table 13.1 Comparison among Star, Snowflake and Fact Constellation Schema

Parameter	*Star*	*Snowflake*	*Fact constellation*
Query Joins	Require simple joins	Requires complicated joins	Requires complicated joins
Data structure	De-normalized data structure	Normalized data structure.	Normalized data structure.
Number of Fact Tables	Single fact table	Single fact table	Multiple fact tables
Query Performance	It gives faster query results due to fewer join operations.	It is slow in query processing due to larger join operations.	It is slow in query processing due to larger join operations.
Dimension	Dimension table does not split into pieces.	Dimension tables are split into many pieces.	Dimension tables are split into many pieces.
Data Redundancy	Data is redundant due to de-normalization.	Data is not redundant as dimensions are normalized.	Data is not redundant as dimensions are normalized.
Data Integrity	Tough to enforce data integrity due to redundancy of data.	Easy to enforce data integrity due to no redundancy of data.	Easy to enforce data integrity due to no redundancy of data.

Remind Me

- Schema is a logical description of database.
- Schema is a blueprint of the whole database that defines data organization and relations among data.
- Dimensions are generally the entities towards which an organization preserves records.
- Measure is the term used for the values that rely on the dimensions. For example, amount sold, quantity sold, etc.
- Fact table is a group of associated data items. It consists of values of dimensions and measures.
- Schemas in data warehouse are classified into three classes: Star, Snowflake, and Fact Constellation schema.
- Star schema looks like a star with points expanding from a center.
- The major difference between Star and Snowflake schema is that Snowflake schema may consist of normalized dimensions while Star schema consists of de-normalized dimensions.
- The main difference between Star/Snowflake and Fact Constellation schema is that Star/Snowflake schema consist of only one fact table while Fact Constellation schema consist of multiple fact tables.

Point Me (Books)

- Conolly, Thomas, and Carolyn Begg. 2015. *Database Systems: A Practical Approach to Design, Implementation, and Management*, 6th ed. New York: Pearson Education.
- Thareja, Reema. 2009. *Data Warehousing*. Delhi: Oxford University Press.

Point Me (Video)

- Understanding Schemas in Datawarehousing | Edureka, https://www.youtube.com/watch?v=uigKK02XGxE

Connect Me (Internet Resources)

- https://www.tutorialspoint.com/dwh/dwh_schemas.htm
- http://www.teradatapoint.com/data-warehousing-schemas
- https://en.wikipedia.org/wiki/Star_schema
- https://en.wikipedia.org/wiki/Snowflake_schema

Test Me

Answer these questions based on your learning in this chapter.

1. Out of Star schema and Snowflake schema, whose dimension table is normalized?
2. Due to normalization in the Snowflake schema, the redundancy is reduced and therefore, it becomes easy to maintain and save the storage space.
   (a) True (b) False
3. Which is also known as galaxy schema?
   (a) Star Schema (b) Snow Flake Schema
   (c) Fact Constellation Schema (d) None of the above
4. List the schema that a data warehouse system can implement.
   (a) Star Schema (b) Snowflake Schema
   (c) Fact Constellation Schema (d) All mentioned above
5. How many fact tables are there in a Star schema?
   (a) One (b) Two (c) Three (d) Four

6. Snowflake schema uses the concept of normalization.
   (a) True (b) False
7. Normalization splits up the data into additional tables.
   (a) Yes (b) No
8. Some dimension tables in the Snowflake schema are not normalized.
   (a) True (b) False
9. Is it possible to share dimension tables between fact tables.
   (a) Yes (b) No
10. A database uses relational model, while a data warehouse uses
    (a) Star (b) Snowflake
    (c) Fact Constellation schema (d) All mentioned above

Answer Keys:

1. Snowflake schema	2. (a)	3. (c)	4. (d)
5. (a)	6. (a)	7. (a)	8. (b)
9. (a)	10. (b)		

14

Online Analytical Processing

Chapter Objectives

- ✓ To understand the need for online analytical processing
- ✓ To distinguish OLAP from OLTP and data mining
- ✓ To comprehend the representation of multi-dimensional view of data
- ✓ To understand and apply the concept of data cube in real world applications
- ✓ To implement multi-dimensional view of data in Oracle
- ✓ To understand different types of OLAP Servers such as ROLAP and MOLAP
- ✓ To able to perform different OLAP Operations on the database

14.1 Introduction to Online Analytical Processing

As there is a huge growth in data warehousing in recent past, the demand for more powerful access tools that help in advanced analytical processing from historical data has increased. Online Analytical Processing (OLAP) and data mining are two types of access tools that have been developed to meet the demands of management users. OLAP and data mining are distinct in what they offer the user and due to this they are complementary technologies.

OLAP is a design paradigm that provides a method to extract useful information from a physical data store. It aggregates information from multiple systems and provides summarized information/ view to the management, while data mining is used to find hidden patterns within the data.

OLAP summarizes data and makes forecasts. For example, it answers operational questions like 'What are the average sales of cycles, by region and by year?' Data mining discovers hidden patterns in data and operates at a detailed level instead of a summary level. For instance, in a telecom industry where customer churn is a key factor, data mining would answer questions like, 'Who is likely to shift service providers and what are the reasons for that?' In conclusion, OLAP answers questions such as 'Is this true?' while data mining answers questions as 'Why is this happening? And what might happen if ...?'

Thus, OLAP and data mining complement each other and help the management in better decision taking. An environment that consists of a data warehouse/data marts together including tools such as OLAP and/or data mining are collectively known as Business Intelligence (BI) technologies.

14.1.1 Defining OLAP

Dr E.F. Codd (1993) has defined OLAP as 'the dynamic synthesis, analysis, and consolidation of large volumes of multi-dimensional data'.

From this definition, it is clear that OLAP deals with multi-dimensional view of data as compared to a simple relational database view. It helps users to get a wider knowledge and understanding about different features of their corporate data through consistent, fast and interactive access to a comprehensive variety of possible views of the data. In next sections, we will discuss in detail about this multi-dimensional view of data.

OLAP is used to response the complex questions shared on data warehouses. The queries like 'who?' and 'what?' can be answered with simple tools but there is need of special tools that can support OLAP to answer advanced queries of the nature of 'what if?' and 'why?'. The decisions about future actions are also supported by OLAP. A typical OLAP computation can be more difficult than simple aggregation of data, e.g., 'What would be the effect on property sales in different regions of Punjab if Government taxes went down by 2% and legal costs went up by 4.5% for properties over Rs 1,00,000?'.

To compare the performances of various OLAP tools, ***Analytical Queries per Minute*** (AQM) is used as a standard benchmark. The syntax of complex queries of OLAP systems should be hidden from users and systems should offer consistent response times for all types of queries including the complex ones.

14.1.2 OLAP applications

The various applications of OLAP in different functional areas are described in Table 14.1 as follows.

Table 14.1 Applications of OLAP

Functional area	*Examples of OLAP applications*
Marketing	Market research analysis, sales forecasting, customer and promotion analysis
Finance	Budgeting, financial modeling and performance analysis
Sales	Sales forecasting and analysis
Manufacturing	Production planning and defect analysis

14.1.3 Features of OLAP

The important features of OLAP are given as follows.

- Multi-dimensional view of data
- Time intelligence
- Complex calculations support

Multi-dimensional view of data

A multi-dimensional view of data offers the support to process the analytical data through flexible access to corporate data. It helps to look at data in several dimensions; for example, sales by region, sales by sales representative, sales by product category, sales by month, etc. It provides the ability to quickly switch between one view of data and another. It allows users to analyze their information in small chunks instead of giant reports, which are confusing.

Time intelligence

Time intelligence is helpful in judging the performance of any kind of analytical application over time, e.g., current month versus last month or current month of year versus the same month of last year, and so on. The concepts such as period-over-period and year-to-date comparisons should be straightforwardly defined in an OLAP system.

Complex calculations support

OLAP systems provide different types of powerful computational methods required to forecast sales such as percentage growth and moving averages.

14.1.4 OLAP Benefits

The key benefits offered by OLAP are:

- Increased productivity of end-users.
- Retention of organizational control over the integrity of corporate data.
- Reduced backlog of applications development for IT staff.
- Improved profitability and potential revenue.
- Reduced query drag and network traffic on the data warehouse or OLTP systems.

14.1.5 Strengths of OLAP

The major strengths of any OLAP are listed below.

- It is a powerful visualization tool.
- OLAP tools are good for analyzing time series.
- It provides fast, interactive response time.
- OLAP tools are offered by many vendors.
- It can be of help in identifying outliers and clusters.

14.1.6 Comparison between OLTP and OLAP

The differences between OLTP and OLAP are summarized in Table 14.2.

Table 14.2 Difference between OLTP and OLAP

Characteristics	*OLTP*	*OLAP*
Type of Users	These systems are developed for office workers.	On the other hand, these systems are developed for decision makers.
Number of Users	Number of users can vary from hundreds or even thousands of users in case of a large organization.	OLAP systems may be accessible to dozens of users or selected group of managers in an organization.
Functions	OLTP systems support day-to-day activities of an organization and are mission-critical.	OLAP systems on the other hand support decision-making functions of an organization using analytical investigations and are management-critical. They are more functionality driven.
Processing	It involves repetitive processing.	OLAP is Ad hoc, Unstructured and uses heuristic processing.
Nature of Query	One record at a time is processed by OLTP systems, e.g., a record of a customer who might be on the phone or in the store.	These systems deal with individual customer records. Many records are processed at a time by OLAP systems and these systems give aggregated data or summary to a manger.
Design	OLTP database systems are application-oriented.	On the other hand OLAP systems are subject-oriented.
Database View	OLTP is based on relational model.	OLAP supports multi-dimensional view of data.
Type of Queries	It allows simple queries.	It allows complex queries.
Transaction throughput (Number of transactions per second)	It involves high level of transaction throughput.	It provides a medium which leads to low level of transaction throughput.

14.1.7 Differences between OLAP and data mining

Both OLAP and data mining fall under Business Intelligence (BI) technologies. BI represents the computer-based methods to extract and identify the important information from business data. Data mining is the field of computer science that deals with mining important patterns from huge sets of data and it is basically a combination of many techniques from statistics, artificial intelligence and database management. On the other hand, OLAP is a collection of methods to query multi-dimensional databases.

Different kinds of analytical problems can be solved using OLAP and data mining. OLAP forecasts values by summarizing data. For example, it responses operational queries such as 'What are the average sales of cars, by region and by year?'

On the other hand, data mining works at a detailed level rather than a summary level and identifies hidden patterns from the data. For example, data mining would provide answers in case of a telecom industry for queries such as, 'Who is likely to shift service providers and what are the reasons for that?'.

OLAP and data mining complement each other, e.g., when OLAP identifies difficulties regarding the sales of a product in a particular section then data mining can be helpful in identifying the behavior of different customers and hence, it indicates the possible solutions. Similarly, when data mining forecasts something like a decrease or increase in sales, OLAP can be useful to find the net income.

14.2 Representation of Multi-dimensional Data

In order to understand the concept of multi-dimensional view of data, let us consider the database of Figure 14.1 (a). If the user generally asks queries such as 'What was the revenue for Patiala in the first quarter?' the query will retrieve only a single value and it works efficiently. However, if the user asks questions of kind 'What is the total annual revenue for each city?' or 'What is the average revenue for each city?', then these queries result in multiple values and their aggregation. If we consider large databases consisting of thousands of cities, the time that it takes a relational DBMS to perform such calculation becomes significant. A typical RDBMS can scan a few hundred records per second.

City	*Time*	*Total Revenue*
Patiala	Q1	27564
Patiala	Q2	32523
Patiala	Q3	32341
Patiala	Q4	29806
Ambala	Q1	40123
Ambala	Q2	48658
Ambala	Q3	56243
Ambala	Q4	46879
Ropar	Q1	52451
Ropar	Q2	32568
Ropar	Q3	41786
Ropar	Q4	52349
...	...	...
...	...	...

(a)

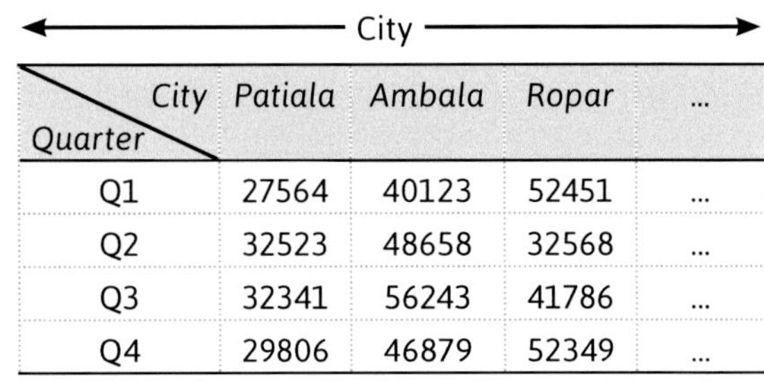
City

Quarter \ *City*	*Patiala*	*Ambala*	*Ropar*	...
Q1	27564	40123	52451	...
Q2	32523	48658	32568	...
Q3	32341	56243	41786	...
Q4	29806	46879	52349	...

(b)

Figure 14.1 (a) Relational model, (b) Two dimensional view

Then, in this case it is better to process this database as a two-dimensional matrix, with the dimensions such as Time (Quarters) and City, as shown in Figure 14.1 (b). By visualizing one observes that data fits naturally into this two-dimensional matrix. Then, the system need not scan the whole database, it just needs to apply aggregation on a particular row or column and efficiency of the system increases as compared to a traditional RDBMS model.

Suppose, one additional dimension such as property type is considered with the revenue data In such case, the total revenue produced will be illustrated by the sale of property type (for simplicity, Flat and House are used), by city, and by time (quarters). This data can be fitted into a four-field table as shown in Figure 14.2 (a), yet the data fits more logically into a three-dimensional cube as shown in Figure 14.2 (b).

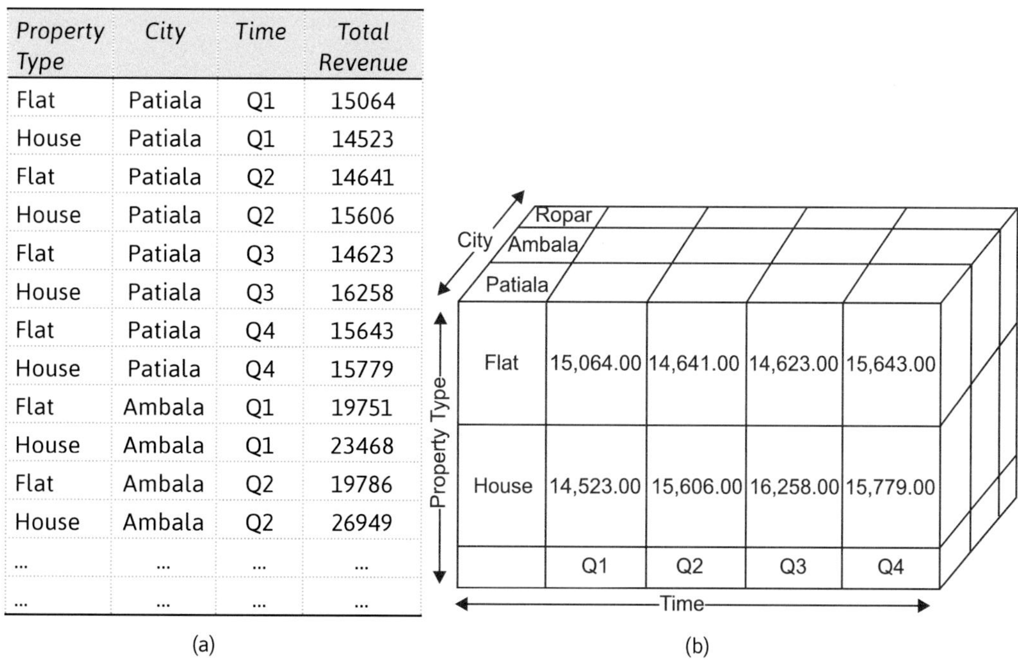

Property Type	City	Time	Total Revenue
Flat	Patiala	Q1	15064
House	Patiala	Q1	14523
Flat	Patiala	Q2	14641
House	Patiala	Q2	15606
Flat	Patiala	Q3	14623
House	Patiala	Q3	16258
Flat	Patiala	Q4	15643
House	Patiala	Q4	15779
Flat	Ambala	Q1	19751
House	Ambala	Q1	23468
Flat	Ambala	Q2	19786
House	Ambala	Q2	26949
...	...	...	...
...	...	...	...

(a) (b)

Figure 14.2 (a) Relational model representation, (b) Three dimensional view

Here, the cube illustrates data as cells in an array by relating the total revenue with the dimensions such as City, Time and Property Type. The concept of the data cube is further discussed in the next sub-section.

14.2.1 Data Cube

A Data Cube is described in terms of dimensions and facts. It represents data in different dimensions. Here, the dimensions are generally the entities which an organization preserves as records. Can you identify the dimensions and facts in Figure 14.1 and Figure 14.2.

Hopefully you have been able to identify that in Figure 14.1, City and Time are dimensions and Total Revenue is the fact. Thus, Figure 14.1 (b) represents two dimensional views of data. While in Figure 14.2 Property Type, City, and Time are dimensions and Total Revenue is the fact. Since the depiction covers three dimensions so it's three dimensional view of data.

In Figure 14.1 (b), the cube shows data as cells in an array by relating the Total Revenue with the dimensions such as Time and Location. And in Figure 14.2 (b), the cube shows data as cells in an array by relating the Total Revenue with the dimensions such as City, Time and Property Type.

Let us further understand the concept of the cube with another example of a company database. Suppose an organization wishes to check sales records corresponding to dimensions such as branch, time, location, and item using a sales data warehouse. These dimensions help in tracking records of monthly sales and branches where the items were sold. For example, the 'item' dimension table may consist of attributes such as item_code, item_type, item_name and item_brand.

In a two dimensional view of data, there are records corresponding to item and time only. The Figure 14.3 illustrates the sales for 'New Delhi' corresponding to item and time dimensions on the basis of type of items sold.

Location = 'New Delhi'				
Time (quarter)	Item (type)			
	Entertainment	Keyboard	Mobile	Locks
Q1	500	700	10	300
Q2	769	765	30	476
Q3	987	489	18	659
Q4	666	976	40	539

Figure 14.3 Two dimensional view of sale data, i.e., Item and Time

If the user wishes to see the data of sales along with one more dimension, let us suppose, the location dimension, then three dimensional view may be helpful in this case. The Figure 14.4 represents the three dimensional view of sales data corresponding to item, time and location.

	Location = 'Gurgaon'			Location = 'New Delhi'			Location = 'Mumbai'		
Time	Item			Item			Item		
	Mouse	Mobile	Modem	Mouse	Mobile	Modem	Mouse	Mobile	Modem
Q1	788	987	765	786	85	987	986	567	875
Q2	678	654	987	659	786	436	980	876	908
Q3	899	875	190	983	909	237	987	100	1089
Q4	787	969	908	537	567	836	837	926	987

Figure 14.4 Three dimensional view of sale data, i.e., Item, Time and Location

This data can be viewed, alternately as shown in Figure 14.5.

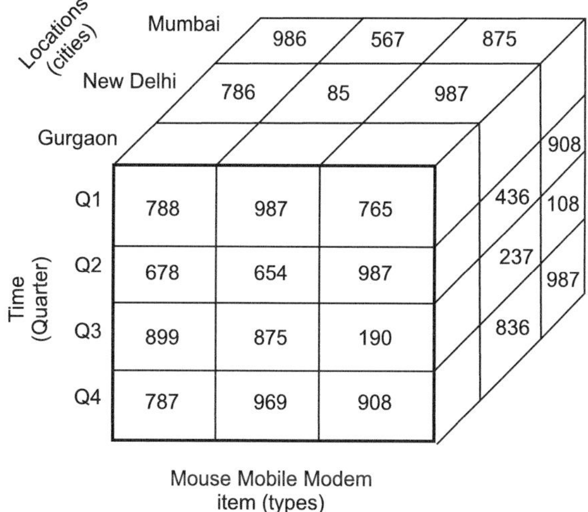

Figure 14.5 Cubical three dimensional view of sale data

Here, Item, Time and Locations are dimensions and the cube shows data as cells in an array by relating these dimensions. A cube may have more than one measure. For example, we may be interested in not only showing total sale value but also the total quantity.

14.3 Implementing Multi-dimensional View of Data in Oracle

The SQL SELECT statement with GROUP BY clause is used for aggregation of data. It divides the table into sub-tables based on the attributes' values in the GROUP BY clause so that each sub-table has the same values for the(se) attribute(s) and then aggregations over each sub-table are carried out. SQL has a variety of aggregation functions including max, min, average, count which are used widely by employing the GROUP BY facility. For data cube implementation extension of GROUP BY clause with ROLLUP and CUBE can be used as discussed below with an example: the emp database as shown in Figure 14.6.

☑ Autocommit Display 50

```
select * from emp
```

Results Explain Describe Saved SQL History

ENO	ENAME	JOB	SAL	DNO
1	RAM	AP	4000	10
2	RAJ	PROF	4000	10
3	RAJESH	ASSOC PROF	8000	20
4	RAJ	ASSOC PROF	9000	20
5	RAJU	PROF	5999	30
10	as	PROF	3444	10
11	as	PROF	8444	10
12	as	AP	3000	10

Figure 14.6 Emp database

Here, the management may be interested in finding the total number of employees in each job within each department, for which we can use the GROUP BY clause over dno, job fields/dimensions to display the total number of employees as shown in Figure 14.7.

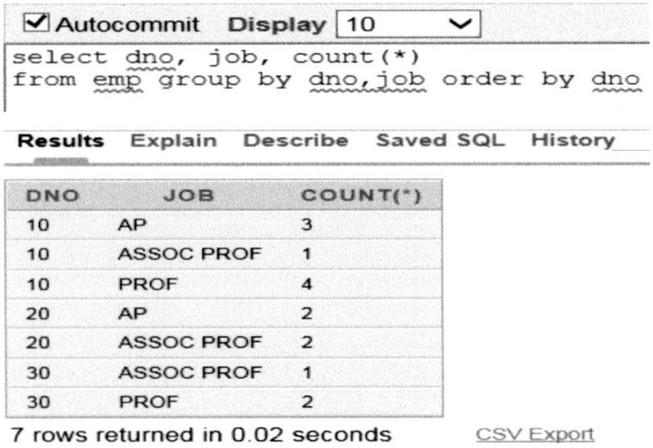

Autocommit Display 10

```
select dno, job, count(*)
from emp group by dno,job order by dno
```

Results Explain Describe Saved SQL History

DNO	JOB	COUNT(*)
10	AP	3
10	ASSOC PROF	1
10	PROF	4
20	AP	2
20	ASSOC PROF	2
30	ASSOC PROF	1
30	PROF	2

7 rows returned in 0.02 seconds CSV Export

Figure 14.7 Total number of employees in each job within each department

This information can be viewed as two dimensional data with dno and job as dimensions and count of employees as fact. In Figure 14.8, the cube illustrates data as cells in an array by relating these dimensions.

DNO / JOB	AP	ASSOC PROF	PROF	Total
10	3	1	4	8
20	2	2	-	4
30	1	1	2	4
Total	6	4	6	16

Figure 14.8 Two dimensional view of employee data

The GROUP BY clause is able to produce counts for each dno and job, but it is unable to produce aggregations. To produce aggregations, we can use the ROLLUP extension of GROUP BY clause as discussed below.

ROLLUP extension of GROUP BY clause

The ROLLUP extension generates group subtotals from right to left as well as a grand total. If there are 'n' numbers of columns listed in the ROLLUP, then there will be 'n+1' level of subtotals. The extension of GROUP BY clause with ROLLUP to generate one level of aggregation is shown in Figure 14.9.

```
select dno, job, count(*)
from emp group by ROLLUP(dno,job) ORDER BY DNO
```

Results Explain Describe Saved SQL History

DNO	JOB	COUNT(*)
10	AP	3
10	ASSOC PROF	1
10	PROF	4
10	-	8
20	AP	2
20	ASSOC PROF	2
20	-	4
30	ASSOC PROF	1
30	PROF	2
30	-	3
-	-	15

Figure 14.9 Use of ROLLUP for aggregation of data

The ROLLUP extension is able to produce aggregation for *n-1* dimensions, *i.e.,* one dimension, dno in this case. In order to produce aggregation for all the dimensions, the CUBE extension of GROUP BY can be used as discussed below.

CUBE extension of GROUP BY clause

Along with the subtotals produced by the ROLLUP extension, the CUBE extension will produce subtotals for all combinations of the dimensions identified. If there are 'n' numbers of columns listed in the CUBE, then there will be 2^n subtotal combinations. The extension of GROUP BY clause with CUBE to produce full aggregation is shown in Figure 14.10.

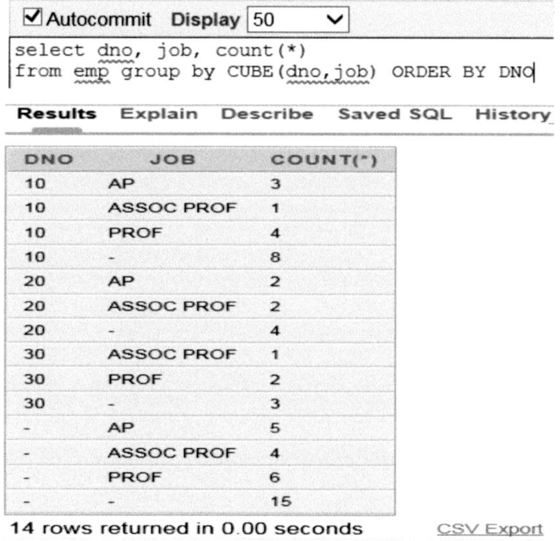

Autocommit Display 50

```
select dno, job, count(*)
from emp group by CUBE(dno,job) ORDER BY DNO
```

Results Explain Describe Saved SQL History

DNO	JOB	COUNT(*)
10	AP	3
10	ASSOC PROF	1
10	PROF	4
10	-	8
20	AP	2
20	ASSOC PROF	2
20	-	4
30	ASSOC PROF	1
30	PROF	2
30	-	3
-	AP	5
-	ASSOC PROF	4
-	PROF	6
-	-	15

14 rows returned in 0.00 seconds CSV Export

Figure 14.10 Use of CUBE for aggregation of data

Let us consider, an extended employee database which has one more dimension as state shown in Figure 14.11.

ENO	JOB	STATE	DNO
1	AP	PB	10
2	AP	HP	10
3	ASSOC PROF	HP	10
4	PROF	HP	10
5	AP	PB	20
6	AP	PB	20
7	PROF	HP	20

7 rows selected.

Figure 14.11 Employee database with third dimension state

Here, the management may be interested in finding the total number of employees from each state within each job within each department number, and for this we can use CUBE over dno, job, state dimensions to display a three dimensional view of the data as shown in Figure 14.12. This means the first grouping is done on department number, then with each department number group, further grouping is done on each job and then within each sub group of job, another grouping is done on the basis of sate.

```
SELECT DNO,JOB,STATE, COUNT(*) FROM PK GROUP BY CUBE (DNO, JOB, STATE)
ORDER BY DNO
```

DNO	JOB	STATE	COUNT(*)
10	AP	HP	1
10	AP	PB	1
10	AP		2
10	ASSOC PROF	HP	1
10	ASSOC PROF		1
10	PROF	HP	1
10	PROF		1
10		HP	3
10		PB	1
10			4
20	AP	PB	2
20	AP		2
20	PROF	HP	1
20	PROF		1
DNO	JOB	STATE	COUNT(*)
20		HP	1
20		PB	2
20			3
	AP	HP	1
	AP	PB	3
	AP		4
	ASSOC PROF	HP	1
	ASSOC PROF		1
	PROF	HP	2
	PROF		2
		HP	4
		PB	3
			7

Figure 14.12 Three dimensional view of the employee database

Here, dno, job and state are three dimensions and count is the fact. The cubical representation of same data is shown in Figure 14.13.

States: PB, HR, HP

D No ↓ Job →	AP	ASSOC PROF	PROF	Total
10	3	1	4	8
20	2	2	–	4
30	1	1	2	4
Total	6	4	6	16

Figure 14.13 Cubical three dimensional representation of the employee database

14.4 Improving efficiency of OLAP by pre-computing the queries

To understand this concept, let us consider the database of a University that has 7 departments, 3 types of jobs titles in each department and it has employees from 10 states. In this scenario, management may be interested in finding the count of employees, and the list of all possible queries on this database is given in Table 14.3.

Table 14.3 Possible number of queries on given scenario

Query	*Possible number of queries*
Total Number of employees in University	1
Query for particular department	7 (one for each department)
Query for particular Job	3 (one for each job)
Query for particular State	10 (one for each state)
Query for particular Department, Job combination	21 (7 X 3 combinations are possible)
Query for particular Department, State combination	70 (7 X 10 combinations are possible)
Query for particular Job, State combination	30 (3 X 10 combinations are possible)
Query for particular Department, Job, State combination	210 (7 X 3 X 10 combinations are possible)
Total Possible Queries	352

In this case, 352 queries are possible but in a real situation one could have a larger number of possible queries, by considering a University of having 100 departments having 10 job titles in each department and having employees from 29 states. Then possible queries will be more than 100 X 10 X 29 =29,000.

To improve the efficency of OLAP systems it is important to work on the option to precompute these queries to be able to run these queries on the fly.

There are three possible ways to address this issue.

Pre-compute and store all

In this strategy all the aggregations will be precomputed and stored. It wil have best query response because all the results are pre-computed and stored, but this startegy is impractical because it requires large resources to compute and store aggregates in large database.

Pre-compute and store none

In this strategy, all the aggregations will be computed on-the-fly on the actual database. This strategy does not require extra space for the cube and always provides updated information but it will have a slow query response time.

Pre-compute and store some

In this strategy, most frequently queries aggregates will be pre-computed and stored in the database and other aggregations will be computed as and when need arises. The selection of pre-compuation aggregations is perfromed in such a manner that the remaining aggregates can be computed from pre-computed aggregations. However, it is not always possible to carry this out and in such cases the source database will be accessed to compute remaining aggregates. This strategy is considered as the most optimal.

In order to implement this solution, it is important to decide about what is the total number of queries that needs to be pre-computed. This is discussed in Table 14.3.

Let us reproduce the list of queries discussed earlier in Table 14.3, and define them as (*d, j, s*) where *d* represents a value of department dimension, *j* specifies job dimension and *s* stands for state dimension. Here, *ALL* at a particular dimension means number of employees in all instances of that dimension. For example, (*ALL*, *j*, *s*), refers number of employees in all departments working for job *j* and from state *s*. Thus, (ALL, Assistant Professor, Punjab) means the number of employees in all departments working as Assistant Professor and from Punjab.

Table 14.4 Pre-computation of query analysis

Number of Queries	*Dimension*	*Representation*	*Remarks*
1	Null	(ALL, ALL, ALL)	Number of employees from all departments, all jobs and all states, i.e., the total number of employees in the University.
7	Department	(d, ALL, ALL)	Number of employees from all jobs and states working in a particular department.

Contd.

Number of Queries	Dimension	Representation	Remarks
3	Job	(ALL, j, ALL)	Number of employees from all departments and states working on a particular job.
10	State	(ALL, ALL, s)	Number of employees from all departments and jobs belonging to a particular state.
21	Department, Job	(d, j, ALL)	Number of employees from all states working in a particular department and on a particular job.
70	Department, State	(d, ALL, s)	Number of employees for all jobs working in a particular department and belonging to a particular state.
30	Job, State	(ALL, j, s)	Number of employees from all departments working for particular job and belonging to a particular state.
210	Department, Job, state	(d, j, s)	Number of employees working in a particular department, on a particular job and belonging to a particular state.

As shown in Figure 14.14, aggregation can be applied on a particular dimension on the fly if we have pre-computed and stored all the queries of (d, j, s) types. Thus, there is a need to pre-compute and store only 210 queries of type (d, j, s) and remaining 142 (i.e., 352-210) queries will run on the fly. With this we are able to develop all 352 queries by using the results of pre-computed 210 queries.

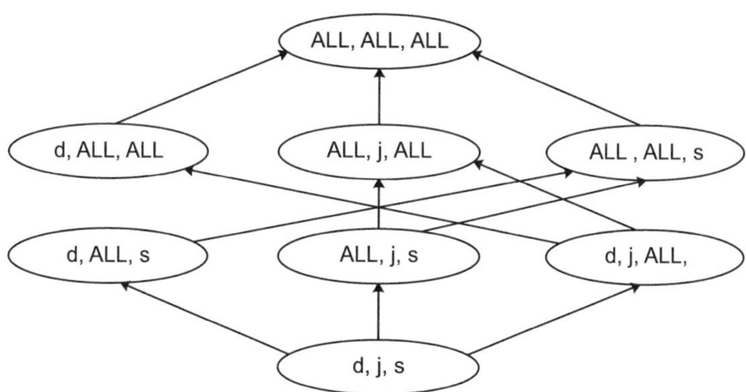

Figure 14.14 Pre-computation of only queries of type (d, j, s)

14.5 Types of OLAP Servers

There are two types of OLAP servers which are given as follows:

- Relational OLAP (ROLAP)
- Multi-dimensional OLAP (MOLAP)

14.5.1 Relational OLAP

ROLAP is based on the relational model of DBMS. The result of GROUP BY queries as discussed in Section 14.4 can be pre-computed and stored in another relational table or view for implementation by the ROLAP server. It is also known as a bottom up approach which uses the star schema of data warehousing.

The major advantages of ROLAP, is the support of existing RDBMS and efficient storage because no zero facts are returned by the SQL query. It means that if there is no record for Professor in department number 20, the SQL query will not return any record for it. Records will be returned for it, if at least one record is found for the given job in a particular dept number as shown in Figure 14.15. It shows that GROUP BY clause doe not return or store zero value fact. While these queries run on the fly and are not pre computed, low efficiency is the issue with ROLAP servers.

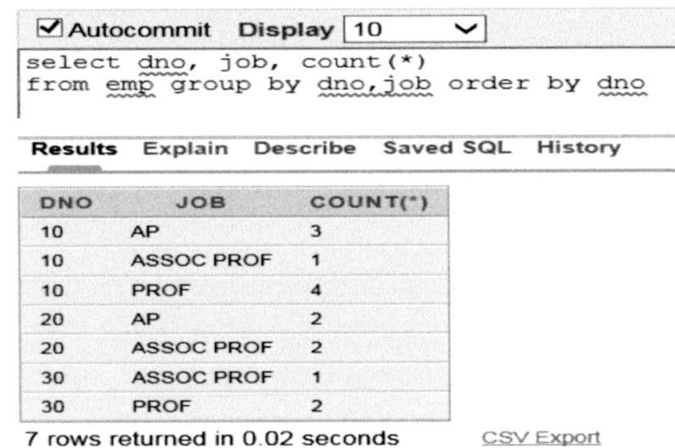


```
select dno, job, count(*)
from emp group by dno,job order by dno
```

DNO	JOB	COUNT(*)
10	AP	3
10	ASSOC PROF	1
10	PROF	4
20	AP	2
20	ASSOC PROF	2
30	ASSOC PROF	1
30	PROF	2

Figure 14.15 No zero value facts returned by Group By query

The ROLAP architecture consists of a Database server, ROLAP server and front-end tool as shown in Figure 14.16.

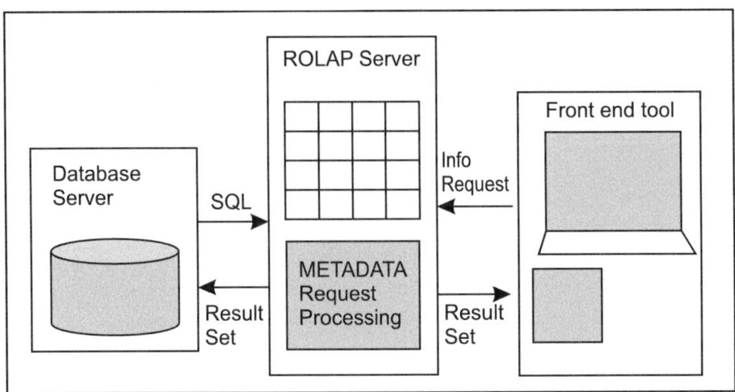

Figure 14.16 ROLAP architecture

The data in ROLAP server is normally in de-normalized form.

Advantages and Disadvantages of ROLAP

The main advantages and disadvantages of using ROLAP server are given as follows.

Advantages

- These can be used with existing RDBMS without any problem.
- As no zero facts can be stored, therefore data is stored efficiently.
- ROLAP servers do not use pre-computed data cubes.

Disadvantages

- Poor query performance.

14.5.2 MOLAP

Multi-dimensional OLAP is based on multi-dimensional DBMS for storage and access of data. It is known as a top-down approach to OLAP. It uses a special purpose file system to store pre-computed values in the cube. Commonly, arrays are used to store the information of cubes as shown in Figure 14.17.

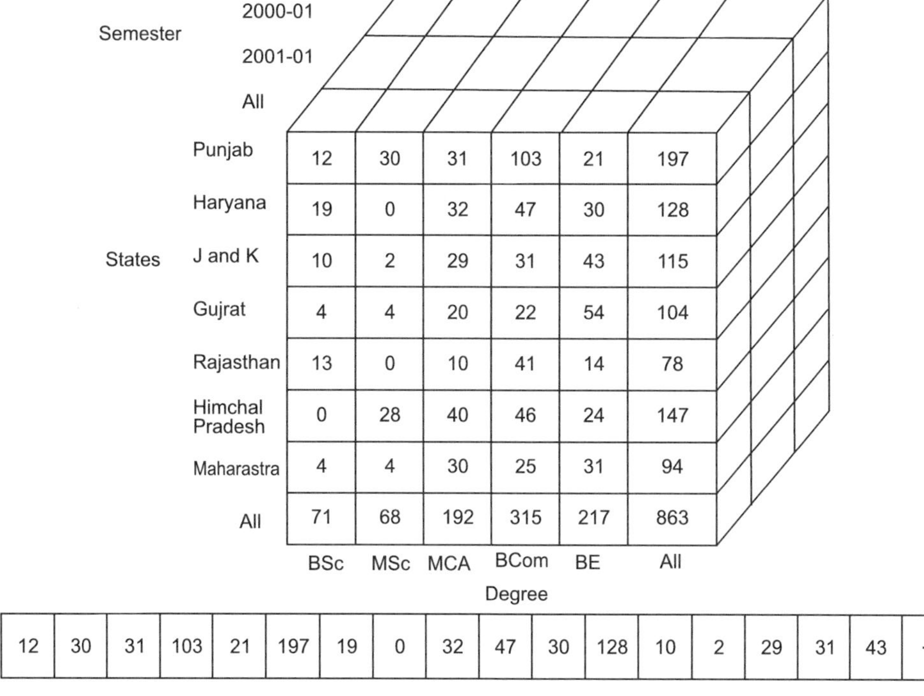

	BSc	MSc	MCA	BCom	BE	All
Punjab	12	30	31	103	21	197
Haryana	19	0	32	47	30	128
J and K	10	2	29	31	43	115
Gujrat	4	4	20	22	54	104
Rajasthan	13	0	10	41	14	78
Himchal Pradesh	0	28	40	46	24	147
Maharastra	4	4	30	25	31	94
All	71	68	192	315	217	863

12	30	31	103	21	197	19	0	32	47	30	128	10	2	29	31	43	···

Figure 14.17 MOLAP Implementation

In this case, cell locations can be inferred from the known dimensions while dimensions can be inferred from cell locations. There are some issues in implementations of MOLAP as arrays are likely to be very large for large multi-dimensional databases. Since, zero facts are stored in MOLAP it produces the case of sparseness of data. To overcome the problem of large sizes, arrays are normally split into chunks so that these can be accommodated in the main memory.To overcome the issue of sparseness, the chunks may be compressed.

The MOLAP architecture consists of a Database server, a MOLAP server and front-end tools as shown in Figure 14.18.

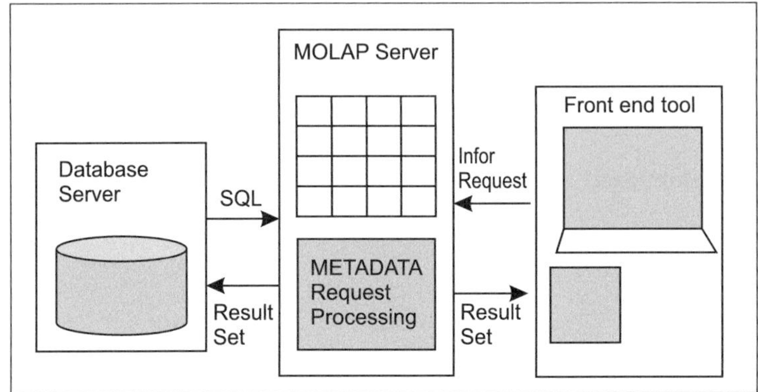

Figure 14.18 MOLAP architecture

Advantages and Disadvantages of MOLAP

The key advantages and disadvantages of using MOLAP servers are:

Advantages

- MOLAP servers allow quickest indexing of pre-computed data.
- It allows users to analyze both large and less-detailed data.
- It is suitable for inexperienced users as MOLAP is easier to use.

Disadvantages

- MOLAP is not able to contain detailed data.
- If the dataset is sparse then the storage utilization may be low.

14.5.3 Comparison of ROLAP and MOLAP

The comparison of ROLAP and MOLAP on basis of identified properties is given in Table 14.5.

Table 14.5 Comparison of ROLAP and MOLAP

Property	*ROLAP*	*MOLAP*
Information retrieval	Information retrieval is comparatively slow.	Information retrieval is fast.
Data Model	Uses relational table.	Uses sparse array to store datasets.
Type of Users	ROLAP is best suited for experienced users.	MOLAP is applicable for inexperienced users as it is easy to use.
Disk Space	It may not require space other than available in data warehouse.	MOLAP maintains an isolated database for data cubes.
Scalability	It is scalable as it easy to add dimension and fact in SQL query.	It has limited scalability as any addition of new dimension requires a complete remapping of values with dimensions in an array.
DBMS Facility	It has strong DBMS facility as it is based on relational model.	It has poor DBMS facility due to its different data structure.

14.6 OLAP Operations

OLAP is implemented with data cubes, on which the following operations may be applied:

- Roll-up
- Drill-down
- Slice and dice
- Pivot (rotate)

14.6.1 Roll-up

Roll-up is similar to zooming out on the data cube. Roll-up is used to provide abstract level details to user. It performs further aggregation of data by reduction in dimension or by stepping up a concept hierarchy for a dimension. Figure 14.19 illustrates the working of roll-up.

Here, aggregation is performed on cities to climb up to state for dimension reduction. The aggregation can also be performed on Time (Quarter) to year, etc. or individual items to group like mobile, modem, etc.

14.6.2 Drill-down

Drill-down is opposite of roll-up. Drill-down is like zooming in on the data and is used to provide detailed data to the user. It provides detailed information by introducing a new dimension or by moving down a concept hierarchy for a dimension. It navigates from less detailed to more detailed data. Figure 14.20 illustrates the working of drill-down.

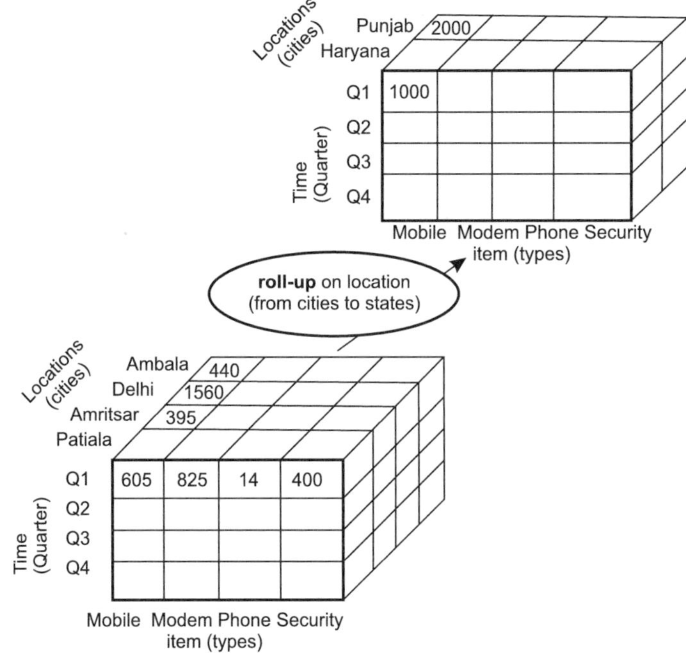

Figure 14.19 Working of the Roll-up operation

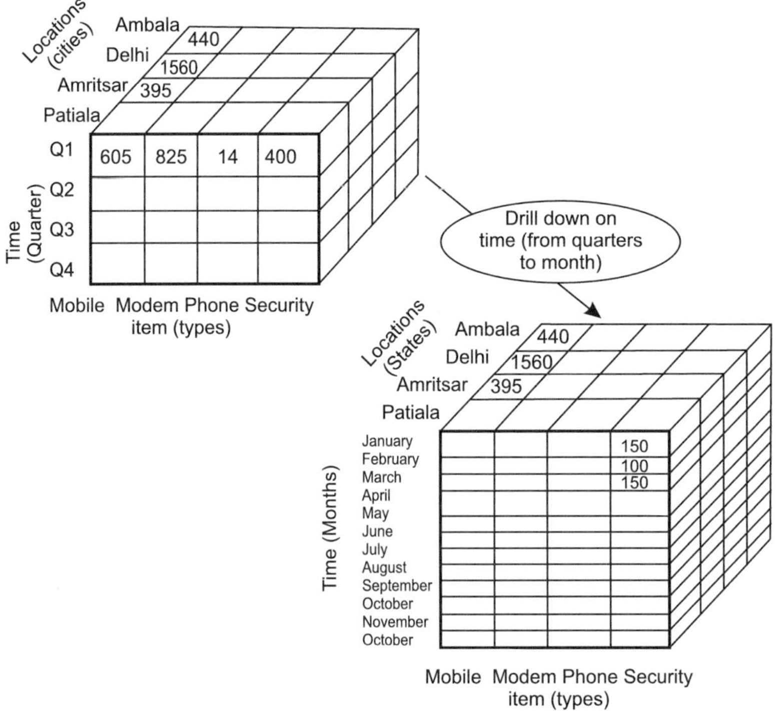

Figure 14.20 Working of the Drill-down operation

In this example, the time dimension runs down from the level of quarter to the level of month on moving down.

14.6.3 Slice and dice

Slice and dice represent the way to view the information from different perspectives. The slice operation gives a new sub-cube by selecting one particular dimension from a specified cube. Thus, a slice is a subset of the cube corresponding to a single value for one or more members of the dimensions. It results in reduction in dimension. So, a slice operation is performed when the user wants to select one dimension of a three-dimensional cube that results in a two-dimensional slice.

The Figure 14.21 shows the working of the slice operation. In this figure, a slice operation is performed using the criterion time 'Q1' for the dimension 'time'. It selects one or more dimensions and gives a new sub-cube.

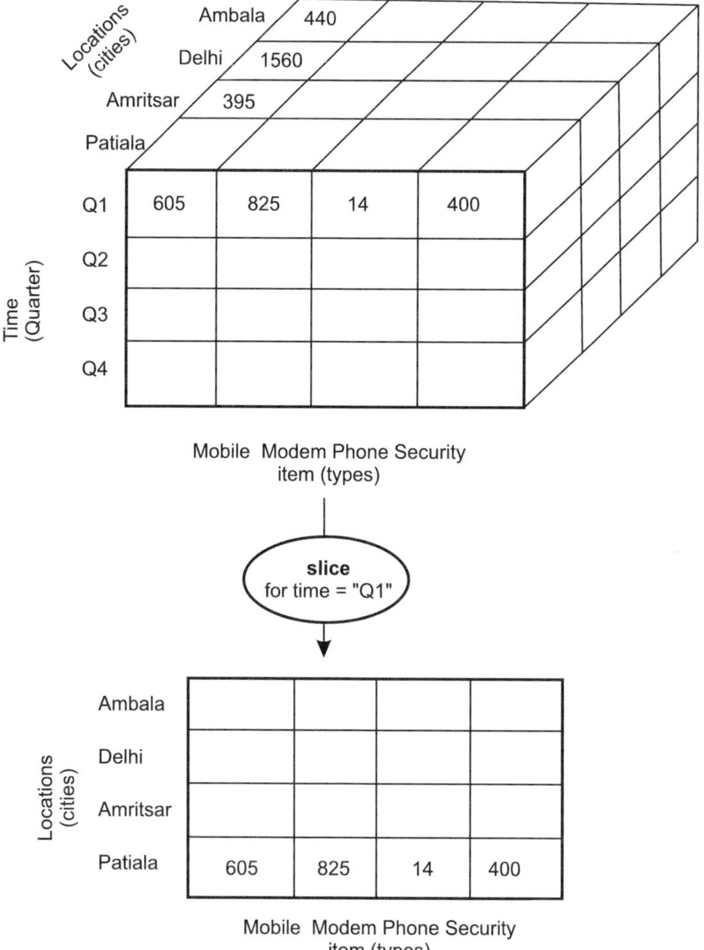

Figure 14.21 Working of the Slice operation

Let us consider another case of a University database system, where we have a count of the number of students from each state in previous semesters in a particular course as shown in Figure 14.22.

Let us suppose management is interested in finding the details of their BE course. So, the degree dimension will be fixed as degree = BE and the slice will be taken out. It will not have any information about other degrees as shown in Figure 14.22.

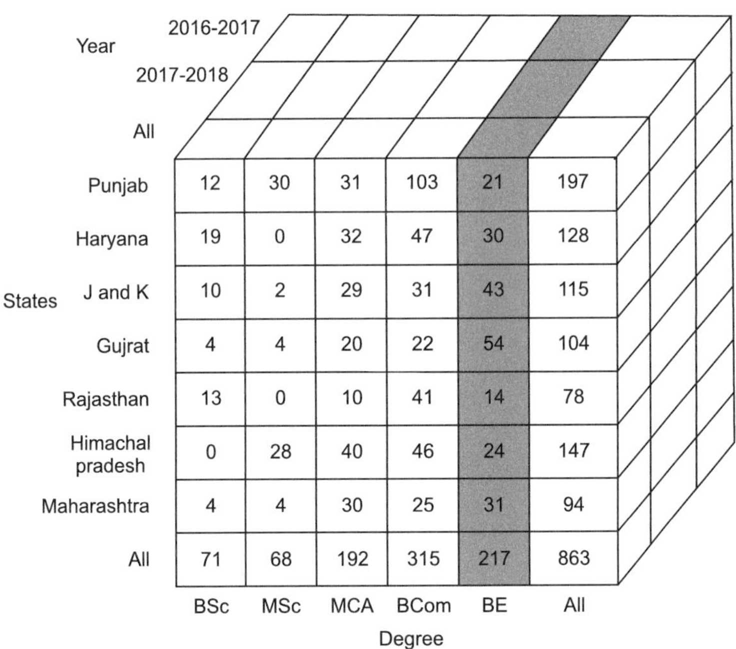

Figure 14.22 The Slice operation

The information retrieved therefore is more like a two-dimensional rectangle than a cube for degree = BE as shown in Table 14.6.

Table 14.6 Result of the slice operation for degree = BE

State \ Year	2014–2015	2015–2016	2016–2017	2017–2018
Punjab	11	5	10	2
Haryana	17	0	13	5
J and K	23	2	20	1
Gujarat	31	4	23	4
Rajasthan	7	0	7	4
Himachal Pradesh	13	8	11	6
Maharashtra	19	4	12	5

14.6.4 Dice

The dice operation is analogous to slice operation without reduction in the number of dimensions. The Dice operation gives a new sub-cube by selecting two or more dimensions from a specified cube. Figure 14.23 shows the workings of the dice operation.

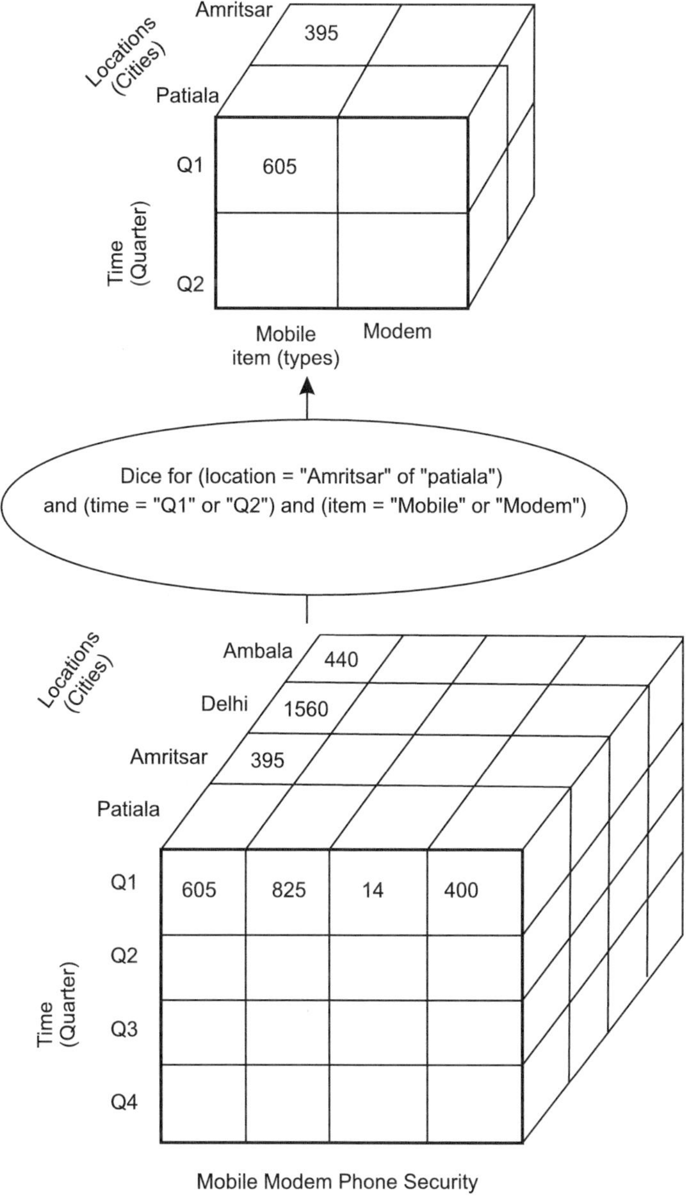

Figure 14.23 Working of the Dice operation

Here, the dice operation is performed on the cube on the basis of the selection criteria of the following three dimensions.

- (location = 'Amritsar' or 'Patiala')
- (time = 'Q1' or 'Q2')
- (item = 'Mobile' or 'Modem')

As discussed, a dice is attained by performing selection on two or more dimensions.

Similarly, in the case of the university database system, a dice operation can be performed to know the number of students enrolled in both BE and BCom degrees from states Punjab, Haryana and Maharashtra as shown in Figure 14.24.

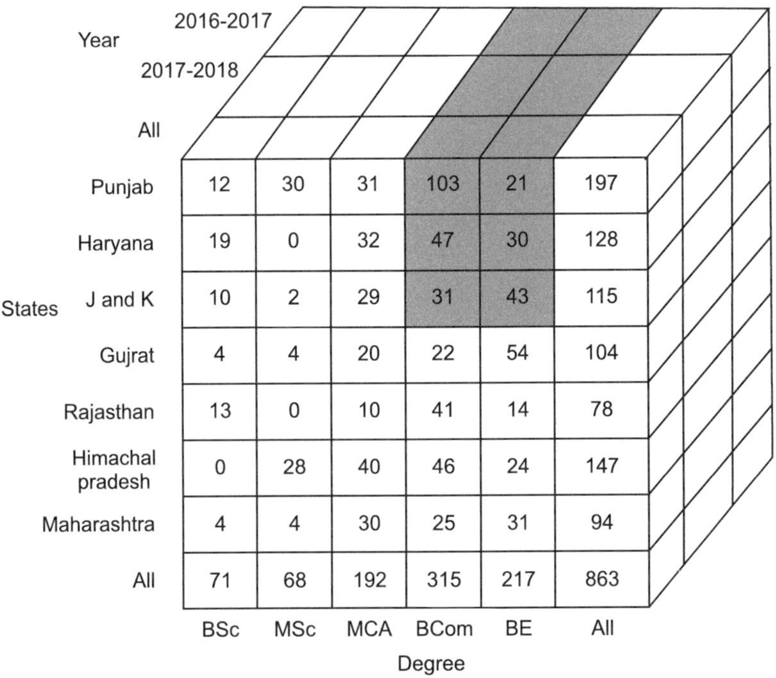

Figure 14.24 Dice operation

14.6.5 Pivot

The pivot operation is also called rotation. This operation rotates the data axes in view to get another presentation of data. It may include swapping of the columns and rows. Figure 14.25 illustrates how of the pivot operation works.

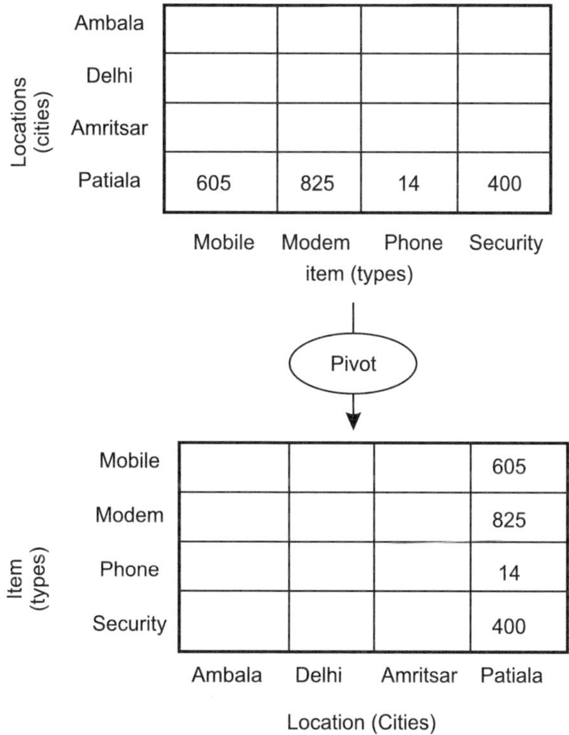

Figure 14.25 Workings of the Pivot operation

Remind Me

- OLAP is a technology that enables analysts to extract and view business data from different points of view.
- The OLAP cube is a data structure optimized for very quick data analysis.
- The OLAP cube consists of numeric facts called measures which are categorized by dimensions.
- The OLAP cube is also called the hypercube.
- The important features of OLAP are multi-dimensional view of data, time intelligence and complex calculations support.
- There are two types of OLAP servers: Relational OLAP (ROLAP) and Multi-dimensional OLAP (MOLAP).
- ROLAP is based on the relational model of DBMS.
- MOLAP is based on the multi-dimensional DBMS for storage and access of data.
- OLAP has four analytical operations called roll-up, drill-down, slice & dice, and pivot.
- Roll-up is similar to zooming out on the data cube.
- Drill-down is opposite of roll-up. Drill-down is like zooming in on the data and is used to provide detailed data to the user.
- Slice and dice represent the way to view the information from different perspectives.
- The dice operation is analogous to slice operation, however it does not include reduction in the number of dimensions.
- The pivot operation is also called rotation.

Point Me (Books)

- Conolly, Thomas, and Carolyn Begg. 2015. *Database Systems: A Practical Approach to Design, Implementation, and Management*, 6th ed. New York: Pearson Education.
- Kimball, Ralph, and Margy Ross. 2013. *The Data Warehouse Toolkit: the complete guide to dimensional modeling*, 3rd ed. Indianapolis: John Wiley & Sons.
- Sharma, Gajendra. 2010. *Data Mining Data Warehousing and OLAP*. Delhi: S. K. Kataria & Sons.

Point Me (Video)

- Data Warehouse Concepts | Data Warehouse Tutorial | Data Warehouse Architecture | Edureka, https://www.youtube.com/watch?v=CHYPF7jxlik
- OLAP Operations Tutorial, https://www.youtube.com/watch?v=0ZMndP_Y32U

Connect Me (Internet Resources)

- https://www.guru99.com/online-analytical-processing.html
- https://www.tutorialspoint.com/dwh/dwh_olap.htm
- https://en.wikipedia.org/wiki/Online_analytical_processing
- http://olap.com/olap-definition/

Test Me

Answer these multiple choice questions based on your learning in this chapter.

1. Construct a data cube from the table given below. Is this a dense or a sparse data cube? If it is sparse, identify the cells that are empty.

Product ID	*Location ID*	*Number Sold*
1	1	10
1	3	6
2	1	5
2	2	22

2. Let us suppose that X university has seven departments, three types of jobs titles in each department and it has employees from 10 states. In this scenario, management is interested in finding the count of employees, what will be the count of all possible queries on this database? What is number of queries which we can pre-compute and store? Justify your answer.
3. Compare ROLAP and MOLP on following parameters:
   Information retrieval, type of users, disk space, scalability and data model
4. Write the SQL query to display top 5 highest paid employees from employee table.
5. An educational psychologist wants to use association analysis to analyze test results. The test consists of 100 questions with four possible answers each. How would you convert this data into a form suitable for association analysis?
6. How many dimensions are selected in a slice operation? How many dimensions are selected in a dice operation? How many fact tables are there in a star schema?
7. Cubes are logical representation of multi-dimensional data.
   (a) True (b) False

8. OLAP is the process of analyzing the data, managing aggregations, partitioning information into cubes for in depth visualization.
   (a) Yes (b) No

Answer Keys:

7. (a) 8. (a)

15

Big Data and NoSQL

Chapter Objectives

- ✓ To discuss the major issues of relational databases
- ✓ To understand the need for NoSQL
- ✓ To comprehend the characteristics of NoSQL
- ✓ To understand different data models of NoSQL
- ✓ To understand the concept of the CAP theorem
- ✓ To discuss the future of NoSQL

After about half a century of dominance of relational database, the current excitement about NoSQL databases comes as a big surprise. In this chapter, we'll explore the challenges faced by relational databases due to changing technological paradigms and why the current rise of NoSQL databases is not a flash in the pan.

Let us start our discussion by looking at relational databases.

15.1 The Rise of Relational Databases

Dr E. F Codd proposed the relational model in 1969. It was soon adopted by the mainstream software industries due to its simplicity and efficiency replacing hierarchical and network models that were prevalent at that time. The timeline showing the rise of the relational model is depicted in Figure 15.1.

The reasons for the success of relational databases were their simplicity, the power of SQL, support for transaction management, concurrency control, and recovery management.

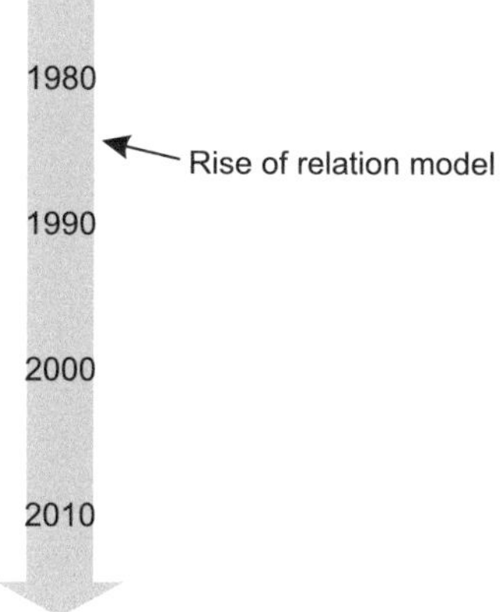

Figure 15.1 Rise of the relational model

15.2 Major Issues with Relational Databases

The relational data model organizes data in rows and columns that are arranged in a tabular form. In the relational model, a row is known as a tuple which is a set of key-value pairs and a relation is a set of these tuples. All operations in SQL consume and return relations. This foundation based on relations provides a certain elegance and simplicity, but it also suffers some limitations. The values in a relational tuple have to be simple (atomic)—they cannot contain any structure, such as a nested record or a list.

This limitation is not true for in-memory data structures, which can take on much richer structures than relations. As a result, if you want to use a richer in-memory data structure, you would have to translate it to a relational representation to store it on disk. This problem is known as impedance mismatch i.e. two different representations that require inter-translation as shown in Figure 15.2.

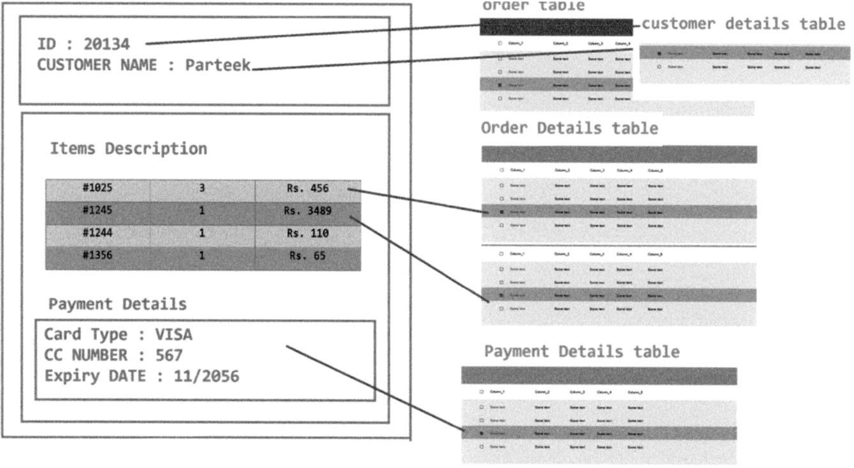

Figure 15.2 An order, which looks like a single aggregate structure in the UI, is split into many rows from many tables in a relational database

The impedance mismatch is a major source of frustration for application developers. In the 1990s many experts believed that impedance mismatch would lead to relational databases being replaced with databases that replicate the in-memory data structures to disk. Later, with the advent of object-oriented programming languages, object-oriented databases were also developed but they could never make their way into the mainstream software development. Figure 15.3 depicts this era.

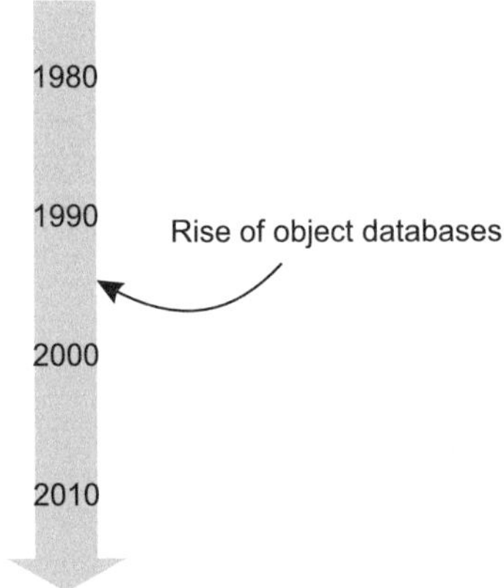

Figure 15.3 Rise of Object databases

While object-oriented languages succeeded in becoming the major programming paradigm, object-oriented databases faded away into darkness. Instead, object-relational mapping (ORM) frameworks were developed which removed a lot of grunt work. However, ORM frameworks were a problem on their own. When developers tried too hard to ignore (abstract away) the database using ORMs, the query performance would suffer.

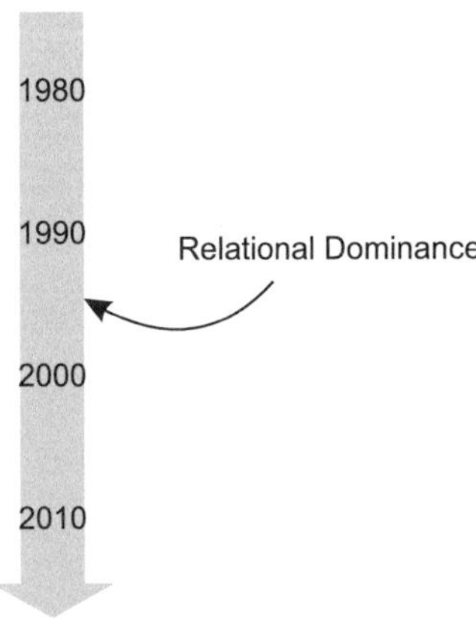

Figure 15.4 Relational dominance in the late 1990s and early 2000s

Nevertheless, relational databases continued to dominate the enterprise computing world in the last decade of 20th century as shown in Figure 15.4, but during the early 2000s, cracks began to open up in their dominance.

15.3 Challenges from the Internet Boom

In late the 1990s the Internet grew at an unimaginable pace. Soon large datasets appeared in the form of social networks, activity logs, scientific data, etc. As the Internet became more accessible, the number of users grew which led to exponential growth of data. This growth of data is depicted in Figure 15.5.

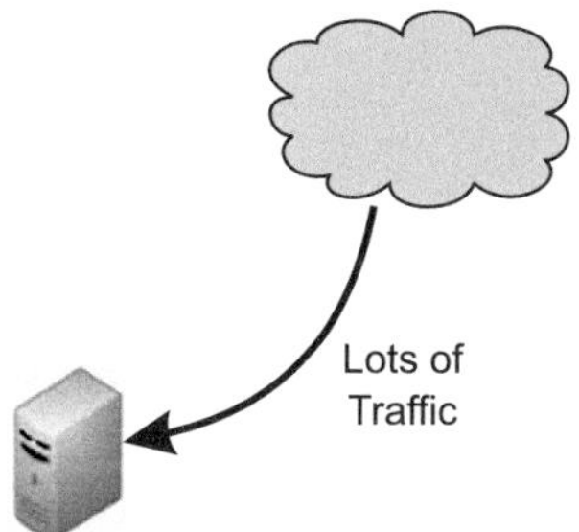

Figure 15.5 Generation of lots of traffic during the internet boom

15.3.1 The rapid growth of unstructured data

With the Internet, there was a rapid growth of unstructured data. The volume of unstructured data can be clearly observed from the following facts and figures.

- Youtube users upload 48 hours of new video every minute of the day.
- 571 new websites are created every minute of the day.
- 90% of world's data has been created in last two years.
- Data production will be 44 times greater in 2020 than it was in 2009.
- Brands and organizations on Facebook receive 34,722 'Likes' every minute of the day.
- 100 terabytes of data is uploaded daily to Facebook.
- According to Twitter's own research in early 2012, it saw roughly 185 million tweets everyday and had more than 465 million accounts.
- 30 Billion independent pieces of content are shared on Facebook every month.
- In late 2011, IDC Digital Universe published a report indicating that about 1.8 zettabytes of data was created that year.

15.3.2 Types of data in the era of the Internet boom

There are three types of data as depicted in Figure 15.6. To elaborate:

i. Structured Data
ii. Semi-Structured Data
iii. Unstructured Data

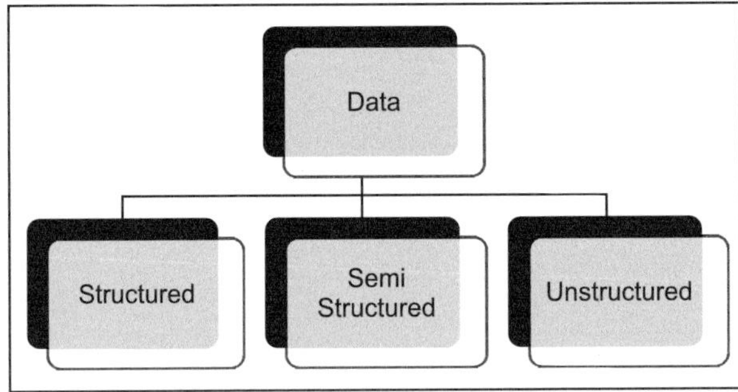

Figure 15.6 Types of data

Let us discuss each type of data one by one.

Structured data

Data that has a fixed structure and can be arranged in rows and columns is known as Structured Data. For example, a database stored in SQL, excel sheets, OLTP (Online Transaction Processing), and such as depicted in Figure 15.7 are all structured.

They have a relational key and can be easily mapped into pre-designed fields. It is the simplest way to manage information. But structured data represents only 5 to 10% of all the data present in the world.

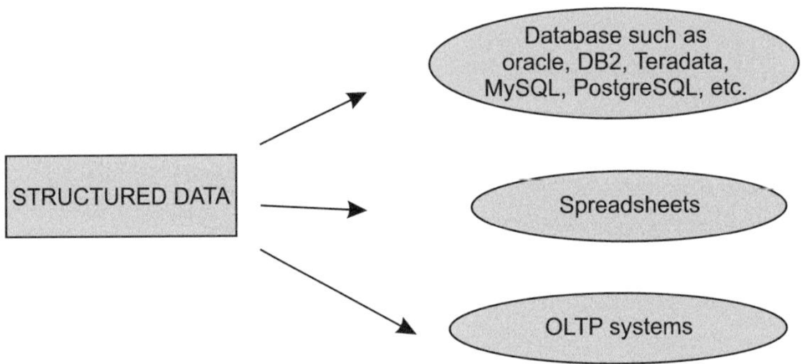

Figure 15.7 Structured data

Semi-Structured data

Semi-structured data doesn't reside in a relational database but has some organizational properties that make it easier to analyze. CSV file, XML and JSON documents are all examples of semi structured documents.

Just like structured data, the semi-structured data also represents only about 5-10% of all data world-wide.

Unstructured data

Unstructured data represents around 80% of data. It often includes text and multimedia content. Examples include e-mail messages, word processing documents, videos, photos, audio files, presentations, web pages and many other kinds of business documents. Unstructured data is everywhere. In fact, most individuals and organizations conduct their lives around unstructured data.

More examples of unstructured data include:

- Satellite images: This includes the weather data or the data that the government captures via satellite surveillance. Search Google Earth to see satellite image data.
- Scientific data: This includes seismic imagery, atmospheric data, and high energy physics (data from particle accelerators).
- Photographs and video: This includes security, surveillance, and traffic video.
- Radar or sonar data: This includes vehicular, meteorological, and oceanographic seismic profiles.
- Text internal to any company: The text within official documents, logs, survey results, and email communications. Enterprise information actually represents a large percentage of the text information in the world today.
- Social media data: This data is generated from the social media platforms such as YouTube, Facebook, Twitter, LinkedIn, and Flickr.
- Mobile data: This includes data such as text messages and location information.
- Website content: This comes from any website delivering unstructured content, like YouTube, Vimeo or Wikipedia.

The distribution of these three types of data is shown in Figure 15.8.

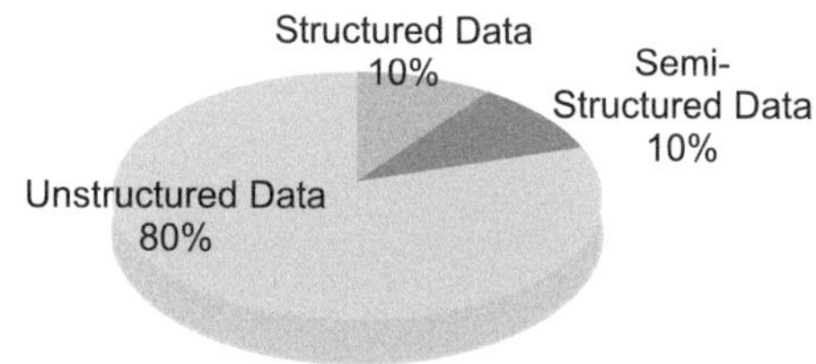

Figure 15.8 Percentage distribution of different types of data

Test Your Skills

Classify the following types of data into structured, unstructured or semi-structured.

• Email • MS Access • IMages • MS Excel • Chat conversations	• Relations / Table • Facebook • Database • XML

The solution is given below:

Structured	Unstructured	Semi-structured
• MS Access • Database • Relations / Table • MS Excel	• Email • Images • Chat conversations • Facebook	• XML

Since 80% of data is unstructured, there is a huge demand for database experts who can process and analyze this data. It is important to note that traditional databases can only process structured data which is merely 10% of the total data being generated. Thus, the Internet boom has produced new challenges and opportunities in terms of technologies and skills.

15.4 Emergence of Big Data due to the Internet Boom

This huge surge in the volume of data gave rise to a new concept known as Big Data. According to Gartner - 'Big data is high-volume, high-velocity and/or high-variety information assets that demand cost-effective, innovative forms of information processing that enable enhanced insight, decision making, and process automation.'

Big Data involves 4 V's as given below.

- Volume: Data size
- Variety: Data formats
- Velocity: Data streaming speeds
- Veracity: Data trustworthiness

Let us discuss each of these terms one by one.

Volume of data

Big data implies an enormous amount of data. This data is generated by machines, networks and human interaction on systems like social media. Big data deals with zettabytes of data.

For reference, data sizes in terms of bytes has been given below.

- 10^3 Bytes- 1 KB (Kilobytes)
- 10^6 Bytes- 1 MB (Megabytes)
- 10^9 Bytes- 1 GB (Gigabytes)
- 10^{12} Bytes- 1 TB (Terabytes)
- 10^{15} Bytes- 1 PB (Petabytes)
- 10^{18} Bytes- 1 EB (Exabytes)
- 10^{21} Bytes- 1 ZB (Zettabytes)

Variety of data

Variety refers to either the sources or types of data. Traditionally, data came from sources like spreadsheets and databases. Now data is being generated in form of emails, photos, videos, monitoring devices, PDFs, audio, and more. This variety of unstructured data creates problems for storage, mining and analyzing data.

Velocity of data

Velocity refers to the speed at which data is being generated. Data flows in from sources like business processes, machines, networks and human interaction with social media sites, mobile devices, sensors and such. This flow of data is massive and continuous. To understand the velocity of data we can consider the case of a driverless car. To make a driverless car we have to deploy thousands of sensors and the frequency at which these sensors are generating data is in milliseconds. We have to process this high-speed data in real time and generate the response in order to make the whole thing work. This example clearly indicates the importance to process high-velocity data.

Veracity of data

Veracity refers to the biases, noise, and abnormality in data. It tells us about the trustworthiness of data. To judge data veracity, we ask a simple question - 'Is the data that is being stored, and mined meaningful to the problem being analyzed?' It is estimated that $3.1 Trillion (2012) a year is wasted in the US economy due to poor data quality. The veracity of data analysis is the biggest challenge when compared to volume and velocity.

These 4 V's of big data are illustrated by the info-graphics as shown in Figure 15.9.

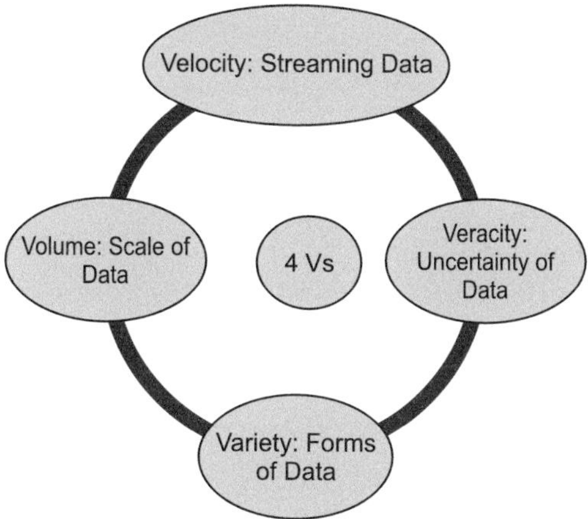

Figure 15.9 Info graphic of 4 V's of big data

15.5 Possible Solutions to Handle Huge Amount of Data

Whenever a new challenge arises, we first try to solve it using existing technologies and skills. During the Internet boom relational database was dominant, and so, solutions to the problem of big data were attempted by using relational databases. The first solution was to scale up resources. Scaling up implies bigger machines, more processors, disk storage and memory as shown Figure 15.10.

Figure 15.10 Scaling up using a large centralized server

But bigger machines get more and more expensive, and finally there are limits to size. This situation is depicted in the diagrams in Figure 15.11.

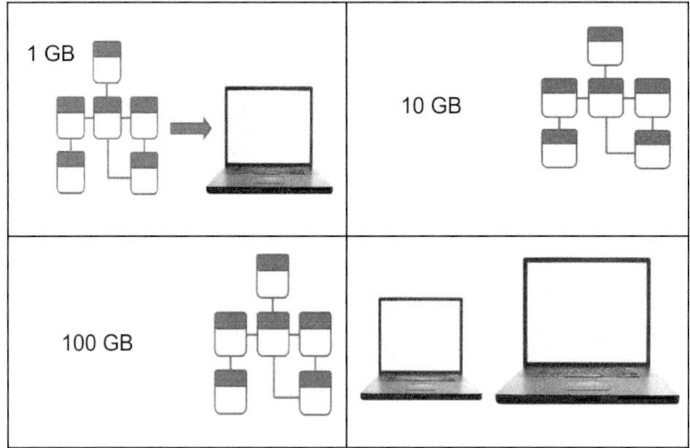

Figure 15.11 Handling of huge data volume through the relational model

Soon we reached our limits. The alternative solution was to scale out i.e. to use lots of small machines in a cluster as shown in Figure 15.12. A cluster of small machines can use commodity hardware and ends up being cheaper than large servers. It is also more resilient — while individual machine failures are common, the overall cluster can be built to keep going despite such failures, providing very high reliability.

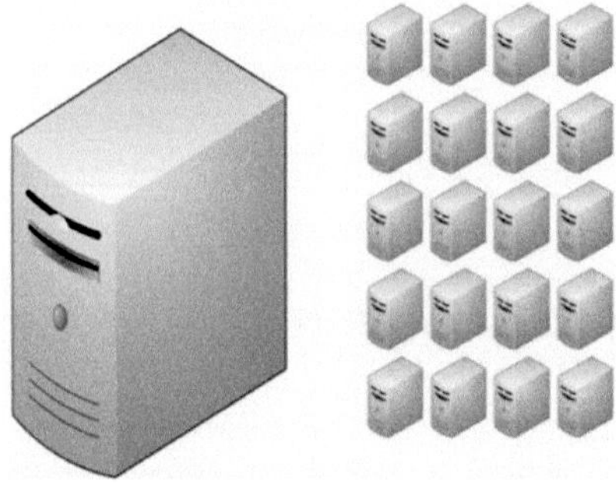

Figure 15.12 Cluster computing emerged as a winner

As large organizations moved towards using clusters, this revealed a new problem — relational databases were not designed to run efficiently on clusters such as depicted in Figure 15.13. Clustered relational databases, such as the Oracle RAC or Microsoft SQL Server, work on the concept of a shared disk subsystem. But, tuning relational databases for cluster environments is considered an 'unnatural act' by computers. This was accompanied by some licensing issues too. Commercial relational databases are usually priced on a single-server assumption, so running them on a cluster raised prices and led to frustrating negotiations with purchase departments.

Figure 15.13 SQL in cluster environment

This mismatch between relational databases and clusters led some organizations to consider an alternative route to data storage.

15.6 The Emergence of Technologies for Cluster Environment

Google and Amazon started their work based on cluster environments and had already tried out various cluster technologies. They were at the forefront of the effort of running large clusters. Furthermore, they were handling huge amounts of data. All this forced them to develop an alternative solution to relational databases. As the 2000s went on, both companies produced brief but highly influential papers about their efforts: BigTable from Google and Dynamo from Amazon as shown in Figure 15.14.

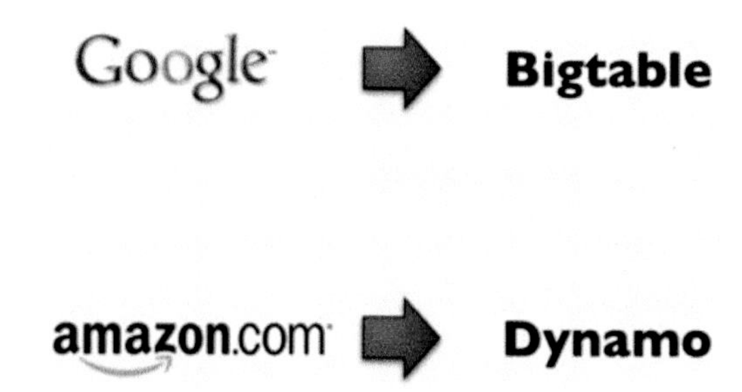

Figure 15.14 BigTable and Dynamo for cluster environments

15.7 Birth of NoSQL

The usage of the term 'NoSQL' that is so common today can be traced back to a developers' meet organized on June 11, 2009, in San Francisco by Johan Oskarsson, a software developer based in London. The example of BigTable and Dynamo had inspired a bunch of projects experimenting with alternative data storage strategies, and discussions about these had become a feature of better software conferences around that time. Johan was interested in finding out more about some of these new databases while he was in San Francisco for a Hadoop summit. Since he had little time there, he felt that it wouldn't be feasible to visit them all, so he decided to host a 'meet-up' where all could come together and present their work.

Johan wanted a nice name for the meet-up—something that would make a good Twitter hashtag: short, memorable, and without too many Google hits so that a search on the name would quickly find the meet. He asked for suggestions on the #cassandra IRC channel. At last, he selected 'NoSQL' based on a suggestion from Eric Evans as illustrated in Figure 15.15. While the selected name had the disadvantage of being negative and not really descriptive these systems, but it did fit the hashtag criteria well. At that time, they were thinking of only a single meeting to name and were not expecting the name to become generic.

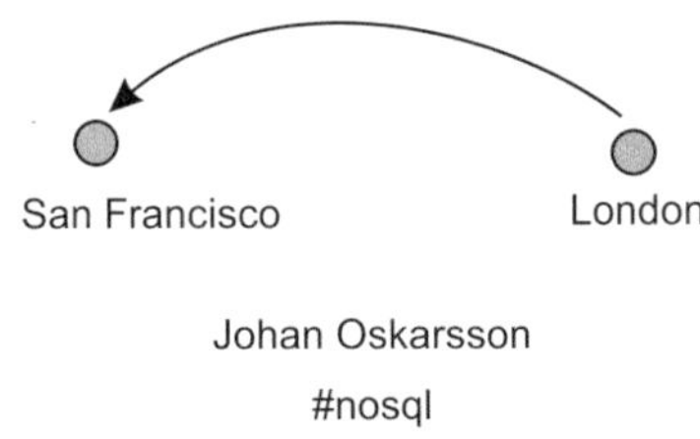

Figure 15.15 NoSQL Meet

The term 'NoSQL' caught on like wildfire, but it never had a strong technical definition. As the original call for the meet-up asked for 'open-source, distributed, non-relational databases' hence NoSQL is attached to all these features. In the meet-up, experts from Voldemort, Cassandra, Dynomite, HBase, Hypertable, CouchDB, and MongoDB participated as shown in Figure 15.16.

Figure 15.16 Participants of NoSQL meet

15.8 Defining NoSQL from the Characteristics it Shares

There is no generally accepted definition of the term NoSQL. It is defined on the basis of some common characteristics of the databases that tend to be called 'NoSQL.'

The important characteristics of NoSQL are given below, are also illustrated in Figure 15.17.

- It is not based on the relational model; thus, it is non-relational.
- These databases are generally open-source.
- Most NoSQL databases are driven by the need to run on clusters. Thus, they are cluster-friendly.
- NoSQL databases are used to address the needs of the early 21st-century web.
- NoSQL databases operate without a schema, allowing you to freely add fields to database records. This is particularly useful when dealing with non-uniform data.

Characteristics of NoSQL

non-relational open-source

cluster-friendly

21st Century Web

schema-less

Figure 15.17 Features of NoSQL

15.9 Some Misconceptions about NoSQL

A general misconception about NoSQL is that it does not use SQL. This is not true. Most of NoSQL databases have their own query language. For example, Cassandra uses CQL which is exactly like SQL.

Another important point to note is that 'NoSQL,' does not mean 'no' to SQL? Rather NoSQL is a smart acronym for 'Not Only SQL' but this interpretation has a couple of problems. Most people write 'NoSQL' whereas 'Not Only SQL' should be written as 'NOSQL.'

15.10 Data Models of NoSQL

A data model allows us to perceive and manipulate our data. The data model describes how we interact with the data in the database. As we know, the dominant data model for the last couple of decades was the relational data model, which is best visualized as a set of tables or rather like a page of a spreadsheet.

One of the most obvious shifts with NoSQL is to move away from the relational model. With NoSQL other data models appeared; mainly categorized as follows:

i. Key-value data model
ii. Document data model

iii. Column-family model
iv. Graph data model

These models and systems based on these models are depicted in Figure 15.18.

Figure 15.18 NoSQL data models

15.10.1 Key-value data model

A key-value is a simple hash table, primarily used when all access to the data is via the primary key. Think of a table in a traditional RDBMS form with two columns, such as ID and NAME, the ID column being the key and NAME column storing the value. In an RDBMS, the NAME column is restricted to storing a data value of single data type, for instance, string. But, in a key-value data model, the VALUE is an aggregate containing the whole information corresponding to the key, i.e., ID as shown in Figure 15.19.

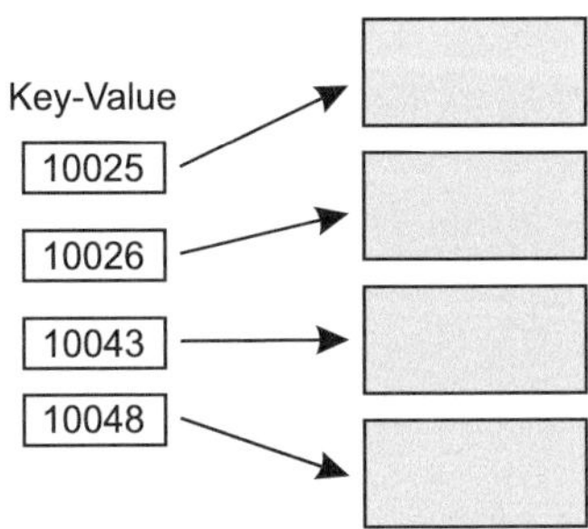

Figure 15.19 Key-value data model

Let us consider a very abstract example of a banking system to understand the concept of a key-value data model. Suppose we are using a relational model to store details about every transaction with respect to the account numbers and we are storing account number, amount, type and date for every transaction in a relational table as shown in Table 15.1.

Now, in order to print an account statement for a particular account number we have to search the whole table to find out the latest transactions for that particular account number. If the database is very huge, containing millions of records then it may be distributed over more than one computer.

In such a case, a query has to run on multiple computers to get the account statement. This may not be the best way to query data in case of a cluster environment.

Table 15.1 The relational model to store account information

Account Number	*Balance*	*Type*	*Date*
10001	20000	Withdraw	12-12-2017
10004	30000	Deposit	12-12-2017
10003	80000	Withdraw	12-12-2017
10008	60000	Deposit	12-12-2017
10009	20000	Withdraw	12-12-2017
10002	90000	Withdraw	12-12-2017
...			
10001	10000	Withdraw	22-12-2017
10009	7000	Withdraw	22-12-2017
10002	80000	Withdraw	22-12-2017
10003	60000	Withdraw	22-12-2017
10004	40000	Deposit	22-12-2017

Now consider an alternative scenario, where we are storing this data using a key-value data model. In this case, every account number will act as a key and the details about its transactions are stored as its value. For example, account number 10001's transactions are stored as its values as shown in Figure 15.20.

Now to print the account statement for any account number we just need to search for the key field of the given account number and after finding that particular key we just need to print its corresponding value. In this case, the data about a single account will be available only on a single computer making it ideal for a cluster environment.

Some of the popular key-value databases are Riak, Redis, Memcached DB, Berkeley DB, HamsterDB and Amazon DynamoDB. Riak is the commonly used key-value based software, Table 15.2 compares, terminologies used in Riak and RDBMS.

Table 15.2 Comparison of terminologies used in Oracle and Riak

Riak	*RDBMS*
Key	Row id
Bucket	Table
Key-value	Row
Riak Cluster	Database instance

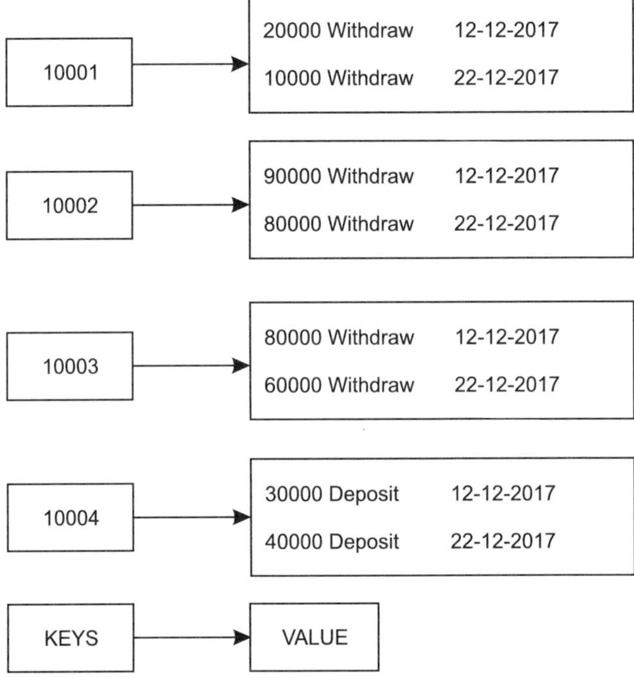

Figure 15.20 Key-value model to store account information

15.10.2 Column-family data model

Column-family based databases, such as Cassandra, HBase, Hypertable, and Amazon SimpleDB, allow you to store data with keys mapped to values and the values are further grouped into multiple column families where each column family is a map of data as shown in Figure 15.21.

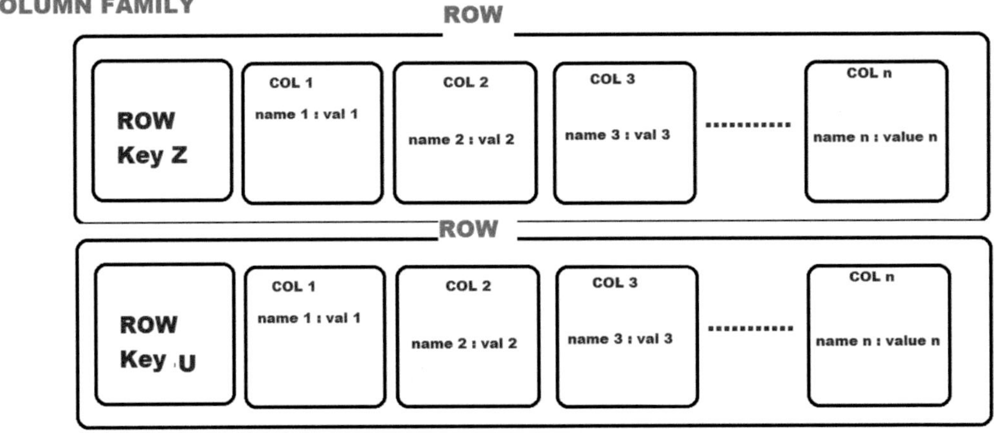

Figure 15.21 Column-family data model

The Column-family model is a two-level aggregate structure. On the first level is the key and the second-level values are referred to as columns. It allows picking out a particular column, so to get a particular customer's name we could do something like: get('1234', 'name') as shown in Figure 15.22.

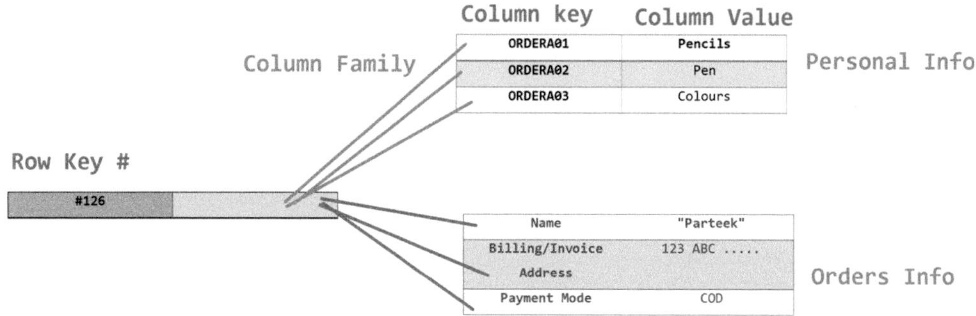

Figure 15.22 Representing customer information in a Column-family structure

Cassandra is the commonly used column-family based database, Table 15.3 compares, terminologies used in RDBMS and Cassandra.

Table 15.3 Comparison of terminologies used in RDBMS and Cassandra

RDBMS	*Cassandra*
Database	Keyspace
Row	Row
Table	Column Family
Database instance	Cluster
Column (same throughout the rows)	Columns (can be unique for each row)

15.10.3 Document data model

Documents are at the core of document databases. To understand the working of document model let us consider, a bill generated by an e-commerce store as shown in Figure 15.23.

The bill contains the following details: order number, customer number, the detail of items purchased and the payments summary. In case of the relational model, to generate this bill we have to join multiple tables. For example, the order number will be extracted from the order table, customer details from the customer table, the detail of items purchased from the order detail table and payment details from the credit card table as shown in Figure 15.23.

In the case of a cluster environment, these tables may exist on different computers and running a join query across multiple computers is not very efficient. Alternatively, we can store this bill document itself in the database on a single computer. Of course, it would not be normalized but it still would be a more efficient approach in case of the cluster environment. This type of storage comes under the Document Data model. It is non-relational and is usually supports the JSON, XML, CSV, OR TSV formats.

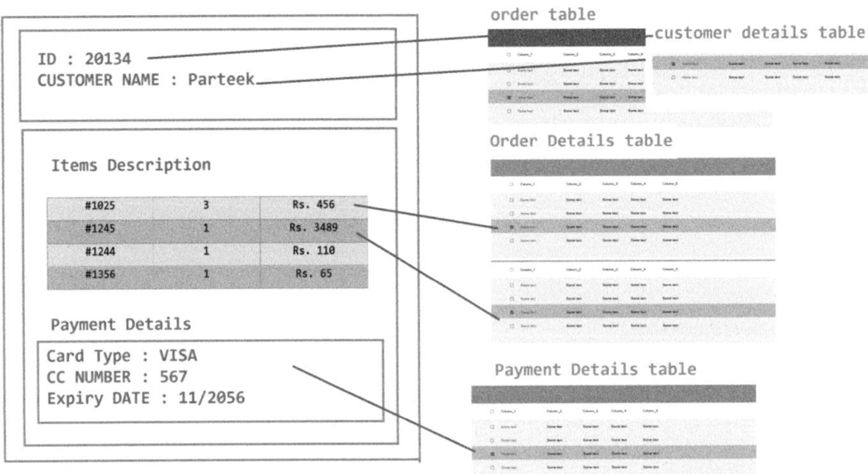

Figure 15.23 Document model

In the Document data model, the database stores and retrieves documents. These documents are self-describing, hierarchical tree data structures which can consist of maps, collections, and scalar values as shown in Figure 15.24.

{ "id" : 2001
"customer_id" : #C4568
"line-items" : | {"product_id": P34, "quantity" : 9 }, {"product_id": P14, "quantity" : 2 }|}
{ "id" : 2002
"customer_id" : #C4569
"line-items" : | {"product_id": P45, "quantity" : 2 }, {"product_id": P14, "quantity" : 1 }|}

No Schema

Figure 15.24 Document data model

MongoDB is the commonly used document data model based software, Table 15.4 compares, terminologies used in MongoDB and RDBMS.

Table 15.4 Comparison of terminologies used in MongoDB and RDBMS

MongoDB	*RDBMS*
Database	schema
Collection	Table
_id	Row id
DBRef	Joins
MongoDB instance	Database instance
document	Row

15.10.4 Graph databases

Graph databases have existed long before the term 'NoSQL' was coined. They have a special place as shown in Figure 15.25. Most NoSQL databases were inspired by the need to do computation on clusters, which led to aggregate-oriented data models of large records with simple connections.

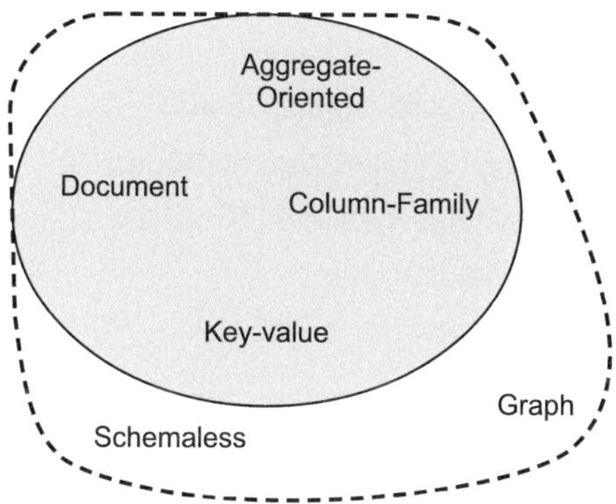

Figure 15.25 NoSQL data models

To understand the working of the Graph model, let us consider the case of a social networking platform such as Facebook that maintains a social graph for each user. In case of the relational model, we can store a friend's information in a FRIEND table that will contain the user id of the friend as shown in Table 15.5.

Table 15.5 Friends database

UserID	*Friend_UserID*
100	102
102	101
101	102
100	103
103	104
104	102
102	105

Now, in order to perform any activity such as fetching updates from the friend's wall, we will need to write a complex query involving multiple joins.

In such a scenario, it is better to store the graph itself in the database. In the graph data database we have nodes that are connected by edges. Once you have built up a graph containing nodes and edges, a graph database allows you to query this network and apply operations that work with a graph data structure. This is the important difference between a graph and relational databases. Although relational databases can implement relationships using foreign keys, the joins required to navigate around can get quite expensive—which means performance is often poor for highly connected data models. Graph databases make traversal along the relationships very light-weight.

Neo4J is a popular database based on the graph data model. Creating a graph is as simple as creating nodes followed by declaring a relationship among nodes.

For instance, let us create two nodes, Rahat and Rishan:

```
Node rahat = graphDb.createNode();
rahat.setProperty("name", "Rahat");
Node rishan = graphDb.createNode();
rishan.setProperty("name", "Rishan");
Creating Relationship
rahat.createRelationshipTo(rishan, FRIEND);
rishan.createRelationshipTo(rahat, FRIEND);
```

In Figure 15.26, we have a web of information whose number of nodes is very small but there is a rich structure of interconnections between them. This is ideal for capturing any data consisting of complex relationships such as social networks, product preferences, or eligibility rules. Thus, Graph databases store entities and relationships between these entities. Entities are also known as nodes which can have various properties. Relations are known as edges that can also have properties. Edges may have directional significance attached to them.

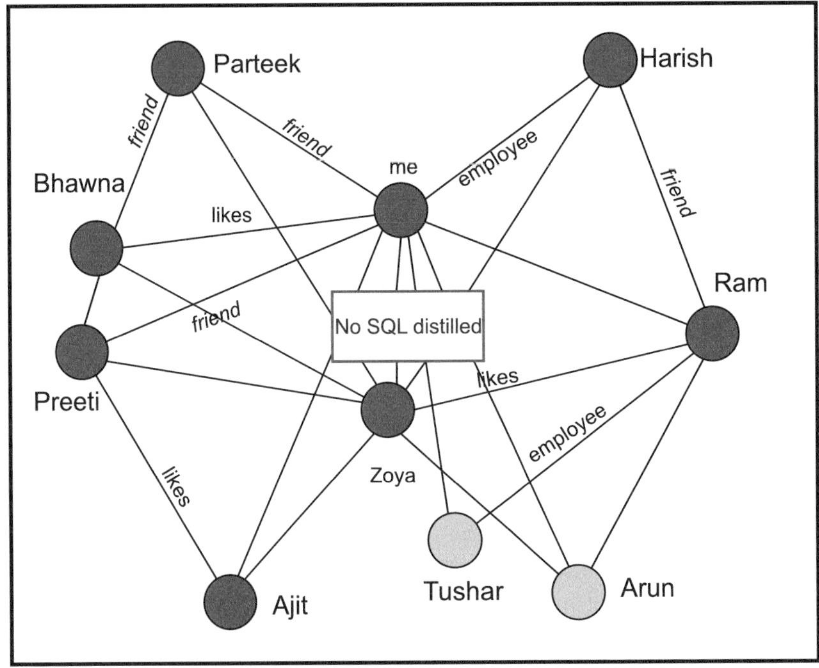

Figure 15.26 An example of the Graph structure

15.11 Consistency in a Distributed Environment

Consistency in the relational model is achieved with the ACID (Atomicity, Consistency, Isolation, Durability) property, while NoSQL follows BASE (Basically Available Soft-state Eventual consistent) as illustrated in Figure 15.27.

RDBMS == ACID

NoSQL == BASE

Figure 15.27 RDBMS versus NoSQL

15.12 CAP Theorem

The CAP (Consistency, Availability, Partition tolerance) theorem, also known as Brewer's theorem, states that it is impossible for a distributed computer system to simultaneously guarantee all three of the following three characteristics.

Consistency (all nodes see the same data at the same time)

Availability (a guarantee that every request receives a response irrespective of whether it was successful or failed)

Partition tolerance (the system continues to operate despite arbitrary message loss or failure of part of the system)

According to the theorem, a distributed system cannot guarantee all three of these characteristics at the same time but may satisfy any two of them; sometimes also known as 'two out of three' concept.

It means that if a system is partitioned in a network environment, then we can achieve either consistency of the system or availability of the system as illustrated in Figure 15.28.

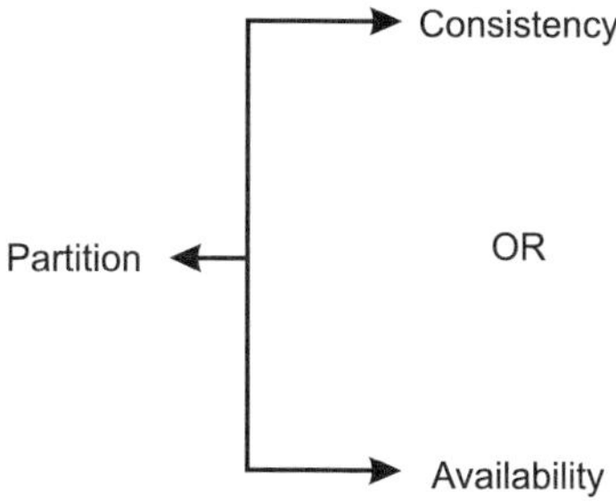

Figure 15.28 CAP theorem

It means if a network link is broken between two sites in a distributed environment as shown in Figure 15.29, then any update operation on site X will not be reflected at site Y. Thus, the system will become inconsistent. In order to avoid that, we have to shut down the service, rendering the system unavailable. Thus, in case of a partitioned network, if we want to achieve consistency then availability cannot be achieved and if want to make our system available in spite of the partition then consistency will be lost. Thus, CAP theorem states that it is impossible for a distributed computer system to simultaneously have consistency, availability, and partition tolerance. Generally, depending upon the need of an application, it is a choice between 'two out of three'.

Figure 15.29 Consistency in a distributed environment

15.13 Future of NoSQL

After discussing features and models of NoSQL, we can conclude that NoSQL makes the process of software development easier and can handle large-scale data. But a billion-dollar question is - 'What will be the future of NoSQL (illustrated in Figure 15.30)?'

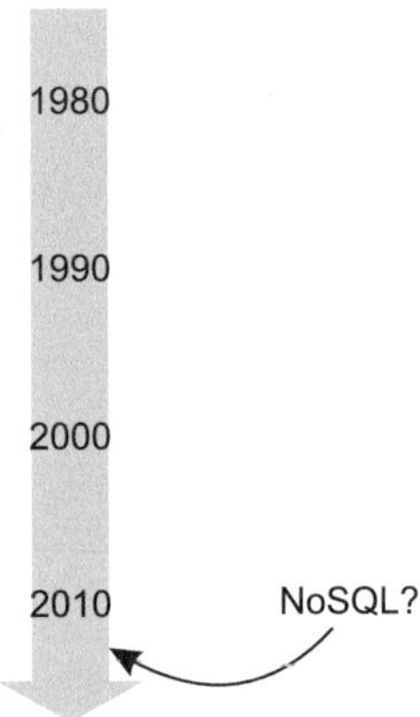

Figure 15.30 Future of NoSQL?

The major strength of the relational model is its ACID properties. It means that data is always consistent, but NoSQL works in the shadow of the CAP theorem. In a financial application, we cannot compromise on the consistency of data, so in future, we will continue to use relational model for all financial applications. But, in applications such as e-commerce, where availability is the major concern, NoSQL data models perform better than relational models because of ease of development and ability to handle large-scale data as illustrated in Figure 15.31.

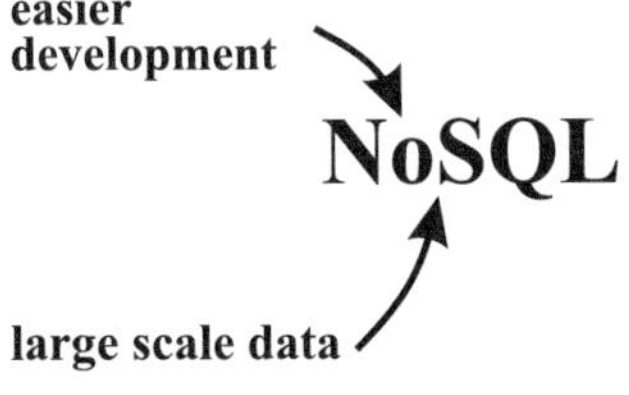

Figure 15.31 Strengths of NoSQL

Similarly, in applications like social networking websites where queries are based on users and their activities, graph-based models perform better. So, in future, we will mix different technologies — that programmers would use the appropriate technology for the specific job at hand. In the field of Big Data field, a new term has emerged called 'polyglot persistence' as illustrated in Figure 32. Polyglot persistence is commonly used to define this hybrid approach.

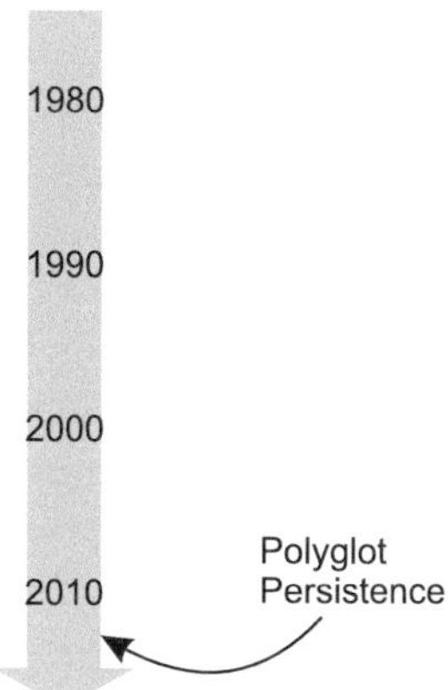

Figure 15.32 The future is Polyglot persistence

For instance, an e-commerce platform may require a hybrid approach to information as shown in Figure 15.33.

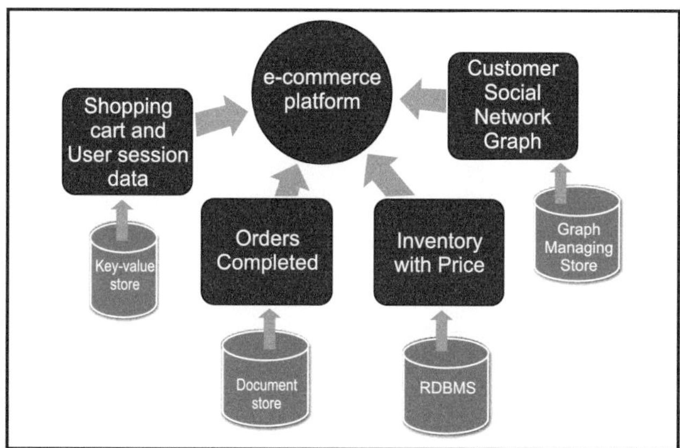

Figure 15.33 Polyglot persistence in a real environment

For shopping cart and session data, the key-value store is the best-suited model; to store completed order information the document model is best; while for inventory and item price the relational model is optimal. For a customer's social graph, a graph-based data model is best suited. In the future, we can expect to see lots of hybrid data models being used. In a nutshell, in future the relational model and NoSQL will both co-exist and will be used in a hybrid manner to provide full e-commerce solutions.

15.14 Difference between NoSQL and Relational Data Models (RDBMS)

There are two major differences between NoSQL and RDBMS. First, RDBMS uses a relational data model whereas NoSQL provides us with many options, each suited for a different scenario. So in RDBMS, we put the data in a bunch of tables and query it using complex join operations in order to present useful information to the user. On the other hand, in NoSQL, the data may be stored in aggregate form keeping software development as simple as possible.

Secondly, RDBMS requires a rigid schema where NoSQL is schema-less. Relational technology requires strict definition of a schema prior to storing any data into a database. Changing the schema once data is inserted is extremely disruptive and to be completely avoided – the exact opposite of the behavior desired in the Big Data era, where application developers need to constantly – and rapidly – incorporate new types of data to enrich their applications. In comparison, NoSQL allows changing the schema or the format of the data being inserted any time, without application disruption.

NoSQL also may not guarantee full ACID (atomicity, consistency, isolation, durability) property but still has a distributed and fault tolerant architecture.

Remind Me

- The reasons for the success of relational databases were their simplicity, power of SQL, support for transaction management, concurrency control, and recovery management.
- The biggest frustration with the relational database is of impedance mismatch. The difference between the relational model and the in-memory data structures is known as impedance mismatch.
- During the Internet boom, to store huge data clusters appeared as a possible solution. But, the mismatch between relational databases and clusters led some organization to consider an alternative route to data storage.
- A NoSQL database provides a mechanism for storage and retrieval of data based on a bunch of data models other than the relational model. Motivations for this approach include simplicity of design, horizontal scaling and finer control over availability.
- The data model (e.g., Key-value data model, Document data model, Column-family model and Graph data model) differs from the RDBMS, and therefore some operations are faster in NoSQL and some are faster in RDBMS.
- The CAP theorem says that if a system is partitioned in a network environment, then we can achieve either consistency of the system or availability of the system.
- In future, 'polyglot persistence' which is a hybrid approach will become popular.

Point Me (Books)

- Sadalage, Pramod J., and Martin Fowler. 2013. *NoSQL Distilled: A Brief Guide to the Emerging World of Polyglot Persistence*. New York: Pearson Education.

Point Me (Video)

- Introduction to NoSQL By Martin Fowler https://www.youtube.com/watch?v=ql_g07C_Q5I
- NoSQL Introduction By Parteek Bhatia https://www.youtube.com/watch?v=6Pp88Qc1CvE&t=336s

Connect Me (Internet Resources)

- https://martinfowler.com/books/nosql.html
- https://www.w3resource.com/mongodb/nosql.php
- https://www.simplilearn.com/introduction-to-nosql-databases-tutorial-video
- https://www.tutorialspoint.com/articles/what-is-nosql-and-is-it-the-next-big-trend-in-databases
- https://intellipaat.com/blog/nosql-database-tutorial/

Test Me

Answer these questions based on your learning in this chapter.

1. Cluster technology followed by Amazon is ....
2. MongoDB is based on .... model
3. Cassandra is based on ....
4. The Graph model in this chapter is ....
5. .... NoSQL model used ACID
6. .... models used aggregate model
7. Different columns in a row are allowed in .... model
8. BASE stands for ....
9. CAP stands for ....
10. For completed orders which model needs to be used ....

Answer Keys:

1. Dynamo 2. Document 3. Column family model 4. neo4j
5. Graph model
6. Key-value data model, Document data model and Column-family model
7. Column-family model
8. Basically Available Soft state Eventual Consistency
9. Consistency, Availability, Partition tolerance 10. Document data model

Index

Colour Plates

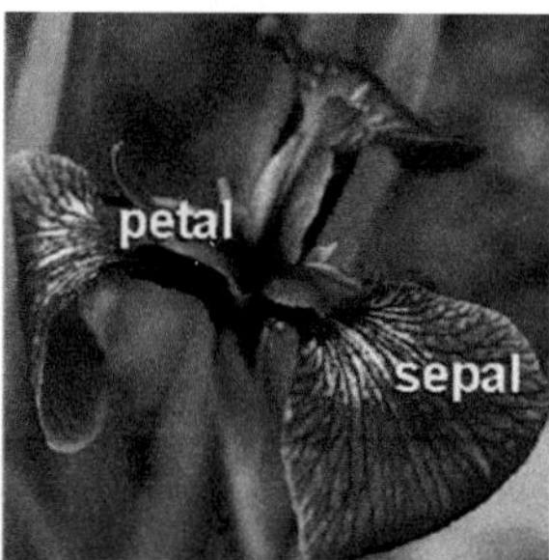

Figure 3.3 Sample of the Iris flower

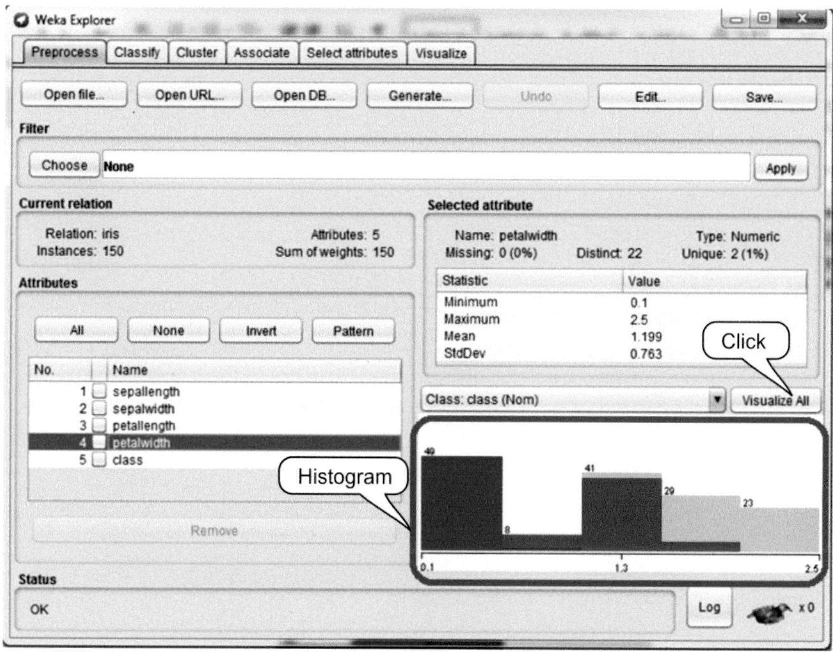

Figure 3.13 Histogram for Petal width

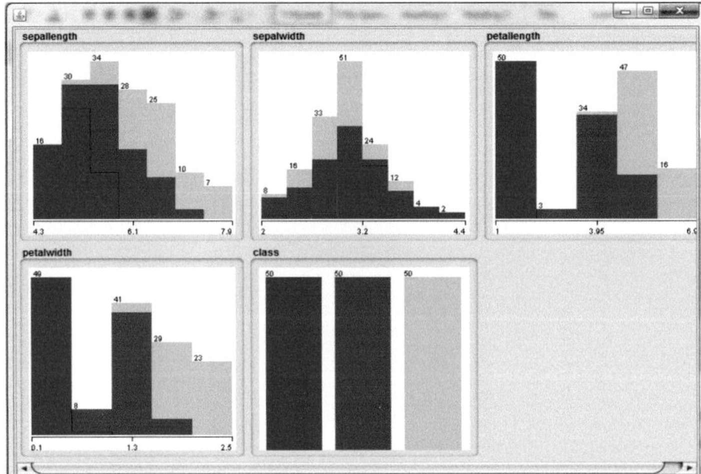

Figure 3.14 Histograms for all attributes of Iris dataset

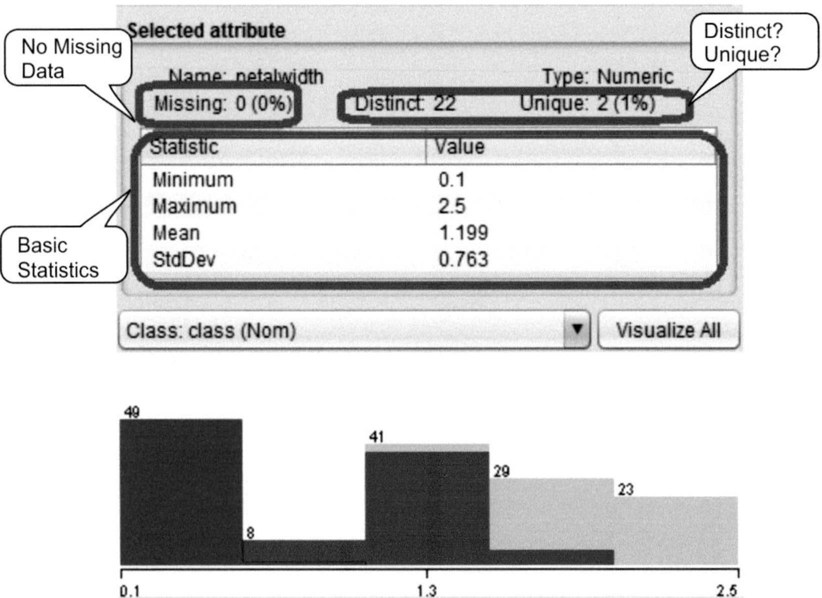

Figure 3.15 Attribute statistics

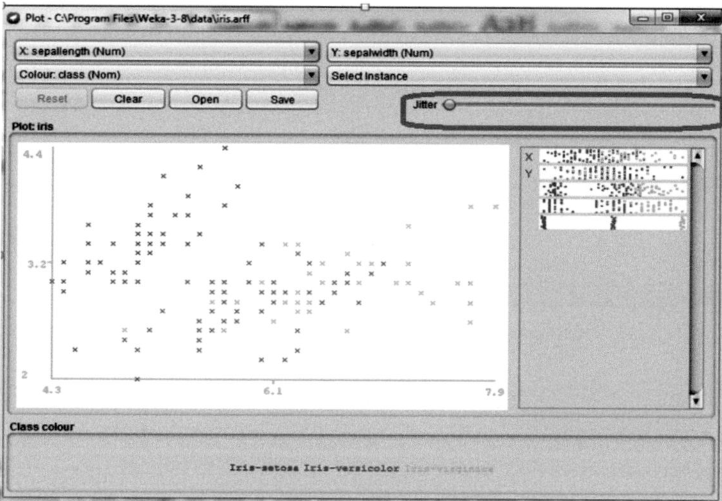

Figure 3.20 Plotting of dataset

Classifier output

```
=== Summary ===

Correctly Classified Instances          49               96.0784 %
Incorrectly Classified Instances         2                3.9216 %
Kappa statistic                          0.9408
Mean absolute error                      0.0396
Root mean squared error                  0.1579
Relative absolute error                  8.8979 %
Root relative squared error             33.4091 %
Total Number of Instances               51

=== Detailed Accuracy By Class ===

                 TP Rate  FP Rate  Precision  Recall   F-Measure  MCC      ROC Area  PRC Area  Class
                 1.000    0.000    1.000      1.000    1.000      1.000    1.000     1.000     Iris-setosa
                 1.000    0.063    0.905      1.000    0.950      0.921    0.969     0.905     Iris-versicolor
                 0.882    0.000    1.000      0.882    0.938      0.913    0.967     0.938     Iris-virginica
Weighted Avg.    0.961    0.023    0.965      0.961    0.961      0.942    0.977     0.944

=== Confusion Matrix ===

  a  b  c   <-- classified as
 15  0  0 |  a = Iris-setosa
  0 19  0 |  b = Iris-versicolor
  0  2 15 |  c = Iris-virginica
```

Confusion Matrix

Figure 6.11 Decision tree accuracy statistics

```
=== Confusion Matrix ===

  a  b  c   <-- classified as
 15  0  0 |  a = Iris-setosa
  0 19  0 |  b = Iris-versicolor
  0  2 15 |  c = Iris-virginica
```

Figure 6.14 Confusion matrix

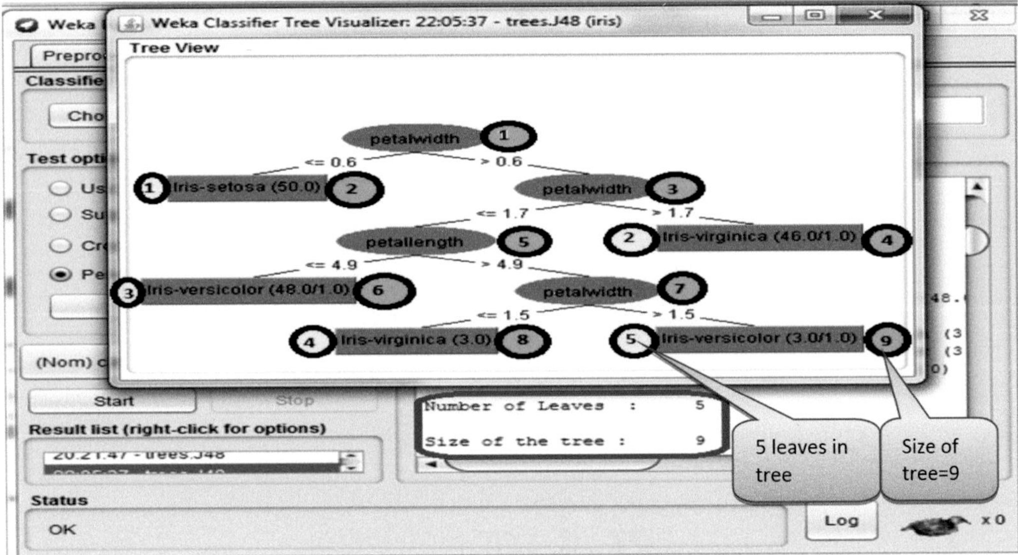

Figure 6.20 Size and leaves of the tree

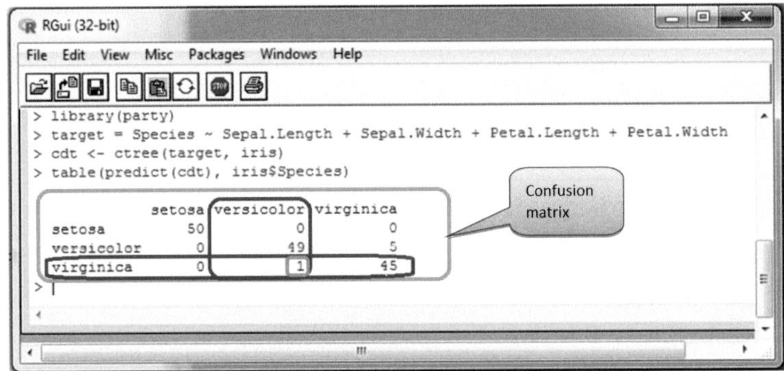

Figure 6.37 Implementation of the decision tree in R

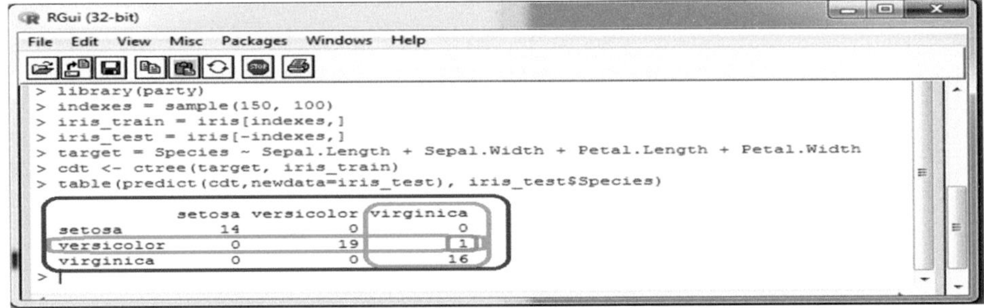

Figure 6.40 Prediction by the decision tree on testing dataset

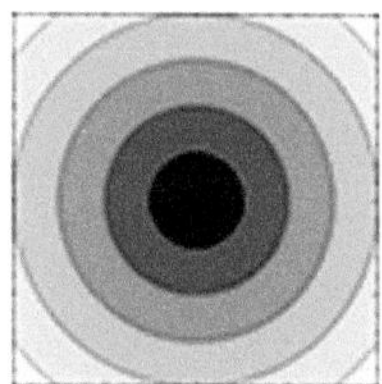

Figure 7.2 Representation of Euclidean distance

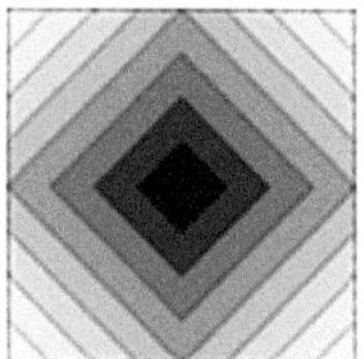

Figure 7.3 Representation of Manhattan distance

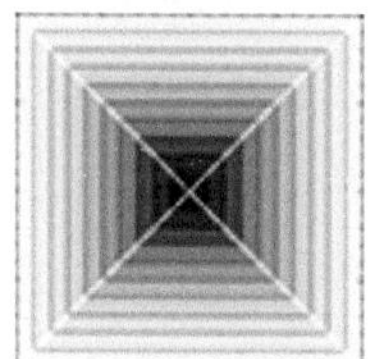

Figure 7.4 Representation of Chebyshev distance

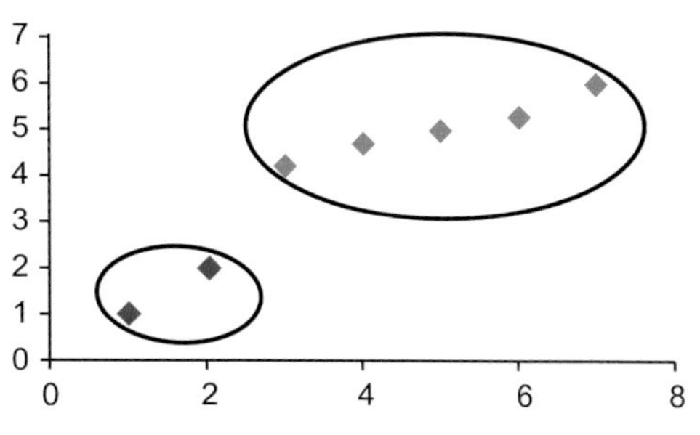

Figure 7.8 Plot of data for k=2

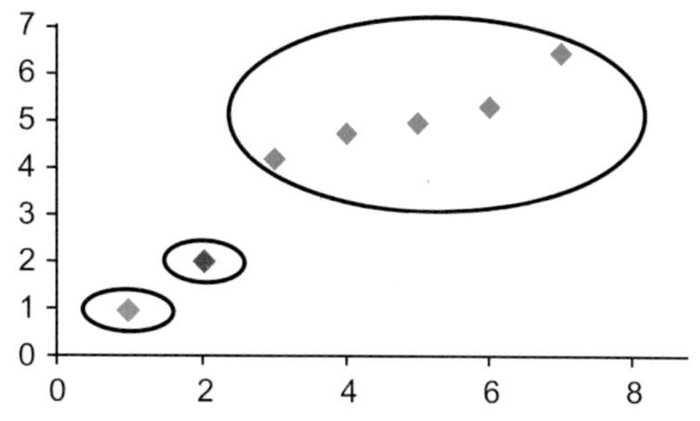

Figure 7.9 Plot of data for k=3

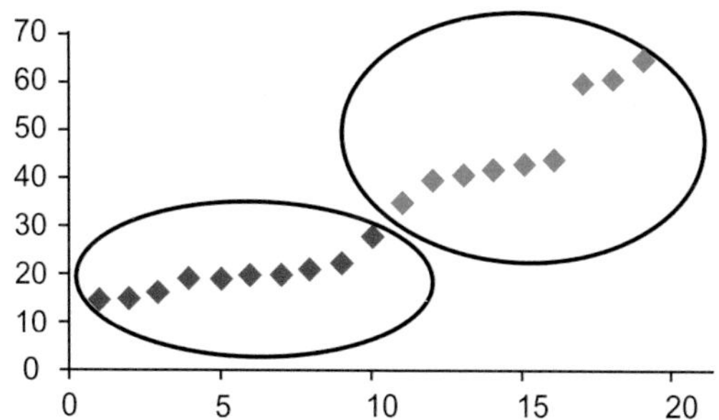

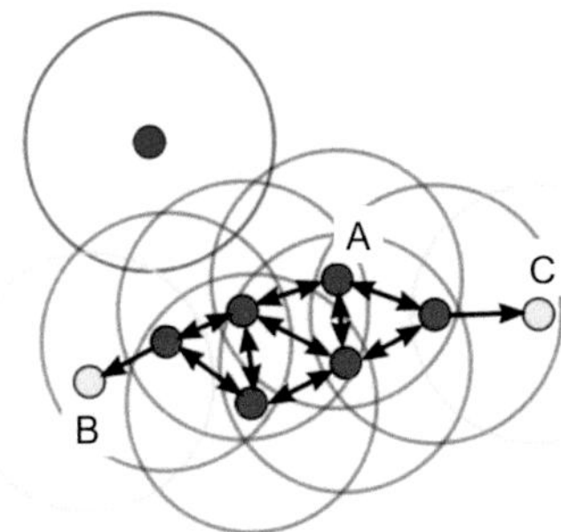

Figure 7.23 Another case of density reachability

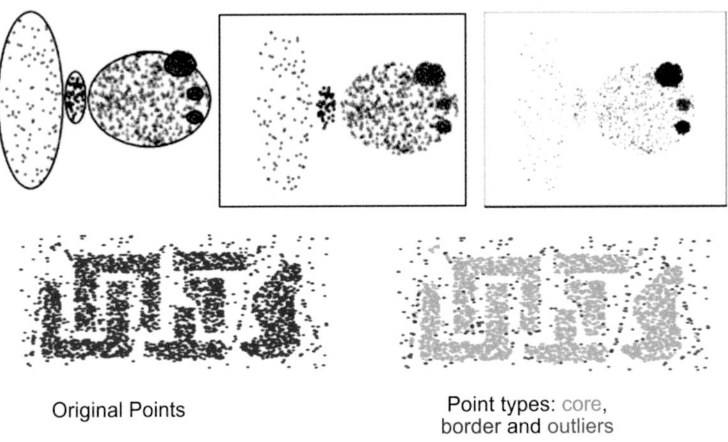

Figure 7.24 Some more examples of DBSCAN

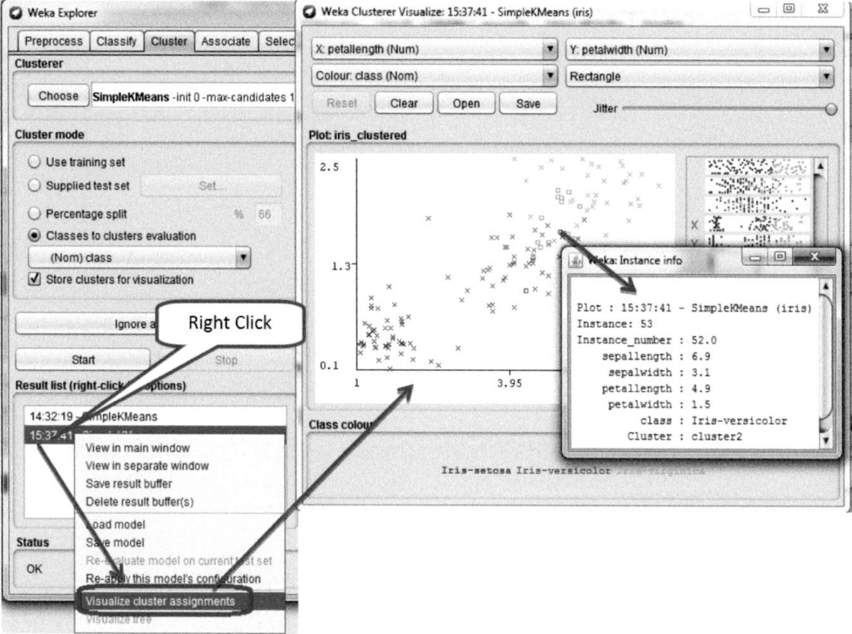

Figure 8.8 Cluster visualization

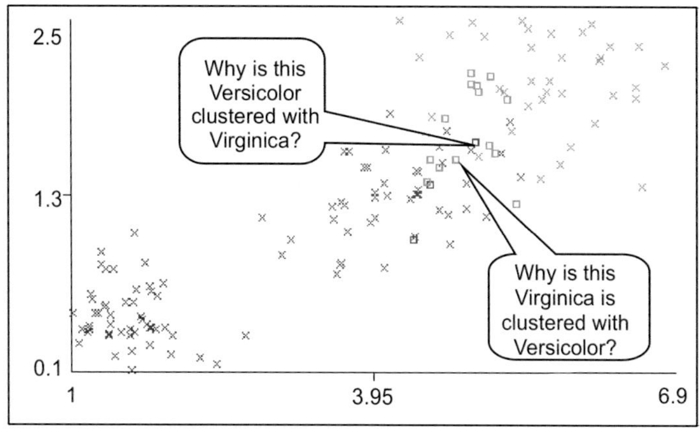

Figure 8.9 Cluster visualization for Petal length vs. Petal width

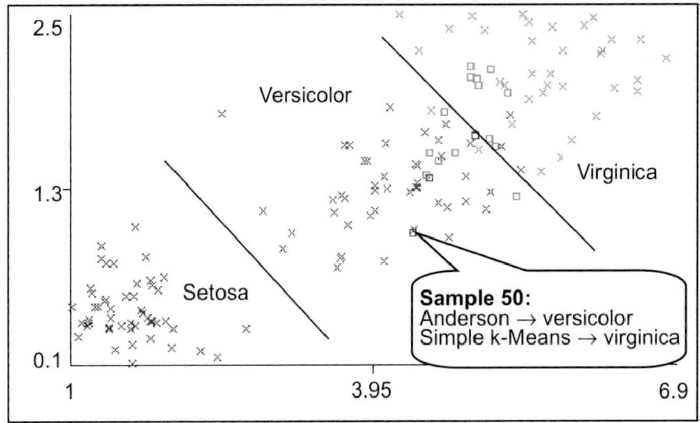

Figure 8.10 Cluster visualization with respect to Petal length vs. Petal width

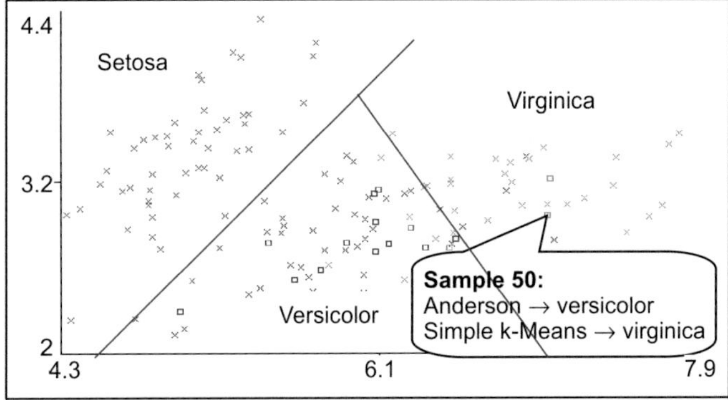

Figure 8.11 Cluster visualization with respect to Sepal length vs. Sepal width

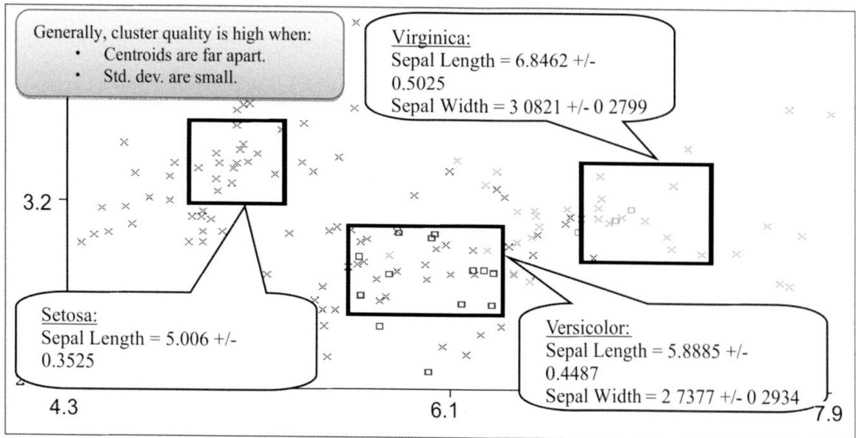

Figure 8.13 Cluster visualization with respect to Sepal length vs. Sepal width

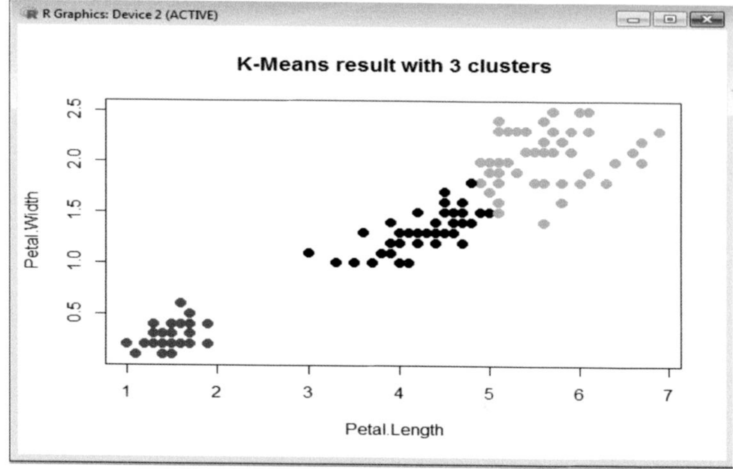

Figure 8.32 Plot of Petal length vs. Petal width after clustering

'Jnited States
- Publisher Services